Admiralty Record®

Volume 4

PUBLISHED ADMIRALTY OPINIONS OF
THE SUPREME COURT OF THE UNITED STATES AND
THE UNITED STATES COURTS OF APPEALS ISSUED DURING
THE CALENDAR YEAR

2016

Cite as: 4 Adm. R. _____

REPORTED BY KIRK N. AURANDT, ESQ.
MEMBER OF THE BAR IN LOUISIANA AND PENNSYLVANIA

ADMIRALTY RECORD PUBLISHING COMPANY, L.L.C.
MANDEVILLE, LOUISIANA, U.S.A.

ISSN 2334-5411
ISBN 978-0-9983853-6-5

Admiralty record: published admiralty opinions of the
Supreme Court of the United States and the United
States Courts of Appeals issued during the calendar
year ... Mandeville, Louisiana, U.S.A.: Admiralty
Record Publishing Company, LLC, 2014-

    KF1104 .A75
    ISSN: 2334-5411

https://lccn.loc.gov/2014200303

PREFACE

Volume 4—the fourth annual edition of the Admiralty Record®—reports the published admiralty opinions of the Supreme Court of the United States and the United States Courts of Appeals that were issued during the calendar year 2016. The opinions reported are the original majority, concurring, and dissenting opinions of the Court, with only minor changes in formatting to better suit a dual-column presentation. The pagination found in the original opinion is indicated by the number contained inside of black brackets. Also, where applicable, I have added parallel citations to opinions reported in this Volume and in prior Volumes of the Admiralty Record®.

The decision to select an opinion to appear in Volume 4 of the Admiralty Record® was made solely by me following an examination of those opinions that each of the above-named courts designated for publication in 2016. Every effort has been made to ensure inclusion of all 2016 federal appellate court admiralty opinions that were designated for publication; however, to the extent that a relevant admiralty opinion has been inadvertently overlooked or otherwise mistakenly omitted, the error is regretted and is solely my own. A few opinions from appeals in civil cases that technically may not have fallen under a federal district court's admiralty or maritime jurisdiction have been reported if they touched upon admiralty matters, or were otherwise deemed to be of potential interest to the admiralty practitioner. Additionally, several opinions from criminal cases involving maritime crimes and civil cases arising under the Federal Employers' Liability Act have been included.

To assist the reader in locating those opinions from 2016 involving subject matters of interest, I have prepared an Index to the opinions. I have also prepared Tables of Authority, which supply page references to the cases, statutes, and rules cited in each opinion. Prior to relying upon any of the opinions reported herein, the reader is reminded to verify the current status of any particular case as valid precedent by checking the case with a reliable citator.

Additional copies of Volume 1 (covering 2013), Volume 2 (covering 2014), Volume 3 (covering 2015), Volume 4 (covering 2016), and succeeding-year Volumes may be ordered at www.admiraltyrecord.com. I hope that the Admiralty Record® will become a valuable and ready reference source for not only the admiralty practitioner, but for anyone who is interested in reading the published admiralty opinions of the federal appellate courts.

KIRK N. AURANDT, ESQ.

This page intentionally left blank

Table of Contents[1]

(Cases arranged chronologically by Court)

PAGE

---

[1] In 2016, there were no published admiralty opinions from the United States Court of Appeals for the Federal Circuit.

This page intentionally left blank

Supreme Court of the United States

Supreme Court of the United States

No. 14-1209

STURGEON

vs.

FROST

On Writ of Certiorari to the United States Court of Appeals for the Ninth Circuit

Decided: March 22, 2016

Citation: 577 U.S. __, 136 S.Ct. 1061, 4 Adm. R. 2 (2016).

ROBERTS, C.J., delivered the opinion of the Court.

[—1—] ROBERTS, C.J.:

For almost 40 years, John Sturgeon has hunted moose along the Nation River in Alaska. Because parts of the river are shallow and difficult to navigate, Sturgeon travels by hovercraft, an amphibious vehicle capable of gliding over land and water. To reach his preferred hunting grounds, Sturgeon must pilot his hovercraft over a stretch of the Nation River that flows through the Yukon-Charley Rivers National Preserve, a 1.7 million acre federal preservation area managed by the National Park Service. 16 U. S. C. §410hh(10).

Alaska law permits the use of hovercraft. National Park Service regulations do not. See 36 CFR §2.17(e) (2015). After Park Service rangers informed Sturgeon that he was prohibited from using his hovercraft within the boundaries of the preserve, Sturgeon filed suit, seeking declaratory and injunctive relief. He argues that the Nation River is owned by the State, and that the Alaska National Interest [—2—] Lands Conservation Act (ANILCA) prohibits the Park Service from enforcing its regulations on state-owned land in Alaska. The Park Service disagrees, contending that it has authority to regulate waters flowing through federally managed preservation areas. The District Court and the Court of Appeals ruled in favor of the Park Service. We granted certiorari.

I

In 1867, Secretary of State William Seward, serving under President Andrew Johnson, negotiated a treaty to purchase Alaska from Russia for $7.2 million. Treaty Concerning the Cession of the Russian Possessions in North America, Mar. 30, 1867, 15 Stat. 539. In a single stroke, the United States gained 365 million acres of land—an area more than twice the size of Texas. Despite the bargain price of two cents an acre, however, the purchase was mocked by contemporaries as "Seward's Folly" and President Johnson's "Polar Bear Garden." See C. Naske & H. Slotnick, Alaska: A History 92–94 (2011) (Naske & Slotnick); S. Rep. No. 1163, 85th Cong., 1st Sess., 2 (1957).

The monikers didn't stick. In 1898, the "Three Lucky Swedes"—Jafet Lindeberg, Eric Lindblom, and Jon Brynteson—struck gold in Nome, Alaska. As word of their discovery spread, thousands traveled to Alaska to try their hand at mining. Once the gold rush subsided, settlers turned to other types of mining, fishing, and trapping, fueling an emerging export economy. See Naske & Slotnick 128–129, 155, 249–251; D. Wharton, The Alaska Gold Rush 186–187 (1972).

Despite newfound recognition of Alaska's economic potential, however, it was not until the 1950's that Congress seriously considered admitting Alaska as a State. By that time, it was clear that Alaska was strategically important both in the Pacific and Arctic, and that the [—3—] Territory was rich in natural resources, including oil. Moreover, the people of Alaska favored statehood. See Naske & Slotnick 201, 224–235. But there was a problem: Out of the 365 million acres of land in Alaska, 98 percent were owned by the Federal Government. As a result, absent a land grant from the Federal Government to the State, there would be little land available to drive private economic activity and contribute to the state tax base. See S. Rep. No. 1163, at 2, 12 ("The expenses of the State of Alaska will be comparatively high, partially due to the vast land areas within the State; but the State would be able to realize revenues from only 2 percent of this vast area unless some provision were made to modify the present land-ownership conditions").

A solution was struck. The 1958 Alaska Statehood Act permitted Alaska to select 103 million acres of "vacant, unappropriated, and unreserved" federal land—just over a quarter of all land in Alaska—for state ownership. §§6(a)–(b), 72 Stat. 340. That land grant included "mineral deposits," which were "subject to lease by the State as the State legislature may direct." §6(i), *id.*, at 342. Upon statehood, Alaska also gained "title to and ownership of the lands beneath navigable waters" within the State, in addition to "the natural resources within such lands and waters," including "the right and power to manage, administer, lease, develop, and use the said lands and natural resources." §3(a), 67 Stat. 30, 43 U. S. C. §1311(a); §6(m), 72 Stat. 343. With over 100 million acres of land now available to the new State, Alaska could begin to fulfill its state policy "to encourage the settlement of its land and the development of its resources by making them available for maximum use consistent with the public interest." Alaska Const., Art. VIII, §1 (2014).

The Statehood Act did not, however, determine the rights of the Alaska Natives, who asserted aboriginal title to much of the same land now claimed by the State. [—4—] Naske & Slotnick 287–289. To resolve the dispute, Congress in 1971 passed the Alaska Native Claims Settlement Act (ANCSA), which extinguished aboriginal land claims in Alaska. 85 Stat. 688, as amended, 43 U. S. C. §1601 *et seq.* In exchange, Congress provided for a $960 million settlement and permitted corporations organized by groups of Alaska Natives to select 40 million acres of federal land to manage within the State. §§1605, 1610–1615; Naske & Slotnick 296–297. Congress sought to implement the settlement "rapidly, with certainty, in conformity with the real economic and social needs" of Alaska Natives. §1601(b).

In addition to settling the claims of the Alaska Natives, ANCSA directed the Secretary of the Interior to select up to 80 million acres of unreserved federal land in Alaska for addition to the National Park,

Forest, Wildlife Refuge, and Wild and Scenic Rivers Systems, subject to congressional approval. §1616(d)(2). When Congress failed to approve the Secretary's selections, however, President Carter unilaterally designated 56 million acres of federal land in Alaska as national monuments. See Presidential Proclamation Nos. 4611–4627, 3 CFR 69–104 (1978 Comp.).

President Carter's actions were unpopular among many Alaskans, who were concerned that the new monuments would be subject to restrictive federal regulations. Protesters demonstrated in Fairbanks, and more than 2,500 Alaskans participated in the "Great Denali-McKinley Trespass." The goal of the trespass was to break over 25 Park Service rules in a two-day period—including by camping, hunting, snowmobiling, setting campfires, shooting guns, and unleashing dogs. During the event, a "rider on horseback, acting the part of Paul Revere, galloped through the crowd yelling, 'The Feds are coming! The Feds are coming!'" N. Y. Times, Jan. 15, 1979, p. A8; Anchorage Daily News, Jan. 15, 1979, pp. 1–2.

Congress once again stepped in to settle the controversy, [—5—] passing the Alaska National Interest Lands Conservation Act. 94 Stat. 2371, 16 U. S. C. §3101 *et seq.* ANILCA had two stated goals: First, to provide "sufficient protection for the national interest in the scenic, natural, cultural and environmental values on the public lands in Alaska." §3101(d). And second, to provide "adequate opportunity for satisfaction of the economic and social needs of the State of Alaska and its people." *Ibid.*

ANILCA set aside 104 million acres of land in Alaska for preservation purposes, in the process creating ten new national parks, preserves, and monuments—including the Yukon-Charley Rivers National Preserve— and tripling the number of acres set aside in the United States for federal wilderness preservation. See §410hh; Naske & Slotnick 315–316. At the same time, ANILCA specified that the Park Service could not prohibit on those lands certain activities of particular importance to Alaskans. See, *e.g.*, §3170(a)

(Secretary must permit reasonable use of vehicles "for travel to and from villages and homesites"); §3201 (Secretary must permit "the taking of fish and wildlife for sport purposes and subsistence uses" within National Preserves in Alaska, subject to regulation and certain exceptions). President Carter's earlier land designations were rescinded. See §3209(a).

Under ANILCA, federal preservation lands in Alaska were placed into "conservation system units," which were defined to include "any unit in Alaska of the National Park System, National Wildlife Refuge System, National Wild and Scenic Rivers Systems, National Trails System, National Wilderness Preservation System, or a National Forest Monument." §3102(4). Congress drew the boundaries of those units to "follow hydrographic divides or embrace other topographic or natural features," however, rather than to map the Federal Government's landholdings. §3103(b). As a consequence, in addition to federal land, over 18 million acres of state, Native Corporation, [—6—] and private land ended up inside the boundaries of conservation system units. See Brief for Petitioner 6.

This brings us back to Sturgeon and his hovercraft.

II

A

One fall day in 2007, Sturgeon was piloting his hovercraft on the Nation River, which rises in the Ogilvie Mountains in Canada and joins the Yukon River within the boundaries of the Yukon-Charley Rivers National Preserve conservation system unit (Yukon-Charley). Sturgeon was headed to a hunting ground upstream from the preserve, just shy of the Canadian border. To reach that hunting ground, dubbed "moose meadows," Sturgeon had to travel on a portion of the river that flows through the preserve.

About two miles into his trip on the Nation River, Sturgeon stopped on a gravel bar to repair the steering cable of his hovercraft. As he was performing the repairs, Sturgeon was approached by three Park Service rangers. The rangers informed him that hovercraft were prohibited under Park Service regulations, and that he was committing a crime by operating his hovercraft within the boundaries of the Yukon-Charley. Despite Sturgeon's protests that Park Service regulations did not apply because the river was owned by the State of Alaska, the rangers ordered Sturgeon to remove his hovercraft from the preserve. Sturgeon complied, heading home without a moose.

Sturgeon now fears that he will be criminally prosecuted if he returns to hunt along the Nation River in his hovercraft. To avoid prosecution, Sturgeon sued the Park Service and several federal officials in the United States District Court for the District of Alaska. He seeks declaratory and injunctive relief permitting him to operate his hovercraft within the boundaries of the Yukon-Charley. Alaska intervened in support of Sturgeon, and the Park [—7—] Service opposed the suit.

The District Court granted summary judgment to the Park Service. *Sturgeon* v. *Masica*, 2013 WL 5888230 (Oct. 30, 2013). The Court of Appeals for the Ninth Circuit affirmed in pertinent part. *Sturgeon* v. *Masica*, 768 F. 3d 1066, 2 Adm. R. 503 (2014).

We granted certiorari. 576 U. S. ___ (2015).

B

The Secretary of the Interior has authority to "prescribe regulations" concerning "boating and other activities on or relating to water located within System units, including water subject to the jurisdiction of the United States." 54 U. S. C. §100751(b) (2012 ed., Supp. II). "System units" are in turn defined as "any area of land and water administered by the Secretary, acting through the Director [of the Park Service], for park, monument, historic, parkway, recreational, or other purposes." §§100102, 100501.

The Park Service's hovercraft regulation was adopted pursuant to Section 100751(b). The hovercraft ban applies not only within "[t]he boundaries of federally owned lands and waters administered by the National Park Service," but also to "[w]aters subject to the jurisdiction of the United States located within the boundaries of the National Park System, including navigable waters . . . without regard to the ownership of submerged lands." 36 CFR §1.2(a). The hovercraft ban is not limited to Alaska, but instead has effect in federally managed preservation areas across the country.

Section 103(c) of ANILCA, in contrast, addresses the scope of the Park Service's authority over lands within the boundaries of conservation system units in Alaska. The first sentence of Section 103(c) specifies the property included as a portion of those units. It states: "Only those lands within the boundaries of any conservation system unit which are public lands (as such term is defined in this [—8—] Act) shall be deemed to be included as a portion of such unit." 16 U. S. C. §3103(c). ANILCA defines the word "land" to include "lands, waters, and interests therein," and the term "public lands" to include "lands the title to which is in the United States after December 2, 1980," with certain exceptions. §3102. In sum, only "lands, waters, and interests therein" to which the United States has "title" are considered "public" land "included as a portion" of the conservation system units in Alaska.

The second sentence of Section 103(c) concerns the Park Service's authority to regulate "non-public" lands in Alaska, which include state, Native Corporation, and private property. It provides: "No lands which, before, on, or after December 2, 1980, are conveyed to the State, to any Native Corporation, or to any private party shall be subject to the regulations applicable solely to public lands within such units." §3103(c).

The third sentence of Section 103(c) explains how new lands become part of conservation system units: "If the State, a Native Corporation, or other owner desires to convey any such lands, the Secretary may acquire such lands in accordance with applicable law (including this Act), and any

such lands shall become part of the unit, and be administered accordingly." *Ibid.*

C

The parties dispute whether Section 103(c) of ANILCA created an Alaska-specific exception to the Park Service's general authority over boating and related activities in federally managed preservation areas. Sturgeon, the Park Service, and the Ninth Circuit each adopt a different reading of Section 103(c), reaching different conclusions about the scope of the Park Service's powers.

Sturgeon, joined by the State, understands Section 103(c) to stand for a simple proposition: The Park Service is prohibited from regulating "non-public" land in Alaska [—9—] as if that land were owned by the Federal Government. He contends that his reading is consistent with the history of federal land management in Alaska, beginning with the Alaska Statehood Act and culminating in ANILCA.

Sturgeon's argument proceeds in two steps. First, he asserts that the Nation River is not "public land" for purposes of ANILCA and is therefore not part of the Yukon-Charley. As discussed, ANILCA defines "public lands" as lands to which the United States has "title." 16 U. S. C. §3102. And Section 103(c) provides that "[o]nly those lands within the boundaries of any conservation system unit which are public lands (as such term is defined in this Act) shall be deemed to be included as a portion of such unit." §3103(c).

Sturgeon argues that the Nation River is not "public land" because it is owned by the State and not by the Federal Government. To support his argument, Sturgeon relies on the Alaska Statehood Act, which granted ownership of the submerged lands beneath the navigable waters in Alaska, and the resources within those waters, to the State. See §6(m), 72 Stat. 343; 43 U. S. C. §1311(a). He also cites this Court's decision in *United States* v. *California*, 436 U. S. 32 (1978), which stated that "the Submerged Lands Act transferred title to and ownership of the submerged lands and waters" to the States. *Id.*, at 40 (internal quotation marks omitted). Because the State and not the Federal Government owns the Nation River, Sturgeon urges, it is not "public" land under ANILCA and is therefore not part of the Yukon-Charley.

Second, Sturgeon asserts that because the Nation River is not part of the Yukon-Charley, the Park Service lacks authority to regulate it. His argument rests on the second sentence of Section 103(c), which states that "[n]o lands which, before, on, or after December 2, 1980, are conveyed to the State, to any Native Corporation, or to any private party shall be subject to the regulations applicable solely [—10—] to public lands within such units." 16 U. S. C. §3103(c).

Sturgeon argues that the phrase "regulations applicable solely to public lands within such units" refers to those regulations that apply "solely" by virtue of the Park Service's "authority to manage national parks." Brief for Petitioner 18, 26–27. The word "solely," Sturgeon contends, simply ensures that "non-public" lands within the boundaries of those units remain subject to laws generally "applicable to both public and private lands (such as the Clean Air Act and Clean Water Act)." Id., at 19. Because the hovercraft regulation was adopted pursuant to the Park Service's authority over federally managed preservation areas, and is not a law of general applicability like the Clean Air Act or the Clean Water Act, Sturgeon concludes that Section 103(c) bars enforcement of the regulation.

The Park Service, in contrast, reads Section 103(c) more narrowly. In its brief in this Court, the Park Service, while defending the reasoning of the Ninth Circuit, relies primarily on very different arguments. The agency stresses that it has longstanding authority to regulate waters within federally managed preservation areas, and that Section 103(c) does not take any of that authority away. In reaching its conclusion, the Park Service disagrees with Sturgeon at each step.

First, the Park Service contends that the Nation River is part of the Yukon-Charley. To support that contention, the agency cites ANILCA's definition of "public lands," which— as noted—includes "lands, waters, and interests therein" to which the United States has "title." 16 U. S. C. §3102. The Park Service argues that the United States has "title" to an "interest" in the water within the boundaries of the Yukon-Charley under the reserved water rights doctrine.

The reserved water rights doctrine specifies that "when the Federal Government withdraws its land from the public domain and reserves it for a federal purpose, the [—11—] Government, by implication, reserves appurtenant water then unappropriated to the extent needed to accomplish the purpose of the reservation." Cappaert v. United States, 426 U. S. 128, 138 (1976). By creating the Yukon-Charley, the Park Service urges, the Federal Government reserved the water within the boundaries of the conservation system unit to achieve the Government's conservation goals. As a result, the Federal Government has "title" to an "interest" in the Nation River, making it "public" land subject to Park Service regulations.

Second, the Park Service contends that even if the Nation River is not "public" land, the agency still has authority to regulate it. According to the Park Service, the second sentence of Section 103(c) imposes only a limited restriction on the agency's power, prohibiting it from enforcing on "non-public" lands only those regulations that explicitly apply "solely to public lands." The hovercraft regulation applies both within "[t]he boundaries of federally owned lands and waters administered by the National Park Service" and to "[w]aters subject to the jurisdiction of the United States located within the boundaries of the National Park System, including navigable waters . . . without regard to the ownership of submerged lands." 36 CFR §1.2(a). Accordingly, the Park Service asserts, the hovercraft regulation does not apply "solely to public lands," and Section 103(c) therefore does not prevent enforcement of the regulation. See Brief for Respondents 56–58.

The Ninth Circuit, for its part, adopted a reading of Section 103(c) different from the primary argument advanced by the Park Service in this Court. The Court of Appeals did not reach the question whether the Nation River counts as "public" land for purposes of ANILCA. Instead, it held that the phrase "regulations applicable solely to public lands within such units" distinguishes between Park Service regulations that apply solely to [—12—] "public" lands *in Alaska,* and Park Service regulations that apply to federally managed preservation areas across the country. In the Ninth Circuit's view, the Park Service may enforce nationally applicable regulations on both "public" and "non-public" property within the boundaries of conservation system units in Alaska, because such regulations do not apply "solely to public lands within such units." The Park Service may not, however, apply Alaska-specific regulations to "non-public" lands within the boundaries of those units.

According to the Ninth Circuit, because the hovercraft regulation "applies to all federal-owned lands and waters administered by [the Park Service] nationwide, as well as all navigable waters lying within national parks," the hovercraft ban does not apply "solely" within conservation system units in Alaska. 768 F. 3d, at 1077, 2 Adm. R. at 510. The Ninth Circuit concluded that the Park Service therefore has authority to enforce its hovercraft regulation on the Nation River. *Id.,* at 1078, 2 Adm. R. at 510. The Ninth Circuit's holding is subject to some interpretation, but Sturgeon, the State, the Alaska Native Corporations, and the Park Service (at least at times) concur in our understanding of the decision below. See Brief for Petitioner 25; Brief for State of Alaska as *Amicus Curiae* 23; Brief for Arctic Slope Regional Corporation et al. as *Amici Curiae* 12–13; Brief for Doyon, Ltd., et al. as *Amici Curiae* 31–32; Brief for Respondents 20; Tr. of Oral Arg. 61; 80 Fed. Reg. 65573 (2015).

III

We reject the interpretation of Section 103(c) adopted by the Ninth Circuit. The court's reading of the phrase "regulations applicable solely to public lands within such units" may be plausible in the abstract, but it is ultimately inconsistent with both the text and context of the statute as a whole. Statutory language "cannot be construed in a vacuum. It is a fundamental canon of statutory construc- [—13—] tion that the words of a statute must be read in their context and with a view to their place in the overall statutory scheme." *Roberts* v. *Sea-Land Services, Inc.,* 566 U. S. ___, ___ (2012) (slip op., at 6) (internal quotation marks omitted).

Under the reading of the statute adopted below, the Park Service may apply nationally applicable regulations to "non-public" lands within the boundaries of conservation system units in Alaska, but it may not apply Alaska-specific regulations to those lands. That is a surprising conclusion. ANILCA repeatedly recognizes that Alaska is different—from its "unrivaled scenic and geological values," to the "unique" situation of its "rural residents dependent on subsistence uses," to "the need for development and use of Arctic resources with appropriate recognition and consideration given to the unique nature of the Arctic environment." 16 U. S. C. §§3101(b), 3111(2), 3147(b)(5).

ANILCA itself accordingly carves out numerous Alaska-specific exceptions to the Park Service's general authority over federally managed preservation areas. For example, ANILCA requires the Secretary of the Interior to permit "the exercise of valid commercial fishing rights or privileges" within the National Wildlife Refuge System in Alaska, including the use of "campsites, cabins, motorized vehicles, and aircraft landings directly incident to the exercise of such rights or privileges," with certain exceptions. 94 Stat. 2393. ANILCA also requires the Secretary to "permit on the public lands appropriate use for subsistence purposes of snowmobiles, motorboats, and other means of surface transportation traditionally employed for such purposes by local residents, subject to reasonable regulation." 16 U. S. C. §3121(b). And it provides that National Preserves "in Alaska shall be administered and managed as a unit of the National Park System in the same manner as a national park *except* as otherwise provided in this Act [—14—] and *except* that the taking of fish and wildlife for sport purposes and subsistence uses, and trapping shall be allowed" pursuant to applicable law. §3201 (emphasis added).

Many similar examples are woven throughout ANILCA. See, *e.g.*, 94 Stat. 2393 (Secretary must administer wildlife refuge "so as to not impede the passage of navigation and access by boat on the Yukon and Kuskokwim Rivers," subject to reasonable regulation); *id.*, at 2388 (Secretary must allow reindeer grazing uses in certain areas, including construction of necessary facilities); 16 U. S. C. §3203(a) (Alaska-specific rules for wilderness management apply "in recognition of the unique conditions in Alaska"); §3170(a) (Secretary must permit reasonable use of snow-machines, motorboats, and airplanes within conservation system units "for travel to and from villages and homesites").

All those Alaska-specific provisions reflect the simple truth that Alaska is often the exception, not the rule. Yet the reading below would prevent the Park Service from recognizing Alaska's unique conditions. Under that reading, the Park Service could regulate "non-public" lands in Alaska only through rules applicable *outside* Alaska as well. Thus, for example, if the Park Service elected to allow hovercraft during hunting season in Alaska—in a departure from its nationwide rule—the more relaxed regulation would apply only to the "public" land within the boundaries of the unit. Hovercraft would still be banned from the "non-public" land, even during hunting season. Whatever the reach of the Park Service's authority under ANILCA, we cannot conclude that Section 103(c) adopted such a topsy-turvy approach.

Moreover, it is clear that Section 103(c) draws a distinction between "public" and "non-public" lands within the boundaries of conservation system units in Alaska. See §3103(c) ("Only those lands within the boundaries of any [—15—] conservation system unit which are public lands . . . shall be deemed to be included as a portion of such unit"); *ibid.* (No lands "conveyed to the State, to any Native Corporation, or to any private party shall be subject to the regulations

applicable solely to public lands within such units"). And yet, according to the court below, if the Park Service wanted to differentiate between that "public" and "nonpublic" land in an Alaska-specific way, it would have to regulate the "non-public" land pursuant to rules applicable outside Alaska, and the "public" land pursuant to Alaska-specific provisions. Assuming the Park Service has authority over "non-public" land in Alaska (an issue we do not decide), that strikes us as an implausible reading of the statute.

Looking at ANILCA both as a whole and with respect to Section 103(c), the Act contemplates the possibility that all the land within the boundaries of conservation system units in Alaska may be treated differently from federally managed preservation areas across the country, and that "non-public" lands within the boundaries of those units may be treated differently from "public" lands within the unit. Under the Ninth Circuit's reading of Section 103(c), however, the former is not an option, and the latter would require contorted and counterintuitive measures.

We therefore reject the interpretation of Section 103(c) adopted by the court below. That reading of the statute was the sole basis for the disposition of this case by the Court of Appeals. We accordingly vacate the judgment of that court and remand for further proceedings.

We do not reach the remainder of the parties' arguments. In particular, we do not decide whether the Nation River qualifies as "public land" for purposes of ANILCA. Sturgeon claims that it does not; the Park Service that it does. The parties' arguments in this respect touch on vital issues of state sovereignty, on the one hand, and federal authority, on the other. We find that in this case those [—16—] issues should be addressed by the lower courts in the first instance.

Given this determination, we also do not decide whether the Park Service has authority under Section 100751(b) to regulate Sturgeon's activities on the Nation River, even if the river is not "public" land, or whether—as Sturgeon argues—any such authority is limited by ANILCA. Finally, we do not consider the Park Service's alternative argument that it has authority under ANILCA over both "public" and "non-public" lands within the boundaries of conservation system units in Alaska, to the extent a regulation is written to apply specifically to both types of land. We leave those arguments to the lower courts for consideration as necessary.

The judgment of the Court of Appeals for the Ninth Circuit is vacated, and the case is remanded for further proceedings consistent with this opinion.

It is so ordered.

This page intentionally left blank

United States Court of Appeals for the First Circuit

United States Court of Appeals
for the First Circuit

No. 14-1733

UNITED STATES
VS.
DÍAZ-DONCEL

Appeal from the United States District Court for the
District of Puerto Rico

Decided: January 27, 2016

Citation: 811 F.3d 517, 4 Adm. R. 12 (1st Cir. 2016).

Before **TORRUELLA**, **HAWKINS,** * and **BARRON**,
Circuit Judges.

* Of the Ninth Circuit, sitting by designation.

[—2—] **BARRON**, Circuit Judge:

This appeal follows defendant Ferrison Díaz-Doncel's straight plea of guilty to all three counts set forth in a criminal indictment. The first two counts were for conspiracy to possess, and aiding and abetting the possession of, cocaine on a vessel subject to the jurisdiction of the United States, in violation of the Maritime Drug Law Enforcement Act ("MDLEA"). 46 U.S.C. §§ 70501 et seq.; 18 U.S.C. § 2. The third count was for aiding and abetting a failure to heave. 18 U.S.C. §§ 2237, 2.[1] On appeal, Díaz argues that Congress exceeded the scope of its Article I powers in enacting the MDLEA and that his MDLEA convictions must therefore be reversed. But precedent makes clear that Díaz waived his right to bring this challenge when he entered his guilty plea.

The undisputed facts can be briefly stated. On June 28, 2013, a United States Coast Guard ("USCG") cutter ordered a cigarette boat in the Caribbean Sea to heave to. Following a chase, a Dutch war ship with USCG personnel on-board interdicted the cigarette boat. The USCG personnel then boarded the cigarette boat, arrested the crew, including Díaz, and seized the vessel.

Following the arrest, Díaz was indicted by a federal grand jury on three counts. He then filed a late motion to dismiss [—3—] the indictment. The motion argued that Congress had exceeded the scope of its powers under Article I of the United States Constitution in enacting the MDLEA. The District Court denied the motion as untimely. The District Court ruled that no exception could be made for Díaz's late filing, because his challenge was not a challenge to the Court's subject matter jurisdiction.

On the second day of the trial, Díaz entered a straight plea of guilty to all three counts. The District Court then sentenced Díaz to 168 months of imprisonment on each of the MDLEA counts, and to 60 months of imprisonment for failing to heave, to be served concurrently. On appeal, Díaz challenges only his MDLEA convictions, which he contends must be reversed because Congress exceeded the scope of its Article I powers in enacting that statute.

"Ordinarily a guilty plea, entered unconditionally—that is, without reserving an issue or issues for appeal—establishes guilt and forfeits all objections and defenses." *United States v. González*, 311 F.3d 440, 442 (1st Cir. 2002) (citing *United States v. Cordero*, 42 F.3d 697, 699 (1st Cir. 1994)). There are, however, "a few exceptions to this principle." *Id.* And the one that Díaz relies on "applies where the claim on appeal is that the district court lacked subject matter jurisdiction over the case." *Id.*[2] [—4—]

---

[1] 18 U.S.C. § 2237 "makes it unlawful for an operator of 'a vessel subject to the jurisdiction of the United States, to knowingly fail to obey' a federal law enforcement officer's order 'to heave to that vessel' (in layman's terms, failing to slow down or stop)." *United States v. $8,440,190.00 in U.S. Currency*, 719 F.3d 49, 53, 1 Adm. R. 18, 19 (1st Cir. 2013).

[2] Another exception to the rule that a guilty plea waives all objections is derived from the Supreme Court's decisions in [—4—] *Blackledge v. Perry*, 417 U.S. 21 (1974), and *Menna v. New York*, 423 U.S. 61 (1975). Those cases involved, respectively, "a due process challenge arising from repetitive, vindictive prosecution" and a double jeopardy challenge. *United States v. Miranda*, 780 F.3d 1185, 1190, 3 Adm. R. 676, 679 (D.C. Cir. 2015). Diaz makes no argument that his case falls into the *Blackledge-Menna* exception. And we note

Our precedent makes clear, however, that this exception does not apply here. As we have held before, a constitutional challenge to Congress's "jurisdiction" to pass the MDLEA pursuant to its Article I powers is not a challenge to a district court's subject matter jurisdiction over a criminal case brought under the MDLEA. *United States v. Nueci-Peña*, 711 F.3d 191, 197 (1st Cir. 2013); *United States v. Cardales-Luna*, 632 F.3d 731, 737-38 (1st Cir. 2011). And the D.C. Circuit recently agreed in concluding that a guilty plea barred a defendant from asserting an Article I challenge to the MDLEA on appeal. *See United States v. Miranda*, 780 F.3d 1185, 1189-91, 3 Adm. R. 676, 678–80 (D.C. Cir. 2015). Thus, whatever the merits of Díaz's constitutional argument, *see Cardales-Luna*, 632 F.3d at 738-51 (Torruella, J., dissenting) (setting forth the argument that Congress exceeded its Article I powers in enacting the MDLEA), Díaz waived his right to assert it when he pled guilty. The convictions are therefore ***affirmed***.

–Dissenting Opinion Follows–

(Reporter's Note: Dissenting opinion follows on p. 14).

---

that the D.C. Circuit recently held that a challenge such as Diaz's does not fit within the *Blackledge-Menna* exception. *Id.*

[—5—] **TORRUELLA,** Circuit Judge, dissenting:

I disagree that the issue of the challenge to Díaz's conviction under the MDLEA has been waived. As I stated in *United States v. Cardales-Luna*, 632 F.3d 731, 738-51 (1st Cir. 2011) (Torruella, J., dissenting), and *United States v. González*, 311 F.3d 440, 444-450 (1st Cir. 2002) (Torruella, J., concurring), this is a constitutional challenge to the government's authority under the MDLEA, which implicates the subject matter jurisdiction of this Court, and, as a result, this issue can be raised by Díaz at any point in the proceeding. His right to assert this argument is not waived by entering an unconditional guilty plea. *See Cardales-Luna*, 632 F.3d at 751; *González*, 311 F.3d at 444. I respectfully dissent for all of the reasons stated in those cases.

United States Court of Appeals
for the First Circuit

No. 13-1496

CASIANO-JIMÉNEZ
vs.
UNITED STATES

Appeal from the United States District Court for the
District of Puerto Rico

Decided: March 29, 2016

Citation: 817 F.3d 816, 4 Adm. R. 15 (1st Cir. 2016).

Before **HOWARD,** Chief Judge, **TORRUELLA,** and
SELYA, Circuit Judges.

[—2—] SELYA, Circuit Judge:

A criminal defendant's right to testify in his own behalf—or, conversely, not to testify—is a critically important right. Given the salience of the right, a defendant is entitled to be fully briefed so that he may make an informed choice. In this case, the defendant did not receive his due. Consequently, the district court erred in denying the defendant's petition for post-conviction relief under 28 U.S.C. § 2255.

I. BACKGROUND

We sketch the factual and procedural terrain in broad strokes. The reader who thirsts for more exegetic details may slake that thirst by consulting our opinion rejecting the petitioner's direct appeal. See *United States v. Angulo-Hernández*, 565 F.3d 2, 4–7 (1st Cir. 2009).

In 2009, petitioner-appellant José Luis Casiano-Jiménez was convicted of conspiring to smuggle narcotics by ship into the United States. At trial, the petitioner's defense was based on lack of knowledge: he maintained that he was unaware that any contraband was clandestine aboard the ship. None of the seven defendants (including the petitioner) took the stand to testify. Rather, they presented a joint defense through a single expert who examined the vessel and opined that—based on the hidden location of the contraband—it

was possible that none of the crew members were aware that drugs were on board. [—3—]

The jury found the captain and the engineer, along with the petitioner (whom the government characterized as the ship's first officer) and one other crew member, guilty of conspiring to possess controlled substances with intent to distribute and aiding and abetting.[1] See 18 U.S.C. § 2(a); 46 U.S.C. §§ 70503(a)(1), 70506(b). The jury acquitted three other crew members (all ordinary seamen). The district court proceeded to sentence the convicted defendants (including the petitioner) to lengthy prison terms.

On direct review, the convicted defendants challenged the jury verdicts on various grounds, including the alleged insufficiency of the evidence. We affirmed, though one member of the panel dissented on the basis that the evidence, though sufficient to support the verdicts against the captain and the engineer, did not suffice to show that the other two convicted defendants (including the petitioner) were aware of any drugs being on board. See *Angulo-Hernández*, 565 F.3d at 13–18 (Torruella, J., concurring in part and dissenting in part). The petitioner unsuccessfully sought both rehearing en banc and a writ of certiorari, and his conviction and sentence became final. [—4—]

The petitioner filed a timeous section 2255 petition for post-conviction relief that raised, inter alia, a claim that his trial counsel was ineffective for failing to advise him of his right to testify in his own behalf.[2] The district court denied the petition and refused to grant a certificate of appealability (COA). See 28 U.S.C. § 2253(c)(2). This court granted a COA, however, limited to the plaint that the petitioner was entitled to an evidentiary hearing on his ineffective assistance of counsel

---

[1] The jury also found this group of defendants guilty of aiding and abetting the possession of a machine gun. See 18 U.S.C. §§ 2(a), 924(c)(1)(B)(ii). The district court, however, wiped out this portion of the jury verdict, granting judgments of acquittal across the board. See Fed. R. Crim. P. 29(c).

[2] The petitioner also put forth other grounds for section 2255 relief, but those grounds have been abandoned and need not concern us.

claim. By unpublished order, we then remanded the case to the district court for such an evidentiary hearing. *See Casiano-Jiménez v. United States*, No. 11-2049 (1st Cir. Nov. 30, 2012) (unpublished order).

The district court held the evidentiary hearing in March of 2013. The petitioner and his trial counsel, Frank Inserni, both testified. They agreed that Inserni had never explained to the petitioner either that he had a right to testify in his own behalf or that the decision to do so belonged exclusively to him. Inserni added that the lawyers for all the defendants collectively decided that "it would be detrimental" to have any of the defendants testify. They chose instead to retain a single expert to present a "lack of knowledge" defense on behalf of all the [—5—] defendants. The lawyers proceeded to communicate this strategy to the defendants at a group meeting.

The petitioner's testimony fit seamlessly with Inserni's testimony. The petitioner acknowledged that he had spoken to Inserni about testifying, but confirmed that Inserni had not advised him of his right to testify. He likewise corroborated Inserni's version of what was said at the group meeting.

In a three-page unpublished order, the district court again rejected the section 2255 petition. It also declined—as it had before—to issue a COA. The petitioner nevertheless filed a notice of appeal. He then requested and received a COA from this court. Briefing and oral argument followed,[3] and we took the matter under advisement.

II. ANALYSIS

Our analysis begins with an overview of the legal landscape and then proceeds to the merits of the petitioner's appeal.

---

[3] Shortly before oral argument in this court, the government informed us that the petitioner had completed his prison term and had been returned to Colombia. He remains subject, however, to a 5-year term of supervised release, and the government concedes that his appeal is not moot.

A. *The Legal Landscape.*

"[T]he appropriate vehicle for claims that the defendant's right to testify was violated by defense counsel is a [—6—] claim of ineffective assistance of counsel." *United States v. Teague*, 953 F.2d 1525, 1534 (11th Cir. 1992). Such a claim may properly be raised by a petition for post-conviction relief under 28 U.S.C. § 2255. *See Owens v. United States*, 483 F.3d 48, 56 (1st Cir. 2007).

Prevailing on an ineffective-assistance claim necessitates two showings: the defendant "must demonstrate that counsel's performance fell below an objective threshold of reasonable care and that this deficient performance prejudiced him." *United States v. Caramadre*, 807 F.3d 359, 371 (1st Cir. 2015); *see Strickland v. Washington*, 466 U.S. 668, 687 (1984). The prejudice prong requires a defendant to establish that, but for counsel's deficient performance, there is a reasonable probability that the outcome of the proceeding would have been different. *See Turner v. United States*, 699 F.3d 578, 584 (1st Cir. 2012).

In any trial, a defendant's right to testify in his own defense is a "fundamental constitutional right" and is "essential to due process of law in a fair adversary process." *Rock v. Arkansas*, 483 U.S. 44, 51, 53 n.10 (1987) (quoting *Faretta v. California*, 422 U.S. 806, 819 n.15 (1975)). The defendant's lawyer, rather than the trial judge, bears the primary responsibility of informing and advising the defendant of this right, including its strategic ramifications. *See Teague*, 953 [—7—] F.2d at 1533. Similarly, the defendant's lawyer bears the primary responsibility of explaining that the choice of whether or not to testify belongs to the defendant. *See id.* It follows inexorably that "[t]he right to testify may not be waived by counsel acting alone." *Owens*, 483 F.3d at 58 (citing cases). If the defendant is unaware of his right to testify and counsel, without consultation, unilaterally declines to call the defendant as a witness in his own behalf, the defendant's right to make an informed decision has been nullified. *See id.* at 59.

Viewed against this backdrop, it is not surprising that we have held that an attorney's failure to inform a defendant of his right to testify comprises constitutionally deficient performance. *See id.* at 58; *see also Teague*, 953 F.2d at 1534 (explaining that such a failure amounts to an attorney's neglect of a "vital professional responsibility"). In determining whether a lawyer has adequately apprised his client of this fundamental right, no particular formulation is required. *See Owens*, 483 F.3d at 60 n.10. There are no magic words; the inquiry is whether "some sort of conversation" has occurred between the attorney and his client, such that "the client can make a knowing and informed decision" regarding whether to testify in his own defense. *Id.*

B. *The Case at Hand.*

We now move from the general to the specific. Where, as here, a petitioner appeals the denial of post-conviction relief [—8—] following an evidentiary hearing, we review the district court's findings of fact for clear error. *See Owens*, 483 F.3d at 57. Under this rubric, credibility determinations are entitled to equal or greater deference. *See Awon v. United States*, 308 F.3d 133, 141 (1st Cir. 2002); *Keller v. United States*, 38 F.3d 16, 25 (1st Cir. 1994). Questions of law, however, engender de novo review. *See Owens*, 483 F.3d at 57.

We start with an appraisal of trial counsel's performance. At the evidentiary hearing, Inserni was asked pointblank whether he had advised the petitioner of his right to testify. The attorney admitted unequivocally that he had not informed the petitioner about this right. Rather, a group meeting transpired at which counsel for all of the defendants "explained to them . . . that it would not be advisable for any of them to take the stand" and that the attorneys had collectively agreed that a single expert would present the rudiments of a "lack of knowledge" defense on behalf of all the defendants. The petitioner's testimony on these points echoed that of his trial counsel.

In a terse rescript, the district court concluded that the petitioner's claim was "inherently incredible." The court made no explicit credibility findings—yet it refused to credit Inserni's and the petitioner's statements that the petitioner had never been apprised of his right to testify. Focusing instead on [—9—] Inserni's description of the joint meeting among the defendants and their counsel, the court held that the petitioner had been sufficiently notified of his fundamental constitutional right to testify.

Although we recognize that the standard of review is deferential, *see Awon*, 308 F.3d at 141, the foundation upon which the district court's holding rests is as insubstantial as a house built upon the shifting sands. The holding assumes that the discussion at the group meeting served as a sufficient surrogate both for the explanation of the right to testify that Inserni owed to the petitioner and for the petitioner's informed decision about whether to testify in his own defense. For aught that appears, those assumptions are plucked out of thin air: their frailty is made readily apparent by a careful examination of the testimony about the joint meeting.

Inserni testified that the assembled defense lawyers told the assembled defendants that the lawyers "thought an expert would be the best way . . . to testify on all their behalf" and explained to them that "it was a consensus . . . it would not be advisable for any of [the defendants] to take the stand." But that consensus was a consensus only among the lawyers. During the meeting, no one told the petitioner, in words or substance, that he had a right to testify; and no one bothered to obtain his informed consent to remaining silent. Plainly, then, the testimony [—10—] about the meeting cannot support the district court's finding that there was a collective and informed decision, reached by all the defendants (including the petitioner), that none of them would testify. The most that can be said is that the defense lawyers unilaterally decided that none of the defendants would testify and presented that decision to the defendants as a fait accompli.

We have admonished that "[t]he right to testify may not be waived by counsel acting alone." *Owens*, 483 F.3d at 58. There must be a focused discussion between lawyer and client, and that discussion must—at a bare minimum—enable the defendant to make an informed decision about whether to take the stand. *See id.* at 60 n.10. Here, there is simply no evidence that Inserni shouldered even this modest burden.

Inserni's failure to discuss the right to testify with the petitioner is especially troubling given the petitioner's profile. After all, the petitioner was an alien who had limited proficiency in English and no experience with the American criminal justice system. Seen in this light, trial counsel's omission verged on the egregious—and there was nothing "inherently incredible" about either the petitioner's or Inserni's testimony at the section 2255 hearing.

The short of it is that the record contains no evidence sufficient to ground a finding either that the petitioner knowingly waived his right to testify or that he was even aware that such a [—11—] right existed. To the contrary, it appears that trial counsel took the bit in his teeth: he decided that the petitioner should not testify and then foisted his decision upon the petitioner without any meaningful dialogue. This usurpation transgressed both the lawyer's professional responsibility to his client and the petitioner's constitutional rights.

The record contains nothing that would suggest a justification for such a gross dereliction of duty. We hold, therefore, that counsel's omission represented constitutionally deficient performance of his duty to his client.

This brings us to the prejudice prong of the ineffective-assistance inquiry. The court below did not address this issue except to state that the petitioner's testimony would have been "the same" as that of the defense expert. We do not agree.

The defense expert testified, based on his experience generally and the concealed placement of the contraband on board the ship,[4] that it was "possible" that none of the defendants knew that the ship contained drugs. Although this testimony aligned with the theme of the defense, it fell far short of what the petitioner, had he testified, could have added. A party's explicit [—12—] disclaimer of knowledge may well have more weight than an expert's theoretical conclusion. *Cf. Rock*, 483 U.S. at 52 (observing that "the most important witness for the defense in many criminal cases is the defendant himself"). That appears to be the case here.

The petitioner's testimony at the evidentiary hearing revealed that he would have been able to tell the jury:

- prior to the voyage, he had never met either the captain or any of the other crew members;

- he had never before set foot on that particular ship;

- he signed on to the voyage only as an "able-bodied seaman";

- he had no knowledge of drugs being brought onto the ship; and

- it was not until he was aboard the ship that (to fill a vacancy) he was pressed into service as "first officer."

Contrary to the district court's avowal, the petitioner's testimony was not "the same" as the expert's testimony, but was materially different (and far more exculpatory). Though the expert testified to the petitioner's hypothetical lack of knowledge, the petitioner would have testified as to what he actually knew. So viewed, the petitioner's testimony could have been a game-changer. *Cf. Owens*, 483 F.3d at 59 (explaining that "[a]

---

[4] The contraband was secreted in a cache below the crew's quarters, covered by multiple layers of plywood and placed underneath a metal hatch. *See Angulo-Hernández*, 565 F.3d at 6. The concealment was so artfully done that, after the vessel was intercepted and seized, it took the Coast Guard almost a week to discover the drugs. *See id.*

defendant's testimony as to non-involvement should not be disregarded lightly"). [—13—]

The bottom line is that a third party's testimony as to what a defendant may have known cannot fairly be equated with the defendant's own first-hand account of what he actually knew. Here, moreover, the petitioner's testimony would have been significant even beyond his direct denial of culpable knowledge. He would have explained away his status as "first officer" of the ship, and made pellucid that he was a stranger to the captain and the crew. These facts would have bolstered the petitioner's claim that he was unaware of the presence of any contraband on the ship.

Given this tableau, prejudice is obvious. The petitioner's conviction depended, in material part, on the government's ability to persuade the jury that he knew the ship was ferrying drugs. *See Angulo-Hernández*, 565 F.3d at 8. The petitioner's testimony would have hit this issue head-on and could very well have turned the tide.

Nor does the record offer any basis for believing that the petitioner, properly informed of his rights, would have made a tactical decision not to take the stand. Nothing in the record militated against the petitioner's testifying in his own defense. He had no criminal history, and Inserni testified that when it was related to him by the petitioner, he found the petitioner's story to be credible. What is more, the petitioner's account was consistent with that of the defense expert and it would not have [—14—] been necessary to alter the joint defense strategy had the petitioner elected to testify.

Last—but far from least—the government's case was thin.[5] The government's proof was almost entirely circumstantial, and three of the petitioner's codefendants—all ordinary seamen—were acquitted. We think that this mixed verdict raises a substantial question as to whether the petitioner's conviction resulted from the government's portrayal of him as the "first officer." The petitioner's explanation of how this status came about may well have had decretory significance.

We conclude, without serious question, that there is a reasonable probability that the petitioner's testimony could have tipped the scales in his favor. *See Owens*, 483 F.3d at 59 (noting that "[a] defendant's testimony could be crucial in any trial"). Had the petitioner been appropriately informed of his right to testify and had he in fact testified and been found credible by the jury, exoneration was a likely prospect.

III. CONCLUSION

We need go no further. Because the record shows with conspicuous clarity both that the petitioner received [—15—] constitutionally ineffective assistance of counsel at his criminal trial and that he was prejudiced as a result, the district court ought to have granted his section 2255 petition. Its failure to do so was reversible error. Consequently, we *reverse* the judgment below and *remand* with instructions to *vacate* the petitioner's conviction and sentence.

Reversed and remanded.

---

[5] Even without the petitioner's testimony, this court divided two-to-one on whether the evidence against the petitioner was sufficient to convict. *See Angulo-Hernández*, 565 F.3d at 14–18 (Torruella, J., concurring in part and dissenting in part). Furthermore, notes sent to the court during jury deliberations indicated strong divisions among the jurors.

United States Court of Appeals
for the First Circuit

No. 15-1234

UNITED STATES

vs.

PEREZ

Appeal from the United States District Court for the
District of Puerto Rico

Decided: April 22, 2016

Citation: 819 F.3d 541, 4 Adm. R. 20 (1st Cir. 2016).

Before **KAYATTA, SELYA,** and **STAHL,** Circuit Judges.

[—2—] **SELYA,** Circuit Judge:

This sentencing appeal embodies four discrete claims of error. Having scrutinized these claims in light of the record as a whole, we affirm the appellant's sentence.

I. BACKGROUND

The critical facts are largely uncontested. Defendant-appellant Englis Pérez, a Dominican national, journeyed to Venezuela in early 2014 to undertake a cocaine-smuggling venture. Shortly after midnight on March 4, 2014, federal authorities intercepted a 30-foot speedboat—operating without lights, powered by two outsized outboard engines, and equipped with 23 extra fuel tanks—that had left port in Venezuela and was approaching the coast of Puerto Rico. The vessel was carrying 38 bales, which contained in the aggregate approximately 1,056 kilograms of cocaine.

Only two persons were aboard the vessel when it was intercepted: the appellant and an individual later identified as Gregorio Rodríguez. A federal grand jury sitting in the District of Puerto Rico returned a six-count indictment against the pair, charging them with conspiracy to import 5 or more kilograms of cocaine into the United States, in violation of 21 U.S.C. §§ 952(a), 960, and 963 (count 1); conspiracy to possess with intent to distribute 5 kilograms or more of cocaine, in violation of 21 U.S.C. §§ 841(a)(1) and 846 (count 2);

aiding and abetting in the possession with intent to distribute 5 kilograms or more of [—3—] cocaine, in violation of 18 U.S.C. § 2 and 21 U.S.C. § 841(a)(1) (count 3); aiding and abetting in the importation of 5 kilograms or more of cocaine, in violation of 18 U.S.C. § 2 and 21 U.S.C. §§ 952 and 960 (count 4); conspiracy to possess with intent to distribute 5 or more kilograms of cocaine on board a vessel subject to the jurisdiction of the United States, in violation of 46 U.S.C. §§ 70502(c)(1)(D), 70503(a)(1), 70504(b)(1) and 70506(a) and (b) (count 5); and aiding and abetting in the possession with intent to distribute 5 kilograms or more of cocaine on board a vessel subject to the jurisdiction of the United States, in violation of 18 U.S.C. § 2 and 46 U.S.C. §§ 70502(c)(1)(D), 70503(a)(1), 70504(b)(1) and 70506(a) (count 6). Although the appellant originally maintained his innocence, he shortly entered a straight guilty plea to all six counts of the indictment.

Following the preparation of a presentence investigation report and some related skirmishing, the district court convened the disposition hearing on January 27, 2015. The November 2014 edition of the sentencing guidelines controlled. *See United States v. Harotunian*, 920 F.2d 1040, 1041-42 (1st Cir. 1990). The court calculated the appellant's guideline sentencing range (GSR) as 135-168 months and imposed a sentence at the bottom of that range: 135 months. This timely appeal ensued. [—4—]

II. ANALYSIS

In this case, the appellant challenges both the procedural underpinnings and the substantive reasonableness of his sentence. Overall, claims of sentencing error are reviewed for abuse of discretion. *See Gall v. United States*, 552 U.S. 38, 51 (2007); *United States v. Martin*, 520 F.3d 87, 92 (1st Cir. 2008). With respect to procedural claims, however, the abuse-of-discretion standard of review is not monolithic. Within it, "we assay the district court's factfinding for clear error and afford de novo consideration to its interpretation and application of the sentencing guidelines." *United States v.*

Flores-Machicote, 706 F.3d 16, 20 (1st Cir. 2013).

Against this backdrop, we turn to the appellant's asseverational array. Because a reviewing court, in the sentencing context, should first address claims of procedural error, *see Martin*, 520 F.3d at 92, we start there.

A. *Mitigating Role.*

The appellant asserts that the district court committed procedural error when it refused to reduce his GSR to compensate for the appellant's role in the offense. This claim was preserved below and, thus, our review is for clear error. *See United States v. Garcia*, 954 F.2d 12, 16 (1st Cir. 1992).

USSG §3B1.2(b) provides for reducing a defendant's base offense level by two levels if the defendant was a minor [—5—] participant in the criminal activity. The appellant argues that he was entitled to the benefit of this adjustment,[1] which would have lowered his GSR (and, presumably, his sentence). We do not agree.

A defendant who seeks a mitigating role adjustment bears the burden of proving, by a preponderance of the evidence, that he is entitled to the downward adjustment. *See United States v. Vargas*, 560 F.3d 45, 50 (1st Cir. 2009). "To qualify as a minor participant, a defendant must prove that he is both less culpable than his cohorts in the particular criminal endeavor and less culpable than the majority of those within the universe of persons participating in similar crimes." *United States v. Torres-Landrúa*, 783 F.3d 58, 65 (1st Cir. 2015) (quoting *United States v. Santos*, 357 F.3d 136, 142 (1st Cir. 2004)). Here, we need go no further than the first prong of this two-part test.

Role-in-the-offense determinations are notoriously fact-specific. *See United States v.*

Meléndez-Rivera, 782 F.3d 26, 28 (1st Cir. 2015); *United States v. Rosa-Carino*, 615 F.3d 75, 81 (1st Cir. 2010). In this instance, the district court explicitly found, as a matter of fact, that the two participants in the smuggle (the appellant and Rodríguez) were "equally culpable." [—6—] This finding is not clearly erroneous: the two men traveled first to Colombia and then to Venezuela, specifically to undertake the unlawful voyage; they shared the work at sea en route to Puerto Rico; and the appellant's special skill set as a mechanic was essential to the success of the venture. The fact that Rodríguez was deemed the "captain" of the craft does not undermine the sentencing court's finding that they were equal partners in the criminal activity. *See, e.g., United States v. Bravo*, 489 F.3d 1, 11 (1st Cir. 2007).

We have said before that "absent a mistake of law, battles over a defendant's status . . . will almost always be won or lost in the district court." *United States v. Graciani*, 61 F.3d 70, 75 (1st Cir. 1995). This case is no exception.

In an effort to blunt the force of this reasoning, the appellant advances two arguments. First, he says that "the district court summarily declined to grant the [minor role] adjustment without outlining any reasoning for its decision." This statement is simply wrong: the district court entertained extensive argument on this very point and explained its reasoning in some detail. The court mentioned the large quantity of drugs, the trust that the drug owners obviously placed in the appellant, and the appellant's expertise in "how to handle the boat." That the appellant resists the district court's explanation for the [—7—] "equal culpability" finding is not a basis for holding that the finding is unexplained.

The appellant also makes a hierarchical argument. He submits that he is a minor participant in the criminal activity, broadly defined, because he played a bit part when compared to those unidentified individuals who "owned" the drugs and those unidentified individuals who presumably were prepared to distribute them in the United States.

---

[1] The appellant originally sought a four-level decrease in his offense level arguing that his role in the offense was no more than minimal. *See* USSG §3B1.2(a). However, he abandoned that position below.

This argument is unavailing. When two persons undertake to transport by themselves a large quantity of drugs in a long and hazardous voyage at sea, it is not clear error for a sentencing court to regard each as a principal and refuse to grant any mitigating role adjustment.[2] *See United States v. Zakharov*, 468 F.3d 1171, 1181 (9th Cir. 2006); *United States v. Coneo-Guerrero*, 148 F.3d 44, 50-51 (1st Cir. 1998).

That ends this aspect of the matter. Where there is more than one plausible view of the circumstances, "the sentencing court's choice among supportable alternatives cannot be clearly erroneous." *United States v. Ruiz*, 905 F.2d 499, 508 (1st Cir. 1990). [—8—]

B. *Failure to Explain.*

Congress has directed every sentencing court to "state in open court the reasons for its imposition of the particular sentence." 18 U.S.C. § 3553(c). Though the court's explanation need not "be precise to the point of pedantry," *United States v. Turbides-Leonardo*, 468 F.3d 34, 40 (1st Cir. 2006), the explanation given should "identify the [relevant] factors driving [the sentencing] determination." *United States v. Sepúlveda-Hernández*, ___ F.3d ___, ___ (1st Cir. 2016) [No. 15-1293, slip op. at 5]; *see United States v. Ruiz-Huertas*, 792 F.3d 223, 226-27 (1st Cir.), *cert. denied*, 136 S. Ct. 258-59 (2015).

The appellant argues that the court below forsook this duty. Since the appellant did not preserve any such claim of error in the district court, our review is for plain error. *See United States v. Montero-Montero*, ___ F.3d ___, ___ (1st Cir. 2016) [No. 15-1405, slip op. at 3]. To establish plain error, an appellant must show "(1) that an error occurred (2) which was clear or obvious and which not only (3) affected the [appellant's] substantial rights, but also (4) seriously impaired the fairness, integrity, or

public reputation of judicial proceedings." *United States v. Duarte*, 246 F.3d 56, 60 (1st Cir. 2001).

The appellant's argument is puzzling. He alleges, without qualification, that "the district court failed to explain its reasons for the 135-month sentence it imposed." Yet, the [—9—] sentencing transcript belies this allegation. The court explicitly stated that "[t]he guideline computations satisfactorily reflect the components of this offense by considering its nature and circumstances. . . ." The court went on to note that it had "considered the other sentencing factors set forth in Title 18, U.S. Code [§] 3553." The court also referred to the appellant's "personal history and characteristics . . . as well as . . . the nature of the circumstances under which [he] was hired to perform this job."

After alluding to the "elements of the offense and [the appellant's] participation in the same," the court stated that it was taking into account "the need to promote respect for the law, protect the public from further crimes by defendant, the need to address issues of deterrence and punishment, as balanced together with the personal history and characteristics of defendant." In the end, the court concluded "that a sentence in this case at the lower end of the guideline range would be a sentence that is just and not greater than necessary."

Where, as here, the court imposes a sentence that comes within the GSR, "the burden of adequate explanation is lightened." *Montero-Montero*, slip op. at 4. We hold that the court's explanation was sufficient to satisfy this lightened burden and to explicate its within-the-range sentence. There was no error, plain or otherwise. [—10—]

C. *National Disparity.*

Citing 18 U.S.C. § 3553(a)(6), the appellant next argues that his sentence was "disproportionate to others found guilty of the same or similar conduct." This argument is unpersuasive.

---

[2] Here, moreover, the district court's choice to define the criminal activity narrowly was consistent with the indictment, which focused on the voyage and the interception of the vessel. Consistent with this focus, the facts of record do not deal either with the provenance of the drugs or with the ultimate plans for their retail distribution.

Section 3553(a)(6) instructs a sentencing court to consider "the need to avoid unwarranted sentence disparities among defendants with similar records who have been found guilty of similar conduct." This provision is aimed, generally, at the minimization of sentencing disparities among defendants nationwide. *See Martin*, 520 F.3d at 94. Because the appellant did not raise this claim of error below, our review is for plain error. *See Duarte*, 246 F.3d at 60.

We see nothing resembling plain error here. The appellant presents this argument in hortatory terms without developing any relevant factual foundation. The lack of developed argumentation is fatal to the claim. *See United States v. Zannino*, 895 F.2d 1, 17 (1st Cir. 1990) ("[I]ssues adverted to in a perfunctory manner, unaccompanied by some effort at developed argumentation, are deemed waived.").

D. *Substantive Reasonableness.*

The appellant's last claim of error targets the substantive reasonableness of his sentence. The standard of review is murky. *See Ruiz-Huertas*, 792 F.3d at 228 & n.4 (noting uncertainty about whether a claim that a sentence is substantively [—11—] unreasonable must be preserved below). Rather than resolving the question, we assume—favorably to the appellant—that our review of this claim is for abuse of discretion. Even so, the appellant's challenge fails.

A sentence will survive a challenge to its substantive reasonableness as long as it rests on a "plausible sentencing rationale" and reflects a "defensible result." *Martin*, 520 F.3d at 96. "A challenge directed at substantive reasonableness is usually a heavy lift, and reversal is 'particularly unlikely when . . . the sentence imposed fits within the compass of a properly calculated [guideline sentencing range].'" *Ruiz-Huertas*, 792 F.3d at 228-29 (quoting *United States v. Vega-Salgado*, 769 F.3d 100, 105 (1st Cir. 2014) (omission and alteration in original)).

So it is here: as recounted above, the district court articulated an eminently

plausible rationale for the sentence. Moreover—given the parameters of the GSR, the large quantity of drugs involved, and the appellant's vital role in the smuggle—a 135-month sentence is defensible.

The appellant's main argument in support of his plaint that his sentence is substantively unreasonable is that his coconspirator, Rodríguez, received a much lighter sentence (48 months).[3] But at the time the appellant was sentenced—January [—12—] 27, 2015—Rodríguez's case was still pending. Rodríguez was not sentenced until March 10, 2015, roughly six weeks *after* the appellant was sentenced. The fact that the disparity argument, as made to us, could not have been made to the sentencing court creates a curious anomaly. *Cf. Cahoon v. Shelton*, 647 F.3d 18, 29 (1st Cir. 2011) (warning that a party cannot expect to obtain relief from an appellate court that he never sought in the trial court); *Beaulieu v. U.S. IRS*, 865 F.2d 1351, 1352 (1st Cir. 1989) (same).

Here, however, we need not grapple with this anomaly. That the appellant and Rodríguez received different sentences tells us nothing about which of those sentences varies from the norm; and the limited record available to us suggests that there are reasons why a sentencing judge could have seen the two situations as quite different.[4] These uncertainties, taken together, preclude any finding that the appellant's within-guidelines sentence is substantively unreasonable. [—13—]

---

[3] Although the appellant's briefs assert that Rodríguez was sentenced to 46 months' imprisonment, the court docket indicates [—12—] that Rodríguez was sentenced to 48 months. *See United States v. Rodríguez*, Crim. Case No. 3:14-cr-00182 (D.P.R. Mar. 10, 2015).

[4] Unlike the appellant, Rodríguez pleaded guilty to only a single count of the indictment; he did not enter a straight plea but, rather, pleaded guilty pursuant to a negotiated plea agreement (the terms of which are not summarized in the appellant's brief or elsewhere in the sentencing record); and there is some indication in the record that Rodríguez may have been experiencing medical complications that influenced the duration of his sentence.

III. CONCLUSION

We need go no further. For the reasons elucidated above, the appellant's sentence is

Affirmed.

United States Court of Appeals
for the First Circuit

No. 15-1576

UNITED STATES

vs.

TRINIDAD

Appeal from the United States District Court for the District of Puerto Rico

Decided: October 14, 2016

Citation: 839 F.3d 112, 4 Adm. R. 25 (1st Cir. 2016).

Before **HOWARD**, Chief Judge, and **TORRUELLA** and **BARRON**, Circuit Judges.

[—2—] **BARRON,** Circuit Judge:

Persis Trinidad was convicted of violating the Maritime Drug Law Enforcement Act ("MDLEA") after his vessel was intercepted by United States authorities. Trinidad appeals the District Court's application of a sentencing enhancement to him.[1] That enhancement applies if the defendant "acted as a pilot, copilot, captain, navigator, flight officer, or any other operation officer" on a vessel carrying controlled substances. U.S.S.G. §2D1.1(b)(3)(C). We conclude that the District Court did not err in

---

[1] Apparently content with the "benefit of his bargain," *United States v. Saxena*, 229 F.3d 1, 6 (1st Cir. 2000), Trinidad does not challenge the validity of his plea agreement, and so does not challenge the Coast Guard's determination that his vessel was a "vessel without nationality," 46 U.S.C. § 70502(c)(1)(A), which the MDLEA defines as a "vessel aboard which the master or individual in charge makes a claim of registry and for which the claimed nation of registry does not affirmatively and unequivocally assert that the vessel is of its nationality," *id.* at § 70502(d)(1)(C). We thus have no reason to question that determination. Moreover, because Trinidad makes no argument that his guilty plea is invalid, he also makes no argument that his plea agreement must be vacated because Congress exceeded its constitutional authority under Article I in enacting the MDLEA. As we have made clear that such a challenge would not implicate our subject-matter jurisdiction, we do not address that issue either. *E.g., United States v. Nueci-Peña*, 711 F.3d 191, 196-97 (1st Cir. 2013).

ruling that Trinidad acted as a "navigator" within the meaning of the enhancement.

I.

On or about September 27, 2014, Trinidad and Algemiro Coa-Peña were intercepted in a 30-foot "go-fast type vessel" by the United States Coast Guard, approximately 80 nautical miles [—3—] south of Lea Beata, Dominican Republic.[2] The vessel bore no indicia of nationality.

Trinidad and Coa-Peña told the Coast Guard that the vessel was coming from Colombia, and one of the men claimed Colombian nationality for the vessel. After the Government of Colombia indicated that it could neither confirm nor deny registry of the vessel, the Coast Guard determined that the vessel was one without nationality within the meaning of the MDLEA, 46 U.S.C. § 70502(c)(1)(A), and boarded the vessel. The Coast Guard found approximately 144 kilograms of cocaine onboard.

On January 8, 2015, Trinidad pleaded guilty to one count of possession with intent to distribute cocaine, in violation of provisions of the MDLEA. *See* 46 U.S.C. §§ 70503(a)(1), 70504(b)(1), 70506(a), and 70506(b). In so doing, Trinidad admitted that he and Coa-Peña took turns driving the vessel. Trinidad also admitted that he and Coa-Peña "set sail for the Dominican Republic utilizing Global Positioning Devices that were provided to them."

The parties agreed to a total offense level of 31, unless Trinidad complied with the requirements set forth in [—4—] U.S.S.G. §2D1.1(b)(17) (the so-called "safety-valve reduction"), in which case the parties agreed that the total offense level would be 29. The agreed-upon offense level did not include the two-level sentencing enhancement for Trinidad's "act[ing] as a pilot, copilot, captain,

---

[2] "Because this appeal follows a guilty plea, we draw the facts from the plea agreement, the change-of-plea colloquy, the unchallenged portions of the presentence investigation report . . . , and the transcript of the disposition hearing." *United States v. Ocasio-Cancel*, 727 F.3d 85, 88 (1st Cir. 2013).

navigator, flight officer, or any other operation officer aboard any craft or vessel." U.S.S.G. §2D1.1(b)(3)(C).

The pre-sentence report ("PSR") put together by the probation office calculated a total offense level of 33. The PSR calculated that level by taking into account the parties' stipulated base offense level and by adding the two-level "pilot-navigator enhancement" set forth in U.S.S.G. §2D1.1(b)(3)(C). The PSR did not account for the two-level safety-valve reduction. The PSR added the enhancement because the probation officer determined that Trinidad "acted as a navigator" in the course of committing the underlying offense. Trinidad objected to the enhancement on the grounds that he was neither the captain nor the navigator of the vessel, as Trinidad only took turns steering the vessel and did not himself handle the vessel's GPS system.

The District Court calculated a total offense level of 31 and sentenced Trinidad to a term of imprisonment of 108 months, at the low end of the applicable Guidelines range. In so doing, the District Court adopted both the two-level safety- [—5—] valve reduction and the two-level pilot-navigator enhancement. The District Court applied the enhancement because it found that Trinidad navigated the vessel under the circumstances.

Trinidad appeals the application of the pilot-navigator sentencing enhancement to him.

II.

We review the District Court's interpretation and application of this sentencing enhancement de novo and the District Court's underlying "factual findings, which must be supported by a preponderance of the evidence, for clear error." *United States v. Lopez*, 299 F.3d 84, 87 (1st Cir. 2002). The government's sole argument to us is that the District Court did not err in finding that the enhancement applies because Trinidad acted as a navigator. We agree.

The undisputed record shows that Trinidad took turns steering the vessel with Coa-Peña,

the only other passenger on board; that the vessel was traveling from Colombia to the Dominican Republic; that he and Coa-Peña "set sail . . . utilizing Global Positioning Devices"; and that the vessel was intercepted after twenty-four hours on the high seas. Given these facts, the District Court reasonably concluded that Trinidad must have been responsible for ensuring that the boat stayed on course for some not insubstantial portion of the trip. [—6—]

Trinidad does contend that he did not "use" the GPS, and that he therefore cannot be said to have been navigating. But the District Court reasonably concluded that Trinidad must have relied on the GPS to keep the boat on course. Unlike on land, the District Court noted, Trinidad could not have been instructed to "[j]ust keep going straight." Thus, the District Court did not clearly err in determining that, even if Trinidad did not himself set or calibrate the GPS device, it was impossible to conclude that he "[got] on a boat," was told "that way," and went. "That's not the way it goes. You will end up God knows where. It's a big ocean up there."

Further supporting the District Court's assessment of Trinidad's onboard role—and reliance on instrumentation in guiding the boat's course—is the portion of the colloquy at sentencing in which Trinidad's counsel did not contest the notion that Trinidad had relied on the GPS to keep the boat on course. In that exchange, Trinidad's counsel, in trying to explain that Trinidad's role was too minimal to make him a navigator, remarked, "If you tell him look at the GPS or the (Remarks in Spanish)—we're going 280 east for example." At that point, the District Court stated: "You have given it in. The moment that you use the compass, if you will, or you're using the GPS as you mention, you are navigating." So, while Trinidad contends that, in order to be deemed a navigator, he [—7—] must have been, at points, "in charge of navigating the vessel and directing it to its ultimate destination," we conclude that the District Court reasonably found Trinidad was in charge of doing just that during some not insubstantial portions of the trip.

We therefore agree that, on this record, Trinidad, who was an experienced fisherman, acted as a navigator during the journey from Colombia to the Dominican Republic. *See The Oxford English Dictionary* 259 (2d ed. 1989) (defining "navigate" to mean, among other things, "to sail, direct, or manage (a ship)" and "to plot and supervise the course of (an aircraft or spacecraft)"); *The Random House Dictionary of the English Language* 1282 (2d ed. 1987) (defining "navigate" to mean, among other things, "to direct or manage (a ship . . .) on its course"); *Webster's Third New Int'l Dictionary* 1509 (1981) (defining "navigate" to mean, among other things, "to steer, direct, or manage in sailing: conduct (a boat) upon the water by the art or skill of seamen").[3] **[—8—]**

In so concluding, we reject Trinidad's contention that a person can only qualify as a navigator if he or she knows how to program or adjust a GPS—or other navigational device—and not if he merely relies on it to keep the boat on course. Nothing in the text or commentary of the enhancement supports such a restricted definition of the term "navigator." *Cf. United States v. Cruz-Mendez*, 811 F.3d 1172, 1176, 4 Adm. R. 370, 372 (9th Cir. 2016) (explaining that appropriate application of the "pilot" portion of the enhancement is "not dependent on a finding of any particular formal training"); *United States v. Cartwright*, 413 F.3d 1295, 1296-99 (11th Cir. 2005) (per curiam) (reviewing the defendant's actions on board the vessel, rather than the extent of his knowledge or training, in applying the "captain" portion of the enhancement).

We also reject Trinidad's contention that he did not act as a navigator because he was a subordinate to the other man on the vessel. By its own terms, the enhancement reaches anyone who "act[s] as *a* navigator," just as it reaches captains and co-pilots alike. U.S.S.G. §2D1.1(b)(3)(C) (emphasis added). Thus, even assuming that Trinidad did not bear "ultimate responsibility" for the vessel's safe passage, as he contends, that fact would not preclude the conclusion that he "act[ed] as **[—9—]** a navigator." *Id.* And to the extent Trinidad contends that the enhancement can only be applied to persons with special authority, he is also wrong. *See United States v. Guerrero*, 114 F.3d 332, 346 & n.16 (1st Cir. 1997), *cert. denied* 522 U.S. 870 & 522 U.S. 924 (1997).

III.

For the reasons given, we ***affirm***.

–Dissenting Opinion Follows–

(Reporter's Note: Dissenting opinion follows on p. 28).

---

[3] The definition of the term "navigate" found in the *Sea Talk Nautical Dictionary* is not inconsistent with the District Court's decision to apply the pilot-navigator enhancement. The District Court's statements during the plea colloquy reflect the District Court's conclusion that Trinidad must have adjusted the course of the vessel by "employing the elements of position, course, and speed" provided to him by the pre-programmed GPS, and thus that Trinidad must have "determin[ed] [his] position, course, and speed" using the GPS, and adjusted the course of the **[—8—]** vessel accordingly. *Sea Talk Nautical Dictionary*, http://www.seatalk.info (last visited September 13, 2016).

[—10—] TORRUELLA, Circuit Judge, dissenting:

The sole issue raised by appellant's counsel before the trial court, and now before this court, is an objection to the sentencing court's enhancement of appellant's sentence pursuant to its finding that he was a "navigator" within the meaning of U.S.S.G. §2D.1(b)(3)(C).[4] Because I disagree with the majority opinion's overly-broad reading of this term, I must respectfully dissent.

If I did not feel bound by my prior decision in *United States v. Bravo*, 489 F.3d 1 (1st Cir. 2007), however, there would be additional grounds which would lead me to further part from my brethren in affirming appellant's conviction. I can no longer support the approach taken by this and our sister circuits in embracing the sweeping powers asserted by Congress and the Executive under the Maritime Drug Law Enforcement Act ("MDLEA"), and I am of the view that the district court acted without jurisdiction over appellant.[5]

My concerns are of a fundamental nature and deal with the power of this court, or rather the lack of power of this court, to penalize appellant for the crimes which he allegedly committed against the United States. That is, first, whether [—11—] the United States has the power to arrest appellant under the circumstances of this case and involuntarily render him into the territory of the United States. Second, whether the United States has the power to retroactively apply to him the criminal laws of the United States for conduct which previous to his arrest and rendition was not subject to those laws, and which only comes into play by the actions of the United States in arresting appellant in international waters and rendering him into United States territory.[6]

I.

To fully consider the issues raised by appellant's conviction, a more detailed fleshing of the record is required than appears in the majority opinion.[7]

Appellant Persis Trinidad was, at the time of the alleged violations, a 46-year-old native and citizen of the Dominican Republic, who lived in the seaside village of Playa [—12—] Las Galeras, Samana, in the northern part of the island, where he eked out a living as a fisherman earning about $150 a month. Although his record shows that he had a sixth-grade education, Trinidad nevertheless expressed being illiterate, a fact that can be confirmed from his "signature" on the plea agreement and other court documents. Furthermore, his primary language is Spanish and he has no fluency in English. Sometime in August, 2014, Trinidad was approached by a Colombian who went by the first name of Andrés, who bought some fish from him. The following day, Andrés hired him for a fishing trip, during which he asked Trinidad if he was interested in another job, earning more money. Upon inquiring as to the nature of the job, Trinidad was told it would require his going to Colombia and bringing back narcotics by sea to Santo Domingo, Dominican Republic, for which he would be paid $20,000. Andrés informed Trinidad that he would help him get his Dominican Republic passport and would pay for his airfare to Colombia. Thereafter, Trinidad accepted the offer.

On September 16, 2014, Andrés picked up Trinidad at Playa Las Galeras and drove him to Santo Domingo where he gave him 2,600 Dominican pesos (RD$) for passport fees, and

---

[4] Which applies if the defendant "acted as a pilot, copilot, captain, navigator, flight officer, or any other operation officer" on a vessel carrying controlled substances. U.S.S.G. §2D1. 1(b)(3)(c).

[5] *Cf., United States v. Cardales-Luna*, 632 F.3d 731, 739 (1st Cir. 2011) (Torruella, J., dissenting).

[6] These are matters that can be raised *motu proprio* by the court at any stage of the proceedings, and I hereby raise them. *See*

Cardales-Luna, 632 F.3d at 740 (Torruella, J., dissenting) (citing *United States v. Madera–López*, 190 F. App'x 832, 834 (11th Cir. 2006)). As in *Cardales-Luna*, I believe that we must address jurisdictional deficiencies as great as this one whenever they present themselves. *Id.* at 750-51.

[7] As with the majority opinion, I take my recount of the relevant facts "from the plea agreement, the change-of plea colloquy, the unchallenged portions of the presentence investigation report. . . ., and the transcript of the disposition hearing," *supra* note 2, at *3, as well as from his co-defendant's pre-sentence report.

approximately RD$1,500 more for government processing. Andrés then helped Trinidad with the passport process and subsequently went with him to the Avianca Airline's office where Andrés paid [—13—] for Trinidad's airline ticket to Barranquilla, Colombia and then gave the ticket to Trinidad. Andrés then gave Trinidad RD$3,600 for his transportation to Punta Cana International Airport and $500 to cover miscellaneous expenses. On that same day Trinidad went to the airport, took the Avianca flight to Bogotá, Colombia, and there connected to a flight to Barranquilla, Colombia.

Upon his arrival at the Barranquilla airport, Trinidad was met by a Colombian couple, who took him to a hotel (at an unknown location) in Barranquilla, where he stayed until September 23, 2014. On this date another Colombian picked him up and transported him to a second hotel in Barranquilla (also at an unknown location), where he sojourned for one more night. While at this second hotel, Trinidad met Algemiro Coa-Peña ("Coa-Peña"), who was to be his companion on the return sea voyage to the Dominican Republic, as well as his eventual codefendant in this case. Coa-Peña is a native of Cartagena, Colombia and a citizen of the Republic of Colombia.

At some time on the 24th, Andrés picked up Trinidad and took him to a store to purchase two pairs of pants for him. Later that night took him to a small pier near the hotel where a so-called "go-fast" boat was docked.[8] Andrés told Trinidad that [—14—] the narcotics would be transported to the Dominican Republic aboard that vessel. Trinidad observed that the boat had twelve blue fuel drums aboard, and saw unidentified Colombian personnel load the boat with six bales, which were placed in the forward part of the vessel. At some point, Coa-Peña arrived at the pier, whereupon two unidentified individuals showed up and handed two Global Positioning System ("GPS") handheld instruments to Coa-Peña and Trinidad, and proceeded to program the instruments with the coordinates of the destination in the Dominican Republic where the drugs were to be delivered. Although they attempted to instruct Trinidad and Coa-Peña on the use of the GPS's, it was Coa-Peña who eventually handled them because of Trinidad's apparent inability to familiarize himself with their use at that time.

Soon thereafter, Coa-Peña and Trinidad left from Barranquilla, Colombia destined for Santo Domingo, Dominican Republic. During the trip towards the Dominican Republic, both took turns steering the vessel, with Coa-Peña "handling" the GPS.[9] On September 26, 2014, the voyage was proceeding normally [—15—] until the boat reached an area approximately 80 miles south of Isla Beata, Dominican Republic. At this point, while the vessel was still in international waters, the vessel's engines experienced trouble and the boat came to a stop. Shortly after, the disabled vessel was approached by a U.S. Coast Guard cutter, which, with the aid of a marine patrol aircraft, had for some time been tracking the vessel Trinidad and Coa-Peña were travelling on, as well as another "suspicious" boat, as they headed in a northerly course towards the Dominican Republic. A boarding team from the cutter soon approached the disabled vessel, which as previously indicated, was dead in the water. The other "suspicious vessel" was nowhere in sight, having disappeared into the expanse of the sea.

The boarding team reported coming upon a 30-foot "go-fast" boat, with no markings or indicia of nationality, and aboard which were two persons later identified as Trinidad and Coa-Peña. Neither claimed to be the master of the vessel, but *one of them orally claimed Colombian nationality for the vessel.* Both indicated that their last port of call was in

---

8 "This is a small boat, customized with additional engines and fuel tanks for added speed and range. Experience tells us [—14—] that such boats play a large role in the drug trade." *United States v. González*, 311 F.3d 440, 444 n.3 (1st Cir. 2002) (Torruella, J., concurring).

9 Considering that the GPS's had been already set up, presumably the "handling" would have only required looking at the instrument's screen, which would indicate the direction to follow, something akin to looking at your watch to see the time [—15—] or looking at the GPS screens on the phone or dashboard of an automobile.

Colombia, and that their next port of call was Santo Domingo. Several bales of cargo could be observed in the forward section of the boat. [—16—]

The Coast Guard put in effect their protocol under the U.S.-Colombia bilateral agreement on maritime smuggling,[10] whereby the government of Colombia was contacted to request confirmation or denial of the registry of the suspect vessel in Colombia. On the next day, September 27, the Colombian government responded that it could neither confirm nor deny registry of the vessel in Colombia (unsurprisingly, given the dearth of information available at that point), whereupon the Coast Guard's Seventh District Commander granted permission to the cutter's boarding crew to consider the vessel as one without nationality, and to conduct a boarding under U.S. law. The boarding party then conducted a field test of the substances found in the bales located on the bow section of the intercepted vessel, which yielded a positive result for the presence of cocaine. Upon this discovery, Trinidad and Coa-Peña were formally detained.

On board the intercepted vessel were found 144.9 kilograms of cocaine packed in bricks inside six bales, which were moved to the Coast Guard cutter as the detained boat could not be safely towed and had to be purposely sunk to prevent it from becoming a hazard to navigation. Trinidad and Coa-Peña [—17—] were brought aboard the U. S. Coast Guard cutter and then transported aboard the cutter to Mayaguez, Puerto Rico, which, according to the Government's euphemistic statement in the indictment, "was where the defendants first entered the United States *after commission of the . . . offense*" (emphasis added), a contention which in itself raises some interesting issues,[11] which will be presently discussed.

---

[10] *See* Agreement between the Government of the United States of America and the Government of the Republic of Colombia to Suppress Illicit Traffic by Sea, U.S.-Colom., Feb. 20, 1997, T.I.A.S. No. 12,835.

[11] Commission of what offense? Against whom? And when?

Appellant pled guilty to Count One of the Indictment which charged possession with the intent to distribute more than five kilograms of cocaine on board a vessel subject to the jurisdiction of the United States, that is, a vessel without nationality, for which he was sentenced to imprisonment for a period of 108 months.[12]

II.

The majority opinion argues that because Trinidad admitted as part of his plea agreement that he took turns "conning the vessel" with Coa-Peña, that he therefore meets the [—18—] definition of a "navigator."[13] In making this argument the majority cites English dictionaries that equate "navigate" with "to steer." *Supra* at *7.

I take issue with what in my view is an obviously unjust result. The majority's opinion relies on an overly broad way of reading this term. To be a navigator contains its own particular subset of skills that are more easily

---

[12] The district court calculated that Trinidad had a total offense level of 31. This number was reached by taking the offense level agreed to as part of the plea agreement (31), subtracting two points because Trinidad complied with the requirements for the safety-valve reduction (U.S.S.G. §2D1.1(b)(17)) and adding two points for the navigator enhancement (U.S.S.G. §2D1.1(b)(3)(C)). Without the navigator enhancement Trinidad's total offense level would have been 29, which carried a recommended range of 87-108 months' imprisonment.

[13] Because this statement was agreed to as part of the plea agreement I am setting aside serious concerns that may be raised about the source of this information. Trinidad was interrogated by Homeland Security Agents who "provided Miranda Warnings to the Defendant." One wonders what meaning Miranda warnings might have to a poor fisherman from the Dominican Republic. One also wonders if the Dominican consulate in Puerto Rico was contacted and informed that a citizen of the Dominican Republic, who surely may not understand his rights under the U.S. Constitution, was being held and interrogated without counsel being present. *See* Vienna Convention on Consular Relations art. 36, Apr. 24, 1963, 21 U.S.T. 77. This is only one of the numerous problems that might arise when foreign nationals are pulled into the United States for criminal prosecution.

summarized by the term "navigator" than merely driving a boat. Although the majority cites common dictionaries of the English language to equate "navigate" with "steer," much more telling, in my view, is the definition of "navigate" found in nautical dictionaries. Here the definition is "[t]o safely operate a vessel employing the elements of position, course and speed" and "[t]o determine position, course and speed using instruments." Definition of "Navigate", *Sea Talk Nautical Dictionary,* *http://www.seatalk.info/ (last visited Oct. 6, 2016).* This [—19—] definition embraces the notion that in nautical terms "to navigate" actually requires extra abilities to determine "position, course and speed using instruments." Yet the facts recited above suggest that the very opposite was true of Trinidad. He specifically did not understand how to use the GPS. It had to be set up for him and it is undisputed that Coa-Peña managed those instruments throughout the trip.

To assume a broader definition of "navigator" suggests that the sheer act of driving somehow enhances the individual's criminal conduct. But would we ever suggest that suburban or rural drug dealers should receive an enhanced sentence simply because they drive a car to the location of their drug transactions rather than walk or take public transportation as their more urban counterparts might? Persis Trinidad was a fisherman who knew how to engage in his trade, which was coastal fishing on a yola (a small open skiff propelled by oars or an outboard motor). *See United States v. Matos-Luchi,* 627 F.3d 1, 2 (1st Cir. 2010). He was offered more money than he could make in ten years of fishing to help manage the boat between Colombia and the Dominican Republic. During the voyage he may have periodically looked at the screen of the handheld GPS he was provided with by his Colombian cohorts, but this is no more an exceptional skill or action than if he had been driving most modern cars which have GPS in their dashboard. *Id.* Nothing in [—20—] this behavior suggests extra-culpability or a justifiable basis for enhancement. If the truth be said he was a water borne "mule," nothing

more than the common "mules" that sit in commercial airlines, transporting contraband in and on their bodies, for which they are not penalized additionally as has been done with Trinidad.

III.

My departure from the majority's opinion is not limited to their reading of the term "navigator," however. The Maritime Drug Enforcement Act (MDLEA), codified as amended at 46 U.S.C. §§ 70501-08, has been used to expand United States *criminal* jurisdiction well beyond U.S. borders to include people and acts that have no connection whatsoever with the United States. This extraterritorial exercise is far in excess of any powers either permitted by international law or granted by Congress to the Executive branch.

Considering that Trinidad is an illiterate, non-English speaking Dominican citizen, with no record of his having ever resided or even visited the United States, without any prior criminal past and unaware of U.S. criminal law until he was captured in the high seas, the question arises whether he can be charged with retroactively violating U.S. law upon his forced rendition into U.S. territory. When and where did Trinidad commit this alleged U.S. crime? Can it be said that [—21—] there was any U.S. crime committed by Trinidad, before the vessel he was navigating was intercepted? That would be a stretch that would be difficult to swallow. Thus we must assume, that if there was a U.S. crime committed, it was only after he was physically apprehended in the high seas. Prior to that Trinidad could not have infringed any U.S. law, and if he did commit any crime for which he could be charged, it would have been against the laws of Colombia and/or the Dominican Republic. This raises the question of how Trinidad's conduct before he was apprehended (which conduct could not then have been a U.S. crime) can become a U.S. crime by the United States Government capturing Trinidad at a time when he had committed no crime against the United States. This enigma is at the heart of the attempt by the United States to exercise universal criminal jurisdiction through means repeatedly and soundly rejected pursuant to customary international law.

This conundrum arises because of the expansive definition Congress has given to statelessness.[14]   There are two [—22—] problems with the MDLEA's treatment of stateless vessels. First, its definition of when a vessel is actually stateless far exceeds anything that exists or is allowed by international law. Second, the degree and type of proof the MDLEA accepts for statelessness risks violating international and domestic law. The MDLEA uses the statelessness of a vessel as the hook by which it allegedly acquires jurisdiction over a vessel and its crew, allowing it to *retroactively* apply U.S. criminal laws to said persons irrespective of their nationality, the place where the alleged crimes were committed, or the lack of any U.S. connection or impact of the charged conduct.

A. Defining when a Vessel is Stateless

According to the MDLEA a vessel without nationality is one "aboard which the master or individual in charge" either "makes a claim of registry that is denied by the nation whose registry is claimed," "fails . . . to make a claim of nationality or registry for that vessel," or

---

[14] Because I take issue with whether Trinidad's boat was actually stateless I am setting aside the question of what type of jurisdiction the Constitution and international law would allow the United States to exercise on stateless vessels. A common view is that "stateless vessels do not fall within the veil of another sovereign's territorial protection" and therefore "all nations can treat them as their own territory and subject them to their laws." *United States v. Moreno-Morillo*, 334 F.3d 819, 828 (9th Cir. 2003) (quoting *United States v. Caicedo*, 47 F.3d 370, 373 (9th Cir. 1995)). Although this view [—22—] recognizes that in exercising jurisdiction the United States is not infringing on the rights of another nation to legislate for the boat in question, this still raises due process and jurisdictional concerns regarding the people on the boat. For this reason I agree with those commentators who have found that "[t]he better view appears to be that there is a need for some jurisdictional nexus in order that a State may extend its laws to those on board a stateless ship and enforce the laws against them." R.R. Churchill & A.V. Lowe, *The Law of the Sea* 214 (3d ed. 1999).

"makes a claim of registry and for which the claimed nation of registry does not [—23—] affirmatively and unequivocally assert that the vessel is of its nationality." 46 U.S.C. § 70502(d)(1)(A)-(C). It is this last provision that is at issue here.[15]

When Trinidad's boat was intercepted by the U.S. Coast Guard, Trinidad and Coa-Peña were questioned as to the nationality of the boat and Coa-Peña answered that the ship was Colombian. Nevertheless, the vessel in question was deemed stateless by the United States after Colombian authorities responded to the inquiry by U.S. authorities to the effect that Colombian registry could be "neither confirm[ed] nor den[ied]." On the basis of this noncommittal statement, based upon the flimsy information available at the time, the Coast Guard was authorized pursuant to the U.S.'s self-promoting legislation to assume jurisdiction over the vessel and its crew, *and to apply U.S. criminal laws to them.* 46 U.S.C. § 70502(d)(1)(C). Of course, we do not know what information was actually provided by the Coast Guard to the Colombian authorities, nor do we know what Colombia's answer would have been had all the circumstantial evidence described previously, pointing to a non- [—24—] U.S. nationality of the vessel and its crew, been available and provided to Colombia.

Under international law, however, the acquisition of jurisdiction in this case on the basis of "statelessness" because of Colombia's failure to make an unequivocal assertion of nationality within the twenty-four hours or so given is a gross overstepping of jurisdictional boundaries. In international maritime law there is the long-established concept of the law of the flag, a principle of customary international law that is adhered to by the

---

[15] There are other grounds for allegedly exercising jurisdiction in the legislation, including "a vessel registered in a foreign nation if that nation has consented or waived objection to the enforcement of United States law by the United States." 46 U.S.C. § 70502(c); *but see Cardales-Luna*, 632 F.3d at 740 (Torruella, J., dissenting). Those grounds are not at issue here.

United States.[16] Under the law of the flag principle, a ship has the nationality of the country whose flag it is *entitled* to fly.[17] Central to this entire regime is the principle that

> [e]ach state under international law may determine *for itself* the conditions on which [—25—] it will grant its nationality to a merchant ship, thereby accepting responsibility for it and acquiring authority over it. . . . The United States has firmly and successfully maintained that the regularity and validity of a registration can be questioned *only by the registering state.*

Lauritzen, 345 U.S. at 584 (emphasis added).[18]

---

[16] Customary international law is part of the federal common law. Restatement (Third) of Foreign Relations Law § 111 (Am. Law Inst. 1987); *see also Kadic v. Karadzic*, 70 F.3d 232, 246 (2d Cir. 1995) (accepting "the settled proposition that federal common law incorporates international law").

[17] *See* United Nations Convention on the Law of the Sea art. 91, Dec. 10, 1982, 1833 U.N.T.S. 397 (UNCLOS). Although the United States has not ratified UNCLOS, Article 91 is part of the customary international law codified by UNCLOS, which is recognized by this country. *United States v. Alaska*, 503 U.S. 569, 588 n.10 (1992); *see also Lauritzen v. Larsen*, 345 U.S. 571, 584 (1953) ("Perhaps the most venerable and universal rule of maritime law . . . is that which gives cardinal importance to the law of the flag."); *see also, United States v. Arra*, 630 F. 2d 836, 840 (1st Cir. 1980) ("Vessels have the nationality of the nation whose flag they are *entitled* to fly . . . ." (emphasis added)).

[18] In support of this argument the Court cited the example of The Virginius, a boat that claimed U.S. registry and was seized by the Spanish while en route to Cuba. *Lauritzen*, 345 U.S. at 584 n.17. Although there were questions regarding the validity of the registration, the United States took the position that it was up to the courts of the United States to determine its status. The Attorney General to the Secretary of State, Dec. 17, 1873, *Foreign Relations of the United States*, 1874 (Washington, DC: GPO, 1874-75), XXXIV: 1113-5. Spain ultimately consented, and paid $80,000 in reparation to the United States. Claims: The Case of the "Virginius," Feb. 27, 1875, 11 U.S.T.I.A. 544 1968.

This means that once a claim of Colombian nationality was made, it was up to Colombia to definitively decide whether the boat was in fact Colombian, not for the United States to unilaterally make that decision in a conclusive manner with the scarcity of information available to it at the time of interception and arrest.[19] It should be noted that under the [—26—] MDLEA it is contemplated that nationality can be asserted orally. 46 U.S.C. § 70502(e)(3) ("A claim of nationality or registry" includes "a verbal claim of nationality or registry by the master or individual in charge of the vessel").[20] This is particularly relevant when considering smaller boats of the type found here because "[m]any states . . . do not issue documents to ships with a tonnage below a given figure" and "a State may not require, or permit, the registration of ships below a certain size . . . but may nonetheless regard such ships as having its nationality if they are owned by its nationals." *Matos-Luchi*, 627 F.3d at 18 (Lipez, J., dissenting) (quoting H. Meyers, *The Nationality of Ships* 160 (1967) and R.R. Churchill & A.V. Lowe, *The Law of the Sea* 213 n.19 (3d ed. 1999)). Indeed, the United States is an example of a nation that extends its nationality to otherwise unregistered ships

---

[19] I note that this is a question that does not admit an easy answer. Although a preliminary investigation into Colombian law reveals that "[n]o ship shall have Colombian nationality unless registered under the statute relating to national merchant shipping" the boat at issue in this case is not of a type or size normally associated with "merchant shipping." U.N. Secretariat, Laws Concerning the Nationality of Ships, U.N. Doc. ST/LEG/SER.B/5 at 25 (1955). It is thus not clear how or when Colombia extends its nationality to recreational vehicles. *See United States v. Matos-Luchi*, 627 F.3d 1, 18 (1st Cir. 2010) (Lipez, J., dissenting) (arguing that many states do not have formal registries for smaller vessels). [—26—] In any event, this is a question to be resolved by Colombian courts, not the uniquely unqualified courts of the United States. *See Lauritzen*, 345 U.S. at 584.

[20] Similarly, under the more recent Drug Trafficking Vessel Interdiction Act of 2008 (DTVIA), which is applicable to submersibles and submersible vessels, a valid claim of the vessel's nationality can be made verbally by the vessel's master or individual in charge. 18 U.S.C. § 2285(d)(3).

that are owned, in whole or part, by one of its citizens. 46 U.S.C. § 70502(b)(2) (defining a vessel of the United States in part as one "owned in any part by an individual who is a citizen of the United [—27—] States," unless said vessel has been granted nationality by another nation).

Given the facts of this case, I am unaware of anything preventing further inquiry into such a crucial factor as was the nationality of the vessel. There is no apparent reason why this matter was not raised or pursued once dry land and legal representation were reached. *Cf. United States v. Greer*, 285 F.3d 158, 175 (2d Cir. 2002) (jurisdictional element of the MDLEA may be inquired into any time before trial); *United States v. Bustos-Useches*, 273 F.3d 622, 627 (5th Cir. 2001) (identifying legitimate deadline to consent to U.S. law any time before trial). The jurisdictional issue was not cast in stone based only on the flimsy information available *in situs* at the time of the interception. Considering the undisputed circumstantial evidence surrounding this sea voyage (*i.e.*, the place where the vessel departed from, the nationality of the personnel that dealt with this enterprise, the nationality of half of the crew that by all appearances was the leading actor aboard the vessel, and *the specific claim of the vessel's Colombian nationality*), it is difficult to deny the vessel's Colombian connection and nationality, which if it had been properly raised and established, should have deprived the court [—28—] of jurisdiction and led to dismissal of the charges against Trinidad.[21]

Nothing in the MDLEA dictates a contrary result. Although the MDLEA does define as a "vessel without nationality" one "aboard which the master or individual in charge makes a claim of registry and for which the claimed nation of registry does not affirmatively and unequivocally assert that the vessel is of its nationality," there is no indication of a timeline according to which the claimed nation of registry must "affirmatively and unequivocally" assert that nationality. 46 U.S.C. § 70502(d) (1)(C). Moreover, although

the MDLEA provides an evidentiary mechanism for the government to demonstrate "[t]he response of a foreign nation to a claim of registry," this provision again does not specify a timeline for the inquiry. 46 U.S.C. § 70502(d)(2) (stating that the response "may be made by radio, telephone, or similar oral or electronic means, and is proved conclusively by certification of the Secretary of State or the Secretary's designee").[22] Given the complex issues of international and municipal law that may be at issue, the costs associated with maintaining a registry, and the [—29—] small size of the boat in question in this case, how can it be expected that an "unequivocal" assertion of nationality could be made by Colombia in twenty-four hours? We have examples in this circuit of countries taking up to five days to provide a definitive response, so imposing an arbitrary timeline of twenty-four hours is something not required by the MDLEA and increases the likelihood of a grave violation of international law. *United States v. Cardales*, 168 F.3d 548, 551-52 (1st Cir. 1999) (On May 31, Venezuela was unable to say if a boat that claimed Venezuelan registry was Venezuelan, but on June 5 "the Venezuelan government notified the State Department that the [boat] was indeed of Venezuelan registry.").

This court is directed to avoid interpreting the MDLEA in a way that would result in a violation of international law. *Murray v. Schooner Charming Betsy*, 6 U.S. (2 Cranch) 64, 117-18 (1804). Reading the MDLEA to permit the half-hearted attempt to establish nationality that was made here to establish statelessness in violation of international law is in direct contradiction to this longstanding notion of statutory construction. *Weinberger v. Rossi*, 456 U.S. 25, 32 (1982) (applying Schooner *Charming Betsy* as a "maxim of statutory construction."). Because nothing in the statute denied the government or Trinidad's attorney the ability to conduct further inquiry into the nationality of the vessel, it is incumbent on [—30—] us to avoid reading into the statute a requirement that

---

[21] I am unaware of any rule that prohibits the establishment of nationality by the use of circumstantial evidence.

[22] The record does not appear to include the required certificate, presumably because Trinidad and Coa-Peña pled guilty and did not challenge the jurisdiction of the court.

the described verification was legally sufficient to establish the statelessness of Trinidad's boat.

Trinidad's shipmate *invoked Colombian nationality for the vessel*, and Colombia could not confirm or deny this assertion within the short time provided. Colombia did not grant U.S. authorities permission to subject the boat to U.S. jurisdiction, and so the United States unilaterally decided that, pursuant to its laws, the vessel was stateless and therefore subject to U.S. criminal laws. I cannot read the MDLEA as permitting such a brazen expansion of U.S. jurisdiction at the expense of international law.

B. The Degree of Proof Necessary to Establish Statelessness

Finally, I further object to this circuit's treatment of this question as one that may be answered by a preponderance of the evidence. *Matos-Luchi*, 627 F.3d at 5; *see also United States v. Vilches-Navarrete*, 523 F.3d 1, 8-10 (1st Cir. 2008) (Torruella, J., dissenting in part). This is done by treating the question of statelessness as one of jurisdiction, but as my analysis above seeks to demonstrate, the status of Trinidad's boat goes far beyond the question of whether United States courts have jurisdiction. It goes to the very heart of whether there has been any crime committed at all. *Matos-Luchi*, 627 F.3d at 14 (Lipez, J., dissenting) ("[A] failure to prove that [—31—] defendants' conduct occurred on board a covered vessel amounts to a failure to prove that the defendants violated the MDLEA."). If Trinidad cannot face any criminal penalty at all in the absence of proof of his vessel's statelessness, how can proof of his vessel's statelessness possibly be subjected to a preponderance of the evidence standard? *See United States v. Perlaza*, 439 F.3d 1149, 1167 (9th Cir. 2006) (holding that when a jurisdictional inquiry into statelessness turns on factual issues, then it "*must* be resolved by a jury").

IV.

With due respect, I cannot join an opinion which validates the blatant violation of international law by the United States.

United States Court of Appeals
for the First Circuit

No. 13-2249

UNITED STATES
vs.
DE LA CRUZ-GARCÍA

Appeal from the United States District Court for the
District of Puerto Rico

Decided: November 16, 2016

Citation: 842 F.3d 1, 4 Adm. R. 36 (1st Cir. 2016).

Before **HOWARD**, Chief Judge, and **TORRUELLA** and
KAYATTA, Circuit Judges.

[—2—] **HOWARD**, Chief Judge:

Appellant Pedro De La Cruz-García pled guilty to illegally bringing aliens into the United States by boat in violation of 8 U.S.C. § 1324(a)(1)(A)(i). The district court sentenced De La Cruz to thirty-eight months in prison based, in part, on a ten-level enhancement for the death of a passenger who jumped from the boat. For the reasons discussed below, we affirm the sentence.

I.

On February 28, 2013, De La Cruz and two fellow citizens of the Dominican Republic crowded twenty-six passengers from Haiti onto their makeshift twenty-five-foot vessel named the "Don Tino." The group set sail for United States soil via the Mona Passage. Ultimately, the journey proved unsuccessful. Law enforcement agents observed the vessel approaching Mona Island, Puerto Rico, and reported the illegal migrant landing to the Department of Homeland Security.

Upon being discovered by law enforcement, several passengers jumped from the Don Tino in a last-ditch effort to reach shore. The authorities apprehended all but one of the passengers. An unaccounted-for Haitian woman, however, remained in the water. After an unsuccessful rescue attempt, the missing passenger's body, later identified as Gedette Benjamin, was recovered off the coast of Mona Island. [—3—]

Once in custody, De La Cruz agreed to speak with authorities and described his plan to illegally enter the United States. The ensuing investigation revealed that the three Dominican Republic nationals, including De La Cruz, were responsible for navigating and operating the Don Tino. De La Cruz agreed to assist with the journey in return for free passage.

De La Cruz ultimately entered into an agreement with the government and pled guilty to one count of bringing or attempting to bring an alien into the United States at a place other than a designated port of entry. *See* 8 U.S.C. § 1324(a)(1)(A)(i). The plea agreement expressly reserved De La Cruz's right to oppose the U.S.S.G. § 2L1.1(b)(7)(D) sentence enhancement, which applies "[i]f any person died" during the commission of the offense. Ultimately, the district court imposed the ten-level enhancement, resulting in a guideline range of forty-one to fifty-one months. The court varied below that range, sentencing De La Cruz to thirty-eight months in prison and a three-year term of supervised release.

On appeal, De La Cruz challenges only the ten-level enhancement pursuant to § 2L1.1(b)(7)(D).

II.

We review the district court's fact-finding under the deferential "clear error" standard and its "resolution of legal [—4—] questions" de novo. *United States v. McCormick*, 773 F.3d 357, 359 (1st Cir. 2014).

The parties disagree as to the appropriate causation standard under § 2L1.1(b)(7). The government urges us to adopt but-for causation, while De La Cruz suggests a foreseeability requirement.[1] We have not

---

[1] De La Cruz does not argue that the appropriate standard is proximate causation. *See United States v. Ramos-Delgado*, 763 F.3d 398, 401 (5th Cir. 2014) (noting circuit split on this issue). Accordingly, we decline to address whether proximate causation is the applicable standard or how, if at all, such a standard would differ from a requirement of reasonable foreseeability.

previously considered this issue, and other circuits have reached divergent results. *Compare United States v. Zaldivar*, 615 F.3d 1346, 1350-51 (11th Cir. 2010) ("[I]t must be reasonably foreseeable to a defendant that his actions or the actions of any other member of the smuggling operation could create the sort of dangerous circumstances that would be likely to result in serious injury or death."), *and United States v. Cardena-Garcia*, 362 F.3d 663, 666 (10th Cir. 2004) (holding that "[a] sufficient nexus" exists where "the death . . . was reasonably foreseeable and Appellants' conduct was a contributing factor"), *with Ramos*, 763 F.3d at 401 (requiring only "actual or but-for causation").

Ultimately, we need not resolve this dispute. Applying De La Cruz's preferred standard, the district court did not clearly [—5—] err in finding, by a preponderance of the evidence, that the passenger's death was a reasonably foreseeable result of De La Cruz's actions. In pleading guilty, De La Cruz admitted to using an unseaworthy and overcrowded vessel to transport passengers through dangerous waters. As the district court articulated, "many things can go wrong" in such a situation. For example, "[y]ou can sink . . . . You can all drown. You can be caught." We agree that, when De La Cruz set sail on an illegal alien smuggling operation, he could have reasonably foreseen the possibility that the vessel would be spotted by the authorities as it approached shore. He also could have foreseen the possibility that some passengers, desperate to avoid apprehension and reach United States soil, might leap into the sea. *See Zaldivar*, 615 F.3d at 1351 (finding it "reasonably foreseeable" that the defendant's coconspirator would "fle[e] at a high rate of speed once th[e] boat had been detected by the Coast Guard"). Indeed, Ms. Benjamin was not the only passenger to have taken this risk, as eleven other people followed her into the water. Finally, in light of De La Cruz's concession that the rough sea conditions were foreseeable, it was hardly a stretch that passengers jumping overboard might drown. Ms. Benjamin's tragic death was reasonably foreseeable in these circumstances. [—6—]

III.

For the foregoing reasons, we **AFFIRM** De La Cruz's sentence.

United States Court of Appeals
for the First Circuit

No. 16-1302

NEVOR
VS.
MONEYPENNY HOLDINGS, LLC

Appeals from the United States District Court for the
District of Rhode Island

Decided: November 22, 2016

Citation: 842 F.3d 113, 4 Adm. R. 38 (1st Cir. 2016).

Before **BARRON, SELYA,** and **STAHL,** Circuit Judges.

[—2—] **SELYA,** Circuit Judge:

In this maritime personal injury case, the district court awarded the plaintiff compensatory damages for past and future harms totaling nearly $1,500,000. Adding insult to injury, the court tacked on prejudgment interest at the Rhode Island state rate of 12% per annum and entered judgment in the plaintiff's favor for $2,318,487. The defendant appeals, challenging both the damages award and the prejudgment interest increment.

After careful consideration, we find the award of damages to be unimpugnable. The award of prejudgment interest, though, presents greater complications: with respect to that award, we tackle a question of first impression within this circuit and, following the resolution of that question, affirm the interest award in part and reverse it in part. The tale follows.

I. BACKGROUND

We rehearse the relevant facts as found by the district court, *see Nevor v. Moneypenny Holdings, LLC,* 2016 WL 183906 (D.R.I. Jan. 14, 2016), consistent with record support. Plaintiff-appellee Kenneth Nevor was once a professional sailor. His experience included sailing, racing, and transporting racing yachts. His skillset extended to maintaining and repairing sailboats, their mechanical equipment, and their electronic gear.

Nevor began sailing as a boy and—by the age of 35—had participated in a number of elite racing events worldwide. At [—3—] the time of the mishap giving rise to this action, Nevor was an employee of defendant-appellant Moneypenny Holdings, LLC (Moneypenny), which owned a 52-foot sailing vessel called the Vesper and a 35-foot motor support vessel called the Odd Job.

In March of 2011, Nevor was part of a crew preparing the Vesper for a regatta in the Caribbean. The Vesper was travelling in the British Virgin Islands when the members of the crew learned that they—but not the boat—needed to return to St. Thomas to clear customs. To facilitate this process, the Odd Job met the Vesper with a view toward carrying some crewmembers back to shore. When the Odd Job pulled up alongside the Vesper, the Vesper's captain directed some of the crew (including Nevor) to transfer from the Vesper to the Odd Job. The wind was blowing at between eight and twelve knots—normal for that time of year—but the sea was choppy. Still, the captain did not lash the Odd Job and Vesper together before proceeding with the transfer.

As Nevor disembarked the Vesper to board the Odd Job, the boats separated. Nevor slipped, grasping the Vesper's lifeline as he reached for the Odd Job with his foot. He was able to complete the transfer, but the stress on his right arm caused his bicep to tear from the bone.

Nevor stayed with the Vesper for two weeks after his injury to assist with race preparations. He then returned stateside to undergo surgery. Once the operation was performed, [—4—] he completed six months of physical therapy. Even after he had finished the prescribed course of therapy, his treating physician found residual atrophy in the reattached muscle. Several months later, Nevor visited another specialist who determined that Nevor's right arm remained weaker than his left and was unlikely to improve. This specialist concluded that Nevor could not do the heavy lifting that his previous job demanded.

In June of 2013, Nevor invoked admiralty jurisdiction, *see* 28 U.S.C. § 1333, and sued Moneypenny in Rhode Island's federal district court.[1] His complaint alleged negligence under the Jones Act, *see* 46 U.S.C. §§ 30101-30106, and unseaworthiness under general maritime law.

Following a four-day bench trial, the district court wrote a thorough and closely reasoned rescript stating its findings of fact and conclusions of law. The court awarded Nevor $1,460,458 in damages ($710,458 for loss of earnings and loss of future earning capacity and $750,000 for pain, suffering, and mental anguish).[2] *See Nevor*, 2016 WL 183906, at *7. The court subsequently granted Nevor's motion to add prejudgment interest to [—5—] the damages award. This increment, which totaled $858,029, brought the aggregate judgment to $2,318,487 (plus costs).

These consolidated appeals ensued.[3] In them, Moneypenny concedes liability but challenges several of the monetary components of the judgment.

II. ANALYSIS

Moneypenny's claims of error fall into two broad categories. First, it offers various reasons why the award of damages should be deemed excessive. Second, it assails the prejudgment interest award as totally inappropriate and, alternatively, says that no prejudgment interest should accrue on damages for future harm. We address these claims sequentially.

---

[1] Nevor's complaint named James R. Swartz, Moneypenny's principal, as a codefendant. Nevor subsequently dropped Swartz as a party, though, and we make no further mention of him.

[2] Nevor's hospital and medical expenses were paid separately as part of the shipowner's obligation of maintenance and cure. *See Whitman v. Miles*, 387 F.3d 68, 71-72 (1st Cir. 2004).

[3] Moneypenny filed notices of appeal on two separate occasions. For simplicity's sake, we treat the appeals as a unit.

A. *Damages.*

As an opening salvo, Moneypenny blasts the district court's stated basis for awarding economic damages (lost wages and prospective loss of earning capacity). In its words, the court's factual findings were "clearly erroneous" and "premised on inadmissible speculation."

In the aftermath of a bench trial, we review the district court's factual findings for clear error. *See Reliance Steel Prods. Co. v. Nat'l Fire Ins. Co.*, 880 F.2d 575, 576 (1st Cir. 1989). We will set aside those findings "only if, on the entire [—6—] evidence, we are left with the definite and firm conviction that a mistake has been committed." *Id.* (citation omitted). Whether we would have reached the same result as the district court is not the issue: "[w]here there are two permissible views of the evidence, the factfinder's choice between them cannot be clearly erroneous." *Id.* at 577 (quoting *Anderson v. City of Bessemer City*, 470 U.S. 564, 574 (1985)).

This deferential standard of review applies with unabated force when a district court's findings depend wholly or in part on expert testimony. When judges act as factfinders, they are given "considerable leeway in choosing among the views of experts and in determining the weight and value to be assigned to the opinions of each expert." *Reilly v. United States*, 863 F.2d 149, 167 (1st Cir. 1988).

At trial, the parties presented detailed information about the sailing industry, as well as expert testimony about Nevor's physical limitations, projected wages, past and future earning capacity, vocational capabilities, and work-life expectancy. With respect to Nevor's projected wages and lost earning capacity— the focal points of the district court's economic damages calculation—Nevor's experts testified that at the time of the accident he was "at the cusp" of joining the ranks of the ultra-elite sailors who earned between $100,000 and $120,000 per year. This evidence was consistent with the fact that, in the [—7—] first three months of 2011 (the year of his injury), Nevor already had earned just shy of

$30,000 working for Moneypenny. The experts went on to explain that Nevor was one of "only maybe a thousand people" competing internationally at an elite level and that he had the skills and strength required to advance. Similarly, they opined that, but for the injuries sustained in the accident, Nevor could have remained employed as a top-echelon sailor for several decades.[4]

Of course, this evidence did not go unrebutted. Moneypenny presented expert testimony that Nevor sustained virtually no loss in earning capacity as a result of the accident and that, even if not injured, he was unlikely to earn more than $100,000 per year as a sailor.

The district court sided with Nevor's experts. It concluded that, but for the injuries sustained in the accident, Nevor "would have continued to be employed in high-level sailing" and "would have advanced as a professional sailor in his chosen field if he had not been injured." *Nevor*, 2016 WL 183906, at *6. [—8—] In reaching these conclusions, the court found persuasive the testimony voiced by Nevor's witnesses regarding his vocational capabilities, earning capacity, and work-life expectancy.

In this venue, Moneypenny asseverates that the compiled record offered "no reliable means of predicting the duration of Nevor's sailing career, the positions which he may have held, or the income which he might have earned." And although Moneypenny concedes that it might have been "possible" for Nevor to reach sailing's upper echelon and earn the wages commensurate with sailing at that level, it insists that the evidence fell well short

of the "reliable demonstration" benchmark set by the Supreme Court. *See Jones & Laughlin Steel Corp. v. Pfeifer*, 462 U.S. 523, 534-35 (1983) (explaining that "[a]lthough it may be difficult to prove when, and whether, a particular injured worker might have received [] wage increases, . . . they may be reliably demonstrated for some workers").

Contrary to Moneypenny's importunings, a reliable demonstration does not demand proof positive. Forecasting future losses necessarily requires the trier to sift through the projections of experts, gauge the credibility of witnesses, and draw reasonable inferences from the facts. *See Johnson v. Watts Regulator Co.*, 63 F.3d 1129, 1138 (1st Cir. 1995); *Reliance Steel*, 880 F.2d at 576. While robes and gavels, not tea leaves or crystal balls, are the tools of a trial judge's trade, some degree of [—9—] speculation is inherent in any such forecast. A reliable demonstration demands only that the court's prediction is reasonable, given the facts in the record. Here, we must give due weight to the court's determinations of witness credibility, its findings as to the relative persuasiveness of various experts, and its appraisal of competing facts. *See Reliance Steel*, 880 F.2d at 576.

Viewed through this prism, we find plentiful support in the record for the court's determination that Nevor had in prospect a top-flight racing career that was likely to be long and successful and lost it due to the injuries sustained in the accident. Consequently, we decline Moneypenny's invitation to second-guess the district court's founded determination that the evidence reliably demonstrated that Nevor was likely to move further up the ranks. In the last analysis, that determination depended upon a weighing of conflicting evidence, and such an appraisal falls peculiarly within the trial court's ken. *See Reilly*, 863 F.2d at 167.

Moneypenny next argues that Nevor's failure to attend a specialized vocational rehabilitation program constituted a breach of his duty to mitigate damages and should have reduced his damages award. The district court saw the matter differently and did not reduce the award on this account. [—10—]

---

[4] In the court below, Moneypenny made several unsuccessful attempts to strike the testimony of Nevor's vocational expert (Michael LaRaia). On appeal, it complains of these denials in but a single sentence in its opening brief: a conclusory assertion that the district court abused its discretion in refusing to strike the testimony. We thus deem the argument undeveloped and consider it waived. *See United States v. Zannino*, 895 F.2d 1, 17 (1st Cir. 1990) ("[I]ssues adverted to in a perfunctory manner, unaccompanied by some effort at developed argumentation, are deemed waived.").

At the threshold, we note that mitigation is in the nature of an affirmative defense. *See Allied Int'l, Inc. v. Int'l Longshoremen's Ass'n*, 814 F.2d 32, 38-39 (1st Cir. 1987). Thus, Moneypenny bore the burden to prove by a preponderance of the evidence that Nevor "failed to take reasonable steps to hold down [his] losses." *Id*. As the proponent of an affirmative defense, Moneypenny also bore "the risk of equipoise." *O'Neal v. McAninch*, 513 U.S. 432, 444 (1995).

On appeal, Moneypenny ascribes two errors to the district court's refusal to credit its mitigation defense. We start with its suggestion that the district court was obligated to give a fuller explanation of its ruling.

The Civil Rules provide that, after a bench trial, "the court must find the facts specially and state its conclusions of law separately." Fed. R. Civ. P. 52(a)(1). This rule, however, has practical limits. A "district court [is] not required to make findings on every detail, [is] not required to discuss all of the evidence that supports each of the findings made, and [is] not required to respond individually to each evidentiary or factual contention made by the losing side." *Addamax Corp. v. Open Software Found., Inc.*, 152 F.3d 48, 55 (1st Cir. 1998). The court's findings are adequate as long as they "make plain the basis for its disposition of the case." *Valsamis v. González-Romero*, 748 F.3d 61, 63 (1st Cir. 2014). **[—11—]**

Here, the district court explained in considerable detail the basis for its findings on liability, concluding that Moneypenny was liable under both the Jones Act (for negligence) and general maritime law (for unseaworthiness). *See Nevor*, 2016 WL 183906, at *4-5. It then set forth (again, in considerable detail) the basis for its calculation of damages. *See id*. at *5-7. Those calculations rejected, albeit implicitly, Moneypenny's mitigation defense.[5] The

upshot is that the court found the facts with particularity, stated its legal conclusions plainly, and explained in no uncertain terms its disposition of the case. No more was exigible to satisfy the requirements of Rule 52(a). *See Damon v. Sun Co.*, 87 F.3d 1467, 1480 (1st Cir. 1996); *see also Banerjee v. Bd. of Trs. of Smith Coll.*, 648 F.2d 61, 66 (1st Cir. 1981).

The second branch of Moneypenny's mitigation defense is its claim that the evidence required a finding of failure to mitigate. We disagree: the district court's implicit conclusion that Moneypenny's mitigation defense did not hold water is adequately supported in the record. **[—12—]**

The relevant facts are susceptible to succinct summarization. Moneypenny introduced evidence that one of Nevor's doctors prescribed a round of vocational rehabilitation sessions that Nevor did not attend. Nevor countered that he was never notified about this proposed regimen. He also introduced evidence that, even if he had been notified, the therapy was unavailable—the rehabilitation center that he was directed to attend treated only injuries (unlike Nevor's) arising under state workers' compensation law. We think it a commonsense proposition that a plaintiff cannot be charged with a failure to mitigate damages when the suggested mitigation measure is unavailable to him.

What is more, the record is replete with testimony that, far from avoiding therapy, Nevor avidly sought it out. On one occasion, he asked his doctor to refer him for an additional round of physical therapy. At other times, he sought therapy on his own.

The short of it is that the district court faced a fact-sensitive determination on the mitigation issue, couched in evidence that lent itself to multiple interpretations. Where, as here, "the conclusions of the [trier] depend on its election among conflicting facts or its choice of which competing inferences to draw from undisputed basic facts, appellate courts should defer to such fact-intensive findings, absent clear error." *Reliance Steel*, 880 F.2d at 576 (alteration in original) (quoting *Irons v.*

---

[5] There is no question, though, that the district court did in fact consider the mitigation defense. At trial, the court acknowledged that the parties had "thoroughly covered" and "valiantly argued" the issue, and vouchsafed that it would "take [the mitigation defense] into consideration."

[—13—] *FBI*, 811 F.2d 681, 684 (1st Cir. 1987)). Such deference is appropriate in this instance, and we discern no clear error in the court's implicit conclusion that Nevor was not guilty of failing to mitigate his damages.

This brings us to Moneypenny's claim that the award of non-economic damages (for pain and suffering, mental anguish, and the like) is excessive and unsupported by the evidence. The court's ultimate conclusion—the monetization of Nevor's noneconomic harms—is assayed for abuse of discretion. *See Limone v. United States*, 579 F.3d 79, 103 (1st Cir. 2009) (describing such a conclusion as a "classic example of a judgment call"). Such an award will stand unless it "shock[s] our collective conscience or raise[s] the specter of a miscarriage of justice." *Id.* at 84.

We conclude that the district court's non-economic damages award finds sufficient purchase in the record. Nevor offered ample evidence showing that he underwent significant pain and suffering, that his quality of life was reduced, and that he experienced lasting physical and emotional distress long after the accident. He submitted to a painful surgery, endured a lengthy recovery, attended months of physical therapy sessions, and was forced to limit his physical activities. Moreover, Nevor faces the prospect of lasting consequences because his injuries (including some residual scarring) have been found to be permanent. [—14—]

Non-economic damages are notoriously difficult to quantify. "[T]here is no scientific formula or measuring device which can be applied to place a precise dollar value" on pain, suffering, and other items of intangible harm. *Limone*, 579 F.3d at 105 (quoting *Wagenmann v. Adams*, 829 F.2d 196, 216 (1st Cir. 1987)). Given what Nevor has experienced and what he predictably faces, we find the district court's award to be within the wide universe of reasonable awards. Though generous, the award is proportional to the weight of the evidence and is neither conscience-shocking nor a harbinger of a miscarriage of justice. Indeed, it is consistent with awards in analogous cases. *See, e.g., Bielunas v. F/V Misty Dawn, Inc.*, 621 F.3d

72, 80-82 (1st Cir. 2010) (affirming award of over $2,000,000 in non-economic damages where plaintiff sustained painful foot injury that resulted in disability).

For these reasons, the district court's damages award must be affirmed in full.

B. *Interest.*

Moneypenny's interest-related assignments of error can be divided into two tranches. First, Moneypenny submits that the successful Jones Act claim should have precluded any award of prejudgment interest. Second, Moneypenny submits that—even apart from his Jones Act argument—the district court should not have granted Nevor any prejudgment interest with respect to damages for [—15—] future harm. We address these matters one by one, affording de novo review to questions of law and abuse-of-discretion review to judgment calls. *See Limone*, 579 F.3d at 102.

We preface our discussion of specific issues with a synopsis of the applicable legal doctrine. A seaman injured during the course of his employment may recover damages under a variety of statutory and common-law theories, including (as pertinent here) the Jones Act and general maritime law. The Jones Act provides a cause of action for a seaman injured through his employer's negligence. *See* 46 U.S.C. §§ 30101-30106. Whether a plaintiff is entitled to prejudgment interest on an award of damages under the Jones Act, however, is open to question. The prevailing view appears to be that, in pure Jones Act suits, recovery of prejudgment interest is not permitted.[6] *See Petersen v. Chesapeake & Ohio Ry. Co.*, 784 F.2d 732, 740

---

[6] There is, however, some play in the joints. *Compare Wyatt v. Penrod Drilling Co.*, 735 F.2d 951, 955 (5th Cir. 1984) (noting that the Fifth Circuit has "disapproved the award of prejudgment interest in a Jones Act case tried to a jury"), *with Williams v. Reading & Bates Drilling Co.*, 750 F.2d 487, 491 (5th Cir. 1985) (holding that when a federal court sits in admiralty jurisdiction, the judge may exercise his discretion to award prejudgment interest on a Jones Act claim).

(6th Cir. 1986). Our court has not squarely addressed this issue.

The situation is quite different with respect to general maritime law. Under that body of law, there is a common-law cause of action for injuries resulting from the unseaworthiness of a [—16—] vessel on which a seaman was employed. *See Poulis-Minott v. Smith*, 388 F.3d 354, 366 (1st Cir. 2004). In that context, "[p]rejudgment interest is generally available." *Borges v. Our Lady of the Sea Corp.*, 935 F.2d 436, 443 n.1 (1st Cir. 1991).

There is a split of authority about whether an injured seaman who prevails on fully aligned claims under both the Jones Act and the unseaworthiness rubric may be awarded prejudgment interest. For example, some courts of appeals have held that a seaman is not entitled to prejudgment interest when he prevails on parallel Jones Act and unseaworthiness claims. *See Petersen*, 784 F.2d at 741; *see also Wyatt v. Penrod Drilling Co.*, 735 F.2d 951, 956 (5th Cir. 1984) (noting that "[i]f the court may not award prejudgment interest on the Jones Act claim, there is no separate pure admiralty item on which to allow interest" (internal alteration and citation omitted)). The Second Circuit has viewed the matter differently. When a seaman prevails on both Jones Act and unseaworthiness claims and there are no exceptional circumstances militating against an award of prejudgment interest, that court has held that the seaman is entitled to prejudgment interest on the total amount of the award. *See Magee v. U.S. Lines, Inc.*, 976 F.2d 821, 822 (2d Cir. 1992). That rule is preferable, the court reasoned, because it permits the plaintiff to "be paid under the theory of liability that provides the most complete recovery." *Id.* [—17—]

It is in this stormy sea that we must anchor our analysis. Moneypenny, though, attempts to circumnavigate the issue entirely. It claims that the district court's damages award was based solely on a finding of Jones Act negligence and, thus, cannot bear the weight of prejudgment interest. The record belies this claim.

In its separate written order awarding prejudgment interest, the district court explicitly found that Nevor was entitled to prejudgment interest because the damages award was, at least in part, under general maritime law (that is, for unseaworthiness). The language of the district court's earlier rescript supports this characterization. There, the court found that Moneypenny's failure to apply a non-skid product to the Odd Job's slippery side "made the [boat] unseaworthy and substantially contributed to" Nevor's injuries. *Nevor*, 2016 WL 183906, at *5. Additionally, the court found that Moneypenny's failure either to provide proper training to its crew or to implement appropriate safety procedures rendered both the Vesper and the Odd Job unseaworthy and further contributed to Nevor's injuries. *See id.*

The district court's conclusion that the damages award was based in part on a finding of unseaworthiness was not clearly erroneous. To begin, a district court's characterization of its own findings is entitled to some deference. *See Martha's Vineyard Scuba Headquarters, Inc. v. Unidentified, Wrecked & Abandoned* [—18—] *Steam Vessel*, 833 F.2d 1059, 1066-67 (1st Cir. 1987) (acknowledging the "special role played by the writing judge in elucidating the meaning and intendment of an order which he authored"). The court below, sitting without a jury, was entitled to weigh the evidence and to draw reasonable inferences. *See Reliance Steel*, 880 F.2d at 576-77. In the circumstances of this case, we conclude, without serious question, that the damages award was a "mixed" award.

Struggling to right a sinking ship, Moneypenny asserts that even if the lack of non-skid product rendered the Odd Job unseaworthy, the record does not establish that this particular unseaworthiness contributed to Nevor's injuries. We need not probe this point too deeply because, even assuming (albeit without deciding) that Moneypenny's assertion may have some force, it would not change our conclusion. The district court's findings regarding Moneypenny's failure to provide proper training and to implement appropriate safety procedures are well-documented, and those findings are alone sufficient to show that the damages award was based at least in part on a viable theory of unseaworthiness. *See Crumady v. The Joachim Hendrik Fisser*, 358 U.S. 423, 427 (1959) (explaining that "[u]nseaworthiness extends not only to the vessel but to the crew"); *Cape Fear, Inc. v. Martin*, 312 F.3d 496, 500 (1st Cir. 2002) (explaining that procedures crewmembers employ may render ship unseaworthy). [—19—]

Having established that the damages award straddles both a successful Jones Act claim and a successful unseaworthiness claim, we turn to Moneypenny's contention that the presence of the Jones Act claim poisons the well and precludes an award of prejudgment interest. We assume for argument's sake—but do not decide—that a successful Jones Act claim, standing alone, would not bear prejudgment interest. Even so, we reject Moneypenny's contention. We hold that when a court, in a bench trial, awards damages based on mixed Jones Act and unseaworthiness claims, prejudgment interest is available.[7] We explain briefly.

To begin, we lay to rest a diversion. Moneypenny asserts that our analysis is controlled by the Supreme Court's decision in *Miles v. Apex Marine Corp.*, 498 U.S. 19 (1990). There, the Court considered whether the estate of a deceased seaman could recover the seaman's future lost earnings under general maritime law. *See id.* at 21. The Court observed that even if it were to create an exception to the traditional rule that unseaworthiness claims do not survive a seaman's death, it would nevertheless bar the recovery of the deceased seaman's lost wages because the Jones Act—which does include a limited survival right—already prohibits such a recovery. Thus, there was no principled basis for expanding [—20—] the remedies available in a general maritime action based on strict liability. *See id.* at 33-36.

The case at hand, however, is a different kettle of fish. The *Miles* plaintiff wanted the Court to create a general maritime law remedy that was previously unavailable. Here, however, Nevor seeks to have us retain a remedy—prejudgment interest on damages awarded in connection with admiralty torts—that was available long before the passage of the Jones Act. *See City of Milwaukee v. Cement Div., Nat'l. Gypsum Co.*, 515 U.S. 189, 195 & n.7, 196 (1995). Seen in this light, this case fits much more closely with *Atlantic Sounding Co. v. Townsend*, 557 U.S. 404 (2009), in which the Court concluded that the passage of the Jones Act did not implicitly deprive plaintiffs of their longstanding right to recover those damages historically available under general maritime law. *See id.* at 408 (holding that the Jones Act did not preclude plaintiffs from seeking punitive damages in combined Jones Act and general maritime law cases); *id.* at 420 (noting that "[u]nlike the situation presented in *Miles*, both the general maritime cause of action . . . and the remedy . . . were well established before the passage of the Jones Act").

With this potential distraction laid to rest, we return to the question of whether the intertwining of Jones Act and unseaworthiness claims precludes Nevor from any access to prejudgment interest. We approach this conundrum mindful that [—21—] "prejudgment interest traditionally has been considered part of the compensation due plaintiff." *Osterneck v. Ernst & Whinney*, 489 U.S. 169, 175 (1989). The "essential rationale for awarding prejudgment interest is to ensure that an injured party is fully compensated for its loss," and "[f]ull compensation has long been recognized as a basic principle of admiralty law." *City of Milwaukee*, 515 U.S. at 195-96. Put simply, an award of prejudgment interest helps achieve the laudable goal of making an injured plaintiff whole. *See id.* at 196. It follows that adopting Moneypenny's grudging approach to prejudgment interest would prevent many prevailing plaintiffs from recovering damages generally considered part of their due compensation. *See Osterneck*, 489 U.S. at 175.

---

[7] We take no view as to the appropriate interest rate to be applied. The court below borrowed the Rhode Island state rate for prejudgment interest in tort actions, *see* R.I. Gen. Laws § 9-21-10, and Moneypenny has not contested the court's use of that rate.

To be sure, a plaintiff who recovers damages for a general maritime law claim, such as an unseaworthiness claim, may lose his right to prejudgment interest if "exceptional circumstances" make an award of interest inequitable. *City of Milwaukee*, 515 U.S. at 194-95 (citation omitted). Such circumstances might include, say, undue delay by the prevailing party, exorbitant over-estimation of damages, or bad faith. *See Anderson v. Whittaker Corp.*, 894 F.2d 804, 809 (6th Cir. 1990) (citation omitted); *Alkmeon Naviera, S.A. v. M/V Marina L*, 633 F.2d 789, 797-98 (9th Cir. 1980) (collecting cases). But the [—22—] record here evinces no such disabling circumstance: Nevor has prosecuted his case forcefully, but not unreasonably so.[8]

Even though our court has not decided the precise question with which we are confronted, a persuasive analogy exists. We have held that when a plaintiff raises claims under parallel causes of action (both federal and state, for example) and receives a damages award straddling both of those fully aligned claims, the defendant may not cite the presence of a more restricted remedy on one claim to deny the plaintiff a more expansive remedy on the other claim. *See Tobin v. Liberty Mut. Ins. Co.*, 553 F.3d 121, 146 (1st Cir. 2009) (explaining that "a successful plaintiff's right to a particular remedy under federal law does not trump his right to a more advantageous remedy under state law"). Thus, "[w]hen federal and state claims overlap, the plaintiff may choose to be awarded damages based on state law if that law offers a more generous outcome than federal law." *Id.*; *accord Freeman v. Package Mach. Co.*, 865 F.2d 1331, 1345 (1st Cir. 1988) (noting that although a prevailing plaintiff in such a situation is "entitled [—23—] to only a single slice of the pie[,] . . . the choice of the slice [is] his").

This same paradigm seems altogether appropriate where, as here, a plaintiff has prevailed on fully aligned Jones Act and unseaworthiness claims. After all, the plaintiff is entitled to interest on the unseaworthiness claim and there is no logical reason why his broader success should strip him of that entitlement.

There is yet another leg to our voyage. Although we hold that the district court was correct in awarding some prejudgment interest (due to the successful unseaworthiness claim), we nonetheless agree with Moneypenny that the court went too far: in fashioning an award of prejudgment interest, the court should first have set to one side the damages attributable to future harm.

In this circuit, the law is well-established that "prejudgment interest should not be awarded on damages for future loss, either liquidated or unliquidated." *Borges*, 935 F.2d at 444-45 (collecting cases). This is a reflection of the commonsense notion that interest should not accrue before the harm itself has occurred. *See id.* at 445.

The law of the circuit doctrine requires this court (and, by extension, all lower courts within this circuit) to respect, in the absence of supervening authority, the decisions of prior panels [—24—] on the same issue. *See San Juan Cable LLC v. P.R. Tel. Co.*, 612 F.3d 25, 33 (1st Cir. 2010). "Once we have decided a legal question and articulated our reasoning, there is usually no need for us to repastinate the same soil when another case presents essentially the same legal question." *Vander Luitgaren v. Sun Life Assur. Co. of Canada*, 765 F.3d 59, 61 (1st Cir. 2014). Although there are a few exceptions to this rule, *see San Juan Cable*, 612 F.3d at 33 (describing narrow exceptions to law of the circuit doctrine), none applies here. We conclude, therefore, that the district court was bound to follow *Borges*, and its failure to do so constitutes reversible

---

[8] The mere fact that Nevor elected to sue simultaneously under both the Jones Act and general maritime law is not itself an exceptional circumstance. *See McAllister v. Magnolia Petrol. Co.*, 357 U.S. 221, 224-25 (1958) (explaining that if a seaman "is to sue for both unseaworthiness [under general maritime law] and Jones Act negligence, he must do so in a single proceeding" and that such an injured seaman will "rarely forego" his right to seek relief under both causes of action).

error.[9] Prejudgment interest must be limited to items of loss that were in the rear-view mirror at the time of the damages award and the concomitant entry of judgment (*e.g.*, wages and earning capacity already lost, pain and suffering already experienced, and the like). Correspondingly, the award of prejudgment interest must omit items of loss not yet accrued as of that date (*e.g.*, future loss of wages and earning capacity, future pain and suffering, and the like). On remand, the district court [—**25**—] must reformulate its award of prejudgment interest in accordance with these principles.

III. CONCLUSION

We need go no further. For the reasons elucidated above, we affirm the damages award; affirm the award of prejudgment interest in part and reverse it in part; and remand for the entry of an amended judgment, nunc pro tunc, consistent with this opinion. The amended judgment shall, of course, carry post-judgment interest at the federal rate, *see* 28 U.S.C. § 1961(a), which will commence to run (by virtue of the nunc pro tunc provision) from the date of the original judgment, *see Fiorentino v. Rio Mar Assocs. LP, SE*, 626 F.3d 648, 652 (1st Cir. 2010).

Affirmed in part, reversed in part, and remanded. Two-thirds costs shall be taxed in favor of the plaintiff.

---

[9] At oral argument, Nevor insisted that our opinion in *Rivera v. Rederi A/B Nordstjernan*, 456 F.2d 970 (1st Cir. 1972), supports his receipt of prejudgment interest on damages for future harms. This is magical thinking: *Rivera* held that trial judges have discretion to award prejudgment interest in some cases, but it did not address the propriety of awarding such interest with respect to damages for future harms. *See id.* at 976.

United States Court of Appeals
for the First Circuit

No. 16-1267

BLOCK ISLAND FISHING, INC.
vs.
ROGERS

Appeals from the United States District Court for the
District of Massachusetts

Decided: December 23, 2016

Citation: 844 F.3d 358, 4 Adm. R. 47 (1st Cir. 2016).

Before **LYNCH, LIPEZ,** and **BARRON,** Circuit Judges.

[—2—] **LYNCH,** Circuit Judge:

This case involves rulings of some significance to seamen and their employers in this circuit, as well as for summary judgment practice. Jamie Rogers, a seaman, was injured on October 3, 2013, on the vessel F/V HEDY BRENNA. Admiralty law entitles seamen who become injured during the course of their service at sea to recover "maintenance and cure" payments from their employers. Block Island Fishing, Inc., is the owner and operator of the fishing vessel. Having made some maintenance and cure payments to Rogers and believing it had overpaid, Block Island brought this suit against Rogers to dispute the duration and amount of maintenance and cure payments that it owed.

Block Island then moved for summary judgment on the ground that its maintenance and cure duties terminated on July 31, 2014. It supported its motion with record evidence showing that Rogers had returned to work as a commercial fisherman on another fishing vessel in July.

The district court rejected July 31 as the proper date of termination. But it went beyond the issue raised by Block Island's summary judgment motion and found November 18, 2014 as the date on which Block Island's obligations ended. That was the date on which a doctor, but not Rogers' primary care physician, found that Rogers no longer needed follow-up care.

The district court also noted that injured seamen are generally entitled to maintenance and cure payments only in the [—3—] amount of their actual living expenses, but it reserved for a jury to determine the exact sum that Block Island owed Rogers, along with other issues not resolved at the summary judgment stage. Relatedly, the district court held on summary judgment that Block Island had overpaid Rogers by calculating its maintenance and cure payments using figures that overestimated Rogers' actual living expenses. It further ruled that Block Island could offset the sum of overpayment against any damages award that Rogers might win at trial. We affirm in part and vacate and remand in part.

As to the exact date on which Block Island's maintenance and cure obligations ended, the district court erred by sua sponte replacing Block Island's proposed date (July 31) with its own (November 18) without giving Rogers sufficient notice or opportunity to make his case against the new date. A summary judgment order is premature where the nonmoving party lacked "notice and a reasonable time to respond" to the grounds on which that motion would be granted. Fed. R. Civ. P. 56(f).

We agree with the district court's implicit recognition that injured seamen like Rogers can generally recover only reasonable expenses through maintenance and cure payments, and that it will be the factually exceptional case where the seaman's actual expenses are not reasonable. Whether this case presents such exceptional circumstances is an issue for the jury. Finally, as a matter of first impression, we adopt the ruling of the Fifth [—4—] Circuit in *Boudreaux v. Transocean Deepwater, Inc.,* 721 F.3d 723, 1 Adm. R. 275 (5th Cir. 2013), and hold that Block Island may offset any overpayment against Rogers' potential damages award, but may not sue for the sum in an independent action. *See id.* at 726–28, 1 Adm. R. at 276–78.

I.

"Because our review of a grant of summary judgment is de novo, we, like the district court, are obliged to review the record in the light most favorable to the nonmoving party, and to draw all reasonable inferences in the nonmoving party's favor." *LeBlanc v. Great Am. Ins. Co.*, 6 F.3d 836, 841 (1st Cir. 1993). Although there are numerous dates at issue, the core of the dispute involves (1) when Block Island's maintenance and cure obligations terminated, and (2) the amount, if any, of the maintenance and cure owed. Block Island takes the position that it overpaid Rogers based on an inflated rent amount that it believed Rogers to be paying when, in fact, Rogers had found less expensive housing. Rogers takes the position that special circumstances dictate that actual expenses are not the appropriate measure here.

A. *Rogers' Injury and His Various Residences from 2013 to 2014*

In August 2013, Rogers and his family moved into a single-family home in Bristol, Rhode Island. He paid the first month's rent of $1,600, which included utilities, but he cannot remember paying rent in subsequent months. In September 2013, Rogers joined the crew of the F/V HEDY BRENNA, a commercial fishing [—5—] vessel owned and operated by Block Island. For a fishing trip in which he participated that month, Rogers was paid $2,892 in his catch share for the trip.

On October 3, 2013, during another fishing voyage, Rogers fell off the top bunk while sleeping and injured himself. Three days later, upon returning from the voyage, Rogers was diagnosed with a fractured rib and received medical treatment. In October 2013, Block Island paid Rogers $1,752.37 in catch share from the October 3 voyage and $475 in maintenance. On November 1, 2013, Block Island supplemented that amount with an additional $175 in maintenance and $1,857.78 in lost wages. The total sum paid from Block Island to Rogers over this period equaled $4,260.15.

In November 2013, Rogers and his family were evicted from the Bristol apartment and moved to a less expensive apartment in Fall River, Massachusetts. He paid $625 in monthly rent, excluding utilities, for the new Fall River apartment. On November 4, 2013, Rogers' treating physician, Dr. Christian Campos, gave him a "fit for duty" slip and cleared him to return to work as a fisherman "without restrictions."

Rogers' health worsened in December, however, when he was diagnosed with pneumonia and was hospitalized for three weeks. Rogers attributes the pneumonia to his rib injury. Block Island [—6—] learned about Rogers' condition and hospitalization on December 19, 2013.

On February 20, 2014, Dr. Campos reported that Rogers' condition was improving and that Rogers could "increase his level of physical activity as tolerated without restrictions" while staying on pain medication. On March 17, 2014, Dr. Campos completed another examination and once again advised Rogers to continue to "increase his level of physical activity as tolerated without restrictions."

In March 2014, Rogers moved to Sparta, Tennessee, where he lived with his brother. Rogers paid his brother $800 per month as rent. Finally, in May or June 2014, Rogers purchased a 38-foot boat for $2,500 and lived on that boat before returning to Fall River in June.

On June 19, 2014, Rogers' primary care physician, Dr. Melanie Cardoza, examined Rogers for pain in his lower back and left leg. During this examination, Rogers told the doctor that he had returned from a fishing trip the previous day and that he was planning to embark on another fishing trip the next day. The conversation demonstrated that Rogers had been working as a fisherman in June. Dr. Cardoza's examination of Rogers' chest and lungs revealed "normal excursion with symmetric chest walls and quiet, even and easy respiratory effort with no use of accessory muscles." [—7—]

By July 2014, Rogers was working on, and was physically fit to captain, another fishing vessel, the KELLY ANN. But Dr. Campos examined Rogers in August 2014 and provided him with a letter stating that he was not yet fit to return to work as a commercial fisherman.

On November 18, 2014, Dr. Campos examined Rogers again and found that "his condition had improved to the point that no 'further formal follow-up' was necessary." At oral argument, Rogers' counsel clarified that although Dr. Campos had discharged Rogers from his care on November 18, he had "transferr[ed] all follow-up care to his primary care physician, Dr. Cardoza, who was also treating Rogers for his illness and injury."

B. *Communications Between Parties Regarding Maintenance and Cure*

In January 2014, after learning about Rogers' pneumonia and hospitalization the previous month as recounted above, Block Island hired Neil Stoddard of Marine Safety Consultants to investigate Rogers' demand for maintenance and cure. From that point, almost a year of correspondence ensued between Stoddard and Danny Alberto, a paralegal employed by Rogers' counsel, regarding the rate of maintenance and cure owed to Rogers.

In a letter dated January 9, 2014, Stoddard requested medical records from Rogers' counsel to support Rogers' claim of ongoing medical treatment. On January 24, 2014, Alberto responded to Stoddard's letter and requested that Block Island pay Rogers [—8—] $72 per day in maintenance and cure. Alberto cited the following as Rogers' monthly expenses: $1,600 for rent, $119.25 for gas, $61.28 for electricity, and $362.50 for food, based on the U.S. Department of Agriculture's Moderate Cost Plan for a person of Rogers' age living in a four-person family home.

Upon Stoddard's objection that Alberto had provided only "cash receipts" with "nothing on them to identify them as a rent payment," Alberto mailed Stoddard a copy of the Bristol lease on March 27, 2014. (Rogers had vacated the Bristol home in November 2013.) This lease indicated that the monthly $1,600 rent included utilities. When Stoddard discovered that Rogers had moved to the Fall River apartment, and he further objected to the $72

daily rate demanded by Alberto, Alberto responded that "he had provided 'all of Mr. Rogers['] living expenses and all of his medical records'" and warned that he would pursue punitive damages on Rogers' behalf if Block Island did not begin making the requested maintenance and cure payments. At some point during this exchange, Alberto also provided Stoddard with two utility invoices that reflected two different addresses in Fall River.

In late June, Block Island paid $68,891.41 in cure to Rogers' health care providers. Then, on July 23, 2014, Block Island sent Rogers a maintenance check for $10,800.06—based on a daily rate of $63.26—covering the period from October 2013 to April 23, 2014, "the date of his last treatment record received." [—9—] The $63.26 rate was calculated based on Rogers' $1,600 monthly rent for his Bristol home and $279.80 per month in food. As the Bristol lease reflected that utilities were included, Block Island did not account for electricity and gas bills in calculating the maintenance and cure rate.

On July 25, 2014, Alberto sent Stoddard a copy of Rogers' Fall River lease, which reflected a monthly rent of $625 excluding utilities. (Rogers had vacated this apartment in March 2014.) After another threat from Alberto that he would seek punitive damages if Block Island did not provide additional maintenance of $72 per day, Block Island sent Rogers a second check for $11,956.14, based on a daily rate of $63.26.

II.

On November 25, 2014, Block Island filed a complaint against Rogers in the U.S. District Court for the District of Massachusetts. Block Island sought a declaratory judgment on the amount of retroactive maintenance owed to Rogers (Count I), on whether it had any continuing obligation to pay maintenance and cure, and on whether it was entitled to reimbursement for overpayments resulting from Rogers' failure to provide accurate and timely information about his living expenses and medical treatment (Count II). On March 6, 2015, Rogers filed a counterclaim alleging negligence under the Jones Act, 46 U.S.C. § 30104 (Count I), unseaworthiness (Count II), continuing [—10—] maintenance and cure (Count III), negligent or intentional failure to provide maintenance and cure (Count IV), and lost wages (Count V).

Block Island moved for summary judgment on its counts for declaratory judgment, and on Counts III and IV of Rogers' counterclaim. Block Island also sought $13,027.80, the amount by which it had allegedly overpaid Rogers.

The district court granted in part and denied in part Block Island's motion. First, as to its demand for reimbursement for its overpayment, the district court agreed with Block Island's premise that it had overpaid Rogers because his actual expenses were lower than what Block Island believed them to be: "The undisputed evidence is that Rogers vacated the Bristol apartment [with $1,600 monthly rent] in November of 2013, and that his monthly rent since leaving Bristol has not exceeded $800. It is also undisputed that in calculating the daily maintenance due[,] Block Island relied on the $1,600 monthly rent figure and that an overpayment resulted." Nonetheless, the court relied on the Fifth Circuit's opinion in *Boudreaux* to rule that, despite the overpayment, Block Island could not seek affirmative recovery of maintenance and cure payments that it had already made. *See* 721 F.3d at 726–28, 1 Adm. R. at 276–78. But the court did allow Block Island to offset the sum of overpayment, to be determined by a jury, against any damages award that Rogers might win at trial. [—11—]

The district court then denied Block Island's summary judgment motion as to Count IV of Rogers' counterclaim, which alleged that "Block Island negligently or intentionally failed to promptly provide maintenance and cure prior to November 3, 2014." "[A]s with most issues of negligence," the court explained, "the issue of the provision of prompt and proper maintenance and cure is a matter for the jury."

With regard to Block Island's summary judgment request for declaratory relief

"establishing a specific date upon which its maintenance and cure obligations to Rogers came to an end," the district court rejected Block Island's proposed date of July 31, 2014 but sua sponte supplied its own date of November 18, 2014 to ultimately grant summary judgment in Block Island's favor. The court noted that "[o]n this issue, the relevant question before the court is not whether Rogers returned to work as a fisherman (which could be explained by necessity as well as by cure)." Accordingly, although Rogers had been working on the KELLY ANN in July 2014, that fact was not dispositive of whether Rogers had reached the point of maximum medical recovery, as Block Island had argued.

The district court then turned to November 18, 2014—the date on which Dr. Campos had found that Rogers' health had so improved that he required no more follow-up visits—as the date on which Rogers had reached maximum medical recovery and thus was [—12—] no longer entitled to maintenance and cure. The court observed that while Rogers protested that he continued to have trouble breathing and to experience pain at the site of his injury, Rogers "offer[ed] no medical evidence that contradict[ed] his own doctor's evaluation that he had achieved the maximum feasible recovery as of November 18, 2014." On that basis, the court granted Block Island's summary judgment motion as to Count III (continuing maintenance and cure) of Rogers' counterclaims.

The court lastly denied Block Island's request for attorney's fees.

Rogers' interlocutory appeal, permissible in admiralty cases under 28 U.S.C. § 1292(a)(3) and our circuit's case law, followed. *See Doyle v. Huntress, Inc.*, 419 F.3d 3, 6–7 (1st Cir. 2005); *P.R. Ports Auth. v. Barge Katy-B*, 427 F.3d 93, 100–01 (1st Cir. 2005); *Martha's Vineyard Scuba Headquarters, Inc. v. Unidentified Vessel*, 833 F.2d 1059, 1063–64 (1st Cir. 1987).

III.

We review de novo the entry of summary judgment. *Hannon v. Beard*, 645 F.3d 45, 47 (1st Cir. 2011).

A. *District Court's Duty to Give Notice Before Entering Summary Judgment on Grounds Not Stated in the Motion*

Rogers' primary argument on appeal is that the district court erroneously entered summary judgment on a ground that Block Island had "never briefed, argued, or raised," thus depriving [—13—] Rogers of due notice or opportunity to contest that ground. We agree.

Under Federal Rule of Civil Procedure 56(f), a district court may grant a summary judgment motion on grounds not raised by the moving party, but may do so only "[a]fter giving notice and a reasonable time to respond" to the opposing party. Fed. R. Civ. P. 56(f). Our circuit has established two criteria that a district court must meet before entering summary judgment sua sponte: First, "discovery [must be] sufficiently advanced that the parties have enjoyed a reasonable opportunity to glean the material facts." *Berkovitz v. Home Box Office, Inc.*, 89 F.3d 24, 29 (1st Cir. 1996) (citations omitted). Rogers does not claim that he did not have a reasonable opportunity for discovery.

Second, the district court must "first give[] the targeted party appropriate notice and a chance to present its evidence on the essential elements of the claim or defense." *Id.* "Notice, in this context, has two aspects: the summary judgment target is entitled to know both the grounds that the district court will consider and the point at which her obligation to bring forth evidence supporting the elements of her claim accrues." *Rogan v. Menino*, 175 F.3d 75, 79 (1st Cir. 1999) (citing *Berkovitz*, 89 F.3d at 31).

Here, Block Island sought summary judgment explicitly and only on the ground that its maintenance and cure obligations [—14—] terminated on July 31, 2014 because Rogers had resumed his job as a commercial fisherman by that point. According to Block Island, Rogers' return to work signaled that it need not make further payments because "[m]aintenance and cure is designed to provide a seaman with food and lodging when he becomes sick or injured in the ship's service; and it extends during the period when he is incapacitated to do a seaman's work and continues until he reaches maximum medical recovery." *Vaughn v. Atkinson*, 369 U.S. 527, 531 (1962).

While the district court rejected the July 31, 2014 date and the return-to-work theory, it independently, and without notice to Rogers, determined that November 18, 2014 should be the date on which Block Island's maintenance and cure obligations ended, based on a theory of maximum medical recovery. November 18 is the date on which Dr. Campos advised that Rogers no longer required follow-up care from him.

As a threshold matter, the district court correctly noted the well-established law that a fishing vessel must continue to make maintenance and cure payments until the point of maximum medical recovery—that is, the point at which an injured seaman's "condition has stabilized and further progress ended short of a full recovery." *Whitman v. Miles*, 387 F.3d 68, 72 (1st Cir. 2004) (quoting *In re RJF Int'l Corp. for Exoneration from or Limitation of Liab.*, 354 F.3d 104, 106 (1st Cir. 2004)). As a matter of [—15—] summary judgment law, we hold that the district court nonetheless erred when it substituted a new date and ground for summary judgment without first notifying Rogers and giving him an opportunity to dispute this new date and ground.

The court's decision to grant summary judgment based on the November 18 date, notwithstanding the fact that Block Island's summary judgment motion had focused exclusively on July 31, deprived Rogers of the opportunity to argue and present evidence that he had not yet reached maximum medical recovery as of November 18. Indeed, Rogers suffered prejudice as a result of the district court's failure to provide notice of the ground on which it would enter summary judgment. Had he known that maximum medical recovery would be an issue at summary judgment, Rogers says that he would have submitted additional evidence (already in his possession) of further treatment with Dr. Cardoza, his primary care physician, after November 18. In light of the lack of notice afforded to Rogers, the district court acted prematurely when it concluded that Rogers had "offer[ed] no medical evidence that contradict[ed] [Dr. Campos's] evaluation that he had achieved the maximum feasible recovery as of November 18, 2014."

Although Block Island concedes that it briefed only the July 31, 2014 date and return-to-work theory, it argues that the district court committed no error in entering summary judgment based on the November 18 date because Rogers had been "fully aware" [—16—] that maximum medical recovery would be a central issue throughout this case. Block Island contends that Rogers had "a reasonable opportunity to glean the material facts" on that issue during discovery. But this argument misses the point. Rogers had no reason to know that he would face the issue at summary judgment. The district court has a duty to notify the nonmoving party of the stage in the litigation at which his "obligation to bring forth evidence supporting the elements of [his] claim accrues." *Rogan*, 175 F.3d at 79. That Rogers knew he would need to dispute that he had reached maximum medical recovery at trial, is not the same as knowing that the issue would be decided at summary judgment.[1]

B. *Calculating the Amount of Maintenance and Cure Payments*

Rogers also complains that the district court erred when it allegedly ruled that the amount of Rogers' maintenance and cure recovery is capped at the actual living expenses that he incurred.[2] [—17—] We understand differently the district court's statements on the law governing the calculation of maintenance and cure.

We do not read the district court's statements on this point as a ruling that limited, as a matter of law, Rogers' maintenance and cure recovery to his actual living expenses. First, the district court stated that an overpayment had resulted in the specific context of determining "whether the court can—or should—do anything about the maintenance overpayment in a restitutionary sense." That is, recognition of the overpayment immediately preceded the court's ruling that Block Island could not affirmatively seek to recover any amount of overpayment but rather could only offset it against any damages that Rogers might win at trial.

Second, our reading is bolstered by the fact that, in the same summary judgment opinion, the district court refused to decide whether Block Island had unduly delayed making maintenance and cure payments to Rogers, an issue that is material to establish whether Block Island's negligence contributed to Rogers' move from [—18—] the Bristol home

---

[1] In vacating the district court's decision on the end date of Block Island's maintenance and cure obligations, we note that we need not and do not reach the question of whether a lack of notice before a summary judgment ruling could ever be per se sufficient for a vacatur absent a further showing of prejudice. Here, there is sufficient evidence in the record to demonstrate that Rogers was prejudiced by the district court's premature summary judgment ruling on the end-date issue. The end date of the obligation to pay maintenance and cure, in turn, affects the issue of the total amount of maintenance and cure owed, and that, in turn, affects the issue of whether there has been an overpayment.

[2] Rogers' argument that the district court imposed such a cap presumably comes from two places in the summary judgment opinion. First, while recounting the governing law applicable to the dispute, the district court cited *Johnson v. United States*, 333 [—17—] U.S. 46, 50 (1948), and noted that a seaman is "entitled to recover maintenance only for his actual living expenses." Then, the district court listed the following three propositions as "undisputed" for the purposes of the summary judgment motion: (1) that Rogers vacated the Bristol apartment with $1,600 monthly rent in November 2013; (2) that Rogers' rent since leaving Bristol has not exceeded $800 per month; and (3) "that in calculating the daily maintenance due[,] Block Island relied on the $1,600 monthly rent figure and that an overpayment resulted."

to a series of less expensive residences. The court reserved this issue for the jury, noting that "as with most issues of negligence, the issue of the provision of prompt and proper maintenance and cure is a matter for the jury." By assigning the decision to the jury, the court left open the possibility that the jury might find that Block Island did negligently delay in paying Rogers. This finding might, in turn, impact the amount of maintenance and cure to which Rogers is entitled.

In this circuit, as in numerous sister circuits, the norm is to award an injured seaman maintenance and cure payments in the amount of his actual living expenses. *See, e.g., Johnson*, 333 U.S. at 50 (affirming circuit court's decision to reject injured seaman's claim for maintenance and cure because "there [wa]s ample evidence . . . that petitioner had incurred no expense or liability for his care and support at the home of his parents"); *Hall v. Noble Drilling (U.S.) Inc.*, 242 F.3d 582, 587 (5th Cir. 2001) ("A seaman is entitled to the reasonable cost of food and lodging, *provided he has incurred the expense.*" (emphasis added)); *Barnes v. Andover Co., L.P.*, 900 F.2d 630, 641 (3d Cir. 1990) ("Because maintenance is intended to substitute for the food and lodging that a seaman enjoyed at sea, it is established that the seaman is entitled only to expenses actually incurred. Thus, if a seaman is not charged for hospitalization or lives with his [—19—] family without incurring any expense or liability for his care, no maintenance is due." (citations omitted)).

But the rule remains that an injured seaman may recover reasonable expenses beyond the amount that he actually incurred, even if it is the exceptional case where the seaman's reasonable expenses will exceed his actual expenses. *See, e.g., McMillan v. Tug Jane A. Bouchard*, 885 F. Supp. 452, 463–67 & n.13 (E.D.N.Y. 1995) (holding that injured seaman was entitled to maintenance and cure payments even though he had paid no rent, after factfinding at trial that the seaman had involuntarily moved in with friends and family because his employer had refused to pay him maintenance), *abrogated on other grounds by Hicks v. Tug PATRIOT*, 783 F.3d

939, 3 Adm. R. 135 (2d Cir. 2015); *cf. Vaughan v. Atkinson*, 369 U.S. 527, 530–31, 533 (1962) (holding that injured seaman was entitled to attorney's fees and to his wages earned as taxi driver without offset, after factfinding that his employer had negligently remained "silen[t,] neither admitting nor denying" its duty to pay maintenance and cure for two years). Rogers argues that this case presents just this kind of exceptional circumstance because Block Island's delayed maintenance and cure payments forced him to vacate the Bristol home and seek cheaper housing. That fact-bound determination, however, is one for the jury. To the extent that the district court could be understood as having ruled otherwise, any such ruling would be error. [—20—]

C. *Method of Recovery for Any Overpayment*

Finally, both parties seek affirmance of the district court's decision that although Block Island cannot affirmatively sue to recover any maintenance and cure payments that it has already made to Rogers, it can offset any overpayment (the exact amount of which should be determined at trial) against any damages that Rogers may win.

The district court properly relied on *Boudreaux v. Transocean Deepwater, Inc.*, 721 F.3d 723, 1 Adm. R. 275 (5th Cir. 2013). There, the Fifth Circuit faced a similar question—namely, whether a Jones Act employer, upon establishing that it overpaid an injured seaman, is "automatically entitled to a judgment against the seaman for benefits already paid." *Id.* at 725, 1 Adm. R. at 276. The court answered this question in the negative, observing that allowing for such affirmative recovery would disturb a central policy of admiralty law, which seeks to "achieve[] a fair reconciliation between protecting seamen in the wake of debilitating on-the-job injury and ensuring that shipowners can protect themselves from liability for sums attributable to concealed preexisting injuries." *Id.* at 728, 1 Adm. R. at 278. By denying the availability of affirmative recoveries but allowing for offset against the injured seaman's damages award, the court in *Boudreaux* strove to strike the proper balance.

We agree with *Boudreaux's* sound rule, as well as the rationale animating it. [—21—]

We thereby adopt the Fifth Circuit's approach in *Boudreaux* that "once a shipowner pays maintenance and cure to the injured seaman, the payments can be recovered only by offset against the seaman's damages award—not by an independent suit seeking affirmative recovery." *Id.* at 728, 1 Adm. R. at 278.

IV.

We *affirm* the district court's ruling that Block Island may offset any overpayment that occurred against any damages that Rogers may win at trial.

We *vacate* the ruling that Block Island's maintenance and cure obligations terminated on November 18, 2014, and *remand* for further proceedings not inconsistent with this opinion. The district court did not provide Rogers with sufficient notice and opportunity to contend otherwise before entering summary judgment. No costs are awarded.

United States Court of Appeals for the Second Circuit

United States Court of Appeals
for the Second Circuit

No. 14-4036

ZURICH AM. INS. CO.
vs.
TEAM TANKERS A.S.

Appeal from the United States District Court for the
Southern District of New York

Decided: January 28, 2016

Citation: 811 F.3d 584, 4 Adm. R. 56 (2d Cir. 2016).

Before **CABRANES, PARKER,** and **LOHIER,** Circuit Judges.

[—3—] **CABRANES,** Circuit Judge:

This appeal presents two questions. The first, which we dispose of in relatively short order, is whether the District Court erred in confirming an arbitration award. The second, which merits fuller discussion, is whether the party that prevailed in arbitration was entitled, by contract or statute, to recoup the fees and costs it incurred in seeking to confirm the arbitral award before the District Court.

Petitioners-appellants are Zurich American Insurance Co. ("Zurich") and Vinmar International, Ltd. ("Vinmar") (jointly, the "petitioner" or the "shipper"). The appeal challenges two orders of the United States District Court for the Southern District of New York (William H. Pauley III, *Judge*). In the first, entered on June 30, 2014, the District Court denied the petitioner's motion to vacate an arbitration award and granted the motion of respondents-appellees Team Tankers A.S. ("Team Tankers"), Eitzen Chemical USA ("Eitzen"), and the M/T Siteam Explorer (the "Siteam Explorer") (jointly, the "respondent" or the "carrier") to confirm it. In the second, entered on September 29, 2014, the District Court awarded the respondent its attorney's fees and costs.

We **AFFIRM** the District Court's June 30, 2014 order denying the petitioner's motion to vacate the arbitral award and granting the [—4—] respondent's motion to confirm it but

REVERSE the District Court's September 29, 2014 order awarding attorney's fees and costs to the respondent because the award was not authorized under relevant law.

BACKGROUND

In June 2008, Vinmar chartered from Team Tankers a ship called the M/T Siteam Explorer to move a large quantity of a chemical called acrylonitrile (ACN) from Houston, Texas to Ulsan, South Korea. J.A. 365; *Zurich Am. Ins. Co. v. Team Tankers A.S.*, No. 13-CV-8404 (WHP), 2014 WL 2945803, at *1 (S.D.N.Y. June 30, 2014). ACN is a versatile raw material that is, in its most valuable form, colorless. J.A. 368-70; *Zurich Am. Ins. Co.*, 2014 WL 2945803, at *1. Contact with other chemicals can cause ACN to "yellow" (i.e., become yellow in color), which is evidence of a change in composition that reduces its value. J.A. 365, 369-70; *Zurich Am. Ins. Co.*, 2014 WL 2945803, at *1-2.

Vinmar planned to find a buyer for its cargo in Ulsan, but the ACN market dropped while the Siteam Explorer was at sea. Accordingly, when the ship arrived in port in August 2008, the ACN was transferred into onshore tanks for storage. J.A. 365-66. At that time, the ACN remained "on specification" for color—that is, it had not begun to yellow. *Zurich Am. Ins. Co.*, 2014 WL 2945803, at *1; *see* J.A. 366.

Six weeks later, Vinmar tested the stored ACN and learned that it had yellowed beyond Vinmar's quality standards. J.A. 366. It [—5—] also tested a sample that had been carried on the Siteam Explorer but never exposed to the Ulsan shore tanks; it too had yellowed. J.A. 370; *Zurich Am. Ins. Co.*, 2014 WL 2945803, at *1. A sample pulled from tanks in Houston that had not been carried on the Siteam Explorer had not yellowed at all. J.A. 370.

Consistent with the charter agreement, Vinmar initiated arbitration before the Society of Maritime Arbitrators, Inc. ("SMA"). J.A. 366; *Zurich Am. Ins. Co.*, 2014 WL 2945803, at *2. Vinmar attempted to show that it had delivered the ACN to Houston in good order but that it had arrived contaminated in Ulsan. *See* J.A. 369-71. It argued that the ACN had been contaminated by a chemical called "pygas" previously carried in the Siteam Explorer's tanks. *See* J.A. 369.

On August 26, 2013, applying the Carriage of Goods by Sea Act ("COGSA"), 46 U.S.C. § 30701 note, the arbitration panel majority held that, for three reasons, Vinmar was not entitled to relief. It held, first, that Vinmar had not made out a *prima facie* case that the ACN had been damaged while aboard the vessel, J.A. 370-73; second, that even if Vinmar had made out a *prima facie* case, Team Tankers had shown that it exercised due diligence in transporting the cargo, J.A. 373-75; and third, that Vinmar had in any event failed to prove damages, J.A. 375-76.

Following the panel's decision, the shipper, Vinmar, petitioned the District Court on November 25, 2013 to vacate the award under section 10 of the Federal Arbitration Act ("FAA"), 9 [—6—] U.S.C. § 1 *et seq.*,[1] arguing

---

[1] Title 9, United States Code, Section 10 provides, in relevant part:

(a) In any of the following cases the United States court in and for the district wherein the award was made may make an order vacating the award upon the application of any party to the arbitration—

(1) where the award was procured by corruption, fraud, or undue means;

(2) where there was evident partiality or corruption in the arbitrators, or either of them;

(3) where the arbitrators were guilty of misconduct in refusing to postpone the hearing, upon sufficient cause shown, or in refusing to hear evidence pertinent and material to the controversy; or of any other misbehavior by which the rights of any party have been prejudiced; or

(4) where the arbitrators exceeded their powers, or so imperfectly executed them that a mutual, final, and definite award upon the subject matter submitted was not made.

that the panel manifestly disregarded COGSA in reaching each of the three conclusions described above. *See* J.A. 13-16. In January 2014, the shipper learned that the panel chairman had died as a result of a brain tumor with which he had been diagnosed during the arbitration, and of which he never informed the parties. *Zurich Am. Ins. Co.*, 2014 WL 2945803, at *3, *8. Vinmar amended its petition to argue that that his failure to do so constituted "corruption" or "misbehavior" as those terms are used in the FAA. J.A. 483-86; *see* 9 U.S.C. § 10(a).

The District Court held that the arbitration panel had not manifestly disregarded the law in determining that Vinmar had not made out a *prima facie* case under COGSA; accordingly, the Court [—7—] declined to address Vinmar's other manifest-disregard arguments. *Zurich Am. Ins. Co.*, 2014 WL 2945803, at *8. It likewise held that the panel chairman had not been guilty of "corruption" or "misbehavior." *Id.* at *8-11. On the authority of a provision in the charter agreement stating that "[d]amages for breach of this Charter shall include all provable damages, and all costs of suit and attorneys [sic] fees incurred in any action hereunder," the District Court awarded the respondent carrier the fees and costs it incurred in connection with the district court proceeding. *Id.* at *11.

On appeal, the petitioner shipper argues that the District Court erred in three respects: (1) concluding that the arbitral panel did not manifestly disregard the law; (2) concluding that the panel chairman had not been guilty of "corruption" or "misbehavior"; and (3) awarding attorney's fees and costs to the respondent carrier. We agree with the District Court's decision to uphold the arbitral award. We conclude, however, that it erred in awarding the respondent carrier its fees and costs.

DISCUSSION

I. The Arbitral Award

"[T]o avoid undermining the twin goals of arbitration, namely, settling disputes efficiently and avoiding long and expensive litigation," arbitral awards "are subject to very limited review." *Folkways Music Publishers, Inc. v. Weiss*, 989 F.2d 108, 111 (2d Cir. 1993). Under the United Nations Convention on the Recognition and Enforcement of Foreign Arbitral Awards, June 10, [—8—] 1958, 21 U.S.T. 2517, 330 U.N.T.S. 38 (the "New York Convention"), which governs this dispute, a court must confirm an arbitral award "unless it finds one of the grounds for refusal or deferral of recognition or enforcement of the award specified in the said Convention." 9 U.S.C. § 207.[2]

The award in this case having been rendered in the United States, available grounds for vacatur include all the express grounds for vacating an award under the FAA. *See Yusuf Ahmed Alghanim & Sons v. Toys "R" Us, Inc.*, 126 F.3d 15, 23 (2d Cir. 1997) ("The [New York] Convention specifically contemplates that the state in which . . . the award is made, will be free to set aside or modify an award in accordance with its domestic arbitral law and its full panoply of express and implied grounds for relief."). As relevant here, the FAA permits a court to vacate an arbitral award "where there was evident partiality or corruption in the arbitrators," 9 U.S.C. § 10(a)(2), or "where the arbitrators were guilty . . . of any . . . misbehavior by which the rights of any party have been prejudiced," *id.* § 10(a)(3). A court may also "set aside an arbitration award if it was rendered in [—9—] manifest disregard of the law." *Schwartz v. Merrill Lynch & Co., Inc.*, 665 F.3d 444, 451 (2d Cir. 2011) (internal quotation marks omitted).

---

[2] Title 9, United States Code, Section 207—which is part of the statutory scheme that "implements the . . . New York Convention," *Schneider v. Kingdom of Thailand*, 688 F.3d 68, 71 (2d Cir. 2012)—reads in full as follows:

Within three years after an arbitral award falling under the Convention is made, any party to the arbitration may apply to any court having jurisdiction under this chapter for an order confirming the award as against any other party to the arbitration. The court shall confirm the award unless it finds one of the grounds for refusal or deferral of recognition or enforcement of the award specified in the said Convention.

We conclude that the shipper has not established any ground for vacating the arbitral award. On this point we agree entirely with the District Court's thorough analysis, *see Zurich Am. Ins. Co.*, 2014 WL 2945803, and thus touch only briefly on the shipper's arguments.

A. Manifest Disregard of the Law

The shipper's first argument—that the arbitral panel manifestly disregarded the substantive law of COGSA—is easily rejected. "A litigant seeking to vacate an arbitration award based on alleged manifest disregard of the law bears a heavy burden . . . ." *T.Co Metals, LLC v. Dempsey Pipe & Supply, Inc.*, 592 F.3d 329, 339 (2d Cir. 2010) (internal quotation marks omitted). A court may vacate an arbitral award on this ground only if the court "finds both that (1) the arbitrators knew of a governing legal principle yet refused to apply it or ignored it altogether, and (2) the law ignored by the arbitrators was well defined, explicit, and clearly applicable to the case." *Wallace v. Buttar*, 378 F.3d 182, 189 (2d Cir. 2004) (alterations omitted).

The shipper's basic argument, briefly stated, is that the arbitration panel majority disregarded COGSA by requiring the shipper to prove the cause of the damage to its cargo, rather than properly applying COGSA's burden-shifting regime. *See Transatlantic Marine Claims v. OOCL Inspiration*, 137 F.3d 94, 98-99 (2d Cir. 1998) (describing COGSA's system of burdens and [—10—] presumptions). We disagree. As the District Court carefully explained, the panel majority recognized that COGSA permits a shipper to make a *prima facie* case by establishing that it delivered goods to a carrier in sound condition, and that the goods arrived in damaged condition following carriage. *See Zurich Am. Ins. Co.*, 2014 WL 2945803, at *5-8. The majority simply found that the shipper's evidence was insufficient to satisfy its initial burden under COGSA. *See* J.A. 373 ("Claimants have not shown, by a preponderance of evidence or otherwise, that the alleged contamination took place while the cargo was in the custody of the Siteam Explorer."); J.A. 371 (discussing weaknesses in the shipper's evidentiary showing). It is arguable that the shipper's evidence could have supported a contrary conclusion, but that does not show that the panel majority manifestly disregarded the law.

B. "Corruption" and "Misbehavior"

The shipper's second argument is that the panel chairman was guilty of "corruption" or "misbehavior" because he failed to disclose his illness to the parties; such disclosure, the shipper argues, was required by the SMA Rules, which governed the conduct of the arbitration. We find this argument no more convincing than did the District Court. We will simply emphasize that the shipper's attempt to secure vacatur based on a violation of private arbitral rules runs headlong into the principle that parties may not expand by contract the FAA's grounds for vacating an award. *See Hall St. Assocs., LLC v. Mattel, Inc.*, 552 U.S. 576, 585-88 (2008). Parties may, of course, "tailor some, even many, features of arbitration by contract," *id.* at [—11—] 586 (citation omitted); but if an arbitrator's failure to comply with arbitral rules, without more, could properly be considered "corruption" or "misbehavior," the FAA's grounds for vacatur would be precisely as varied and expansive as the rules private parties might choose to adopt. We accordingly reject this argument.

In sum, the shipper has established no ground on which to vacate the arbitral award. Accordingly, the District Court did not err in denying the shipper's motion to vacate the award and granting the carrier's motion to confirm it.

II. The Award of Attorney's Fees & Costs

We conclude, however, that the District Court erred in awarding the respondent carrier the fees and costs it incurred in seeking to confirm the award, and pause to explain why we think the award untenable.

"Our basic point of reference when considering the award of attorney's fees is the bedrock principle known as the American Rule: Each litigant pays his own attorney's fees, win or lose, unless a statute or contract

provides otherwise." *Baker Botts L.L.P. v. ASARCO LLC*, 135 S. Ct. 2158, 2164 (2015). In the proceeding below, the District Court determined that this "default rule," *id.* at 2168, was displaced by contract. The Court awarded fees and costs to the respondent carrier under a provision of the charter agreement which reads: "BREACH. Damages for breach of this Charter shall include all provable damages, and all costs of suit and attorney fees incurred in any action hereunder." J.A. 31. [—12—]

We hold that this result was in error. By its terms, this provision authorizes a fee award *against* a party that breaches the charter agreement, as part of the non-breaching party's damages. There was no finding below, nor indeed any suggestion, that the petitioner shipper breached the charter agreement.

The respondent carrier argues that the award may be sustained on the theory that the shipper breached the parties' contract not through any conduct related to the transport of the shipper's cargo to South Korea, but through its conduct in litigation. The carrier reasons that the parties agreed to be bound by the arbitral panel's decision, and the shipper breached that understanding by resisting entry of judgment on the award.

For two reasons, we are unconvinced. First, the parties agreed to arbitrate, but they also consented to confirmation of the arbitral award in any court of competent jurisdiction. *See* J.A. 31. In so doing, they agreed that a federal court would have authority to confirm the award under the standards provided in the FAA. *See* 9 U.S.C. § 9 ("If the parties in their agreement have agreed that a judgment of the court shall be entered upon the award made pursuant to arbitration, . . . any party to the arbitration may apply to the court . . . for an order confirming the award, and thereupon the court must grant such an order unless the award is vacated, modified, or corrected as prescribed in sections 10 and 11 of this title."); *Phoenix Aktiengesellschaft v. Ecoplas, Inc.*, 391 F.3d 433, 436 (2d Cir. 2004). The parties having effectively incorporated FAA review into their contract, the argument that the shipper breached that [—13—] contract by making arguments the FAA permits is unconvincing. *See I/S Stavborg v. Nat'l Metal Converters, Inc.*, 500 F.2d 424, 426 (2d Cir. 1974) ("One purpose of [9 U.S.C. § 9] is to ensure that the parties have affirmatively agreed to the application of the federal substantive law contemplated by the Act to the interpretation of the arbitration agreement into which they have entered.").[3]

Second, even if the contract *did* oblige the shipper to forbear from resisting confirmation of the award, it would be to that extent unenforceable. Read that way, the contract would authorize a federal court to confirm the arbitral award while effectively preventing that court from ensuring that the award complied with the FAA. We have held that "[p]arties seeking to enforce arbitration awards through federal-court confirmation judgments may not divest the courts of their statutory and common-law authority to review both the substance of the awards and the arbitral process for compliance with § 10(a) and the manifest disregard standard." *Hoeft v. MVL Grp., Inc.*, 343 F.3d 57, 66 (2d Cir. 2003), *abrogated on other grounds by Hall St. Assocs.*, 552 U.S. at 584–85. Accordingly, we reject **[—14—]** the argument that the shipper breached the charter agreement by seeking to vacate the award.

The carrier argues in the alternative that the award can be sustained under 28 U.S.C. § 1927,[4] which authorizes a court to assess "costs, expenses, and attorneys' fees" against any attorney who "so multiplies the pro-

ceedings in any case unreasonably and vexatiously." But an award under § 1927 is proper only "when there is a finding of conduct constituting or akin to bad faith." *State St. Bank v. Inversiones Errazuriz*, 374 F.3d 158, 180 (2d Cir. 2004) (internal quotation marks omitted). The attorney's actions must be "so completely without merit as to require the conclusion that they must have been undertaken for some improper purpose such as delay." *Id.*

A finding of bad faith or improper purpose is not warranted on this record. The petitioner shipper's arguments on appeal (which mirror its arguments below) are not convincing. Yet the shipper ties its reasoning, however flawed, to recognizable legal concepts. Its manifest-disregard argument relies on the proposition, not on its face absurd, that arbitrators manifestly disregard the law when the facts they find flatly and obviously preclude the legal conclusions they reach. Its "corruption" and "misbehavior" arguments rely on the disclosure-based framework we have applied in evident- **[—15—]** partiality cases. *See, e.g., Applied Indus. Materials Corp. v. Ovalar*, 492 F.3d 132, 137-38 (2d Cir. 2007). These are, as we say, unconvincing arguments, but not so unconvincing as to *require* the conclusion that they are made for an improper purpose.

Perhaps something in the record could support a fee award under § 1927. But we have not found it, and the respondent carrier has made no effort to identify it. Accordingly, we must reverse the District Court's award of attorney's fees and costs.

CONCLUSION

In sum, we hold that:

(1) The District Court did not err in denying the petitioner shipper's motion to vacate the arbitral award and granting the respondent carrier's motion to confirm it; but

(2) The District Court erred in awarding attorney's fees and costs to the respondent carrier.

---

[3] This is not to suggest that the parties' affirmative consent to confirmation was required before a federal court could confirm the arbitral award. It was not: the award in this case fell under the New York Convention, which (unlike the FAA) "does not in any way condition confirmation on express or implicit consent." *Phoenix Aktiengesellschaft*, 391 F.3d at 436; *see also* 9 U.S.C. § 207, note 2, *ante*. We simply conclude that the parties' decision to expressly include a consent-to-confirmation term in their contract convincingly demonstrates their intent to incorporate principles of FAA review into their agreement.

[4] More accurately, the carrier states in conclusory fashion that the award can be upheld under 28 U.S.C. § 1927. *See* Respondent's Br. 51.

We thus **AFFIRM** the District Court's order of June 30, 2014 confirming the arbitral award but **REVERSE** the District Court's order of September 29, 2014 awarding fees and costs.

**United States Court of Appeals
for the Second Circuit**

No. 15-97

**HAPAG-LLOYD AKTIENGESELLSCHAFT
VS.
U.S. OIL TRADING LLC**

Appeal from the United States District Court for the
Southern District of New York

Decided: February 24, 2016

Citation: 814 F.3d 146, 4 Adm. R. 62 (2d Cir. 2016).

Before **KEARSE, STRAUB,** and **WESLEY,** Circuit
Judges.

[—2—] WESLEY, Circuit Judge:[1]

T his action presents, as the District Court aptly put it, "interesting and apparently novel questions regarding the interplay among the United States bankruptcy law, maritime law and the federal interpleader statutes." *UPT Pool Ltd. v. Dynamic Oil Trading (Sing.) PTE. Ltd.*, Nos. 14-CV-9262 (VEC) et al., 2015 WL 4005527, at *1 (S.D.N.Y. July 1, 2015). It is just one of at least twenty-five other interpleader actions in the United States District Court for the Southern District of New York (Valerie E. Caproni, *Judge*), concerning similar issues among overlapping parties.

Plaintiff-Appellee Hapag-Lloyd Aktiengesellschaft ("Hapag-Lloyd"), based in Hamburg, Germany, owns or charters a fleet of shipping vessels, three of which—the M/V *Seaspan Hamburg*, the M/V *Santa Roberta*, and the M/V *Sofia* [—3—] *Express*—are involved in this case.[2] Hapag-Lloyd contracted with non-appealing Defendant O.W. Bunker Germany GmbH ("O.W. Germany") to purchase fuel bunkers for these three ships, among others, for the calendar year 2014.[3]

Pursuant to this contract, Hapag-Lloyd would place orders with O.W. Germany for delivery of bunkers to the vessels and then remit payment as invoiced.

In October 2014, Hapag-Lloyd placed orders with O.W. Germany for bunkers to be supplied in Tacoma, Washington, to the three vessels in question; the fuel was actually delivered to the vessels by U.S. Oil Trading LLC ("USOT").[4] One month later, O.W. Germany's parent company, O.W. Denmark, filed for bankruptcy—followed by similar bankruptcy filings by affiliated [—4—] entities, including some in the United States Bankruptcy Court for the District of Connecticut.[5] As a result, in this action multiple parties assert claims to payment by Hapag-Lloyd for the bunkers—some sounding in contract (the O.W. Entities), and others

---

[1] All *amici curiae* are referred to collectively as the "Vessel Interests."

[2] Hapag-Lloyd owns the M/V *Sofia Express* and is the time charterer of the M/V *Seaspan Hamburg* and the M/V *Santa Roberta*, but the nature of its interest in each vessel is not significant to this case.

[3] "Bunker fuel," or even commonly just "bunker," is the term for fuel oil used to power

modern vessels; it derives from the tank in which the fuel is stored, whose name is itself a holdover term from coal bunkers used in early steam vessels. *See generally Garanti Finansal Kiralama A.S. v. Aqua Marine & Trading Inc.*, 697 F.3d 59, 62 (2d Cir. 2012); *In re Sea Bridge Marine, Inc.*, 412 B.R. 868, 871 n.1 (Bankr. E.D. La. 2008).

[4] USOT informs us in briefing that it entered into contracts with O.W. Bunker & Trading A/S ("O.W. Denmark") to provide bunkers to the vessels, the delivery of which occurred on various dates in October 2014. The vessels accepted delivery and stamped the bunker delivery receipts. USOT then issued invoices to O.W. Denmark in the amounts of $1,507,408.99 (M/V *Seaspan Hamburg*), $1,315,507.80 (M/V *Sofia Express*), and $1,481,860.28 (M/V *Santa Roberta*). Hapag-Lloyd alleges it has received invoices from O.W. Germany for each of the three orders in the amounts of $1,516,809.83 (M/V *Seaspan Hamburg*), $1,318,668.24 (M/V *Sofia Express*), and $1,495,860.94 (M/V *Santa Roberta*).

[5] The affiliated entities in the bankruptcy proceedings in Connecticut are O.W. Bunker Holding North America Inc., O.W. Bunker North American Inc., and O.W. Bunker USA Inc. *See In re O.W. Bunker Holding N. Am. Inc. et al.*, No. 14-51720 (JAM) (Bankr. D. Conn. filed Nov. 13, 2014). None of these entities were initially named in this action, but O.W. Bunker USA Inc. ("O.W. USA") has since been added as a defendant through an amended complaint. *See infra* note 6. We refer to O.W. Germany, O.W. Denmark, and O.W. USA collectively as "the O.W. Entities."

sounding in statutory maritime liens (the O.W. Entities and USOT).[6]

In December, the litigation frenzy began. On December 17, USOT instituted *in rem* actions on the basis of its asserted maritime liens against the M/V *Sofia Express* in the United States District Court for the Western District of Washington and [—5—] against the M/V *Santa Roberta* and the M/V *Seaspan Hamburg* in the United States District Court for the Central District of California.[7] As part of these actions, USOT obtained *ex parte* arrest warrants for the vessels, which it intended to execute when the vessels arrived in their respective ports at some point within the next several days. However, on the same day and the opposite coast, Hapag-Lloyd filed its Interpleader Complaint below and moved *ex parte* for an anti-suit injunction under 28 U.S.C. § 2361. Understandably uneasy to act without notice to the defendants, the District Court held a hearing on Hapag-Lloyd's motion the following day. USOT's counsel was present at the hearing but informed the District Court that he had not been authorized by USOT to appear on their behalf. The District Court adjourned for an hour to give USOT's counsel time to speak with his client, but when it reconvened, USOT still did not enter an appearance.

The District Court then granted Hapag-Lloyd's motion and enjoined the named defendants from

> instituting or prosecuting any proceeding or action anywhere, affecting the property and res involved in this action of interpleader, including but not limited to the arrest, attachment or other restraint of the subject Vessels pursuant to Supplemental Admiralty Rule C or Rule B or other laws to enforce claimants' alleged maritime lien claims arising from the bunker deliveries until the further order of the Court. [—6—]

Order at 2, *Hapag-Lloyd*, No. 14-cv-9949 (S.D.N.Y. Dec. 19, 2014), ECF No. 5. The District Court then ordered Hapag-Lloyd to post an initial bond, with a six-percent increase if the litigation lasted longer than a year. *Id.* at 3.[8] That same day, the District Court directed the parties to submit briefs concerning the propriety of Hapag-Lloyd's interpleader action. *See* Order at 4, *Hapag-Lloyd*, No. 14-cv-9949 (S.D.N.Y. Dec. 19, 2014), ECF No. 8. USOT later appeared and filed a motion to vacate or modify the injunction, which the District Court denied. *See* Order, *Hapag-Lloyd*, No. 14-cv-9949 (S.D.N.Y. Dec. 30, 2014), ECF No. 17.[9]

---

[6] The initial complaint named both Crédit Agricole S.A. and ING Bank, N.V., as alleged assignees or creditors of various claimants. However, the parties have shifted somewhat since USOT took its appeal. On July 14, 2015, Hapag-Lloyd filed an amended complaint, adding O.W. USA as a defendant and replacing Crédit Agricole S.A. with Crédit Agricole CIB, which then executed a stipulation dismissing the case against them. *See* First Am. Cmpl. for Interpleader and Declaratory J., *Hapag-Lloyd Aktiengesellschaft v. U.S. Oil Trading LLC et al.*, No. 14-cv-9949 (S.D.N.Y. July 14, 2015), ECF No. 84; Stipulation and Notice of Dismissal of Crédit Agricole CIB, *Hapag-Lloyd*, No. 14-cv-9949 (S.D.N.Y. Sept. 15, 2015), ECF No. 115. ING Bank remains a named defendant. We have amended the caption in the instant appeal accordingly, but the change in non-appealing players has no significance to our decision today.

[7] *See U.S. Oil Trading LLC v. M/V Vienna Express*, No. 3:14-cv-05982 (W.D. Wash. filed Dec. 17, 2014); *U.S. Oil Trading LLC v. M/V Santa Roberta*, No. 2:14-cv-09662 (C.D. Cal. filed Dec. 17, 2014).

[8] Hapag-Lloyd posted bond in the following amounts with respect to each vessel: $1,607,818.41 (M/V *Seaspan Hamburg*); $1,397,788.33 (M/V *Sofia Express*); and $1,507,771.89 (M/V *Santa Roberta*). *See* Underwriter's Interpleader and Declaratory J. Surety Bond, *Hapag-Lloyd*, No. 14-cv-9949 (S.D.N.Y. Dec. 22, 2014), ECF No. 9. These amounts exceed the costs for the fuel bunkers invoiced to the various parties. *See supra* note 4.

[9] Accordingly, USOT's arrest warrants in the other districts have never been executed. One of those actions has been transferred to the Southern District of New York, *see U.S. Oil Trading, LLC v. M/V Vienna Express*, No. 14-5982 RJB, 2015 WL 4714838, at *11 (W.D. Wash. Aug. 7, 2015), and the other has been stayed pending the resolution of this appeal, *see* Order Removing Case from Active Caseload by Virtue of Stay at 1, *U.S. Oil Trading v.*

USOT took its appeal, and the parties completed their appellate briefing, before the District Court issued its written decision on subject matter jurisdiction. *See UPT Pool Ltd.*, 2015 WL 4005527. Although this order of the District Court is not formally before us on appeal,[10] we instructed the parties to brief [—7—] their respective positions on the District Court's conclusions. *See* Order, *Hapag-Lloyd Aktiengesellschaft v. U.S. Oil Trading LLC*, No. 15-97 (2d Cir. Oct. 26, 2015), ECF No. 135.[11] With the benefit of this supplemental briefing and oral argument, we turn to subject matter jurisdiction and the merits. [—8—]

M/V Santa Roberta, No. CV 14-09662-AB (SSx) (C.D. Cal. June 29, 2015), ECF No. 36.

[10] "[E]very federal appellate court has a special obligation to 'satisfy itself not only of its own jurisdiction, but also that of the lower courts in a cause under review,' even though the parties are prepared to [—7—] concede it." *Bender v. Williamsport Area Sch. Dist.*, 475 U.S. 534, 541 (1986) (quoting *Mitchell v. Maurer*, 293 U.S. 237, 244 (1934)). "'And if the record discloses that the lower court was without jurisdiction,'" the appellate court has "'jurisdiction on appeal, not of the merits but merely for the purpose of correcting the error of the lower court in entertaining the suit.'" *Id.* (quoting *United States v. Corrick*, 298 U.S. 435, 440 (1936)). Since we have jurisdiction over this appeal from the injunction under 28 U.S.C. § 1292(a)(1), we must address the subject matter jurisdiction of the District Court even though its later order ruling on its jurisdiction is not technically before us.

[11] On the same day, we granted a motion by the Vessel Interests—interpleader plaintiffs in related proceedings before the District Court—to participate as *amici curiae*. *See* Order, *Hapag-Lloyd*, No. 15-97 (2d Cir. Oct. 26, 2015), ECF No. 136. *Amici* Vessel Interests then also filed a letter brief in response to our supplemental briefing Order. *See* Mem. Br., *Hapag-Lloyd*, No. 15-97 (2d Cir. Nov. 2, 2015), ECF No. 144. However, non-intervenor *amici curiae* are not "parties" to this appeal, *cf. Wilder v. Bernstein*, 965 F.2d 1196, 1203 (2d Cir. 1992) (citing *Morales v. Turman*, 820 F.2d 728, 732 (5th Cir. 1987)), and therefore were neither ordered nor entitled to participate in the supplemental briefing. Thus, we consider only the Vessel Interests' initial brief as *amici curiae*—and not their letter brief—on this appeal.

DISCUSSION[12]

The federal interpleader statute confers original jurisdiction on federal district courts where "[t]wo or more adverse claimants [of at least minimally] diverse citizenship" may or do claim entitlement to "money or property of the value of $500 or more," or any benefit arising from an "instrument of value or amount of $500 or more" or an "obligation written or unwritten to the amount of $500 or more," provided that the plaintiff "has deposited such money or property" into the registry of the court or "has given bond payable to the clerk of the court in such amount and with such surety as the court or judge may deem proper." 28 U.S.C. § 1335(a). Where the other requirements are met, the statute makes it irrelevant that "the titles or claims of the conflicting claimants do not have a [—9—] common origin." *Id.* § 1335(b). USOT contends that these statutory requirements are not met. Its principal argument is that, because its claims to payment arise from statutory *in rem* liens against Hapag-Lloyd's vessels while the O.W. Entities' claims arise from the supply contracts (and thus are

---

[12] If the jurisdictional issue is presented on the face of the complaint, we accept as true all of the complaint's material factual allegations, along with the reasonable inferences that can be drawn from them, but if the issue is presented on the basis of controverting evidence outside of the complaint, we review the district court's factual findings for clear error and its rulings of law *de novo*. *See, e.g.*, *Tandon v. Captain's Cove Marina of Bridgeport, Inc.*, 752 F.3d 239, 243, 2 Adm. R. 57, 59 (2d Cir. 2014). "For purposes of ruling on a motion to dismiss for want of standing, both the trial and reviewing courts must accept as true all material allegations of the complaint, and must construe the complaint in favor of the complaining party." *Warth v. Seldin*, 422 U.S. 490, 501 (1975); *see also Lujan v. Defenders of Wildlife*, 504 U.S 555, 561 (1992) ("The party invoking federal jurisdiction bears the burden of establishing [standing] . . . in the same way as any other matter on which the plaintiff bears the burden of proof, *i.e.*, with the same manner and degree of evidence required at the successive stages of the litigation."). With respect to a district court's grant of injunctive relief pursuant to 28 U.S.C. § 2361, we review for abuse of discretion. *See Nat'l Union Fire Ins. Co. of Pittsburgh, Pa. v. Karp*, 108 F.3d 17, 23 (2d Cir. 1997).

correctly characterized by USOT as being *in personam* in nature), its codefendants are not claiming entitlement to the *same* money, property, or benefit of the instrument or obligation. USOT is of the view that its maritime liens do not arise out of the Hapag-Lloyd–O.W. Entities contracts but rather from the fact that USOT "provid[ed] necessaries to a vessel on the order of the owner or a person authorized by the owner." *See* Maritime Commercial Instruments and Liens Act, 46 U.S.C. § 31342.[13] In the context of this case, however, USOT focuses on a difference that is not material to the availability of interpleader.

It is well established that the interpleader statute is "remedial and to be liberally construed," particularly to prevent races to judgment and the unfairness of multiple and potentially conflicting obligations. *State Farm Fire & Cas. Co. v. Tashire*, 386 U.S. 523, 533 (1967). Though this matter presents a novel factual situation, we think the case before us fits squarely within the language and purpose of the interpleader statute. Like the District Court, we find instructive *Royal School Laboratories, Inc. v. Town of Waterman*, 358 F.2d 813 (2d Cir. 1966). There, we upheld an interpleader complaint by the Town, naming a supplier of equipment and furniture to the Town and the assignee of the general contractor who purchased but did not pay for the materials. *Id.* at 815. The supplier's equitable unjust enrichment claims against the Town arose from materialman claims while **[—10—]** the general contractor's assignee asserted claims against the Town for payment for the equipment arising from a contract. Judge Friendly, writing for the court, explained that "nothing could be more palpably unjust than to permit two recoveries against [the interpleader plaintiff] for the same enrichment." *Id.*[14] We conclude that the

claims alleged in this action concern the same enrichment to Hapag-Lloyd—*i.e.*, the value of the bunkers, payment for which is the entitlement claimed by all parties[15]—and are thus likewise "inextricably interrelated." *Id.* Although the claims may have different legal origins, we have previously held that there is no requirement that interpleader claims arise "out of a common source of right or entitlement." *Ashton v. Josephine Bay Paul & C. Michael Paul Found., Inc.*, 918 F.2d 1065, 1069 (2d Cir. 1990); *see also* 28 U.S.C. § 1335(b). **[—11—]**

The interconnection of the claims is evident. To recover under a maritime lien, USOT must demonstrate that it provided necessaries "on the order of the owner or a person authorized by the owner." 46 U.S.C. § 31342(a); *see also id.* § 31341 (listing persons "presumed to have authority to procure necessaries for a vessel"). We have no reason at this time to test USOT's assertion that an O.W. entity had the authority the lien statute requires, but it is difficult to see how USOT could prove authorization without reference to the chain of contractual relationships beginning with Hapag-Lloyd and passing through the O.W. Entities to itself. This chain of contracts is, of course, also the source of at least some of the claims by the O.W. Entities—others of which are competing *in*

---

[13] For the purposes of § 31342, bunkers are "necessaries." 1 Thomas J. Schoenbaum, Admiralty & Maritime Law § 9-3 (5th ed. 2014) (citing *Gulf Oil Trading Co. v. M/V Caribe Mar*, 757 F.2d 743 (5th Cir. 1985)).

[14] Concern over double recovery was similarly addressed in a non-interpleader case cited by both parties, *Central Hudson Gas & Electric Corp. v. Empresa Naviera Santa S.A.*, 56 F.3d 359 (2d Cir.

1995). In that case, we concluded *in rem* and *in personam* claims were distinct, and thus, a judgment in an *in rem* action was not a res judicata bar to a subsequent *in personam* action—in part because plaintiff "did not seek duplicative or additional damages" and instead in essence sought merely to treat the vessel operator as jointly liable with the vessel itself. *Id.* at 367. It is also worth noting that the considerations underlying whether a claim is precluded by *res judicata*—a judicial doctrine—are distinct from the considerations underlying the federal interpleader statutes, and thus *Central Hudson*'s analysis is of limited value in this case.

[15] The amounts alleged to be owed differ slightly between each claimant, because the contractual prices in the interlocking chain seem to incorporate some level of profit. *See supra* note 4. This is not fatal to an interpleader claim; the statute expressly applies to "titles or claims of the conflicting claimants" that "are not identical." 28 U.S.C. § 1335(b).

rem liens asserted under the same statutory entitlement claimed by USOT.[16]

USOT attempts to distinguish the entitlements by arguing that a payment by Hapag-Lloyd to O.W. Germany under its contracts would not discharge the maritime lien held by USOT. Indeed, that may be true.[17] But an interpleader action does not [—12—] abrogate USOT's right to be paid (if it has one); it merely requires USOT to litigate its claim in the context of the same proceeding as competing claimants, so that the District Court can minimize or eliminate the risk of double payment to the extent the governing law permits.[18] Adjudication of Hapag-Lloyd's obligation to pay for the fuel bunkers involves inextricably intertwined claims, and inter-

pleader jurisdiction is proper under the broad and remedial nature of § 1335.[19] [—13—]

USOT also challenges the sufficiency of the District Court's *in rem* jurisdiction.[20] However, USOT's arguments fail here as well. It relies on cases in which the person possessing the *in rem* claim initiates the proceeding without the vessel owner's consent, which would necessitate the court obtaining jurisdiction over the *res. See In re Millenium Seacarriers, Inc.,* 419 F.3d 83, 94 (2d Cir. 2005) (Sotomayor, J.); *Dluhos v. Floating & Abandoned Vessel,* 162 F.3d 63, 68–69 (2d Cir. 1998). USOT's argument—that *both* parties' consent is necessary in cases where the party initiating suit is the owner of the *res* that the lienholder seeks to arrest—relies on cases holding that where a lienholder brings a claim, both parties' consent is "sufficient" for a court to exercise *in rem* jurisdiction without seizure of the *res. E.g., Panaconti Shipping Co. v. M/V Ypapanti,* 865 F.2d 705, 707–08 (5th Cir. 1989). That is not inconsistent,

---

[16] *See* Verified Answer, Interpleader Claims, and Countercls. of O.W. Bunker Ger. GmbH at 14, ¶ 83, *Hapag-Lloyd,* No. 14-cv-9949 (S.D.N.Y. July 17, 2015), ECF No. 93; Answer, Countercls. and Cross-Claim of ING Bank N.V. to the First Am. Cmpl. for Interpleader and Declaratory J. at 11–12, ¶¶ 6–13, *Hapag-Lloyd,* No. 14-cv-9949 (S.D.N.Y. July 28, 2015), ECF No. 98.

[17] USOT's maritime lien certainly would be extinguished if USOT received payment from O.W. Denmark pursuant to its invoices. *See Mullane v. Chambers,* 438 F.3d 132, 138 (1st Cir. 2006) (after repayment, "any maritime lien had been extinguished by satisfaction"); *see also World Fuel Servs., Inc. v. Magdalena Green M/V,* 464 F. App'x 339, 341 (5th Cir. 2012) (per curiam) (same). In such a case, USOT could not recover both through its contract with O.W. Denmark *and* through its lien on Hapag-Lloyd's vessels, thereby further demonstrating that the [—12—] entitlements arising from the maritime lien and the interlocking contracts are inextricable.

[18] The various relationships in this case may, for example, require the District Court to untangle complicated questions of subrogation and set-offs among the parties as it determines payment obligations. *See Pearlman v. Reliance Ins. Co.,* 371 U.S. 132, 136–37, 136 n.12 (1962) (discussing the doctrine of subrogation); *Am. Fid. Co. v. Nat'l City Bank of Evansville,* 266 F.2d 910, 914 (D.C. Cir. 1959) (discussing equitable liens as a form of subrogation in the context of material suppliers). Because of the complexity of the questions presented by these competing claims, the District Court's interpleader jurisdiction over the parties and attendant issues meets the goals of efficiency and fairness motivating the statute.

[19] USOT's second argument as to interpleader jurisdiction—that the amount of the bond is insufficient under § 1335—patently fails. While USOT's arguments focus exclusively on the statutory clause that refers to deposit of the money or amount of obligation itself, it ignores that the statute *alternatively* permits posting of a bond "in such amount and with such surety as the court or judge may deem proper." 28 U.S.C. § 1335; *see also Aetna Cas. & Sur. Co. v. B.B.B. Constr. Corp.,* 173 F.2d 307, 309 (2d Cir. 1949) (noting that the interpleader statute was expressly amended to contain the bond as an alternative to payment of a deposit). The District Court clearly made a determination that the amount posted was sufficient, and we see no abuse of discretion in its conclusion. *See also supra* note 8.

[20] Hapag-Lloyd argues that USOT conflates subject matter and *in rem* jurisdiction, which are distinct. *See Mattel, Inc. v. Barbie-Club.com,* 310 F.3d 293, 298 (2d Cir. 2002) (Sotomayor, J.) (distinguishing between subject matter jurisdiction and *in rem* jurisdiction). While it is true that some elements of the arguments overlap, USOT in fact makes two arguments: first, the amount of the bond is insufficient under § 1335 to confer subject matter jurisdiction—which we addressed *supra* note 19—and second, even if it is sufficient under § 1335, it is insufficient to constitute a substitute *res* for the vessels themselves, which we address here.

however, with other cases indicating that only the owner's consent is necessary. *In rem* jurisdiction is "'a customary elliptical way of referring to jurisdiction over the interests of persons in a thing.'" *Shaffer v. Heitner*, 433 U.S. 186, 207 (1977) (quoting RESTATEMENT (SECOND) OF CONFLICT OF LAWS § 56, intro. note (1971)). To obtain jurisdiction over that interest, a court must either seize the *res* or obtain the consent of the owner or other person asserting a right of possession. This principle is demonstrated by the many cases in which *in rem* [—14—] jurisdiction has been held waived without seizure when the owner appears without contesting jurisdiction. *See, e.g., United States v. Republic Marine, Inc.*, 829 F.2d 1399, 1402 (7th Cir. 1987); *Cactus Pipe & Supply Co. v. M/V Montmartre*, 756 F.2d 1103, 1107–08 (5th Cir. 1985); *cf. Continental Grain Co. v. The FBL-585*, 364 U.S. 19, 22–27 (1960) (construing the owner's consent as sufficient for venue transfer of both *in personam* and *in rem* claims). By initiating an interpleader concerning certain *in rem* claims and posting adequate security for those claims, Hapag-Lloyd consented to the District Court's jurisdiction over its interests, which is sufficient to confer jurisdiction. *See Cactus Pipe*, 756 F.2d at 1107; *Reed v. Steamship Yaka*, 307 F.2d 203, 204 (3d Cir. 1962), *rev'd on other grounds*, 373 U.S 410 (1963).[21]

Next, USOT contends that the interpleader injunction issued in this case is in violation of the requirements of 28 U.S.C. § 2361.[22] USOT

argues that § 2361 does not expressly authorize [—15—] an interpleader injunction to extend to foreign suits. While the statute itself has no extraterritorial reach, federal courts have long possessed the inherent power to restrain the parties before them from engaging in suits in foreign jurisdictions. *See China Trade & Dev. Corp. v. M.V. Choong Yong*, 837 F.2d 33, 35 (2d Cir. 1987). This Circuit has articulated a test for when such injunctions are warranted: First, an anti-foreign-suit injunction may be imposed only if the parties are the same and resolution of the case before the enjoining court is dispositive of the action to be enjoined; if this threshold is met, the District Court must then examine five factors:

(1) frustration of a policy in the enjoining forum; (2) the foreign action would be vexatious; (3) a threat to the issuing court's in rem or quasi in rem jurisdiction; (4) the proceedings in the other forum prejudice [—16—] other equitable considerations; or (5) adjud-

---

§ 2361 conflicts with the 1983 revisions to Rule 4, which allow any adult non-party to complete service in the district in which a claimant resides."); *see also* Fed. R. Civ. P. 22(b) ("An action under [28 U.S.C. §§ 1335, 1397, and 2361] must be [—15—] conducted under these rules."). As USOT has not argued service was defective under Federal Rule of Civil Procedure 4, we treat service as sufficient. *See Norton v. Sam's Club*, 145 F.3d 114, 117 (2d Cir. 1998).

USOT makes an additional argument that the injunction was improper because it prevented USOT from executing arrest orders obtained in other federal courts. That USOT had obtained arrest orders prior to entry of the injunction is of no significance—interpleader injunctions clearly may restrain claimants "from instituting or *prosecuting*" actions in another jurisdiction. 28 U.S.C. § 2361 (emphasis added). In any event, USOT's arrest actions were not "first filed" because they were apparently filed later on the same day that Hapag-Lloyd filed its interpleader complaint. Moreover, some courts have found inapplicable the first-filed rule where filings were made on the same day, regardless of their order. *E.g., Ontel Prods., Inc. v. Project Strategies Corp.*, 899 F. Supp. 1144, 1150, 1153 (S.D.N.Y. 1995). *But see, e.g., Alden Corp. v. Eazypower Corp.*, 294 F. Supp. 2d 233, 235 n.2 (D. Conn. 2003).

---

[21] Similarly, USOT's argument that the bond is insufficient as a substitute *res* is unavailing. First, as we have just explained, no *res* is necessary when the owner consents; second, USOT's cited sources deal with the method by which a vessel's owner can free it from seizure through posting a bond and thus have no applicability in a case where seizure neither occurred nor is required.

[22] USOT also argues that service was not by U.S. Marshal and thus ineffective. Service of process is a question of "practice and procedure" governed by the Federal Rules of Civil Procedure; statutory requirements to the contrary were voided by the Rules Enabling Act. *See Henderson v. United States*, 517 U.S. 654, 656 (1996); *Aisner v. Penn. Mut. Life Ins. Co.*, 53 F.3d 1282, 1995 WL 295968, at *2 (5th Cir. 1995) (per curiam) (unpublished) ("Rule 4 of the Federal Rules of Civil Procedure supersedes § 2361 to the extent that

ication of the same issues in separate actions would result in delay, inconvenience, expense, inconsistency, or a race to judgment.

Id. at 35–36 (internal quotation marks omitted); *accord Ibeto Petrochemical Indus. Ltd. v. M/T Beffen*, 475 F.3d 56, 64 (2d Cir. 2007). Our review of the record does not reveal any such analysis by the District Court of the factors, which leaves us without a sufficient record of the District Court's exercise of its discretion. *See Gasperini v. Ctr. for Humanities, Inc.*, 149 F.3d 137, 142, 144 (2d Cir. 1998).

However, if we were merely to vacate and remand on this ground, Hapag-Lloyd would remain free to seek an anti-foreign suit injunction under *China Trade*, and the order granting or denying that injunction would then be immediately appealable under 28 U.S.C. § 1292(a)(1). In the interests of judicial economy and orderly resolution of the matter, therefore, we think it more prudent to order a limited remand pursuant to our Circuit's practice under *United States v. Jacobson*, 15 F.3d 19, 22 (2d Cir. 1994). The remand permits the District Court to make its determinations under the correct standard and return its determinations to us for consideration without the need for reassignment to a new panel and full briefing.

Accordingly, we remand to the District Court with instructions to enter an order, within ninety days of the issuance of our mandate, that eliminates or retains the foreign scope of the injunction, with specific determinations applying the *China Trade* test. If the District Court retains the scope of the injunction, either party may restore jurisdiction to this panel by filing a letter with the Clerk of this Court within thirty days after entry of such order; if the District Court eliminates the foreign scope of [—17—] the injunction and Hapag-Lloyd wishes to challenge that decision, it will be required to file a notice of appeal in order to do so. *See generally Jennings v. Stephens*, 135 S. Ct. 793, 798 (2015) ("[A]n appellee who does not cross-appeal may not attack the decree with a view . . . to enlarging his own rights

thereunder . . . ." (internal quotation marks omitted)). In either event, briefing of the issue may be by letter, not to exceed ten double-spaced pages, setting forth the grounds for claiming error in the District Court's decision and attaching a copy of the order. Upon the filing of such a letter, the opposing party may file a response of the same maximum length within fourteen days. Oral argument will be scheduled at the panel's discretion. If neither party files an initial letter—or notice of appeal, if required—the order entered by the District Court on remand will not be reviewed.

Finally, USOT challenges the District Court's exercise of personal jurisdiction over it as well as interpleader venue. However, we conclude that USOT has waived these issues, excluding them from appellate review in this case. The instances to which USOT points as asserting its personal jurisdiction arguments to the District Court are cursory, often one-sentence statements, which we have long held are generally insufficient to preserve an issue for appeal. *See Wal-Mart Stores, Inc. v. Visa U.S.A., Inc.*, 396 F.3d 96, 124 n.29 (2d Cir. 2005) (holding that under established law of the Circuit, a one-sentence challenge to a fee award was not sufficient to preserve the issue for appeal). Similarly, USOT's purported "objections" to venue at the District Court are minimal. Though one colloquy at a hearing could possibly be interpreted to raise the question of venue, we note from Hapag-Lloyd's supplemental briefing and our own review of the District Court docket that the deadline for motions to dismiss on the basis of personal jurisdiction and venue passed [—18—] without any submission from USOT. Thus, we decline to decide these issues for the first—and apparently only—time on appeal.[23]

---

[23] USOT argues that, even if its arguments were forfeited, we should consider them to avoid "manifest injustice." *Magi XXI, Inc. v. Stato della Città del Vaticano*, 714 F.3d 714, 724 (2d Cir. 2013) (internal quotation marks omitted). As we stated above, USOT had the opportunity to submit briefing on these issues to the District Court and chose not to do so. Such a decision bespeaks more waiver than forfeiture, *see Hamilton v. Atlas Turner, Inc.*, 197 F.3d 58, 61–62 (2d Cir. 1999),

CONCLUSION

We have considered USOT's remaining arguments and find them to be without merit. Accordingly, we AFFIRM in part the District Court's orders of December 19 and 30, 2014, but REMAND the case to the District Court with instructions to enter an order, within ninety days of the issuance of our mandate, that eliminates or retains the foreign scope of its injunction according to specific conclusions under the *China Trade* test. Either party may seek review of such order by filing a letter or notice of appeal, as prescribed above. In the interests of judicial economy, any such reinstated appeal will be assigned to this panel. The mandate shall issue forthwith.

---

which eliminates our discretion to reach the issue, *see Wood v. Milyard*, 132 S. Ct. 1826, 1832 (2012). Even assuming we possessed the discretion, we generally exercise it when presented with "a question of law" for which "there is no need for additional factfinding." *Magi XXI*, 714 F.3d at 724 (internal quotation marks omitted). Given the lack of development of the factual record below, we are not persuaded this case would present an appropriate vehicle to exercise our discretion in any event.

United States Court of Appeals
for the Second Circuit

No. 14-1346

FIREMAN'S FUND INS. CO.
vs.
GREAT AM. INS. CO. OF N.Y.

Appeals from the United States District Court for the
Southern District of New York

Decided: May 20, 2016

Citation: 822 F.3d 620, 4 Adm. R. 70 (2d Cir. 2016).

Before **CABRANES, POOLER,** and **DRONEY,** Circuit
Judges.

[—3—] **DRONEY,** Circuit Judge:

Plaintiffs-Appellants are Fireman's Fund Insurance Company, One Beacon Insurance Company, National Liability and Fire Insurance Company, and QBE Marine & Energy Syndicate 1036 (collectively "Fireman's Fund"), insurance companies that provided marine general liability and marine excess liability policies to Defendant–Appellant Signal International, LLC ("Signal").[1] [—4—] Fireman's Fund and Signal appealed from a judgment of the United States District Court for the Southern District of New York (Oetken, *J.*), granting summary judgment to Defendants-Appellees Great American Insurance Company of New York ("Great American") and Max Specialty Insurance Company ("MSI").

Fireman's Fund, Great American, and MSI issued insurance policies that provided

_____

[1] Fireman's Fund Insurance Company and One Beacon Insurance Company each agreed to cover fifty percent of the total amount insured under the marine general liability policy. Fireman's Fund Insurance Company and National [—4—] Liability and Fire Insurance Company each agreed to cover thirty-four percent of the total amount insured under the marine excess liability policy, and QBE Marine & Energy Syndicate 1036 agreed to cover the remaining thirty-two percent. The premiums for these two policies were also divided among the respective insurers. In this opinion, we refer to both the marine general liability policy and marine excess liability policy as issued by Fireman's Fund.

various coverages for a dry dock in Port Arthur, Texas owned by Signal. After the dry dock sank in 2009, Signal and Fireman's Fund sought contributions from Great American and MSI for the loss of the dry dock and resulting environmental cleanup costs. The district court ruled in adjudicating a number of summary judgment motions that the Great American and MSI policies were void in light of Signal's failure to [—5—] disclose when it applied for those policies that the dry dock had significantly deteriorated and that repairs recommended by a number of consultants and engineers over several years had not been made.

After submission of this appeal, MSI and Signal reached a settlement and obtained a dismissal of the case between them. Therefore, Signal no longer appeals the grant of summary judgment to MSI. Nonetheless, Fireman's Fund asserts that it may still pursue appeal of the issues relating to the policy issued to Signal by MSI based on our decision in *Maryland Cas. Co. v. W.R. Grace & Co. See* 218 F.3d 204, 211 (2d Cir. 2000) ("[T]he contract of settlement an insurer enters into with the insured cannot affect the rights of another insurer who is not a party to it. Instead, whatever obligations or rights to contribution may exist between two or more insurers of the same event flow from equitable principles."). Fireman's Fund was granted summary judgment below against MSI [—6—] on a contribution claim based on MSI's policy, and we assume without deciding that Fireman's Fund is correct that it may pursue this appeal of the district court's decision finding the MSI policy void, based on Fireman's Fund's interest in the unappealed summary judgment decision on contribution.

We agree with the district court's orders. We hold that the Great American policy was a marine insurance contract subject to the doctrine of *uberrimae fidei* and that Signal's nondisclosure violated its duty under that doctrine, permitting Great American to void the policy. We further hold that MSI's policy was governed by Mississippi law; that, under that law, Signal materially misrepresented the dry dock's condition; and that MSI was entitled to void the policy on that basis. Accordingly, we **AFFIRM**. [—7—]

BACKGROUND

I. Factual Background

A. The Operation and Loss of the Dry Dock

Signal is a marine construction firm involved principally in building and repairing ocean-going structures such as offshore drilling rigs, platforms, and barges. In 2003, Signal purchased six facilities—two in Mississippi and four in Texas—for use in its business of repairing, upgrading, and converting offshore drilling rigs.[2] One of the Texas facilities was a dockyard in Port Arthur, Texas. In acquiring that facility, Signal assumed an existing lease of a dry dock ("the dry dock") located along the Sabine-Neches [—8—] Waterway near the Gulf of Mexico.[3] The dry dock was built in 1944 at the direction of the United States Navy to repair Navy ships. In early 2005, Signal accepted an offer from the lessor to purchase the dry dock, which Signal had been using in its operations since it assumed the lease.

Throughout its lease and ownership of the dry dock, Signal received a number of reports on the dry dock's deteriorated condition. These included the following:

- The Heger Reports: The dry dock engineering firm Heger Dry Dock, Inc. ("Heger") of Holliston, Massachusetts, periodically inspected the dry dock between 2002 and 2009. In 2002, Freide Goldman Offshore—the operator of the dry dock before Signal—asked Heger to inspect the dry dock in order to provide an estimate of its fair market value.[4] In a December [—9—] 2002 appraisal, Heger described "the dry dock [as being] . . . in fair to good condition, with the exception of the pontoon deck . . . , which [was] in poor condition and should be replaced, and section H, which showed markedly more corrosion internally . . . ."[5] J.A. 4215. Heger estimated that the dry dock would have "10 years of remaining useful life if the pontoon deck [was] completely repaired," but the costs of making these "extensive repairs" in the United States rendered the dry dock's value "below zero."[6] J.A. 4215, 4216. In a series of subsequent reports from 2007 through 2009 commissioned by Signal to assist it in prolonging the existing life of the dry dock, Heger found that the dry dock had continued to deteriorate and that long-term repairs had not been made. Instead, Signal had simply patched damaged areas with "doublers."[7] J.A. 688. Heger provided

---

[2] These rigs included jack-ups, semi-submersibles, and mobile offshore production units. "A *jack-up* is a rig that is towed to a location, where the legs are 'jacked' down to the ocean floor allowing the work area to be raised about 50 feet above the water level." 1 Thomas J. Schoenbaum, *Admiralty and Maritime Law* § 3-9, at 169 n.8 (5th ed. 2011). "A *semi-submersible* is a cross between a submersible and a barge . . . [that] is submerged about 50 feet after which special anchors are lowered to complete the mooring of the rig." *Id.* A mobile offshore production unit is "a jackup rig that has been converted to an offshore production platform" and "can be moved and is reusable." Norman J. Hyne, *Dictionary of Petroleum Exploration, Drilling & Production* 327 (2d ed. 2014).

[3] A dry dock is a large structure used to lift ships and other ocean-going vessels out of water for repairs and construction. The dry dock is lowered into the water by flooding its pontoons with water, and then, after an object is loaded onto the dry dock, it is raised by pumping water out of the pontoons.

[4] Although the 2002 Heger Report was created before Signal assumed the dry dock lease, Freide Goldman Offshore's President of Texas Operations, John Haley—who became Signal's Senior Vice President of Texas Operations when Signal acquired the Port Arthur dockyard—received a copy of the report in December 2002, and Haley shared this report with other employees at Signal by (at the latest) January 2005.

[5] The dry dock consisted of eight pontoons designated "A" through "H."

[6] Alternatively, assuming that the dry dock was transported for repairs abroad, Heger estimated that the dry dock's fair market value would be approximately $800,000.

[7] "Doublers," or doubler plates, are steel plates that "offer a temporary solution for steel plate

recommendations for extensive repairs that would be required for the dry dock to continue to operate safely. However, Heger repeatedly advised that "the expected life extension for [—10—] the dock . . . [would] only be a few years" and therefore "the cost, time and effort to perform this work [was] not economically justifiable." J.A. 689. Heger also provided Signal with plans for converting the dry dock to a seven-pontoon configuration (by removing Pontoon H) but warned that "the dry dock structure . . . should be satisfactorily restored before using the dock or proceeding with any modifications." J.A. 4513-14.

- The ABS Audits: Auditor ABS Consulting ("ABS") of Houston, Texas, a maritime risk management firm, was designated by the Port of Port Arthur to review and report on Signal's maintenance and repair programs at the dry dock. In 2003, ABS observed "the rapidly increasing rate of overall deterioration" of the dry dock, which was "largely due to the drydock's age . . . , and . . . lack of adequate maintenance and/or repair." J.A. 4166. ABS noted that, although it had notified the dry dock's owners and operators in January 2000 of the "advanced state of . . . deterioration," they had "made no apparent efforts" to implement ABS's recommended repairs. J.A. 4168. Instead, "more than a hundred doubler plates ha[d] been welded over severely wasted/holed . . . platings." J.A. 4167. Six months later, ABS reported that Pontoon H was "leaking severely," and

Pontoons E and G were "leaking significantly" as well. J.A. 4161. ABS concluded that "it appeared that unsafe drydock operations were being conducted" and recommended that "additional drydockings [not be conducted] until substantial hull repairs [were] made to 'H' pontoon and the repairs [were] verified." J.A. 4162 (emphases omitted).

- Internal Staff Study: In April 2003, Signal conducted an internal "staff study" to determine whether to purchase the [—11—] leased dry dock from the Port Commission of Port Arthur. The study found that, "without major renewal costs," the dry dock's remaining useful life was "only 3 to 5 years." J.A. 4188. The study concluded that it would cost $21.88 million to extend the life of the dry dock's pontoons "for maybe 10 to 15 years." J.A. 4186-87. The study ultimately advised against purchasing the dry dock in light of its "relatively short remaining useful life and extreme costs of renewal/life extension." J.A. 4188.

- The DLS Surveys: The marine appraiser, surveyor, and consulting firm Dufour, Laskay & Strouse, Inc. ("DLS") of Houston, Louisiana, and Florida was hired to inspect and appraise Signal's Texas and Mississippi facilities "for the purpose of asset allocation and financial review" by GE Commercial Finance, Signal's financing company. J.A. 526. Between 2005 and 2007, DLS observed that the dry dock "had significant water in most compartments . . . [that] require[d] pumping and trimming every four hours," which was "indicative of some wastage holes in the bottom." J.A. 551, 4437; see also J.A. 5314. Each year, DLS noted that "[t]he deck plating . . . ha[d] significant doubler plates where plating ha[d] either wasted or separated from internal framing" and that "there was . . . a 12' long tear in the plating extending along a transverse frame" that "reportedly . . . w[ould] be fitted with a proper doubler in the near

---

damage" on marine structures. Ibrahim A. Assakkaf, *Reliability Design of Doubler Plates for Sea Tankers, in* Advances in Civil Engineering and Building Materials 823, 823 (Shuenn-Yih Chang et al. eds. 2013). The plates provide "an inexpensive method of repairing corroded plating, cracked plates, or defective welds." *Id.* Doubler plates are "added [on] top of [a] defective area and welded around the plate's perimeter." *Id.* "This temporary repair method [is intended to] maintain structural integrity until . . . permanent repairs [are] made to the original corroded structure." *Id.*

future." J.A. 551, 4437, 5314. In 2007, DLS concluded that the dry dock was in "fair to good condition" but recommended that its pontoons be dry-docked and repaired "[a]s soon as practical within the succeeding eighteen months . . . to render [it] in good stable operating condition and provide a life extension." J.A. 4437. [—12—]

- The 2009 Heller Property Risk Assessment Report: Stephen Heller & Associates Inc. ("Heller") of Houston—a loss prevention consulting firm—was hired by Signal in 2008 to conduct a risk review of Signal's Mississippi and Texas facilities in order to "assist [insurance] underwriters in evaluating the exposures, operations, and loss prevention" for those facilities. J.A. 2267. In a January 2009 report, Heller rated the Mississippi and Texas facilities "[o]verall" as "Above Average," meaning that they met "[a]cceptable standards including some industry best practices." J.A. 2270. Heller found that "[t]he maximum foreseeable loss (MFL) or worst case scenario for these facilities [included] a sinking or structural collapse of [the] dry dock at . . . Port Arthur." J.A. 2269. The maximum foreseeable loss was described as "one of extremely low probability and frequency based on previous industry experience." J.A. 2298-99.

Signal never replaced the dry dock's pontoons or pontoon decks. Instead, Signal continued to use inserts and doublers to patch holes in the decks.

In 2009, Signal decided to implement the seven-pontoon configuration by removing Pontoon H. On August 20, 2009, it attempted to remove that pontoon, but during that procedure the entire dry dock sank. [—13—]

Shortly after the sinking, Signal notified the Texas General Land Office ("GLO"), which regulates pollution affecting Texas shoreline waters, about what had occurred. In September 2009, the GLO advised Signal to "initiate immediate action to recover the . . .

dry dock from Texas coastal waters."[8] J.A. 3516. In June 2010, Signal hired Weeks Marine, Inc., to manage removal of the sunken dry dock and cleanup of the site. Removal and cleanup efforts were not completed until March 2012 and resulted in $12,395,026 in costs.

B. The Insurance Policies Covering the Dry Dock

Signal had obtained five insurance policies that insured against risks related to the dry dock at the time of its sinking: (1) a marine general liability policy issued by Fireman's Fund; (2) a marine excess liability policy issued by Fireman's Fund; (3) a pollution policy issued by Great American (the "Pollution Policy"); [—14—] (4) a primary property insurance policy (the "PPI Policy") issued by Westchester Surplus Lines Insurance Company ("Westchester"); and (5) an excess property insurance policy issued by MSI, which provided coverage in excess of the PPI Policy (the "EPI Policy"). Only the Great American Pollution Policy and the MSI EPI Policy are at issue here.

Great American first underwrote the Pollution Policy in 2004 and renewed it annually through 2009. To obtain the renewal of the policy for 2009, Signal completed and submitted Great American's standard "Vessel Pollution Liability Application" along with a "Schedule of Vessels," which included the dry dock and approximately twenty-five tugboats and barges owned by Signal. The Pollution Policy insured Signal against losses of up to $5 million for each property in the Schedule resulting from pollution discharges into navigable waters. The policy specifically insured against claims under the "Oil Pollution Act of 1990, . . . 33 U.S.C. [—15—] [§] 2701 et seq." ("OPA"), the "Comprehensive Environmental Response, Compensation[,] and Liability Act, 42 U.S.C. [§] 9601, et seq." ("CERCLA"), and the "Federal Water Pollution Control Act Amendments of 1972, 33 U.S.C. [§] 1321, et seq." ("FWPCA"), and the costs of "on-water removal of materials of a

---

[8] The dry dock contained substantial amounts of asbestos and related contaminants.

non-OPA and non-CERCLA nature which has been mandated by an authorized public authority and [was] the result of a defined single, sudden and accidental event." J.A. 737. An endorsement to the policy also extended coverage to "all Vessels while under repair, alteration, construction, conversion or rebuilding" within 100 miles of the Port Arthur dockyard. J.A. 738.

MSI underwrote the EPI Policy in January 2009. To apply for the policy, Signal submitted its "2009-2010 Property Insurance Submission." This document included a "Statement of Values" that described the dry dock's value as $13.6 million and the 2009 Heller Report, but it did not include other information—such as the Heger [—16—] reports, the ABS audits, or the DLS surveys—suggesting that the dry dock was in need of repair. The EPI Policy insured against loss of or damage to properties listed in the Statement of Values, as well as business interruption costs and "[e]xtra [e]xpense[s]" associated with the loss of those properties. The policy provided $15 million coverage for losses in excess of the underlying PPI Policy, which covered losses up to $10 million.

C. Post-Loss Insurance Claims

In January 2010, Westchester paid Signal its total coverage amount of $10 million pursuant to the PPI Policy for losses related to the dry dock. MSI paid Signal $3.6 million of its total coverage amount of $15 million under the EPI Policy based on the $13.6 million value of the dry dock, as represented in the Statement of Values. Great American refused to make any payments under its Pollution Policy.

In meetings between Signal and its insurers in early 2010, MSI and Great American argued that their policies did not cover the [—17—] costs of removing the dry dock from the Sabine-Neches Waterway and cleaning up the site. Fireman's Fund agreed to fund Signal's removal and cleanup efforts but reserved its right to seek reimbursement later from MSI and Great American.

II. Procedural Background

On March 2, 2010, Fireman's Fund commenced this action against Signal, Great American, and MSI, seeking a declaration as to the obligations of Signal and its insurers for losses associated with the sinking of the dry dock. MSI asserted cross-claims against Signal for the $3.6 million it had paid, and also sought to void the EPI Policy on the ground of misrepresentation after discovery revealed the various reports on the dry dock's poor condition that Signal had not provided to MSI when applying for the policy. Signal cross-claimed against MSI for cleanup and removal costs and additional damages. Great American filed claims against Signal and Fireman's Fund, seeking a declaration that the Pollution Policy was void under [—18—] the maritime doctrine of *uberrimae fidei*, which imposes a duty of utmost good faith on the insured,[9] or alternatively under the policy's "Misrepresentation" clause.[10]

On October 15, 2010, Signal assigned to Fireman's Fund its rights under the Great American Pollution Policy, and Fireman's Fund continued to pursue coverage against Great American. Both Signal and Fireman's Fund maintained their claims against MSI; Signal opposed MSI's efforts to obtain from Signal the $3.6 million it had already paid, and both Signal and Fireman's Fund sought additional payments from MSI under its EPI Policy.

This appeal arises out of eight motions that were filed after the close of discovery. Fireman's Fund, Signal, Great American, and [—19—] MSI moved or cross-moved on the coverage issues for the Pollution Policy and EPI Policy.[11]

---

[9] The doctrine of *uberrimae fidei* is discussed in more depth later in this opinion.

[10] The Pollution Policy's "Misrepresentation" clause provides that "[a]ny concealment or misrepresentation by [the insured] of any material fact . . . will void this policy completely . . . , whether such concealment or misrepresentation is deliberate, negligent, inadvertent, innocent, or otherwise." J.A. 727.

[11] Fireman's Fund and Signal jointly moved for summary judgment against Great American, and

On March 25, 2013, the district court granted partial summary judgment, holding that under the EPI Policy, MSI was required to contribute to the payments that Fireman's Fund had made to Signal. *Fireman's Fund Ins. Co. v. Great Am. Ins. Co. of New York*, No. 10 Civ. 1653 (JPO), 2013 WL 1195277, at *8-9 (S.D.N.Y. Mar. 25, 2013). However, on March 31, 2014, the district court ruled—also on summary judgment—that the Great American Pollution Policy and the MSI EPI Policy were void *ab initio* because of Signal's failure to disclose the dry dock's deteriorated state. *See Fireman's Fund Ins. Co. v. Great Am. Ins. Co. of New York*, 10 F. Supp. 3d 460, 466 (S.D.N.Y. 2014). The court concluded that the Great American Pollution Policy [—20—] was a marine insurance contract subject to the doctrine of *uberrimae fidei* and that Signal had breached its duty of utmost good faith to Great American by withholding material information about the dry dock's condition when it applied for coverage. *See id.* 476-93. The district court also held that the EPI Policy was void under Mississippi law because Signal had materially misrepresented the dry dock's condition in its 2009-2010 Property Insurance Submission. *Id.* at 494-503. The court therefore denied Fireman's Fund's and Signal's motions for summary judgment and partial summary judgment, granted MSI's and Great American's motions for summary judgment declaring the policies void, and denied the remaining motions, including MSI's motion for reconsideration of the March 25, 2013 decision on contribution. *Id.* at 493 & n.19, 503-04 & n.25. Fireman's Fund and Signal appealed.

After submission of this appeal, MSI and Signal reached a settlement and obtained dismissal of the case between them. We [—21—] still must address the validity of the EPI policy, however, because, notwithstanding the recent settlement between Fireman's Fund and Signal, the EPI policy is still the basis for Fireman's Fund's claim for contribution against MSI.

DISCUSSION[12]

I. Great American's Pollution Policy

Fireman's Fund argues that Great American's Pollution Policy is not subject to the doctrine of *uberrimae fidei*. It further argues that, [—22—] even if the doctrine applies, Signal did not breach its duty to Great American because it provided all information that Great American requested about the dry dock on its insurance application.

A. Admiralty Jurisdiction and the Doctrine of *Uberrimae Fidei*

Great American argues—and the district court concluded—that the Pollution Policy is void under the maritime doctrine of *uberrimae fidei*. For the doctrine to apply, Fireman's Fund's suit against Great American "must . . . be sustainable under the [court's] admiralty

---

Great American cross-moved for summary judgment against them, on Great American's cross-claims and counterclaims. Fireman's Fund also moved for summary judgment, and Great American cross-moved for summary judgment, as to whether cleanup and removal costs were covered by the Pollution Policy. Signal moved for partial summary judgment against MSI, seeking a declaration that the EPI Policy was not void. MSI cross-moved for summary judgment against Signal on the same issue.

---

[12] A district court's grant of summary judgment is reviewed *de novo*. *See Aulicino v. N.Y.C. Dep't of Homeless Servs.*, 580 F.3d 73, 79 (2d Cir. 2009). Summary judgment should be granted "if the movant shows that there is no genuine dispute as to any material fact and the movant is entitled to judgment as a matter of law." Fed. R. Civ. P. 56(a). A fact is material if it might affect the outcome of the case under governing law. *Anderson v. Liberty Lobby, Inc.*, 477 U.S. 242, 248 (1986). A dispute is genuine "if the evidence is such that a reasonable jury could return a verdict for the nonmoving party." *Id.* In making this determination, the Court "must 'construe the facts in the light most favorable to the non-moving party and must resolve all ambiguities and draw all reasonable inferences against the movant.'" *Beyer v. Cty. of Nassau*, 524 F.3d 160, 163 (2d Cir. 2008) (quoting *Dallas Aerospace, Inc. v. CIS Air Corp.*, 352 F.3d 775, 780 (2d Cir. 2003)). Where "parties file[] cross-motions for summary judgment[,] . . . each party's motion must be examined on its own merits, and in each case all reasonable inferences must be drawn against the party whose motion is under consideration." *Morales v. Quintel Entm't, Inc.*, 249 F.3d 115, 121 (2d Cir. 2001).

jurisdiction." *Norfolk S. Ry. Co. v. Kirby*, 543 U.S. 14, 23 (2004) (emphasis omitted). This is because federal courts' "authority to make decisional law for the interpretation of maritime contracts stems from the Constitution's grant of admiralty jurisdiction to federal courts." *Id.*; *see* U.S. Const. art. III, § 2, cl. 1 (providing that the federal judicial power "shall extend . . . to all Cases of admiralty and maritime Jurisdiction"). Thus, "the grant of admiralty jurisdiction and the power to make admiralty law are mutually [—23—] dependent." *Kirby*, 543 U.S. at 23.

"Title 28 U.S.C. § 1333(1) grants federal district courts the power to entertain '[a]ny civil case of admiralty or maritime jurisdiction.'" *Atl. Mut. Ins. Co. v. Balfour Maclaine Int'l Ltd.*, 968 F.2d 196, 199 (2d Cir. 1992). "[T]his grant includes jurisdiction 'over all contracts which relate to the navigation, business, or commerce of the sea.'" *Id.* (ellipsis omitted) (quoting *DeLovio v. Boit*, 7 F. Cas. 418, 444 (C.C.D. Mass. 1815)).

"[T]here are few 'clean lines between maritime and non-maritime contracts.'" *Folksamerica Reinsurance Co. v. Clean Water of N.Y., Inc.*, 413 F.3d 307, 311 (2d Cir. 2005) (quoting *Kirby*, 543 U.S. at 23). "The boundaries of admiralty jurisdiction over contracts are conceptual rather than spatial, and defined by the purpose of the jurisdictional grant—to protect maritime commerce." *Id.* (citations omitted). "[W]hether a contract is a maritime one . . . 'depends upon the nature and character of the contract,' and the true criterion [—24—] is whether it has 'reference to maritime service or maritime transactions.'" *Kirby*, 543 U.S. at 23-24 (ellipsis omitted) (quoting *N. Pac. S.S. Co. v. Hall Bros. Marine Ry. & Shipbuilding Co.*, 249 U.S. 119, 125 (1919)). Our inquiry focuses on "whether the principal objective of a contract is maritime commerce." *Id.* at 25. "Therefore, the contract's subject matter must be our focal point." *Folksamerica*, 413 F.3d at 312.

"[A]dmiralty jurisdiction will exist over an insurance contract where the primary or principal objective of the contract is the establishment of 'policies of marine insurance.'" *Id.* at 315 (quoting *Ins. Co. v. Dunham*, 78 U.S. (11 Wall.) 1, 35 (1870)). "[W]hether an insurance policy is marine insurance depends on 'whether the insurer assumes risks which are marine risks.'" *Id.* at 316 (quoting *Jeffcott v. Aetna Ins. Co.*, 129 F.2d 582, 584 (2d Cir. 1942)). "[A]n insurance policy's predominant purpose, as measured by the dimensions of the contingency insured against and the risk [—25—] assumed, determines the nature of the insurance." *Id.* at 317 (quoting *Acadia Ins. Co. v. McNeil*, 116 F.3d 599, 603 (1st Cir. 1997)). Thus, "[u]ltimately, coverage determines whether a policy is 'marine insurance,' and coverage is a function of the terms of the insurance contract and the nature of the business insured." *Id.*

The question of whether an insurance contract is subject to the court's admiralty jurisdiction "ha[s] implications beyond conferring federal jurisdiction." *Id.* at 310. In particular, "[w]hen a contract is a maritime one, and the dispute is not inherently local, federal law controls the contract inter-pretation." *Kirby*, 543 U.S. at 22-23.

Under federal law, a marine insurance contract is subject to "the federal maritime doctrine of *uberrimae fide*, or utmost good faith." *Folksamerica*, 413 F.3d at 310; *see also Knight v. U.S. Fire Ins. Co.*, 804 F.2d 9, 13 (2d Cir. 1986) ("[T]he substantive law governing marine insurance . . . . [includes the] well-established [principle that] under the doctrine of *uberrimae fidei* . . . the parties to a marine [—26—] insurance policy must accord each other the highest degree of good faith."). The doctrine is a recognition that "the [insured] is more likely to be aware of . . . information" that "materially affects the risk being insured," *N.Y. Marine & Gen. Ins. Co. v. Tradeline (L.L.C.)*, 266 F.3d 112, 123 (2d Cir. 2001), and that "[o]ften the insurer lacks the practicable means to verify the accuracy or sufficiency of facts provided by the insured for purposes of establishing the contractual terms," 2 Thomas J. Schoenbaum, *Admiralty and Maritime Law* § 19-14, at 404-05 (5th ed. 2011). For example, the vessel to be insured may be at some great distance on the high seas, impossible to inspect at the time the application for insurance is filed. *See* Warren

J. Marwedel & Stephanie A. Espinoza, *Dagger, Shield, or Double-Edged Sword?: The Reciprocal Nature of the Doctrine of Uberrimae Fidei*, 83 Tul. L. Rev. 1163, 1168-69 (2009).

Accordingly, under the doctrine, "the party seeking insurance is required to disclose all circumstances known to it which [—27—] materially affect the risk." *Folksamerica*, 413 F.3d at 311 (quoting *Atl. Mut. Ins. Co. v. Balfour MacLaine Int'l Ltd. (In re Balfour MacLaine Int'l Ltd.)*, 85 F.3d 68, 80 (2d Cir. 1996)); *see also Knight*, 804 F.2d at 13 ("Since the [insured] is in the best position to know of any circumstances material to the risk, he must reveal those facts to the underwriter, rather than wait for the underwriter to inquire."). "If [the insured] acquires material information after having applied for insurance, he is required to communicate that information to the proposed insurer" as well. *Puritan Ins. Co. v. Eagle S.S. Co. S.A.*, 779 F.2d 866, 870 (2d Cir. 1985). Thus, "[t]he [insured] is bound, although no inquiry be made, to disclose every fact within his knowledge that is material to the risk." 2 Schoenbaum, *supra*, § 19-14, at 405-06. "The standard for disclosure is an objective one, that is, whether a reasonable person in the [insured's] position would know that the particular fact is material." *Knight*, 804 F.2d at 13.

"Failure by the [insured] to disclose all available information [—28—] will allow the insurer to avoid the policy," regardless of "whether such omission is intentional or results from mistake, accident, forgetfulness, or inadvertence."[13] 2 Schoenbaum, *supra*,

---

[13] The district court concluded that, under *uberrimae fidei*, the Pollution Policy was void *ab initio*, "meaning that there was never an enforceable contract to begin with." *Catlin (Syndicate 2003) at Lloyd's v. San Juan Towing & Marine Servs., Inc.*, 778 F.3d 69, 83 n.19, 3 Adm. R. 24, 34 n. 19 (1st Cir. 2015). However, we agree with the First Circuit that, "as the Supreme Court has described it, . . . *uberrimae fidei* renders a marine insurance contract *voidable*—the contract is deemed valid until being voided at the election of the insurer." *Id.*, 3 Adm. R. at 34 n. 19 (emphasis in original); *see Stipcich v. Metro. Life Ins. Co.*, 277 U.S. 311, 316 (1928) (noting that, for insurance

§ 19-14, at 406; *see Sun Mut. Ins. Co. v. Ocean Ins. Co.*, 107 U.S. 485, 510 (1883) ("The concealment, whether intentional or inadvertent, . . . avoids the policy . . . . In respect to the duty of disclosing all material facts, . . . [t]he obligation . . . is one *uberrimae fidei*. The duty of communication, indeed, is independent of the intention, and is violated by the fact of concealment even where there is no design to deceive."); *Puritan Ins. Co.*, 779 F.2d at 870-71; *see also Catlin (Syndicate 2003) at Lloyd's v. San Juan Towing & Marine Servs., Inc.*, [—29—] 778 F.3d 69, 83, 3 Adm. R. 24, 34 (1st Cir. 2015) ("Under *uberrimae fidei*, when the marine insured fails to disclose to the marine insurer *all* circumstances known to it and unknown to the insurer which 'materially affect the insurer's risk,' the insurer may void the marine insurance policy at its option." (emphasis in original) (quoting *Windsor Mount Joy Mut. Ins. Co. v. Giragosian*, 57 F.3d 50, 55 (1st Cir. 1995))). However, "[t]he principle of *uberrimae fidei* does not require the voiding of the contract unless the undisclosed facts were material and relied upon." *Puritan*, 779 F.2d at 871.

B. The Pollution Policy is a Marine Insurance Contract

1. The "Threshold Inquiry": The Maritime Nature of the Dispute

In determining whether a contractual dispute falls within our admiralty jurisdiction, "[s]everal of our cases . . . [have] require[d] that, prior to inquiring into the subject matter of the contract, we first make a 'threshold inquiry' into the subject matter of the dispute." *Folksamerica*, 413 F.3d at 312. Those cases hold that "a [—30—] federal court must initially determine whether the *subject matter of the dispute* is so attenuated from the business of maritime commerce that it does not implicate the concerns underlying

---

policies subject to the doctrine of *uberrimae fidei*, "a failure by the insured to disclose conditions affecting the risk, of which he is aware, makes the contract voidable at the insurer's option"). As Great American seeks a declaration that the Pollution Policy is void, the distinction makes no practical difference here.

admiralty and maritime jurisdiction." *Id.* (quoting *Balfour*, 968 F.2d at 200).

"[S]ome uncertainty [exists] as to the extent to which this Court's 'threshold inquiry' test survives the Supreme Court's . . . decision [in *Kirby*] . . . . [where,] [f]ocusing on the contract subject matter, the [*Kirby*] Court found admiralty jurisdiction." *Id.* at 313. "[T]he absence of any discussion by the Supreme Court [in *Kirby*] of a 'threshold inquiry' akin to that found in our precedents is notable."[14] *Id.* at 314. [—31—]

However, we need not resolve that uncertainty here. Assuming the continued vitality of the "threshold inquiry" into the subject matter of the dispute, this case survives it. The dispute over the Pollution Policy concerns insurance coverage for the costs of removing the dry dock and the pollutants it produced upon sinking in navigable waters. The sinking of the dry dock created potential dangers to public health and safety and the environment—matters that would directly impact those who conducted maritime commerce in those waters.

Moreover, the parties' dispute here concerns information provided to an insurer for pollution coverage for a structure used in vessel repair and maintenance. These questions directly implicate the business of maritime commerce. *See Folksamerica*, 413 F.3d at 313 ("The business of ship maintenance has long been recognized as maritime . . . ."); *id.* at 321 ("Pollution coverage is widely recognized as marine in nature."); *cf. Sirius Ins. Co. (UK) Ltd. v. Collins*, 16 F.3d [—32—] 34, 36 (2d Cir. 1994)

---

[14] "The Supreme Court introduced [*Kirby*] as 'a maritime case about a train wreck.'" *Folksamerica*, 413 F.3d at 313 (quoting *Kirby*, 543 U.S. at 18). "That decision involved a contract for the transportation of goods from Australia to Alabama." *Id.* (citation omitted). "The dispute concerned a railroad's liability for machinery damaged during a train derailment. The machinery had been transported by ship from . . . Australia, to Savannah, Georgia, and was en route from Savannah to Huntsville, Alabama, when the train derailed." *Id.* (citation omitted). "The Court focused entirely on the underlying contract . . . . [in] f[inding] admiralty jurisdiction." *Id.*

("There are few objects—perhaps none—more essentially related to maritime commerce than vessels.").

Thus, "the insurance claim [here] . . . has more than a 'speculative and attenuated' connection with maritime commerce." *Folksamerica*, 413 F.3d at 313 (quoting *Balfour*, 968 F.2d at 200). Assuming that the threshold inquiry survives *Kirby*, the dispute here is sufficiently maritime in nature to withstand that inquiry.

2. The Maritime Nature of the Pollution Policy

Our next inquiry is whether the Pollution Policy itself is sufficiently "marine" to warrant application of federal maritime law, including the doctrine of *uberrimae fidei.*

Fireman's Fund urges us to consider only the policy's coverage of the dry dock in determining whether the contract is marine insurance. It maintains that such a "fixed structure drydock" is not a vessel, and thus pollution coverage for the dry dock is not subject to maritime jurisdiction. Fireman's Fund Br. at 17. Fireman's Fund argues that this coverage is severable from the [—33—] policy's coverage of other structures and vessels, as evidenced by the fact that each object listed in the policy's Schedule of Vessels is subject to a separate premium.

Prior to *Kirby*, this Court had held that admiralty jurisdiction was limited to "contracts, claims, and services [that were] *purely* maritime." *Folksamerica*, 413 F.3d at 314 (quoting *Rea v. The Eclipse*, 135 U.S. 599, 608 (1890)). "A 'mixed' contract, i.e., a contract that contain[ed] both admiralty and non-admiralty obligations [was], therefore, usually not within admiralty jurisdiction." *Transatlantic Marine Claims Agency, Inc. v. Ace Shipping Corp.*, 109 F.3d 105, 109 (2d Cir. 1997). "[T]he general rule that 'mixed' contracts f[e]ll outside admiralty jurisdiction" was subject to two exceptions: (1) cases where the "claim [arose] from a breach of maritime obligations that [were] severable from the non-maritime obligations of the contract" ("the severability exception"), and (2) cases "where the non-maritime elements of a contract [were] merely incidental to the [—34—] maritime ones" (" the incidental exception"). *Folksamerica*, 413 F.3d at 314 (citations and internal quotation marks omitted).

After *Kirby*, however, we "amended our jurisprudence on maritime contracts." *Williamson v. Recovery Ltd. P'ship*, 542 F.3d 43, 49 (2d Cir. 2008). We held that "[i]n applying what we have previously called the 'incidental' exception, we should focus 'on whether the principal objective of a contract is maritime commerce,' rather than on whether the non-maritime components are properly characterized as more than 'incidental' or 'merely incidental' to the contract." *Folksamerica*, 413 F.3d at 315 (citation omitted) (quoting *Kirby*, 543 U.S. at 25).

We have not yet addressed the impact of *Kirby* on the severability exception.[15] The Ninth Circuit has held that the exception "collapses in the wake of the [*Kirby*] Court's conceptually-based 'primary objective' test." *Sentry Select Ins. Co. v. Royal Ins. Co.* [—35—] *of Am.*, 481 F.3d 1208, 1218 (9th Cir. 2007). We need not to resolve the issue here, however. Assuming *arguendo* that the Pollution Policy is severable and that its coverage of the dry dock should be viewed in isolation, we nonetheless find that the policy is a maritime contract.

To reach this conclusion, we consider whether "the primary or principal objective of the [Pollution Policy's dry dock coverage] is the establishment of policies of marine insurance," which "depends on whether the insurer assumes risks which are marine risks." *Folksamerica*, 413 F.3d at 315, 316 (citations and internal quotation marks omitted). This requires consideration of "the terms of the insurance contract and the nature of the business insured." *Id.* at 317.

As it pertains to the dry dock, the Pollution Policy insures against liability for "accidental discharge or substantial threat of a discharge" from the dry dock "into the navigable waters

of the [—36—] United States." J.A. 724. Coverage includes liability arising under the OPA[16] and the FWPCA,[17] statutes that hold parties responsible for the release of pollutants into navigable waters. *See* 33 U.S.C. §§ 1321(b)(3), 2702(a). It also extends to "the on-water removal of materials . . . [as] mandated by an authorized public authority." J.A. 737.

In addition to emissions from the dry dock itself, the policy insures against liability for emissions from "all Vessels while under repair" within "a 100 nautical mile radius" of the Port Arthur dockyard. J.A. 738. Thus, the policy provides coverage for vessels located at the dry dock in connection with Signal's repair business— [—37—] the type of business which has "long been recognized as maritime."[18] *Folksamerica*, 413 F.3d at 313. There is no indication that coverage for vessels located at the dry dock was obtained through the payment of separate premiums. Rather, coverage for such vessels is an extension of the policy's coverage of the dry dock. *See Sirius*, 16 F.3d at 37 (noting that the existence of "separately calculated premiums" is relevant in determining severability of insurance contract provisions). We therefore cannot

---

[15] In *Folksamerica*, the plaintiff did not assert that the severability exception applied. *See Folksamerica*, 413 F.3d at 314.

[16] The OPA holds parties that are responsible for "a vessel or a facility from which oil is discharged, or which poses the substantial threat of a discharge of oil, into or upon the navigable waters or adjoining shorelines" liable for "removal costs and damages." 33 U.S.C. § 2702(a).

[17] The provision of the FWPCA cited in the Great American Pollution Policy prohibits "[t]he discharge of oil or hazardous substances . . . into or upon the navigable waters of the United States, adjoining shorelines, or into or upon the waters of the contiguous zone . . . in such quantities as may be harmful." 33 U.S.C. § 1321(b)(3).

[18] Fireman's Fund argues that Signal's dry dock operations should be considered non-maritime because, in 2009, sixty percent of Signal's revenue came from ship construction, a non-maritime activity. *See Kossick v. United Fruit Co.*, 365 U.S. 731, 735 (1961) ("[A] contract to repair or to insure a ship is maritime, but a contract to build a ship is not." (citations omitted)). However, Christopher Scott Cunningham, Signal's Chief Financial Officer, testified that Signal's construction projects took place at sites other than Port Arthur, and Fireman's Fund has cited no evidence to the contrary.

agree with Fireman's Fund that the policy's provisions related to the dry dock "did not provide coverage for any potential liabilities associated with the actual repair or maintenance of vessels."[19] Fireman's Fund [—38—] Br. 20.

We conclude that the primary object of the Pollution Policy's coverage of the dry dock was to insure against the risk of liability for pollutants emitted during Signal's ship repair and maintenance operations there. Insurance policies protecting against such risks have long been considered marine in nature. *See Folksamerica*, 413 F.3d at 321 (finding pollution coverage provisions to be marine, given that "[p]ollution coverage is widely recognized as marine in nature," marine insurance contracts often include pollution coverage, and "[t]he insured's business operations in oil and cargo transportation render[ed] pollution coverage potentially significant"); *see also Certain Underwriters at Lloyds v. Inlet Fisheries Inc.*, 518 F.3d 645, 654 (9th Cir. 2008) ("One type of insurance [—39—] typifying marine insurance is protection and indemnity ('P & I') insurance . . . . P & I insurance historically included pollution liability . . . . Vessel pollution policies mirror P & I policies in their general terms, but cover liability under the OPA and other environmental statutes. That vessel pollution insurance covers new statutory liabilities . . . does not alter the fact that the risks of incurring that liability stem from the same vagaries of marine life that have shaped maritime insurance law for centuries." (citation omitted)). We hold that the Pollution Policy is a marine insurance policy, subject to

___

[19] We are also not persuaded by Fireman's Fund's argument that the Pollution Policy is not marine insurance because the dry dock bore no relation to a vessel [—38—] or to maritime commerce. *Kirby* makes clear that the involvement of a vessel (or lack thereof) is not dispositive in determining whether a contract is marine. *See Kirby*, 543 U.S. at 23 ("To ascertain whether a contract is a maritime one, we cannot look to whether a ship or other vessel was involved in the dispute, as we would in a putative maritime tort case."). Moreover, given its use in repairing and maintaining vessels, the dry dock itself bore a significant relationship to vessels and to maritime commerce.

our admiralty jurisdiction and federal maritime law, including the doctrine of *uberrimae fidei*.[20] [—40—]

C. Signal Violated Its Duty of Utmost Good Faith by Failing To Disclose the Dry Dock's Condition

We turn next to the questions of whether Signal violated its duty of utmost good faith

___

[20] We also conclude that the Great American Pollution Policy is not so "inherently local" as to require the application of state law. *Kirby*, 543 U.S. at 22-23 (citing *Kossick*, 365 U.S. at 735). This analysis asks "whether . . . the application of state law would . . . disturb the uniformity of maritime law." *Kossick*, 365 U.S. at 738. The Supreme Court has recognized that in contract cases, which implicate parties' voluntary agreements, local interests are generally minimized. *See id.* at 741. Moreover, application of state law here would disturb the uniformity of maritime law by upsetting parties' expectations that marine insurance policies are subject to the doctrine of *uberrimae fidei*. This expectation has significant implications for how both insurers and insureds negotiate such policies and conduct themselves for the duration of those policies. *Cf.* Jeremy A. Herschaft, [—40—] *Not Your Average Coffee Shop: Lloyd's of London—A Twenty-First-Century Primer on the History, Structure, and Future of the Backbone of Marine Insurance*, 29 Tul. Mar. L.J. 169, 180-81 (2005). The doctrine provides insurers with assurances that the party in the best position to provide information material to the risk—the insured—will bear the burden of providing such information. *See Tradeline*, 266 F.3d at 123 ("*Uberrimae fidae* . . . requires an [insured] to disclose any information that materially affects the risk being insured, because the [insured] is more likely to be aware of such information."); 2 Schoenbaum, *supra*, § 19-14, at 404-05 ("Often the insurer lacks the practicable means to verify the accuracy or sufficiency of facts provided by the insured for purposes of establishing the contractual terms."). The interest in uniform application of the doctrine is especially strong given that marine insurance policies, like the Great American Pollution Policy, frequently provide coverage for properties located in various states and throughout the world. *See Kirby*, 543 U.S. at 29 ("Confusion and inefficiency will inevitably result if more than one body of law governs a given contract's meaning."). Because here "state interests cannot be accommodated without defeating a federal interest [in the uniformity of maritime law], . . . federal substantive law should govern." *Id.* at 27.

under the doctrine of *uberrimae fidei* and whether this breach permits Great American to void the Pollution Policy. Under the doctrine, Signal was "bound, although no inquiry be made, to disclose every fact within [its] knowledge that [was] material to the risk [insured against]." 2 Schoenbaum, *supra*, § 19-14, at 405-06; *see Puritan*, 779 F.2d at 870. [—41—]

We have held that the doctrine "does not require the voiding of the contract unless the undisclosed facts were material and relied upon." *Puritan*, 779 F.2d at 871. While both parties acknowledge the materiality requirement, they disagree as to whether reliance is an independent requirement and whether that requirement should apply here. Great American notes that reliance has not been widely discussed in this Circuit since *Puritan*. It also contends that, to the extent reliance may be required in some circumstances, it should not be required here, because this case involves a "complete non-disclosure," as opposed to a partial, misleading disclosure. 14-1346-cv Dkt. No. 264.

Citing our decision in *Puritan*, the Eighth Circuit recently held that materiality and reliance are "distinct elements," both of which must be proven for the doctrine to apply. *See St. Paul Fire & Marine Ins. Co. v. Abhe & Svoboda, Inc.*, 798 F.3d 715, 720-22, 3 Adm. R. 522, 524-26 (8th Cir. 2015). "[M]ateriality examines whether a fact would have influenced the [—42—] judgment of a *reasonable and prudent* underwriter," *id.*, 3 Adm. R. at 526, in deciding whether "to insure at all or at a particular premium," *Tradeline*, 266 F.3d at 123; *see also Sun Mut. Ins. Co.*, 107 U.S. at 509-10 (holding that nondisclosure permitted avoidance of the contract where, "[h]ad [the undisclosed information] been known, it [was] reasonable to believe that a prudent underwriter would not have accepted the proposal as made"). Reliance, however—according to the Eighth Circuit—requires "a causal connection between the misrepresentation or concealment of that material fact and the *actual* underwriter's decision to issue the policy." *St. Paul Fire*, 798 F.3d at 722, 3 Adm. R. at 526; *see Puritan*, 779 F.2d at 871 ("[A] marine insurance policy

'cannot be voided for misrepresentation where the alleged misrepresentation was not relied upon and did not in any way mislead the insurer.'" (quoting *Rose & Lucy, Inc. v. Resolute Ins. Co.*, 249 F. Supp. 991, 992 (D. Mass. 1965))). [—43—]

We need not decide here whether subjective reliance is required in all cases in order for the doctrine to apply. Even assuming that it is, we find that Signal breached its duty to Great American and that no genuine disputes of fact exist as to either the materiality of Signal's non-disclosures or Great American's reliance.

In applying for the 2009-2010 Pollution Policy, Signal's insurance broker submitted only Great American's standard "Vessel Pollution Liability Application" along with a "Schedule of Vessels," which listed the dry dock. It appears that the only information in those materials related to the dry dock's condition was that it was built in 1945, that it was constructed from steel, and that its gross tonnage was less than 27,000 tons; neither Signal nor Fireman's Fund has argued otherwise. Signal did not provide any surveys to Great American when it applied for coverage for the dry dock.

Notwithstanding the paucity of relevant information furnished by Signal to Great American, it is undisputed that by 2009 [—44—] Signal had in its possession numerous surveys and reports concluding that the dry dock had substantially deteriorated and that necessary long-term repairs were not being made. At least one survey estimated that the dry dock's value was "below zero." J.A. 4216. Signal's own internal documents and communications with the Heger engineering firm demonstrate its awareness of these concerns. Nevertheless, Signal did not disclose this information to Great American.

This undisclosed information was clearly material—that is, it "would have influenced the judgment of a reasonable and prudent underwriter." *St. Paul Fire*, 798 F.3d at 722, 3 Adm. R. at 526 (emphasis omitted). That multiple engineers and Signal's own internal staff study described considerable deterioration of the dry dock and Signal's failure to make recommended repairs over several years was precisely the type of information that would have affected a reasonable insurer's decision "to insure [the dry dock] at all or [at least] at a particular [—45—] premium." *Tradeline*, 266 F.3d at 123. If disclosed, this information would have raised significant concerns about the likelihood of pollutant emissions from the dry dock. Given the nature and abundance of this information and the high likelihood that it would have impacted coverage, there can be no genuine dispute that "a reasonable person in [Signal's] position would [have] know[n] that [these] particular fact[s] [were] material" and that Signal therefore had a duty to disclose them. *Knight*, 804 F.2d at 13; *see Catlin*, 778 F.3d at 82, 3 Adm. R. at 33–34 ("[A] hull inspector who surveyed the [drydock] testified that he found 'heavy wastage' in the drydock's hull during an . . . inspection. . . . [The insured's] failure to disclose . . . the [drydock's] level of deterioration [when it applied for insurance] . . . [is a] material fact[], the nondisclosure of which violates *uberrimae fidei*.").

There is also no genuine dispute that in "decid[ing] to issue the policy," *St. Paul Fire*, 798 F.3d at 720, 3 Adm. R. at 525, the underwriters at Great [—46—] American in fact relied upon the absence of this undisclosed information from Signal's application materials. Cindy Stringer, the Great American underwriter who evaluated the Pollution Policy applications from 2005 to 2010,[21] testified at her deposition that, "had I been able to read [the] [undisclosed] surveys, I definitely would have been concerned . . . . If I had known [the dry dock] was in bad shape, and Signal told me they were going to fix it up, . . . more than likely, I would have told them I didn't want to cover that vessel until they completed all the recommendations." J.A. 6440. She further stated that, "[i]f I knew that the wing walls were in poor condition, I definitely [would have] want[ed] to know what was being done about it." J.A. 6445.

Stringer's testimony also established that, in agreeing to underwrite the policy, she was acting on the understanding that [—47—] Signal was complying with its duty of utmost good faith. She testified as follows:

> If the insured had information that could materially affect our policy, it would be their obligation to furnish us with that information. . . . [F]or example, if you were to read a survey that said that you had a vessel that was about ready to collapse or something like that, that would be something that you should bring to the attention of your broker, who would then bring it to our attention.

J.A. 6443. She also opined that "it would be common sense if you had a vessel that was about ready to collapse or in danger of sinking or something like that, you would definitely want to let somebody know about it," because "if a prudent insured [is] aware of a condition that would put a vessel in jeopardy, . . . they owe the duty to let underwriters know of that condition." J.A. 6444.

Reese Lever, an underwriter who worked with Stringer on the 2009 renewal of the Pollution Policy,[22] similarly testified that, if Signal was "doing repairs on a vessel, . . . if they're major repairs, it's [—48—] something we'd want to know about," and that "it's common sense you'd want to let your insurers know that you're repairing these vessels." J.A. 6431. Lever explained that, in his view, "it goes back to the duty of utmost good faith. If there are vessels that have problems, the underwriter should be aware of it." J.A. 6431.

Fireman's Fund argues that Signal did not have an obligation to provide the undisclosed information because Great American did not request surveys or additional information about the dry dock's condition as part of its underwriting criteria or application. However, under the doctrine of *uberrimae fidei*, Great American was not obligated to request such information. *See Knight*, 804

---

[21] Another underwriter, Charles Dillon, underwrote the original Pollution Policy in 2004. Stringer took over the account when Dillon left Great American in 2005.

[22] According to Stringer, Lever compiled the renewal and Stringer approved it.

F.2d at 13 ("Since the [insured] is in the best position to know of any circumstances material to the risk, he must reveal those facts to the underwriter, *rather than wait for the underwriter to inquire.*" (emphasis added)). Instead, Great American was entitled make its decision to underwrite the policy based on the information that Signal **[—49—]** provided, secure in the knowledge that Signal was under a duty of utmost good faith that required it to disclose all information material to the risk insured against. *See Tradeline*, 266 F.3d at 123; 2 Schoenbaum, *supra*, § 19-14, at 404-06.

Fireman's Fund also argues that a genuine dispute exists as to whether the undisclosed information was material because Great American agreed to insure another dry dock owned by Signal ("the Bender dry dock") under the Pollution Policy after the Port Arthur dry dock sank, despite receiving a survey that "raised concerns" about the Bender dry dock's condition. J.A. 6019. For several reasons, we are not persuaded. First, although Lever testified that he considered several points in the Bender dry dock survey significant to his underwriting analysis,[23] none of those conditions rose to the level of extensive dilapidation described in the undisclosed reports regarding the Port Arthur dry dock. Moreover, **[—50—]** unlike the Bender dry dock, the available information regarding the Port Arthur dry dock's condition was not limited to an isolated survey. Rather, the undisclosed information at issue here consisted of reports by multiple engineers and risk management professionals (and Signal itself) over a period of more than seven years that contained corroborating accounts of extensive dry dock deterioration and Signal's continued failure to make recommended long-term repairs. In light of these significant distinctions, Great American's decision to insure the Bender dry dock does not raise any genuine dispute as to whether the undisclosed information regarding the Port Arthur dry dock was material and relied upon.

We conclude that Signal breached its duty of utmost good faith by failing to disclose information about the dry dock's condition to Great American. Because this information was both material and relied upon, Great American is entitled to void the Pollution Policy. *See Puritan*, 779 F.2d at 871; *see also Catlin*, 778 F.3d **[—51—]** at 83, 3 Adm. R. at 34 ("[T]he evidence conclusively shows that [the insured] failed to disclose material information about the [dry dock's] actual value and preexisting deteriorated condition prior to [the insurer] determining whether it would accept the risk. [The insurer] was free, therefore, to void the policy."). We affirm the district court's grant of Great American's motion for summary judgment and its denial of Fireman's Fund and Signal's cross-motions.

II. MSI's Excess Property Insurance Policy

We next consider the EPI Policy issued by MSI. The district court held that the EPI Policy was not a maritime contract, *Fireman's Fund Ins. Co. v. Great Am. Ins. Co. of New York*, No. 10 Civ. 1653 (JPO), 2013 WL 311084, at *5 (S.D.N.Y. Jan. 25, 2013), a conclusion that is not challenged on appeal.[24] Nevertheless, the court found that the

---

[23] The survey of the Bender dry dock does not appear in the record. The only evidence of its contents is Lever's deposition testimony.

---

[24] The district court concluded that the dry dock was not a "vessel" under *Lozman v. City of Riviera Beach*, -- U.S. --, 133 S. Ct. 735, 1 Adm. R. 2 (2013), *see Fireman's Fund*, 2013 WL 311084, at *3-5, and that "the vessel status of the Drydock was relevant [to the question of whether the EPI Policy was a marine insurance contract] because it informed the primary purpose of the PPI and EPI Policies[] and . . . was *dispositive* because the Drydock was 'by far' the largest piece of property **[—52—]** insured" under those policies, *Fireman's Fund*, 10 F. Supp. 3d at 479. The court did not find the dry dock's status to be similarly dispositive of the question of whether the Great American Pollution Policy was a marine insurance contract. *See id.*

We need not review the district court's conclusion that the EPI Policy was a nonmaritime contract. Although MSI originally filed a cross-appeal challenging that conclusion, MSI later moved to withdraw its cross-appeal without prejudice to re-filing if we ordered a remand in the appeals considered here. We granted the motion, and therefore the question of whether the EPI Policy is a maritime contract is not before us.

[—52—] policy was void under Mississippi law for material misrepresentation. *Fireman's Fund*, 10 F. Supp. 3d at 503.

Fireman's Fund argues that the district court erred in holding that the EPI Policy was governed by Mississippi law rather than Texas law. Alternatively, it contends that, even if Mississippi law applies, the court erred in its application of that state law. For the reasons below, we reject both arguments. [—53—]

A. Mississippi Law Governs the EPI Policy

1. New York Choice of Law Rules

"We review the district court's choice of law *de novo.*" *Fin. One Pub. Co. v. Lehman Bros. Special Fin., Inc.*, 414 F.3d 325, 331 (2d Cir. 2005).

"A federal court sitting in diversity . . . must apply the choice of law rules of the forum state." *Rogers v. Grimaldi*, 875 F.2d 994, 1002 (2d Cir. 1989). "Generally, [New York] courts will enforce a choice-of-law clause so long as the chosen law bears a reasonable relationship to the parties or the transaction." *Welsbach Elec. Corp. v. MasTec N. Am., Inc.*, 859 N.E.2d 498, 500 (N.Y. 2006) (citation omitted). This is because "[a] basic precept of contract interpretation is that agreements should be construed to effectuate the parties' intent." *Id.* (citations omitted).

Where a choice of law clause is not dispositive, "[t]he first step . . . is to determine whether there is an actual conflict between the laws of the jurisdictions involved." *In re Allstate Ins. Co. (Stolarz)*, [—54—] 613 N.E.2d 936, 937 (N.Y. 1993); *see* 28 Glen Banks, *New York Practice Series: New York Contract Law* § 8:4 (2015) ("If the contract has no choice-of-law clause and the laws of different jurisdictions could apply, New York courts may undertake a choice-of-law analysis. The first step in any case presenting a potential choice-of-law issue is to determine whether there is an actual conflict between the laws of the jurisdictions involved."). If an actual conflict exists, New York applies "[t]he 'center

of gravity' or 'grouping of contacts' choice of law theory." *Stolarz*, 613 N.E.2d at 939.

[A]pplication of the "grouping of contacts" theory to choice-of-law disputes "gives . . . the place having the most interest in the problem paramount control over the legal issues arising out of a particular factual context, thus allowing the forum to apply the policy of the jurisdiction most intimately concerned with the outcome of the particular litigation[.]"

In re Liquidation of Midland Ins. Co., 947 N.E.2d 1174, 1179 (N.Y. 2011) (quoting *Auten v. Auten*, 124 N.E.2d 99, 102 (N.Y. 1954)). "[B]y stressing the significant contacts, [this analysis] enables the court, not only to reflect the relative interests of the several jurisdictions [—55—] involved, but also to give effect to the probable intention of the parties and consideration to 'whether one rule or the other produces the best practical result[.]'" *Auten*, 124 N.E.2d at 102 (citations omitted) (quoting *Swift & Co. v. Bankers Trust Co.*, 19 N.E.2d 992, 995 (N.Y. 1939)).

"Under this approach, the spectrum of significant contacts—rather than a single possibly fortuitous event—may be considered[.]" *Stolarz*, 613 N.E.2d at 939 (citation omitted). "[T]he New York Court of Appeals has endorsed the following factors (identified in the Restatement [(Second) of Conflict of Laws]): 'the places of negotiation and performance; the location of the subject matter; and the domicile or place of business of the contracting parties.'" *Schwartz v. Liberty Mut. Ins. Co.*, 539 F.3d 135, 151-52 (2d Cir. 2008) (quoting *Zurich Ins. Co. v. Shearson Lehman Hutton, Inc.*, 642 N.E.2d 1065, 1068 (N.Y. 1994)). [—56—]

"Critical to a sound analysis, however, is selecting the contacts that obtain significance in the particular contract dispute." *Stolarz*, 613 N.E.2d at 939. The New York Appellate Divisions have repeatedly recognized that "'where the insured risk is scattered throughout multiple states, [New York] courts . . . deem the risk to be located principally in one state,' namely, in the state of the *insured's domicile* at the time the policy was issued," and thus have held that "the state of the insured's domicile should be regarded as a proxy for the principal location of the insured risk." *Certain Underwriters at Lloyd's v. Foster Wheeler Corp.*, 822 N.Y.S.2d 30, 35, 36 (App. Div. 1st Dep't 2006) (emphasis added) (quoting *Md. Cas. Co. v. Cont'l Cas. Co.*, 332 F.3d 145, 153 (2d Cir. 2003)), *aff'd*, 876 N.E.2d 500 (N.Y. 2007).[25] These courts have noted that "[t]he state of the [—57—] insured's domicile is a fact known to the parties at the time of contracting, and . . . application of the law of that state is most likely to conform to their expectations." *Id.* at 34-35.

2. Choice of Law Governing the EPI Policy

Fireman's Fund argues that the district court erred by treating "the state of the insured's domicile [as] determinative" of the choice of law analysis, *Fireman's Fund*, 10 F. Supp. 3d at 496, and by alternatively holding that the grouping-of-contacts analysis favors

---

[25] *Accord Jimenez v. Monadnock Constr., Inc.*, 970 N.Y.S.2d 577, 580-81 (App. Div. 2d Dep't 2013) ("Where the covered risks are spread over multiple states, 'the state of the insured's domicile should be regarded as a proxy for the principal location of the insured risk[.]'" (quoting *Midland*, 947 N.E.2d at 1179)); *FC Bruckner Assocs., L.P. v. Fireman's Fund Ins. Co.*, 944 N.Y.S.2d 84, 85 (App. Div. 1st Dep't 2012) ("[A]s we noted in *Foster Wheeler* with respect to a choice-of-law analysis [—57—] for insurance policies covering multistate risks, '[t]he state of the insured's domicile is a fact known to the parties at the time of contracting, and (in the absence of a contractual choice-of-law provision) application of the law of that state is most likely to conform to their expectations[.]'" (quoting *Foster Wheeler*, 822 N.Y.S.2d at 34-35)); *Liberty Surplus Ins. Corp. v. Nat'l Union Fire Ins. Co. of Pittsburgh, Pa.*, 888 N.Y.S.2d 35, 36 (App. Div. 1st Dep't 2009); *Travelers Cas. & Sur. Co. v. Honeywell Int'l, Inc.*, 880 N.Y.S.2d 66, 67 (App. Div. 1st Dep't 2009); *Appalachian Ins. Co. v. Riunione Adriatic Di Sicurata*, 875 N.Y.S.2d 57, 58 (App. Div. 1st Dep't 2009); *cf. Lapolla Indus., Inc. v. Aspen Specialty Ins. Co.*, 566 F. App'x 95, 97 (2d Cir. 2014) (summary order) (citing *Foster Wheeler*, 822 N.Y.S.2d at 34, 37; *Midland*, 947 N.E.2d at 1179.

application of Mississippi law over Texas law.[26] [—58—]

As a preliminary matter, we must determine if the district court looked to the wrong "insured" in its choice of law analysis. Signal claimed that its subsidiary, Signal International Texas L.P. ("Signal-Texas"), which is domiciled in Texas, owned and operated the dry dock, so the relevant domicile of the insured is therefore Texas.

However, contrary to this claim, there is no genuine dispute that Signal International, LLC, was the relevant insured under the EPI Policy. Signal's consultant and former Senior Vice President of Texas Operations, John Haley, stated in his affidavit that "Signal International, L.L.C. . . . was the owner and operator of the AFDB-5 Drydock." J.A. 1852. Furthermore, the EPI Policy itself names [—59—] "Signal International, LLC" as the "Insured[]," with an address in Pascagoula, Mississippi. J.A. 168. Although the PPI Policy identifies "[t]he First Named Insured" as "Signal International, LLC and any owned . . . subsidiary," J.A. 283, the PPI Policy identifies only Signal International, LLC, by name and lists a Mississippi address for the First Named Insured. Both the EPI Policy and the PPI Policy therefore evince the parties' understanding that the insured was Signal

---

[26] The district court found that Mississippi law and Texas law are in conflict regarding the circumstances under which a contract may be voided for misrepresentation. *Fireman's Fund*, 10 F. Supp. 3d at 494-95. We agree. *Compare Carroll v. Metro. Ins. & Annuity Co.*, 166 F.3d 802, 805 (5th Cir. 1999) ("Under [—58—] Mississippi law, if an applicant for insurance is found to have made a misstatement of material fact in the application, the insurer that issued a policy based on the false application is entitled to void or rescind the policy . . . . Whether the misrepresentation was intentional, negligent, or the result of mistake or oversight is of no consequence."), *with Mayes v. Mass. Mut. Life Ins. Co.*, 608 S.W.2d 612, 616 (Tex. 1980) ("It is now settled law in this state that . . . before [an] insurer may avoid a policy because of the misrepresentation of the insured . . . [the insurer must prove] the intent to deceive on the part of the insured in making [the representation] . . . .").

International, LLC, which was domiciled in Mississippi.

Moreover, an analysis that would look to a subsidiary of the insured based on the particular loss that triggered coverage would be at odds with New York's choice of law rules. Under New York law, "barring extraordinary circumstances, only one state's law should govern an insurance agreement." *Md. Cas. Co.*, 332 F.3d at 153. New York courts have declined to look to the location of an insured's subsidiaries in determining choice of law, because "applying multiple states' laws to the enforcement of a single [—60—] insurance policy 'defies the law as well as the traditional concerns of judicial economy and uniformity.'" *See FC Bruckner Assocs., L.P. v. Fireman's Fund Ins. Co.*, 944 N.Y.S.2d 84, 85-86 (App. Div. 1st Dep't 2012) (ellipses omitted) (quoting *Wausau Bus. Ins. Co. v. Horizon Admin. Servs. LLC*, 803 F. Supp. 2d 209, 216 (E.D.N.Y. 2011)).

We therefore conclude that, in determining what law governs the EPI Policy, the relevant insured is Signal International LLC, and its domicile is Mississippi.[27]

Fireman's Fund argues that the district court erred by treating the insured's domicile as dispositive of the choice of law analysis.

---

[27] Fireman's Fund claims that Signal was domiciled both in Mississippi—"its principal office" at the time of contracting—and Delaware, "its place of incorporation." Fireman's Fund Br. at 57. However, where "the state of [a corporate insured's] principal place of business [and] the state of its incorporation . . . are not the same state[,] . . . the state of the principal place of business takes precedence over the state of incorporation" for the choice of law analysis. *Foster Wheeler*, 822 N.Y.S.2d at 36; *see Honeywell*, 880 N.Y.S.2d at 67 ("[F]or [choice of law] purposes, a corporate insured's domicile is the state of its principal place of business, not the state of its incorporation." (citations omitted)); *cf. Certain Underwriters at Lloyds of London v. Ill. Nat'l Ins. Co.*, 553 F. App'x 110, 111-12 (2d Cir. 2014) (summary order) (citing *Foster Wheeler* and applying law of the insured's principal place of business); Restatement (Second) of Conflict of Laws § 188 cmt. e (1971) ("At least with respect to most issues, a corporation's principal place of business is a more important contact than the place of incorporation . . . .").

[—61—] To the contrary, though, under New York law, the law of Signal's domicile governs the EPI Policy since the policy covers risks spread across multiple states. *See, e.g., Lapolla*, 566 F. App'x at 97; *Foster Wheeler*, 822 N.Y.S.2d at 34-36; *cf. Midland*, 947 N.E.2d at 1179.

Nevertheless, even if the totality of the relevant contacts is considered, the result is the same. The EPI Policy's "Declarations" page states that "[t]his Insurance policy is issued pursuant to Mississippi law covering surplus lines insurance." J.A. 168. The same page contains information specific to the Signal policy, including the insured, the covered property, and the policy premium.[28] Signal's 2009-2010 Property Insurance Submission also [—62—] listed Mississippi as the choice of law for the property policies. In addition, in its preliminary claim statement for coverage after the dry dock sank, Signal

---

[28] Fireman's Fund argues that another page of the EPI Policy supports the application of Texas law. The page states that "[t]his insurance contract is with an insurer not licensed to transact insurance in this state and is issued and delivered as surplus line coverage under the Texas Insurance statutes." J.A. 166. "Surplus lines insurance allows a person who seeks to insure a Texas risk but is unable to obtain that insurance from a Texas-licensed insurer to seek the insurance from an insurer who is not licensed in Texas but is an 'eligible' surplus lines insurer." *Strayhorn v. Lexington Ins. Co.*, 128 S.W.3d 772, 775 (Tex. App. 2004) (quoting Tex. Ins. Code Ann. § 981.001), *aff'd*, 209 S.W.3d 83 (Tex. 2006). "A surplus lines insurer is, by definition, not authorized to issue insurance in Texas. [However,] Texas law permits surplus line insurers to provide insurance in Texas [—62—] if the insurer . . . meets certain requirements" under the Texas Insurance Code. *Chandler Mgmt. Corp. v. First Specialty Ins. Corp.*, 452 S.W.3d 887, 893 (Tex. App. 2014) (citations omitted). The fact that Signal was able to obtain the EPI Policy as surplus lines insurance from MSI in accordance with Texas law does not answer the question of what state's law the parties intended to govern the substance of the policy itself. The designation of Mississippi law on the "Declarations" page of the policy, combined with Signal's designation of Mississippi as the applicable choice of law in its 2009-2010 Property Insurance Submission and preliminary claim statement after the loss of the dry dock, demonstrates that the parties intended Mississippi law to govern the policy.

stated that the EPI Policy was "issued to a Mississippi insured," " delivered to Signal's offices in Mississippi," and "subject to Mississippi law and jurisdiction." J.A. 6462. These documents demonstrate the parties' understanding that Mississippi law would apply to the policy.

The balance of the other choice of law factors does not clearly favor the law of one state over another. The EPI Policy was negotiated in Virginia and New York. Performance of the contract was to take place in Texas and Mississippi, and the value of the assets insured by the EPI Policy was split almost evenly between [—63—] those two states. Signal is domiciled in Mississippi, and MSI is domiciled in Virginia.

The mere presence of the dry dock in Texas does not give Texas an overriding interest in having its law govern the policy. "[T]his is merely a dispute over who—[the insured or the insurer]—must bear the cost[s]" related to the loss of the dry dock. *Md. Cas. Co.*, 332 F.3d at 155. "[T]he interest [of a state in which a covered item is located] diminishes when the question is not whether someone will or can pay for the cleanup but rather who will pay." *Id.* (internal quotation marks omitted).

Because the parties' understanding and the insured's domicile favor application of Mississippi law, while the other choice of law factors do not favor the law of any one particular state, Mississippi has the "most significant relationship to the transaction and the parties," such that Mississippi law governs the EPI Policy. *Midland*, 947 N.E.2d at 1179 (quoting *Zurich Ins. Co.*, 642 N.E.2d at 1068). [—64—]

B. MSI Was Entitled to Void the EPI Policy under Mississippi Law

Fireman's Fund next argues that, even if Mississippi law governs the EPI Policy, the district court's grant of summary judgment to MSI was error. It contends that MSI failed to show that the requirements to void a contract for material misrepresentation were met, or

that, at the very least, genuine disputes of fact preclude summary judgment.

1. Material Misrepresentation under Mississippi Common Law

"Under Mississippi law, if an applicant for insurance is found to have made a misstatement of material fact in the application, the insurer that issued a policy based on the false application is entitled to void or rescind the policy."[29] *Carroll v. Metro. Ins. & Annuity Co.*, [—65—] 166 F.3d 802, 805 (5th Cir. 1999). Thus, "[i]n making . . . underwriting decisions, insurers have the right to rely on the information supplied in the application." *Id.* at 805-06. "To establish that, as a matter of law, a material misrepresentation has been made in an insurance application, (1) it must contain answers that are false, incomplete, or misleading, and (2) the false, incomplete, or misleading answers must be material to the risk insured against or contemplated by the policy." *Id.* at 805 (emphasis omitted).

"Whether the misrepresentation was intentional, negligent, or the result of mistake or oversight is of no consequence." *Id.*

> If the applicant for insurance undertakes to make a positive statement of a fact, if it be material to the risk, such fact must be true. It is not sufficient that he believes it true, but it must be so in fact, or the policy will be avoided, provided, always, that the

---

[29] Although the district court and several courts applying Mississippi law have concluded that material misrepresentation renders a contract void *ab initio*, see *Fireman's Fund*, 10 F. Supp. 3d at 465, 495; *Republic Fire & Cas. Ins. Co. v. Azlin*, No. 4:10-CV-037-SA-JMV, 2012 WL 4482355, at *6 (N.D. Miss. Sept. 26, 2012); *Dukes v. S.C. Ins. Co.*, 590 F. Supp. 1166, 1169 (S.D. Miss. 1984), *aff'd*, 770 F.2d 545 (5th Cir. 1985), the Mississippi Supreme Court has recently stated that "the longstanding, well-established law of this State renders voidable a policy issued [—65—] as a result of material misrepresentations," *Jones-Smith v. Safeway Ins. Co.*, 174 So. 3d 240, 242 (Miss. 2015). As MSI sought a declaration that the EPI Policy is void, the distinction makes no practical difference here.

misstatement be about a material matter. [—66—]

Prudential Ins. Co. of Am. v. Estate of Russell, 274 So. 2d 113, 116 (Miss. 1973) (emphasis omitted) (quoting *Fid. Mut. Life Ins. Co. v. Miazza*, 46 So. 817, 819 (Miss. 1908)); *see also Miazza*, 46 So. at 819 ("If the misstatement is material, it can make no difference as to whether or not it was made in good faith.").

"A misrepresentation in an insurance application is material if knowledge of the true facts would have influenced a prudent insurer in determining whether to accept the risk." *Carroll*, 166 F.3d at 805. "Stated differently, a fact is material if it might have led a prudent insurer to decline the risk, accept the risk only for an increased premium, or otherwise refuse to issue the exact policy requested by the applicant." *Id.*

2. The EPI Policy's Concealment Clause Did Not Require MSI to Prove "Intent to Deceive"

Fireman's Fund argues that, in order to void the EPI Policy, MSI was required to prove that Signal intended to deceive MSI [—67—] when it applied for insurance, regardless of whether Mississippi common law would require such intent. We disagree.

The EPI policy's "Concealment, Misrepresentation or Fraud" clause ("the concealment clause") provides that "[t]his Coverage Part is void in any case of fraud by the Insured as it relates to this Coverage Part at any time. It is also void if the named insured or any other insured, at any time, *intentionally* conceal or misrepresent a material fact . . . ." J.A. 172 (emphasis added).

However, although the policy's concealment clause permits the insurer to void the policy where concealment or misrepresentation is intentional, it does not state that this is the *exclusive* ground upon which the contract may be voided. Under Mississippi law, "[w]hether the misrepresentation was intentional, negligent, or the result of mistake or oversight is of no consequence" in determining whether an insurer may void a policy for mis-

representation or concealment. *Carroll*, 166 F.3d at 805. Nothing [—68—] in the EPI Policy indicates that the concealment clause was intended to foreclose MSI's right to void a policy for material misrepresentation as provided under Mississippi law, and we decline to read such a limitation into the policy. *Cf. Ivison v. Ivison*, 762 So. 2d 329, 336 (Miss. 2000) ("It is fundamental in contract law that courts cannot make a contract where none exists, nor can they modify, add to, or subtract from the terms of a contract already in existence.").[30] We therefore conclude that MSI was not required to prove that Signal intended to deceive it in order to void the policy.

3. MSI Was Not Required To Request "Answers" on an "Application" To Void the Policy for Material Misrepresentation

Fireman's Fund next argues that MSI could not void the EPI Policy on grounds of material misrepresentation because MSI did not demonstrate that Signal made any false or misleading "answers" [—69—] on an insurance "application." *See, e.g., Carroll*, 166 F.3d at 805 ("To establish that . . . a material misrepresentation has been made in an insurance application, . . . it must contain answers that are false, incomplete, or misleading . . . ."). It argues that MSI did not receive any false "answers" from Signal, since it did not require Signal to complete a standard application in order to obtain the policy. Instead, Signal provided a property insurance submission of its own creation (the 2009-2010 Property Insurance Submission), which included the 2009 Heller Report and a "Statement of Values." The Statement of Values described the dry dock's value as $13.6 million, and the Heller Report described the

---

[30] We note that at least one court applying Mississippi law, when confronted with a concealment clause nearly identical to the clause present here, permitted the insurer to seek to void the insurance policy under alternative theories of material misrepresentation and breach of the concealment clause, while recognizing that the latter required the statements to be "knowingly and willfully made" and the former did not. *See Azlin*, 2012 WL 4482355, at *5-12.

possibility of the dry dock sinking as a "worst case scenario" "of extremely low probability." J.A. 2269, 2298-99. Fireman's Fund claims that Signal had no affirmative duty to provide further information about the dry dock in the absence of a request from MSI.

We are not persuaded by these arguments. While Mississippi [—70—] has frequently addressed the doctrine of material misrepresentation in the context of traditional insurance applications, the Mississippi Supreme Court has recognized that the doctrine arises from "a principle of general application"—"the universal rule that any contract induced by misrepresentation or concealment of material facts may be avoided by the party injuriously affected thereby." *Prudential*, 274 So. 2d at 116 (emphasis omitted) (quoting *Miazza*, 46 So. at 819); *cf. Dukes v. S.C. Ins. Co.*, 590 F. Supp. 1166, 1169 (S.D. Miss. 1984) ("[T]he Plaintiff's suit must fail in that the policy of insurance should be declared void *ab initio* [for material misrepresentation under Mississippi law]. This is simply a general principal of contract law which *the special nature of insurance contracts does not alter*." (emphasis added)), *aff'd*, 770 F.2d 545 (5th Cir. 1985). "The omission or concealment of material facts can constitute a misrepresentation, just as can a positive, direct assertion." *Davidson v. Rogers*, 431 So. 2d 483, 484-85 (Miss. 1983). [—71—]

It would be inconsistent with these principles to hold—as Fireman's Fund suggests—that Signal could not misrepresent the dry dock's condition simply because MSI accepted a submission of Signal's own creation in agreeing to underwrite the policy. Although MSI did not require Signal to complete a standardized application, Signal nonetheless made affirmative representations about the dry dock (by providing MSI with the Statement of Values and the 2009 Heller Report) in order to induce MSI to insure it.[31]

---

[31] This case is therefore distinguishable from those cited by Fireman's Fund which hold that, under Mississippi law, an "[insurance] company has no right to rescind [a] policy because there was information, not asked for on the application and *not volunteered* by the applicant, the knowledge of which would have caused the company to refuse to

When Signal provided this information, it was required to do so in a way that was not misleading, because "[i]n making [its] underwriting decision[], [MSI] ha[d] the right to rely on the information supplied." *Carroll*, 166 F.3d at 805; *see also Golden Rule Ins. Co. v. Hopkins*, 788 F. Supp. 295, 301 (S.D. Miss. 1991) ("[T]he [—72—] 'innocent misrepresentation' standard [under Mississippi law] . . . operates to the benefit of the misinformed insurance company."); *cf. Prudential*, 274 So. 2d at 116 ("If the applicant for insurance undertakes to make a positive statement of a fact, if it be material to the risk, such fact must be true." (emphasis omitted) (quoting *Miazza*, 46 So. at 819)).

By providing MSI with the Statement of Values and only the 2009 Heller Report, Signal represented (1) that the dry dock was valued at $13.6 million, (2) that Signal was operating its facilities—including the Port Arthur dockyard—in accordance with "[a]cceptable standards including some industry best practices," J.A. 1318, and (3) that the likelihood of the dry dock sinking was a "worst-case scenario . . . of extremely low probability," J.A. 2298-99. Signal made these representations despite knowing that (1) multiple engineers—and its own employees—had concluded over several years that the dry dock was in poor condition, in need of extensive [—73—] and costly repairs, and nearing the end of its useful life, (2) several engineers had concluded that the dry dock was not operating safely and that extensive repairs would be required before Signal could attempt to reconfigure the dry dock to extend its life, and (3) Signal was not undertaking the long-term repairs that these engineers had recommended. By selectively providing only positive information about the dry dock's condition, while failing to disclose the substantial and multiple sources of information in its possession that called these positive reports into question, Signal's representations to MSI amounted to a misrepresentation of the dry dock's

---

insure." *Mattox v. W. Fid. Ins. Co.*, 694 F. Supp. 210, 216 (N.D. Miss. 1988) (emphasis added). Here, although it was not requested on a standardized application, Signal volunteered information about the dry dock's condition.

condition.[32] *See Davidson*, 431 So. 2d at 484-85. If material, this [—74—] misrepresentation provided a basis for MSI to void the policy under Mississippi law.

4. Signal's Misrepresentation Was Material and Induced MSI To Issue the EPI Policy

Fireman's Fund argues that MSI failed to show that any misrepresentation that Signal might have made regarding the dry dock was material or relied upon in MSI's decision to underwrite the EPI Policy. It also argues that, at the very least, there are genuine disputes of fact that should have precluded summary judgment on these issues.

We disagree. The EPI Policy insured against business interference and extra expenses resulting from the loss of specific properties, including the dry dock. Information that the dry dock had been appraised as having a negative value, had been described as dilapidated and nearing the end of its useful life, and had not undergone long-term repairs (despite the recommendations of [—75—] multiple engineers over several years) would be highly relevant to a "prudent insurer['s]" decision to underwrite the policy, since such information—if investigated and discovered to be true—would indicate an increased risk of loss. *See Carroll*, 166 F.3d at 805.

---

[32] Fireman's Fund argues that the 2009-2010 Property Insurance Submission was sufficient to put MSI on notice that it should inquire about possible deficiencies in the dry dock's condition. *See Mass. Mut. Life Ins. Co. v. Nicholson*, 775 F. Supp. 954, 960 (N.D. Miss. 1991) ("[T]he insurance company has the right to rely on the information contained in the application, as long as the insurance company did not have 'sufficient indications that would have put a prudent man on notice.'" (citation omitted) (quoting *N.Y. Life Ins. Co. v. Strudel*, 243 F.2d 90, 93 (5th Cir. 1957))). We disagree. Nothing in Signal's submission suggested that the dry dock was dilapidated, that repairs were not being made, or that it was nearing the end of its useful life. The Heller Report's reference to the sinking of the dry [—74—] dock as a worst case scenario did not put MSI on notice of the need to inquire more fully about its condition before agreeing to underwrite the policy.

Signal's experience in applying for hull insurance prior to applying for the EPI Policy also demonstrates the materiality of the undisclosed information and Signal's knowledge that it was material. In 2005, Signal's insurance broker, Willis of Alabama, Inc., applied for hull insurance for the dry dock by submitting the 2002 Heger Report to two insurance providers—Fireman's Fund Insurance Company ("FFIC") and Trident Marine ("Trident"). The FFIC underwriter inquired as to what repairs had been made, observing that "[t]he [a]ppraisal [in the 2002 Heger report] reflects an 'Inside the United States' net value of ($1,150,00) less than zero" and that he was "going have a tough time convincing anybody" to provide the requested insurance. J.A. 4251. Trident's underwriter [—76—] similarly questioned whether any repairs had been made, noting that, according to the 2002 Heger report, "the pontoon deck of all sections was found to be in poor condition and should be replaced" and "Section H was also in poor condition." J.A. 4253. The underwriter stated that Trident "would need confirmation from the [insured] that this was taken care of before [Trident] could commit to cover [the dry dock]." *Id.* Thus, in both instances, the underwriters considered the 2002 Heger Report's documented concerns about the dry dock significant to their underwriting decisions. Signal's disclosure of the report permitted these insurers—unlike MSI—to undertake a further investigation of the dry dock's condition before agreeing to underwrite the policy and at a particular premium.

We therefore find that there is no genuine dispute that Signal's misrepresentation to MSI—which presented only positive information regarding the dry dock's condition while omitting [—77—] contrary information like the 2002 Heger Report—was material. *See Carroll*, 166 F.3d at 805; *cf. King v. Aetna Ins. Co.*, 54 F.2d 253, 254-55 (2d Cir. 1931) ("[The insured's broker] was informed . . . by [another insurer] that he must ascertain what [the insured] paid for the boat, and, when [the broker] reported that [the insured] would not say, he was told by [the other insurer] that [it] would not place the insurance. If this information was material to the [other insurer], [the broker] must have appreciated that it would be equally material to the [insurer that issued the policy].").

There is also no genuine dispute that MSI was, in fact, induced to underwrite the policy based on this misrepresentation. *See Carroll*, 166 F.3d at 805 ("[T]he insurer that issued a policy *based on the false application* is entitled to void or rescind the policy." (emphasis added)); *see also Republic Fire & Cas. Ins. Co. v. Azlin*, No. 4:10-CV-037-SA-JMV, 2012 WL 4482355, at *6 (N.D. Miss. Sept. 26, 2012) ("[M]isstatements of material fact in an application for [—78—] insurance provide grounds for declaring a policy *issued in reliance thereon* void ab initio." (emphasis added) (quoting *GuideOne Mut. Ins. Co. v. Rock*, No. 1:06-CV-218-SA-JAD, 2009 WL 1854452, at *2 (N.D. Miss. June 29, 2009))).

James F. Morano, III, the MSI underwriter responsible for the EPI Policy, testified at his deposition that MSI "relied upon the [2009] Heller report," which "gave a favorable overview of the condition of the properties," for information regarding the dry dock's condition. J.A. 3241. He further testified that, if other surveys had "told [him] information that was different from the information that was being provided to [him], [he] would like to see it" when making his underwriting decision. J.A. 3264. In particular, "if [Signal] had surveys to indicate [the dry dock's] deteriorated condition, [or] repairs that ha[d] been done, that would be helpful." *Id.* In a sworn declaration, Morano further stated as follows: [—79—]

> Had the conflicting information regarding the condition of the drydock been provided to [MSI] before the Policy was issued, I would have either declined to bind coverage, or offered coverage that expressly excluded claims arising out of the drydock, because the full picture regarding the condition of the drydock, as revealed in the many [undisclosed] engineer reports . . . , portrayed a material risk of imminent catastrophic failure.

J.A. 5629. Having reviewed Morano's account and the remainder of the record, we conclude that there is no genuine dispute that Signal's misrepresentation regarding the dry dock in its 2009-2010 Property Insurance Submission induced MSI to underwrite the EPI Policy.

Because there is no genuine dispute that Signal induced MSI to underwrite the EPI Policy by materially misrepresenting the dry dock's condition when it applied for coverage, the district court correctly held that MSI was entitled to void the EPI Policy under Mississippi law. Consequently, Fireman's Fund may not succeed on its claim for equitable contribution against MSI that it was granted on summary judgment below, as the validity of the EPI policy is a [—80—] prerequisite to such a claim.

CONCLUSION

We hold that Great American's Pollution Policy is a marine insurance contract and that Great American was entitled to void the policy under the doctrine of *uberrimae fidei* due to Signal's failure to disclose material information indicating that the dry dock was in a deteriorated condition and that recommended long-term repairs were not being made. We also hold that MSI was entitled to void the EPI Policy under Mississippi law because Signal materially misrepresented the dry dock's condition when it disclosed to MSI only reports reflecting positively on the dry dock, while failing to disclose numerous other reports indicating that the dry dock was in a dilapidated state and nearing the end of its useful life. Because no genuine disputes of fact exist as to these issues, the district court properly granted Great American's and MSI's motions for summary [—81—] judgment. Accordingly, the judgments of the district court are **AFFIRMED**.

United States Court of Appeals
for the Second Circuit

No. 15-665

IN RE PETITION OF BRUCE GERMAIN

Appeal from the United States District Court for the Northern District of New York

Decided: June 1, 2016

Citation: 824 F.3d 258, 4 Adm. R. 92 (2d Cir. 2016).

Before **KATZMANN**, Chief Judge, and **SACK** and **LOHIER**, Circuit Judges.

[—2—] **KATZMANN**, Chief Judge:

In broad strokes, this case concerns a tort involving a vessel on navigable waters. More specifically, the case involves a diving accident off a recreational vessel anchored in shallow but navigable lake waters. Before the 1970s, it would have been beyond doubt that such facts would place this case squarely in the jurisdiction of the federal courts, because the traditional test for admiralty tort [—3—] jurisdiction simply asked whether the tort occurred on navigable waters.

But in 1972, the Supreme Court began refining the situs rule, or locality test, for admiralty tort jurisdiction to weed out "absurd" cases that had little to do with maritime commerce, such as planes crashing into lakes or swimmers colliding into each other. In three subsequent cases, the Court further developed this test, creating a multi-part inquiry designed to address cases at the margin of admiralty jurisdiction. In addition to location, the prevailing test now focuses on whether the incident giving rise to the tort, defined at an "intermediate level of possible generality," has a "potentially disruptive effect on maritime commerce, and whether the general character of the activity giving rise to the incident bears a substantial relationship to traditional maritime activity." *Tandon v. Captain's Cove Marina of Bridgeport, Inc.*, 752 F.3d 239, 247–48, 2 Adm. R. 57, 63 (2d Cir. 2014).

Applying this test, the United States District Court for the Northern District of New York (Sannes, J.) held that admiralty jurisdiction was lacking here. The district court reasoned that a recreational injury occurring on a recreational vessel anchored in a shallow recreational bay of navigable waters could not disrupt maritime commerce and did not bear a sufficient relationship to traditional [—4—] maritime activity. Although we believe the district court correctly articulated the Supreme Court's modern test for admiralty tort jurisdiction, we respectfully disagree with its conclusion that jurisdiction is lacking here. Indeed, the Supreme Court has instructed us that, "ordinarily," "every tort involving a vessel on navigable waters falls within the scope of admiralty jurisdiction." *Jerome B. Grubart, Inc. v. Great Lakes Dredge & Dock Co.*, 513 U.S. 527, 543 (1995). Accordingly, we REVERSE and REMAND for further proceedings consistent with this opinion.

Standard of Review

"When reviewing a district court's determination of subject matter jurisdiction pursuant to Rule 12(b)(1), we review factual findings for clear error and legal conclusions *de novo*." *Tandon*, 752 F.3d at 243, 2 Adm. R. at 59 (brackets omitted) (quoting *Close v. New York*, 125 F.3d 31, 35 (2d Cir. 1997)). "It is . . . well established that when the question is subject matter jurisdiction, the court is permitted to rely on information beyond the face of the complaint." *St. Paul Fire & Marine Ins. Co. v. Universal Builders Supply*, 409 F.3d 73, 80 (2d Cir. 2005); *see also Kamen v. Am. Tel. & Tel. Co.*, 791 F.2d 1006, 1011 (2d Cir. 1986) ("[W]hen, as here, subject matter [—5—] jurisdiction is challenged under Rule 12(b)(1), evidentiary matter may be presented by affidavit or otherwise.").[1]

---

[1] As discussed in the procedural history section, the present appeal concerns one of two separate but related actions that the district court collectively addressed in a single memorandum-decision and order. Because of the semi-consolidated nature of the two actions and their overlapping issues, the district court relied on "uncontroverted facts in the complaints in each case," i.e., the negligence complaint and the limitation petition (which in turn referenced the negligence complaint), and it

Factual Background

The district court found that, on July 30, 2011, Petitioner-Appellant Bruce Germain, Claimant-Appellee Matthew Ficarra, and three others left Brewerton, New York, on the shore of Lake Oneida, for an excursion on Germain's 38-foot motor boat, *Game Day*. *See Ficarra v. Germain*, 91 F. Supp. 3d 309, 312 (N.D.N.Y. 2015). Lake Oneida is connected to and part of the New York State Erie Canal System. *Id.* Using a federal shipping lane, the five headed to the shallow Three Mile Bay, a popular spot for recreational swimming on Lake Oneida that is less than a nautical mile from the federal shipping lane. *Id.* When Germain, Ficarra, and the three other guests anchored at around 12:30 p.m., the bay was already crowded with other boats. *Id.* [—6—]

Around 6:00 p.m., Germain began preparing for the return trip to Brewerton, and Ficarra and the other passengers[2] began returning to the boat. *Id.* At some point while Germain and the other passengers were preparing the vessel for the return trip, Ficarra dived[3] off the port side into the water. *Id.* Ficarra climbed back on board and entered the water again, this time doing a back flip from the back of the boat that resulted in his striking his head on the lake floor. *Id.* at 312–13. Germain and others then jumped into the water to assist Ficarra. *Id.* Local rescue and police boats later arrived at the scene, and they took Ficarra back across Lake Oneida to

---

also considered the facts presented in the parties' affidavits that were filed in both actions. *See Ficarra v. Germain*, 91 F. Supp. 3d 309, 312 n.2 (N.D.N.Y. 2015).

[2] As in *Tandon*, "[w]e use the term 'passenger' throughout in its broad general sense of 'a person who travels in a conveyance . . . without participating in its operation,'" 752 F.3d at 241 n.2, 2 Adm. R. at 57 n.2 (quoting *passenger, n.*, The American Heritage Dictionary 1285 (4th ed. 2000)), rather than its more technical sense under admiralty and maritime law, *see, e.g.*, 1 Thomas J. Schoenbaum, *Admiralty and Maritime Law* § 5-5 at 269–70 (5th ed. 2011).

[3] "Although *dove* is fairly common in [American English] (on the analogy of drove), *dived* is the predominant past-tense form—and the preferable one." Bryan A. Garner, *Garner's Modern American Usage* 269 (3d ed. 2009).

Brewerton via the federal shipping lane.[4] *Id.* at 313. Doctors [—7—] later determined that Ficarra suffered a serious spinal cord injury causing paralysis and quadriplegia. *Id.*

Procedural History

On June 16, 2014, Ficarra filed suit against Germain in New York State Supreme Court, asserting claims for negligence under New York law. Ficarra's complaint alleges, among other things, that Germain was negligent for failing: (1) to operate, captain, anchor, maintain, or control his vessel in a safe and reasonably prudent manner to protect the safety and welfare of his boat's passengers; (2) to properly and adequately instruct his passengers on safe boating and diving practices; (3) to properly and adequately inspect the area in which his boat was anchored; and (4) to adequately warn his passengers of the dangerous conditions existing at the time of the aforementioned incident.

On July 17, 2014, Germain removed Ficarra's negligence suit to the United States District Court for the Northern District of New York. On August 18, 2014, Ficarra moved to remand the action back to state court for lack of subject matter jurisdiction, arguing that the claims alleged in his complaint were not within the scope of admiralty jurisdiction. [—8—]

On August 14, 2014, Germain filed a petition in the United States District Court for the Northern District of New York seeking exoneration from or limitation of liability under the Limitation of Liability Act of 1851, 46 U.S.C. §§ 30501–12, and Rule F of the Supplemental Rules for Admiralty or Maritime Claims and Asset Forfeiture Actions

---

[4] At oral argument, Ficarra's attorney disputed whether Ficarra had been taken back to Brewerton by boat, but he candidly admitted that he could not provide a record citation for his view of events. We rely on the facts found by the district court, which are not clearly erroneous. In any event, whether Ficarra was actually taken back to Brewerton by boat or other means does not affect our analysis.

("Rule F").[5] On August 20, 2014, the district court (Kahn, *J.*) issued an order in the limitation proceeding directing Germain "to submit a brief explaining why his [petition] should not be dismissed for lack of subject matter jurisdiction." App. 38. As ordered, Germain filed a brief, affidavit, and related exhibits in support of his limitation petition, and he also filed these same papers in opposition to Ficarra's motion to remand in the separate negligence action.

Both the negligence action and limitation proceeding were then transferred to a different judge on December 29, 2014. In a single memorandum-decision and order, the district court (Sannes, *J.*) concluded that Ficarra's claims did not meet the modern test for admiralty tort jurisdiction. *See Ficarra*, 91 F. Supp. 3d at 313– [—9—] 17.[6] And because the district court held that it lacked jurisdiction to hear either action, it remanded the negligence suit and dismissed the limitation petition. *Id.* at 318.

Germain filed notices of appeal in both actions, but he voluntarily withdrew the notice of appeal in the remanded negligence suit, recognizing that, under 28 U.S.C. § 1447(d), "[a]n order remanding a case to the State court from which it was removed is not reviewable on appeal or otherwise," unless the case was removed pursuant to 28 U.S.C. §§ 1442 or 1443. Accordingly, the only appeal presently before us is the district court's dismissal of Germain's limitation petition.

Discussion

The key issue on appeal is whether federal courts have admiralty jurisdiction over claims for injury to a passenger who jumped from a vessel on open navigable waters. They do. But before we reach this question, we must first [—10—] address Ficarra's primary argument that the present appeal is an improper attack on the district court's remand order. It is not.

I.

Ficarra's primary argument in opposition to Germain's appeal is that Germain's appeal of the limitation petition's dismissal is an improper attack on the district court's remand order, which Germain did not—indeed, could not—appeal. In short, and as discussed in greater detail below, because admiralty cases involving petitions for limitation of liability may proceed on dual tracks in state and federal court, Germain is entitled to appeal the dismissal of his limitation petition.

The Constitution provides that "[t]he judicial Power shall extend . . . to all Cases of admiralty and maritime Jurisdiction." U.S. Const. art. III, § 2. Congress codified this constitutional grant of admiralty and maritime jurisdiction in 28 U.S.C. § 1333(1), which provides that "[t]he district courts shall have original jurisdiction, exclusive of the courts of the States, of . . . [a]ny civil case of admiralty or maritime jurisdiction, saving to suitors in all cases all other remedies to which they are otherwise entitled." The interaction between the exclusivity [—11—] clause and the saving-to-suitors clause of § 1333(1) has caused much confusion. *See, e.g., Lewis v. Lewis & Clark Marine, Inc.*, 531 U.S. 438, 444 (2001) ("What the drafters of the Judiciary Act intended in creating the saving to suitors clause is not entirely clear and has been the subject of some debate.").

Adding to the confusion is a separate statute, the Limitation of Liability Act of 1851, 46 U.S.C. §§ 30505–12, which Congress enacted "to encourage shipbuilding and to induce capitalists to invest money in this branch of industry." *Tandon*, 752 F.3d at 243–44, 2 Adm. R. at 60 (quoting *Lewis*, 531 U.S. at 446). As we explained in *Tandon*, "[u]nder the present version of this statute, 'the liability of the owner of a vessel for any claim, debt, or liability [covered by the Act] shall not exceed the value of the vessel and pending

---

[5] As in *Tandon*, "we adhere to the more common practice of using the terms 'petition' and 'petitioner'" under the Limitation of Liability Act rather than "complaint" and "plaintiff." 752 F.3d at 240 n. 1, 2 Adm. R. at 57 n.1 (citing 3 *Benedict on Admiralty* § 1 (7th ed. rev. 2009)).

[6] The district court also rejected Germain's untimely argument for diversity jurisdiction, *see Ficarra*, 91 F. Supp. 3d at 317–18, a rejection that Germain does not challenge on appeal.

freight." *Id.* at 244, 2 Adm. R. at 60 (quoting 46 U.S.C. § 30505(a)).

More specifically, the Limitation of Liability Act creates "a form of action peculiar to the admiralty and maritime context," allowing the owner of a vessel to file a petition in federal court seeking total exoneration from or limitation of liability for "damages caused by the negligence of his captain or crew." *Id.* at 243–44, 2 Adm. R. at 60; *see also* 46 U.S.C. § 30511(a); Rule F. Typically, "[o]nce the owner files a petition for limitation, 'all [other] claims and proceedings against the owner related to the [—12—] matter in question shall cease.'" *Tandon*, 752 F.3d at 244, 2 Adm. R. at 60 (quoting 46 U.S.C. § 30511(c)). Notice is then sent to all persons asserting claims affected by the limitation proceeding, who may file claims and challenge the petitioner's right to limitation or exoneration. *See id.*, 2 Adm. R. at 60. "If the petition for limitation of liability is granted, the owner can be liable on the covered claims only up to the total value of his vessel and its pending freight; that amount will then be distributed pro rata among the proven claims." *Id.*, 2 Adm. R. at 60.

As this brief discussion reveals, "[s]ome tension exists between the saving to suitors clause and the Limitation Act. One statute gives suitors the right to a choice of remedies, and the other statute gives vessel owners the right to seek limitation of liability in federal court." *Lewis*, 531 U.S. at 448. To resolve this tension, "the Courts of Appeals have generally permitted claimants to proceed with their claims in state court where there is only a single claimant . . . or where the total claims do not exceed the value of the limitation fund." *Id.* at 451. In *Lewis*, the Supreme Court endorsed this practice, and it further clarified that

> [t]he district courts have jurisdiction over actions arising under the Limitation Act, and they have discretion to stay or dismiss Limitation Act proceedings to allow a suitor to pursue his claims in state court. If the district court concludes that the vessel owner's [—13—] right to limitation will not be adequately protected—where for example a group of claimants cannot agree on appropriate stipulations or there is uncertainty concerning the adequacy of the fund or the number of claims—the court may proceed to adjudicate the merits, deciding the issues of liability and limitation. But where . . . the District Court satisfies itself that a vessel owner's right to seek limitation will be protected, the decision to dissolve the injunction [staying the state court proceeding] is well within the court's discretion.

Id. at 454 (citations omitted). "In sum, [the] Court's case law makes clear that state courts, with all of their remedies, may adjudicate claims . . . against vessel owners so long as the vessel owner's right to seek limitation of liability is protected." *Id.* at 455; *see also* 3 *Benedict on Admiralty* § 13 (7th ed. rev. 2015); 2 Thomas J. Schoenbaum, *Admiralty and Maritime Law* § 15-5 (5th ed. 2011); 13 Charles A. Wright *et al.*, *Federal Practice and Procedure* § 3527 (3d ed. 2008).

Because cases that involve limitation petitions may proceed on dual tracks in state and federal court, there is nothing impermissible about Germain's present appeal. The district court concluded that admiralty jurisdiction was lacking for either proceeding, a conclusion that necessitated remanding Ficarra's negligence suit and dismissing Germain's limitation petition. But since the district court may still be able to adjudicate his limitation petition if admiralty jurisdiction is present, Germain's appeal of the limitation petition's dismissal is proper, even if that [—14—] appeal presses the existence of subject matter jurisdiction, contrary to the premise of the district court's remand order that jurisdiction was absent.

II.

Having addressed the propriety of the present appeal, we must now decide whether the appeal has any merit. As a threshold matter, "[a]lthough the Limitation of Liability Act provides a federal cause of action for a vessel owner seeking exoneration or limitation, it 'does not provide an independent foundation for federal admiralty jurisdiction.'" *Tandon*, 752 F.3d at 244, 2 Adm. R. at 60 (quoting *MLC Fishing, Inc. v. Velez*, 667 F.3d 140, 143 (2d Cir. 2011) (per curiam)). In other words,

> that a vessel owner may file a petition for limitation does not mean the district court necessarily has jurisdiction to hear it. Instead, the district court will only have admiralty jurisdiction to hear a petition for limitation if it already has admiralty jurisdiction over the underlying claims that the petition seeks to limit.

Id., 2 Adm. R. at 60. As in *Tandon*, our present task is therefore limited to determining "whether the underlying claims raise a 'civil case of admiralty or maritime jurisdiction' that the district court could hear under 28 U.S.C. § 1333(1)." *Id.*, 2 Adm. R. at 60.

In answering this question, we first discuss the history of the modern test for admiralty tort jurisdiction, placing that test in the context of the problem it was designed to address. We then apply that test to the facts of this case, bearing **[—15—]** in mind this jurisprudential history. Although we disagree with the district court's application of the modern test, the test is far from a model of clarity and it is more than understandable how the district court, in its thoughtful opinion, could have gone off course.

A.

Traditionally, admiralty jurisdiction "over tort actions was determined largely by the application of a 'locality' test." *Sisson v. Ruby*, 497 U.S. 358, 360 (1990). That is, "[t]he traditional test for admiralty tort jurisdiction asked only whether the tort occurred on navigable waters. If it did, admiralty jurisdiction followed; if it did not, admiralty jurisdiction did not exist." *Grubart*, 513 U.S. at 531–32; *see also The Plymouth*, 70 U.S. 20, 36 (1866) ("Every species of tort, however occurring, and whether on board a vessel or

not, if upon the high seas or navigable waters, is of admiralty cognizance.").

In 1948, however, Congress expanded this narrow rule when it enacted the Extension of Admiralty Jurisdiction Act, which provides that

> [t]he admiralty and maritime jurisdiction of the United States extends to and includes cases of injury or damage, to person or property, caused by a vessel on navigable waters, even though the injury or damage is done or consummated on land. **[—16—]**

46 U.S.C. § 30101(a). As the Supreme Court explained, "[t]he purpose of the Act was to end concern over the sometimes confusing line between land and water, by investing admiralty with jurisdiction over 'all cases' where the injury was caused by a ship or other vessel on navigable water, even if such injury occurred on land." *Grubart*, 513 U.S. at 532.

"After this congressional modification to gather the odd case *into* admiralty," a series of four Supreme Court cases tinkered with the traditional locality test to "keep[] a different class of odd cases *out*." *Id.* (emphasis added). In the first case, *Executive Jet Aviation, Inc. v. City of Cleveland*, a plane crashed into Lake Erie after its jet engines inhaled a flock of seagulls shortly after takeoff from Burke Lakefront Airport in Cleveland, Ohio. 409 U.S. 249, 250 (1972). Because the plane crashed into navigable waters, admiralty jurisdiction arguably existed under the locality test.[7] But the Court observed "that 'a purely mechanical application of the locality test' was not always 'sensible' or 'consonant with the purposes of maritime law,' as when (for example) the literal and universal **[—17—]** application of the locality rule would require admiralty courts to adjudicate tort disputes between colliding swimmers."

---

[7] We say arguably because the Court did not decide precisely where the tort (as opposed to the crash) occurred for purposes of applying the locality test. *See Exec. Jet*, 409 U.S. at 267 ("In the view we take of the question before us, we need not decide who has the better of this dispute.").

Grubart, 513 U.S. at 533 (citation omitted) (quoting *Exec. Jet*, 409 U.S. at 261).

In light of this concern, the Court decided to pull back on the locality test, at least in the aviation context. The Court noted that, "[u]nlike waterborne vessels, [aircraft] are not restrained by one-dimensional geographic and physical boundaries. For this elementary reason, [the Court] conclude[d] that the mere fact that the alleged wrong 'occurs' or 'is located' on or over navigable waters— whatever that means in an aviation context— is not of itself sufficient to turn an airplane negligence case into a 'maritime tort.'" *Exec. Jet*, 409 U.S. at 268. Rather, the *Executive Jet* Court believed "[i]t [was] far more consistent with the history and purpose of admiralty to require also that the wrong bear a significant relationship to traditional maritime activity." *Id.* It therefore held "that unless such a relationship exists, claims arising from airplane accidents are not cognizable in admiralty in the absence of legislation to the contrary." *Id.* In so holding, the Court adopted, at least in the aviation context, the position of several lower courts that "a maritime locality is not sufficient to bring the tort within [—18—] federal admiralty jurisdiction, but that there must also be a maritime nexus—some relationship between the tort and traditional maritime activities, involving navigation or commerce on navigable waters." *Id.* at 256.

Although the Court clearly limited *Executive Jet*'s holding to the "aviation context," that did not stop lower courts from extending its reasoning—particularly the maritime nexus requirement—to other circumstances, an extension the Court expressly endorsed in *Foremost Insurance Co. v. Richardson*, 457 U.S. 668 (1982). In that case, two pleasure boats collided on the Amite River in Louisiana. *Id.* at 669. Although the Court "conceded that pleasure boats themselves had little to do with the maritime commerce lying at the heart of the admiralty court's basic work," it "nonetheless found the necessary relationship," i.e., maritime nexus, "in '[t]he potential disruptive impact [upon maritime commerce] of a collision between boats on navigable waters, when coupled with

the traditional concern that admiralty law holds for navigation.'" *Grubart*, 513 U.S. at 533 (alterations in original) (quoting *Foremost*, 457 U.S. at 675). The Court elaborated that "if these two boats collided at the mouth of the St. Lawrence Seaway, there would be a substantial effect on maritime commerce, without [—19—] regard to whether either boat was actively, or had been previously, engaged in commercial activity." *Foremost*, 457 U.S. at 675.[8]

The Court thus held that *Executive Jet*'s maritime nexus requirement could be satisfied if the incident in question has a *potentially* disruptive effect on maritime commerce, which would be the case for the recreational-vessel collision in *Foremost*. *See Grubart*, 513 U.S. at 533 (explaining *Foremost*). This conclusion was based at least in part on the Court's view that, "[a]lthough the primary focus of admiralty jurisdiction is unquestionably the protection of maritime commerce, ... [t]he federal interest in protecting maritime commerce . . . can be fully vindicated only if *all* operators of vessels on navigable waters are subject to uniform rules of conduct." *Foremost*, 457 U.S. at 674–75. In a footnote, however, the Court remarked that "[n]ot every accident in navigable waters that might disrupt maritime commerce will support federal admiralty jurisdiction." *Id.* at 675 n.5. Rather, it is only "when this kind of potential hazard to maritime commerce arises out of activity that bears a substantial relationship to traditional maritime [—20—] activity, as [did] the navigation of the boats in [*Foremost*], [that] admiralty jurisdiction is appropriate." *Id.*

Eight years later, this footnote would morph into the modern multi-part test for admiralty tort jurisdiction. In *Sisson v. Ruby*, the Court was called upon to decide whether admiralty jurisdiction extends to tort claims arising after a defective washer/dryer caught

---

[8] As one district court later pointed out, "[s]ince the mouth of the St. Lawrence Seaway is miles wide and the colliding pleasure boats were small, [*Foremost*'s] example of a potential disruptive effect upon maritime commerce takes the concept about as far as it can go." *Roane v. Greenwich Swim Comm.*, 330 F. Supp. 2d 306, 315 (S.D.N.Y. 2004).

fire on a pleasure boat docked at a marina, with the resulting fire burning the pleasure boat, other boats docked nearby, and the marina itself. 497 U.S. at 360. In concluding that admiralty jurisdiction covered the claims related to this fire, the Court separated *Foremost*'s footnote discussing the maritime nexus requirement into two components. *See Grubart*, 513 U.S. at 533. Under the *Sisson* test, after determining that the location test is satisfied, courts must first "determine the potential impact of a given type of incident by examining its general character" and whether this type of incident is "likely to disrupt [maritime] commercial activity." *Sisson*, 497 U.S. at 363. Second, "the party seeking to invoke maritime jurisdiction must show a substantial relationship between the activity giving rise to the incident and traditional maritime activity." *Id.* at 364. [—21—]

The Court explained that the first part of the connection "inquiry does not turn on the *actual* effects on maritime commerce" of a particular incident; "[r]ather, a court must assess the general features of the type of incident involved to determine whether such an incident is likely to disrupt commercial activity." *Id.* at 363. For example, the Court described the general features of the incident in *Sisson* as "a fire on a vessel docked at a marina on navigable waters," in *Executive Jet* as "an aircraft sinking in the water," and in *Foremost* as "a collision between boats on navigable waters." *Sisson*, 497 U.S. at 363.

The Court further explained that, under the second part of the connection inquiry, "the relevant 'activity' is defined not by the particular circumstances of the incident, but by the general conduct from which the incident arose." *Id.* at 364. For example, in *Sisson*, "the relevant activity was the storage and maintenance of a vessel at a marina on navigable waters," in *Executive Jet*, "the relevant activity was not a plane sinking in Lake Erie, but air travel generally," and in *Foremost*, the "relevant activity [was] navigation of vessels generally." *Sisson*, 497 U.S. at 364–65. Under this second prong, the *Sisson* Court reiterated *Foremost*'s lesson that "[t]he fundamental interest giving rise to maritime jurisdiction is the protection of

[—22—] maritime commerce and . . . that interest cannot be fully vindicated unless *all* operators of vessels on navigable waters are subject to uniform rules of conduct." *Id.* at 367 (citations and quotation marks omitted). Moreover, "[t]he need for uniform rules of maritime conduct and liability is not limited to navigation, but extends at least to any other activities traditionally undertaken by vessels, commercial or noncommercial." *Id.* The *Sisson* Court "conclude[d] that, just as navigation, storing and maintaining a vessel at a marina on a navigable waterway is substantially related to traditional maritime activity." *Id.*

Finally, in *Jerome B. Grubart, Inc. v. Great Lakes Dredge & Dock Co.*, the Court considered whether admiralty jurisdiction extended to claims related to flooding in the downtown Chicago Loop after operators of a crane sitting on a barge in the Chicago River drove piles into the riverbed above an underwater tunnel, allegedly weakening the tunnel and causing the flooding. 513 U.S. at 529. Before upholding admiralty jurisdiction on such facts, the Court affirmed and further developed the *Sisson* test, explaining that, under "*Sisson*, . . . a party seeking to invoke federal admiralty jurisdiction . . . over a tort claim must satisfy conditions both of location and of connection with maritime activity." *Id.* at 534. First, "[a] [—23—] court applying the location test must determine whether the tort occurred on navigable water or whether injury suffered on land was caused by a vessel on navigable water." *Id.*[9] Second, in applying the connection test, the court examines two issues: (1) the court "must assess the general features of the type of incident involved to determine whether the incident has a potentially disruptive impact on maritime commerce"; and (2) the "court must determine whether the general character of the activity giving rise to the incident shows a substantial relationship to traditional maritime activity."

---

[9] The location part of the modern test effectively incorporates the traditional locality rule, which does not turn on the involvement of a vessel, *see The Plymouth*, 70 U.S. at 36, plus the Extension of Admiralty Jurisdiction Act, which does, *see* 46 U.S.C. § 30101(a).

Id. at 534 (citations and quotation marks omitted).

The *Grubart* Court further explained that the first connection prong "turns . . . on a description of the incident at an intermediate level of possible generality," *id.* at 538, focusing on "the 'general features' of the incident," *id.* at 539. The Court elaborated that, "[a]lthough there is inevitably some play in the joints in selecting the right level of generality when applying the *Sisson* test, the [—24—] inevitable imprecision is not an excuse for whimsy." *Id.* at 542.[10] In *Grubart*, the Court concluded, "the 'general features' of the incident at issue here may be described as damage by a vessel in navigable water to an underwater structure." *Id.* at 539.

In contrast, the second connection prong turns on "whether the general character of the activity giving rise to the incident shows a substantial relationship to traditional maritime activity," and courts should "ask whether a tortfeasor's activity, commercial or noncommercial, on navigable waters is so closely related to activity traditionally subject to admiralty law that the reasons for applying special admiralty rules would apply in the suit at hand." *Id.* at 539–40. "Navigation of boats in navigable waters clearly falls within the substantial relationship, *Foremost*; storing them at a marina on navigable waters is close enough, *Sisson*; whereas in flying an airplane over the water, *Executive Jet*, as in swimming, the relationship is too attenuated." *Id.* at 540 (citations omitted). In *Grubart*, "the 'activity giving rise to the incident' . . . [was] characterized as repair or maintenance work on a navigable waterway performed from a vessel," which, [—25—] the Court concluded, also fell within the substantial relationship. *Id.* (quoting *Sisson*, 497 U.S. at 364).

In affirming the complicated *Sisson* test, however, the *Grubart* Court also cautioned that *Sisson* should be viewed as "a test to weed out torts without a maritime connection," not "an arbitrary exercise for

---

[10] Whimsy, like beauty, is often in the eye of the beholder, but the Court provided no additional guidance as to how lower courts should select the right level of generality.

eliminating jurisdiction over even vessel-related torts connected to traditional maritime commerce." *Id.* at 542 n.4. In other words, "[a]lthough the [modern test] tempers the locality test with the added requirements looking to potential harm and traditional activity, it reflects customary practice in seeing jurisdiction as the norm when the tort originates with a vessel in navigable waters, and in treating departure from the locality principle as the exception." *Id.* at 547.

To drive this point home, the Court devoted considerable attention to the criticism that "[i]f the activity at issue [in *Grubart*] [was] considered maritime related, . . . then virtually 'every activity involving a vessel on navigable waters' would be 'a traditional maritime activity sufficient to invoke maritime jurisdiction.'" *Id.* at 542 (quoting Grubart Br. 6). The Court responded bluntly that "this is not fatal criticism," because the Court "ha[d] not proposed any radical [—26—] alteration of the traditional criteria for invoking admiralty jurisdiction in tort cases." *Id.* Rather, the Court explained that it "ha[d] simply followed the lead of the lower federal courts in rejecting a location rule so rigid as to extend admiralty to a case involving an airplane, not a vessel, engaged in an activity far removed from anything traditionally maritime." *Id.* It further remarked:

> In the cases after *Executive Jet*, the Court stressed the need for a maritime connection, but found one in the navigation or berthing of pleasure boats, despite the fact that the pleasure boat activity took place near shore, where States have a strong interest in applying their own tort law, or was not on all fours with the maritime shipping and commerce that has traditionally made up the business of most maritime courts. Although we agree with petitioners that these cases do not say that every tort involving a vessel on navigable waters falls within the scope of admiralty jurisdiction no matter what, *they do show that ordinarily that will be so.*

Id. at 543 (emphasis added) (citations omitted).

We recently applied the *Executive Jet* line of cases in *Tandon*, which involved a brawl on a marina dock, with some of the brawlers falling into the surrounding navigable waters—the type of "perverse and casuistic borderline situation[]" that could have satisfied the locality test and that the modern test was designed to exclude. *Tandon*, 752 F.3d at 248, 2 Adm. R. at 63 (quoting *Exec. Jet*, 409 U.S. at 255). Applying the *Grubart* test, we held that admiralty jurisdiction did not reach the claims relating [—27—] to this brawl "because this type of incident does not have a potentially disruptive effect on maritime commerce." *Id.* at 240, 2 Adm. R. at 57.

After summarizing the *Executive Jet* line of cases, we restated the *Grubart* test as follows:

First, we ask whether the alleged tort meets the location test: that is, whether it occurred on navigable water or was caused by a vessel on navigable water. Second, we ask whether the alleged tort meets both subparts of the connection test: that is, whether the general type of incident involved has a potentially disruptive effect on maritime commerce, and whether the general character of the activity giving rise to the incident bears a substantial relationship to traditional maritime activity. Only if the location test and both subparts of the connection test are met will admiralty tort jurisdiction be proper under 28 U.S.C. § 1333(1).

Id. at 248, 2 Adm. R. at 63 (citation omitted). Later in that opinion, we explained that "[t]he first part of the connection test looks to the nature of the incident that immediately caused the underlying injury; the second part, by contrast, looks to the nature of the broader activity giving rise to that incident." *Id.* at 250–51, 2 Adm. R. at 65.

Applying the first part of the connection test, we noted that "[t]he overall purpose of the exercise is to determine 'whether the incident could be seen within a class of incidents that pose[] more than a fanciful risk to commercial shipping.'" *Id.* at 249, 2 Adm. R.

at 64 (quoting *Grubart*, 513 U.S. at 539). "We conclude[d] that the incident at [—28—] issue in [that] case [was] best described as a physical altercation among recreational visitors on and around a permanent dock surrounded by navigable water." *Id.*, 2 Adm. R. at 64.

After so defining the incident, "[w]e conclude[d] that this type of incident does not realistically pose a threat to maritime commerce," for four reasons: (1) "a fistfight on and around a dock cannot immediately disrupt navigation"; (2) "a fistfight on a dock cannot immediately damage nearby commercial vessels"; (3) "the class of incidents we consider[ed] [t]here include[d] only fights on permanent docks" that "d[id] not pose the same risks to maritime commerce as a fistfight occurring on a vessel on navigable water"; and (4) "the class of incidents we consider[ed] [t]here involve[d] only physical altercations among recreational visitors, not persons engaged in maritime employment." *Id.* at 249–50, 2 Adm. R. at 64–65. Because we concluded that the incident failed to satisfy the first part of the *Grubart* connection inquiry, we ended our analysis there. *Id.* at 253 n.10, 2 Adm. R. at 67 n.10.

Responding to the argument that "the struggling bodies could themselves pose a navigational hazard," *id.* at 251, 2 Adm. R. at 66, we noted that, "[a]t worst, an incident of this sort might temporarily prevent commercial vessels from mooring at the [—29—] permanent dock around which the fight occurred. But the potential impact of such a temporary disruption is simply too meager to support jurisdiction," *id.* at 252, 2 Adm. R. at 66 (citation omitted). And in response to the argument that "a fight on a dock surrounded by navigable water may require emergency responders to come to the dock by boat and leave by boat, potentially snarling naval traffic in nearby waters[,] [w]e recognize[d] that other courts have found the potentially disruptive impact of a maritime emergency response enough to satisfy the first part of the connection test in some cases," but "[t]hose cases . . . generally dealt with incidents occurring either aboard a vessel or else in open water." *Id.*, 2 Adm. R. at 66–67.

We further acknowledged that "[w]here such an incident takes place on a vessel or in open water far from the shore, the potential danger to commercial shipping posed by a maritime emergency response may be more significant." *Id.*, 2 Adm. R. at 67.

B.

The alleged tort here involves a vessel on navigable waters—factors the Supreme Court has reminded us will ordinarily place a case within the bounds of admiralty jurisdiction. *See Grubart*, 513 U.S. at 543. Nonetheless, the district court applied the *Grubart* test and concluded that admiralty jurisdiction was lacking, [—30—] emphasizing the recreational nature of the vessel and its passengers as well as the location of the incident in shallow waters. We disagree that these factors remove the case from admiralty jurisdiction.

1.

Working through the *Grubart* test, the district court began by noting that "the parties agree the location test has been met since the alleged tort occurred on a navigable body of water, Oneida Lake." *Ficarra*, 91 F. Supp. 3d at 313.

Turning to the first step of the connection test—whether the general type of incident involved has a potentially disruptive effect on maritime commerce—the district court set forth a general description of the incident, which, as noted, must be described at an "intermediate level of possible generality." *Grubart*, 513 U.S. at 538. The district court found "that the incident is best described as an injury to a recreational passenger who jumped from a recreational vessel in a shallow recreational bay of navigable waters." *Ficarra*, 91 F. Supp. 3d at 314.

This description is hardly a fit of "whimsy," *Grubart*, 513 U.S. at 542, but we explained in *Tandon* that the description of the incident at an intermediate level of possible generality should be "neither too general to distinguish different cases [—31—] nor too specific to the unique facts of the particular case," 752 F.3d at 247, 2 Adm. R. at 63. An overly par-ticularized description will invite future litigation over even the smallest change to the fact pattern, even if that change has little bearing on whether federal courts should or should not exercise admiralty jurisdiction. The description should therefore be "general enough to capture the possible effects of similar incidents on maritime commerce." *Id.* at 249, 2 Adm. R. at 64. In this regard, we respectfully believe the district court's description is unnecessarily specific.

First, the Supreme Court has consistently stated that it does not matter for purposes of admiralty tort jurisdiction whether the vessel involved was used for commercial or recreational purposes. *See Foremost*, 457 U.S. at 674–75; *see also Yamaha Motor Corp., U.S.A. v. Calhoun*, 516 U.S. 199, 206 (1996) (holding admiralty jurisdiction extends to jet ski accident). This is so because the federal "interest can be fully vindicated only if *all* operators of vessels on navigable waters are subject to uniform rules of conduct." *Foremost*, 457 U.S. at 675; *see also* 1 Thomas J. Schoenbaum, *Admiralty and Maritime Law* § 3-3 at 130–31 (5th ed. 2011) ("Thus, the current test extends admiralty jurisdiction to pleasure craft, but only if they are [—32—] operating on a waterway with *commercial* navigability."). The district court's emphasis on the recreational nature of Germain's vessel is therefore misplaced.

Second, the Supreme Court has never indicated that it matters whether the navigable waters at issue were shallow or deep. That the Court has not discussed the depth of navigable waters is unsurprising because "[t]he basic test of navigability for purposes of admiralty jurisdiction is the formula of *The Daniel Ball*, [77 U.S. 557 (1870),]" and that formula requires, among other things, "proof of present or potential *commercial* shipping." 1 Schoenbaum, *supra*, § 3-3 at 125–27. "As long as such commercial activity is proved, the particular mode of travel or type of craft—flatboat, barge, power vessel, or other method—is unimportant . . . ." *Id.* § 3-3 at 127. If navigability is satisfied, then, it should matter very little for purposes of the first connection prong whether the navigable waters were shallow or deep.

We noted in *Tandon* that, "in considering the type of incident involved, the location of the incident may be relevant," 752 F.3d at 251, 2 Adm. R. at 66, but there we focused on the distance from shore or, more accurately, the distance from the nearest dock or marina, rather than the depth of the waters. Specifically, in assessing the potential [—33—] effects on maritime commerce, we noted that "[a]n emergency response to an incident on and around a floating dock is . . . much less likely to ensnarl maritime traffic than an emergency response to an incident on a vessel or an incident in open water." *Id.* at 252, 2 Adm. R. at 67 (citation and quotation marks omitted). The incident here, unlike the incident on and around a dock in *Tandon*, occurred on a vessel and in open water.

Third, the district court also relied on *Tandon*'s observation that "the roles of the persons involved . . . can be relevant to the potential effect on maritime commerce." *Ficarra*, 91 F. Supp. 3d at 314 (quoting *Tandon*, 752 F.3d at 249, 2 Adm. R. at 64). But, as noted, the focus under the first prong of the modern test is on capturing possible effects of similar incidents on maritime commerce. Where similar incidents involving different types of persons produce similar effects that have a potentially disruptive effective on maritime commerce, the type of person involved should be omitted from the incident's description. As discussed in greater detail below, the potential effects on maritime commerce of an injury to a passenger who jumped from a vessel on open navigable waters include collisions with commercial vessels caused by distracted crews and disruption to maritime traffic caused by [—34—] maritime rescue. These potential effects may be the same whether the injured passenger was recreational or employed in maritime commerce, and they are also sufficient to satisfy the test. Of course, the loss of a maritime employee may have an additional effect on maritime commerce. *See Tandon*, 752 F.3d at 250, 2 Adm. R. at 65 (collecting cases). But, at least here, that additional effect does not change the outcome of the first connection prong, which would be satisfied regardless of the type of persons involved.

Accordingly, we think a more appropriate description of the incident, described at an intermediate level of possible generality and general enough to capture the possible effects of similar incidents on maritime commerce, is injury to a passenger who jumped from a vessel on open navigable waters. "This description accurately captures the nature of the event giving rise to this suit, and the type of risks that the incident could pose to maritime commerce." *Id.* at 249, 2 Adm. R. at 64.

"[L]ook[ing] not to the particular facts of the case before us—i.e., whether maritime commerce was actually disrupted here—but to whether similar occurrences are likely to be disruptive," *id.*, 2 Adm. R. at 64, we conclude that the incident satisfies the first connection prong. First, the district court concluded that the incident [—35—] would not pose more than a fanciful threat to maritime commerce largely because the location of the incident was in "shallow, recreational bays—waters unsuitable for commercial shipping. Therefore, even if the crew of the vessel was distracted by the passenger jumping overboard, there would be no risk of collision with commercial vessels." *Ficarra*, 91 F. Supp. 3d at 314.[11] To begin with, the district court appears to have assumed that commercial means large, but commercial vessels could include small or flat-bottom vessels used for commercial purposes (e.g., fishing boats or boats taking paying passengers to shallow, hard-to-reach bays for snorkeling, diving, etc.). *Cf. Sinclair v. Soniform, Inc.*, 935 F.2d 599, 600 (3d Cir. 1991) (holding that scuba diver's claims against the crew of the vessel that transported him to a diving site fell within admiralty jurisdiction).

Moreover, the Supreme Court has taken an expansive view of the possible commercial effects caused by collisions of even small recreational vessels on navigable waters,

---

[11] If the shallow waters were in fact unsuitable for commercial shipping, we do not see how the navigability component of the location test would be satisfied because, as noted, navigability for admiralty purposes requires "proof of present or potential *commercial* shipping." 1 Schoenbaum, *supra*, § 3-3 at 127.

regardless of the precise location of those vessels in relation to commercial traffic. In *Foremost*, for example, the Court "supported [its] finding of [—36—] potential disruption . . . with a description of the likely effects of a collision at the mouth of the St. Lawrence Seaway, an area heavily traveled by commercial vessels, even though the place where the collision actually had occurred apparently was 'seldom, if ever, used for commercial traffic.'" *Sisson*, 497 U.S. at 363 (citation omitted) (quoting *Foremost*, 457 U.S. at 670 n.2). We similarly conclude that the crew of a vessel, commercial or recreational, on open navigable waters could become distracted when a passenger is injured from jumping overboard and that the distraction could risk collision with a commercial vessel. *See Roane v. Greenwich Swim Comm.*, 330 F. Supp. 2d 306, 315 (S.D.N.Y. 2004) ("[T]hose on board a boat . . . giving their full attention to the saving of the life of a swimmer in difficulty may well be distracted from hazards posed by the approach of other boats unaware of the rescue in progress, or coming at speed in an effort to assist.").

Second, the district court rejected Germain's argument "that this type of incident may still potentially disrupt maritime commerce because an injured passenger in navigable waters invites rescue." *Ficarra*, 91 F. Supp. 3d at 315 (quotation marks omitted). Although the district court recognized that some [—37—] courts have accepted this argument, it found that "those cases typically involve rescue at sea or far from shore where the potential risk of an emergency response to snarl commercial shipping traffic is more realistic." *Id.* (citing *Roane*, 330 F. Supp. 2d at 314; *Szollosy v. Hyatt Corp.*, 208 F. Supp. 2d 205, 212 (D. Conn. 2002)).

But the incident on open navigable waters here is more comparable to a rescue at sea than a rescue at or near a dock. One of the reasons we held in *Tandon* that rescue of brawlers on or near a dock was unlikely to ensnarl maritime traffic was that "[e]mergency responders may have to travel by boat to reach persons injured near a permanent dock, but they will never have to travel far. And once the emergency responders arrive at the scene, they can moor their vessel at the permanent dock, rather than having to focus simultaneously on navigating their vessel and rescuing the injured." 752 F.3d at 252, 2 Adm. R. at 67. In contrast, rescue of passengers injured on a vessel on open navigable waters will often come not from shore, dock, or docked vessels but from other vessels on those same navigable waters. Here, for example, Ficarra was allegedly rescued by boat and rushed five nautical miles across Lake Oneida back to Brewerton through a federal shipping lane. Such maritime rescues on open navigable waters could divert resources that [—38—] would be called upon in the event of an incident involving a commercial vessel, require commercial boats themselves to aid in the rescue efforts, or otherwise disrupt commercial shipping by, for example, using federal shipping lanes to transport injured passengers to safety. *See Craddock v. M/Y The Golden Rule*, 110 F. Supp. 3d 1267, 1275 (S.D. Fla. 2015); *Polly v. Estate of Carlson*, 859 F. Supp. 270, 272 (E.D. Mich. 1994); *In re Complaint of Bird*, 794 F. Supp. 575, 580 (D.S.C. 1992); *cf. Foremost*, 457 U.S. at 675.

Based on similar reasoning, at least three circuits have relied on the potentially disruptive effect of a maritime emergency response to sustain admiralty jurisdiction, even when the activity or vessels at issue were recreational. *See, e.g., In re Mission Bay Jet Sports, LLC*, 570 F.3d 1124, 1129–30 (9th Cir. 2009); *Ayers v. United States*, 277 F.3d 821, 827–28 (6th Cir. 2002); *Sinclair*, 935 F.2d at 602. We distinguished these cases in *Tandon* on the grounds that they "generally dealt with incidents occurring either aboard a vessel or else in open water," and we further noted that "[w]here such an incident takes place on a vessel or in open water far from the shore, the potential danger to commercial [—39—] shipping posed by a maritime emergency response may be more significant." 752 F.3d at 252, 2 Adm. R. at 67. As discussed above, those factors are present here.

We therefore conclude that the general type of incident involved here—injury to a passenger who jumped from a vessel on open navigable waters—has a potentially disruptive effect on maritime commerce.

2.

The district court further concluded that even if it went to the next step—whether the general character of the activity giving rise to the incident shows a substantial relationship to traditional maritime activity—"admiralty jurisdiction would still not lie." *Ficarra*, 91 F. Supp. 3d at 315. We respectfully disagree.

Under this second step, the district court properly began by "describ[ing] the 'general character' of the alleged tortfeasor's activity which gave rise to the incident." *Id.* (quoting *Grubart*, 513 U.S. at 539). The district court described "Germain's alleged activity which gave rise to the incident . . . as anchoring a recreational vessel in a shallow recreational bay without adequately warning a passenger about the risks of diving in." *Id.* at 316. It then concluded that this activity "is not 'so closely related to activity traditionally subject to admiralty law **[—40—]** that the reasons for applying special admiralty rules would apply in the suit at hand.'" *Id.* at 316 (quoting *Grubart*, 513 U.S. at 539).

We believe a more accurate description of the "general character" of Germain's activity was the transport and care of passengers on board a vessel on navigable waters, which more generally captures the many aspects of Germain's activity that Ficarra alleges gave rise to his injury (e.g., Germain's failure to: operate, captain, anchor, maintain, or control his boat in a manner necessary to protect the safety of his passengers; instruct passengers on safe boating and diving; inspect the area where the boat was anchored; and warn passengers about the conditions where the boat was anchored). And contrary to the district court's suggestion, the activity in question need not be "on all fours with the maritime shipping and commerce that has traditionally made up the business of most maritime courts," particularly when the activity in question concerns a vessel on navigable waters. *Grubart*, 513 U.S. at 543.

In any event, we conclude that the activities at issue here—whether it is the more general transport and care of passengers on a vessel on navigable waters or the more specific anchoring of a vessel without warning of the attendant **[—41—]** dangers—are substantially related to traditional maritime activity. *Cf. Sinclair*, 935 F.2d at 602 ("[T]he transport and care of passengers bears a substantial relationship to traditional maritime activity . . . ."); *Kelly v. Smith*, 485 F.2d 520, 526 (5th Cir. 1973) ("Admiralty has traditionally been concerned with furnishing remedies for those injured while traveling navigable waters."), *abrogated on other grounds as stated in Grubart*, 513 U.S. at 544; *Bird*, 794 F. Supp. at 581 ("The court finds . . . that the anchoring of a boat in navigable waters is a traditional maritime activity and that therefore, the second prong is also satisfied."); 1 *Benedict on Admiralty* § 171 at 11-20 (7th ed. rev. 2015) ("Injuries to passengers on excursion boats or other vessels for hire arising out of the fault of the vessel operator or owner are maritime even though there is nothing uniquely maritime about the type of injury." (collecting cases)).[12] **[—42—]**

In sum, we hold that the claims related to the alleged facts here fall within the scope of admiralty tort jurisdiction. First, the underlying claim meets the location test as it occurred on navigable waters. Second, the underlying claim meets both parts of the connection test: (1) The general type of incident—injury to a passenger who jumped from a vessel on open navigable waters—has a

---

[12] In concluding that Germain's activity lacked a substantial relationship to traditional maritime activity, the district court relied on two cases that have been called into doubt: *Delta Country Ventures, Inc. v. Magana*, 986 F.2d 1260 (9th Cir. 1993), and *Foster v. Peddicord*, 826 F.2d 1370 (4th Cir. 1987). The Ninth Circuit held that "the *Delta Country Ventures* approach is flatly inconsistent with the Supreme Court's subsequent decision in *Grubart* and hence is no longer good law." *Taghadomi v. United States*, 401 F.3d 1080, 1087 (9th Cir. 2005). Although the Fourth Circuit has not overruled *Foster*, its approach also seems inconsistent with subsequent Supreme Court authority and lower courts in the Fourth Circuit have declined to follow it for that reason. *See Bird*, 794 F. Supp. at 580.

potentially disruptive effect on maritime commerce; and (2) the general character of the activity giving rise to the incident—whether described as the transport and care of passengers on a vessel on navigable waters or the anchoring of a vessel without warning of the attendant dangers—bears a substantial relationship to traditional maritime activity.

C.

At oral argument, Germain urged us to adopt a simpler rule and hold that admiralty jurisdiction extends to all torts originating on a vessel on navigable waters. We agree that, in general, courts should strive to adopt clear legal rules, particularly in the context of jurisdiction—fewer things are more wasteful to litigate than where you can litigate. *Cf. Grubart*, 513 U.S. at 549 (Thomas, J., concurring) ("The faults of balancing tests are clearest, and perhaps most [—43—] destructive, in the area of jurisdiction."). And in this respect, the modern test for admiralty tort jurisdiction leaves something to be desired.

Lower courts have exerted considerable effort to make sense of the test, while lamenting its complexity and lack of clarity. *See, e.g., Bird*, 794 F. Supp. at 581 n.9 ("Although the test is broad-based, it is by no means a bright line rule and therefore fails to serve as the type of clear jurisdictional rule that is so important when determining subject matter jurisdiction. The nexus test as defined in *Sisson* instead will invite confusion and inconsistent application on the part of lower courts seeking to apply it." (citation omitted)). As Judge Haight aptly observed: "Just what sort of conduct satisfies the apparently two-pronged 'connection test' the Court articulated in *Grubart* remains for consideration by district courts on a case-by-case basis, and I may perhaps be excused for saying that the Court's chart does not reveal the precise location of every hazard to jurisdictional navigation." *Roane*, 330 F. Supp. 2d at 313. The district court's thoughtful analysis here and our lengthy explanation of why it was erroneous provide only further evidence that this is so. [—44—]

But the Supreme Court is well aware of the modern test's difficulties and the advantages of a simpler rule, both of which Justice Thomas fully set forth in his concurring opinion in *Grubart*. *See* 513 U.S. at 549–556 (Thomas, J., concurring). We need not repeat those arguments here, but they do inform our decision not to adopt the simpler rule that Germain urged us to consider. Most obviously, Justice Thomas's concurrence in *Grubart* advocated a rule similar to the one that Germain seeks here. *See id.* at 555 (Thomas, J., concurring) ("When determining whether maritime jurisdiction exists under § 1333(1), a federal district court should ask if the tort occurred on a vessel on the navigable waters."). However persuaded we might be by Justice Thomas's concurrence, a majority of the *Grubart* Court was not so persuaded, and it is the majority's opinion that we must follow. We therefore decline Germain's invitation to adopt a simpler rule, and we instead apply the test set forth by the *Grubart* majority.

Conclusion

For the foregoing reasons, we conclude that Germain's appeal of the dismissal of his petition seeking exoneration from or limitation of liability was proper, and we also conclude that the district court has jurisdiction over that [—45—] petition. We therefore REVERSE and REMAND for further proceedings consistent with this opinion.

United States Court of Appeals
for the Second Circuit

No. 15-2776

MAGO INT'L
vs.
LHB AG[*]

Appeal from the United States District Court for the
Southern District of New York

Decided: August 15, 2016

Citation: 833 F.3d 270, 4 Adm. R. 106 (2d Cir. 2016).

Before **STRAUB, WESLEY,** and **LIVINGSTON,** Circuit
Judges.

[—2—] **WESLEY,** Circuit Judge:

Mago International ("Mago") appeals
from an order and judgment of the
United States District Court for the
Southern District of New York (McMahon, *J.*),
in which judgment was entered in favor of
LHB AG ("LHB") after resolution of cross-
motions for summary judgment. The central
question concerns whether Mago complied
with terms of a standby letter of credit
("SLOC") issued by LHB—specifically,
whether the submission of unsigned copies of
bills of lading complied with the letter's
requirement that Mago provide a "photocopy
of [a bill of lading] [—3—] evidencing
shipment of the goods to the applicant." App.
101. The District Court concluded that the
unsigned copies did not evidence shipment
and thus Mago did not strictly comply. We
agree and accordingly affirm the order and
judgment of the District Court.

BACKGROUND

In 2011, Mago—a company based in New
York—entered into a contract to sell chicken,
beef, and other meat products to NTP Genita
("Genita"), a company based in Pristina,
Kosovo. As is common in international
transactions, in order to ensure it received
payment, Mago required Genita to obtain an
SLOC, issued by Bank for Business, a Kosovar

bank, and confirmed by LHB. Under the
terms of the letter, if Genita failed to pay
Mago within forty-five days after the date of
an invoice, Mago could present a defined set of
documents to LHB and obtain payment on the
SLOC. Among the documents LHB required
was a "photocopy of B/L evidencing shipment
of the goods to the applicant." App. 101.

Mago shipped twelve containers of products
to Genita under four invoices, designated
199(1-5), 199(6-7), 208(1-2), and 208(3-5),
respectively. Genita defaulted on all four
invoices. Mago tendered its first set of
documents to LHB on September 19, 2012,
including two unsigned bills of lading for each
of the two 199 invoices. App. 114–21. LHB
rejected this tender for, *inter alia*, not
containing signed bills of lading. App. 129.
Mago's second tender cured other deficiencies
identified by LHB but contained the same
unsigned bills of lading for the two 199
invoices. App. 139–44. LHB again rejected the
tender, emailing Mago's managing director
that the unsigned bills of lading were not in
conformity with the terms of the letter. Mago's
third tender occurred on October 8, 2012,
the last day possible to [—4—] submit a
demand for payment. As all previous tenders
had done, this one contained signed bills of
lading for the 208 invoices—but instead of
unsigned bills of lading for the 199 invoices,
Mago provided two telexes from the shipping
company, Mediterranean Shipping Company
("MSC"). These telexes announced that MSC
had retained the original, signed bills of
lading in its files and authorized release of the
shipments to Genita without the latter
presenting the original bill of lading. App. 160,
166. LHB rejected this tender as well. Finally,
on October 11, 2012, Mago tendered a set of
documents containing signed bills of lading for
each invoice. App. 172–84. LHB rejected this
tender as untimely. App. 185.

Mago then filed suit in the Southern
District alleging wrongful dishonor of the
SLOC and naming both LHB and Bank for
Business as defendants.[2] On April 1, 2015,
both LHB and Mago cross-moved for summary

---

[*] The Clerk of Court is respectfully directed to
amend the caption as set forth above.

[2] However, Bank for Business was never served
with the complaint, and the District Court
dismissed it from the case. App. 238.

judgment. The District Court issued its order granting LHB's motion and denying Mago's motion on August 4 and entered judgment on August 6. Mago timely appealed from both the order and the judgment.

DISCUSSION

An SLOC is an agreement by a bank to pay a beneficiary on behalf of a customer who obtains the letter, if the customer defaults on an obligation to the beneficiary. *See, e.g., Tudor Dev. Grp. v. U.S. Fid. & Guar. Co.*, 968 F.2d 357, 360 (3d Cir. 1992). "Originally devised to function in international trade, a letter of credit reduced the risk of nonpayment in cases where credit was extended to strangers in distant places" *Voest-Alpine Int'l Corp. v. Chase Manhattan Bank, N.A.*, 707 F.2d 680, 682 (2d Cir. 1983). "The [—5—] issuing bank, or a bank that acts as confirming bank for the issuer, takes on an absolute duty to pay the amount of the credit to the beneficiary, so long as the beneficiary complies with the terms of the letter." *Beyene v. Irving Tr. Co.*, 762 F.2d 4, 6 (2d Cir. 1985). However, "[i]n order to protect the issuing or confirming bank, this absolute duty does not arise unless the terms of the letter have been complied with strictly." *Id.* "Adherence to this rule ensures that banks, dealing only in documents, will be able to act quickly, enhancing the letter of credit's fluidity. Literal compliance with the credit therefore is also essential so as not to impose an obligation upon the bank that it did not undertake and so as not to jeopardize the bank's right to indemnity from its customer." *Voest-Alpine*, 707 F.2d at 682–83. Therefore, "[i]n determining whether to pay, the bank looks solely at the letter and the documentation the beneficiary presents[] to determine whether the documentation meets the requirements in the letter." *Marino Indus. Corp. v. Chase Manhattan Bank, N.A.*, 686 F.2d 112, 115 (2d Cir. 1982). "The corollary to the rule of strict compliance is that the requirements in letters of credit must be explicit and that all ambiguities are construed against the bank. Since the beneficiary must comply strictly with the requirements of the letter, it must know precisely and unequivocally what those requirements are." *Id.* (citations omitted).

As the District Court noted, resolution of this case turns on whether Mago strictly complied with the terms of the SLOC— specifically, whether presentation of unsigned copies of bills of lading satisfy the credit's requirement that Mago submit a "photocopy of B/L evidencing shipment of the goods to the applicant." App. 101.[3] Mago argues principally that, under the [—6—] Uniform Customs and Practice for Documentary Credits (the "UCP") and interpretive guidance issued by the International Chamber of Commerce Banking Commission, where a letter of credit requires "copies" of transport documents like bills of lading, those copies do not need to be signed. Although the letter does explicitly incorporate the UCP and even assuming Mago interprets the UCP correctly, Mago's argument fails for the simple reason that LHB's letter did not simply require a copy of a bill of lading, but required one that "evidenc[ed] shipment of the goods to the applicant." App. 101. Thus, whatever general guidelines are applicable, the copies here were required to evidence shipment. Because the bill of lading at issue required a signature to evidence shipment, the presentation of those documents did not strictly comply with the terms of the letter.

Even though the unsigned copies of the bills of lading here reflect the name of a ship and purported date of shipment, absent the carrier's signature, there is no evidence that the shipping information on the bill of lading reflects the actual shipment of the goods— precisely the information that the SLOC requires. Notably, the signature block on the bills where the carrier would have signed is immediately preceded by language to that effect:

---

[3] We review *de novo* a district court's grant of summary judgment, and "[w]here there are no disputed issues of material fact, our task is to [—6—] determine whether the district court correctly applied the law." *Mario v. P&C Food Mkts., Inc.*, 313 F.3d 758, 764 (2d Cir. 2002) (internal quotation marks omitted). "We must resolve any documentary ambiguity in [Mago's] favor at this stage of the proceedings, because in ruling upon a motion for summary judgment, we construe ambiguous contractual terms in favor of the party opposing the motion." *Bouzo v. Citibank, N.A.*, 96 F.3d 51, 58 (2d Cir. 1996).

RECEIVED by the Carrier in apparent good order and condition (unless otherwise stated [—7—] herein) the total number or quantity of Containers or other packages or units indicated in the box entitled Carrier's Receipt for carriage subject to all the terms and conditions thereof from the Place of Receipt or Port of Loading to the Port of Discharge or Place of Delivery, which-ever is applicable.

App. 181. Without the carrier's signature, the presented copy of the bill of lading does not appear to fulfill the terms of the SLOC. While copies of bills of lading may not generally require signatures, *see* INTERNATIONAL STANDARD BANKING PRACTICE FOR THE EXAMINATION OF DOCUMENTS UNDER DOCUMENTARY CREDITS SUBJECT TO UCP 600 ("ISBP") ¶ 20, the copies of the bill of lading here appear to require such a signature to satisfy the SLOC's requirement that the document "evidenc[e] shipment of the goods to the applicant." App. 101; *see also* UCP 600, Art. XIV ("[B]anks will accept the document as presented if its content *appears* to fulfill the function of the required document." (emphasis added)). Although Mago presented telexes that it claimed also evidenced shipment, those telexes cannot satisfy the letter's requirement that such evidence be contained in a bill of lading. For the same reason, Mago's argument that the SLOC did not explicitly require a signature is unavailing; it explicitly required evidence of shipment in the bill of lading, and the bill of lading at issue required a signature for confirmation of shipment. Accordingly, neither the unsigned bills of lading nor the telexes tendered by Mago in its presentations to LHB satisfied the requirement of strict compliance, and LHB was entitled to reject the presentations. *See Beyene*, 762 F.2d at 6–7.

Mago finally argues that the District Court erred in granting summary judgment to LHB on the entire amount of the SLOC since Mago presented conforming documents with respect [—8—] to the 208 invoices covering five containers of food products. Instead, Mago contends, the District Court should have not have granted summary judgment to LHB on

those invoices. But Mago's complaint does not present invoice-specific claims to the District Court, nor does it anywhere request at least partial payment on the 208 invoices. App. 18–21, 45–47. During oral argument on the summary judgment motions, the District Court expressly asked for clarification on the differences between the 199 and 208 invoices—Mago still did not contend it was owed at least partial payment on the SLOC. Supp. App. 177–86. In its summary judgment order, the District Court expressly noted that Mago had briefed nothing regarding the 208 invoices and further noted that that it did not know whether that was "because Mago was paid with respect to the 208 invoices or because the failure to present conforming documents for the 199 invoices meant that Mago forfeited payment even for invoices that did on their face confirm to the terms of Item 46A." App. 242. Mago did not move for re-consideration or otherwise argue this point; it simply filed a notice of appeal.

"We have repeatedly held that if an argument has not been raised before the district court, we will not consider it . . . ." *Kraebel v. N.Y.C. Dep't of Hous. Pres. & Dev.*, 959 F.2d 395, 401 (2d Cir. 1992) (citation omitted). We have, on occasion, permitted new arguments in support of "a proposition presented below." *Eastman Kodak Co. v. STWB, Inc.*, 452 F.3d 215, 221 (2d Cir. 2006). But Mago is not making a new argument for a proposition made below; it never requested this relief from the District Court. In fact, Mago still has not made an argument that the law permits (much less requires) partial payment on an SLOC.[4] It has cited [—9—] no case law on appeal, merely requesting vacatur and remand to the District Court for consideration in the first instance—on the basis of what theory we have not been told. Where a party has had such numerous occasions to request certain relief from the

---

[4] LHB's briefing argues that while the UCP permits partial draws on the SLOC, Mago never made a request for a partial draw and thus [—9—] LHB could only evaluate the presentation as a whole. Because we hold Mago forfeited its claims to partial payment, we need not address whether LHB has correctly stated the law governing partial draws.

District Court and, failing to do so, has presented no legal argument of error to us on appeal, we will not set aside the District Court's judgment.

CONCLUSION

We have considered all of Mago's arguments and find them to be without merit. For the reasons stated in this opinion, we AFFIRM the order and judgment of the District Court.

This page intentionally left blank

United States Court of Appeals for the Third Circuit

United States Court of Appeals
for the Third Circuit

No. 14-4292

UNITED STATES EX REL. MOORE & CO.
VS.
MAJESTIC BLUE FISHERIES, LLC

Appeal from the United States District Court for the
District of Delaware

Decided: February 2, 2016

Citation: 812 F.3d 294, 4 Adm. R. 112 (3d Cir. 2016).

Before **VANASKIE, NYGAARD,** and **RENDELL,** Circuit
Judges.

[—3—] **RENDELL,** Circuit Judge:

Under the South Pacific Tuna Treaty
("SPTT"), a limited number of licenses to
fish the tuna-rich waters of the Pacific
Island nations are available to vessels under
the control and command of U.S. citizens.
Moore & Company, P.A. ("Moore"), a law firm,
commenced this False Claims Act ("FCA")
action against Korean nationals and LLCs
formed by them, alleging that the LLCs
acquired two of these SPTT licenses by
fraudulently certifying to the U.S. government
that they were controlled by U.S. citizens and
that their fishing vessels were commanded by
U.S. captains. Moore first learned of this
alleged fraud through discovery in a wrongful
death action that it litigated in federal court
against two of the defendants in this case. The
issue before us is whether the District Court,
in dismissing Moore's action, properly
interpreted the FCA's public disclosure bar
and its "original source" exception,
particularly the 2010 amendments to these
provisions.

The FCA empowers a person, or "relator,"
to sue on behalf of the United States those
who defraud the government, and to share in
any ultimate recovery.[1] But the FCA's public
disclosure bar forecloses a relator's action
when the alleged fraud has been publicly
disclosed in at least [—4—] one of several
enumerated sources—*unless* the relator is an
original source of certain information underlying the action.

In 2010, Congress amended the public
disclosure bar as part of the Patient
Protection and Affordable Care Act
("PPACA"). In doing so, it removed the
language that explicitly stated that a court
was deprived of "jurisdiction" over the FCA
action if the bar applied to that action;
reduced the number of enumerated public
disclosure sources; and expanded the
definition of "original source" by allowing a
relator who "materially adds" to the publicly
disclosed information to qualify.

Each of these three changes is implicated
in this case, as Moore argues that the District
Court erred by (1) construing the amended
bar as a jurisdictional limitation, so that it
improperly dismissed the action under Rule
12(b)(1) rather than Rule 12(b)(6); (2) ruling
that the allegations or transactions of the
alleged fraud were publicly disclosed; and (3)
concluding that Moore was not an original
source. We agree that the public disclosure
bar is no longer jurisdictional and that the
motion therefore should have been decided
under Rule 12(b)(6) rather than Rule 12(b)(1).
We further conclude that the alleged fraud
was publicly disclosed, but that Moore was
nevertheless an original source of information
underlying the action.

At issue on appeal is *not* whether Moore
has alleged an actionable fraud.[2] Rather,
what is contested is whether the [—5—]
alleged fraud was disclosed through any of the
qualifying public disclosure sources, and if so,
whether Moore has materially added to those
public disclosures by contributing details of
the alleged fraud that it independently
uncovered through discovery in the wrongful
death action in federal court. The answers to
these questions turn on how we apply the

---

[1] This type of action is commonly referred to as
a *qui tam* suit.

[2] In addition to moving under Rule 12(b)(1) to
dismiss the complaint for lack of jurisdiction, the
defendants moved under Rule 12(b)(6) to dismiss
the complaint as not alleging [—5—] an actionable
fraud. The District Court, however, did not reach
this issue, as it granted the defendants' Rule
12(b)(1) motion based on the public disclosure bar.

public disclosure bar as amended by the PPACA. We will begin with a discussion of the significance of the bar's new provisions.

I. The 2010 Amendments to the FCA's Public Disclosure Bar

The FCA is a relic of the Civil War, but its public disclosure bar was engrafted on the Act more recently. The original FCA did not require a relator to possess firsthand knowledge of a previously unknown fraud. As a result, in the early 1940s, some enterprising individuals filed FCA actions based not on their own independent knowledge of a fraud but on information revealed in the government's criminal indictments. S. Rep. No. 99-345, at 10–11 (1986). To counteract these "parasitic lawsuits," Congress added a provision in 1943 that denied jurisdiction over FCA actions that were "based upon evidence or information in the possession of the United States, or any agency, officer or employee thereof, at the time such suit was brought." 31 U.S.C. § 232(C) (1946). But this "government knowledge defense" did not just eradicate the parasitic lawsuits; it [—6—] eliminated most FCA lawsuits, for courts strictly interpreted § 232(C) as barring FCA actions even when the government knew of the fraud only because the relator had reported it. *See United States ex rel. Findley v. FPC-Boron Employees' Club*, 105 F.3d 675, 680 (D.C. Cir. 1997) ("[B]y restricting *qui tam* suits by individuals who brought fraudulent activity to the government's attention, Congress had killed the goose that laid the golden egg and eliminated the financial incentive to expose fraud against the government.").

Against this backdrop, Congress amended the FCA in 1986, replacing the government knowledge defense with the less restrictive public disclosure bar. This bar precluded a relator from bringing an action that was based on allegations or transactions of fraud that had been publicly disclosed in certain enumerated sources, but added an exception if the relator was an "original source" of the information underlying the action:

(4)(A) No court shall have jurisdiction over an action under this section based upon the public disclosure of allegations or transactions in [i] a criminal, civil, or administrative hearing, [ii] in a congressional, administrative, or Government Accounting Office report, hearing, audit, or investigation, or [iii] from the news media, unless the action is brought by the Attorney General or the person bringing the action is an original source of the information.

31 U.S.C. § 3730(e)(4)(A) (2006). An "original source" was defined as "an individual who has direct and independent knowledge of the information on which the allegations are [—7—] based and has voluntarily provided the information to the Government before filing an action under this section which is based on the information." *Id.* § 3730(e)(4)(B).

Although the original public disclosure bar was less restrictive than the government knowledge defense, it was by no means a low bar for relators to clear. Indeed, given its broad language, as well as different courts' varying interpretations of that language, relators faced a formidable hurdle.

In 2010, Congress amended the bar as part of the PPACA so that it now reads as follows:

(4)(A) *The court shall dismiss an action or claim under this section, unless opposed by the Government,* if substantially the same allegations or transactions as alleged in the action or claim were publicly disclosed—

(i) in a *Federal* criminal, civil, or administrative *hearing in which the Government or its agent is a party*;

(ii) in a congressional, Government Accountability Office, or other Federal report, hearing, audit or investigation; or

(iii) from the news media,

unless the action is brought by the Attorney General or the person bringing the action is an original source of the information. [—8—]

(B) For purposes of this paragraph, "original source" means *an individual who either (i) prior to a public disclosure under subsection (e)(4)(A), has voluntarily disclosed to the Government the information on which allegations or transactions in a claim are based, or (2) who has knowledge that is independent of and materially adds to the publicly disclosed allegations or transactions*, and who has voluntarily provided the information to the Government before filing an action under this section.

31 U.S.C. § 3730(e)(4)(A), (B) (2012) (emphases added).

The italicized language has radically changed the "hurdle" for relators. First, the bar's preliminary language no longer explicitly states that a court is deprived of "jurisdiction" over the FCA action if the bar applies. *Compare* 31 U.S.C. § 3730(e)(4)(A) (2006) ("No court shall have jurisdiction over an action under this section . . . ."), *with id.* § 3730(e)(4)(A) (2012) ("The court shall dismiss an action or claim under this section, unless opposed by the Government . . . ."). Second, information that was disclosed in a criminal, civil, or administrative hearing now qualifies as a public disclosure only if the information was disclosed in a federal case to which the government was a party. *Compare* 31 U.S.C. § 3730(e)(4)(A) (2006) (listing a "criminal, civil, or administrative hearing" as a public disclosure source), *with id.* § 3730(e)(4)(A)(i) (2012) (listing "a Federal criminal, civil, or administrative hearing in which the Government or [—9—] its agent is a party" as a public disclosure source). As a result, information that was disclosed in a federal case between private parties no longer constitutes publicly disclosed information.

Lastly, Congress expanded the definition of "original source" in § 3730(e)(4)(B). The salient question is no longer whether the relator has "direct and independent knowledge" of the information on which the allegations in the complaint are based. 31 U.S.C. § 3730(e)(4)(B) (2006). Rather, original source status now turns on whether the relator has "knowledge that is independent of and materially adds to the publicly disclosed allegations or transactions." *Id.* § 3730(e)(4)(B) (2012). Significantly, a relator no longer must possess "direct . . . knowledge" of the fraud to qualify as an original source. *See United States ex rel. Stinson, Lyons, Gerlin & Bustamante, P.A. v. Prudential Ins. Co.*, 944 F.2d 1149, 1160 (3d Cir. 1991) (holding under the pre-PPACA bar that a law-firm relator lacked direct knowledge because it had learned of the fraud "through two intermediaries," one of which was "the discovery procedure by which the memoranda [exposing the alleged fraud] were produced"). The focus now is on what independent knowledge the relator has added to what was publicly disclosed.

In short, with its 2010 amendments, Congress overhauled the public disclosure bar. Although no direct legislative history seems to exist, the textual changes alone evince Congress's intent to lower the bar for relators, at least [—10—] as to some of its components. With these changes in mind, we turn to the issues presented in this case.[3]

II. Nonjurisdictional Character of the Amended Public Disclosure Bar

We first address Moore's contention that, by virtue of Congress's change to the bar's preliminary language, the District Court should have decided the case under Rule 12(b)(6) for failure to state a claim rather than under Rule 12(b)(1) for lack of jurisdiction.[4]

---

[3] The District Court had jurisdiction under 28 U.S.C. § 1331, and we have jurisdiction under 28 U.S.C. § 1291. We review de novo the District Court's decision on a motion to dismiss. *McTernan v. City of York, Penn.*, 577 F.3d 521, 526 (3d Cir. 2009).

[4] In considering a Rule 12(b)(1) motion to dismiss for lack of jurisdiction, "the court may [usually] consider and weigh evidence outside the pleadings to determine if it has jurisdiction," and "[t]he plaintiff has the burden of persuasion to convince the court it has jurisdiction." *Gould Electronics Inc. v. United States*, 220 F.3d 169, 178

While the pre-PPACA bar stated that "[n]o court shall have jurisdiction over an action under this section based upon the public disclosure of allegations or transactions [in certain enumerated sources]," 31 U.S.C. § 3730(e)(4)(A) (2006), the post-PPACA bar states that "[t]he court shall dismiss an action or claim under this [—11—] section, unless opposed by the Government, if substantially the same allegations or transactions as alleged in the action or claim were publicly disclosed [in certain enumerated sources]," *id.* § 3730(e)(4)(A) (2012). With little analysis, the District Court declared that this amended provision, like its predecessor, presented a jurisdictional bar. We disagree and join the other circuits that have ruled that the amended version does not set forth a jurisdictional bar. *See United States ex rel. Osheroff v. Humana, Inc.*, 776 F.3d 805, 810 (11th Cir. 2015) ("We conclude that the amended § 3730(e)(4) creates grounds for dismissal for failure to state a claim rather than for lack of jurisdiction."); *United States ex rel. May v. Purdue Pharma L.P.*, 737 F.3d 908, 916 (4th Cir. 2013) ("It is apparent . . . that the public-disclosure bar is no longer jurisdictional.").

As our sister circuits have reasoned, first, the amended bar makes no mention of jurisdiction, and unless Congress has "'clearly state[d]' that the [statutory limitation] is jurisdictional . . ., 'courts should treat the restriction as nonjurisdictional in character.'" *Sebelius v. Auburn Reg'l Med. Ctr.*, 133 S. Ct. 817, 824 (2013) (quoting *Arbaugh v. Y & H Corp.*, 546 U.S. 500, 515–16 (2006)). Second, in amending the bar, Congress removed the jurisdictional language that prohibited a court from entertaining the suit if the public disclosure bar applied. *See Brewster v. Gage*, 280 U.S. 327, 337 (1930) ("The deliberate selection of language so differing from that used in the earlier acts indicates that a change of law was intended."). Third,

Congress left undisturbed similar jurisdictional language in neighboring provisions. *See, e.g.*, 31 U.S.C. § 3730(e)(1) (2012) ("No court shall have jurisdiction over an action brought by a former or present member of the armed services under [—12—] subsection (b) of this section against a member of the armed forces arising out of such person's service in the armed forces."). Finally, if a court holds that a relator's claim is publically disclosed, the amended bar nonetheless permits the government to oppose the court's dismissal of the action, an option that effectively dispels any notion that the bar is still jurisdictional. *See Gonzalez v. Thaler*, 132 S. Ct. 641, 648 (2012) ("Subject-matter jurisdiction can never be waived or forfeited.").

For these reasons, we conclude that the amended bar is not jurisdictional. Accordingly, the District Court should have decided the defendants' motion to dismiss on public disclosure grounds under Rule 12(b)(6), not Rule 12(b)(1).

III. Public Disclosure

We next address whether the fraud alleged by Moore was publicly disclosed. Moore brought this FCA action against Majestic Blue Fisheries, LLC; Pacific Breeze Fisheries, LLC; and Joyce Jungmi Kim, alleging they defrauded the government in that, in order to procure the SPTT fishing licenses, the LLCs fraudulently certified to the U.S. Coast Guard that they were controlled by U.S. citizens and that their eponymous fishing vessels ("F/V Majestic Blue" and "F/V Pacific Breeze") were commanded by U.S. captains.[5] According to Moore, the LLCs, in fact, were controlled by Dongwon Industries, a South Korean tuna company, and their vessels, F/V Majestic Blue and F/V [—13—] Pacific Breeze, were commanded by Korean fishing masters who worked for Dongwon.[6]

(3d Cir. 2000). By contrast, in considering a Rule 12(b)(6) motion to dismiss for failure to state a claim, a court generally considers only the allegations in the complaint, accepting them as true, and the defendant bears the burden of showing that the plaintiff has not stated a claim. *Id.*

[5] Moore also brought this action against Dongwon Industries Co., Ltd., Jayne Songmi Kim, and Jaewoong Kim, but they were never served and have not entered appearances.

[6] To obtain an SPTT license, a vessel must be granted a U.S. Coast Guard certificate of documentation. This certificate is available only to

We must decide whether "substantially the same allegations or transactions [of fraud] as alleged in [Moore's] action or claim were publicly disclosed" in any of the enumerated public disclosure sources. 31 U.S.C. § 3730(e)(4)(A) (2012). We first consider whether the sources on which the defendants rely in arguing that the alleged fraud was publicly disclosed qualify as public disclosure sources under § 3730(e)(4)(A). We next determine whether "substantially the same allegations or transactions" of fraud alleged by Moore were publicly disclosed through these qualifying sources. *Id.*

As stated earlier, to be publicly disclosed, the alleged fraud must have been revealed through at least one of three sources: (1) "a Federal criminal, civil, or administrative hearing in which the Government or its agent is a party"; (2) "a congressional, Government Accountability Office, or other Federal report, hearing, audit, or investigation"; or (3) "news media." *Id.* § 3730(e)(4)(A)(i)–(iii). Here, the defendants argue, as they did in the District Court, that the alleged fraud was publicly disclosed in "news media" and "Federal report[s]."

As "news media," the defendants proffered a mixture of two Internet news articles, a podcast, and a blog, but the [—14—] District Court concluded that only the two news articles qualified. The first article, "Flogging and Mutiny in the 21st Century, Proudly Waving the Stars and Stripes," which was posted on maritimeaccident.org, describes the experience of Doug Pine, an American who had served as a "captain" of the F/V Majestic Blue ("Maritime Accident article"). (App. 726.) The second, "Coast Guard Probes Island Mariner's Account of Fiasco at Sea," which was posted on vashonbeachcomber.com, also describes Pine's experience aboard the F/V Majestic Blue ("Vashon Beachcomber article"). (App. 731.) Moore concedes that these two articles qualify as "news media."[7] [—15—]

The District Court also decided that certain information that Moore had obtained through Freedom of Information Act ("FOIA") requests constituted "Federal report[s]." This information included the LLCs' allegedly fraudulent certifications to the U.S. Coast Guard that they were controlled by U.S. citizens and that their vessels, F/V Majestic Blue and F/V Pacific Breeze, were commanded by U.S. captains, as well as certain emails sent by a man named "K.Y. Hwang" of "Dongwon Industries."[8] (App. 608.)

In deciding that these FOIA documents constituted federal reports, the District Court relied on *Schindler Elevator Corp. v. United States ex rel. Kirk*, 563 U.S. 401 (2011). There, the Court analyzed whether FOIA documents constitute "report[s]" under the *pre*-PPACA bar and decided that "[a] written agency response to a FOIA request falls within the ordinary meaning of 'report,'" and that "[a]ny records the agency produces along with its written FOIA response are part of that response." *Id.* at 410–11. The District Court concluded that *Schindler*'s interpretation of "report" in the pre-PPACA bar applied with equal force to the post-PPACA bar because a "report" is also a public disclosure source in the post-PPACA bar.

---

blog consisted mostly of posted "Responses" by various individuals to Pine's story about his experience on the F/V Majestic Blue. We need not address whether these sources qualify as news media because we conclude that the alleged fraud was publicly disclosed through the two news articles and the documents obtained by Moore through Freedom of Information Act requests.

We also recognize that the defendants attached the two news articles to their motion to dismiss, and that because these articles were not attached to Moore's complaint, a court would not usually consider such evidence in deciding a Rule 12(b)(6) motion. Moore, however, has conceded that these news articles qualify as news media and has not challenged their authenticity, and so we will judicially notice them for the limited purpose of determining "what was in the public realm at the time, not whether the contents of those articles [—15—] were in fact true." *Benak ex rel. Alliance Premier Growth Fund v. Appliance Capital Mgmt. L.P.*, 435 F.3d 396, 401 n.15 (3d Cir. 2006).

---

vessels that are under the control and command of U.S. citizens.

[7] On appeal, the defendants argue that the District Court erred in deciding that the podcast and the blog did not qualify as news media. The podcast was an interview with Doug Pine, and the

[8] Moore attached this information to its complaint.

Compare 31 U.S.C. § 3730(e)(4)(A) (2006) (listing "a congressional, administrative, or Government Accounting office *report*" as a public disclosure source (emphasis added)), *with id.* § 3730(e)(4)(A)(ii) (2012) (listing "a congressional, [—16—] Government Accountability Office, or other Federal *report*" as a public disclosure source (emphasis added)).

While Moore recognizes that a government "report" is also a public disclosure source in the post-PPACA bar, it contends that the Court's interpretation of that word in *Schindler* does not apply to the post-PPACA bar because the pre-PPACA bar is "a much different statute." (Moore's Br. 26.) It further urges us to follow the "guiding philosophy" behind the 2010 amendments to the public disclosure bar, which, it asserts, is that the bar applies only when federal officials are likely to see the public disclosures. (*Id.*)

We reject Moore's argument. The PPACA did not alter the bar in any way that would render *Schindler*'s interpretation of "report" inapplicable to the FOIA documents under consideration here. Moreover, even before *Schindler* was decided, many courts, including our own, had similarly interpreted "report" in the pre-PPACA bar. *See, e.g., United States ex rel. Mistick PBT v. Housing Auth. of Pittsburgh*, 186 F.3d 376, 383 (3d Cir. 1999) (concluding that FOIA documents "fell within the ordinary meaning of the term 'report'"); *United States ex rel. Grynberg v. Praxair, Inc.*, 389 F.3d 1038, 1051 (10th Cir. 2004) ("It is generally accepted that a response to a request under the FOIA is a public disclosure."). When Congress overhauled the bar in 2010, it could have reacted to these cases by excluding FOIA documents as "report[s]." *Cf. Merck & Co., Inc. v. Reynolds*, 559 U.S. 633, 648 (2010) ("We normally assume that, when Congress enacts statutes, it is aware of relevant judicial precedent."). But it did not: it left "report" largely unaltered [—17—] as a public disclosure source.[9] Congress thus did not amend this source in any way that would cast doubt on the view held by many courts that a "report" includes

FOIA documents, a view later confirmed by the Court in *Schindler*.

In addition, Moore's "guiding philosophy" argument rings hollow when we consider that § 3730(e)(4)(A) includes many documents that the government will likely never see. For example, "news media" is a source that "include[s] a large number of local newspapers and radio stations" and therefore "likely describes a multitude of sources that would seldom come to the attention of the Attorney General." *Graham Cty. Soil & Water Conservation Dist. v. United States ex rel. Wilson*, 559 U.S. 280, 300 (2010).

We next consider whether substantially the same "allegations or transactions" of fraud alleged by Moore were publicly disclosed via the two news articles and the FOIA documents. "An allegation of fraud is an explicit accusation of wrongdoing. A transaction warranting an inference of fraud is one that is composed of a misrepresented state of facts plus the actual state of facts." *United States ex rel. Zizic v. Q2Administrators, LLC*, 728 F.3d 228, 235–36 (3d Cir. 2013). Formulaically this appears as follows: "X (misrepresented state of facts) + Y (true state of facts) = Z (fraud)." *United States ex rel. Dunleavy v. Cty. of Del.*, 123 F.3d 734, 741 (3d Cir. 1997). A defendant must therefore show that substantially the same "allegation[]" of fraud (Z) *or* "transaction[]" of fraud (X + Y) was publicly disclosed through the sources enumerated in § 3730(e)(4)(A). [—18—]

Here, Moore's "allegation" of fraud (Z) is that the defendants fraudulently procured certificates of documentation from the U.S. Coast Guard so that they could obtain the SPTT fishing licenses. As for the "transaction" of that fraud, it alleges that the defendants certified to the U.S. Coast Guard that U.S. citizens controlled the LLCs and commanded their vessels (the mispresented state of facts, or X) when in fact Dongwon both controlled the LLCs and commanded their vessels (the true state of facts, or Y). The defendants have shown that substantially this same "transaction" was publicly disclosed.

---

[9] Congress did amend this source so that only "Federal" reports qualify. The FOIA is, of course, a federal statute.

In the applications for certificates of documentation that the LLCs filed with the U.S. Coast Guard and that were obtained by Moore through FOIA requests, Majestic Blue LLC and Pacific Breeze LLC certified that "non-citizens do not have authority within a management group, whether through veto power, combined voting, or otherwise, to exercise control over the LLC[s]," and that their eponymous fishing vessels "will at all times remain under the command of a U.S. citizen." (App. 233–34, 236–37.)

However, the two news articles indicate that Majestic Blue LLC is not controlled by U.S. citizens, nor is its vessel commanded by a U.S. captain. The Vashon Beachcomber article describes how Doug Pine accepted a position on the F/V Majestic Blue "as captain of the Korean-managed ship," states that the F/V Majestic Blue is "operated by a Korean company," and even names that company as "Korea's Dongwon Corporation." (App. 731.) The Maritime Accident article reveals how the Korean fishing master, not Captain Pine, commanded the vessel: [—19—]

When the [F/V Majestic Blue] was registered in the US, the Korean captain became the fishmaster and Captain Pine joined as Captain. It was an uncomfortable relationship.

. . . .

Pine found it difficult to exercise his authority almost from the moment he first boarded the vessel: "The first day I was aboard I asked for the crew list[.] It was ordered by rank. I was Number Two, the fishmaster was number 1. The second officer refused a direct order to change it. The Korean officers refused to obey any routine command activity.

In fact, Pine was supposed to simply be a "paper captain" to meet the requirements of the US flag and to accept the authority of the fishmaster, the former captain. Pine was unable to manoeuver the vessel or use the navigation equipment on the bridge.

(App. 726.)

Less apparent, though still publicly disclosed, is the true state of facts (the "Y") for Pacific Breeze LLC and its vessel, revealed through emails sent by K.Y. Hwang of Dongwon Industries and obtained by Moore via FOIA requests. (Notably, these emails also support the true state of facts for Majestic Blue LLC and its vessel.) In one email, K.Y. Hwang informs the recipient that he is "from Dongwon Industries" and is "in charge of care for F/V Majestic Blue & Pacific Breeze." (App. 608.) He writes that he has received a [—20—] message from the LLCs' general manager and that he is worried about the looming expiration of the vessels' SPTT licenses. In a second email, addressed to the LLCs' general manager, he states that "[w]e [Dongwon] are studying the possibility of our US flagged fishing vessel' [sic] operation in Atlantic Ocean." (App. 609–10.) Relying on these emails, Moore itself alleges in its complaint that "[c]learly, Dongwon, rather than any U.S. Citizen, maintained operational control over the LLCs and made all major decisions for Majestic Blue and Pacific Breeze." (App. 47.) It further contends that "[b]y Dongwon's own admission [], the Vessels are part of Dongwon's 'US flagged fishing vessel operation' and were not really owned or controlled by U.S. Citizens despite Defendants' contrary certifications to the U.S. Government." (App. 48.)

In sum, we have little difficulty concluding that the transaction setting forth the alleged fraud was publicly disclosed via the two news articles and the FOIA documents.

IV. Original Source

Moore can nonetheless clear the bar if it qualifies as an "original source." The post-PPACA bar defines an original source as one "who has knowledge that is independent of and materially adds to the publicly disclosed allegations or transactions." 31 U.S.C. § 3730(e)(4)(B) (2012). In support of its case for original source status, Moore relies on information that it obtained from discovery in a federal civil case. In June 2010, the F/V Majestic Blue sank in the South Pacific, resulting in the death of its captain, David Hill. Moore represented Hill's wife in a wrongful death action in federal court against Majestic Blue LLC and Dongwon. In discovery [—21—] in that litigation, Moore obtained documents and deposed individuals including K.Y. Hwang, and Joyce Kim and Jayne Kim, the LLCs' sole shareholders. From this discovery, Moore not only first learned of the alleged fraud but also uncovered details as to how it unfolded. Moore argues, as it must, that this information that it obtained in the wrongful death action is independent of, and materially adds to, the publicly disclosed transaction of fraud. We agree.

A. Independent of

The District Court held that Moore was not an original source because the information that it had obtained through discovery in the wrongful death action did not constitute "independent knowledge." In doing so, it analyzed Moore's knowledge according to our jurisprudence under the pre-PPACA bar whereby we had required that a relator's knowledge must be independent not just from information that qualified as a public disclosure under § 3730(e)(4)(A), but also from information readily available in the public domain. *See United States ex rel. Atkinson v. Pa. Shipbuilding Co.*, 473 F.3d 506, 522 (3d Cir. 2007) (stating that while "reliance solely on 'public disclosures' under § 3730(e)(4)(A) is *always* insufficient under § 3730(e)(4)(B) to confer original source status, reliance on public information that does not qualify as a public disclosure under § 3730(e)(4)(A) may also preclude original source status depending on . . . . the availability of the information and the amount of labor and deduction required to construct the claim" (citation and quotation marks omitted)). Informed by this pre-PPACA interpretation, the District Court concluded that Moore's knowledge was not independent because the information [—22—] obtained in the civil litigation was in the "public domain" and not "obscure." (App. 23.)

Although the District Court was correct in interpreting our pre-PPACA jurisprudence, it erred in concluding that this interpretation of independent knowledge should also apply to the post-PPACA bar. As noted earlier, the pre-PPACA bar defined an original source as "an

individual who has direct and independent knowledge of the information on which the [complaint's] allegations are based." 31 U.S.C. § 3730(e)(4)(B) (2006). This definition does not indicate what the knowledge must be independent from and makes no reference to the public disclosure sources enumerated in § 3730(e)(4)(A). Accordingly, we reasoned that the relator's knowledge needed to be independent from information readily available in the public domain. *See Atkinson*, 473 F.3d at 522–23.

But the PPACA's new definition of original source requires an entirely different analysis. An original source is now defined as one "who has knowledge that is independent of and materially adds to *the publicly disclosed allegations or transactions*." 31 § 3730(e)(4)(B) (2012) (emphasis added). This definition therefore states that a relator's knowledge must be independent of, and materially add to, not all information readily available in the public domain, but, rather, only information revealed through a public disclosure source in § 3730(e)(4)(A).

Indeed, the text plainly requires courts to compare the relator's knowledge with the information that was disclosed through the public disclosure sources enumerated in § 3730(e)(4)(A). By using the definite article "the" before [—23—] "publicly disclosed allegations or transactions" in § 3730(e)(4)(B), Congress has referred back to the public disclosures in § 3730(e)(4)(A). *See New Oxford American Dictionary* 1748 (2d ed. 2005) (defining "the" as a word "denoting one or more people or things already mentioned"). Congress also tied the definition of "original source" in § 3730(e)(4)(B) to public disclosures in § 3730(e)(4)(A) by employing the identical phrases "allegations or transactions" and "publicly disclosed" in both provisions. *Compare* 31 U.S.C. § 3730(e)(4)(A) (2012) ("The court shall dismiss an action . . . if substantially the same *allegations or transactions* as alleged in the action or claim were *publicly disclosed* [in the following enumerated sources]." (emphases added)), *with id.* § 3730(e)(4)(B) (defining original source as one "who has knowledge that is independent of and materially adds to the *publicly disclosed allegations or trans-actions."* (emphasis added)); *cf. Rockwell Int'l Corp. v. United States*, 549 U.S. 457, 471 (2007) (deciding that the word "allegations" that was used in both § 3730(e)(4)(A) and § 3730(e)(4)(B) of the *pre*-PPACA bar meant different things because § 3730(e)(4)(B) did not also refer to "transactions" and "[h]ad Congress wanted to link original-source status to information underlying the public disclosure, it would surely have used the identical phrase, 'allegations or trans-actions'").[10] [—24—]

Applying this new definition of original source to the information that Moore gained through discovery in the wrongful death action as to how Dongwon established and controlled the LLCs, information that we will describe in more detail below, we conclude that Moore possesses knowledge that is "independent of . . . the publicly disclosed allegations or transactions." 31 U.S.C. § 3730(e)(4)(B) (2012).

B. Materially Adds

Through the wrongful death action, Moore contends that it learned, and thus alleged, numerous details that "materially add[]" to the publicly disclosed transaction of fraud, as is required for the original source exception to apply. As we will describe in more detail below, Moore discovered information such as what specific individuals were involved in the alleged fraud and how they initiated and perpetrated the alleged transgression.

---

[10] It would also make little sense to apply our interpretation of "independent knowledge" under the pre-PPACA bar to the post-PPACA bar. In addition to "independent of," "materially adds to" modifies "the publicly disclosed allegations or transactions." So if "the publicly disclosed allegations or transactions" included not just public disclosures under § 3730(e)(4)(A) but also other information in the public domain, we would ask whether the relator's knowledge [—24—] materially adds to that information in the public domain. This would often lead to circular inquiries. Here, for example, we would ask whether Moore's knowledge that it gleaned from discovery in the wrongful death action materially adds to that same information.

We have not previously interpreted "materially adds." The word "add" means to "put (something) in or on something else so as to improve or alter its quality or nature." *New Oxford Dictionary, supra,* at 18. And "material" is defined as "significant, influential, or relevant." *Id.* at 1045. So to "materially add[]" to the publicly disclosed allegation or [—25—] transaction of fraud, a relator must contribute significant additional information to that which has been publicly disclosed so as to improve its quality.

The defendants concur with this definition but argue that Moore falls outside of it. Citing cases from other circuits, they contend that the information that Moore obtained through the wrongful death action merely provides additional details that are immaterial because they only support the transaction of fraud that was already publicly disclosed. *See, e.g., United States ex rel. Osheroff v. Humana, Inc.,* 776 F.3d 805, 815 (11th Cir. 2015) (holding relator was not original source because he provided only additional background information to the publicly disclosed fraud). According to the defendants, because the essential elements of the fraud's transaction were publicly disclosed in the news articles and the FOIA documents, Moore's additional details as to how the fraud originated and transpired do not materially add to the publicly disclosed transaction of fraud.

Yet that cannot be the meaning of the term, for that would read out of the statute the original source exception. The exception, of course, comes into play only when some facts regarding the allegation or transaction have been publicly disclosed. The salient issue, then, is how to distinguish additional but immaterial information from information that "materially adds" to the publicly disclosed allegation or transaction of fraud.

Rule 9(b)'s pleading requirement is of some assistance. Under Rule 9(b), which applies to FCA actions, "[i]n alleging fraud or mistake, a party must state with particularity the circumstances constituting fraud or mistake." [—26—] *Foglia v. Renal Ventures Mgmt., LLC,* 754 F.3d 153, 155 (3d Cir. 2014) (quoting Fed. R. Civ. P. 9(b)). A plaintiff alleging fraud must therefore support its allegations "with all of the essential factual background that would accompany the first paragraph of any newspaper story—that is, the who, what, when, where and how of the events at issue." *In re Rockefeller Ctr. Props., Inc. Securities Litig.*, 311 F.3d 198, 217 (3d Cir. 2002) (citation and quotation marks omitted). In our view, this standard also serves as a helpful benchmark for measuring "materially adds." Specifically, a relator materially adds to the publicly disclosed allegation or transaction of fraud when it contributes information—distinct from what was publicly disclosed—that adds in a significant way to the essential factual background: "the who, what, when, where and how of the events at issue."[11] *Id.*

Moore has satisfied that standard with certain information that it learned through discovery in the wrongful death action. Indeed, with this information, it has contributed significant, specific details that were not publicly disclosed as to how Dongwon surreptitiously established and controlled Majestic Blue LLC and Pacific Breeze LLC.

For example, based on the discovery that it obtained in the wrongful death action, Moore alleged that in 2008, Jawoong Kim, a former Dongwon executive and brother of the company's chairman, approached his daughters, Joyce and Jayne Kim, who are U.S. citizens, and asked them to form U.S. LLCs to "buy" two fishing vessels from Dongwon. [—27—] The Kim sisters then formed Majestic Blue LLC and Pacific Breeze LLC and assumed from Dongwon record ownership of the F/V Majestic Blue and the F/V Pacific Breeze. But the Kim sisters served only as straw owners of the two LLCs: they capitalized each LLC with a mere $50.00, and they knew nothing about the business operations of the LLCs, relying entirely on their father Jawoong Kim to manage the companies.[12]

Moore also alleged that Dongwon never actually "sold" the vessels to the LLCs. To "buy" the vessels from Dongwon, the Kim sisters signed agreements in which the LLCs agreed to pay $4.4 million for each vessel. Yet these agreements did not hold the Kim sisters personally responsible for paying the LLCs' debt, despite the LLCs' negligible capital. Nor did Dongwon take out a mortgage on the vessels. And neither the Kim sisters nor the LLCs ever paid any money to Dongwon for these vessels. [—28—]

Moore further alleged that Dongwon created a fake "manager" of the LLCs to initiate the SPTT license application process. At one point, "William Phil," who claimed to be the LLCs' manager, emailed the National Marine Fisheries Service and the U.S. Coast Guard about obtaining the SPTT licenses. (App. 43.) "William Phil," though, was "a pseudonym for three Korean nationals who are also employees of Dongwon who operated under the false name in order to sound more like an American citizen." (*Id.*) In fact, Joyce Kim testified in a 2011 deposition that she had never even heard of him.

We conclude that this information added to the publicly disclosed information in a material way. While the information set forth in the two news articles and the FOIA documents publicly disclosed the basic elements of the fraud's transaction (i.e, the "X + Y"), the information that Moore acquired from discovery in the wrongful death action added significant details to the essential factual background of the fraud—the who,

---

[11] To be clear, this standard is intended to apply when a relator's original source status is at issue at any stage of the litigation—not just at the motion to dismiss stage.

[12] In footnote 7 *supra*, we declined to say whether the podcast interview with Doug Pine

qualified as "news media." In that interview, Pine stated generally that two sisters with U.S. citizenship owned the LLCs and that their U.S. citizenship was being exploited by Dongwon. But even if the podcast qualified as news media, the specific information that Moore obtained in discovery about the Kim sisters and Dongwon is distinct from, and adds significantly to, the vague information disclosed by the podcast. Unlike the podcast, Moore's discovery documents revealed the sisters' names and their lack of knowledge about the LLCs; their father's name, his affiliation with Dongwon, and his initiation of the alleged fraud; and details as to how the LLCs were structured and poorly capitalized.

what, when, where, and how of the alleged fraud—that were not publicly disclosed.

V. Conclusion

Having alleged information that is independent of and materially adds to the publicly disclosed information, Moore is an original source under the post-PPACA public disclosure bar. We will accordingly reverse the District Court's September 23, 2014, order dismissing Moore's action insofar as that order applied to Moore's claims arising under the post- [—29—] PPACA FCA and will remand the case for further proceedings.[13]

---

[13] We note that there will remain pending in the District Court on remand the defendants' Rule 12(b)(6) motion to dismiss for failure to state a claim that the District Court did not rule on in light of its grant of the defendants' Rule 12(b)(1) motion.

United States Court of Appeals
for the Third Circuit

No. 14-4043

HAVENS
vs.
MOBEX NETWORK SERVS., LLC

Appeal from the United States District Court for the
District of New Jersey

Decided: April 14, 2016

Citation: 820 F.3d 80, 4 Adm. R. 123 (3d Cir. 2016).

Before **FUENTES**, ***SLOVITER**, and **ROTH**, Circuit
Judges.

* The Honorable Dolores K. Sloviter assumed inactive
status on April 4, 2016 after the argument and conference
in this case, but before the filing of the opinion. The
opinion is filed by a quorum of the panel pursuant to 28
U.S.C. § 46(d) and Third Circuit I.O.P. Chapter 12.

[—3—] **ROTH**, Circuit Judge:

Warren Havens and five entities under
his control brought this suit against
competitors Mobex Network Services,
LLC, Mobex Communications, Inc., Maritime
Communications/Land Mobile, LLC (MCLM),
Paging Systems, Inc. (PSI), and Touch Tel
Corporation for allegedly violating the Federal
Communications Act (FCA) and the Sherman
Antitrust Act. The District Court dismissed
the two FCA claims for failure to state a
claim. After a nine-day bench trial, the
District Court entered judgment for MCLM on
the basis that no conspiracy existed. We will
affirm.

I.

A. FACTS [—4—]

Marine radio providers enable vessels to
communicate while on waterways and on the
high seas. An Automated Maritime Tele-
communications System (AMTS) station is a
special type of radio station in the United
States that provides communication services
between land and vessels in navigable
waterways. The AMTS spectrum is 217 to 218

MHz and 219 to 220 MHz.[1] Advances in
wireless technology have greatly expanded the
potential uses of AMTS's, including systems
for public transportation safety, such as
"Positive Train Control."

The FCC originally issued licenses to use
AMTS-designated frequencies on a site-based
system. In this system, the site is a small
geographic region defined by location and the
waterway served. These "site-based" licenses
were provided at no cost on a first-come, first-
served basis. In 2000, the FCC stopped
issuing site-based licenses and began issuing
AMTS licenses on a geographic basis through
a competitive bidding process. Under the new
procedure, the FCC divided the United States
into ten regions and, at two public auctions,
sold "geographic" licenses for two blocks of
AMTS frequencies (A block and B block) in
each region. Both site-based and geographic
licensees are subject to buildout and service
requirements to remain valid.[2]

Although geographic licensees may
generally place stations anywhere within their
allotted region, they may not interfere with
the functioning of existing site-based stations.
Specifically, 47 C.F.R. § 80.385(b)(1) requires
that an "AMTS geographic area licensee must
locate its stations at least 120 kilometers from
the stations of co-channel site- [—5—] based
AMTS licensees" to avoid radio interference
with site-based usage. In other words, the
location of a site-based station creates a gap in
a geographic licensee's coverage area in which
the geographic licensee is barred from
transmitting on AMTS frequencies. If a site-
based license is terminated, revoked, or found
invalid, however, the spectrum will revert
automatically to the geographic licensee.[3]

Plaintiffs and defendants are holders of
various AMTS licenses in the United States.
Out of the twenty geographic licenses in the
United States that were available at auction,
plaintiffs obtained thirteen, MCLM obtained
four, and PSI obtained two. None of the
defendants sought to bid on licenses in the
same block and region in which the other

---

[1] *See* 47 C.F.R. §§ 2.106, 30.385.
[2] *See* 47 C.F.R. §§ 1.946(c), 1.955(a), 80.49(a)(3).
[3] *See id.* § 80.385(c).

defendants held a pre-existing site-based license. But plaintiffs obtained geographic licenses in areas overlaying many of Mobex, MCLM, and PSI's pre-existing site-based licenses. At the center of this dispute is MCLM's refusal to disclose to plaintiffs the location of MCLM's operating site-based stations within plaintiffs' geographic regions. Unable to agree on who should turn over their geographic coordinates first, the parties did not exchange information. This action, along with various FCC administrative proceedings, followed.

B. PROCEEDINGS

On June 20, 2008, plaintiffs brought claims against MCLM, Mobex Network Services, PSI, and Touch Tel. The parties then agreed to dismiss the case without prejudice in light of a pending action in California state court. On [—6—] February 18, 2011, Havens filed a Second Amended Complaint under a new docket number and added Mobex Communications as a defendant. Plaintiffs assert three claims in the Second Amended Complaint. In Count I, they seek a mandatory injunction under § 401(b) of the FCA to force defendants to comply with 47 C.F.R. § 80.385 and with the directives set out in three FCC documents, which plaintiffs refer to as the "Cooperation Orders."[4] Specifically, plaintiffs request that the court require defendants to provide plaintiffs with the operating contours for their site-based locations that are located within plaintiffs' geographic locations. In Count II, plaintiffs allege that defendants violated § 201(b) of the FCA by taking actions that are "unjust and unreasonable" and seek monetary damages under §§ 206 and 207. Plaintiffs also allege in Count III that defendants violated § 1 of the Sherman Act by conspiring among themselves and with non-named parties, in unreasonable restraint of trade or commerce in the AMTS market, as evidenced by defendants' coordination of the purchase of A and B block licenses, their agreement to "warehouse" licenses by failing to construct site-based stations and by

refusing to disclose the operating stations' contours, and their false representations to the industry and the FCC.[5] [—7—]

Plaintiffs attached the three "Cooperation Orders" to the Second Amended Complaint. The first document is an April 8, 2009, FCC declaratory ruling in response to MCLM's request for clarification regarding § 80.385(b)(1), in which the Commission declared that a geographic licensee's co-channel interference protection obligations should be based on actual operating parameters, rather than maximum permissible operating parameters. In a footnote, the FCC then stated: "As we noted in [a prior] decision, we expect incumbent AMTS licensees to cooperate with geographic licensees in order to avoid and resolve interference issues. This includes, at a minimum, providing upon request sufficient information to enable geographic licensees to calculate the site-based station's protected contour."[6]

The second Cooperation Order, dated March 20, 2009, concerns a marine radio provider's application to modify its AMTS geographic license and PSI's petition to dismiss the application on the basis that the geographic licensee had not afforded PSI's site-based location adequate protection. In dismissing PSI's petition, the FCC noted that the application had to make certain assumptions regarding PSI's site-based location. In the immediately following footnote, the FCC then stated that "AMTS site-based incumbents · are expected to cooperate with geographic licensees in order to avoid and resolve interference issues. . . . This includes, at a minimum, providing upon request sufficient information to enable

---

[4] We use this term simply to refer to the documents described by Plaintiffs, and not to imply that they constitute "orders" within the meaning of § 401(b). See infra Part II.A.

[5] Count III also includes claims under § 2 of the Sherman Act based on the "Essential Facilities Doctrine." These claims were dismissed by the District Court pursuant to Rule 12(b)(6) and are not at issue in this appeal.

[6] Dennis C. Brown, Esq., Letter, 24 FCC Rcd. 4135, 4136 n.9 (2009) (Letter) (internal quotations omitted).

[—8—] geographic licensees to calculate the site-based station's protected contour."[7]

The last Cooperation Order is an April 16, 2010, FCC denial of reconsideration of its declaratory ruling at issue in the first Cooperation Order. In reaffirming its decision that actual parameters should be used for determining co-channel interference protection, the FCC observed that "AMTS site-based licensees are expected to cooperate with geographic licensees in avoiding and resolving interference issues, and . . . this obligation requires, at a minimum, that the site-based licensee 'provid[e] upon request sufficient information to enable geographic licensees to calculate the site-based station's protected contour.'"[8]

On December 22, 2011, the District Court dismissed plaintiffs' FCA claims pursuant to Federal Rule of Civil Procedure 12(b)(6).[9] On Count I, the District Court held that 47 C.F.R. § 80.385 and the Cooperation Orders do not constitute "orders" under the meaning of § 401(b) because they do not require defendants to engage in any particular disclosure of their contour information. On Count II, the [—9—] District Court held that the FCC had not yet addressed whether the precise type of conduct at issue here was "unjust or unreasonable" and therefore plaintiffs had no private right of action under §§ 206 and 207.

MCLM subsequently moved for summary judgment on the remaining claim. Plaintiffs sought to reopen discovery pursuant to Rule 56(d). At this point, the other defendants had stopped actively litigating the case. Mobex had become defunct and had had default entered against it in February 2013; PSI and

Touch Tel entered into a settlement agreement with plaintiffs on April 8, 2013. On March 20, 2014, the District Court denied both MCLM's motion for summary judgment and plaintiffs' Rule 56(d) motion.

The bench trial began on May 20, 2014, and proved contentious. Prior to trial, plaintiffs sought to admit 6,500 trial exhibits but then revised the list to 522 exhibits, and were eventually ordered to limit the list further. Six witnesses testified, including two plaintiffs' experts who described advances in accident avoidance in railroad transportation. Warren Havens also testified on behalf of all plaintiffs. Additional witnesses were Sandra DePriest, MCLM founder; Donald DePriest, her husband and a communications business-man; and John Reardon, former Mobex Communications president, CEO, and general counsel. The parties also submitted excerpts of deposition testimony of David Kling, a Touch Tel engineer; David Predmore, a former Mobex Communications and Mobex Network in-house attorney; and Robert Cooper, Touch Tel's president. The nine-day bench trial concluded on June 10, 2014.

Almost a month after the parties had submitted proposed findings of fact and conclusions of law, plaintiffs [—10—] wrote to the District Court to appraise it of "certain new and material information." Plaintiffs attached MCLM's responses to interrogatories served by the FCC, in which MCLM stated that it had abandoned many of its sites prior to May 12, 2012, and December 2, 2013. Plaintiffs claim that, had MCLM disclosed this previously, plaintiffs would have been significantly less hindered in their build-out plans for their geographic stations. According to plaintiffs, "the only credible reason for MCLM not so advising plaintiffs was to uphold, and keep hidden, MCLM's contribution to its antitrust conspiracy with PSI."

On September 2, 2014, the District Court found in favor of MCLM on the basis that plaintiffs had failed to show by a preponderance of the evidence that a

---

[7] In re Applications of Ne. Utils. Serv. Co. to Modify License for Station WQEJ718, 24 FCC Rcd. 3310, 3311 n.12 (2009) (NUSCO Order).

[8] In re Maritime Commc'ns/Land Mobile, LLC Warren Havens, Envtl. LLC, Intelligent Transp. & Monitoring LLC, Skybridge Spectrum Found., 25 FCC Rcd. 3805, 3807 ¶ 6 (2010) (Reconsideration Order) (quoting Letter, 24 FCC Rcd. at 4136 n.9).

[9] See Havens v. Mobex Network Servs., LLC, No. 11-993, 2011 WL 6826104 (D.N.J. Dec. 22, 2011).

conspiracy existed.[10] "Put another way, were the Court as factfinder presented with [this] question in a typical verdict sheet given to the jury in a Sherman Act § 1 case, . . . the Court would answer, easily, No."[11] Because plaintiffs lost on the merits, the court dismissed the default judgment against Mobex as well.

II.[12] [—11—]

A. PRIVATE ENFORCEMENT OF FCC ORDERS

Section 401(b) of the FCA gives private individuals an express right to enforce FCC "orders." This provision authorizes injunctive relief for any party injured where another party "fails or neglects to obey any order of the Commission other than for the payment of money."[13] Plaintiffs seek a court order directing MCLM to provide them with contour information for its site-based AMTS stations. However, plaintiffs are entitled to a remedy only if the provisions of 47 C.F.R. § 80.385(b)(1) or the so-called Cooperation Orders constitute "orders" within the meaning of § 401(b).

---

[10] *See Havens v. Maritime Commc'ns/Land Mobile, LLC*, No. 11-993, 2014 WL 4352300 (D.N.J. Sept. 2, 2014).

[11] *Id.* at *30.

[12] The District Court had subject matter jurisdiction pursuant to 28 U.S.C. §§ 1331 and 1337, and we exercise jurisdiction pursuant to 28 U.S.C. § 1291. We exercise plenary review over a district court's grant of a motion to dismiss for failure to state a claim under Rule 12(b)(6). *See Farber v. City of [—11—] Paterson*, 440 F.3d 131, 134 (3d Cir. 2006). "A motion to dismiss pursuant to Rule 12(b)(6) may be granted only if, accepting all well pleaded allegations in the complaint as true, and viewing them in the light most favorable to plaintiff, plaintiff is not entitled to relief." *In re Burlington Coat Factory Sec. Litig.*, 114 F.3d 1410, 1420 (3d Cir. 1997). "We review the District Court's factual finding from the non-jury trial under a clearly erroneous standard . . .." *Gordon v. Lewistown Hosp.*, 423 F.3d 184, 201 (3d Cir. 2005). When we are confronted with mixed questions of law and fact, however, "we apply the clearly erroneous standard except that the District Court's choice and interpretation of legal precepts remain subject to plenary review." *Id.*

[13] 47 U.S.C. § 401(b).

We previously addressed the definition of an "order" under § 401(b) in *Mallenbaum v. Adelphia Communications Corp.*[14] There, the plaintiffs challenged Adelphia's monthly [—12—] fee to cable subscribers who received programming on more than one television set. The monthly fee was based on 47 C.F.R. § 76.923, which requires that charges for multiple outlets be based on actual cost.[15] In analyzing whether the plaintiffs had an express right of action under § 401(b), we began by considering the Supreme Court's decision in *Columbia Broadcasting System, Inc. v. United States.*[16] Although *CBS* interpreted a different provision of the FCA, we identified from it the general principle that "an agency regulation should be considered an 'order' if it requires a defendant to take concrete actions."[17] We then outlined the circuit split in applying this principle,[18] but declined to [—13—] choose between the two approaches because the plaintiffs lost under either test.[19] Specifically, 47 C.F.R. § 76.923

---

[14] 74 F.3d 465 (3d Cir. 1996).

[15] *Id.* at 467.

[16] 316 U.S. 407 (1942).

[17] *Mallenbaum*, 74 F.3d at 468 (citing *CBS*, 316 U.S. at 416-25).

[18] Currently, the Fourth, Fifth, Sixth, Seventh, and Ninth Circuits expressly or implicitly hold that "order" encompasses both FCC adjudicatory and rulemaking orders, *see Lansdowne on the Potomac Homeowners Ass'n, Inc. v. OpenBand at Lansdowne, LLC*, 713 F.3d 187, 200-01 (4th Cir. 2013); *Alltel Tenn., Inc. v. Tenn. Pub. Serv. Comm'n*, 913 F.2d 305, 308 (6th Cir. 1990); *Hawaiian Tel. Co. v. Pub. Utils. Comm'n*, 827 F.2d 1264, 1271 (9th Cir. 1987); *Ill. Bell Tel., Co. v. Ill. Commerce Comm'n*, 740 F.2d 566, 571 (7th Cir. 1984); *S. Cent. Bell Tel. Co. v. La. Pub. Serv. Comm'n*, 744 F.2d 1107, 1115-19 (5th Cir. 1984), *vacated and remanded on other grounds by* 476 U.S. 1166 (1986), whereas, the First Circuit requires that an "order" be judicial in nature, *see New England Tele. and Tele. Co. v. Pub. Utils. Comm'n*, 742 F.2d 1, 4-8 (1st Cir. 1984). Much of this disagreement stems from the question of whether a court [—13—] should rely on the Administrative Procedure Act's definition of "order," which is limited to "a final disposition . . . in a matter other than rule making." *See* 5 U.S.C. § 551(6).

[19] *Mallenbaum*, 74 F.3d at 468 n.5 ("We need not choose between the First Circuit and Ninth Circuit approaches, for, even assuming *arguendo*

does not order cable operators to charge specific rates; rather, it offers "guidelines to be followed by local franchising authorities" and "[did] not itself require particular actions to be taken by defendant Adelphia."[20]

As in *Mallenbaum*, we will not adopt either approach to defining "order" under § 401(b) because 47 C.F.R. § 80.385(b)(1) and the Cooperation Orders fail under both standards. For its part, § 80.385 does not address a site-based licensee's duty to provide contour information. In fact, it is focused solely on the obligation of a geographic licensee to protect the site-based licensee's rights by adhering to certain requirements, and imposes no obligations on site-based licensees.[21] While the rule may "presuppose" that a site-based licensee will provide a geographic licensee its coordinates to safeguard its own interests, such an assumption cannot form the basis of an enforceable "order" under § [—14—] 401(b). Since 47 C.F.R. § 80.385(b)(1) imposes no duties on MCLM, it does not afford plaintiffs a remedy.[22]

Similarly, the Cooperation Orders do not impose any obligations on MCLM. Most of the language highlighted by plaintiffs describes the FCC's mere expectation that site-based and geographic licensees will cooperate with one another.[23] This makes sense considering

that the documents were not intended to address a site-based licensee's obligations. Like § 80.385, the Cooperation Orders describe a geographic licensee's duty to a site-based licensee: the first and third documents provide the procedure for determining the necessary level of interference protection and the second document resolves a dispute concerning interference. Only in dicta—indeed, relegated mostly to footnotes—did the FCC describe any duty owed by site-based licensees. We do not view this language as creating any binding or enforceable requirement under § 401(b). [—15—]

Furthermore, even if the Cooperation Orders require MCLM to take some action, that action is not sufficiently concrete. The FCC requested that site-based licensees, "at a minimum, provid[e] upon request sufficient information to enable geographic licensees to calculate the site-based station's protected contour."[24] This language says nothing about how any alleged obligation should be undertaken: When, and in what matter, must the information be provided? In fact, the FCC described cooperation as needed "in order to avoid and resolve interference issues,"[25] implying that disclosure of contour information may occur only *after* an interference issue arises.

We therefore reiterate that vague statements by the FCC, particularly when made in dictum, cannot form the basis of an "order" under § 401(b). Because neither 47 C.F.R. § 80.385(b)(1) nor the so-called Cooperation Orders constitute an "order," we

---

that some rules may be considered orders under § 401(b), the FCC rule at issue here may not.").

[20] *Id.* at 469.

[21] 47 C.F.R. § 80.385(b)(1) ("[E]ach AMTS geographic area licensee may place stations anywhere within its region without obtaining prior Commission approval provided: (1) The AMTS geographic area licensee must locate its stations at least 120 kilometers from the stations of co-channel site-based AMTS licensees . . . .").

[22] *See Mallenbaum*, 74 F.3d at 469; *see generally CBS*, 316 U.S. at 416-25.

[23] *See, e.g., Letter*, 24 FCC Rcd. at 4136 n.9 ("[W]e expect incumbent AMTS licensees to cooperate with geographic licensees in order to avoid and resolve interference issues." (internal quotations omitted)); *NUSCO Order*, 24 FCC Rcd. at 3311 n.12 ("AMTS site-based incumbents are expected to cooperate with geographic licensees in order to avoid and resolve interference issues."); *Reconsideration Order*, 25 FCC Rcd. at 3807 ¶ 6 ("AMTS site-based licensees are expected to

cooperate with geographic licensees in avoiding and resolving interference issues . . . .").

[24] *Letter*, 24 FCC Rcd. at 4136 n.9; *NUSCO Order*, 24 FCC Rcd. at 3311 n.12; *see Reconsideration Order*, 25 FCC Rcd. at 3807 ¶ 6.

[25] *Letter*, 24 FCC Rcd. at 4136 n.9; *NUSCO Order*, 24 FCC Rcd. at 3311 n.12; *see Reconsideration Order*, 25 FCC Rcd. at 3807 ¶ 6; *see also In re Amendment of the Commission's Rules Concerning Maritime Communications, Second Memorandum Opinion and Order and Fifth Report and Order*, 17 FCC Rcd. 6685, 6704 ¶ 39 (2002) ("In instances where interference occurs, we will expect the licensees to coordinate among themselves to minimize such interference and to cooperate to resolve any interference problems that may arise.").

will affirm the District Court's dismissal of Count I. [—16—]

B. PRIVATE ACTIONS UNDER SECTION 207.

Under 47 U.S.C. § 207, any person damaged by a common carrier may either make a complaint to the FCC or sue in district court for "the recovery of the damages for which such common carrier may be liable under the provisions of this chapter." Common carriers, such as MCLM, are liable if they "do, or cause or permit to be done, any act, matter, or thing in this chapter prohibited or declared to be unlawful, or shall omit to do any act, matter, or thing in this chapter required to be done."[26] Plaintiffs claim that MCLM violated § 201(b), which declares that all practices in connection with common carrier service shall be "just and reasonable" and that any "unjust or unreasonable [practice] is declared to be unlawful."[27]

A plaintiff is not entitled to a cause of action under § 207 simply on the basis of its own determination that conduct was "unjust or unreasonable." In *Global Crossing Telecommunications, Inc. v. Metrophones Telecommunications, Inc.*, the Supreme Court considered whether a payphone operator could bring a federal claim under § 207 on the basis of the FCC's determination that "a carrier's refusal to pay the compensation ordered amounts to an 'unreasonable practice' within the terms of § 201(b)."[28] [—17—] The Court held that a private lawsuit is proper under § 207 only "*if* the FCC could properly hold that a carrier's failure to pay compensation is an 'unreasonable practice' deemed 'unlawful' under § 201(b)."[29] Here, plaintiffs do not rely on any regulation determining that the particular type of actions taken by MCLM were "unjust or unreasonable" under the

meaning of § 201(b). Instead, plaintiffs assert that such a finding is unnecessary based on the FCA's grant of a broad private remedy and "the Supreme Court's intentional use of the phrase '*could* properly hold' instead of '*did* properly hold'" in *Global Crossing*.[30] We do not agree.

In creating § 201(b), Congress "delegated to the agency authority to 'fill' a 'gap,' *i.e.*, to apply § 201 through regulations and orders with the force of law."[31] Although § 201(b)'s language is certainly broad, its purpose is to empower the FCC to declare unlawful certain common carrier practices.[32] Nothing in the statute implies that violations of [—18—] all FCC regulations amount to unjust or unreasonable practices, and plaintiffs point to no authority supporting such an interprettation. Furthermore, adopting plaintiffs' approach would "put interpretation of a finely-tuned regulatory scheme squarely in the hands of private parties and some 700 federal district judges, instead of in the hands of the Commission."[33] It strains reason to believe that Congress intended such a result. A more common sense reading of the statute is that the FCC must first determine that a particular type of practice constitutes an "unjust or unreasonable" practice under § 201(b) before a plaintiff may bring a cause of

---

[26] 47 U.S.C. § 206.

[27] Plaintiffs identify many other FCC rules and orders that Defendants allegedly violated, but they confine their appeal to the question of whether the conduct underlying these violations was "unjust or unreasonable" under § 201(b).

[28] 550 U.S. 47, 52 (2007) (internal quotations omitted).

[29] *Id.* at 52-53.

[30] *See* Pls.' Br. at 55-57 (emphasis added in brief).

[31] *Global Crossing*, 550 U.S. at 57; *see Nat'l Cable & Telecomms. Ass'n v. Brand X Internet Servs.*, 545 U.S. 967, 980-81 (2005) ("[Section 201(b)] give[s] the Commission the authority to promulgate binding legal rules . . . .").

[32] *See* 47 U.S.C. § 201(b) ("All charges, practices, classifications, and regulations for and in connection with such communication service, shall be just and reasonable, and any such charge, practice, classification, or regulation that is unjust or unreasonable is declared to be unlawful. . . . *Provided*, That communications by wire or radio subject to this chapter may be classified . . . as the Commission may decide to be just and reasonable . . . . The Commission may prescribe such rules and regulations as may be necessary in [—18—] the public interest to carry out the provisions of this chapter.").

[33] *N. Cnty. Comm'ns Corp. v. Cal. Catalog & Tech.*, 594 F.3d 1149, 1158 (9th Cir. 2010) (internal quotations omitted).

action under § 207 on the basis of that conduct.

Although *Global Crossing* did not state that there must be an FCC ruling deeming the conduct at issue "unjust or unreasonable," an FCC determination was critical to its analysis. The Court first noted that "the FCC has long implemented § 201(b) through the issuance of rules and regulations."[34] It then considered the more "difficult question" of "whether the particular FCC regulation . . . lawfully implements § 201(b)'s 'unreasonable practice' prohibition."[35] Applying the *Chevron* framework, the Court held that the FCC properly implemented § 201(b) due to its reasonable determination that failure to abide by its rate [—19—] determinations was an unjust or unreasonable action.[36] In other words, the question of lawful implementation was premised on there being an FCC finding in the first place. Moreover, the Court carefully limited its holding by stating that not "every violation of FCC regulations is an unjust and unreasonable practice."[37] Although the Court used the phrase "if the FCC could properly hold" instead of "if the FCC did properly hold," its emphasis in the sentence—and throughout the opinion—was on "*if*" the FCC's determination was proper.[38] We therefore do not agree that, by using one turn of phrase, the Court sanctioned such an expansive reading of the FCA.

We will affirm the District Court's dismissal of Count II because plaintiffs do not identify any particular actions taken by MCLM that have been determined by the FCC to be unreasonable or unjust. Therefore,

plaintiffs do not possess a private right of action under § 207.[39] [—20—]

C. CONCERTED ACTION.

Section 1 of the Sherman Act provides that "[e]very contract, combination in the form of trust or otherwise, or conspiracy, in restraint of trade or commerce among the several States, or with foreign nations, is hereby declared to be illegal."[40] "The existence of an agreement is the hallmark of a Section 1 claim."[41] For liability under § 1 to exist, there must be a "unity of purpose or a common design and understanding or a meeting of the minds in an unlawful arrangement."[42] This can be shown by putting forth direct evidence of concerted action, such as "a document or conversation explicitly manifesting the existence of the agreement in question,"[43] or circumstantial evidence of [—21—] conscious parallel conduct and other "plus factors."[44] The term "plus factors" refers to circumstances demonstrating that the wrongful conduct "was conscious and not the result of independent business decisions of the competitors."[45]

---

[34] *Global Crossing*, 550 U.S. at 53.

[35] *Id.* at 54-55.

[36] *Id.* at 55-57; *see id.* at 60 ("[T]he FCC properly implements § 201(b) when it reasonably finds that the failure to follow a Commission, *e.g.*, rate or rate-division determination made under a *different* statutory provision is unjust or unreasonable under § 201(b).").

[37] *Id.* at 56.

[38] *See id.* at 53 ("Insofar as the statute's language is concerned, to violate a regulation that lawfully implements § 201(b)'s requirements *is* to violate the statute.").

[39] The FCC need not have declared a particular defendant's actions unreasonable in a prior adjudication. In *Demmick v. Cellco Partnership*, Verizon argued that claims under § 201(b), prior to being filed in federal court, "must be brought to the Federal Communications Commission . . . for a [—20—] determination regarding the reasonableness of the challenged conduct." No. 06-2163, 2011 WL 1253733, at *2 (D.N.J. Mar. 29, 2011). The court rejected this argument based, in part, on the fact that there was no prior adjudication in *Global Crossing*. *Id.* at *4-5. But, in *Global Crossing*, the FCC announced through general rulemaking that a particular type of practice was unjust or unreasonable. This, too, is all our holding today requires in order to maintain a cause of action.

[40] 15 U.S.C. § 1.

[41] *In re Baby Food Antitrust Litig.*, 166 F.3d 112, 117 (3d Cir. 1999).

[42] *Alvord-Polk, Inc. v. F. Schumacher & Co.*, 37 F.3d 996, 999 (3d Cir. 1994) (internal quotations omitted).

[43] *See In re Ins. Brokerage Antitrust Litig.*, 618 F.3d 300, 324 n.23 (3d Cir. 2010).

[44] *See In re Flat Glass Antitrust Litig.*, 385 F.3d 350, 360 & n.11 (3d Cir. 2004).

[45] *Baby Food*, 166 F.3d at 122.

Plaintiffs' direct evidence of concerted action at trial was an alleged agreement that was reached during a conversation over twenty-five years ago between Touch Tel's president Cooper and a businessman named Fred Daniel. Daniel is the founder of Regionet, a marine radio provider that was later acquired by Mobex. According to plaintiffs, Cooper and Daniel agreed to split up the market for geographic licenses, whereby Regionet would only bid on A block licenses and PSI and Touch Tel would only bid on B block licenses. Plaintiffs further alleged that knowledge of this conspiracy passed to Mobex employees after Regionet was acquired in 2000, and then to MCLM after it purchased Mobex's licenses in 2005. Plaintiffs also sought to prove the existence of concerted action by virtue of certain plus factors, including that defendants refused to provide contour information, did not construct or operate their stations, and took actions not in their individual economic interests.

On appeal, plaintiffs mainly quibble with the District Court's conclusion that no agreement existed. Notably absent from this discussion is any recitation or application of the clearly erroneous standard of review, which must guide our analysis. A finding of fact is clearly erroneous only if it is "completely devoid of minimum evidentiary support [—22—] displaying some hue of credibility or bears no rational relationship to the supportive evidentiary data."[46] In an extensive 59-page opinion, the District Court examined all of the evidence and provided more than ample support for its conclusion that no concerted action existed. The District Court first found that Daniel and Cooper's early conversation illustrated only "a course of action that Daniel and his company intended to take, which arguably warned Cooper off of pursuing the same course" and did not amount to direct evidence of market-allocation.[47] As to any evidence that such an agreement continued, the District Court found the evidence speculative, only showing an opportunity for, not the existence of, an

unlawful agreement.[48] Lastly, the District Court determined that the alleged plus factors did not amount to evidence that a meeting of the minds existed.[49] We find no clear error in the District Court's factual findings.

Plaintiffs argue that the District Court applied an improper standard of proof in its treatment of the plus factors. Specifically, plaintiffs cite cases in which we found that the sharing of confidential information between horizontal competitors could indicate that a conspiracy existed.[50] But, in those cases, we were asked to review a district court's grant of summary judgment, when the facts must be viewed in the [—23—] light most favorable to the non-moving party and all reasonable inferences must be drawn in that party's favor. In other words, we held that the sharing of confidential information *may* be evidence of a conspiracy, not that it *must* be. Here, the District Court properly denied summary judgment and allowed the claims to proceed to trial. At trial, the court was then tasked with evaluating the credibility of the witnesses and weighing the evidence that plaintiffs actually put forth. The court's findings were made on this basis.

Plaintiffs claim that the District Court erred further by crediting the testimony of MCLM's key witnesses despite plaintiffs' after-trial submission, which allegedly demonstrates that those witnesses lied at trial. As a preliminary matter, plaintiffs do not clarify how the District Court should have treated this evidence. They included no formal request for relief in their August 22, 2014, letter, seeking only consideration of MCLM's interrogatory responses as additional evidence of conspiracy. It appears that the District Court did just that but was not persuaded. And rightfully so: Rather than offering "new and material" information, this submission repeated the same unsubstantiated and largely irrelevant arguments plaintiffs made at the bench trial. We therefore find no clear

---

[46] *Berg Chilling Sys., Inc. v. Hull Corp.*, 369 F.3d 745, 754 (3d Cir. 2004) (internal quotations omitted).

[47] *Havens*, 2014 WL 4352300, at *17.

[48] *See id.* at *20-22.

[49] *See id.* at *22-30.

[50] *See, e.g., Flat Glass*, 385 F.3d 350; *Baby Food*, 166 F.3d 122; *Petruzzi's IGA Supermarkets, Inc. v. Darling-Delaware Co.*, 998 F.2d 1224 (3d Cir. 1993).

error in the District Court's decision to credit the testimony of MCLM's witnesses.

III. CONCLUSION.

For the foregoing reasons, we will affirm the District Court's dismissal of Counts I and II pursuant to Rule 12(b)(6) and its entry of judgment in favor of MCLM on Count III.

United States Court of Appeals
for the Third Circuit

No. 15-1498

IN RE WORLD IMPORTS, LTD.

Appeal from the United States District Court for the
Eastern District of Pennsylvania

Decided: April 20, 2016

Citation: 820 F.3d 576, 4 Adm. R. 132 (3d Cir. 2016).

Before **McKEE,** Chief Judge, **JORDAN,** and
VANASKIE, Circuit Judges.

[—3—] JORDAN, Circuit Judge:

In a bankruptcy proceeding, OEC Group, New York ("OEC") asserted maritime liens on goods then in its possession, and it now appeals a ruling of the United States District Court for the Eastern District of Pennsylvania that certain contractual modifications to those liens were unenforceable. Because we conclude that the modifications were enforceable as to goods then in OEC's possession, we will reverse and remand for the District Court to craft an appropriate remedy.

I. Background

Although the parties dispute the legal consequences of the facts, what happened is not in dispute. World Imports, Ltd., World Imports Chicago, LLC, World Imports South, LLC, and 11000 LLC (collectively, "World Imports")[1] are business entities **[A 206]** that buy furniture wholesale and sell it to retail distributors. OEC provided non-vessel-operating common carrier transportation services[2] to World Imports for approximately five years, including services to ensure that cargo was delivered from countries of origin to World Imports' warehouse or to other United States destinations designated by World Imports. [—4—]

A. Supporting Documents

On or about January 26, 2009, World Imports, Ltd. entered into an Application for Credit with OEC (the "Application"). Page two of the Application, titled "Notice Concerning Limitation of Liability," was signed by the vice president of World Imports, Ltd. and included the following language:

> [OEC] has adopted general terms and conditions of service. These terms and conditions are printed on the back of or accompany every invoice issued by [OEC] and are incorporated herein by reference. … When [OEC] is acting as a carrier, the exact limits of liability and the other terms and conditions of carriage can be located on the ocean bill of lading or other shipping document such as the airway bill issued by the carrier (which is the contract between the parties). Unless modified or superseded by the terms of the bill of lading or other contract of carriage, [OEC's] general terms and conditions of service will also apply to the transaction. However, the terms of the bill of lading prevail in all cases.

(A 40.)

Page three of the Application, titled "Terms for Credit Accounts," was signed by the bookkeeper of World Imports, Ltd. and said: [—5—]

> Specific terms and conditions of service … apply to the services performed by [OEC]. These terms and conditions are established by contract as set forth in the governing instrument or by operation of law. [OEC's] standard payment terms require receipt of cash in advance of performance. In the event that [OEC] extends credit to [World Imports], which is defined as permitting [World Imports] to pay for service within a specified period of time after

---

[1] For convenience we refer to the several World Imports debtor-entities together in the singular.

[2] A non-vessel-operating common carrier "is a consolidator who acts as a carrier by arranging for the transportation of goods from port to port." *Logistics Mgmt., Inc. v. One (1) Pyramid Tent Arena*, 86 F.3d 908, 911 n.1 (9th Cir. 1996) (internal quotation and editorial marks omitted).

performance by [OEC], [World Imports] agrees that the following additional terms are applicable. ...

As security for *any existing and future indebtedness* of [World Imports] to [OEC], including claims for charges, expenses or advances incurred by [OEC] in connection with any shipment or transaction of [World Imports], and whether or not presently contemplated by [World Imports] and [OEC], [World Imports] hereby grants to [OEC] a general lien and security interest in any and all property of [World Imports] (including goods and documents relating thereto) then or thereafter in [OEC's] possession, custody or control or en route (the "Collateral"). This general lien and security interest shall be in addition to any other rights [OEC] has or may acquire under other agreements and/or applicable law, *and shall survive delivery or release of any specific property* of [World Imports]. ... **[—6—]**

(A 37 (emphasis added).)

For each container of goods it transported for World Imports, OEC provided to World Imports an invoice (the "Invoice") which contained, in its "Terms and Conditions of Service," the following provisions:

These terms and conditions constitute a legally binding contract between the "Company" [*i.e.,* OEC] and the "Customer" [*i.e.,* World Imports].

...

14. General Lien and Right to Sell Customer's Property.

(a) Company shall have a general and continuing lien on any and all property of Customer coming into Company's actual or constructive possession or control for monies owed to Company with regard to the shipment on which the lien is claimed, *a prior shipment*(s) and/or both ... .

(A 42 (emphasis added).)

As required by federal law, OEC also publishes a tariff (the "Tariff") with the Federal Maritime Commission, which governs its shipments. Included with the Tariff is a Bill of Lading whose terms and conditions provide, in pertinent part, as follows: **[—7—]**

17. CARRIER'S LIEN

The Carrier shall have a lien on the Goods, inclusive of any Container owned or leased by the Merchant and on all equipment and appurtenances thereto, as well as on any Charges[3] due any other person, and on any documents relating thereto, *which lien shall survive delivery, for all sums due under this contract or any other contract or undertaking to which the Merchant was party* or otherwise involved, including, but not limited to, General Average contributions, salvage and the cost of recovering such sums, inclusive of attorney's fees. Such lien may be enforced by the Carrier by public or private sale at the expense of and without notice to the Merchant.

(A 54-55 (emphasis added).)[4] **[—8—]**

---

[3] As defined in the Tariff, "Goods" referred to "the cargo received from the shipper" and "Charges" referred to "freight, deadfreight, demurrage and all expenses and money obligations incurred and payable by the Merchant." (A 43.)

[4] The record does not reflect the relationship of the various World Imports entities to one another, nor whether representatives from all of those entities signed credit applications similar to the Application executed by World Imports, Ltd. Indeed, World Imports has argued that, because one page of the Application was signed by a bookkeeper, none of the World Imports entities is bound by that document. However, in the briefing and argument before us, World Imports has never taken issue with OEC's assertion that all **[—8—]** the World Imports entities are effectively bound by the contractual provisions of the Invoice and Tariff, both of which grant, like the Application, a continuing lien as security for past debts. For purposes of our analysis, therefore, we take it as given that all of the World Imports entities are bound, at the very least, by the Invoice and the

B. Procedural Background

On July 3, 2013 (the "Petition Date"), World Imports filed voluntary petitions for relief in the Bankruptcy Court pursuant to Chapter 11 of Title 11 of the United States Code (the "Bankruptcy Code"). OEC promptly filed a motion for relief from the automatic stay imposed by Bankruptcy Code § 362(a). It argued that it was a secured creditor with a possessory maritime lien on World Imports' goods in its possession and was entitled to refuse to release such goods unless and until certain prepetition claims were satisfied. As exhibits to its motion, OEC provided documentation that, as of July 10, 2013, the total amount owed to OEC by World Imports was $1,452,956. Of that amount, $458,251 was the estimated freight and related charges due on containers then in OEC's possession (the "Landed Goods"). The remaining $994,705 consisted of freight and related charges associated with goods for which OEC had previously provided transportation services (the "Prepetition Goods"). OEC estimated the total value of World Imports' goods then in OEC's possession was approximately $1,926,363.

World Imports responded by filing an adversary proceeding against OEC and a motion for an expedited [—9—] hearing to compel OEC to turn over all of World Imports' "Current Goods," which World Imports defined to include both the Landed Goods and goods then in transit for which OEC was to provide delivery in the near future. (A 60.) World Imports represented its willingness to pay OEC for the freight charges on those Current Goods but not for the outstanding charges associated with the Prepetition Goods. After a hearing, the Bankruptcy Court granted the injunctive relief sought by World Imports, ordering that:

> Pursuant to 11 U.S.C. §[]542, [World Imports is] entitled to immediate delivery and possession of the Current Goods and Defendant OEC shall immediately account for and deliver the Current Goods to [World Imports];
>
> ...
>
> Upon Defendant OEC's delivery of the Current Goods to [World Imports], [World Imports] shall pay Defendant OEC: (a) the regular freight charges on the Current Goods; (b) documented demurrage/retention charges.

(A 105.) After OEC timely filed its notice of appeal from the Bankruptcy Court's order, that court issued an opinion in support of its order. *See In re World Imports, Ltd. Inc.*, 498 B.R. 58 (Bankr. E.D. Pa. 2013).

OEC did not seek a stay of the Bankruptcy Court's order. Rather, on appeal to the District Court, it requested entry of an order requiring World Imports to pay all outstanding amounts due for OEC's transportation services or, in the alternative, providing OEC with "valid, fully [—10—] enforceable replacement liens on assets of [World Imports] in the amount of $1,926,363." (A 243.) The District Court ordered the parties to brief "whether the specific contract at issue between the parties created a maritime lien ... ." (A 299.) After that briefing, the Court entered an order on January 22, 2015, affirming the order of the Bankruptcy Court. Specifically, the District Court held that OEC did not possess a valid maritime lien on the Prepetition Goods because "the provisions in OEC's contract with [World Imports] purporting to give OEC a lien on goods in its possession for freight charges for the Prepetition Goods [are] unenforceable." *World Imports, Ltd. v. OEC Group New York*, 526 B.R. 127, 135 (E.D. Pa. 2015). Accordingly, OEC could not assert a maritime lien to supersede interests secured according to the Uniform Commercial Code as adopted in various jurisdictions. *Id.* at 136. OEC timely appealed. [—11—]

Tariff, and that the primary issue is the legal effect of the agreements reflected in those documents.

II. DISCUSSION[5]

OEC frames its appeal as a single question, namely, whether the Bankruptcy Court and District Court erred in holding that the contract provisions at issue, which purported to give OEC maritime liens on goods in its possession both for freight charges on those goods and for unpaid charges on prior shipments, were unenforceable. In its response, World Imports has added the further question of whether OEC's failure to obtain a stay of the Bankruptcy Court's order renders the appeal moot. We address the latter question first.

A. Mootness

World Imports argues that OEC's appeal should be dismissed as constitutionally moot because OEC failed to obtain a stay of the Bankruptcy Court's order and, instead, fully complied with that order by releasing the Current Goods [—12—] to World Imports in exchange for payment for the charges on those goods. That argument, however, fails to account for remedies that may still be granted to OEC. As we observed in *In re Continental Airlines,*

> an appeal is moot in the constitutional sense only if events have taken place during the pendency of the appeal that make it impossible for the court to grant any effectual relief whatsoever. An appeal is not moot merely because a court cannot restore the parties to the

status quo ante. Rather, when a court can fashion some form of meaningful relief, even if it only partially redresses the grievances of the prevailing party, the appeal is not moot.

91 F.3d 553, 558 (3d Cir. 1996) (internal quotation marks omitted); *see also Church of Scientology of California v. United States,* 506 U.S. 9, 12 (1992). In this case, although OEC complied with the Bankruptcy Court's order by delivering the Current Goods, it has asked for relief that would remedy its loss from the surrender of those goods, specifically, a court order either requiring World Imports to pay its outstanding debts to OEC or granting OEC enforceable replacement liens on other assets of World Imports. Because we are not precluded from granting any effective relief, OEC's appeal is not moot.[6] [—13—]

B. Whether OEC Held a Valid Maritime Lien

The District Court concluded, and World Imports does not dispute, that a valid maritime lien would supersede any UCC security interests that may exist in the World Imports cargo. World Imports also concedes that OEC possessed a valid maritime lien on the Current Goods "for the actual freight charges associated with the Current Goods."[7]

---

[5] Pursuant to 28 U.S.C. § 1334(b), the Bankruptcy Court had jurisdiction over the adversary proceeding, which was a core proceeding under 28 U.S.C. §§ 157(b)(2)(A), (E), and (O). Pursuant to 28 U.S.C. §§ 158(a) and 1292(a), the District Court had jurisdiction over the appeal from the Bankruptcy Court's order granting injunctive relief. We have appellate jurisdiction to review the decision of the District Court pursuant to 28 U.S.C. § 1291. In our review, we "exercise the same standard of review as the District Court when it reviewed the original appeal from the Bankruptcy Court. Thus, we review the Bankruptcy Court's findings of fact for clear error and exercise plenary review over the Bankruptcy Court's legal determinations." *In re Handel,* 570 F. 3d 140, 141 (3d Cir. 2009) (citation omitted).

[6] Although World Imports cites *Continental Airlines* for the authority that failure to seek a stay may, in some circumstances, justify dismissal of an appeal, the language on which it relies was describing not constitutional but equitable [—13—] mootness, *see Continental,* 91 F.3d at 558, which is not at issue here.

[7] OEC cites numerous authorities to establish that, as a non-vessel-operating common carrier contracting primarily to transport goods by sea, its contracts with World Imports were maritime contracts. Moreover, OEC argues that, although it does not physically transport goods, it takes legal responsibility for their transportation and thus "is treated by the law as a bona fide carrier entitled to assert a maritime lien on cargo." (Appellant's Br. 13 n.4 (citing *Logistics Mgmt.,* 86 F.3d at 913-15).) Although World Imports disputes that its contracts with OEC, by themselves, created maritime liens, it does not dispute that OEC's role as a non-vessel-operating common carrier created maritime liens arising by operation of law.

(Appellees' Br. 10 n.5.) Thus, the only dispute is whether OEC held a valid maritime lien for charges associated with the Prepetition Goods.

1. Maritime Liens Generally

"A maritime lien is a privileged claim upon maritime property, such as a vessel, arising out of services rendered to [—14—] or injuries caused by that property." 1 Thomas J. Schoenbaum, *Adm. and Mar. Law* § 9-1, at 683 (5th ed. 2011). Maritime liens are a security device intended "to keep ships moving in commerce while preventing them from escaping their debts by sailing away." *Id.* at 684-85. Thus, such a lien attaches to the maritime property from the moment a debt arises, and adheres, even through changes in the property's ownership, until extinguished by operation of law. *Id.* at 683.

Because maritime liens enjoy a special priority status and may operate without notice, courts are hesitant to recognize new forms of them or new circumstances under which such liens may arise. *See Osaka Shosen Kaisha v. Pacific Export Lumber Co.*, 260 U.S. 490, 499 (1923) ("The maritime privilege or lien, though adhering to the vessel, is a secret one which may operate to the prejudice of general creditors and purchasers without notice and is therefore stricti juris and cannot be extended by construction, analogy or inference." (citing *Vandewater v. Mills, Claimant of Yankee Blade*, 60 U.S. 82 (1856))). Federal courts nevertheless "have full authority to update old doctrines and to recognize new forms of liens if warranted by new conditions." *Logistics Mgmt., Inc. v. One (1) Pyramid Tent Arena*, 86 F.3d 908, 913 n.7 (9th Cir. 1996) (internal quotation omitted) (collecting cases).

In much the same way that traditional maritime liens against a ship were based on the legal fiction that the ship was the wrongdoer, *see* 1 Schoenbaum, *supra*, § 9-1, at 683-84, maritime law recognizes a reciprocal claim against the ship's cargo for debts associated with it. [—15—]

Subject to the exception that the lien of the shipowner may be displaced by an

unconditional delivery of the goods before the consignee is required to pay the freight, or by an inconsistent and irreconcilable provision in the charter-party or bill of lading, the rule is universal as understood in the decisions of the Federal courts, that the ship is bound to the merchandise and the merchandise to the ship for the performance on the part of the shipper and shipowner of their respective contracts.

The Maggie Hammond, 76 U.S. (9 Wall.) 435, 449-50 (1869). As the Supreme Court acknowledged in its influential opinion in a case captioned simply *The Bird of Paradise*, such liens on cargo may arise out of contracts to pay freight. 72 U.S. (5 Wall.) 545 (1866); *see also* 2 Thomas A. Russell, *Benedict on Admiralty* § 44, at 3-50 n.2 (7th ed. rev. 2010) (collecting cases).

2. Waiver of Liens for Unpaid Freight

A lien for unpaid freight "arises from the right of the ship-owner to retain the possession of the goods until the freight is paid," and thus is lost upon "*unconditional* delivery to the consignee." *Bird of Paradise*, 72 U.S. at 555 (emphasis added). Yet, because it would frustrate commerce to require shipowners to retain their liens only by actual possession of the implicated cargo,[8] a

---

[8] *See In re 4,885 Bags of Linseed*, 66 U.S. (1 Black) 108, 114 (1861) (emphasis added):

It is in the interest of the ship-owner that his [—16—] vessel should discharge her cargo as speedily as possible after her arrival at the port of delivery. And it would be a serious sacrifice of his interests if the ship was compelled, in order to preserve the lien, to remain day after day with her cargo on board, waiting until the consignee found it convenient to pay the freight, or until the lien could be enforced in a court of admiralty. The consignee, too, in many instances, might desire to see the cargo unladen before he paid the freight, in order to ascertain whether all of the goods mentioned in the bill of lading were on board, and not damaged by the fault of the ship. ... *And if the cargo cannot be unladen and placed in the*

shipowner enjoys a strong [—16—] presumption that, absent a clear indication to the contrary, he has not waived his cargo lien upon delivery of that cargo.⁹ To [—17—] overcome the presumption against waiver, a court determining whether a cargo lien has been waived by unconditional delivery may consider, among other things, whether there was an understanding between the parties regarding retention of the lien either before or at the time the consignee took possession of the cargo,¹⁰ whether there was a [—18—]

---

warehouse of the consignee, without waiving the lien, it would seriously embarrass the ordinary operations and convenience of commerce, both as to the ship-owner and the merchant.

⁹ *See Bird of Paradise*, 72 U.S. at 556 (emphasis added):

Where the stipulation is, that the goods are to be delivered at the port of discharge before the freight is paid, without any condition or qualification, it seems to be agreed that the lien of the ship-owner for the payment of the freight is waived and lost, as the right of lien is inseparably associated with the possession of the goods. Unless the stipulation is, that the [—17—] delivery shall precede the payment of the freight, and the language employed as applied to the subject-matter and the surrounding circumstances is such as clearly to show that the change of possession is to be absolute and unconditional, *the lien is not displaced, as the presumption of law is the other way,* which is never to be regarded as controlled, except in cases where the language employed in the instrument satisfactorily indicates that such is the intention of the parties.

See also N.H. Shipping Corp. v. Freights of the S/S Jackie Hause, 181 F. Supp. 165, 169 (S.D.N.Y. 1960) ("This right of the vessel [to a cargo lien] is so strong in the eyes of the admiralty that it will only be considered relinquished by the most unequivocal and express terms or the most absolute and unconditional surrender." (citing *Bird of Paradise*, 72 U.S. 545)); 1 Schoenbaum, *supra*, § 9-7, at 728-29 ("A lienholder may waive his lien either expressly or by implication, but waiver is not favored, and the courts will require a clearly manifested intention to forego the lien." (internal footnote omitted)).

¹⁰ *See The Eddy*, 72 U.S. (5 Wall.) 481, 495-96 (1866) (affirming that courts will uphold the

stipulation in the contract of affreightment inconsistent with the exercise of a lien, or whether other security was taken when the cargo was discharged. 2 Russell, *supra*, § 44, at 3-52.

Both the Bankruptcy Court and the District Court appear to have assumed, without analysis, that OEC did not merely deliver the Prepetition Goods to World Imports, but did so unconditionally and thus in waiver of its liens on those goods.¹¹ Given the strong presumption against waiver, and in the absence of clear evidence of unconditional delivery, we cannot agree with that assumption. The evidence appears to us to be very much to the contrary. Consistent with the presumption against waiver, both the Application and the Tariff expressly state the understanding of the parties that OEC would hold liens against any World Imports goods in OEC's possession as security for (among other things) charges incurred for any shipment of World Imports goods, and that such liens would "survive delivery." (A 37, 54.) Independent of the question of whether those provisions are fully enforceable in and of themselves, they are compelling evidence that OEC did not clearly intend to waive its cargo liens on the Prepetition Goods by making an unconditional [—19—] delivery of such goods. They show instead that there was an agreement between the parties, for the purpose of perpetuating any such lien, to apply unwaived and unsatisfied liens toward cargo currently in OEC's possession, the cargo essentially taking the place of cargo previously delivered out of OEC's possession. Moreover, this case is akin to *Capitol Transportation, Inc. v. United States*, in which the First Circuit rejected the argument that a

---

parties' agreement that a cargo lien shall survive delivery).

¹¹ See *In re World Imports, Ltd. Inc.*, 498 B.R. 58, 62 (Bankr. E.D. Pa. 2013) (rejecting OEC's reliance on *Bird of Paradise*, emphasizing that that case "*nowhere* explicitly states that a *maritime* lien may be extended by contract to secure goods already shipped and unconditionally released to an owner" (original emphasis)); *World Imports, Ltd. v. OEC Group N.Y.*, 526 B.R. 127, 133 (E.D. Pa. 2015) (referring to the Prepetition Goods as "those already unconditionally delivered").

carrier had waived its liens on prior shipments when it released shipping containers "without providing notice of a continuing lien," noting that "the relevant tariffs in effect in this case provide that such liens survive delivery of the goods." 612 F.2d 1312, 1324-25 (1st Cir. 1979). Those tariffs, the court affirmed, "are considered binding and in essence carry the force of law." *Id.* at 1325. In light of the express language of OEC's Tariff, that case squarely supports the position that OEC did not unconditionally deliver the Prepetition Goods, and hence retained its liens on those goods.

We further note that the persistence of a lien through substitution is not a novel practice, as "[i]t is familiar doctrine of the admiralty courts that a maritime lien attaches not only to the original subject of the lien, but also to whatever is substituted for it, and that the lienholder may follow the proceeds wherever he can distinctly trace them." *Bank of British N. Am. v. Freights, etc., of the Hutton*, 137 F. 534, 536 (2d Cir. 1905). *Cf. N.H. Shipping Corp. v. Freights of the S/S Jackie Hause*, 181 F. Supp. 165, 171 (S.D.N.Y. 1960) (holding that a shipowner had not waived its cargo lien when its release of the cargo was conditioned on the substitution of freight money, held in escrow, for such cargo). [—20—]

World Imports disputes that the parties could have created valid maritime liens entirely through contract, but it has not attempted to dispute that, as a general proposition, OEC's carrier services created enforceable maritime liens by operation of law. Indeed, World Imports' consistent acknowledgment that "OEC possessed a maritime lien on the Current Goods for the actual freight charges associated with the Current Goods" is also, by implication, a tacit concession that OEC, at least initially, must have possessed comparable maritime liens on the Prepetition Goods for freight charges associated with *those* goods. (Appellees' Br. 10.) Hence, if one concludes, as we do, that OEC never waived those liens on the Prepetition Goods, then the question of whether the parties could and did create the liens solely through contract is a red herring.

Instead, the dispositive questions are whether liens arising by operation of maritime law may be modified or extended by agreement, and whether such an agreement may extend an unwaived lien onto property currently in the lienholder's possession.

3. Enforceability of Maritime Lien Provisions

World Imports argues against the enforceability of the parties' contractual lien modifications by pointing to portions of the Supreme Court's opinion in *Bird of Paradise* which state that maritime liens on cargo are established by operation of law rather than agreement of the parties and arise from the shipowners' possessory interest in the cargo. Attempting to place on OEC the burden of proving both that the parties intended to preserve the maritime liens for the Prepetition Goods and that the delivery of those goods was not [—21—] unconditional,[12] World Imports argues that OEC has failed to produce "any evidence whatsoever to demonstrate that the delivery of the Prepetition Goods was anything but unconditional." (Appellees' Br. 14 n.9.) Insisting that OEC made such an unconditional delivery of the Prepetition Goods, World Imports essentially argues that *Bird of Paradise* does not authorize the parties to reassert waived liens from the Prepetition Goods onto the Current Goods. Both the District Court and Bankruptcy Court accepted that argument and declined to interpret *Bird of Paradise* as authorizing the parties' contractual extension of OEC's maritime liens.

---

[12] Specifically, World Imports cites *Logistics Mgmt.*, 86 F.3d at 914-15, as supportive of their position that "OEC bears the burden to produce evidence which shows that the parties intended to preserve the maritime lien." (Appellees' Br. 14 n.9.) Although *Logistics Mgmt.* reiterates that a maritime lien is lost on unconditional delivery, we discern nothing in that case placing on the lienholder the burden of proving that the parties intended to preserve the lien. Rather, as noted above, the presumption falls heavily in the opposite direction.

To recap, our analysis of the facts begins from a very different premise than that adopted by the District Court and Bankruptcy Court. They assumed that OEC waived its liens on the Prepetition Goods through unconditional delivery but nevertheless tried, through contract, to revive those liens and place them on the Current Goods. We conclude that OEC did not waive its previous liens but rather agreed with World Imports in advance that such liens would survive delivery and would be applied to any of World Imports' goods currently in [—22—] OEC's possession. On that foundation, we hold that their agreement to extend the liens is enforceable.

Despite World Imports' contentions, the opinion in *Bird of Paradise* made clear that there is no internal contradiction in recognizing a lien as a creature of maritime law that, once created by operation of law, may be extended or modified by agreement of the parties. In that case, the Court affirmed that a maritime lien "arises from the usages of commerce, independently of the agreement of the parties … ." *Bird of Paradise*, 72 U.S. at 555; *see also Osaka*, 260 U.S. at 499-500 (clarifying that "[t]he contract of affreightment itself creates no lien, and this court has consistently declared that the obligation between ship and cargo is mutual and reciprocal and does not attach until the cargo is on board or in the master's custody"); *Krauss Bros. Lumber Co. v. Dimon S.S. Corp.*, 290 U.S. 117, 121 (1933) (affirming that, while contracts may form the basis of a maritime lien, it is "[o]nly upon the lading of the vessel or at least when she is ready to receive the cargo" that the lien arises or attaches). In other words, a traditional maritime lien cannot be created by contract alone, but that does not mean that such liens, once created, are beyond contractual modification.

On the contrary, immediately after recognizing that a cargo lien, being possessory, "is lost by an unconditional delivery to the consignee," *Bird of Paradise* used broad language supporting contractual modification and extension of the lien beyond delivery, stating:

Parties, however, *may frame their contract of affreightment as they please*, and *of course may employ words to affirm the existence of the* [—23—] *maritime lien, or to extend or modify it*, or they may so frame their contract as to exclude it altogether. They may agree that the goods, when the ship arrives at the port of destination, shall be deposited in the warehouse of the consignee or owner, and that the transfer and deposit shall not be regarded as the waiver of the lien; and *where they so agree, the settled rule in this court is, that the law will uphold the agreement and support the lien.*

72 U.S. at 555 (emphasis added)

The Bankruptcy Court interpreted that passage more narrowly than the language calls for, hanging great weight on the opinion's prior use of the definite article "the" before the word "freight" to conclude that a maritime lien was limited to the immediate circumstances in which it arose:

[In *Bird of Paradise*], the High Court stated that the "[l]egal effect of such a lien is that the ship-owner, as carrier by water, may retain the goods until *the* freight is paid … " *Id.* at 555. It added that the lien "arises from the right of the shipowner to retain the possession of the goods until *the* freight is paid, and is lost by an unconditional delivery to the consignee." *Id.* This Court places emphasis on the definite article ("the") preceding the word "freight." It reads those statements to limit the extent of a maritime lien to the freight charges for *those goods* on *that vessel* at *that time*. It does not share OEC's reading of the case to allow the [—24—] parties to unconditionally extend the lien to unpaid freight for *prior cargo deliveries*. *See also Newell* [*v. Norton*, 70 U.S. (3 Wall.) 257, 262 (1865)] ("Indeed, the only power the contracting parties have respecting such liens as attach as consequences to certain contracts is, that the creditor may waive the lien, and may by express stipulation, or by his manner of dealing in certain cases, give credit exclusively to those who would also have been bound to him personally by the same contract which would have given rise to the lien.").

In re World Imports, 498 B.R. at 61-62 (original emphasis). Besides its underlying assumption that OEC waived its prior liens through unconditional delivery, we think the Bankruptcy Court's analysis is flawed by two significant oversights. First, it overlooks the context and sequence in which the supposedly limiting language appeared in the *Bird of Paradise* opinion. As mentioned above, the Supreme Court's opinion began by describing the origins and traditional form of maritime liens, but then, in its transition between paragraphs, signaled that the parties may depart from the norm by contractual agreement. *See Bird of Paradise*, 72 U.S. at 555 ("[T]he lien ... arises from the right of the shipowner to retain the possession of the goods until the freight is paid, and is lost by an unconditional delivery to the consignee. *Parties, however, may frame their contract of affreightment as they please*, and of course may employ words to affirm the existence of the maritime lien, *or to extend or modify it ...* ." (emphasis added and footnote omitted)). Had the order of the statements been reversed —that is, had the Supreme Court stressed the traditional form of [—25—] maritime liens *after* discussing contractual modification— that might provide a stronger basis from which to argue that the Supreme Court intended to limit (albeit only implicitly) the scope of contractual modifications of liens to something closely resembling the traditional form. However, read in proper sequence, the Supreme Court's opinion signals the opposite message, namely, that despite the non-contractual origins and traditional form of maritime liens, parties are free to contractually extend or modify an existing lien "as they please." *Id.*, 72 U.S. at 555.

The Bankruptcy Court's second oversight is its casual citation to language appearing in the report of another Supreme Court case, *Newell v. Norton*, language that is not the Supreme Court's but is merely a summary of one party's position in the syllabus of that

case, on a point which ultimately played no role in the Court's analysis. *See Newell*, 70 U.S. at 261-62 (documenting the arguments of counsel for the appellants in that case). World Imports has pushed that erroneous reliance on *Newell's* syllabus at every stage of the proceedings (*see* A 65, 258, 318; Appellees' Br. 13), even after OEC has repeatedly, and correctly, drawn attention to the citation's complete absence of authoritative value (*see* A 223, 227, 231, 274, 280, 307; Appellant's Br. 22, 25 n.8; Reply Br. 8-9). The dogged determination of World Imports to perpetuate a clear error of citation is both troubling and revealing.

Especially in light of the "familiar doctrine" that a maritime lien may attach to property substituted for the original object of the lien, *Bank of British N. Am.*, 137 F. at 536, we see no sound reason why the parties' contractual transfer of the unwaived liens to the Current Goods should [—26—] not have been enforceable.[13] *See also Logistics Mgmt.*, 86 F.3d at 914 ("Contractual provisions regarding liens on cargo for freight are enforceable in admiralty." (citing *Bird of Paradise*, 72 U.S. at 555)); *id.* ("[A] lien on the cargo is normally expressly granted in the bills of lading and

---

[13] Despite the seemingly broad scope of contractual modification contemplated by *Bird of Paradise*, there must of course be some limiting principal that would prevent contracting parties from unilaterally altering the rights of bona fide purchasers whose interests would otherwise be affected by a continuing lien on cargo that has passed into the stream of commerce. The facts of this case, however, do not implicate that concern, as OEC has only sought to enforce its liens on goods that were still in its possession, and has conceded that the case may be resolved on those more limited grounds. Hence, while we understand the Bankruptcy Court's resistance to "the proposition that the freight charges for goods upon their release from a warehouse and entry into the hands of others in the ordinary course of commerce remain secured by a pre-existing *maritime* lien," *In re World Imports*, 498 B.R. at 62 (original emphasis), we emphasize that the disposition of this case concerns only the enforceability of a contractual transfer of a lien from previously released goods to currently held goods. In short, the enforceability of a provision asserting a maritime lien on goods that have already been released into the stream of commerce is not at issue in this case.

charter parties. If so, the extent of the relevant lien is governed by the terms of the lien clause." (quoting Eric M. Danoff, *Provisional Remedies in Adm. U.S.*, 4 U.S.F. Mar. L.J. 293, 299 (1992))). [—27—]

Both the District Court and World Imports raise the policy argument that an extended maritime lien on cargo could hurt innocent third parties. In doing so, they rely primarily on *Atlantic Richfield Co. v. Good Hope Refineries, Inc.*, 604 F.2d 865 (5th Cir. 1979), in which the Fifth Circuit concluded that a transportation provider could not assert a lien on undelivered cargo to secure unpaid charges on already delivered cargo. After concluding, as a matter of contractual interpretation, that the applicable lien clause did not guarantee this right "[o]n its face" and was not otherwise ambiguous, *id.* at 871, the court opined, in dicta, that a broader construction of the contractual language might also have unfavorable consequences to third parties:

> [An] expansive interpretation of this maritime lien clause ... would have consequences far beyond the situation where the cargo belonged to the charterer and was seized before it left the vessel. The lien for the debts of past voyages would extend to cargo owned by others, and might, if all the other terms of the entire clause were literally enforced, follow that cargo after delivery, even if all freights due for its carriage were paid. We *decline to sanction reinterpretation of words apparently clear* to permit this result.

Id. at 873 (emphasis added).

The Fifth Circuit's policy concerns were apparently ancillary to what the court considered a question of contractual interpretation, but the District Court in the present case decided that the lien clauses now at issue are [—28—] unenforceable on policy grounds alone. Specifically, it worried that "[a] third-party purchaser of the undelivered goods would have no notice that the goods it purchased could be withheld pursuant to a maritime lien on previously-shipped goods." *World Imports*, 526 B.R. at 134.

Putting aside the real and immediate harm of depriving OEC of the benefit of its bargain with World Imports, at least three other considerations weigh against the District Court's policy concern. First, any risk to third parties is mitigated by the fact that, unlike the voyage charter at issue in *Atlantic Richfield*, OEC's Tariff not only specifies the applicability of the maritime lien to unsatisfied debts of previous shipments in unambiguous language, but does so in a published document.

Second, the potential of harm to third parties is implicated regardless of whether the maritime lien is intended to satisfy the consignee's immediate charges or past ones. In either case, the lien creates the danger that the consignee's failure to meet its obligations to the carrier will impede its ability to put the cargo into the hands of a third party. "[T]his is a characteristic of all maritime liens." *Usher v. M/V Ocean Wave*, 27 F.3d 370, 374 (9th Cir. 1994). Any marginal increase in the risk to third parties (above the risk inherent in a traditional lien on cargo) is limited in this case because, as already noted *supra* n.13, the goods to which the previous liens attached were still in the carrier's possession. In other words, the type of lien asserted in this case was still, at bottom, a possessory lien over goods that had not yet entered the stream of commerce.

Third, we must consider the potential benefits to commerce of enforcing the parties' voluntary decision to [—29—] enter into this type of credit arrangement. Although World Imports has argued that commerce is hindered by allowing a current shipment of goods "to be held hostage" to secure the payment of prior shipments, that argument ignores the commercial benefit implicit in that or any other credit arrangement that facilitates the exchange of goods or services with a guarantee of future payment. The relevant fact is not simply that the most recent shipment was held up, but that numerous prior shipments were *not* held up because the shipper had assurances that it could release those shipments conditionally, without surrendering its liens. In other words, while the traditional cargo lien promotes commerce by ensuring that a particular ship can assert a secured claim even after the cargo has conditionally left the ship, OEC's contractually modified lien further promotes commerce over a series of transactions by ensuring that the carrier can retain its secured claims in an ongoing business relationship.[14] [—30—]

Besides its public policy argument, the District Court also relied on the oft-cited principle that maritime liens should be strictly construed, reasoning that

> [n]o Supreme Court decision has addressed whether parties may contractually modify a maritime lien to make the delivery of existing shipments contingent on the consignee's payment for already-delivered shipments. As maritime liens are to be strictly construed, this Court declines OEC's invitation to extend or modify maritime liens beyond the circumstances

indicated by Supreme Court precedent. *See Osaka Shosen Kaisha*, 260 U.S. at 499 … .

World Imports, 526 B.R. at 132-33.

The case which the District Court cited, *Osaka Shosen Kaisha v. Pacific Export Lumber Co.*, reaffirmed that "[t]he maritime privilege or lien … is a secret one which may [—31—] operate to the prejudice of general creditors and purchasers without notice and is therefore strict juris and cannot be extended by construction, analogy or inference." 260 U.S. at 499. And while that principle is sound, we think the District Court has misapprehended its import. The principle does not restrain the private modification of liens arising out of the traditional relationship between ship and cargo—*e.g.*, the lien of the cargo owner on the ship or the lien of the shipowner on the cargo—but rather limits the judicial creation of new circumstances, outside that reciprocal relationship, under which liens may attach in the first instance. The language proscribing the expansion of the lien universe "by construction, analogy or inference" curtails a court's ability to recognize, by mere legal implication, previously unanticipated circumstances under which liens may arise by operation of maritime law, but says nothing about private parties' ability to modify traditional liens by express agreement. Reading that language to limit private lien modifications to those forms previously and specifically blessed by the Supreme Court renders meaningless the same Court's affirmation that parties may extend or modify liens and otherwise frame their contracts of affreightment as they please. *Compare Osaka*, 260 U.S. at 499-500 (finding inadequate legal authority to recognize a new type of lien upon a ship for damages resulting from a failure to accept all the intended cargo),[15] *with Bird of*

---

[14] OEC also points to *Eagle Marine Transp. Co. v. A Cargo of Hardwood Chips*, 1998 WL 382141 (E.D. La. July 8, 1998), as persuasive authority that a lien purporting to enforce freight charges on past shipments is enforceable. In that case, the district court noted that the contract giving rise to the lien provided as follows: "Seller has a maritime lien on all cargo which it may assert and enforce to ensure payment of the freight and demurrage on all current en route shipments and earlier completed shipments. Waiver of such lien on prior shipments does not constitute a waiver as to the cargo covered by this agreement." *Id.* at *1. OEC essentially argues that that case tacitly approved the type of contractual extension of a cargo lien as is implicated here, because "if the court had believed that such a lien provision was not enforceable, it would have so indicated … ." (Appellant's Br. [—30—] 37.) However, as the District Court pointed out, the issue in that case was whether the transporter had discharged the lien by unconditional delivery, and the court's opinion did not specify "whether the lien at issue was asserted to enforce payment of freight charges to previous shipments" as opposed to the current shipment. *World Imports*, 526 B.R. at 135. Thus, the opinion did not squarely address the enforceability of a lien for charges incurred on past shipments. Nevertheless, the circumstances of that case give at least some indication that the type of contractual modification at issue in this case is not novel.

[15] The *Osaka* court stressed that, under well-established law, the reciprocal obligations between ship and cargo, from which maritime liens arise, do not attach until the cargo is physically loaded on the ship; hence, the court declined to recognize, by inference alone, a lien on the ship for cargo that was contractually anticipated but never actually [—32—] loaded aboard. *See Osaka Shosen Kaisha v. Pacific Export Lumber Co.*, 260 U.S. 490, 497-500

Paradise, 72 U.S. at 555 [—32—] (recognizing that parties "of course" may agree "to extend or modify" a lien "aris[ing] from the usages of commerce"). The District Court appears to have blurred the distinction between judicial enforcement of a private contract and more comprehensive judicial rule-making, interpreting OEC's enforceability argument as an invitation for the court itself to "extend or modify maritime liens" beyond their traditional forms. *World Imports, Ltd.*, 526 B.R. at 132. In this case at least, there is a material difference between judicial expansion of a legal doctrine and judicial enforcement of a private agreement to vary from a legal default. [—33—]

One last argument against enforceability of OEC's liens is embodied in the Bankruptcy Court's conclusion that the contractual arrangement presented here cannot stand because, if permitted, it would effectively negate the utility of general lien laws adopted by the states. According to the Bankruptcy Court: "[I]f OEC's position were correct, parties would *never* need recourse to the *general* lien laws of the several states. An agreement to extend the shipper's maritime lien to any unpaid debt would co-opt the field and suffice to render any further security arrangements wholly unnecessary." *In re World Imports, Ltd. Inc.*, 498 B.R. at 62 (original emphasis). Besides being overstated,

---

(1923); *see also Vandewater v. Mills, Claimant of Yankee Blade*, 60 U.S. 82; 89-90 (1856) (invoking the principle of *stricti juris* in concluding that, where the ship does not receive the cargo, no maritime lien or privilege attaches). That is a very different situation from the one presented here, where the question is whether the parties can contractually preserve an existing lien (that is, for cargo that was actually loaded and conditionally delivered) and then apply that surviving lien to subsequent cargo that was also loaded and still in the carrier's possession. Upholding a lien in *Osaka* would have required recognition of a new type of maritime lien incompatible with the theoretical underpinnings of the reciprocal lien relationship – *i.e.*, it would have created a new class of lien for cargo that never touched the ship. By contrast, the present case does not require the recognition of any liens other than those arising through the traditional ship-and-cargo relationship, all based on cargo actually loaded and shipped.

that conclusion rests on a faulty premise. Implicit in the stated concern is, once again, an assumption that all previous liens on goods from prior shipments were unconditionally waived. In that view, OEC is attempting a *post hoc* resurrection of liens that it had already surrendered by unconditional delivery —a contractual cheat that would allow it to essentially jump back to the front of the creditor line after relinquishing its spot.

Given the express agreement that OEC would not waive its liens upon delivery, however, the parties' contractual modification is better regarded as an *ex ante* agreement that OEC would simply retain the position already afforded to it by operation of maritime law. Put differently, the contractual extension of OEC's outstanding liens from the Prepetition Goods onto the Current Goods allowed OEC, at most, to do in the aggregate what maritime law already permitted it to do piecemeal with individual shipments, and World Imports' other creditors are only disadvantaged to the same extent they would have been had OEC engaged in the more protracted, commerce-restrictive process of withholding [—34—] each shipment until its attendant lien was satisfied. If parties to a maritime contract, through negotiation and private ordering, opt to streamline that process by retaining and consolidating liens arising by operation of longstanding maritime law, at least as such liens apply to goods still in the shipper's possession, there is no compelling argument to undo such an agreement.[16]

---

[16] We are sympathetic to the Bankruptcy Court's concern that permitting the extension of maritime liens necessarily preempts the operation of state-based commercial law, and thus disadvantages—or at least *maintains* at a disadvantage—all creditors whose claims arise under such law. The question of whether centuries of federal admiralty law favoring the claims of the carrier above other creditors should give way to more modernized statutory schemes may be open to legitimate debate. But the debate is not for us. Congress is free to change policy in this area at any time. Unless and until it does, the federal common law of admiralty still prevails over state-based claims, and the traditions of that law are sufficiently well-established to allow carriers holding advantageous maritime liens to make

In sum, we do not think the policy concerns roused by World Imports and accepted by the Bankruptcy Court and District Court are sufficient to either outweigh the benefits to commerce of allowing two sophisticated businesses to contract for a mutually agreeable transportation and credit arrangement, or to curtail the broad contractual freedom that *Bird of Paradise* on its face allows. [—35—]

III. Conclusion

Given the strong presumption that OEC did not waive its maritime liens on the Prepetition Goods, the clear documentation that the parties intended such liens to survive delivery, the familiar principle that a maritime lien may attach to property substituted for the original object of the lien, and the parties' general freedom to modify or extend existing liens by contract, we conclude that the parties' agreement to apply those unwaived liens toward the Current Goods is enforceable. Thus, we will reverse and remand so that OEC may be granted relief appropriate to its valid maritime liens.

---

private agreements to preserve, modify and extend those liens through the substitution of currently held goods.

United States Court of Appeals
for the Third Circuit

No. 14-3956

NEW YORK SHIPPING ASS'N
vs.
WATERFRONT COMM'N OF N.Y. HARBOR

Appeal from the United States District Court for the District of New Jersey

Decided: August 30, 2016

Citation: 835 F.3d 344, 4 Adm. R. 145 (3d Cir. 2016).

Before **FUENTES, NYGAARD,** and **ROTH,** Circuit Judges.

[—6—] NYGAARD, Circuit Judge:

The District Court ruled that the Appellee, Waterfront Commission of New York Harbor (Commission or Waterfront Commission),[1] was within its statutory authority [—7—] to require shipping companies and other employers to certify that prospective employees had been referred for employment pursuant to federal and state nondiscrimination policies. The District Court also rejected claims that the Commission had unlawfully interfered with collective bargaining rights, holding that such rights were not completely protected under the language of the Waterfront Commission Compact (Compact), which was entered into by the states of New Jersey and New York in 1953. We will affirm.

I.

Factual and Procedural Background

This appeal takes us deep into the hiring practices and procedures utilized on the New York/New Jersey waterfront. We will start with some history, which to varying degrees, has been reported elsewhere. *See, e.g., De*

Veau v. Braisted, 363 U.S. 144 (1960); *Waterfront Comm'n of N.Y. Harbor v. Sea Land Serv., Inc.,* 764 F.2d 961 (3d Cir. 1985); *Hazleton v. Murray,* 21 N.J. 115 (1956); *Waterfront Comm'n of N.Y. Harbor v. Constr. & Marine Equip. Co., Inc.,* 928 F. Supp. 1388 (D.N.J. 1996). Years of criminal activity and corrupt hiring practices on the waterfront were first brought to light in 1949 in a series of 24 articles published in the *New York Sun* by journalist Malcolm Johnson. Entitled "Crime on the Waterfront," these articles won Johnson the Pulitzer Prize, and formed the basis for the 1954 film "On the Waterfront."[2] [—8—]

Hiring practices on the waterfront also caught the attention of the New York State Crime Commission (Crime Commission), which issued a report in 1953 relating in detail the pervasive influence of crime and corruption on waterfront hiring practices. *See Fourth Report of the New York State Crime Commission,* N.Y.S. Leg. Doc. No. 70 (1953). The Crime Commission singled-out the "shape-up" hiring system for particular scorn. The term connotes a hiring method whereby the applicants appeared daily at the docks or other locations and a hiring boss would select those who would be given work. *Id.* at 37.[3] The foundation of this practice was the union foreman's unfettered control over the process and his unchecked power to select whomever he desired for employment.

The Crime Commission report led to public hearings on its findings. Then-New York Governor Thomas E. Dewey held hearings, the goal of which was to come up with a legislative plan to address the Commission's concerns. Representatives of the State of New Jersey were also present for and participated in these hearings. The "shape-up" hiring system was identified by the Commission as a vector for corruption and criminal practices on the

---

[1] Appellee Waterfront Commission of New York Harbor is a bi-state corporate and political entity created by interstate compact. N.J.S.A. § 32:23-1; N.Y. Unconsol. Laws § 9801 (McKinney). All statutory citations to the Compact [—7—] provisions will be to the New Jersey statute, unless otherwise noted.

[2] For detailed historical information on the New York waterfront and its association with criminal activity, see [—8—] Nathan Ward, Dark Harbor: The War for the New York Waterfront (2010); *see also* Jonathan Eig, 'Waterfront' Jungle, N.Y. Times, Sept. 24, 2010.

[3] *See also Levias v. Pac. Maritime Ass'n,* 760 F. Supp. 2d 1036, 1050 (W.D. Wash. 2001).

docks. So as "to investigate, deter, combat and remedy" this criminality and corruption, the states of New Jersey and New York entered into the Compact in 1953. *Gonzalez v. Waterfront Comm'n* [—9—] *of N.Y. Harbor*, 755 F.3d 176, 177 (3d Cir. 2014); *see also* N.J.S.A. § 32:23-1, et seq. Pursuant to Art. I., § 10 of the United States Constitution, Congress approved the Compact in August of 1953.[4] The Compact created the Waterfront Commission to, among other things, eliminate corrupt hiring practices on the waterfront. *Waterfront Comm'n of N.Y. v. Elizabeth-Newark Shipping Inc.*, 164 F.3d 177, 180 (3d Cir. 1980) (citing *Hazelton*, 21 N.J. at 120-23). In enacting the Compact, the legislatures of both states noted:

> that the conditions under which waterfront labor is employed with the Port of New York district are depressing and degrading to such labor, resulting from the lack of any systemic method of hiring, the lack of adequate information as to the availability of employment, corrupt hiring practices, and the fact that persons conducting such hiring are frequently criminals and persons notoriously lacking in moral [—10—] character and integrity and neither responsive or responsible to the employers nor to the uncoerced will of the majority members of the labor organizations of the employees; that as a result waterfront laborers suffer from irregularity of employment, fear and insecurity, inadequate earnings, an unduly high accident rate, subjection to borrowing at usurious rates of interest, exploitation and extortion as the price of securing employment.

N.J.S.A. § 32:23-2.

---

[4] The Compact Clause of the Constitution provides that "[n]o State shall, without the Consent of Congress, . . . enter into any Agreement or Compact with another State." Art. I, § 10, cl. 3. Accordingly, before a compact between two States can be given effect it must be approved by Congress. *See Virginia v. Maryland*, 540 U.S. 56, 66 (2003). Once a Compact receives such approval, it is "transform[ed] . . . into a law of the United States." *Id.* (internal quotation marks omitted).

One way the Compact sought to rein in the corruption associated with hiring on the waterfront was by requiring the Commission to regulate longshoremen and stevedores. Employment Information Centers were to be operated by the Commission to handle all hiring of longshoremen. Further, the Compact charged the Commission with registering all individuals who were qualified to work as longshoremen and specifically provided that "no person shall act as a longshoreman within the Port of New York district unless at the time he is included in the longshoremen's register." N.J.S.A. § 32:23-27. The Compact also provided a definition of a longshoreman:

> [A] natural person, other than the hiring agent, who is employed for work at a pier or other waterfront [—11—] terminal, either by a carrier of freight by water or by a stevedore (a) physically to move waterborne freight on vessels berthed at piers, on piers or at other waterfront terminals, or (b) to engage in direct and immediate checking of any such freight or of the custodial accounting therefore, or in the recording or tabulation of the hours worked at piers or other waterfront terminals by natural persons employed by carriers of freight by water or stevedores, or (c) to supervise directly and immediately others who are employed as in subdivision (a) of this definition.

N.J.S.A. § 32:23-6. This definition was expanded in 1957 to include workers who performed labor that was incidental to the movement of waterborne freight. N.J.S.A. § 32:23-85(6). A longshoreman who fits either the original or expanded definition was known as a "deep sea" longshoreman.[5] Further, the Compact gave the Commission the authority to license stevedoring companies that wanted to operate at the Port. A 'stevedore,' according to the Compact, is a contractor [—12—] hired by a carrier of waterborne freight to move

---

[5] These longshoremen are sometimes referred to as "five-digit" longshoremen in light of the five digit registration number assigned them by the Commission. *See Bozzi v. Waterfront Comm'n of N. Y. Harbor*, No. 90-cv-0926 (MGC), 1994 WL 606043 at *2 (S.D.N.Y. Nov. 3, 1994).

freight in ships that are berthed at piers, or at other waterfront terminals. *See* N.J.S.A. § 32:23-6.

By 1969, new developments in shipping technology required changes to hiring procedures on the waterfront. The New Jersey Supreme Court has summarized this new technology:

> Containerization involves the loading of cargo by a shipper into a box-like object called a container. The cargo-laden container is loaded onto a truck frame that transports it to a pier where it is hoisted aboard a ship designed to carry containers. At the port of discharge, the process is simply reversed. Container-ization contrasts sharply with the traditional "break-bulk" shipping method, which involved loading trucks item by item, emptying them piece by piece at the pier, and then loading the ship in the same fashion.

Waterfront Comm'n of N.Y. v. Mercedes-Benz of N. Am., Inc., 99 N.J. 402, 411-12 (1985). Containerization and other new technologies dramatically decreased the need for manual labor at the port. This decrease in the size of the labor force led, in turn, to the enactment of an amendment to the Compact: Section 5-p. Known as the "closed register [—13—] statute," Section 5-p authorized the Commission to open or close the Longshoreman's Register so as to balance the workforce with the demand for labor. *See, e.g., Nat'l Org. of Women, N.Y. Chapter v. Waterfront Comm'n of N.Y. Harbor*, 468 F. Supp. 317, 319 (S.D.N.Y. 1979); *see also* N.J.S.A. § 32:23-114. The prevalence of containerization in the shipping industry also led to the creation of a new class of dock worker: longshoremen who did not load or unload ships, but instead performed services that were incidental to those tasks. This new class of longshoremen were registered with the Commission and commonly referred to as "A-registrants," to distinguish them from deep sea longshoremen.[6] A-registrants were not

permitted to do any work that involved the discharge or unloading of cargo vessels. New classifications of stevedores were also created to cover those contactors that were involved in the loading and unloading of the containers, cargo storage, cargo repairing, coopering, general maintenance and other miscellaneous work.

The Commission codified these worker classifications in Section 4.4 of its Rules and Regulations. Section 4.4 divided the Longshoreman's Register into two sections, reflecting these two classifications of labor:

> (b) The register shall be divided as follows: (1) A "deep sea" register which shall include all persons registered by the [—14—] commission as longshore-men and checkers except those persons registered as longshoremen pursuant to the 1969 amendments to the Act (NY Laws 1969, ch. 953; NJ Laws 1969, ch. 128); (2) An "A" or "1969 amendment" register which shall include all persons registered by the commission as longshoremen pursuant to the 1969 amendments to the act (NY Laws 1969, ch. 953; NJ Laws 1969, ch. 128).

N.Y. Comp. Codes R. & Regs. Tit. 21 § 4.4 (2013). This resulted in the bifurcation of the labor force: members of the New York Shipping Association (NYSA) represented the deep sea registrants while Metropolitan Marine Maintenance Contractor's Association (MMMCA) members employed the A-registrants. In the 1980s, the Commission clarified the status of these two workforces as they related to the closed register. Section 5-p was amended to now provide that "[n]otwithstanding any other provision of this act, the commission may include [A-registrants] in the longshoremen's register under such terms and conditions as the commission may prescribe." N.J.S.A. § 32:23-114(4).

Section 5-p was again amended in 1999. Increased business in the port and attrition in

---

[6] The "A" classification comes from the "A" prefix attached before these worker's multi-digit registration number, which appear on licenses

issued by the Commission to those workers. *See Bozzi*, 1994 WL 606043 at *3.

the labor force, among other things, necessitated changes to the procedures that had previously been used to open the longshoreman's register. Public hearings were held in which the Commission and [—15—] several of the Appellants participated. As amended, Section 5-p required that

> [t]he sponsoring employer shall certify that the selection of the persons so sponsored was made on a fair and non-discriminatory basis in accordance with the requirements of the laws of the United States and the States of New York and New Jersey dealing with equal employment opportunities.

N.J.S.A. § 32:23-114(1).

The dispute before us today arose from the Commission's decision to open the longshoremen's register in December of 2013. The NYSA, an organization representing marine terminal operators, stevedoring companies and ship operators in the Port of New York and New Jersey, along with the MMMCA, and the International Long-shoremen's Association, AFL-CIO (ILA), filed a complaint against the Commission in November of 2013.[7] The NYSA and the ILA had, three months earlier, asked the [—16—] Commission to add, on its own initiative, more than 600 employees to the deep sea register. The NYSA and the ILA also told the Commission that they would recruit, train, and hire individuals pursuant to the terms of the Recruitment and Hiring Plan, which was agreed to under a new collective bargaining agreement between the NYSA and the ILA.[8] After meeting with representatives of the NYSA, MMMCA and others, the Commission issued Determination 35 in December of 2013

which, among other things, stated that the Commission would open the Register to accept applications for 225 new positions. The Commission's Determination also required:

> . . . that prior to the Commission's acceptance of any application for inclusion in the Longshoremen's Register pursuant to this Determination, a representative of the NYSA–ILA Contract Board directly involved with the administration of the Hiring Plan shall submit a letter setting forth the name and address of the recommended individual, and certifying that:

>> (1) he or she has personal knowledge of the facts concerning the recruitment, [—17—] referral, selection and sponsorship of [the applicant] and (2) the selection of the person so sponsored was made in a fair and nondiscriminatory basis in accordance with the requirements of the laws of the United States and the States of New York and New Jersey dealing with equal employment opportunities.

Commission Determination 35 (Dec. 3, 2013).[9]

The Appellants sued the Commission in November of 2014. They asked for declaratory and injunctive relief pursuant to the Declaratory Judgments Act, 28 U.S.C.A. §§ 2201-2202 (2006). They also asked the District Court for a preliminary injunction prohibiting the Commission from implementing its antidiscrimination certification requirements. The District Court denied the request for a preliminary injunction, finding that the Appellants failed to show irreparable harm and a likelihood of success on the merits. The Commission then filed a motion to dismiss. Appellants amended their complaint in January of 2015, which the District Court ultimately dismissed. Appellants have timely appealed that dismissal. [—18—]

---

[7] The MMMCA represents maintenance contractor employers and the ILA represents longshoremen and other waterfront workers employed by the NYSA's members. Also parties to this dispute are two local chapters of the ILA—Local 1804-1 and Local 1814. Where appropriate, we will refer to all Appellants collectively.

[8] Under this plan, 51% of new hires were to consist of honorably discharged military veterans, 25% of new hires would be referrals from the ILA and 24% would be referrals from the NYSA.

[9] A copy of Determination 35 is available at http://www.waterfrontcommission.org/news/determination35.pdf

III.

We have jurisdiction to review the District Court's October 9, 2014 order dismissing the Appellants' amended complaint under 28 U.S.C. § 1291. We exercise plenary review of an order granting a motion to dismiss under Rule 12(b)(6) and apply the same standard as the District Court. *Fowler v. UPMC Shadyside*, 578 F.3d 203, 206 (3d Cir. 2009). "To survive a motion to dismiss, a complaint must contain sufficient factual matter, accepted as true, to 'state a claim to relief that is plausible on its face.'" *Ashcroft v. Iqbal*, 556 U.S. 662, 678 (2009) (quoting *Bell Atl. Corp. v. Twombly*, 550 U.S. 544, 570 (2007)).

IV.

Appellants NYSA, ILA and the ILA Locals filed a joint brief while Appellant MMMCA opted to brief us separately. Appellants collectively question the validity of the antidiscrimination certification procedure added to Section 5-p in 1999, and, by extension, Rule 4.4. They also claim that they have successfully pleaded the Commission's unlawful interference with their collective bargaining rights. The NYSA, ILA and ILA Locals further claim that the Commission violated their due process rights in promulgating its certification amendment in Rule 4.4. For organizational purposes, we will address these issues with reference to the specific counts of the Amended Complaint in which they were raised.

A.

Dismissal of Counts I and II [—19—]

The Compact permits "amendments and supplements" as long as those changes implement the Compact's purposes and are concurred in by the legislatures of New Jersey and New York. N.J.S.A. § 32:23-70; N.Y. Unconsol. § 9870. Such amendments have the pre-approval of Congress.[10] Here, Count I of

the Amended Complaint challenges the Commission's amendment to Rule 4.4 on the basis that the Compact provision under which it was promulgated—the 1999 amendment to Compact Section 5-p—is not consistent with the purposes of the Compact, and is therefore invalid due to a lack of Congressional approval. Therefore, to resolve this issue, we must determine whether the anti-discrimination certification requirement of Section 5-p is a valid amendment which implements the purposes of the Compact. The parties agree that the resolution of this issue turns on whether one of the purposes of the Compact was the elimination of racial discrimination in the hiring of longshoremen. Meanwhile, Count II of the Amended [—20—] Complaint turns on the scope of the 1999 amendment to Section 5-p itself; that is, whether that amendment applies to A-registrants. The resolution of these questions requires us to interpret provisions of the Compact. To so do, we treat the Compact like any other federal statute, and interpret it accordingly. *See Texas v. New Mexico*, 482 U.S. 124, 128 (1987).

Appellants argue that because the Compact did not specifically mention racial dis-crimination at the time it was enacted, any amendment designed to ensure fair and non-discriminatory hiring practices cannot further the Compact's purposes and is, therefore, unconstitutional. They base this argument on their belief that the phrase "corrupt hiring practices" (which they admit the Commission was formed to combat) does not include the purposeful exclusion of racial minorities. Therefore, the Appellants conclude, the Commission cannot require them to certify that their hiring practices comply with federal

---

[10] Congress' pre-approval of such amendments is certainly rare. As the Supreme Court has noted: "Congress expressly gave its consent to such implementing legislation not formally part of the compact. This provision in the consent by Congress

to a compact is so extraordinary as to be unique in the history of compacts. Of all the instances of congressional approval of state compacts . . . we have found no other in which Congress gave its consent to implementing legislation. It is instructive that this unique provision has occurred in connection with approval of a compact dealing with the prevention of crime where, because of the peculiarly local nature of the problem, the inference is strongest that local policies are not to be thwarted." *De Veau v. Braisted,* 363 U.S. 144, 154 (1960).

and state laws dealing with equal opportunity. This argument is meritless. Like the District Court, we also conclude that Count I of the Amended Complaint fails to state a claim as matter of law because one of the purposes of the Compact is the elimination of racial discrimination in hiring. Section 5-p's certification requirement furthers this purpose and is thus, constitutional.

The stated purpose of the Compact, as set out in Article I, is to rid the docks of "corrupt hiring practices," "depressing and degrading" labor conditions, and "irregularity of employment." N.J.S.A. § 32:23-2; *see also Elizabeth-Newark Shipping, Inc.*, 164 F.3d at 180 ("The Compact was enacted to eliminate corrupt hiring practices on [—21—] the . . . waterfront.").[11] Can it seriously be argued that racial discrimination in hiring (or anywhere, for that matter), is not a corrupt practice? We questioned counsel for the NYSA at oral argument on this very point and counsel conceded that the antidiscrimination certification requirement was "a good thing." Oral Argument Tr. at 8-9. When pressed further, and mirroring the arguments raised in their brief, counsel maintained that racial discrimination may be a corrupt hiring practice, but that it was not one of the

practices considered corrupt when the Compact was enacted in 1953. This argument belies the Compact's legislative history and we [—22—] have little difficulty concluding that such a corrupt practice was indeed contemplated by the state legislatures and Congress in enacting and approving the Compact.

Racial discrimination in hiring was a concern brought to the attention of the state legislatures in 1953. Testimony provided by Cleophus Jacobs, the secretary-treasurer of ILA Local 968, a predominately African-American local, revealed that of its 500 members, only 100 had been getting work at that time. Jacobs specifically pointed to the shape-up system as an instrument of racial discrimination:

> Our opposition to the shape-up, therefore, is not of recent origin, nor are we jumping on the bandwagon of an outraged public opinion. To the members of our local the shape-up had produced an even greater evil than that which the public generally has now come to recognize. It has been the instrument of racial discrimination against our members and consequently has further reduced job opportunities for them.

WC-ADD at 301. This testimony was not the only instance where racial discrimination was discussed prior to the enactment of the Compact. Special Counsel to the Dewey hearings, Theodore Kiendl, followed-up on Jacob's statements by asking him: [—23—]

> Q: And you think [the shape-up] system leads to racial discrimination?
>
> A: It does. Whether crime might have been produced or not, but the system of shape-up really facilitates the exercise of racial discrimination.

WC-ADD at 305. Counsel also produced a March 1952 edition of the "Negro Longshoreman," a newsletter written and edited by the rank-and-file membership of Local 968. Counsel called attention to the

---

[11] Appellant MMMCA argues that Article I of the Compact is "the least likely place to find the 'purposes' of the Compact," and that "Congress did not treat 'the purposes of the Compact' as a coded reference to Article I." MMMCA Br. at 37, 48. Instead, the MMMCA maintains that Article I is merely a preamble or introduction for the "substantive provisions of the Compact." MMMCA Br. at 47-48. As the Commission points out, however, this argument quickly withers when confronted with testimony offered when the Compact was discussed in the United States Senate in July of 1953. Speaking about the Compact, New Jersey Senator Robert C. Hendrickson, who had introduced a bill granting the consent of Congress to the Compact, stated that "the purpose of this bill can be best stated by referring to article I of the compact, which sets forth the findings which shook and rocked the American people on the occasion of their recent public disclosure." WC-ADD at 448. In support of their arguments on appeal, the Appellee submitted an addendum containing Commission reports and extensive legislative history materials. We refer to that addendum hereinafter as "WC-ADD."

following statement: "We Negro longshoremen are discriminated against first of all by our own International officials of the ILA who deny us representation or jurisdiction over any piers on the waterfront." *Id.* at 306. Finally, the record of the state hearings clearly demonstrates that racial discrimination was one of the corrupt hiring practices the Compact strove to eliminate. Counsel directly asked Jacobs:

> Q: Now, don't you think that the programs presented by the State Crime Commission eliminate the shape-up entirely and substituting a new form of hiring is highly desirable to obtain the very ends that your union wants to accomplish, to wit, the elimination of racial discrimination entirely? [—24—]
>
> A. I agree the Commission has made an effort . . .

Id.

The subsequent federal Congressional hearings on the Compact likewise contain discussions about the problem of racial discrimination in waterfront hiring practices. During a 1953 hearing on the Compact before the United States Senate, New Hampshire Senator Charles W. Tobey scathingly criticized ILA hiring practices of the time as racially discriminatory. Senator Tobey first noted the ILA's practice of charging African-American union members double the amount of initiation fees they charged to white members. WC-ADD at 445. Then, the Senator continued his statements decrying the racial discrimination inflicted upon the ILA's African-American members:

> Man's inhumanity to man is being exemplified in certain labor circles. Such labor unions had better take cover. They are riding for a fall. The time cannot come too soon. Let us clean them out. Who is running this country anyway, I ask—honest, God-fearing people, or crooked labor union leaders? We can give names and addresses. Cry out, America, "Unclean, unclean."

Id. The "corrupt hiring practices" language used in the Compact embodies the concerns both the state and federal [—25—] legislatures had in confronting racial discrimination in hiring on the docks. Given this legislative history, we easily conclude that the 1999 Amendment to Section 5-p reflected the legislatures' belief that ending racial discrimination in employment was part of the Compact's core purposes. As such, it had Congressional approval. We, therefore, agree with the District Court that Count I fails to state a claim.[12]

We also will affirm the District Court's dismissal of Count II. As we indicated earlier, the issues raised in this Count invoke the scope of Rule 4.4, that is, to which workers it applies. Under the framework in place for hiring of A-registrants, the ILA has the exclusive right to recruit and select potential employees to be referred for employment as A-registrants. The Commission maintains that this practice is no better than the shape-up system of old. In amending Rule 4.4, the Commission's purpose was to hold employers accountable for any racial discrimination that may have infected the ILA's selection and referral of A-registrants. Put another way, the amendment was an attempt by the Commission to ensure that the NYSA and the MMMCA's hiring of A-registrants was done in a nondiscriminatory manner.

Appellants argue that the Rule's certification requirement is improper because Section 5-p, on which it was [—26—] based, only applies to deep-sea longshoremen, not A-registrants. Appellant MMMCA goes further, arguing that the Commission has repeatedly stated that the Section 5-p does not apply to maintenance and repair workers, an overwhelming majority of whom are A-registrants. A look at the language of Section 5-p itself quickly defeats this argument. Section 5-p of the Compact contains five

---

[12] The NYSA and the ILA argue, in a brief footnote, that the District Court's dismissal of Count V should be reversed for the same reasons as Count I. NYSA-ILA Br. at 45 n.10. They point to no other grounds for reversal of this Count. Inasmuch as we will affirm the dismissal of Count I, we likewise will affirm the dismissal of Count V.

subdivisions, the fourth of which states that "[n]otwithstanding any other provision of this act, the commission may include in the longshoremen's register under such terms and conditions as the commission may prescribe: . . . [a] person defined as a 'longshoreman' in subdivision (6) of section 1(5-a) of P.L.1954, c. 14 (C.32:23-85), who is employed by a stevedore as defined in paragraph (b) or (c) of subdivision (1) of the same section (C.32:23-85) and whose employment is not subject to the guaranteed annual income provisions of any collective bargaining agreement relating to longshoremen." N.J.S.A. § 32:23-114(4). These persons, in other words, are A-registrants and under the Compact, the Commission may include them in the register under whatever terms and conditions it wishes.

Appellants offer us little contrary argument, pointing only to an unreported ruling of the United States District Court for the Southern District of New York as support for their position. In *Bozzi, supra.,* two A-registrant workers had mistakenly been working as deep-sea longshoremen in the holds of general cargo vessels. The Commission, after learning of this error, told the two workers to cease performing general longshore work, except for those jobs they had been approved to perform. The A-registrants sued, asking for a declaratory judgment that the Commission had the authority under Section 5-p(5)(b) of the Compact to [—27—] include them in the closed deep-sea register. The Commission argued that the closed register provision has always been interpreted to apply only to deep-sea longshoreman and the Commission has consistently viewed Section 5-p(5)(b) as a housekeeping provision, which merely clarifies the status of A-registrants. The District Court, after an extensive discussion of Section 5-p(5)(b)'s legislative history, agreed with the Commission, and held that the two A-registrants could not individually be added to the closed deep-sea register. The individual workers asked for a declaratory judgment that the Commission had the authority to include them in the closed deep-sea register.

The Appellants seize upon the Commission's position in *Bozzi*—that the closed register provisions of Section 5-p only apply to deep-sea longshoremen, not A-registrants—to argue that the nondiscrimination certification requirements of Section 5-p only apply to deep-sea longshoremen. This contention is baseless and misconstrues *Bozzi*. While A-registrants may not be included in the closed register provisions of Section 5-p, they are subject to Section 5-p's other provisions, like the nondiscrimination provisions at issue here. As the District Court noted, the Commission has been interpreting Section 5-p(5)(b) this way for decades, and that interpretation is entitled to great weight. *See Chevron, U.S.A., Inc. v. Nat'l Res. Def. Council, Inc.,* 467 U.S. 837, 844 (1984).

In sum, Compact Section 5p-(5)(b) clearly provides that A-registrants may be included in the deep-sea register under "such terms and conditions as the [C]ommission may prescribe." N.J.S.A. § 32:23-114(4). The District Court did [—28—] not err in dismissing Count II of the Amended Complaint for failure to state a claim.

B.

Dismissal of Counts III, IV and VII

We will also affirm the District Court's dismissal of Counts III, IV, and VII of the Amended Complaint. Taken together, these three counts accuse the Commission of unlawfully interfering with the Appellants' collective bargaining rights by implementing the nondiscrimination certification provisions. The Appellants also maintain that the Commission's actions violate national labor policy by dictating the terms of their collective bargaining agreements. We reject both contentions.

We take these claims out of numerical order, and start our discussion with Count VII. The District Court dismissed Count VII for an inadequacy in pleading under Fed. R. Civ. P. 8(a), and we review such a ruling for an abuse of discretion. *In re Westinghouse Sec. Litig.,* 90 F.3d 696, 702 (3d Cir. 1996). We see no abuse of the District Court's discretion in its dismissal of this count. At the outset, the NYSA and ILA acknowledge this count's lack of a specific demand for relief. NYSA-ILA Br. at 61. This omission, in and of itself, justifies a dismissal of the count. *See Simmons v. Abruzzo*, 49 F.3d 83, 86 (2d Cir. 1995). Further, we share the District Court's conclusion that Count VII is little more than a collection of conclusory statements and a recitation of Commission Determination 35. Given this, the District Court's conclusion that the Appellants failed to connect their allegations to a violation of Compact Article XV was not unreasonable and [—29—] therefore, its decision to dismiss this count for a failure to adequately allege facts sufficient to state a claim for relief was not an abuse of its discretion.

Turning now to Counts III and IV, we note that the Appellants argue, with more specificity, that the Commission's actions violate Article XV of the Compact, which states, among other things, that:

> This compact [was] not designed . . . to limit in any way any rights granted or derived from any other statute or any rule of law for employees to organize in labor organizations, to bargain collectively and to act in any other way individually, collectively, and though labor organizations or other representatives of their own choosing.

> ****

> This compact is not designed and shall not be construed to limit in any way rights of longshoremen, hiring agents, pier superintendents or port watchmen or their employers to bargain collectively . . ..

N.J.S.A. § 32:23-68, -69. Appellants argue that this Article guarantees them "unfettered collective bargaining" and gives [—30—] them "freedom of choice in the selection of employees." NYSA-ILA Br. at 9-10. This position is untenable, however, because the language of Article XV is not absolute. Indeed, in this very context, we have held that collective bargaining rights cannot supersede "the Commission's supervisory role regarding practices that might lead to corruption." *Sea Land*, 764 F.2d at 966-67. That is, Article XV "guarantees that [collectively bargained] hiring procedures will not be displaced where they comport with the Compact." *Id.* at 963. Obviously, the converse is true as well: where actions are not in furtherance of the original purposes of the Compact, collective bargaining rights may be infringed upon.

Here, as we previously determined, the eradication of racial discrimination in hiring was one of the original purposes of the Compact. The Commission's actions in requiring certification that prospective employees were selected in a nondiscriminatory manner certainly further the Compact's purposes of rooting out corrupt hiring practices such as racial discrimination. Therefore, the Commission's certification regulation cannot be viewed as an improper intrusion into Appellants' collective bargaining rights.

Appellant MMMCA takes a slightly different tact on this issue, arguing that the Commission cannot undertake any action that would limit the ability of labor and management to agree to a mutually satisfactory way of selecting employees. The MMMCA maintains that "the Compact treats as inviolable whatever method the bargaining parties arrive at." MMMCA Br. at 56. While the Compact does safeguard the Appellants' collective bargaining rights, it does so only to the extent those rights do not conflict with the purposes of the Compact. We held as much in *Sea Land, supra*. There, in [—31—] order to resolve a conflict between a Commission regulation and an existing CBA, we proposed a modification, noting that this change "maintains both the Commission's supervisory role regarding practices that might lead to corruption and the union's collectively-bargained hiring procedures." 764 F.2d at 966-67. We reject, therefore, the argument that Appellants' collective bargaining rights are absolute and will affirm the District Court's dismissal of these counts.

C.

Due Process Issues

Appellants' last issue will not detain us long. The Appellants contend that their due process rights were violated because the Commission did not conduct public hearings before implementing the nondiscrimination amendment. This argument does not hold up under scrutiny because the Commission's actions were legislative and procedural due process does not extend to legislative action. *See Rogin v. Bensalem Twp.*, 616 F.2d 680, 693 (3d Cir. 1980) (citing *Bi-Metallic Inv. Co. v. State Bd. of Equalization of Colo.*, 239 U.S. 441 (1915); *see also Acierno v. Cloutier*, 40 F.3d 597, 610 (3d Cir. 1994) (en banc)).

First, and contrary to their own argument, the Appellants note that the Amended Complaint alleged that the nondiscrimination amendment was "enacted," which connotes legislative action. Second, the Amended Complaint fails to allege that the Commission acted in some way that was contrary to statutory procedures. Indeed, amending the Commission's own rules is legislative action. [—32—]

More importantly, the Commission gave the NYSA-ILA ample notice and opportunity vis-à-vis the nondiscrimination amendment. The Appellants were notified of the proposed amendments and indeed, submitted comments in opposition during the pertinent time period. We see no procedural due process violation here simply because the Commission did not hold a public hearing before amending its own rules. Neither did the District Court and we will affirm that determination.

V.

Like the District Court, we conclude that the Amended Complaint fails to state any claim upon which relief may be granted. Therefore, we see no error in the District Court's dismissal.

United States Court of Appeals
for the Third Circuit

No. 15-3635

HARGUS
VS.
FEROCIOUS AND IMPETUOUS, LLC

Appeal from the District Court of the Virgin Islands

Decided: October 18, 2016

Citation: 840 F.3d 133, 4 Adm. R. 155 (3d Cir. 2016).

Before **FUENTES, VANASKIE,** and **RESTREPO,** Circuit Judges.

[—2—] VANASKIE, Circuit Judge:

Appellants Kyle Coleman and the M/V One Love (the "One Love")[1] appeal the District Court's judgment in favor of Appellee Greg Hargus on his negligence claim following a bench trial. For the reasons discussed below, we conclude that the tortious act giving rise to Hargus' claim was insufficient to invoke maritime jurisdiction because the act was not of the type that could potentially disrupt maritime commerce. Therefore, the District Court lacked subject matter jurisdiction over Hargus' personal injury claim. Accordingly, we will vacate the judgment of the District Court and remand the matter with instructions that the District Court dismiss the case. [—3—]

I.

On May 19, 2012, Hargus and a group of individuals rented the One Love to travel from St. Thomas to various destinations throughout the United States Virgin Islands.[2] Ferocious and Impetuous, LLC ("F&I") owned the One Love and had hired Coleman as a captain. One of the stops on the tour was Cruz Bay, St. John, where Coleman anchored the One Love in "knee deep" water close to the shore. (App. 30, 271.) Most of the passengers then disembarked from the One Love. Later in the day, two members of the group—who were standing on the beach approximately 25 feet away from the One Love—threw beer cans at Hargus while he was standing on the deck of the anchored One Love. Upon seeing this, Coleman, who was standing on the beach next to the other two individuals, threw an empty insulated plastic coffee cup at Hargus. The plastic cup hit Hargus in the temple on the left side of his head. Hargus, however, did not lose consciousness and did not complain of any injury at that time. One Love resumed its journey without further incident.

On May 21, 2012, two days after the incident, Hargus, who had experienced pain and vision impairments after being hit by the coffee cup, sought medical attention. He was diagnosed with a concussion and a mild contusion.[3] The treating physician did not prescribe any medication and [—4—] allowed Hargus to return to work that day without restrictions.

Hargus did not seek further medical treatment until more than a year later. From June of 2013 until October of 2013, he was examined by at least three doctors for complaints of headaches, memory loss, mood swings, and neck pain. He last sought treatment for his headaches and other symptoms in October of 2013.

On November 20, 2013, Hargus filed the instant lawsuit in the District Court of the Virgin Islands against Coleman, F&I, Joseph Trattner (owner of F&I), Brent Hazzard, St. Thomas Sport and Social Club, and the One Love, *in rem.* In his Amended Complaint, Hargus asserted five claims: (1) a maritime lien against the One Love; (2) negligence and negligent entrustment against F&I, Trattner, Hazzard, and the St. Thomas Sport and Social Club; (3) negligence against Coleman; and (5) vicarious liability against F&I, Trattner, Hazzard, and the St. Thomas Sport and Social Club. The District Court held a two-day bench trial on Hargus' claims on February 24 and 25, 2015.

---

[1] The One Love is a twenty-six foot recreational vessel.

[2] The factual recitation is based largely upon the Findings of Fact made by the District Court following the Bench Trial. (App. 29-33.)

[3] Hargus had a history of head trauma, having previously suffered 10 to 12 head injuries or concussions.

On September 30, 2015, the District Court issued its opinion, explaining that it had admiralty jurisdiction over Hargus' claims because "[c]laims such as these for personal injury to the passenger of a vessel caused by the captain of the vessel meet the situs and nexus requirements for admiralty tort jurisdiction of this Court." (App. 44.) The District Court further concluded that Coleman was negligent and that the One Love was jointly and severally liable *in rem*. However, the District Court found that F&I and Trattner were not liable for negligence or negligent entrustment and were not vicariously liable. Thereafter, the District Court entered [—5—] judgment in favor of Hargus and against Coleman and the One Love, jointly and severally, in the amount of $50,000. Coleman and the One Love timely filed this appeal.[4]

II.

We have appellate jurisdiction to review a final order of the District Court under 28 U.S.C. § 1291. We exercise de novo review over the District Court's determination of its own admiralty jurisdiction. *Maher Terminals, LLC v. Port Auth. of N.Y. & N.J.*, 805 F.3d 98, 104, 3 Adm. R. 164, 166 (3d Cir. 2015); *Sinclair v. Soniform, Inc.*, 935 F.2d 599, 601 (3d Cir. 1991).

Under the United States Constitution, the federal judicial power encompasses "all Cases of admiralty and maritime Jurisdiction." U.S. Const. art. III, § 2, cl. 1. Congress codified that jurisdiction at 28 U.S.C. § 1333(1), which provides that federal district courts have original jurisdiction over "[a]ny civil case of admiralty or maritime jurisdiction." 28 U.S.C. § 1333(1). "The fundamental interest giving rise to maritime jurisdiction is 'the protection of maritime commerce.'" *Sisson v. Ruby*, 497 U.S. 358, 367 (1990) (quoting *Foremost Ins. Co. v. Richardson*, 457 U.S. 668, 674 (1982)).

When a party seeks to invoke federal admiralty jurisdiction over a tort claim, the claim "must satisfy conditions both of location and of connection with maritime activity." *Jerome B. Grubart, Inc. v. Great Lakes Dredge & [—6—] Dock Co.*, 513 U.S. 527, 534 (1995). The location aspect is satisfied if "the tort occurred on navigable water" or the "injury suffered on land was caused by a vessel on navigable water." *Id.* The connection aspect is a conjunctive two-part inquiry. First, we "must 'assess the general features of the type of incident involved' to determine whether the incident has 'a potentially disruptive impact on maritime commerce.'" *Id.* (quoting *Sisson*, 497 U.S. at 363, 364 n.2). Second, we "must determine whether 'the general character' of the 'activity giving rise to the incident' shows a 'substantial relationship to traditional maritime activity.'" *Id.* (quoting *Sisson*, 497 U.S. at 364 n.2, 365). Federal admiralty jurisdiction is only proper when the location test and both prongs of the connection test are satisfied. *Id.*

Here, even assuming the location test is satisfied, we find that admiralty jurisdiction is lacking because the first prong of the connection test is not met. The first prong of the connection test analyzes whether "the general features of the type of incident involved" have "a potentially disruptive impact on maritime commerce." *Id.* (quoting *Sisson*, 497 U.S. at 363, 364 n.2). This analysis requires us to assess the "potential" disruptive effects that the type of incident involved could have on maritime commerce, not whether the particular incident at hand actually disrupted maritime commerce. *Id.* at 538–39. In so doing, we must describe the incident "at an intermediate level of possible generality." *Id.* at 538. The purpose of this exercise is to ascertain "whether the incident could be seen within a class of incidents that posed more than a fanciful risk to commercial shipping." *Id.* at 539.

Several cases illustrate the proper analysis. In *Sisson*, a fire broke out on a recreational vessel that was docked at a [—7—] marina, destroying that vessel and damaging several recreational vessels nearby and the marina. 497 U.S. at 360. The Supreme Court described the incident as "a fire on a vessel docked at a marina on navigable waters," and concluded

---

[4] It bears noting that no entry of appearance was made on behalf of Hargus. Nor was a brief filed on his behalf and neither Hargus nor an attorney acting on his behalf participated in oral argument.

that this type of incident has the potential to disrupt maritime commerce because the fire could have spread to a nearby commercial vessel or made the marina inaccessible for commercial vessels. *Id.* at 362-63.

Likewise, in *Grubart,* a construction company that was using a crane on a barge in the Chicago River allegedly cracked a freight tunnel running under the river, causing water to pour into the tunnel and flood buildings downtown. 513 U.S. at 530. The Supreme Court described that incident as "damage by a vessel in navigable water to an underwater structure," and concluded that this type of incident has the potential to disrupt maritime commerce because it "could lead to a disruption in the water course itself" or "could lead to restrictions on the navigational use of the waterway during required repairs." *Id.* at 539; *see also Foremost Ins. Co.,* 457 U.S. at 675 (describing a collision between two pleasure boats as "a collision between boats on navigable water" and concluding that such an incident has the potential to disrupt maritime commerce because a collision between boats in an area with heavy commercial boat traffic would have a "substantial effect on maritime commerce"); *id.* at 675 n.5 (explaining that, in *Executive Jet Aviation, Inc. v. City of Cleveland,* 409 U.S. 249 (1972), the Supreme Court concluded that a plane crashing into the water had the potential to disrupt maritime commerce because "an aircraft sinking in the water could create a hazard for the navigation of commercial vessels in the vicinity"). [—8—]

On the other hand, in *Tandon v. Captain's Cove Marina of Bridgeport, Inc.,* 752 F.3d 239, 2 Adm. R. 57 (2d Cir. 2014), the court concluded that a brawl on a permanent floating dock between passengers of two boats did not have the potential to disrupt maritime commerce. In that case, two separate groups of individuals (the "Tandon group" and the "Genna group") traveled by separate boats to a marina restaurant for dinner and drinks. *Id.* at 241, 2 Adm. R. at 57–58. As both groups left the restaurant and boarded their boats, a member of the Tandon group fell into the water. *Id.,* 2 Adm. R. at 58. Members of the Genna group laughed at the mishap, leading members of the Tandon group to yell

unspecified comments in response. *Id.,* 2 Adm. R. at 58. Both groups then proceeded by boat to the South Dock—a floating dock accessible only by water—and docked their respective vessels. *Id.* at 242, 2 Adm. R. at 58. Once both groups disembarked from their vessels onto the South Dock, a fistfight broke out, during which one member of the Genna group was knocked off the South Dock and into the water. *Id.,* 2 Adm. R. at 58. The individual also alleged that he was then held underwater to the point of asphyxia and suffered severe injuries as a result. *Id.,* 2 Adm. R. at 58.

In analyzing the potential for this type of incident to disrupt maritime commerce, the Second Circuit described the incident as "a physical altercation among recreational visitors on and around a permanent dock surrounded by navigable water." *Id.* at 249, 2 Adm. R. at 64. The Court explained that, unlike *Grubart,* this type of incident cannot disrupt navigation because "it does not create any obstruction to the free passage of commercial ships along navigable waterways. Nor can it lead to a disruption in the course of the waterway itself." *Id.,* 2 Adm. R. at 64. Furthermore, the Court noted that, unlike *Sisson,* this incident "cannot immediately damage nearby commercial vessels" and "threatens only its participants." *Id.,* 2 Adm. R. at 65. Moreover, the Court [—9—] found that because the incident did not occur while the parties were at sea, the incident could not "distract the crew from their duties, endangering the safety of the vessel and risking collision with others on the same waterway" or force the vessel "to divert from its course to obtain medical care for the injured person." *Id.* at 250, 2 Adm. R. at 65. Finally, the Court noted that the injured individual was not "employed in maritime commerce." *Id.,* 2 Adm. R. at 65. Accordingly, the Second Circuit concluded that "this type of incident does not realistically pose a threat to maritime commerce." *Id.* at 249, 2 Adm. R. at 64.

Here, the activity in question can be described as throwing a small inert object from land at an individual onboard an anchored vessel. Like the fistfight in *Tandon,* we find that this type of incident "does not realistically pose a threat to maritime commerce." *Id.*, 2 Adm. R. at 64. First, unlike damage to an underwater structure, *see Grubart*, 513 U.S. at 538–39, or a collision between two vessels, *see Foremost Insurance Co.*, 457 U.S. at 675, throwing an inert object from land onto an anchored vessel does not create any potential for disrupting the course of the waterway or obstructing the free passage of commercial ships on the waterway. Second, unlike a fire on a marina, *see Sisson*, 497 U.S. at 363, or a plane crashing into the water, *see Foremost Insurance Co.*, 457 U.S. at 675 n.5, throwing an inert object from land onto an anchored vessel has no potential to damage nearby commercial vessels.

In sum, throwing an object like a coffee cup from land at an individual standing on an anchored vessel does not threaten a disruptive effect on maritime commerce because it does not have the potential of disrupting navigation, damaging nearby commercial vessels, or causing a commercial vessel to divert from its course. Accordingly, Hargus' claims do not satisfy the first prong of the two-prong [—10—] connection test, rendering the invocation of federal admiralty jurisdiction inappropriate.

III.

For the foregoing reasons, we will vacate the District Court's judgment of September 30, 2015 and remand the matter with instructions that the District Court dismiss the case.

United States Court of Appeals for the Fourth Circuit

United States Court of Appeals
for the Fourth Circuit

No. 15-4383

UNITED STATES
VS.
SERAFINI

Appeal from the United States District Court for the
Eastern District of Virginia, at Newport News

Decided: June 10, 2016

Citation: 826 F.3d 146, 4 Adm. R. 160 (4th Cir. 2016).

Before **WILKINSON**, **MOTZ**, and **SHEDD**, Circuit
Judges.

[—2—] **WILKINSON**, Circuit Judge:

Appellant Brian Serafini pleaded guilty to one count of communicating a false distress message to the United States Coast Guard, in violation of 14 U.S.C. § 88(c). He was sentenced to fourteen months imprisonment and required to pay restitution for the costs incurred by the Coast Guard in responding to the specious communication. His sole argument on appeal is that the district court lacked the statutory authority to issue a restitution order. For the reasons that follow, we reject Serafini's claim and affirm the judgment of the district court.

I.

A.

The facts giving rise to this case are not in dispute. On May 11, 2014, Newport News Police Department and Virginia Marine Resources Commission officers responded to a report that an unauthorized boat had drifted into a restricted marine area at the Newport News Shipbuilding Company ("the shipyard"). J.A. 39. When they arrived at the shipyard, the officers discovered Brian Serafini intoxicated in a twenty-four foot Shamrock motor vessel. *Id.*

The officers questioned Serafini about how the vessel came to be in the restricted area of the shipyard. He explained that he had provided assistance to a man who was casting off the Shamrock from a pier located along the Pagan River. Serafini [—3—] told the officers that once the boat left the pier he could not safely return to shore and thus remained onboard. As they exited the mouth of the river, the two men purportedly started fighting and eventually Serafini threw the other man overboard. Upon hearing Serafini's "very detailed" version of events, the Coast Guard and other local agencies immediately set out to find the person Serafini allegedly tossed into the water. *Id.* at 39-40.

During the search, law enforcement determined that the Shamrock motor vessel had in fact been stolen. They also spoke with a witness who saw Serafini alone on the pier prior to the reported theft. *Id.* at 40. Police thereafter arrested Serafini for public intoxication and took him to the Newport News jail for booking. While he was in custody, Serafini disclosed that he had taken some medication that may have caused him to imagine that another man was on the boat. The search was eventually called off—the Coast Guard could not find any evidence indicating that someone had been thrown off the Shamrock. In total, the rescue efforts cost the Coast Guard $117,913. *Id.* at 41.

B.

A grand jury in the Eastern District of Virginia returned a one-count indictment against Serafini charging him with knowingly and willfully communicating a false distress message, in violation of 14 U.S.C. § 88(c). J.A. 6. With the advice of [—4—] counsel, Serafini pleaded guilty on December 30, 2014. *Id.* at 38. Although Serafini and the government did not enter a formal plea agreement, the parties agreed on a stipulated "Statement of Facts," wherein Serafini admitted that his "statements were a false distress call which caused the United States Coast Guard to attempt to save lives when no help was actually needed." *Id.* at 40. Following a sentencing hearing on June 15, 2015, the district court sentenced Serafini to fourteen months imprisonment, to be followed by three years of supervised release. *Id.* at 120-23. The court also ordered Serafini to pay the Coast Guard $117,913 in restitution for the costs it incurred responding to the false distress call. *Id.* at 124. The district court reasoned that the award was statutorily authorized. Serafini now appeals the district court's ruling with respect to the order of restitution.

II.

In this appeal, Serafini contends that the cost provision of Section 88(c) permits the Coast Guard to seek only civil redress against those who communicate false distress messages. We disagree. In our view, Section 88(c)(3) was designed to hold individuals "liable" in either criminal or civil proceedings for "all costs the Coast Guard incurs as a result of the individual's action." We shall first set forth Section 88(c)'s [—5—] remedial scheme and then proceed to address Serafini's particular arguments.

A.

At its core, 14 U.S.C. § 88(c) serves two purposes. First, Congress sought to protect the Coast Guard's limited budget by imposing punishment on those who intentionally send false distress calls. Section 88(c) reflects the view that essential resources should not be squandered at the whim of pranksters or, even worse, by those who would deliberately divert the Coast Guard's attention from their own nefarious activities. Second, and equally important, Section 88(c) reflects Congress's desire to avoid needlessly risking the lives of Coast Guard personnel, whose search and rescue operations can be highly dangerous and are too often accompanied by tragic consequences.

To that end, Section 88(c) provides:

An individual who knowingly and willfully communicates a false distress message to the Coast Guard or causes the Coast Guard to attempt to save lives and property when no help is needed is—

(1) guilty of a class D felony;
(2) subject to a civil penalty of not more than $10,000; and

(3) liable for all costs the Coast Guard incurs as a result of the individual's action.

14 U.S.C. § 88(c). Here, the parties dispute whether subsection (3) permits an order of restitution as part of a criminal sentence. [—6—]

B.

"A restitution order that exceeds the authority of the statutory source is no less illegal than a sentence of imprisonment that exceeds the statutory maximum." *United States v. Davis*, 714 F.3d 809, 812 (4th Cir. 2013). We thus must examine closely the alleged authorizing provision. "We begin, as always, with the text of the statute." *Permanent Mission of India to the U.N. v. City of N.Y.*, 551 U.S. 193, 197 (2007). The statute before us does not define the phrase "liable for all costs the Coast Guard incurs." Accordingly, we apply the "fundamental canon of statutory construction" that "words will be interpreted as taking their ordinary, contemporary, common meaning." *Perrin v. United States*, 444 U.S. 37, 42 (1979). "To determine a statute's plain meaning, we not only look to the language itself, but also the specific context in which that language is used, and the broader context of the statute as a whole." *Country Vintner of N.C., LLC v. E. & J. Gallo Winery, Inc.*, 718 F.3d 249, 258 (4th Cir. 2013).

Serafini asserts that, when read "in context, the phrasing 'liable for costs' connote[s] civil liability, rather than a criminal sanction." Appellant's Br. at 21. According to Serafini, "[t]he text and structure of the statute . . . make this [reading] clear." *Id.* at 13. [—7—]

We fail to see why the phrase "liable for all costs the Coast Guard incurs" would authorize only civil remedies. First of all, Congress did not limit "liability" to a particular form of proceeding. Moreover, the argument for a narrow reading of Section 88(c)(3) is undermined by the language in the preceding subsection (c)(2). Section 88(c)(3) speaks broadly of liability "for all costs the Coast

Guard incurs," while (c)(2) subjects violators solely to a "civil penalty." As the Supreme Court has reiterated: "Where Congress includes particular language in one section of a statute but omits it in another section of the same Act, it is generally presumed that Congress acts intentionally and purposely in the disparate inclusion or exclusion." *See Russello v. United States,* 464 U.S. 16, 23 (1983). Simply put, if Congress wanted to limit subsection 88(c)(3) to civil proceedings, it presumably would have done so explicitly, as it did in subsection (c)(2).

Serafini responds by urging us to draw a negative inference from the fact that Congress "could have specified, as it did with the 'civil penalty' in § 88(c)(2), that it intended the defendant to be 'criminally liable' under § 88(c)(3)." Appellant's Br. at 23. But that argument ignores a critical feature of the statute itself. Most importantly, 14 U.S.C. § 88(c) is a criminal provision; it makes "knowingly and willfully" communicating false distress messages a class D [—8—] felony. Thus, unlike the civil carve out specified in subsection (c)(2), Congress had no need to state in what is generally a criminal statute that subsection (c)(3) authorizes criminal liability.

Serafini also makes much of the fact that Section 88(c)(3) does not use the word "restitution." He maintains that "Congress easily could have used language that clearly called for criminal restitution orders, including, most obviously, the word 'restitution.' Or, it could have referred expressly to the [relevant] restitution statute." *Id.* at 23. Absent an explicit legislative authorization, the argument goes, the federal courts are without authority to award restitution in criminal cases.

We also find this argument unpersuasive. Congress had no need to use the particular word "restitution" when the statutory text made its restitutionary intent so clear. In Section 88(c)(3), Congress subjected individuals to liability "for *all costs* the Coast Guard incurs as a result of the individual's action." 14 U.S.C. § 88(c)(3) (emphasis added). The import of this language is not difficult to

discern. "[T]he use of the word 'all' [as a modifier] suggests an expansive meaning because 'all' is a term of great breadth." *Nat'l Coal. For Students with Disabilities Educ. & Legal Def. Fund v. Allen,* 152 F.3d 283, 290 (4th Cir. 1998). Congress's decision to use the words "liable for all costs" and omit "restitution" was thus anything but a [—9—] bar to a restitutionary order in a criminal case. Rather, by employing the broad language of Section 88(c)(3), Congress intended to include "all" the different items and varieties of expense the Coast Guard might incur "as a result of the individual's action," not to limit the forum in which it might recover them. We note that our reading of the statute is consistent with decisional law from our sister circuits. *See United States v. Kumar,* 750 F.3d 563, 566-68, 2 Adm. R. 443, 443–46 (6th Cir. 2014) (affirming the district court's restitution order of $277,257.70 to the Coast Guard); *United States v. James,* 986 F.2d 441, 444 (11th Cir. 1993) (reversing the lower court's decision because it failed to award the Coast Guard "the costs of the operation from beginning to completion").

Serafini further attempts to bolster his interpretation of Section 88(c) by relying on other provisions in the criminal code. "The fact that [Congress] has [explicitly referred to restitution] in other statutes," Serafini contends, "strongly suggests that it did not intend to do so in § 88(c)(3)." Appellant's Reply Br. at 5-6 (citing 42 U.S.C. § 1383a(b); 38 U.S.C. § 6108(b); 21 U.S.C. § 853(q)).

This kind of exercise, however, leads us far afield. Our task in interpreting the meaning of Section 88(c) "begins where all such inquiries must begin: with the language of the statute itself." *United States v. Ron Pair Enterprises, Inc.,* 489 U.S. [—10—] 235, 241 (1989). "In this case it is also where the inquiry should end, for where, as here, the statute's language is plain, 'the sole function of the courts is to enforce it according to its terms.'" *Id.* (quoting *Caminetti v. United States,* 242 U.S. 470, 485 (1917)). We recognize, of course, that there is no strict rule against the use of other sections of the code as an aid to statutory construction. *See Train v. Colorado Pub. Interest Research Grp., Inc.,* 426 U.S. 1, 10 (1976). Nevertheless we conclude that Section 88(c)'s language, which is by far the most relevant for our purposes, is sufficiently clear to obviate the need for transpositional interpretation.

Finally, Serafini invokes the rule of lenity. Appellant's Reply Br. at 9. He claims that because the statute does not "'plainly and unmistakably' mandate[] criminal restitution," *id.*, the rule of lenity requires that we vacate the district court's decision to impose such liability.

To apply the rule of lenity here would mark a sharp departure from the rulings of the Supreme Court and our own. It is not the case that a provision is "'ambiguous' for purposes of lenity merely because it [is] *possible* to articulate a construction more narrow than that urged by the Government." *Moskal v. United States,* 498 U.S. 103, 108 (1990). Rather, in order to invoke the rule there must be a "grievous ambiguity or uncertainty in the language and structure of the [—11—] Act, such that even after a court has seize[d] everything from which aid can be derived, it is still left with an ambiguous statute." *Chapman v. United States,* 500 U.S. 453, 463 (1991); *see also United States v. Kahoe,* 134 F.3d 1230, 1234 (4th Cir. 1998). Given that the language and structure of Section 88(c) support the government's position, *see ante* at 6-9, it is no surprise that the statute's use of the phrase "liable for all costs the Coast Guard incurs" does not rise to the level of grievousness that would warrant application of the rule of lenity in this case.

In sum, the text and all reasonable inferences from it provide a clear rebuttal to Serafini's proposed construction of Section 88(c)(3). Our interpretation, to repeat, is in no way meant to suggest that the Coast Guard cannot recover the costs associated with a false distress call in a civil action. The sole question before us, however, is whether an order of restitution may issue under Section 88(c)(3) as part of a criminal sentence. We hold that it may. As described above, a primary purpose of the statute was to preserve for legitimate purposes the Coast Guard's finite budget. It would defeat that purpose to mandate that the Coast Guard

expend even more resources in separate civil actions to recoup false distress call costs. *See Federal Trade Commission v. Fred Meyer, Inc.,* 390 U.S. 341, 349 (1968) ("we cannot, in the absence of an [—12—] unmistakable directive, construe the Act in a manner which runs counter to the broad goals which Congress intended it to effectuate").

III.

For the foregoing reasons, we affirm the judgment of the district court.

AFFIRMED

United States Court of Appeals
for the Fourth Circuit

No. 15-4498

UNITED STATES
vs.
SAUNDERS

Appeals from the United States District Court for the Eastern District of North Carolina, at Greenville and Wilmington

Decided: July 5, 2016

Citation: 828 F.3d 198, 4 Adm. R. 164 (4th Cir. 2016).

Before TRAXLER, Chief Judge, WYNN, Circuit Judge, and MOON, Senior United States District Judge for the Western District of Virginia, sitting by designation.

[—4—] PER CURIAM:

Four commercial boat captains were charged with violating the Lacey Act after they caught Atlantic striped bass in federal waters and later sold them. The Lacey Act, through its incorporation of a federal regulation, criminalizes the taking and selling of Atlantic striped bass from federal waters. The Act, however, exempts from prosecution fishing that is "regulated by a fishery management plan in effect" under the Magnuson-Stevens Fishery Conservation and Management Act ("Magnuson-Stevens Act"). 16 U.S.C. § 3377(a). Citing that exception, the captains moved to dismiss the indictments.

The district court granted the motions based on two premises. It first found that a fishery management plan created by the Atlantic States Marine Fisheries Commission ("Commission") and referenced in the Atlantic Striped Bass Conservation Act ("Bass Act") must be treated as a plan in effect under the Magnuson-Stevens Act.[1] Next, the district court [—5—] reasoned that the Commission's plan regulated the boat captains' activity in federal waters. Thus, the district court found that the exception applied.

We conclude, however, that the text of the plan created by the Commission and referenced by the Bass Act in fact regulates only state coastal waters, and accordingly does not regulate fishing in federal waters. The only possible hook to federal waters in the Commission's plan is the general statement that the Secretary of Commerce has authority to regulate bass fishing in federal waters. Even if this statement was enough to say that the plan regulated federal waters (which it is not), the provision would be invalid, because the Commission—a collection of state representatives—has no authority to delegate power over *federal* waters to the Secretary of Commerce.

Accordingly, we remand these cases to the district court with instructions to reinstate the indictments.

I. THE INDICTMENTS

The Appellees Gaston Saunders, Bryan Daniels, Michael Potter, and Stephen Daniels (hereinafter referred to as "Captains") are the captains of commercial fishing vessels. During 2009 and 2010, the captains each harvested several tons [—6—] of bass from federal waters (known as the "exclusive economic zone," or EEZ[2]), which they subsequently transported and sold to commercial seafood dealers.[3]

---

[1] The Government asserts error on that point, arguing that 16 U.S.C. § 5158(c)—which catalyzed the district court's reasoning—contains a scrivener's error. That is, Section 5158(c)'s reference to "any plan issued under subsection (a)" is a textual anomaly, because subsection (a) in fact authorizes only regulations by the Secretary of Commerce, not plans. The Government attributes this dissonance to a drafting oversight in 1991 that

left the "any plan" language in the statute while excising related verbiage. *Compare* Pub. L. No. 100-589, 102 Stat. 2984, at § 6 (Nov. 3, 1988) *with* Pub. L. No. 102-130, 105 Stat. 626, at § 4(1)-(2) (Oct. 17, 1991).
(Continued) [—5—]

Because this appeal can be resolved without deciding whether 16 U.S.C. § 5158(c) contains a scrivener's error, we do not reach the issue.

[2] On the eastern seaboard, the EEZ extends from three to 200 miles offshore. *See* 16 U.S.C. § 1802(11); 50 C.F.R. § 600.10; 48 Fed. Reg. 10,605, 1983 WL 506851 (Mar. 10, 1983).

[3] The indictment charged that these bounties involved bass with a market value greater than

Based on these actions, on January 15, 2015, the Government brought separate indictments containing multiple Lacey Act counts against each captain. The Government now appeals the district court's dismissal of the indictments against Captains Potter and Stephen Daniel in full and against Captains Saunders and Bryan Daniels in part.[4] We consolidated the four cases.

II. THE REGULATORY FRAMEWORK

A. The Lacey Act

The Lacey Act makes it a crime to take wildlife in violation of some other federal law. Specifically, it is illegal to, *inter alia*, transport, acquire, or sell any fish "taken possessed, transported, or sold in violation of any law, treaty, or regulation of the United States . . . ." 16 U.S.C. § 3372(a)(1). If one does so "by knowingly engaging in conduct [—7—] that involves" the sale of such ill-gotten fish having a market value over $350, then he may be imprisoned, fined, or both. *Id.* § 3373(d)(1)(B).

Because the Bass Act, described below, forbids anyone from harvesting, retaining, possessing, or fishing for bass in the EEZ, the captains allegedly violated the Lacey Act when they caught several tons of bass in the EEZ during 2009 and 2010.

B. The Bass Act and the Commission

Congress has found that Atlantic striped bass are commercially, economically, and recreationally important. 16 U.S.C. § 5151(a)(1). Due to their migratory nature, "[n]o single government entity has full management authority" over bass. *Id.* § 5151(a)(2). Congress enacted the Bass Act "to support and encourage the development, implementation, and enforcement of effective interstate action regarding the conservation and management of the Atlantic striped bass."

$350, as required by the Lacey Act. *See* 16 U.S.C. 3373(d)(1)(B).

[4] The indictments against Captains Saunders and Bryan Daniels also included counts for making false statements and aiding and abetting. Those counts are not before us.

Id. § 5151(b). To accomplish this goal, the Bass Act divides regulatory authority over Atlantic striped bass into two distinct, but interrelated, schemes: (1) federal waters and (2) state coastal waters.

First, Congress outlined the regulation of bass in federal waters. 16 U.S.C. § 5158; *see id.* §§ 5152(6), 1802(11); *supra* footnote 2. Section 5158(a) commands the Secretary of Commerce to "promulgate regulations governing fishing for Atlantic [—8—] striped bass in the exclusive economic zone . . . ." The Secretary of Commerce must "consult" with, among others, the Commission when preparing her rules. *Id.* § 5158(b). In addition to other standards, her regulations must be "compatible with the *Plan* and each *Federal moratorium* in effect on fishing for Atlantic striped bass within the coastal waters of a coastal State." *Id.* § 5158(a)(2) (emphasis added).

A state coastal waters "plan" under the Bass Act is a plan (or amendment to such plan) for managing bass "that is prepared and adopted by the Commission." 16 U.S.C. §§ 5152(5), 5152(10). The Bass Act instructs the Commission to annually determine whether its member-States have adopted measures for their "coastal waters" (*i.e.*, zero to three miles offshore) that fully implement and satisfactorily enforce the Commission's plan. *Id.* § 5153(a); *see id.* § 5152(3). The Commission then notifies both the Secretary of Commerce and Secretary of Interior ("Secretaries") of each such "negative determination." *Id.* § 5153(c); *see id.* § 5152(3). At that point, the Secretaries jointly determine whether the particular State is, in fact, in compliance with the Commission's plan. If not, the Secretaries "declare jointly a moratorium on fishing for Atlantic striped bass within the coastal waters of that coastal State," violation of which is punishable civilly. *Id.* §§ 5154(a), (c). The prospect of this federally-imposed moratorium therefore acts as [—9—] an enforcement mechanism against recalcitrant States that refuse to abide by the

Commission's plan governing state coastal waters.[5]

A brief comment on the Commission's history further illuminates the genesis and structure of the Bass Act. States cannot enter into any agreement or compact without the consent of Congress. U.S. Const. art. I, § 10, cl. 3. In 1941, Congress approved the interstate compact that created the Commission and endeavored to better manage fish populations on the Atlantic seaboard. Pub. L. No. 77-539, 56 Stat. 267 (May 4, 1942); *see also* Pub. L. No. 81-721, 64 Stat. 467 (Aug. 19, 1950) (approving addition of new States and repealing limitation on the life of the compact); *New York v. Atl. States Marine Fisheries Comm'n*, 609 F.3d 524, 528 (2d Cir. 2010); *Rhode Island Fishermen's All., Inc. v. Rhode Island Dep't of Envtl. Mgmt.*, 585 F.3d 42, 46 (1st Cir. 2009). Under the compact, each State appoints members to the Commission, which is charged with investigating conservation measures, offering suggestions for coordination of the States' police powers, and presenting [—10—] recommended legislation to the member-States. 56 Stat. 267-68; *New York*, 609 F.3d at 528.

Exercising these powers, the Commission in 1981 issued its first plan for Atlantic striped bass fishing in state coastal waters. Atlantic States Marine Fisheries Commission, *Fisheries Mgmt. Rep. No. 1: Interstate Fisheries Mgmt. Plan of the Striped Bass* (Oct. 1981) ("1981 Plan"). Faced with declining bass populations, the 1981 Plan put forth several "recommended management measures." *Id.* at 1-1 & 1-4. But "attempts at implementing the plan failed due to [the Commission's] lack of direct regulatory authority over the individual Atlantic states." Note, Thomas Rapone, *The EEZ Solution to Striper Management: Why the Federal Government Should Ban the Commercial Harvest of Striped Bass Once and*

---

[5] *See* Note, Joseph A. Farside, Jr., *Atlantic States Marine Fisheries Commission: Getting A Grip on Slippery Fisheries Management*, 11 Roger Williams U. L. Rev. 231, 242 (2005) (explaining that "threat of a moratorium" and corresponding "millions of dollars of lost business" encourages States to comply with Commission's plan).

for All, 44 Suffolk U. L. Rev. 567, 569 (2011); *see id.* at 577 (observing that as the product of "a mere interstate compact, the [Commission] still lacked the regulatory authority to force individual states to comply"); *New York*, 609 F.3d at 528; *see also* Atlantic States Marine Fisheries Commission, *Fishery Mgmt. Rep. No. 41, Amend. 6 to the Interstate Fishery Mgmt. Plan for Atl. Striped Bass*, at p.39 § 5.0 (Feb. 2003) ("Amendment 6") (observing that "Commission does not have the authority to directly compel state/jurisdictional implementation of the measures" proposed). [—11—]

Against the backdrop of this collective action problem, Congress passed the Bass Act in 1984, Pub. L. No. 98-613, 98 Stat. 3187 (Oct. 31, 1984), which functions as the cooperative federalism scheme explained above and summarized in the chart below.

	State coastal waters (0-3 miles offshore)	Federal waters (EEZ) (3-200 miles offshore)
States' regulatory role (via Commission)	*Primary.* Commission designs plan for state coastal waters and annually notifies the Commerce and Interior Secretaries of non-compliance. § 5153.	*Secondary.* Commission provides input to Secretary of Commerce as she formulates regulations for the EEZ. § 5158(b).
Federal regulatory role	*Secondary.* Secretaries of Commerce and Interior make final determinations of non-compliance with plan and declare moratorium in offending State's coastal waters. § 5154(a).	*Primary.* Secretary of Commerce issues regulations for the EEZ, which must be "compatible with" Commission's plan for coastal waters. §5158(a)(2).

C. The Lacey Act Exemption

The Lacey Act exempts conduct from prosecution if it was "*activity regulated* by a fishery management *plan in effect under*" the Magnuson-Stevens Act. 16 U.S.C. § 3377(a) (emphasis added). A Magnuson-Stevens Act plan is quite different from a [—12—] plan created by the Commission. Magnuson-Stevens Act plans are created by one of eight regional councils (or occasionally the

Secretary of Commerce) composed of various state and federal officials. *Id.* §§ 1852(a)(1), (b)-(c), 1854(c). The regional councils themselves are creatures of the Magnuson-Stevens Act, *id.* § 1852(a)(1), not an interstate compact like the Commission. And unlike Commission plans, regional councils' plans must include federally-mandated provisions and are subject to final approval by the Secretary of Commerce. *Id.* §§ 1853(a), 1854(a).

In any event, to resolve these appeals we need only decide whether the Commission's plan (which the district court treated as a Magnuson-Stevens Act plan) regulates the captains' activity of bass fishing in federal waters. *See supra* footnote 1. To that question we now turn.

III. DISCUSSION

"We review a district court's decision to grant a motion to dismiss an indictment *de novo.*" *United States v. Good*, 326 F.3d 589, 591 (4th Cir. 2003).

A. The Commission's plan

The district court concluded that the Commission's plan *authorizes* the Secretary of Commerce to regulate striped bass in federal waters, the EEZ. It further noted that the Secretary of Commerce promulgated a regulation—50 C.F.R. § 697.7(b)—"prohibiting fishing for Atlantic striped bass in the EEZ," [—13—] which is "the same regulation under which [defendants are] being prosecuted." Thus, the district court held the Commission's plan regulates the captains' conduct (by way of the Secretary of Commerce's rule that the plan "authorized"), and the Lacey Act exemption applies. We disagree.

1. The plan does not authorize the Secretary of Commerce's regulation

As an interpretive manner, the Commission's plan does not authorize the Secretary of Commerce to issue the regulation banning fishing for bass in federal waters.

The text of the Commission's plan does not purport to grant any power to regulate federal waters to the Secretary of Commerce. In fact, a portion of a 2003 amendment to the Commission's plan reads:

> Management of striped bass in the EEZ is within the Jurisdiction of the Secretary of Commerce. The responsibilities of the Secretary of Commerce are detailed in the Atlantic Striped Bass Conservation Act.

Amendment 6, at p.38 § 4.8.8.1. This provision is a simple acknowledgement by the Commission of the Secretary of Commerce's independent authority under the Bass Act. *See* 16 U.S.C. § 5158(a); 55 Fed. Reg. 40,181, 1990 WL 351745 (Oct. 2, 1990); 50 C.F.R. § 697.1. Moreover, Section 2.4 of *Amendment 6* defines the plan's "management unit" to expressly "exclud[e] the Exclusive Economic Zone (3-200 nautical miles offshore)." *Id.* [—14—] at v & 20; *see id.* at vii & 39 § 4.9 (recognizing that "management of striped bass in the exclusive economic zone (EEZ) is the responsibility of the Secretary [of Commerce]," while also making non-binding recommendations to the Secretary of Commerce regarding federal waters as contemplated by 16 U.S.C. §§ 5158(a)(3), (b)). In other words, the Commission's plan disclaimed any regulatory role over federal waters and instead recognized the regulation of federal waters as part of the powers granted to the Secretary of Commerce by the Bass Act.

In sum, nothing in the Commission's plan purports to grant authority over federal waters to the Secretary of Commerce.

2. The plan cannot authorize the Secretary of Commerce's regulation

Even had the Commission tried to endow the Secretary of Commerce with some form of power over federal waters, the attempt would have been legally meaningless.

The Secretary of Commerce is the head of an executive department of the United States and a member of the President's cabinet. *See* 5 U.S.C. § 101; U.S. Const. Art. II, § 2, cl.2. In other words, she derives her authority from federal sources—acts of Congress and the inherent Article II powers of the Executive Branch. As it pertains to this case, her power to regulate federal waters comes directly from the Bass Act. 16 U.S.C. § 5158(a). [—15—]

The Commission, by contrast, is the creature of an interstate compact that binds only the sovereign States that are parties to it. *See* Pub. L. No. 77-539, 56 Stat. 267 (May 4, 1942); *New York*, 609 F.3d at 526. It is, for instance, "not a federal agency within the meaning of the" Administrative Procedure Act, *i.e.*, not an "authority of the Government of the United States." *New York*, 609 F.3d at 527. "The fact that the [Commission] was created by an interstate compact and approved by Congress does not alter th[e] analysis." *Id.* at 532; *see id.* at 533 ("we cannot escape the fact that the entity itself is an aggregation of states").

Simply put, the Commission, as a compilation of State representatives, is charged with regulating the States' own waters. *See id.* at 527; *Medeiros v. Vincent*, 431 F.3d 25, 27 (1st Cir. 2005). The Secretary of Commerce regulates federal waters because that is what Congress told her to do in the Bass Act. The Secretary of Commerce needs nothing further, and the Commission has nothing to bestow on her.

B. Void for Complexity

As an alternative ground for affirming the district court, the captains ask us to find that the statutory scheme here is void for vagueness. We disagree with the captains' argument.

A statute is unconstitutionally vague if it "(1) 'fails to provide people of ordinary intelligence a reasonable opportunity [—16—] to understand what conduct it prohibits' or (2) 'authorizes or even encourages arbitrary and discriminatory enforcement.'" *United States v. Shrader*, 675 F.3d 300, 310 (4th Cir. 2012) (quoting *Hill v. Colorado*, 530 U.S. 703, 732 (2000)). The captains present only the first theory. In assessing the existence of fair notice, we consider "whether a statute's

prohibitions are set out in terms that the ordinary person exercising ordinary common sense can sufficiently understand and comply with." *Id.* (internal quotation omitted).

The captains' vagueness argument contains an oddity and an irony. The oddity is that vagueness challenges usually target a particular word or phrase as critically deficient.[6] Here, however, the captains launch a broadside attack on the entire "statutory framework" as unconstitutionally "convoluted and confusing."

The irony is that this claimed convolution is mainly the product of the exceptionally novel (and ultimately unsupported) reading of the Lacey Act, Bass Act, and the Commission's plan [—17—] that the captains urged below. The Government's theory in the indictments was straightforward: the Lacey Act criminalizes taking wildlife in violation of a federal regulation; a federal regulation under the Bass Act makes it illegal to fish for bass in federal waters; the captains fished for bass in federal waters; therefore, the captains committed Lacey Act crimes.

To support their position, the captains tally the number of statutes, plans, and regulations they say must be consulted to divine whether their conduct was illegal. But counting the number of laws in a case is a poor way to decide a due process challenge: Our sister circuits have squarely held that regulatory complexity does not render a statute (or set of statutes) unconstitutionally vague.

> We recognize that putting together the pieces of this regulatory puzzle is not easy. To understand the crime with which Defendant was charged, one must look at four sources and read them together . . . . But a statute does not fail

---

[6] *See, e.g., Johnson v. United States*, -- U.S. --, 135 S. Ct. 2551 (2015) (voiding "residual clause" in Armed Career Criminal Act); *United States v. Shrader*, 675 F.3d 300, 310-12 (4th Cir. 2012) (evaluating statutory terms "harass," "intimidate," and "course of conduct"); *Martin v. Lloyd*, 700 F.3d 132, 136 (4th Cir. 2012) (courts must place particular "phrases or words" in context when considering a vagueness challenge).

the vagueness test simply because it involves a complex regulatory scheme, or requires that several sources be read together, and Defendant has not directed us to a single case in which we have held otherwise.

United States v. Zhi Yong Guo, 634 F.3d 1119, 1122 (9th Cir. 2011); *see United States v. Griffith*, 85 F.3d 284, 288 (7th Cir. 1996) ("The statutory structure involved is admittedly somewhat *complicated*—it takes three steps to get from state prostitution to federal money laundering. But complication is not tantamount to unconstitutional vagueness. Here, each step in the statutory [—18—] analysis is well-defined.") (emphasis in original). We think the principle of law in these cases is sound. Moreover, a "statute need not spell out every possible factual scenario with 'celestial precision' to avoid being struck down on vagueness grounds." *United States v. Whorley*, 550 F.3d 326, 334 (4th Cir. 2008).

We hasten to add that the straightforward prohibition here—colloquially, "don't fish for bass in federal waters"—has been on the books and readily comprehensible to those in the fishing industry (much less the general population) for over a quarter-century. 55 Fed. Reg. 40,181, 1990 WL 351745 (Oct. 2, 1990); *see* Atlantic States Marine Fisheries Commission, *Addendum IV to Amend. 6 to the Interstate Fishery Mgmt. Plan*, at p.5 § 2.3.3 (Oct. 2014) ("Federal waters . . . ha[ve] been closed to the harvest, possession and targeting of striped bass since 1990"). Further, "economic regulation is subject to a less strict vagueness test because its subject matter is often more narrow," and because market participants "can be expected to consult relevant legislation in advance of action." *Vill. of Hoffman Estates v. Flipside, Hoffman Estates, Inc.*, 455 U.S. 489, 498 (1982); *see United States v. Sun*, 278 F.3d 302, 309 (4th Cir. 2002). [—19—]

The Lacey Act also contains a *scienter* requirement (two of them, in fact), thus forcing the Government to prove the captains' knowledge.

Any person who violates [*inter alia*, 16 U.S.C. § 3372(a)] by *knowingly* engaging in conduct that involves the sale or purchase of, the offer of sale or purchase of, or the intent to sell or purchase, fish or wildlife or plants with a market value in excess of $350, *knowing* that the fish or wildlife or plants were taken, possessed, transported, or sold in violation of, or in a manner unlawful under, any underlying law, treaty or regulation, shall be fined not more than $20,000, or imprisoned for not more than five years, or both.

16 U.S.C. § 3373(d)(1)(B). A "*scienter* requirement alone tends to defeat" vagueness challenges to criminal statutes. *United States v. Jaensch*, 665 F.3d 83, 90 (4th Cir. 2011); *see Gonzales v. Carhart*, 550 U.S. 124, 149 (2007) ("*scienter* requirements alleviate vagueness concerns"); *Colautti v. Franklin*, 439 U.S. 379, 395 & n.13 (1979) (recognizing "that the constitutionality of a vague statutory standard is closely related to whether that standard incorporates a requirement of *mens rea*"); *United States v. McLean*, 715 F.3d 129, 137 (4th Cir. 2013); *United States v. Shrader*, 675 F.3d 300, 311 (4th Cir. 2012); *see also United States v. Lee*, 937 F.2d 1388, 1394-95 (9th Cir. 1991) (sustaining Lacey Act conviction against vagueness challenge due [—20—] to *scienter* requirement). Consequently, we find no merit to the captains' vagueness argument.[7]

* * *

We conclude that the Lacey Act, 16 U.S.C. § 3377(a), does not except from prosecution the captains' conduct alleged in the indictments. We also reject the contention that the regulatory regime governing the captains' actions is unconstitutionally vague. Accordingly, we reverse the orders of the district court dismissing the indictments and

---

[7] The captains' overbreadth argument (in truth, a single mention of the term) is insufficiently presented and thus waived. The same conclusion applies to their passing reference to the rule of lenity, which—like their vagueness challenge—does not direct us to any particular statutory words or phrases that we should interpret leniently.

remand the cases with instructions that the indictments be reinstated.

REVERSED AND REMANDED

United States Court of Appeals for the Fifth Circuit

United States Court of Appeals
for the Fifth Circuit

No. 15-30324

SEAHAWK LIQUIDATING TRUST
VS.
CERTAIN UNDERWRITERS AT LLOYDS LONDON

Appeal from the United States District Court for the
Middle District of Louisiana

Decided: January 19, 2016

Citation: 810 F.3d 986, 4 Adm. R. 172 (5th Cir. 2016).

Before SMITH, WIENER, and GRAVES, Circuit Judges.

[—2—] SMITH, Circuit Judge:

This appeal follows a bench trial and judgment for the defendant insurers on the claims of Seahawk Liquidating Trust ("Seahawk") for payment of insurance proceeds. There is no error, so we affirm.

I.

Seahawk[1] operated a fleet of drilling rigs, one of which was the J/U SEAHAWK 3000 (the "Rig"), a three-legged, mat-supported jack-up drilling rig with 375-foot legs used to perform drilling contracts in the Gulf of Mexico beginning in 1974.[2] In February 2010, while moving between drilling locations, the Rig encountered severe weather and jacked up out of the water for several days to avoid the harsh seas. Despite those efforts, the rough seas still caused the legs to become misaligned.

Between February and April, Seahawk repaired the hydraulic-jacking system on several occasions, actions that were consistent with the Rig's history: It had had consistent wear-and-tear problems with, and required repairs to, its hydraulic-jacking system for more than twenty years. In April, the Rig traveled to perform a drilling contract for Hilcorp Drilling Company ("Hilcorp"), but Seahawk still did not know that the legs were misaligned. The Rig [—3—] failed to jack up to a sufficient height to perform the Hilcorp contract because of other problems with the hydraulic-jacking system, leading Hilcorp to request that Seahawk provide a replacement rig, which it did at a cost of $1,092,000.

Though Seahawk brought in a replacement, the Rig became stuck for several days at the Hilcorp location after an incident during the jacking-down process caused further damage to the hydraulic-jacking system. That incident required temporary repairs to the jacking system while the Rig was stuck and further such repairs once it successfully jacked down and moved to a dry dock. At some point in May, while the Rig was in dry dock, Seahawk learned the legs were misaligned but did not fix them because doing so would be too expensive.

After that dry-dock period, the Rig departed in early July to perform another drilling contract, which it completed in calm weather, though the crew used an unorthodox method to jack it up—the Rig essentially jacked up one side of the hull at a time, rather than jacking up the entire hull uniformly. Seahawk's expert, Crane Zumwalt, testified that the crew developed that procedure to compensate for the misaligned legs and that the Rig always succeeded in jacking up if—as with this drilling contract—the weather and seas were calm.

On July 21, 2010, the weather and seas were not calm as the Rig arrived to perform a drilling contract at East Cameron Island. In those conditions, the Rig's operating manual forbade its crew from jacking it into or out of

---

[1] Seahawk Drilling, Inc. filed for bankruptcy, and its trustee pursued these claims against Lloyds. We refer to both as "Seahawk."

[2] A jack-up drilling rig drills for oil offshore at exploratory and developmental wells. These rigs must be towed between drilling locations. Mat-supported jack-up rigs have a hull that usually floats on the surface and connects to three or four legs that attach to a mat that must be extended to the sea floor to raise the hull out of the water in order for the rig to drill. A hydraulic-jacking system extends the legs and mat down and elevates the hull using a mechanism by which pins that are attached to the hull enter the legs, push the legs down, come out of the legs, re-enter, and push down again. The hydraulic-jacking system repeats this process until the hull reaches the necessary height.

the water, but the crew attempted to jack it out of the water nonetheless. The hydraulic-jacking system became disengaged when the Rig attempted to jack up, causing the hull to slide down the legs and float in the sea. The crew, before evacuating, attempted to jack the Rig back up to no avail, and the Rig floated in the rough seas, sustaining further damage, for nearly thirty hours. Zumwalt testified that the Rig would have been able to jack up—and jack back up after sliding [—4—] down—without incident if the weather had been calm.

After the July 21 storm, the Rig went to dry dock for further repairs until December 2010. The repairs again focused on the hydraulic-jacking system instead of the misaligned legs; Seahawk never repaired the legs. While the Rig was in dry dock, Seahawk submitted a claim to the insurers to cover the cost of repairs, alleged to be $16,969,860. The insurers rejected the claim.

II.

Seahawk sued the insurers for proceeds covering the physical damage to the Rig and the loss on the Hilcorp contract. Seahawk's insurance policy (the "Policy")[3] included several key provisions:

- The general-coverage provision: "This insurance is against all risks of direct physical loss of or physical damage to the property insured, subject to the terms, conditions, and exclusions contained herein . . . . This Insurance covers all the hull and machinery of the drilling unit(s) . . . ."

- The $10,000,000-deductible provision: "For the purpose of this [Deductible] Clause, each occurrence shall be treated

separately, but it is agreed that a sequence of losses or damages arising from the same occurrence shall be treated as one occurrence."

- The wear-and-tear exclusion: "There shall be no recovery under this Insurance in respect of . . . [the] Cost of repairing or replacing any part which may be lost, damaged or condemned solely due to . . . wear and tear . . . ."

- The loss-of-contract provision (the "Contract Provision"): "[C]overage hereunder shall include the loss of charter hire resulting from the termination and/or cancellation of [Seahawk's] drilling contract(s) caused by the insured drilling units being unable to operate following a claim recoverable under [the general-coverage provision] if the deductible were nil." [—5—]

Seahawk sought to recover the nearly $17 million for repairs made between February and December 2010. After a three-day bench trial, the district court determined that the insurers had properly rejected the claim because they found that there were two occurrences, meaning two $10 million deductibles had to be met, so Seahawk could recover nothing.[4] There were two occurrences, the court reasoned, because the sequence of losses (i.e., the damages and subsequent repairs) between February and July was proximately caused by the February storm, but the sequence of losses after the July storm was proximately caused by that latter storm. There were two separate proximate causes of two different series of losses, so there were two occurrences.

Seahawk also sought to recover under the Contract Provision. It maintained that the misalignment of the legs caused the Rig to be unable to operate and thereby occasioned the loss of the Hilcorp contract; the misalignment was caused by a severe weather event and would have been recoverable if the deductible

---

[3] Each incident took place during one of two separate policy periods; one ended and the other began on June 30, 2010. The content of the policies is identical; Swiss Re International SE was an underwriter of the first policy only, and Hudson Specialty Insurance Company, Navigators Insurance Company, New York Marine & General Insurance Company, and Torus Insurance were underwriters on the second policy only.

[4] The parties stipulated after trial that Seahawk could not recover if there was more than one occurrence.

were nil; thus, the loss on the Hilcorp contract was recoverable.

The district court found, to the contrary, that the misaligned legs (a theoretically covered loss) at most contributed to the defective hydraulic-jacking system (an excluded loss, as it was caused by wear-and-tear) in causing the loss of the contract. That finding required that the court apply the concurrent-cause doctrine.

III.

The Policy provides that it is governed by Texas law, under which the interpretation of an insurance policy is a question of law, which we review *de novo*. *Ran-Nan Inc. v. Gen. Accident Ins. Co. of Am.*, 252 F.3d 738, 739 (5th [—6—] Cir. 2001). The parties agree that Texas substantive law applies. We review any underlying factual findings for clear error. *Theriot v. United States*, 245 F.3d 388, 394–95 (5th Cir. 1998). A factual finding, such as a causation determination, is clearly erroneous only "when the appellate court, viewing the evidence in its entirety, is left with the definite and firm conviction that a mistake has been made." *Manderson v. Chet Morrison Contractors, Inc.*, 666 F.3d 373, 376 (5th Cir. 2012). "Re-stated, our court may not find clear error if the district court's finding is plausible in light of the record as a whole, even if this court would have weighed the evidence differently." *Id.* at 376–77 (alterations omitted).

IV.

Because there were two occurrences, the district court properly denied Seahawk's claim for the cost of repairs between February and December 2010. That court's proximate-cause analysis was the correct legal standard for determining the number of occurrences, and the court did not clearly err in finding that the February storm was not the proximate cause of the sequence of losses following the July storm.

A.

Under Texas law, we must construe the Policy according to the general rules of contract construction to give effect to the intent. *Gilbert Tex. Constr., L.P. v. Underwriters at Lloyd's London*, 327 S.W.3d 118, 126 (Tex. 2010).[5] We begin with the policy language, giving the terms their "ordinary and generally-accepted meaning unless the policy shows the words are meant in a technical or different sense." *Id.* When an issue of state law is unclear, a federal court [—7—] must make an "*Erie* guess" as to what the state's highest court would decide.[6]

Seahawk's first claim turns entirely on the meaning of "occurrence," which, according to its ordinary and generally-accepted meaning, is "something that occurs"[7] or "something that takes place; *esp*: something that happens unexpectedly and without design."[8] The parties appear not to contest that the February storm was an occurrence; under that ordinary meaning, the July storm would appear to be an occurrence too.

Seahawk, however, contends that the Policy gives "occurrence" a technical meaning by defining it to include "a sequence of losses or damages arising from the same occurrence." The February storm, according to Seahawk, was an occurrence that damaged the Rig's legs and was a but-for cause of the damages suffered after the July storm because the damaged legs slowed down the jacking-up process. Because the Rig's damaged legs contributed to the damages after the July storm, Seahawk characterizes all of the losses between February and December as "arising from the same [February] occurrence."

---

[5] Our decisions often refer to Certain Underwriters at Lloyd's as "Lloyd's." In their briefs, however, these parties use "Lloyds."

[6] *Farm Credit Bank v. Guidry*, 110 F.3d 1147, 1149 (5th Cir. 1997), *overruled on other grounds by Canfield v. Orso (In re Orso)*, 283 F.3d 686 (5th Cir. 2002).

[7] *"Occurrence,"* WEBSTER'S NINTH NEW COLLEGIATE DICTIONARY (1984).

[8] *"Occurrence,"* WEBSTER'S THIRD NEW INTERNATIONAL DICTIONARY (1986).

The insurers maintain, to the contrary, that any damages after the July storm arose from that storm, not the February storm. Like the district court, the insurers interpret the phrase "arising from" to require that the occurrence be the proximate cause of the "sequence of losses or damages." Thus, even if the February storm damaged the legs and thereby contributed to the losses after July, the July storm would be the proximate cause of—and the occurrence giving rise to—the sequence of losses thereafter.

The real issue, then, is how to interpret the term "arising from" when [—8—] used to determine the number of occurrences under the Policy. Seahawk claims the term requires only a causal link between the occurrence and subsequent losses because Texas law construes "arising from" broadly in favor of coverage. The Texas Supreme Court has stated that "arise out of" requires "simply a causal connection or relation, which is interpreted to mean that there is but for causation, though not necessarily direct or proximate causation."[9] But the court broadly interpreted "arising from"—or relied on cases broadly interpreting that term—only in different contexts in which a broad interpretation would *increase* coverage.[10] The court seems not to have addressed the term when used to determine the number of occurrences, so we must make an *Erie* guess as to how the

court would interpret "arising from" in this context.

For two reasons, that court likely would adopt the proximate-cause analysis applied by the district court. First, as the insurers point out, interpreting "arising from" broadly to require only a causal link when determining the number of occurrences can expand coverage in one case while contracting it in another. For example, Seahawk desires a recognition of only one occurrence to avoid the application of multiple deductibles—a broad construction would increase coverage. But in another case with identical facts but a slightly different insurance policy, an insured may desire multiple occurrences to avoid [—9—] the application of a single policy limit—a narrow construction would increase coverage. Although Texas favors broadly construing policies to provide for coverage, there is no reason to predict—given the conflicting effects on coverage—that the Texas Supreme Court would broadly construe "arising from" in this context.

Second, the proximate-cause analysis is at least implicitly consistent with our and Texas's precedent. Three cases in particular illustrate this point.[11] In each, the policy defined an occurrence as losses "arising out of" a single event or continuous exposure to a condition. And, in each, the court ignored a but-for cause and focused on the direct, immediate, and proximate cause of the losses to determine the number of occurrences.

In *Goose Creek*, an arsonist set fire to two schools in the same school district. Although the same arsonist was the but-for cause of both fires, the fires occurred several blocks and at least two hours apart, and neither caused the other. The school district claimed there was one occurrence and thus one deductible. According to the court, though, there were two occurrences because the "two fires [were] distinguishable in space and time

---

[9] *Utica Nat'l Ins. Co. of Tex. v. Am. Indem. Co.*, 141 S.W.3d 198, 203 (Tex. 2004). We interpret identically the terms "arising out of" and "arising from." *Am. States. Ins. Co. v. Bailey*, 133 F.3d 363, 370 n.7 (5th Cir. 1998).

[10] *See, e.g., Utica Nat'l Ins.*, 141 S.W.3d at 203 (interpreting "arising out of" broadly to reduce the scope of a policy's exclusionary provision); *Mid-Century Ins. Co. of Tex. v. Lindsey*, 997 S.W.2d 153, 156–59 (Tex. 1999) (broadly interpreting the term "arise out of" with regard to the use of a motor vehicle to cover the accidental discharge of a weapon after an attempt to enter the vehicle); *Amerisure Ins. Co. v. Navigators Ins. Co.*, 611 F.3d 299, 312–13 (5th Cir. 2010) (interpreting "arise out of" broadly to find that a conditional exclusion did not apply); *Red Ball Motor Freight, Inc. v. Emp'rs Mut. Liab. Ins. Co. of Wis.*, 189 F.2d 374, 378 (5th Cir. 1951) (interpreting "arising out of" the use of a truck broadly to provide coverage for damages from the driver's negligent refueling).

[11] *Goose Creek Consol. Indep. Sch. Dist. v. Cont'l Cas. Co.*, 658 S.W.2d 338 (Tex. App.—Houston [1st Dist.] 1983, no writ); *U.E. Tex. One-Barrington, Ltd. v. Gen. Star Indem. Co.*, 332 F.3d 274 (5th Cir. 2003); *H.E. Butt Grocery Co. v. Nat'l Union Fire Ins. Co.*, 150 F.3d 526 (5th Cir. 1998).

[and] one did not cause the other." *Goose Creek*, 658 S.W.2d at 341. Though the fires were traced back to the same but-for cause, there were two occurrences because the damages directly arose from two separate fires.

In *U.E. Texas*, nineteen buildings in an apartment complex suffered damage from plumbing leaks. Hoping to pay one deductible, the owner contended there was only one occurrence because the leaks allegedly arose from [—10—] one defective installation of plumbing. The parties stipulated, however, that each leak affected only the specific building under which it occurred. Although there was ostensibly one "overarching cause"—the installation—the court instead focused on the "specific event[s] that caused the loss," *U.E. Tex.*, 332 F.3d at 278—the individual leaks—to conclude there were nineteen occurrences:

> To point to the installation of the pipes as a single event which gave rise to the damage to the nineteen buildings proves too much. Of course it is true that had the plumbing system never been installed the leaks would not have occurred. In this sense, it is true that the leaks which independently damaged the nineteen buildings arose from the same event. However, to look this far back would render any damage to the complex occurring at any time related to the plumbing as arising from the same event.

Id.

In *H.E. Butt*, one employee sexually abused two children in the same bathroom at the same grocery store but on different occasions. Hoping to limit liability under its self-insurance, the insured claimed there was only one occurrence because both incidents arose from its negligent supervision of the employee. The court said that "[t]he question under Texas law becomes whether HEB's negligent employment relationship with its pedophilic employee, rather than the two acts of sexual abuse, 'caused' the injuries to the two children and gave rise to HEB's liability."

H.E. Butt, 150 F.3d at 530. Although negligent supervision plainly was a but-for cause of the children's injuries, there would be no injury or exposure to liability without the intervening sexual abuse. *Id.* at 531. There were two occurrences because

> [w]hile a single occurrence may result in multiple injuries to multiple parties over a period of time . . . [,] *if one cause is interrupted and replaced by another intervening cause, the chain of causation is broken and more than one occurrence has taken place.* Here, it is clear that each child's injuries are independent and caused by the separate acts of sexual abuse.

Id. at 534 (alterations in original) (emphasis added) (internal citations [—11—] omitted).[12] The court discounted a but-for cause and explicitly used the proximate-cause analysis to determine the number of occurrences.

The proper conclusion here follows naturally from the three above-cited decisions: When an occurrence is technically defined to include a series of losses arising from the same event, it includes only those losses *proximately caused* by that event. The Policy defines an occurrence as a series of losses "arising from" the same occurrence and thereby incorporates the proximate-cause analysis.[13] Thus, the district court applied the

---

[12] The court relied on *Appalachian Insurance Co. v. Liberty Mutual Insurance Co.*, 676 F.2d 56, 61 (3d Cir. 1982), which held that to determine the number of occurrences "the court asks if there was but one proximate, uninterrupted, and continuing cause which resulted in all of the injuries and damage." (Alteration and internal quotation marks omitted.)

[13] Seahawk points to *All Metals, Inc. v. Liberty Mutual Fire Insurance Co.*, No. 3-09-CV-0846-BD, 2010 WL 3027045, at *1 (N.D. Tex. 2010), for the proposition that we nonetheless might broadly interpret "arising from." *All Metals* does not support Seahawk's argument, because the policy there defined "occurrence" to include all damages at least indirectly stemming from the same event. By explicitly defining "occurrence" to include indirect causes, the parties had rejected the proximate-cause analysis. *Cf. Fed. Ins. Co. v. Bock*, 382 S.W.2d 305, 307 (Tex. App.—Corpus Christi 1964,

correct legal standard in determining the number of occurrences by analyzing whether the February storm was the *proximate cause*—not just a contributing or but-for cause—of the sequence of losses between February and December 2010.

B.

The task remains to review the district court's factual finding that the July storm—rather than the February storm—was the proximate cause of the sequence of losses after July. Again, we review the district court's causation determinations only for clear error and uphold the same if plausible in light of the record as whole. *Manderson*, 666 F.3d at 376–77. [—12—]

The court noted that a proximate cause is "that cause which in a natural and continuous sequence unbroken by any new and intervening cause, produces a loss, and without which the loss would not have occurred." *Bock*, 382 S.W.2d at 307. There was significant evidence to support the determination that the July storm, not the February storm, was the proximate cause of the sequence of losses after July. Zumwalt testified that the misaligned legs, caused by the February storm, did not prevent the Rig from jacking up in calm weather—testimony that was further bolstered by the Rig's successful completion of a contract in calm weather in early July despite its misaligned legs. Moreover, Zumwalt testified that the Rig continued to jack up without incident for at least three and one-half years after the events at issue, despite Seahawk's never having repaired the legs. The evidence also showed that the weather was severe on July 21 before the crew attempted to jack up in violation of the operating manual. Finally, the court noted that five months elapsed between the February and July storms, and Seahawk knew of the misaligned legs for at least two

---

writ ref'd n.r.e.) ("A proper definition of *direct* loss is loss proximately caused by the peril insured against." (emphasis added)); *Utica Nat'l*, 141 S.W.3d at 203 (equating direct causation with proximate causation). Unlike the parties in *All Metals*, Seahawk and the insurers did not expressly reject the proximate-cause analysis, so we apply it.

months before the July storm yet did not repair them.

We cannot say that, given this evidence, the court clearly erred by finding the February storm alone, "in a natural and continuous sequence unbroken by any new and intervening cause," would not have produced the sequence of losses after the July storm. *See id.* The July storm was thus an intervening and proximate cause of the losses.

V.

The district court did not err in rejecting Seahawk's claim under the Contract Provision. The concurrent-cause doctrine applies, and Seahawk could not recover because it failed to comply with the requirements of that doctrine.

Under Texas law, the concurrent-cause doctrine applies any time "covered and non-covered perils combine to create a loss" and limits an insured's [—13—] recovery to the "portion of the damage caused solely by the covered peril(s)." *Wallis v. United Servs. Auto. Ass'n*, 2 S.W.3d 300, 302–03 (Tex. App.–San Antonio 1999, pet. denied). The doctrine is "a rule which embodies the basic principle that insureds are entitled to recover only that which is covered under their policy . . . ." *Id.* at 303. Therefore, "[i]t is essential that the insured produce evidence which will afford a reasonable basis for estimating . . . the proportionate part of damage caused by a risk covered by the insurance policy." *Travelers Indem. Co. v. McKillip*, 469 S.W.2d 160, 163 (Tex. 1971). "[A]n insured's . . . burden of proof on allocation . . . is central to the claim for coverage." *Wallis*, 2 S.W.3d at 303. "Where a loss, however, is caused by a covered peril and an excluded peril that are *independent* causes of the loss, the insurer is liable." *Guar. Nat'l Ins. Co. v. N. River Ins. Co.*, 909 F.2d 133, 137 (5th Cir. 1990) (emphasis added). Thus, the concurrent-cause doctrine applies to limit recovery only when the loss is caused by two concurrent causes instead of two independent causes.

The district court made a factual finding that the misaligned legs (a covered peril) at most combined with the defective hydraulic-jacking system (an excluded peril)[14] to cause the loss of the Hilcorp contract. We review that factual finding only for clear error, *Manderson*, 666 F.3d at 376–77, and conclude there was sufficient evidence to support it. For example, Hilcorp requested that Seahawk replace the Rig specifically because malfunctions with the hydraulic-jacking system were visible; Hilcorp, apparently, did not notice the misaligned legs. Further, Zumwalt testified that nobody at Seahawk even knew the legs were misaligned at this point and that the Rig had experienced problems with its hydraulic-jacking system continuously for over twenty years. [—14—] Additionally, the court noted that the Rig continued to complete drilling contracts over the next three and one-half years without Seahawk's ever repairing its misaligned legs. Given that evidence, the court did not clearly err by finding the misaligned legs were at most a contributing cause—and certainly not an independent cause—of the loss of the Hilcorp contract.

Seahawk advances several unpersuasive theories that even if the misaligned legs and defective hydraulic-jacking system combined to cause the loss of the contract, the concurrent-cause doctrine should not apply. First, according to Seahawk, the doctrine should not apply because the Contract Provision does not explicitly invoke it. That is a non-starter, because the concurrent-cause doctrine applies whenever a policy delineates covered and excluded perils and such perils combine to cause a loss.

Second, Seahawk avers that the loss of a contract is different from physical damages to which the doctrine typically applies. That notion, for which no caselaw is cited, overlooks the fact that the Contract Provision requires that the loss of contract be the result of physical damages that are recoverable under the general-coverage provision. It would be entirely consistent with the concurrent-cause doctrine for Seahawk to prove what proportion

of the physical damages that led to the loss of contract are attributable to a covered peril and for the insurers to pay out the Contract Provision according to that proportion.

Finally, Seahawk avers that the concurrent-cause doctrine would require it to prove a claim "payable" under the Policy's general coverage provision rather than one "recoverable . . . if the deductible were nil." Seahawk contends that all it must show to recover is some theoretically covered physical damage that contributed to a loss of contract. Seahawk elides the principle that compliance with the concurrent-cause doctrine, under Texas law, is a prerequisite [—15—] to any recovery whatsoever. *See Wallis*, 2 S.W.3d at 303 (noting that allocation of damages is central to the insured's claim). When, as here, a covered peril and excluded peril combine to cause a loss, no amount of damages is even *recoverable*[15]—let alone payable—until the insured complies with the concurrent-cause doctrine. *Id.* at 302–03 ("[T]he insured is entitled to *recover* only that portion of the damage caused solely by the covered peril(s)." (emphasis added)). The district court properly applied the concurrent-cause doctrine to the Contract Provision.

The final point, that Seahawk did not meet its burden under the concurrent-cause doctrine, is without controversy. Seahawk presented no evidence to segregate the damage attributable solely to the misaligned legs (the covered peril) as compared to the defective hydraulic-jacking system (the excluded peril). "Although [an insured] is not required to establish the amount of his

---

[14] Seahawk does not challenge the finding that the hydraulic-jacking system's problems were caused by wear-and-tear and were thus excluded from coverage.

[15] *See* BRYAN A. GARNER, DICTIONARY OF LEGAL USAGE 758 (3d ed. 2011) ("recoverable= compensable. . . . 'capable of being legally obtained.'"). Seahawk's reference to *California Insurance Guarantee Association v. Liemsakul*, 193 Cal. App. 3d 433 (Cal. Ct. App. 1987), does not change this conclusion; it stands for the uncontroversial proposition that "recoverable" means "recovery that might have been possible" rather than that which is "actually recovered." Agreeing as we do with that proposition, a claim for damages under Texas law, where a covered peril and excluded peril combine to cause the loss, is not even *recoverable* unless and until the insured complies with the concurrent-cause doctrine.

damages with mathematical precision, there must be some reasonable basis upon which the [fact finder's] finding rests." *Id.* at 304. Seahawk failed to meet its burden under the concurrent-cause doctrine because it presented no evidence to apportion damages between covered and excluded perils, so the district court properly denied the claim under the Contract Provision.

AFFIRMED.

United States Court of Appeals
for the Fifth Circuit

No. 15-30369

GROGAN
VS.
W & T OFFSHORE, INC.

Appeal from the United States District Court for the
Western District of Louisiana

Decided: January 27, 2016

Citation: 812 F.3d 376, 4 Adm. R. 180 (5th Cir. 2016).

Before **HIGGINBOTHAM**, **OWEN**, and **ELROD**, Circuit
Judges.

[—1—] HIGGINBOTHAM, Circuit Judge:

W&T Offshore hired Triton Diving Services to provide a vessel, staff, and equipment for W&T's offshore pipeline project. W&T also hired a safety contractor, Tiger Safety, to provide safety monitoring and training. Tiger personnel came aboard Triton's vessel to furnish these services, and one of them, a technician named Jakarta Grogan, was injured while on board. W&T and Triton now dispute which party must pay for Grogan's injuries. The court [—2—] below interpreted the parties' Master Service Contract to place this burden on W&T alone. We affirm.

I

W&T Offshore ("W&T") is a pipeline and platform operator in the Gulf of Mexico. In October 2011, it hired Triton Diving Services ("Triton") to participate in an offshore pipeline recommissioning project. The project required flushing the pipeline of impurities, which Triton accomplished by pumping fluids flushed from the pipeline to the TRITON ACHIEVER, a dive support vessel (DSV) that Triton captained, crewed, and operated. W&T provided detailed instructions for the filtering operation in a work order that Triton was obliged to follow pursuant to the Master Service Contract ("MSC") between Triton and W&T.

While Triton was performing this service, it detected potentially unsafe levels of hydrogen sulfide ("H_2S") being filtered out of the pipeline fluids and suspended its operations in accordance with its safety manual. Triton then consulted with a W&T facilities engineer, Alan Greig, who recommended that Triton hire Tiger Safety ("Tiger") to help resolve the H_2S problem. A Triton representative made some of the arrangements with Tiger, and Greig also contacted Tiger to discuss the services it would provide, approve the equipment it would use, and confirm how much the services would cost W&T. Because Triton's work order with W&T would require W&T to pay "cost plus 10%" to Triton for any charges for third-party services not addressed in the work order, W&T opted to pay for Tiger's services directly. The contract and job tickets Tiger prepared for its work on the project listed W&T as "Customer" and were signed by W&T representatives.

Tiger personnel, including Jakarta Grogan, came aboard the ACHIEVER to provide H_2S monitoring and safety training. Grogan testified that his job was to take samples when instructed to do so by W&T's [—3—] representative and to provide measurements to that representative.[1] The H_2S problem was eventually resolved, and W&T decided to discharge Grogan and Tiger.

Shortly thereafter, Grogan fell on the deck of the ACHIEVER while attempting to board a personnel basket. He sued Triton and W&T in federal district court over the resulting injuries. W&T and Triton answered and filed cross-claims against each other for indemnity and defense of Grogan's claims. Under the MSC, W&T had agreed to indemnify Triton for personal injury claims brought by members of the "W&T Group," and Triton had agreed to indemnify W&T from personal injury claims brought by members of the "Contractor Group." The MSC defines these groups as follows:

---

[1] More generally, although a W&T representative on the ACHIEVER monitored Tiger's activities, Tiger personnel were directed by Triton personnel with respect to where they were allowed to go on board the vessel and where they were allowed to set up equipment.

1.1.2 "Contractor Group" shall mean: Contractor, its parent, subsidiary and affiliated companies, and their respective parents, subsidiary and affiliated companies, and all of their respective officers, directors, representatives, employees *and invitees on the Work sites* and insurers of all of the foregoing.

1.1.3 "W&T Group" shall mean: W&T, its parent, subsidiary and affiliated or related companies, its and their working interest owners, co-lessees, co-owners, partners, farmors, farmees, joint operators, and joint venturers, if any, and all of their respective officers, directors, representatives, employees *and invitees on the Work sites* and insurers of all of the foregoing.[2]

Each side claimed a right to indemnification under these provisions.[3] W&T claimed that Grogan was Triton's invitee or, in the alternative, that he [—4—] was an invitee of both Triton and W&T.[4] Triton argued that Grogan was W&T's invitee alone. The parties agreed to a bench trial on this issue.[5]

The district court sided with Triton. It rejected W&T's argument that a "dual invitee" situation existed. Rather, it found, ""[b]ased on the facts of [the] case," that Grogan was W&T's invitee, and "decline[d] the invitation to find Triton a 'co-invitor.'" In turn, it concluded that W&T owed Triton indemnity. W&T appealed.

---

[2] Emphases added.

[3] Each side also seeks its defense costs from the other.

[4] Pursuant to stipulations between the two parties, if both W&T and Triton were found to have invited Grogan, then liability would be allocated 63% to Triton and 37% to W&T. Because each party funded half of the settlement with Grogan, such a finding would obligate Triton to reimburse W&T for the amount it overpaid.

[5] With the consent of both parties, the district court used only the briefs and summary judgment record in the case to reach its ruling.

II

"Interpretation of the terms of a contract, including an indemnity clause, is a matter of law, reviewable *de novo* on appeal."[6] However, "[a] district court's factual findings, including those on which the court based its legal conclusions, are reviewed for clear error."[7] "A finding is clearly erroneous when, although there is evidence to support it, the reviewing court based on all of the evidence is left with the definite and firm conviction that a mistake has been committed."[8]

We use the six-factor framework set forth in *Davis & Sons, Inc. v. Gulf Oil Corp.* to determine whether federal maritime law, rather than state law, [—5—] applies to the interpretation and application of a contract.[9] Here, the district court correctly ruled that the MSC is a maritime contract under that framework, a conclusion the parties do not dispute.

"A maritime contract containing an indemnity agreement . . . should be read as a whole and its words given their plain meaning unless the provision is ambiguous."[10] In this case, the district court's interpretation of the MSC turned on the definition of the word

---

[6] *Offshore Marine Contractors, Inc. v. Palm Energy Offshore, L.L.C.*, 779 F.3d 345, 348, 3 Adm. R. 282, 283 (5th Cir. 2015) (quoting *Duval v. N. Assur. Co. of Am.*, 722 F.3d 300, 303, 1 Adm. R. 270, 271 (5th Cir. 2013)); *see Luhr Bros., Inc. v. Crystal Shipowning, PTE. Ltd. (In re Luhr Bros., Inc.)*, 325 F.3d 681, 684 (5th Cir. 2003) (specifically addressing bench trials in admiralty actions).

[7] *Superior MRI Servs., Inc. v. Alliance Healthcare Servs., Inc.*, 778 F.3d 502, 504 (5th Cir. 2015) (quoting *St. Paul Fire & Marine Ins. Co. v. Labuzan*, 579 F.3d 533, 538 (5th Cir. 2009)); *see Luhr Bros.*, 325 F.3d at 684.

[8] *Luhr Bros.*, 325 F.3d at 684 (quoting *Walker v. Braus*, 995 F.2d 77, 80 (5th Cir. 1993)).

[9] 919 F.2d 313, 316 (5th Cir. 1990); *see generally id.* ("What constitutes maritime character is not determinable by rubric. The Supreme Court has resorted to the observation that a contract is maritime if it has a 'genuinely salty flavor.'") (quoting *Kossick v. United Fruit Co.*, 365 U.S. 731, 742 (1961)).

[10] *Hardy v. Gulf Oil Corp.*, 949 F.2d 826, 834 (5th Cir. 1992) (quoting *Weathersby v. Conoco Oil Co.*, 752 F.2d 953, 955 (5th Cir. 1984)).

"invitee." The MSC itself does not define this term. When a maritime contract uses but does not define "invitee," courts in this circuit apply the definition articulated in *Blanks v. Murco Drilling Corp.*[11] In that case, drawing on Louisiana law, we defined "invitee" as "a person who goes onto premises with the expressed or implied invitation of the occupant, on business of the occupant or for their mutual advantage."[12] The court below used the *Blanks* definition without objection from either party.

III

We first consider the district court's determination that Grogan was W&T's invitee. The court found that "W&T satisfies all of the elements necessary to be Tiger's [and therefore Grogan's] invitor." On appeal, W&T disputes only the finding, made as part of the court's *Blanks* analysis, that W&T was an occupant of the ACHIEVER. W&T objects that it did not "charter, [—6—] man, or operate the vessel" and that Triton was an "independent contractor" according to the MSC.

These objections, whether right or wrong, are not dispositive. The MSC does not define the term "occupant" for purposes of determining invitee status, nor does *Blanks* or any other published case from our court. However, in an unpublished case, we applied "the customary meaning of 'occupant,'" namely, "'[o]ne who has possessory rights in, or control over, certain property or premises.'"[13] The district court found that W&T occupied the ACHIEVER because "[w]hile [Triton's] crew . . . retained control

---

[11] *See, e.g., Brown v. Sea Mar Mgmt., LLC,* 288 F. App'x 922, 924 (5th Cir. 2008) (unpublished); *Alex v. Wild Well Control, Inc.,* No. 07-9183, 2009 WL 2599782, at *9 (E.D. La. Aug. 18, 2009) ("When a contract does not specifically define 'invitee,' courts adopt the *Blanks* definition."); *Clayton Williams Energy, Inc. v. Nat'l Union Fire Ins. Co. of La.,* No. 03-2980, 2004 WL 2452780, at *5 (E.D. La. Nov. 1 2004), aff'd, 161 F. App'x 378 (5th Cir. 2006); *Reynaud v. Rowan Companies, Inc.,* No. 98-1326, 1999 WL 65022, at *3 (E.D. La. Feb. 5, 1999).

[12] 766 F.2d 891, 894 (5th Cir. 1985).

[13] *Brown v. Sea Mar Mgmt.,* LLC, 288 F. App'x 922, 925 (5th Cir. 2008) (quoting BLACK'S LAW DICTIONARY 1108 (8th ed. 2004)).

over decisions related to the safe operation of the vessel . . . the direction, command, and control of the vessel as it pertained to the work on the pipeline recommissioning project itself came from W&T or its company representative."

W&T claims this finding lacks support in the record. We disagree. The record indicates that Triton did what W&T paid it to do pursuant to the MSC and an ensuing work order. The work order incorporated documents that provided detailed instructions for every step of Triton's work on recommissioning the pipeline and specified when and where Triton's vessel was to be "mobilize[d]," "relocate[d]," and "demobilized." Under the MSC, Triton warranted that "all Work provided by [Triton] hereunder will conform, in all particulars, to the specifications set forth in the relevant Order," and it agreed that "in the event [Triton's] Work fails to conform to said specifications, W&T may . . . direct [Triton] to repair, replace or re-accomplish (as applicable) the non-conforming Work." Moreover, although the ACHIEVER's crew mostly consisted of Triton employees and invitees, a W&T consultant was on board for much of the time that Triton's was performing work for W&T. [—7—]

Given this evidence, we cannot conclude that the district court clearly erred in determining that W&T occupied the ACHIEVER. W&T does not claim that the district court otherwise erred in applying *Blanks* to it, and we find no other error. The district court correctly determined that Grogan was W&T's invitee.

IV

We next consider the district court's determination that Grogan was *not* Triton's invitee. W&T argues that this determination arose purely from a misreading of the MSC. According to W&T, the district court erroneously held that a "dual invitee" situation could not exist under the MSC. Accordingly, once the district court determined W&T invited Grogan, it concluded that Grogan could not have been Triton's invitee by simple operation of the contract. In

W&T's telling, then, the district court's finding as to Triton was not factual in nature and is entitled to no deference. Triton disputes W&T's reading of the opinion below. We find W&T's reading plausible,[14] but see no need to resolve this debate. Nor need we determine whether the MSC admits the possibility of a "dual invitee" situation. Even if the district court believed it could not deem Triton an invitor because it had already deemed W&T an invitor, and even if [—8—] this belief resulted from a misinterpretation of the MSC, the district court still found facts sufficient to sustain its holding that Grogan was not Triton's invitee.[15]

---

[14] The district court repeatedly suggested that it could not deem Triton an invitor because it had already deemed W&T an invitor: *"Having found that W&T satisfies all of the elements necessary to be Tiger's invitor, this Court declines the invitation to find Triton a "co-invitor." . . . The Court finds that it would be absurd to conclude that . . . there are two invitors since this would eviscerate the indemnity provisions of a contract like the one in this case . . . . Accordingly*, the Court concludes that Grogan was not the invitee of both Triton and W&T. . . . Based on the facts of this case, the Court concludes that Tiger was W&T's invitee, and therefore, that Grogan, Tiger's employee, was a member of the W&T Group. *Having reached this conclusion*, it is the ruling of this Court that W&T owes Triton indemnity for its defense costs and the amounts paid in settlement of Grogan's claims." (Emphases added.) On the other hand, the court observed that "the facts in [another Fifth Circuit case] are analogous to the facts found by this Court to conclude that a 'dual invitor' situation simply did not exist" and that "most cases that have analyzed the concept of invitee status have facts in common with the facts of this case, which when taken together, militate in favor of finding W&T to be the invitor."

[15] *See Bickford v. Int'l Speedway Corp.*, 654 F.2d 1028, 1031 (5th Cir. Unit B 1981) ("[R]eversal is inappropriate if the ruling of the district court can be affirmed on any grounds, regardless of whether those grounds were used by the district court."). To be clear: we do not reach the issue of whether W&T accurately characterizes the district court's reasoning, nor do we determine whether the MSC allows a "dual invitee" situation. We note, however, that even if the district court had erroneously rejected the possibility of a "dual invitee," this may not have affected its result. In *Blanks*, the contract at issue explicitly contemplated and allocated liability in case of a "dual invitee" situation;

The district court found that Triton did not induce Tiger's and Grogan's participation in W&T's project. Rather, although Triton "coordinate[d] logistics" with Tiger and "impliedly consented to Tiger working from the [ACHIEVER]," "it was W&T . . . that directly contracted with Tiger for a specific scope of work, funded and directed all of Tiger's work, and was the entity that explicitly invited Tiger to work on the 'overall' pipeline recommissioning project." The conduct of the parties over the course of the project further demonstrated that W&T was ultimately responsible for Tiger's presence and that of its employees. "Tiger's operations manager, David Lacombe, considered his customer to be W&T, and he corresponded directly with [W&T's project manager Alan] Greig when changes were made to the number of Tiger personnel or regarding the return of equipment." Tiger and Grogan were subject to the "oversight and project management of . . . Greig . . . and his on-site representatives"; W&T representatives "gave Grogan his day-to-day instructions," approved his work tickets, and decided when he would be sent back to shore.

Under the *Blanks* standard, these facts justify the district court's conclusion that Grogan was not Triton's invitee. *Blanks* presented closely [—9—] analogous facts, and in that case, we declined to extend invitor status to the party in Triton's position. In *Blanks*, a well operator, ANR, hired a service company, Murco. ANR and Murco each indemnified the other for claims brought by the other's invitees. ANR also hired a subcontractor, Consolidated, to work on the same project. Consolidated's employee, Blanks, was injured while assisting a Murco employee on Murco's rig. We held that Blanks was ANR's invitee alone, and emphasized that he "was invited onto the drilling site by ANR through his employee status with Consolidated and was there performing services for ANR's benefit."[16] Our analysis in

---

nevertheless, we held, on similar facts, that only the party analogous to W&T could be considered an invitor. 766 F.2d at 893-94.

[16] *Blanks*, 766 F.2d at 894. We also pointed out that "[a]lthough there was no written contract between ANR and Consolidated, Consolidated was

Blanks thus focused on the party ultimately responsible for the invitee's presence.[17] In this case, that party was W&T, not Triton.

In disputing the district court's *Blanks* analysis as to Triton, W&T focuses solely on the court's observation that "the presence of H_2S did not preclude the operation of Triton's vessel . . . . The vessel could have been reassigned to another job where there was no H_2S threat." In the district court's view, this showed that "W&T was the party that stood to benefit from Tiger's H_2S services." W&T argues that the record is devoid of evidence of "another job" available to Triton and that the court's invitee determination as to Triton was therefore clearly erroneous.

Again, we disagree. The district court's "another job" hypothetical merely illustrates the undeniable nature of the parties' relationship: W&T's project was the ultimate reason for Triton and Tiger's presence on the work site, and [—10—] any benefit to Triton from Tiger's presence was indirect. Under our case law, a contractor may incidentally benefit from the presence of a subcontractor without having invited the subcontractor onto the project for purposes of liability.[18] Such was the case here. As the district court explained, although Tiger's presence may have indirectly benefited Triton, it was *crucial* for W&T: "The [ACHIEVER] could have been reassigned to another job where there was no H_2S threat, but W&T's project could not move forward at all until the H_2S situation was addressed." The district court did not err in reasoning that this fact, alongside others, was consistent with a finding that Grogan and Tiger were not Triton's invitees.

V

The district court properly determined that Grogan was W&T's invitee. Moreover, its valid factual findings compel the conclusion that Grogan was not Triton's invitee. The district court was therefore correct to hold W&T liable under the MSC for Triton's settlement and defense costs related to Grogan's claims. We AFFIRM the ruling of the district court.

---

clearly working directly for ANR . . . . Weekly reports and service tickets for Consolidated's services were signed by an on-site representative of ANR. Consolidated's invoices were presented to ANR for payment." *Id.* at 893.

[17] *See also id.* ("[I]nvitee status is determined by who invites the injured party onto the premises.").

[18] In *Blanks*, the injured party, Blanks, was found to be ANR's invitee, and not Murco's, even though he was assisting Murco's employee on Murco's rig at the time he was injured. *See* 766 F.2d at 893-95.

United States Court of Appeals
for the Fifth Circuit

No. 15-30446

TETRA TECHNOLOGIES, INC.
vs.
CONTINENTAL INS. CO.

Appeal from the United States District Court for the
Eastern District of Louisiana

Decided: February 24, 2016

Citation: 814 F.3d 733, 4 Adm. R. 185 (5th Cir. 2016).

Before **STEWART**, Chief Judge, and **REAVLEY**, and
DAVIS, Circuit Judges.

[—1—] PER CURIAM:

Defendant-Appellant Continental Insurance Co. ("Continental") appeals the district court's final judgment in favor of Plaintiffs-Appellees Tetra Technologies, Inc. ("Tetra") and Maritech Resources, Inc. ("Maritech"), requiring Continental and its co-defendant insured, Vertex Services ("Vertex"), to indemnify them.[1] For the reasons set out below, we affirm in part, reverse in part, and remand. [—2—]

I. Background

This dispute arises from injuries sustained by a platform worker, Abraham Mayorga, employed by Vertex. Mayorga sued Tetra and Maritech (hereinafter collectively "Tetra" unless separately identified) for personal injury, and Tetra sought indemnity from Vertex and its insurer, Continental, pursuant to certain agreements and an insurance policy. On cross motions for summary judgment, the district court concluded that Tetra is entitled to indemnity from Continental and Vertex. Continental appeals.

---

[1] Although Vertex is a co-defendant with Continental, and the outcome concerns both Continental and Vertex, only Continental filed the motions for summary judgment and brought both appeals.

A. Facts

Tetra and Vertex entered into a Master Service Agreement (the "MSA"), under which Vertex's employees would perform work for Tetra. The MSA required Vertex to indemnify Tetra for injuries sustained by Vertex's employees while working for Tetra. Pursuant to the MSA, Vertex was also required to list Tetra as an additional insured under its general liability insurance policy issued by Continental (the "Policy").

Tetra entered into an agreement (the "Salvage Plan") with Maritech to salvage a decommissioned oil production platform located at Eugene Island 129 ("EI129"). Tetra retained Vertex to perform at least some aspects of the salvage operation. Mayorga served as a rigger for the project, working from a Tetra-owned barge, the *D/B Arapaho*. On May 22, 2011, Mayorga was assigned to assist in removing a bridge connecting two sections of the EI129 platform. In his complaint, Mayorga alleged that he was injured when the bridge collapsed, causing him and other workers on it to fall 70–80 feet into the Gulf of Mexico. Mayorga filed suit against Tetra, alleging that it had been negligent in performing the salvage operation.

B. Procedural History

Tetra filed this indemnity action against Vertex and Continental. Tetra [—3—] and Continental filed cross motions for summary judgment. Continental asserted that it was not required to indemnify Tetra, because (1) the Outer Continental Shelf Lands Act ("OCSLA") made Louisiana law applicable as surrogate federal law; (2) the indemnity agreement was void under the Louisiana Oilfield Indemnity Act ("LOIA"); and (3) in any event, Tetra's claims were excluded under Exclusion d of the Policy. Tetra argued that neither LOIA nor the Policy precluded recovery against Continental or Vertex. On the initial cross motions for summary judgment, the district court found that Continental and Vertex are required to indemnify Tetra because LOIA did not apply and that Exclusion d did not preclude coverage. Continental appealed, but that appeal was dismissed for lack of jurisdiction.

On remand, the parties entered stipulations as to the two issues that prevented resolution of the prior appeal. Tetra also claimed that it was entitled to additional attorneys' fees, while Continental re-urged its motion for summary judgment. The district court denied both Tetra's motion for additional fees (which Tetra does not appeal) and Continental's re-urged motion for summary judgment, entering a final judgment against Continental and Vertex. Continental appeals the grant of summary judgment in favor of Tetra and the denial of its own motion for summary judgment.

II. DISCUSSION

This court "review[s] the district court's judgment on cross motions for summary judgment de novo, addressing each party's motion independently, viewing the evidence and inferences in the light most favorable to the nonmoving party."[2]

Because the dispute in this case stems from events that occurred in the [—4—] Gulf of Mexico above the outer Continental Shelf ("OCS"), OCSLA applies.[3] Under OCSLA, federal law generally applies to such disputes and state law is applied "only as federal law and then only when not inconsistent with applicable federal law."[4] When there are "gaps in the federal law,"[5] OCSLA adopts the law of the adjacent state, here Louisiana, as surrogate federal law "[t]o the extent that [the adjacent state's law is] applicable and not inconsistent with [OCSLA] or with other Federal laws and regulations."[6]

OCSLA is important to this dispute because Continental contends that LOIA applies as surrogate federal law and voids the MSA's indemnity agreement. LOIA renders void, under certain conditions relating generally to the petroleum industry, any agreement that purports to indemnify a party for damages resulting from death or bodily injury caused by the indemnitee's own negligence or fault.[7] If LOIA voids the indemnity agreement, then Tetra is not entitled to indemnity from Continental or Vertex. If LOIA does not void the indemnity agreement, however, then we must determine whether the Continental Policy itself excludes coverage.

Accordingly, we must address three issues: (1) whether OCSLA requires the court to adopt Louisiana law as surrogate federal law; (2) if (or assuming, as did the district court) Louisiana law must be adopted as surrogate federal law, whether LOIA voids the indemnity agreement here; and (3) if LOIA does not void the indemnity agreement, whether the Policy excludes coverage. [—5—]

A. The Summary Judgment Record Is Inadequate To Determine Whether OCSLA Requires The Adoption Of Louisiana Law As Surrogate Federal Law.

1. Applicable Law

"Under *Union Texas Petroleum Corp. v. PLT Engineering, Inc.* [("*PLT*")], three requirements must be met for state law to apply as surrogate federal law under the OCSLA."[8] First, "[t]he controversy must arise on a situs covered by OCSLA (i.e., the subsoil, seabed, or artificial structures permanently or temporarily attached thereto)."[9] Second, "[f]ederal maritime law must not apply of its

---

[2] *Morgan v. Plano Ind. Sch. Dist.*, 589 F.3d 740, 745 (5th Cir. 2009).

[3] *See Rodrigue v. Aetna Cas. & Sur. Co.*, 395 U.S. 352, 355–56 (1969) ("The purpose of the [OCSLA] was to define a body of law applicable to the seabed, the subsoil, and the fixed structures such as those . . . on the outer Continental Shelf.").

[4] *Id.*

[5] *Id.* at 356.

[6] 43 U.S.C. § 1333(a)(1), (a)(2)(A); *see also Rodrigue*, 395 U.S. at 356–57; *Fruge ex rel. Fruge v. Parker Drilling Co.*, 337 F.3d 558, 560 (5th Cir. 2003) ("[T]he law applicable is federal law,

---

supplemented by state law of the adjacent state." (internal quotation marks omitted)).

[7] La. Rev. Stat. Ann. § 9:2780(A).

[8] *ACE Am. Ins. Co. v. M-I, L.L.C.*, 699 F.3d 826, 830 (5th Cir. 2012).

[9] *PLT*, 895 F.2d 1043, 1047 (5th Cir. 1990).

own force."[10] Third, "[t]he state law must not be inconsistent with Federal law."[11]

2. We Cannot Determine Whether There Is an OCSLA Situs.

Under the first requirement of the *PLT* test, "the controversy at issue must arise on an OCSLA situs, namely the seabed, subsoil, and fixed structures of the outer Continental Shelf."[12] When dealing with contractual disputes, this circuit applies a focus-of-the-contract test to determine whether a controversy arises on an OCSLA situs.[13] Under the focus-of-the-contract test, "a contractual indemnity claim (or any other contractual dispute) arises on an OCSLA situs if a majority of the performance called for under the contract is to be performed on stationary platforms or other OCSLA situses enumerated in 43 U.S.C. § 1333(a)(2)(A)."[14] [—6—]

As this court has discussed, "it is a common practice for companies contracting for work in the oilfield to enter into contracts in two stages," first signing a blanket contract and then "issu[ing] work orders for the performance of specific work."[15] Here, Tetra and Vertex followed this common practice: first entering into the MSA, which functions as a "blanket agreement" between the parties, and then Tetra issuing specific work orders for the completion of particular tasks. In a situation "where the contract consists of two parts, a blanket contract followed by later work order, the two must be interpreted together."[16] But generally, "in determining situs in a contract case such as this, courts should ordinarily look to the location where the work is to be performed pursuant to the specific work order rather than the long term blanket contract."[17]

Continental argues that the evidence in the record—namely the MSA, the Salvage Plan, and Mayorga's deposition testimony—establishes that the controversy arose on an OCSLA situs. Continental also asserts that the "entire goal" of the work Tetra hired Vertex to perform was the deconstruction, decommissioning, and salvaging of parts of the platform on the OCS. Tetra counters that there is no record evidence as to where the majority of Vertex's work for Tetra was to be performed but contends that most of the work was to be performed on lift barges and material barges—not on an OCS platform.

Tetra's specific work order to Vertex that resulted in Mayorga's assignment to the job is absent from the record. However, the absence of a specific work order is not fatal to Continental's assertion that the controversy arose on an OCSLA situs.[18] Here, the primary non-contractual evidence was [—7—] Mayorga's deposition testimony. In his deposition, Mayorga testified that he worked as a rigger for Vertex and that he had been on the barge where the accident occurred for two years. Much of Mayorga's work-specific testimony focused on his actions the night of the accident and does reveal that Mayorga worked extensively on the fixed platform. However, as the district court concluded, it is difficult to extrapolate Mayorga's testimony to determine the scope of the entire work order.

Continental also points to the MSA to show that the controversy arose on an OCSLA situs. However, the terms of the MSA provide little guidance in helping to determine where the majority of the work was to be performed under the contract. Instead, the MSA merely states that Tetra may "obtain certain services [from Vertex], including but not limited to, inspection, maintenance, fabrication, surveying, diving, repair and/or other general oilfield services." Thus, the MSA does not

---

[10] *Id.*

[11] *Id.*

[12] *ACE Am. Ins. Co.*, 699 F.3d at 830.

[13] *Grand Isle Shipyard, Inc. v. Seacor Marine, LLC*, 589 F.3d 778, 787 (5th Cir. 2009) (en banc).

[14] *Id.* at 787–88.

[15] *Grand Isle*, 589 F.3d at 787 n.6 (citing *Davis & Sons v. Gulf Oil Corp.*, 919 F.2d 313, 315–17 (5th Cir. 1990)).

[16] *Grand Isle*, 589 F.3d at 787 n.6 (internal quotation marks omitted).

---

[17] *Id.*

[18] *See ACE Am. Ins. Co.*, 699 F.3d at 831 (noting that service tickets and time sheets [—7—] could provide evidence of the location where work was to be performed).

show that Vertex's work was to be performed on the platform.

Finally, Continental argues that the Salvage Plan is "especially relevant" in determining where the majority of the work was to be completed. First, the Salvage Plan is captioned "Bridge and Bridge Support Salvages, Eugene Island 129 Complex." Next, the work described in the Salvage Plan does largely relate to the EI129 platform. For example, a barge was to be set up at the EI129 Complex and attached to the EI129 platform, and the removed bridges were, of course, on the EI129 Complex and platform. Based on these descriptions of the work and the plan itself, Continental contends that every portion of the work to be completed was located at, adjacent to, or on the platform on the outer Continental Shelf.

The problem with Continental's argument is that the Salvage Plan [—8—] explains the work that Tetra was to perform for Maritech. As the district court observed, the Salvage Plan contains no information related to what services Tetra retained Vertex to perform. While Mayorga was injured deconstructing a bridge platform on the EI129 complex, it does not follow that the majority of Vertex's work was performed in that location. Rather, that one "snapshot" does not explain what the entire work order might have contemplated. In fact, the Salvage Plan itself (which relates to the work Tetra would perform for Maritech) also describes a number of tasks that would be performed on the barge—not on the platform.

Viewing Mayorga's deposition testimony, the MSA, and the Salvage Plan together does suggest that much of Tetra's work was to be performed on the EI129 platform. The relevant question, however, is where a majority of Vertex's performance was to occur under the contract, as the district court explained.[19] The record does not definitively answer that question. Though Continental contends that "Tetra hired Vertex employees to perform the Salvage Plan," there are a number of aspects of that Salvage Plan that were not to be performed on the EI129

platform. Further, the MSA provides no guidance, and Mayorga's testimony and allegations do not establish the scope of the services for which Tetra retained Vertex. In sum, we conclude that neither party is entitled to judgment as to *PLT*'s first prong: whether the controversy arose on an OCSLA situs.

3. We Cannot Determine Whether Federal Maritime Law Applies.

Under *PLT*'s second requirement, in order for the OCSLA choice of law provision to apply, "[f]ederal maritime law must not apply of its own force."[20] [—9—] "Determining whether maritime law applies of its own force involves a two-step inquiry—first, an examination of the historical treatment of contracts of that type in the jurisprudence and second, a six-factor 'fact-specific' inquiry into the nature of the contract."[21] The court "must analyze whether the particular work order . . . is maritime in nature."[22] This court

consider[s] six factors in characterizing the contract: 1) what does the specific work order in effect at the time of injury provide? 2) what work did the crew assigned under the work order actually do? 3) was the crew assigned to work aboard a vessel in navigable waters; 4) to what extent did the work being done relate to the mission of that vessel? 5) what was the principal work of the injured worker? and 6) what work was the injured worker actually doing at the time of injury?[23]

Continental argues that *PLT*'s second prong is met because the work at issue involved decommissioning, deconstructing, or salvaging a fixed platform used for oil and gas exploration on the OCS. Such contracts are not "historically treated" as maritime contracts, and maritime law thus generally would not apply of its own force.[24] The flaw in

---

[19] *Grand Isle*, 589 F.3d at 787.

[20] *PLT*, 895 F.2d at 1047.
[21] *ACE Am. Ins. Co.*, 699 F.3d at 831.
[22] *Id.* at 832.
[23] *Davis & Sons, Inc.*, 919 F.2d at 316.
[24] *See Hufnagel v. Omega Serv. Indus., Inc.*, 182 F.3d 340, 352 (5th Cir. 1999) ("Construction work

Continental's argument, as was the case under *PLT*'s first prong, is the paucity of summary judgment evidence. There is little evidence to guide an analysis of "whether the particular work order" was maritime—and of course, the work order itself is absent from the record.

Continental points out that work primarily performed on a fixed platform is not maritime in nature. While true, Continental's overstates what [—10—] can be gleaned from the Salvage Plan. That agreement between Tetra and Maritech does relate in large part to a fixed platform. However, there are aspects of the Salvage Plan that would not be performed on the EI129 platform.

Moreover, the critical question is the nature of the contract between Tetra and Vertex. There appears to be no evidence that Tetra hired Vertex *solely* to perform the Salvage Plan for Maritech, nor any evidence that Vertex's performance related to only, or even mostly, platform-specific tasks. Because the scope of the work Vertex performed for Tetra is unclear, we may not say whether the "particular work order" was maritime or non-maritime in nature.

The only *Davis* factor for which there is clear record evidence is the sixth—the work the injured worker was actually doing at the time of injury. Here, Mayorga was assisting in removing a bridge connecting two platforms at the EI129 complex. The evidence is insufficient or inconclusive as to the other five factors.

As to the first two factors—the nature of the specific work order and the actual work done by the crew—the evidence is inconclusive as to whether the contract was non-maritime.

Continental relies on the Salvage Plan, Mayorga's deposition testimony, and the complaints filed in the underlying lawsuit, but those sources do not describe the nature of the entire work order. They merely show the work that Mayorga and others were performing at the time.

Continental faces a similar problem with the third, fourth, and fifth factors—the relationship to a navigable vessel, the nature of the actual work, and the injured worker's primary work. Continental concedes that Mayorga partially worked on the *D/B Arapaho* but contends that his actual work was not related to a vessel in navigation. Again, there is little evidence as to the total scope of Mayorga's duties.

In sum, we conclude that the evidence is insufficient to determine whether federal maritime law does not apply of its own force. Accordingly, [—11—] neither party is entitled to summary judgment on *PLT*'s second prong.

4. LOIA Is Consistent with Federal Law.

Finally, under *PLT*'s third prong, "[t]he state law must not be inconsistent with Federal law."[25] Nothing in LOIA is inconsistent with federal law,[26] and Tetra does not argue otherwise.[27] Thus, we conclude that *PLT*'s third prong is satisfied.

5. In Sum, We Must Remand On The OCSLA Issue.

Because the summary judgment evidence is insufficient to determine the first two *PLT* prongs, neither party is entitled to summary judgment as to whether LOIA must be

_____

on fixed offshore platforms bears no significant relation to traditional maritime activity."); *see also ACE Am. Ins. Co.*, 699 F.3d at 832 (holding that maritime law did not apply of its own force where "the relevant contract . . . was performed on a stationary platform"); *Grand Isle*, 589 F.3d at 789 (agreeing with the district court's conclusion that contract, "which called for maintenance work on a stationary platform located on the OCS," was not a maritime contract).

[25] *PLT*, 895 F.2d at 1047.
[26] *See Grand Isle*, 589 F.3d at 789 (agreeing with district court's conclusion that this court "has specifically held that nothing in LOIA is inconsistent with federal law" (internal quotation marks and citation omitted)).
[27] *See Strong v. B.P. Expl. & Prod., Inc.*, 440 F.3d 665, 668 (5th Cir. 2006) ("By not contesting [plaintiff's] arguments that [*PLT*'s second and third requirements] are satisfied, B.P. implicitly concedes that those conditions have been met.").

adopted as surrogate federal law under OCSLA. That was not a problem under the district court's analysis because it concluded that if Louisiana law did apply, LOIA would not void the indemnity agreement under these circumstances, and if Louisiana law did not apply, the Policy would not exclude coverage. Because the outcome would be the same either way under the district court's interpretation, it was unnecessary for it to resolve the OCSLA issue. Because, as explained below, we conclude below that LOIA *would* void the indemnity agreement but the Policy itself would not exclude coverage, we remand for the district court to determine the now dispositive issue of whether Louisiana law must be adopted as surrogate federal law. [—12—]

B. LOIA Would Void the Indemnity Agreement.

1. Applicable Law

If OCSLA requires the adoption of Louisiana law as surrogate federal law, the next question is whether LOIA applies to this dispute. LOIA provides, in relevant part:

A. The legislature finds that an inequity is foisted on certain contractors and their employees by the defense or indemnity provisions, either or both, contained in some *agreements pertaining to wells* for oil, gas, or water, or drilling for minerals which occur in a solid, liquid, gaseous, or other state, to the extent those provisions apply to death or bodily injury to persons. It is the intent of the legislature by this Section to declare null and void and against public policy of the state of Louisiana any provision in any agreement which requires defense and/or indemnification, for death or bodily injury to persons, where there is negligence or fault (strict liability) on the part of the indemnitee, or an agent or employee of the indemnitee, or an independent contractor who is directly responsible to the indemnitee.

B. Any provision *contained in, collateral to, or affecting an agreement pertaining to a well* for oil, gas, or water, or drilling for minerals which occur in a solid, liquid, gaseous, or other state, is void and unenforceable to the extent that it purports to or does provide for defense or indemnity, or either, to the indemnitee against loss or liability for damages arising out of or resulting from death or bodily injury to persons, which is caused by or results from the sole or concurrent negligence or fault (strict liability) of the indemnitee, or an agent, employee, or an independent contractor who is directly responsible to the indemnitee.

C. The term "agreement," as it pertains to a well for oil, gas, or water, or drilling for minerals which occur in a solid, liquid, gaseous, or other state, as used in this Section, means any agreement or understanding, written or oral, *concerning any operations related to the exploration, development, production, or transportation of oil, gas, or water, or drilling for minerals which occur in a solid, liquid, gaseous, or other state, including but not limited to drilling, deepening, reworking, repairing, improving,* [—13—] *testing, treating, perforating, acidizing, logging, conditioning, altering, plugging, or otherwise rendering services in or in connection with any well* . . . .

. . .

G. Any provision in any agreement arising out of the operations, services, or activities listed in Subsection C of this Section of the Louisiana Revised Statutes of 1950 *which requires waivers of subrogation, additional named insured endorsements, or any other form of insurance protection* which would frustrate or circumvent the prohibitions of this Section, shall be null and void and of no force and effect.[28]

---

[28] La. Rev. Stat. Ann. § 9:2780 (emphasis added).

Thus, if LOIA applies, it will void not only Vertex's indemnity obligation but also Continental's insurance obligation under the Policy to Tetra as an additional named insured.

This court has adopted a two-part test to determine if LOIA applies. "First, there must be an agreement that 'pertains to' an oil, gas or water well. If the contract does not pertain to a well, the inquiry ends."[29] In determining whether an agreement pertains to a well, "[t]he decisive factor in most cases has been the functional nexus between an agreement and a well or wells."[30]

If the agreement "has the required nexus to a well," the court examines "the contract's involvement with operations related to the exploration, development, production, or transportation of oil, gas, or water."[31] Thus, "if (but only if) the agreement (1) pertains to a well *and* (2) is related to exploration, development, production, or transportation of oil, gas, or water, will the Act invalidate any indemnity provision contained in or collateral to that agreement."[32] This inquiry "requires a fact intensive case by case [—14—] analysis."[33]

2. Analysis

Although the inquiry is usually fact intensive, the question before us here is one of law. The district court seems to have concluded that the salvage of a fully decommissioned production platform does not have the "required nexus to a well" because the well is not in use. Thus, the question before us is whether salvaging a decommissioned platform has a sufficient nexus to a well for LOIA to apply.

Continental contends that this court's decision in *Verdine*, which considered the

extent of LOIA's nexus to a well requirement, shows the district court's error. There, Ensco agreed to provide a fixed platform rig to Amerada Hess Corporation for use on wells located off the Louisiana coast.[34] Specifically, before the platform rig could be used, it required "extensive refurbishment work," which Ensco retained Centin to perform at its onshore fabrication yard.[35] The court observed that "[c]ourts have not addressed whether an agreement for work on a dismantled drilling platform pertains to a well."[36]

The court first noted that at the time Centin's employees worked on the platform, it sat idle in a fabrication yard and "was not participating in in-field exploration, pro-duction, or transportation of oil or gas."[37] Such facts made it "difficult to find a sufficient geographical and functional nexus between the [platform] and a well or wells."[38] However, "while [the platform] was not involved in exploration or production activities at the time Centin performed its contract obligations, the platform was designated for use on particular [—15—] wells."[39] In other words, the platform had been used on active wells before and would again be used on active wells following refurbishment. Refusing "to interpret the legislature's requirement that an agreement pertain to a well in such a restrictive manner that we overlook agreements to which the Act was intended to apply," the court found the requisite nexus to a well because the services "were performed on a structure intended for use in the exploration and production of oil and gas."[40]

Continental argues that under *Verdine*, a platform salvaging operation has the required nexus to a well. This court has not yet considered the extent of *Verdine*'s holding, and *Verdine* itself does not answer this question. The *Verdine* court found it "difficult to find a sufficient geographical and functional nexus

---

[29] *Transcon. Gas Pipe Line Corp. v. Transp. Ins. Co.*, 953 F.2d 985, 991 (5th Cir. 1992).

[30] *Verdine v. Ensco Offshore Co.*, 255 F.3d 246, 252 (5th Cir. 2001).

[31] *Transcon. Gas*, 953 F.2d at 991 (internal quotation marks omitted).

[32] *Id.*

[33] *Verdine*, 255 F.3d at 251.

[34] 255 F.3d at 248–49.

[35] *Id.*

[36] *Id.* at 252–54.

[37] *Id.* at 253.

[38] *Id.*

[39] *Id.* at 254.

[40] *Id.*

between the [platform] and a well or wells" where the platform was not being used for in-field exploration, production, or transportation and instead was sitting idle.[41] Instead, the court concluded that the agreement had a sufficient nexus to a well once it considered the additional fact that the "platform was designated for use on particular wells," namely six particular wells located off the Louisiana coast.[42] That is, *Verdine* suggests that the sufficient nexus to a well arose because the platform was being refurbished for use in future oil exploration.[43]

That does not end our inquiry, however. Continental argues that salvaging a platform from a decommissioned well necessarily has the required [—16—] nexus to a well, relying on district court cases that have interpreted *Verdine* broadly: *Wilcox v. Max Welders, L.L.C.*,[44] *Howell v. Avante Servs., LLC*,[45] *Teaver v. Seatrax of La.*[46]

Howell involved an agreement to cut and pull casings from the wellbores on an oil platform as part of a plan to "plug and abandon" the oil well.[47] The plaintiff argued that the agreement did not relate to a well because the well was not functioning at the time of performance.[48] The district court disagreed, first observing that removing the casings from the wellbore was "collateral to plugging the well" and covered under a straightforward reading of LOIA.[49] Further, "the purpose of the casings was to assist in oil

and gas production."[50] The district court also rejected the plaintiff's argument that "where a structure is no longer involved in or capable of hydrocarbon production, an agreement for services pertaining to that structure is *not* an agreement that pertains to a well."[51] Instead, applying *Verdine*, the court held that such a restrictive reading "would exclude plugging and activities collateral to plugging," which LOIA expressly covers.[52] The court also observed that removing the casings could not be "logically severed from the overall plug and abandonment operation."[53] Thus, the district court concluded that the agreement pertained to a well.[54]

Similarly, in *Teaver*, the plaintiffs argued that the relevant agreement [—17—] did not pertain to a well because the work related to dismantling a platform crane and because the well itself had been dry for several years.[55] Observing that the crane was used "to assist with the plugging and abandoning of the wells," the *Teaver* court found "that the scope of the agreement necessarily pertains to the wells."[56] The court rejected the plaintiffs' argument that the nexus to a well was negated because the wells were non-producing and the platform was thus not an in-field production platform.[57] Relying on *Verdine*, the court concluded that the "wells had previously produced oil and the platform had previously been an in-field production platform." Further, because the crane was used in plugging the well, it fell within the scope of LOIA's broad language.[58]

In *Wilcox*, the district court found that an agreement to, *inter alia*, "provide welding services in connection with the decommissioning of oil and gas platforms" pertained to a well because it was an "agreement to perform an act that is collateral

---

[41] 255 F.3d at 253.

[42] *Id.* at 253–54.

[43] *See Labove v. Candy Fleet, L.L.C.*, No. 11-1405, 2012 WL 3043168, at *6 (E.D. La. July 20, 2012) (characterizing *Verdine* as "holding that a contract for repairs on a dismantled fixed oil platform rig pertained to a well because services rendered were performed on a structure intended for *future use* in the exploration and production of oil and gas" (emphasis added)).

[44] 969 F. Supp. 2d 668, 680–83 (E.D. La. 2013).

[45] Nos. 12-293 & 12-2448, 2013 WL 1681436, at *3–7 (E.D. La. Apr. 17, 2013).

[46] No. 10-1523, 2012 WL 5866042, at *4–5 (E.D. La. Nov. 19, 2012).

[47] 2013 WL 1681436, at *1, *4.

[48] *Id.* at *4.

[49] *Id.*

[50] *Id.* at *5.

[51] *Id.*

[52] *Id.* at *6.

[53] *Id.* at *8.

[54] *Id.* at *6.

[55] 2012 WL 5866042, at *2.

[56] *Id.* at *4–5.

[57] *Id.* at *5.

[58] *Id.*

to plugging the well."[59] The court observed that the platforms were part of the well production system, assisted in oil and gas production, had a geographic nexus to the well, and had a functional nexus because they provided the "physical structure that housed and protected the well conductor."[60] The defendants, however, argued that "[w]here there is no functional or geographic nexus between a live well and the structure in question," LOIA does not apply.[61] Relying heavily on *Howell* and *Verdine*, the *Wilcox* court rejected this argument.[62] Instead, the court noted that the [—18—] platform at issue in *Verdine* was already decommissioned but was still found to be related to a well.[63]

We conclude that these cases properly interpret LOIA. Each case involved agreements to perform work in connection with "plugging and abandoning" the wells at issue. Accepting the argument that LOIA could never apply to a nonproducing well would have required the district courts to interpret LOIA in such a manner as to exclude an expressly covered activity.[64] Those district courts were certainly correct to reject such a restrictive view.

Tetra argues that this case is distinguishable because the wells at issue were decommissioned long before the Salvage Plan came into effect. Tetra asserts that salvaging a decommissioned platform is not collateral to plugging or decommissioning the well but is effectively one step further removed. We reject that argument because it ignores the fact that regulations generally require the removal of an oil platform in connection with a decommissioning operation.[65]

Based on all the above, we conclude that a contract for salvaging a platform from a decommissioned oil well has a sufficient nexus to a well under LOIA. Thus, LOIA would void Vertex's indemnity obligation as well as Continental's obligation to indemnity Tetra as an additional insured. Consequently, if the district court determines on remand that Louisiana law must be adopted as surrogate federal law, Tetra will not be entitled to indemnity from Continental or Vertex. If the district court instead determines that Louisiana law does not apply, then the outcome depends on whether the [—19—] Policy itself excludes coverage.

C. The Policy Does Not Exclude Coverage.

1. Applicable Law

"Texas courts interpret insurance policies according to the rules of contract construction."[66] This court "evaluate[s] the contract based on its plain meaning, determining what the words of the contract say the parties agreed to do."[67] The court "must examine the policy as a whole, seeking to harmonize all provisions and render none meaningless."[68]

"If policy language is worded so that it can be given a definite or certain legal meaning, it is not ambiguous,"[69] and the court must "construe [the policy] as a matter of law and enforce it as written."[70] "An ambiguity does not exist . . . simply because the parties interpret a policy differently."[71] Instead, a policy is ambiguous "if the contractual language is susceptible to two or more

---

[59] 969 F. Supp. 2d at 682–84 (internal quotation marks omitted).

[60] *Id.* at 682.

[61] *Id.*

[62] *Id.*

[63] *Id.* at 682–83.

[64] *See* La. Rev. Stat. Ann. § 9:2780(C) (including plugging or "any act collateral thereto" as activities pertaining to a well).

[65] *See* 30 C.F.R. § 250.1703 (listing general requirements for decommissioning) ("When your facilities are no longer useful for operations, you must . . . [r]emove all platforms and other facilities,

except as provided in §§ 250.1725(a) and 250.1730. . . .").

[66] *Likens v. Hartford Life & Accident Ins. Co.*, 688 F.3d 197, 199 (5th Cir. 2012) (quoting *de Laurentis v. U.S. Auto Ass'n*, 162 S.W.3d 714, 721 (Tex. App.—Houston [14th Dist.] 2005)).

[67] *Id.*

[68] *In re Deepwater Horizon*, 470 S.W.3d 452, 464 (Tex. 2015).

[69] *Am. Int'l Specialty Lines Ins. Co. v. Rentech Steel LLC*, 620 F.3d 558, 562 (5th Cir. 2010).

[70] *In re Deepwater Horizon*, 470 S.W.3d at 464.

[71] *Am. Home Assurance Co. v. Cat Tech L.L.C.*, 660 F.3d 216, 220 (5th Cir. 2011).

reasonable interpretations."[72] Ambiguous policy language—in particular, exclusionary language—must be construed "strictly against the insurer and liberally in favor of the insured."[73] "If the insured's construction of an ambiguous exclusionary provision is reasonable, the court must adopt it, even if it is not the most reasonable position."[74]
[—20—]

2. The Relevant Policy Language

Exclusion d, at issue here, provides:

2. Exclusions
This insurance does not apply to: . . .

d. Any obligation of the insured under a workers compensation, United States Longshoremen's and Harbor Workers' Compensation Act, Jones Act, Death on the High Seas Act, General Maritime Law, Federal Employers' Liability Act, disability benefits or unemployment compensation law or any similar law
. . . .

The district court found that Exclusion d is ambiguous because it is subject to multiple reasonable interpretations. Specifically, the district court concluded that Exclusion d is ambiguous because of: (1) the "any similar law" language; (2) the limiting clause in another provision, Exclusion e; and (3) the seeming illusoriness of coverage under Continental's interpretation. We conclude that Exclusion d is ambiguous because of the "any similar law" language.

As the district court observed, the inclusion of the phrase "any similar law" prompts the court to ask how the enumerated laws are similar. Tetra argues that each of the enumerated laws in Exclusion d contains elements of employers' liability, so "any similar law" should be reasonably read to refer to employers' liability. We agree that the employer/employee relationship is the

"similar" thread throughout each enumerated law.[75] We also conclude that Continental's construction of Exclusion d, which would apply it to a general tort claim, renders the policy ambiguous.

Continental argues on appeal that the laws contained in Exclusion d are not merely employers' liability laws. Specifically, Continental contends that [—21—] the Policy excludes Tetra's coverage because Mayorga's complaint for damages invoked "General Maritime Law," and Exclusion d explicitly includes the phrase "General Maritime Law." Though superficially plausible, that argument is inadequate. We are required to "examine the policy as a whole, seeking to harmonize all provisions and render none meaningless."[76] Continental's construction fails to account for the phrase "any similar law" in Exclusion d, while Tetra's construction does account for it.

This court's decision in *Amerisure Insurance Co. v. Navigators Insurance Co.*, while not on all fours, also lends support to Tetra's argument that "any similar law" renders Exclusion d ambiguous.[77] In *Amerisure*, two workers sued for negligence under the Jones Act, and the insurer argued that the policy did not apply due to a provision excluding coverage for "[a]ny obligation for which the insured . . . may be held liable under any workers compensation, disability benefits or unemployment compensation law or any similar law."[78] This court observed that Jones Act claims are not similar to workers' compensation claims, because "the former is based on the employer's negligence while the latter is not."[79] Thus, "the operative phrase [in the insurance contract] . . . , 'any similar law,' is ambiguous with respect to the Jones Act claims."[80] The logic of *Amerisure* supports a finding of ambiguity here.

---

[72] *Rentech Steel*, 620 F.3d at 562 (internal quotation marks omitted).

[73] *Id.* at 563–64; *see also Likens*, 688 F.3d at 199.

[74] *Likens*, 688 F.3d at 199.

[75] Notably, Exclusion d is phrased in a similar manner as most "workers' compensation" or similar exclusions. *See* 9 Couch on Ins. § 129:11 (3d ed. 2015).

[76] *In re Deepwater Horizon*, 470 S.W.3d at 464.

[77] 611 F.3d 299 (5th Cir. 2010).

[78] *Id.* at 310.

[79] *Id.* at 310.

[80] *Id.*

Because we find that Exclusion d's "any similar law" language suffices to render the exclusion ambiguous, we need not reach the two alternative or additional grounds for finding ambiguity, namely the effect of certain limiting language in Exclusion e, and whether or not Continental's construction of the Policy renders coverage illusory. "In light of this ambiguity, the court must **[—22—]** interpret the [provision] so that it does not exclude coverage."[81] Accordingly, we conclude that the Policy does not exclude coverage. Thus, if the district court determines that Louisiana law does not apply under OCSLA, Tetra will be entitled to indemnity.

III. CONCLUSION

In sum, we REVERSE with respect to the district court's interpretation of LOIA, AFFIRM with respect to the Policy interpretation, and REMAND for a determination of whether Louisiana law applies as surrogate federal law under OCSLA. On remand, if the district court concludes that Louisiana law applies to this dispute, LOIA will void the indemnity agreement, and Continental and Vertex will be entitled to judgment. If the district court concludes that Louisiana law does not apply, then Tetra and Maritech will be entitled to judgment against Continental and Vertex because the Policy does not exclude coverage.

---

[81] *Amerisure Ins. Co.*, 611 F.3d at 310.

United States Court of Appeals
for the Fifth Circuit

No. 15-30381

IN RE DEEPWATER HORIZON

LAKE EUGENIE LAND & DEV., INC.
vs.
BP EXPLORATION & PROD., INC.

Appeal from the United States District Court for the
Eastern District of Louisiana

Decided: February 25, 2016

Citation: 814 F.3d 748, 4 Adm. R. 196 (5th Cir. 2016).

Before **HIGGINBOTHAM, OWEN,** and **ELROD,** Circuit
Judges.

[—1—] PER CURIAM:

In mid-2012, defendants BP Exploration & Production Inc., BP America Production Co., and BP, P.L.C. (collectively, "BP") entered into a court-supervised settlement agreement with a class of parties harmed by the 2010 [—2—] Deepwater Horizon oil spill. The settlement agreement is described at greater length in our previous decision in *In re Deepwater Horizon*, 739 F.3d 790, 2 Adm. R. 140 (5th Cir. 2013). Pertinent to the present case, the agreement provides for compensation to landowners within the "Wetlands Real Property Claim Zone" (Claim Zone), which encompasses coastal Louisiana.

A class member seeking compensation under the agreement must submit a claim form specific to the Claim Zone that requires documentation including a tax assessment and a copy of the deed for the land parcel in the Claim Zone. This form can be submitted through an on-line portal. To screen claims, the on-line portal uses a parcel database that purports to contain "the best available parcel boundary data for real property in the" Claim Zone and data regarding which parcels are oiled. The settlement agreement acknowledges that "[i]n some instances," the parcel boundary data in the database "may be incomplete or out of date." Accordingly, even if the database does not recognize a parcel as

being within the Claim Zone, the Claims Administrator must deem a parcel eligible for compensation "provided the claimant documents the . . . [a]ctual presence of the parcel in the [Claim Zone]." All parcels within the Claim Zone are eligible for compensation; whether a parcel is oiled impacts the compensation amount. A parcel outside the Claim Zone may be added to the Claim Zone, rendering it eligible for compensation, but "only if the parcel is documented as containing the presence of oil."

Once a class member is compensated on any claim, a six-month limitations period begins running within which the class member must submit all additional claims. The administrator of the settlement program has implemented a policy—"Policy 251"—by which the administrator may grant [—3—] relief from deadlines in the settlement agreement.[1] Policy 251 provides, in relevant part:

> The Claims Administrator shall have the discretion to consider and grant or deny Deadline Relief Requests relating to any deadline prescribed by a provision in the Settlement Agreement on the following terms: . . . The claimant shall present the Deadline Relief Request to the Claims Administrator no later than 60 days after the expiration of the deadline concerned. The Claims Administrator shall reject any Request for Relief made after such time expires.

Policy 251 also provides that the party requesting relief from a deadline must show "circumstances that constitute excusable neglect under Fed. R. Civ. P. 60(b)" and enumerates other factors the Claims Administrator may consider. A claimant may appeal the "final determination of a claim" to a panel created by the settlement agreement within thirty days of receiving written notice of the final determination.

---

[1] BP contests that Policy 251 is a valid exercise of the Claims Administrator's authority, but expressly waives that issue for the purposes of this appeal.

Claimants Mary Willkomm, Martin Schoenberger, Clifford Phillip Bein, and Kevin Schoenberger own seven parcels of land in coastal Louisiana and seek compensation under the settlement agreement. In July 2012, Kevin Schoenberger—acting as counsel for himself and the other three claimants—inputted parcel numbers for all seven parcels into the on-line portal for claim submissions. The portal indicated that two of the seven parcels were in the Claim Zone and thus eligible for compensation, and Schoenberger submitted on-line claim forms for those two parcels. The portal indicated that the other five parcels were not in the Claim Zone and did not prompt Schoenberger to submit claim forms for those parcels. Schoenberger did not attempt to document the actual presence of those five parcels in the Claim Zone by [—4—] submitting a parcel eligibility request form, and did not attempt to submit claim forms by mail when not prompted to do so on the on-line portal. Claimants were paid in connection with one of the two eligible parcels in April 2013, and Claimants concede that under the six-month rule, their deadline to file all additional claims expired in late 2013.

In June 2014, Schoenberger learned that other (nonparty) co-owners of two of the five parcels that the portal indicated were ineligible had been compensated for claims on those parcels. Schoenberger attempted to submit on-line claims for those two parcels, but the portal would not allow the claims to be submitted because the six-month deadline had passed. On June 25, 2014, Schoenberger wrote to the Claims Administrator recounting his initial attempt to submit claims on the parcels that were deemed ineligible, reporting his subsequent discovery that the parcels were eligible, and attaching tax bills for the two parcels in question. Schoenberger also uploaded paper claim forms onto the on-line portal in October 2014, but they were not deemed "submitted" and have no claim number. Because the claims could not be submitted and thus have not been formally denied, there is no "final determination" for Claimants to appeal under the settlement agreement's appeal procedure.

Claimants filed a "Motion for Authority to File Wetlands Claims" with the district court, invoking the court's supervisory authority over the interpretation and implementation of the settlement agreement. Claimants asked the court to either determine that all seven of their claims were formally submitted in July 2012 before the six-month deadline had passed or excuse the missed six-month deadline and allow them to file claims anew. The district court denied the motion in a summary order, and Claimants appealed.

We decline to deem Claimants to have submitted claims on the parcels at issue in July 2012. The settlement agreement clearly designates the claim [—5—] form as the manner in which claims should be submitted, and no claim forms were submitted for the two parcels at issue in July 2012, or at any time before the six-month window had closed. We are not persuaded by Claimants' argument that "[t]here is no point in submitting the claim form" once the on-line portal indicates that a parcel is not in the Claim Zone and is thus ineligible for compensation. The settlement agreement clearly provides that "[i]n some instances," the parcel boundary data in the database "may be incomplete or out of date." Claimants were thus on notice that the on-line portal was not a perfect indicator of eligibility, and if they disagreed with its determination, the settlement agreement left it to them to "document[] the . . . [a]ctual presence of the parcel[s] in the [Claim Zone]" by submitting a parcel eligibility request form. Claimants did not do so, and we decline to nullify their failure to exhaust the procedures provided by the settlement agreement.

We also will not exercise any discretion we may have to excuse Claimants' failure to meet the six-month deadline. Even assuming *arguendo* that enacting Policy 251 was a proper exercise of the Claims Administrator's authority and that Policy 251 evidences discretion in the district court or this court to extend deadlines in the settlement agreement, Policy 251 applies only under "circumstances that constitute excusable neglect under Fed. R. Civ. P. 60(b)." Such circumstances do not exist here. If the Claims Administrator's database indicates that a particular property is not eligible for compensation, the onus is on the claimant to obtain and provide any documentation that could show otherwise. Claimant's failure to do so—despite notice that the on-line portal's initial eligibility determination was imperfect and that all claims had to be submitted within six months of first payment—was not excusable neglect under Rule 60(b)(1). *See Wooten v. McDonald Transit Assocs., Inc.*, 788 F.3d 490, 500–01 (5th Cir. 2015). [—6—]

Claimants' final argument is that the on-line portal for claim submissions denied them due process by preventing them from obtaining a final determination of their claims and thus barring them from the appeal process under the settlement agreement. Claimants did not make this argument in their memorandum in support of their motion before the district court, and it is accordingly forfeited. *See Cent. Sw. Tex. Dev., L.L.C. v. JPMorgan Chase Bank, Nat'l Ass'n*, 780 F.3d 296, 300–01 (5th Cir. 2015). Regardless, the enforcement of a properly noticed deadline generally does not effect a due process violation. *See Wainwright v. Torna*, 455 U.S. 586, 588 n.4 (1982).

For the foregoing reasons, the district court's order denying Claimants' Motion for Authority to File Wetlands Claims is AFFIRMED.

United States Court of Appeals
for the Fifth Circuit

No. 14-20589

PETROBRAS AM., INC.
vs.
VICINAY CADENAS, S.A.

Appeals from the United States District Court for the
Southern District of Texas

Decided: March 7, 2016

Citation: 815 F.3d 211, 4 Adm. R. 199 (5th Cir. 2016).

Before **JOLLY**, **JONES**, and **BENAVIDES**, Circuit Judges.

[—1—] **JONES**, Circuit Judge:

Petrobras America, Inc. ("Petrobras") and the Underwriters of its construction all-risks insurance policy ("Underwriters") sued Vicinay Cadenas, S.A. ("Vicinay"), the manufacturer of an underwater tether chain that broke just after being installed to secure the piping system for oil production from the Outer Continental Shelf of the Gulf of Mexico. When the chain ruptured, it caused the pipeline riser and related equipment to collapse to the sea floor, severing the connection between the wellhead and the surface thousands of feet above. Petrobras alleges four hundred million dollars in damage. Acting on all parties' misunderstanding that the case sounds in admiralty, the district [—2—] court granted summary judgment for Vicinay based upon the maritime law economic loss doctrine. The Underwriters then sought leave to amend their complaint, alleging, for the first time, that Louisiana law, not maritime law, applied to this dispute under the Outer Continental Shelf Lands Act ("OCSLA"). 43 U.S.C. §1333(a)(2). The magistrate judge denied the motion, and the district court affirmed that decision. We hold that the choice of law prescribed by OCSLA is statutorily mandated and is consequently not waivable by the parties. On further analysis, we also hold that the applicable law is that of the adjacent state of Louisiana, not admiralty law. *Id.* Consequently, we reverse and remand for application of Louisiana law.

BACKGROUND

In October 2007, Petrobras contracted with Technip USA, Inc. ("Technip"), to construct five "free-standing hybrid riser" ("FSHR") systems that move crude oil from wellheads on the seabed to "Floating Production Storage and Offloading" ("FPSO") facilities on the surface of the sea. The FPSO facilities are independently moored to the seabed and store and offload, but do not transport, the production. The risers are fixed in place at the wellhead. From above, tether chains connect the upper risers to huge nitrogen-filled "buoyancy cans," which are designed to keep tension in the risers so that they will not kink and impede the flow of oil. The buoyancy cans float 660 feet beneath the water surface; their tether chains play no role in securing the FPSO facilities.

Technip subcontracted to Vicinay the manufacture of these tether chains, and Vicinay agreed to produce chains without welded-over cracks and defects. Vicinay, however, supplied chains that contained welded-over cracks. Shortly after installation in March 2011, one of the chains broke, causing the loss of the associated FSHR system, loss of use of the FPSO facility, and lost oil and gas production. [—3—]

Petrobras and the Underwriters sued Vicinay in March 2012 in federal district court asserting negligence, products liability, and failure to warn claims. They alleged subject matter jurisdiction based on admiralty or, alternatively, under OCSLA; they did not assert that Louisiana law applied. Vicinay moved for summary judgment, arguing that it was entitled to prevail under the maritime law's economic loss doctrine announced in *East River Steamship Corp. v. Transamerica Delaval, Inc.*, 476 U.S. 858, 106 S. Ct. 2295 (1986).[1] Notably, while opposing the motion, Petrobras and the Underwriters did not contest the application of maritime law; in fact, they moved to add a fraud claim as an

---

[1] The economic loss doctrine, distinguishing tort from contract law in admiralty cases, disallows recovery of tort damages to the product itself. *See East River*, 476 U.S. at 871-74, 106 S. Ct. at 2302-04.

exception to the economic loss doctrine. The district court, assuming that maritime law applied, granted summary judgment to Vicinay in August 2014 but also granted the motion to amend. Both parties filed interlocutory appeals of the district court's order. Only the Underwriters added a fraud claim.

Approximately two months later, the Underwriters filed another motion for leave to amend and asserted for the first time that Louisiana law, not maritime law, applied to this dispute under OCSLA. The magistrate judge denied the Underwriters' motion for untimeliness and lack of good cause. The district court affirmed the magistrate judge's ruling and denied the motion, provoking another appeal by the Underwriters. All of the parties' appeals have been consolidated before us. [—4—]

DISCUSSION

We review *de novo* a district court's decision to grant summary judgment. *Grand Isle Shipyard, Inc. v. Seacor Marine, LLC*, 589 F.3d 778, 783 (5th Cir. 2009) (en banc). We consider two issues on appeal.[2] The first issue is whether the Underwriters waived their OCSLA choice of law argument by failing to raise it until after summary judgment was granted on the merits. The second is whether, under OCSLA, maritime law or Louisiana law, the law of the state adjacent to the OCSLA situs, applied.[3]

I. Waiver

As a threshold matter, Vicinay argues that the Underwriters waived their choice of law argument by not raising it in the district court

until the eleventh-hour motion to amend their complaint, which was filed after summary judgment was granted. Vicinay contends that the Underwriters confuse OCSLA subject-matter jurisdiction, which is conferred on federal courts in 43 U.S.C. § 1349(b)(1)(A) and cannot be waived, with OCSLA choice of law, 43 U.S.C. §1333(a), which allegedly can be waived and therefore should not be raised for the first time on appeal. It is Vicinay that is confused.

There is no dispute that, as Petrobras and the Underwriters originally pled, OCSLA provides a basis for subject matter jurisdiction in this case. The incident occurred on the Outer Continental Shelf, and the statutory grant of subject matter jurisdiction over cases and controversies "arising out of or in connection with" operations involving resource exploitation on the Shelf is [—5—] straightforward and broad. 43 U.S.C. § 1349 (b)(1)(A); *See, e.g. EP Operating Ltd. P'ship v. Placid Oil Co.*, 26 F.3d 563, 569 (5th Cir. 1994). Although federal courts may have jurisdiction pursuant to OCSLA, however, "they must then turn to the OCSLA choice of law provision to ascertain whether state, federal, or maritime law applies to a particular case." *In re DEEPWATER HORIZON*, 745 F.3d 157, 164, 2 Adm. R. 171, 173 (5th Cir. 2014). OCSLA's choice of law provision asserts federal jurisdiction over the subsoil and seabed of the Outer Continental Shelf, over all "artificial islands," and over installations and devices used in the exploitation of offshore resources, "other than a ship or vessel." 43 U.S.C. §1333(a)(1). In the following subsection, OCSLA adopts as surrogate federal law the "civil and criminal laws of each adjacent State" to govern the aforementioned areas (generally speaking) "[t]o the extent that [State laws] are applicable and not inconsistent . . . with other Federal laws and regulations . . . ." 43 U.S.C. §1333(a)(2)(A).

Vicinay's argument that the OSCLA provisions are waivable runs headlong into this court's precedents rejecting parties' ability to make a "litigation choice" between maritime and adjacent state law. *In re DEEPWATER HORIZON*, 745 F.3d at 165

---

[2] The parties raise two additional issues: (1) assuming that maritime law applies to this dispute, whether the district court erred in its application of the *East River* economic loss doctrine; and (2) whether the district court abused its discretion in denying the Underwriters' motion for leave to amend. In light of our conclusions, the first issue is irrelevant, and the second issue is moot.

[3] We consider this choice of law issue because it is alleged that Louisiana state law does not apply the economic loss doctrine.

n.7, 2 Adm. R. at 174 n.7; *see also Alleman v. Omni Energy Servs. Corp.*, 580 F.3d 280, 283 n.2 (5th Cir. 2009) ("parties cannot choose to be governed by maritime law when OCSLA applies"). Because OSCLA's choice of law scheme is prescribed by Congress, parties may not voluntarily contract around Congress's mandate. *Texaco Exploration & Production, Inc. v. AmClyde Engineered Prods. Co., Inc.*, 448 F.3d 760, 772 n.8 (5th Cir. 2006); *see also Union Tex. Petroleum Corp. v. PLT Eng'g, Inc.*, 895 F.2d 1043, 1050 (5th Cir. 1990) ("We find it beyond any doubt that OCSLA is itself a Congressionally mandated choice of law provision requiring that the substantive law of the adjacent state is to apply even in the presence of a choice of law provision in the contract to the contrary."). [—6—]

Further, the Supreme Court has held that Section 1333(a) "supersede[s] the normal choice of law rules that the forum would apply." *In re DEEPWATER HORIZON*, 745 F.3d at 166, 2 Adm. R. at 175 (citing *Gulf Offshore Co. v. Mobil Oil Corp.*, 453 U.S. 473, 480-81 (1981)). If parties cannot choose to avoid Congress's choice of law provision under OCSLA, then *a fortiori* the provision cannot be waived by failure to raise the issue below. Vicinay's reliance upon *Fruge v. Amerisure Mutual Insurance Co.*, 663 F.3d 743, 777 (5th Cir. 2011), is misplaced. Although that decision upheld waiver of a choice of law argument not raised in the district court, the case did not involve a statutorily mandated choice of law. Because Congress has delineated among admiralty, federal law and adjacent state law in OCSLA, the parties may not avoid, whether voluntarily or inadvertently, the statutory choice. The Underwriters' choice of law argument is not waived.

II. Admiralty or State Law under OCSLA

As has been noted, the OCSLA prescribes the applicability of either maritime law or adjacent state law as "surrogate federal law" to govern the Outer Continental Shelf. *Hufnagel v. Omega Serv. Indus., Inc.*, 183 F.3d 340, 349 (5th Cir. 1999). These regimes are alternative, not overlapping. *In re DEEP-WATER HORIZON*, 745 F.3d at 166, 2 Adm.

R. at 175; *Baker v. Hercules Offshore, Inc.*, 713 F.3d 208, 218, 1 Adm. R. 206, 211–12 (5th Cir. 2013); *Tenn. Gas Pipeline v. Hous. Cas. Ins.*, 87 F.3d 150, 154 (5th Cir. 1996) (noting that OCSLA "was not intended to displace general maritime law").

The Underwriters and Petrobras contend that the district court was required to apply Louisiana law, the law of the adjacent state, while Vicinay argues that maritime law applies to the dispute. This court has interpreted the statute to compel borrowing adjacent state law if three conditions are met: "(1) The controversy must arise on a situs covered by OCSLA (i.e. the subsoil, seabed, or artificial structures permanently or temporarily attached thereto). [—7—] (2) Federal maritime law must not apply of its own force. (3) The state law must not be inconsistent with Federal law." *PLT Eng'g,* 895 F.2d at 1047 (construing §1333(a)(2)(A)).

The decisive question thus becomes whether maritime law "applies of its own force," based on the twin tests of location and connection with maritime activity. *Jerome B. Grubart, Inc. v. Great Lakes Dredge & Dock Co.*, 513 U.S. 527, 534, 115 S. Ct. 1043, 1048 (1995). The location prong asks whether the incident occurred on "navigable waters" or, if injury occurred on land, whether it was caused by a vessel on navigable waters. *In re La. Crawfish Producers*, 772 F.3d 1026, 1029, 2 Adm. R. 375, 376 (5th Cir. 2014). The court must consider where the wrong "took effect" rather than the locus of the tortious conduct. *Id.* (citing *Egorov, Puchinsky, Afanasiev & Juring v. Terriberry, Carroll & Yancey*, 183 F.3d 453, 456 (5th Cir. 1999) (per curiam)).

Under the connection test, the incident giving rise to the alleged tort must be analyzed at an intermediate level of generality by "assess[ing] the general features of the type of incident involved." *Grubart*, 513 U.S. at 534, 115 S. Ct. at 1048 (citing *Sisson v. Ruby*, 497 U.S. 358, 363, 110 S. Ct. 2892, 2896 (1990)). Further, the court must consider whether the general character of the activity giving rise to the plaintiff's injury is substantially related to traditional maritime activity. *Id.* We address each test in turn.

A. Location Test

The Underwriters argue that the location test is not met, principally because the tether chain connected the floating buoyancy can to the riser, which in turn was affixed to the seabed. Under the specific terms of OCSLA, adjacent state law should apply—to the exclusion of admiralty law—to these "fixed structures erected" on the subsoil and seabed. 43 U.S.C. §1333(a)(2)(A). This is a significant argument. *Cf. Hufnagel*, 183 F.3d at 351-52 (location test not met where plaintiff was struck by a chain and hook while engaged in [—8—] repairs on a fixed offshore drilling platform).[4] The critical distinction between *Hufnagel* and this case, of course, is that the tether chain failed deep in the waters of the Gulf of Mexico, whereas the injury to the plaintiff in *Hufnagel* occurred on the deck of a drilling platform and not on or in the sea. Thus, it can be argued that the tortious activity here "took effect" in navigable waters with the severance of the riser string. *See In re La. Crawfish Producers*, 772 F.3d at 1029, 2 Adm. R. at 376. We do not address this prong further, however, because the breaking of the tether chain fails the admiralty connection test.

B. Connection Test

Vicinay argues that the connection test is satisfied because maritime commerce was disrupted by the tether chain's failure, and that failure was "substantially related to traditional maritime commerce." Further, Vicinay reinforces its substantial relationship contention by noting that the FPSO is a vessel and the tether chain and buoyancy can are "unique to the maritime world and do not exist on land-based operations." We disagree.

To show disruption of maritime commerce, Vicinay points out that Petrobras had to suspend all oil and gas development operations in the area to investigate the cause of the chain's failure. The Supreme Court has cautioned, however, that the type of incident involved must not be defined at too high or too low a level of generality; instead the question is "whether the incident could be seen within a class of incidents that posed more than a fanciful risk" to maritime commerce. *Grubart*, 513 U.S. at 538-39, 115 S. Ct. at 1051. The proper focus is on "potential effects, not the 'particular facts of the incident.'" *Id.* at 538, 115 S. Ct. at 1051. Cases from the Supreme Court and this circuit interpret potential disruption of maritime commerce in terms of the incident's [—9—] effect on the navigability of the waterways. *See, e.g., id.* at 539, 115 S. Ct. at 1051 (noting that damage to an underwater freight tunnel may imperil "the water course itself," and "navigational use" could be restricted during repair); *Sisson*, 497 U.S. at 362, 110 S. Ct. at 2896 (a fire on a noncommercial vessel in a marina may disrupt maritime commerce because the fire "can spread to nearby commercial vessels or make the marina inaccessible to such vessels"); *In re La. Crawfish Producers*, 772 F.3d at 1029, 2 Adm. R. at 376 (maritime commerce would be disrupted by the "obstruction of water flows" in Louisiana's Atachafalaya Basin caused by dredging activities).

Here, expressed in general terms, a component failed on an underwater structure in an offshore production installation and caused the structure to fall to the sea floor. Such an incident does not have the potential to disrupt maritime commercial or navigational activities on or in the Gulf of Mexico. Vicinay's emphasis that Petrobras halted its development operations for some period following the failure of the FHSR erroneously relies on the "particular facts of the incident," *Grubart*, 513 U.S. at 538, 115 S. Ct. at 1051, rather than general maritime and commercial activity. Moreover, the disruption affected oil and gas production and development activities rather than navigation or traditional maritime commerce. Even the involvement of the FPSO, technically a vessel, is unrelated to the disruption of navigation or maritime commerce activity because the FPSO's only purpose was to store and process the oil in a fixed location for later transport. Finally, the fact that the buoyancy can

---

[4] Far less persuasive, however, and without legal support is the Underwriters' broader contention that the incident did not occur on "navigable waters" because it took place more than 660 feet below the Gulf of Mexico.

eventually floated to the surface and had to be recovered provides, under the circumstances taken as a whole, no more than a de minimus potential to disrupt maritime commerce or navigation. *See id.* at 538-39, 115 S. Ct. at 1051 (more than a fanciful risk to commercial shipping is required).

Vicinay's argument that the second prong of the connection test is met is squarely foreclosed by *Texaco Exploration & Production v. AmClyde* [—10—] *Engineered Products Co., Inc.* In *AmClyde*, Texaco brought negligence and products liability causes of action against a crane manufacturer arising from the failure of a barge-mounted construction crane that caused the deck of a production platform to collapse into the sea. 448 F.3d 760, 766 (5th Cir. 2006). Critically, the platform was affixed to the Outer Continental Shelf. *Id.* This court held that the tort claims were not substantially related to traditional maritime activity because they were "inextricably connected with the development of the Outer Continental Shelf and an installation for production of resources there," and the development of resources on the Outer Continental Shelf is not a traditional maritime activity. *Id.* at 771; *see also PLT Eng'g*, 895 F.2d at 1048 ("the principal obligation of PLT and the subcontractors was to build the gathering line and connect it to the platform and the transmission line. These activities are not traditionally maritime. Rather they are the subjects of oil and gas exploration."). The *Amclyde* court distinguished *Grubart* as arising from a traditional maritime activity: "repair or maintenance work on a navigable waterway performed from a vessel." 448 F.3d at 771 (citing *Grubart*, 513 U.S. at 540, 115 S. Ct. at 1043).

As in *AmClyde*, Petrobras's products liability, negligence, and failure to warn tort claims resulting from the failure of the tether chain are all "inextricably intertwined" with its oil and gas production and development operations on the Outer Continental Shelf. Further, as *AmClyde* confirms, development on the Outer Continental Shelf is not a traditional maritime activity. Contrary to Vicinay's argument, Petrobras's development of resources on the Outer Continental Shelf was not transformed into a maritime activity because it involved the use of the FPSO facility and a buoyancy can. That the crane in *AmClyde* was mounted on a barge did not alter the conclusion that the resource development activities on a fixed production platform were not maritime in nature; so it is here, particularly because the FPSO facility was [—11—] permanently moored to the Outer Continental Shelf and was not used for transportation. Likewise, the buoyancy can simply kept tension in the risers to prevent kinks that would impede the flow of oil. The can and tether chain had nothing to do with any traditional maritime activities.

In sum, the rupture of the tether chain was neither potentially nor actually disruptive to navigation and maritime commerce, nor did it bear a substantial relation to traditional maritime activity. Maritime law does not apply of its own force. Because the other criteria of OCSLA choice of law are satisfied, Louisiana law applies to this dispute.

CONCLUSION

In light of the erroneous adjudication based on maritime law, we **REVERSE and REMAND** for further proceedings under Louisiana law. The Underwriters' appeal of the district court's denial of its motion for leave to amend is **DISMISSED** as moot.

United States Court of Appeals
for the Fifth Circuit

No. 15-30146

UNITED STATES
VS.
FAFALIOS

Appeal from the United States District Court for the
Eastern District of Louisiana

Decided: March 14, 2016

Citation: 817 F.3d 155, 4 Adm. R. 204 (5th Cir. 2016).

Before **JOLLY** and **JONES**, Circuit Judges, and
MILLS,* District Judge.

* District Judge of the Northern District of
Mississippi, sitting by designation.

[—1—] JOLLY, Circuit Judge:

Matthaios Fafalios appeals his conviction for failing to maintain an oil record book aboard a foreign-flagged merchant sea vessel, in violation of 33 U.S.C. § 1908(a) and 33 C.F.R. § 151.25. Fafalios moved for a judgment of acquittal under Rule 29 of the Federal Rules of Criminal Procedure. For the following reasons, we reverse the district court's denial of Fafalios's Rule 29 motion. We vacate the judgment of conviction, and remand this action for entry of a judgment of acquittal. **[—2—]**

I.

Fafalios is a 65-year-old Greek citizen who has been a merchant seafarer for over forty years. Most recently, Fafalios was the chief engineer on the *M/V Trident Navigator*, a merchant cargo ship registered under the flag of the Marshall Islands. Like many large cargo ships, the *Trident Navigator* gradually collects water in the base of the ship, which is referred to as the "bilge." Bilge water must be dumped periodically to prevent it from overtaking the engine rooms and other on-board machinery. Because bilge water often mixes with oil runoff from the ship's engine room, various international treaties require that the water be filtered before it is returned to the sea. Under the implementing federal statute, the Act to Prevent Pollution from Ships (APPS), and its accompanying regulations, all discharges of bilge water are to be documented in an "oil record book." *See* 33 U.S.C. § 1908(a); 33 C.F.R. § 151.25(a). As chief engineer, Fafalios was responsible for making record book entries regarding the dumping of bilge water.

In December 2013, while in international waters, Fafalios noticed that the *Trident Navigator*'s bilge tank was almost full. Fearing that the bilge water would damage engine components before it could be properly filtered for disposal, Fafalios ordered that the oily bilge water be pumped directly into the ocean without treatment. To conceal his actions, Fafalios did not record this bilge water dumping in the *Trident Navigator*'s oil record book. Several weeks later, the *Trident Navigator* arrived at port in New Orleans. Soon after the ship's arrival, a whistleblower contacted the U.S. Coast Guard and informed them that the untreated bilge water had been pumped overboard. The Coast Guard conducted an investigation, which uncovered Fafalios's actions.

The government indicted Fafalios for failing to maintain an oil record book, in violation of 33 U.S.C. § 1908(a); obstruction of justice under 18 U.S.C. § 1505; and witness tampering under 18 U.S.C. § 1512(b)(3). Fafalios's case **[—3—]** went to trial in December 2014. Before the case was submitted to the jury, Fafalios moved for a judgment of acquittal under Rule 29 of the Federal Rules of Criminal Procedure. Fafalios's Rule 29 motion concerned only the charge for failing to maintain an oil record book in violation of 33 U.S.C. § 1908(a). Fafalios urged that the government had failed to prove that he was the "master" of the ship, which, according to Fafalios, is an element of the offense. The district court reserved ruling on this motion until a later time.

The jury convicted on all three charges on December 16, 2014. Fafalios renewed his Rule 29 motion. The district court denied the motion. Fafalios appealed to this court, and challenges only his conviction under 33 U.S.C.

§ 1908(a) for failure to maintain an oil record book.

II.

Fafalios's Rule 29 motion asserted that the government failed to offer evidence regarding an element of the statute of conviction.[1] This court reviews de novo a district court's denial of a motion for a judgment of acquittal, and views the evidence in the light most favorable to the government. *United States v. Dickinson*, 632 F.3d 186, 188–89 (5th Cir. 2011).

III.

As stated, Fafalios appeals only his conviction under 33 U.S.C. §1908(a) for "failure to maintain a record book." Section 1908(a) states that "[a] person who knowingly violates [international treaty provisions], this chapter, or the regulations issued thereunder commits a class D felony." Foreign-flagged [—4—] ships may be prosecuted under 33 U.S.C. § 1908 only for violations that occur within the navigable waters of the United States, or while at a port or terminal under the jurisdiction of the United States. 33 U.S.C. § 1902(a); *see also United States v. Jho*, 534 F.3d 398, 403 (5th Cir. 2008).

Because Fafalios dumped the dirty bilge water while the *Trident Navigator* was still in international waters, that action, although a violation of international law, did not allow for prosecution under APPS. Thus, the government relied on the statute's accompanying regulations to prosecute Fafalios for failure to maintain an accurate oil record book once the ship entered U.S. waters. *See* 33 U.S.C. § 1908(a) (stating that an

---

[1] In characterizing Fafalios's appeal as a challenge to the sufficiency of the evidence, we reject the government's contention that Fafalios's Rule 29 motion was actually an untimely attack on the indictment, and thus should be reviewed for plain error. Fafalios does not contend that the indictment categorically fails to state an offense, but instead that the government failed to prove the elements of the offense alleged. That Fafalios knew at the time the indictment was served that the government would likely be unable to prove its case does not convert his Rule 29 motion into an untimely attack on the indictment.

individual who "knowingly violates . . . the regulations issued thereunder commits a class D felony"). The regulations, which are promulgated by the Coast Guard, state in relevant part that:

> [e]ach . . . ship of 400 gross tons and above . . . shall maintain an Oil Record Book . . . . Entries shall be made in the Oil Record Book on each occasion [that bilge water is discharged]. . . . Each operation . . . shall be fully recorded without delay in the Oil Record Book so that all the entries in the book appropriate to that operation are completed. Each completed operation shall be signed by the person or persons in charge of the operations concerned and each completed page shall be signed by the master or other person having charge of the ship. . . . The master or other person having charge of a ship required to keep an Oil Record Book shall be responsible for the maintenance of such record.

33 C.F.R. §§ 151.25(a), (e), (h), (j).

Fafalios contends that, under the plain language of the regulations, only the "master or other person having charge of [the] ship" is responsible for the continued maintenance of the oil record book. According to Fafalios, the government's failure to offer any evidence showing that he was the "master" of the *Trident Navigator* means that the government failed to prove an element of the charged offense. [—5—]

This court interprets regulations in the same manner as statutes, looking first to the regulation's plain language. *Lara v. Cinemark USA, Inc.*, 207 F.3d 783, 787 (5th Cir. 2000). "Where the language is unambiguous, we do not look beyond the plain wording of the regulation to determine meaning." *Anthony v. United States*, 520 F.3d 374, 380 (5th Cir. 2008) (citing *Copeland v. Comm'r*, 290 F.3d 326, 332–33 (5th Cir. 2002)); *see also S.D. ex rel. Dickson v. Hood*, 391 F.3d 581, 595 (5th Cir. 2004) ("We have consistently held that a regulation should be construed to give effect to the natural and plain meaning of its words.").

Furthermore, the court "consider[s] the regulation as a whole, with the assumption that the [agency at issue] intended each of the regulation's terms to convey meaning." *Lara*, 207 F.3d at 787 (citing *Bailey v. United States*, 516 U.S. 137, 143–45 (1995)).

We agree with the appellant that, under the plain language of the regulations, only the "master or other person having charge of the ship" is responsible for maintenance of the oil record book. Section 151.25 asserts that each ship is required to maintain an oil record book, and then immediately thereafter explicitly and exclusively designates the "master" of the ship as the individual "responsible" for maintaining such a record book. *See* 33 C.F.R. §§ 151.25(a), (j). The regulations mention only the "master" when assigning responsibility for maintaining the oil record book, which plainly indicates that the responsibility does not extend to others on the vessel. *See Thompson v. Goetzmann*, 337 F.3d 489, 499 (5th Cir. 2003) (invoking the "well-known interpretative canon, *expressio unius est exclusio alterius*—'the expression of one thing implies the exclusion of another'").

Our conclusion is bolstered by the fact that, with respect to other record book obligations, the regulations explicitly contemplate liability for a crew member in Fafalios's position. The subsection addressing the logging and signature requirements extends criminal liability to the "person or persons in [—6—] charge of the operations concerned." *See* 33 C.F.R. § 151.25(h); *see also BFP v. Resolution Trust Corp.*, 511 U.S. 531, 537 (1994) ("'[I]t is generally presumed that Congress acts intentionally and purposely when it includes particular language in one section of a statute but omits it in another'" (quoting *Chicago v. Envtl. Def. Fund*, 511 U.S. 328, 338 (1994)).[2]

The government concedes that Fafalios was not the "master or other person having charge" of the *Trident Navigator*, but offers several reasons why, it its view, Fafalios

nevertheless violated 33 C.F.R. § 151.25. First, the government contends that Fafalios was the "person . . . in charge of the operations concerned [i.e., the dumping of bilge water]," and thus had an obligation to record the dumping of dirty bilge water and sign the oil book entry. *See* 33 C.F.R. § 151.25(h) (Each operation [i.e., dumping of bilge water] . . . shall be fully recorded without delay [and] shall be signed by the person or persons in charge of the operations concerned."). According to the government, the signing and recording obligations found in the regulations are continuing in nature, such that Fafalios's failure to record a bilge water dumping became a prosecutable offense once Fafalios's ship entered U.S. waters.

In making this argument, the government conflates a failure to "record" a dumping in the oil record book with a failure to "maintain" the oil record book going forward. Under 33 C.F.R. § 151.25(h), Fafalios no doubt was required to record the dumping of the untreated bilge water; Fafalios ignored that requirement when he failed to make such an entry. This action, however, occurred while Fafalios was still in international waters, and nothing in the regulations indicates that a failure to sign a record entry is a continuing [—7—] offense. In fact, our past precedents show that a failure to sign an oil record book while still in international waters, standing alone, is not a violation of either APPS or its attendant regulations. *See Jho*, 534 F.3d 398.

The facts in *Jho* are similar to the facts of this case. Like Fafalios, the defendant in *Jho* was a chief engineer who failed to sign the oil record book after an improper bilge-water discharge. The defendant's ship later entered U.S. waters. After the ship docked in a U.S. port, the defendant was charged with aiding and abetting the failure to maintain the oil record book under 33 U.S.C. § 1908(a) and 33 C.F.R. § 151.25. *See id.* at 401; *id.* at 402 n.1. The district court dismissed the indictment on the ground that the unrecorded dumping occurred outside U.S. waters. *Id.* at 402.

The Fifth Circuit reversed the district court's dismissal. The *Jho* court emphasized that 33 C.F.R. § 151.25 criminalizes a failure

---

[2] That *BFP* concerns interpretation of a statute instead of a regulation does not affect its value. As stated, absent a special exception, this court interprets regulations in the same manner as it does statutes. *See Anthony*, 520 F.3d at 380.

to *maintain* oil record books and that, upon entering U.S. waters, a foreign-flagged vessel may expose itself to liability by carrying with it knowingly inaccurate oil record books. At no point, however, did the *Jho* court suggest that the defendant's mere failure to sign the book while still in international waters was an independent ground for liability. In fact, the *Jho* court explicitly held that "Jho['s] argume[nt] that he is not the 'master or other person having charge of [the] ship' . . . is inapposite [because] the government charged Jho with aiding and abetting the oil record book offense[] [of failure to maintain]." *Jho*, 534 F.3d at 402 n.1.

Beyond *Jho*, several independent reasons support the conclusion that Fafalios's failure to sign the record book is not a continuing offense. First, the regulation imposes a duty to record and sign the operation "without delay." This phrase implies that Fafalios committed the offense as soon as he failed to sign the record book and that the offense thus was completed before Fafalios entered U.S. waters. If the regulations were meant to impose a continuing [—8—] duty, they could have done so with different language, for example by requiring that Fafalios, as chief engineer, "maintain" the record book. *Cf. id.* at 403 ("[W]e read the requirement that an oil record book be 'maintained' as imposing a duty upon a foreign-flagged vessel to ensure that its oil record book is accurate (or at least not knowingly inaccurate) upon entering the ports of navigable waters of the United States.").

The government also argues that, even assuming that Fafalios's position as the "person in charge of the operations concerned" does not independently subject him to criminal liability for failure to complete and sign an oil record, the regulations separately required that Fafalios "maintain" an accurate oil record book once the ship entered U.S. waters. Specifically, the government points out that, in addition to imposing on the master a duty to "maintain" the oil record book, the regulations also impose a duty to "maintain" the record book on the ship itself. 33 C.F.R. § 151.25(a) ("Each . . . ship of 400 gross tons and above . . . shall maintain an Oil Record Book."). According to the government,

the ship's duty to maintain the record book applies to Fafalios individually, at least for the records he must sign as the chief engineer.

Of course, in making this argument, the government must account for the fact that 33 C.F.R. § 151.25 uses the word "maintain" twice in close proximity, stating that "[e]ach . . . ship of 400 gross tons and above . . . shall maintain an Oil Record Book" and that "[t]he master or other person having charge of a ship required to keep an Oil Record Book shall be responsible for the maintenance of such record." *See* 33 C.F.R. §§ 151.25(a), (j). The government contends that the word "maintain" has a different meaning in subsection (a), when discussing the ship itself, than it does in subsection (j), when discussing the "master" of the ship individually. According to the government, the only duty to "maintain" the record book—in the sense of keeping it accurate—attaches to the ship (and thus, to anyone on the ship who [—9—] is charged with signing the record book). Conversely, when the regulation states that the master must "maintain" the record book, it simply means that he is in charge of the physical custody of the record book, not that he bears any special duty to ensure that the record book is accurate.

This argument is foreclosed by traditional rules of statutory construction, not to mention common sense. Nothing in 33 C.F.R. § 151.25 suggests that "maintain" should have two totally different meanings as the word is used in the regulations. A longstanding canon of statutory construction holds that "'identical words used in different parts of the same act are intended to have the same meaning.'" *United States v. Cooper*, 135 F.3d 960, 962 (5th Cir. 1998) (quoting *Atlantic Cleaners & Dyers, Inc. v. United States*, 286 U.S. 427, 433 (1932)). Furthermore, the rule of lenity cautions against adopting the government's strained reasoning regarding why the duty to "maintain" the oil record book should extend to Fafalios. *See United States v. Kaluza*, 780 F.3d 647, 669, 3 Adm. R. 287, 302 (5th Cir. 2015) (stating that the rule of lenity requires that "ambiguous criminal laws be interpreted in favor of the defendants subjected to them" (internal quotations omitted)). Finally, even ignoring the portion of the regulation regarding the master's obligations, the government offers no convincing explanation for why § 151.25(a)'s requirement that the ship maintain a record book should be delegated to Fafalios specifically, especially given that the ship itself may be held liable *in rem* for any violation of the regulations, and thus have a bond fixed on it and its departure clearance withheld pending payment of a fine. *See* 33 U.S.C. § 1908(d).[3] [—10—]

Next, the government argues that the Coast Guard has a well-known practice of enforcing the oil record book regulations against chief engineers and that this practice is entitled to at least some deference. This argument is without merit, however, given that the interpretation at issue is in no way inconsistent with prosecutions of chief engineers. As stated, chief engineers can be prosecuted for failure to sign an oil record book when that failure occurs on U.S.-flagged vessels or in U.S. waters. They apparently may be prosecuted for aiding and abetting the failure to maintain an accurate record book, as the defendant in *Jho* was. They can be prosecuted for making false statements to a Coast Guard investigator, as Fafalios was. Chief engineers on foreign-flagged vessels cannot, however, be prosecuted simply for having previously failed to maintain an oil record book once a ship enters U.S. waters, since 33 C.F.R. § 151.25 assigns that duty explicitly and exclusively to the "master or other person having charge of the ship." The Coast Guard's past practices in applying its regulations do not provide a convincing reason to deviate from the plain language of the regulation itself.

Finally, in what amounts to a pure policy argument—an unusual argument to make with respect to the interpretation of a criminal statute—the government argues that reading the regulation as imposing the duty to maintain the record book only on the "master" of the ship would allow chief engineers to falsify records and conceal their falsification from the master. In this scenario, according to the government, neither the chief engineer nor the master would be liable, since only "knowing" violations are criminalized. We are unpersuaded. First, even if this were true, contrived hypotheticals provide little reason to depart from the plain language of the statute and regulations. [—11—] Second, as has already been explained, any Coast Guard investigation will likely involve asking the chief engineer whether the oil record book is accurate; any engineer who stands by his falsified records will expose himself to an obstruction charge, just as Fafalios did.[4]

IV.

In sum, the plain language of 33 C.F.R. § 151.25 states that only the "master or other person having charge of the ship" has a duty to maintain the record book. The government concedes that Fafalios was not the "master or other person having charge" of the *Trident Navigator*. Accordingly, the district court's denial of Fafalios's Rule 29 motion is REVERSED. The judgment of conviction is VACATED, and this case is REMANDED for entry of a judgment of acquittal regarding the charge under 33 U.S.C. § 1908(a).

REVERSED, VACATED, and REMANDED.

---

[3] The government also argues that "maintain" must have two different meanings because, if the requirement that the master "maintain" the record book meant that he must ensure that it was accurate, then there would be no reason to require the master to sign the record book. This contention is without merit. Requiring the master to physically sign the record book increases the odds that the master would detect any irregularities and makes [—10—] proving his involvement in any fraud easier. This provides ample reason to require the master to sign even though he is already obliged to ensure the accuracy of the record.

---

[4] The court also notes that it is the Coast Guard's regulations, and not APPS itself, that limits the scope of prosecution here. If the Coast Guard remains concerned that 33 C.F.R. § 151.25 creates a loophole for individuals such as Fafalios, the agency could amend its regulations in accordance with the applicable procedures.

United States Court of Appeals
for the Fifth Circuit

No. 15-60148

BIS SALAMIS, INC.
vs.

DIRECTOR, OFFICE OF WORKERS' COMPENSATION
PROGRAMS

Petition for Review of an Order of the Benefits
Review Board

Decided: March 17, 2016

Citation: 819 F.3d 116, 4 Adm. R. 209 (5th Cir. 2016).

Before **PRADO**, **OWEN**, and **HAYNES**, Circuit Judges.

[—1—] **HAYNES**, Circuit Judge:

BIS Salamis, Inc. ("Salamis") and Signal Mutual Indemnity Association (collectively, "Petitioners") appeal from the final order of the Benefits Review Board (the "Board"), which granted Joseph Meeks ("Meeks" or "Claimant") benefits under the Longshore Harbor Workers' Compensation Act ("LHWCA"), 33 U.S.C. §§ 901–950.[1] This case has a lengthy procedural history. Essentially, after two remands, the Board vacated the ALJ's findings in favor [—2—] of Petitioners, reversed the ALJ's decision, and rendered a decision in favor of Meeks. For the reasons that follow, we REVERSE in part the award of benefits to Meeks and REINSTATE the ALJ's second order, dated June 28, 2013 ("ALJ's June 2013 Order"), except for the portion of that order denying Meeks's dental costs for his loose and later missing tooth; as to the loose/missing tooth, we AFFIRM the Board's judgment.

I. Background

In 2009, Meeks worked briefly for Salamis as a sandblaster and painter on offshore rigs. He was involved in an offshore accident during that employment, which the parties agree places his claim within the bounds of the LHWCA. The parties dispute solely the nature and extent of Meeks's injuries and whether the incident during Meeks's employment with Salamis caused any compensable injury to Meeks.

A. Factual Background

1. The Incident

On April 9, 2010, a short time after beginning work with Salamis, Meeks was being transferred with several other men from an oil rig to a vessel while attached to a personnel platform and basket ("personnel basket" or "basket"). Meeks claims the basket collided with the vessel near the bulwarks and bounced, knocking him and the other men off the platform on which they were standing and nearly throwing him overboard but for the intervention of one of the men. Meeks alleges he hit the deck on his feet, knocking his teeth together, and then hit his shoulder on the railing of the boat, or bulwark, as he fell.[2] [—3—]

Immediately after the incident, Meeks stated that he was all right. But he avers that within thirty minutes, he began to feel pain in his lower back, neck, and mouth. He alleged the same during his depositions, and that his mouth was bleeding and the accident knocked

---

[1] The respondents in this case include Joseph Meeks and the Director of the Office of Workers' Compensation Programs, but the Office has chosen not to participate in this appeal.

[2] The parties disagree about exactly what happened, but agree that some incident caused the basket to collide with the boat. In reports made contemporaneously or soon after the accident by Salamis and Meeks, Meeks reported that as he was being lowered in the personnel basket onto a boat, the "basket hit [the] deck of [the boat] very hard," and he "f[e]ll out of [the] basket," resulting in neck and back pain. To his physical therapists in the weeks following the incident, Meeks described the personnel basket as having "jolted" onto the ship. [—3—] Meeks later told multiple health care providers that the basket had fallen 6–10 feet and hit the deck of the vessel. Salamis reported Meeks was "[b]eing lowered in a personnel basket which collided with a boat during high seas," and that Meeks reported neck and back pain. The captain's incident report noted a miscommunication between the crane operator and the deck hand, resulting in "lower[ing] the basket into the cargo rail on port side of vessel and collaps[ing] the basket as a swe[l]l was rolling through."

some teeth out. The ALJ apparently credited a statement from Meeks's supervisor that Meeks told him shortly after the incident that Meeks had been "hurt before but . . . never got anything for it." When asked about this statement during the hearing before the ALJ, Meeks could not recall whether he had uttered it.

2. Emergency Care

Meeks filled out an accident report and was given a neck brace, attached to a spine board, and transported ashore in a helicopter. An ambulance ultimately took Meeks to Terrebonne General Medical Center ("Terrebonne"). The report from the ambulance ride notes Meeks alleged pain to his lower back and neck and also listed injury to his "face and/or neck."

Records from Meeks's brief stay at Terrebonne do not indicate that Meeks reported any damage to his teeth or mouth, except a report to a company representative on April 10 that he thought he might have a loose tooth. The nursing assessment from his arrival at Terrebonne noted Meeks had a normal gait, with purposeful movement, no tenderness or paralysis, and a full range of motion in all his joints. Meeks reported falling and having "lower back and neck pain," according to the records. Reports from a CT scan and other evaluations observed no evidence of fractures or traumatic injuries in Meeks's [—4—] spine, but the scans detected "extensive degenerative changes" in both his cervical and lumbar spinal regions.

From his emergency stay, Meeks was diagnosed with a back sprain or strain. The report from that night noted "no acute distress" and "no evidence of trauma." Meeks was discharged to Salamis, which put him up in a hotel and brought him to the company physician, Dr. Gidman, on April 13, 2009. Dr. Gidman had also performed pre-employment physicals on Meeks for Salamis.

3. Treatment with Dr. Gidman

Dr. Gidman evaluated Meeks based on Meeks's complaints of neck, lower back, and right leg pain and found that while the lower back pain was severe, the neck symptoms were only moderate. Based on the April 10 x-rays and separate x-rays Dr. Gidman ordered, the doctor noted advanced degenerative changes in the cervical and the lumbar spine areas, plus moderate scoliosis in Meeks's lumbar spine. Dr. Gidman found no fractures. Meeks reported to Dr. Gidman that he had not had similar problems in the past and had not seen any doctors, received treatment, or lost work for neck, lower back, or right leg problems. After performing a physical examination on Meeks, Dr. Gidman noted no tenderness to the touch, spasms, scars, scrapes, scratches, bruising or swelling in examining Meeks's spine. He found Meeks had a normal gait and did not detect pain upon having Meeks perform straight-leg raises. Based on these findings, Dr. Gidman prescribed Vicodin for pain, muscle relaxers, and anti-inflammatories, and he instructed home therapies of stretching, soaks, rubdowns, heating pad, and only light activities at on-shore work. Dr. Gidman released Meeks to light duty on April 13, 2009.

Meeks returned to Dr. Gidman on April 15, 2009, after performing light work in Salamis's office on land, "complaining of stiffness in his neck and lower back" and "of a cramping and a sleep sensation" in his legs. Straight-leg raising tests were again negative for any symptoms of lower back pain. Dr. Gidman [—5—] prescribed two days of physical therapy, rest during Meeks's previously-scheduled week off, and a follow-up appointment on May 12, 2009. Dr. Gidman released Meeks to regular duty, to follow his time off.

Meeks attended physical therapy on April 16 and 17, 2009, as prescribed. Reports from therapy state that Meeks reported feeling better but still stiff in his neck and back, with sharp pain in his lower back. After Meeks's weeklong break to rest, he returned to performing light duty, and then regular duty work, for Salamis. But Meeks allegedly continued to experience significant pain, so he stopped work and began reporting to Dr. Esses in Houston in May 2009, upon the recommendation of his attorney. In one of the many inconsistencies noted by the ALJ, Meeks admitted during the hearing that, when asked about it at his deposition, Meeks claimed not to remember who referred him to Dr. Esses. Meeks also admitted that on another occasion he had suggested that his daughter referred him to Dr. Esses.

4. Treatment with Dr. Um

In May 2009, Meeks visited Dr. Um, a dentist. Although Meeks's complaints of pain following the incident mostly related to his back and neck, he told a company representative who interviewed him in the emergency room on April 10, 2009, that he thought he had a "loose tooth." He claimed later that his teeth had been jarred together when he collided with the deck of the vessel. Meeks claims his tooth fell out, so he went to see Dr. Um on May 20, 2009. Dr. Um made a partial denture for the missing tooth and capped the others.

5. Treatment with Doctors Esses and Dent

Dr. Esses, an orthopedic surgeon and Meeks's treating physician, began seeing Meeks on May 19, 2009. Meeks told Dr. Esses he "was dropped 10 feet in a personnel basket," resulting in neck and lower back pain. In contrast to the examination by Dr. Gidman, Dr. Esses reported a "marked paravertebral spasm" upon examining Meeks's lower back and found limited range of motion [—6—] in that area. Dr. Esses also recorded that Meeks experienced pain while performing straight-leg raises. Dr. Esses ordered an MRI of the spine, which revealed degenerative changes of stenosis and disc herniation, but no evidence of compression fractures, dislocation, or other traumatic injuries. In June 2009, Dr. Esses prescribed a lumbar epidural steroid injection ("ESI").

Meeks was referred to Dr. Dent for this injection, and received one on July 8, 2009. Meeks complained to Dr. Dent of stiffness in his neck and lower back, weakness in his legs, that he was dragging his right foot by the end of the day, and that his hands and feet tingled. Meeks told Dr. Dent that he was

injured when the personnel basket dropped 10 feet and hit the deck, and that Meeks "was on his feet when the impact occurred." Meeks described his pain to Dr. Dent as between an 8 and 10 on a scale of 10, including sharp, dull, burning pain that radiated from his lower back to his legs and feet. Dr. Dent noted Meeks reported "problems with cooking, cleaning, bathing, and dressing" during this time period. Dr. Dent reported tenderness to the touch along the spine, muscle spasms in the lower back, and pain on attempting to flex the back. Meeks reported pain in the right leg on a straight-leg raising exercise.

Dr. Dent diagnosed Meeks with lumbago, cervical facet syndrome, cervicalgia, cervical neuritis, and lumbar neuritis. He prescribed pain killers, anti-inflammatories, and muscle relaxers, and he further recommended home exercises. Dr. Dent found Meeks was "unable to work," and provided his "medical opinion that the injuries evaluated . . . were the direct result of the patient's work-related injury."

Meeks reported relief for only a couple of days. On July 21, 2009, Dr. Esses noted that Meeks claimed continued and intense pain, with reduced range of motion in his lumbar spine and pain on his right side on straight-leg raising. Dr. Esses thus recommended surgery, and Meeks agreed to schedule one. Salamis would not approve the surgery, so Meeks continued to treat every [—7—] couple of months with Dr. Dent for pain medication and with Dr. Esses for follow-up until September 17, 2010, when Dr. Esses performed the surgery. During these appointments, both Dr. Esses and Dr. Dent documented worsening pain and leg symptoms, including "marked limitation in range of motion" with pain reported on the right side during straight-leg raises. Dr. Dent's records reflect that Meeks denied any illegal drug use in his history and denied the use of tobacco products, although reports to other doctors and Dent's separate notes acknowledge that Meeks smokes one pack of cigarettes each day, and it is undisputed that Meeks once used illegal drugs. Meeks could not explain why he denied past illegal drug use to Dr. Dent and another doctor.

On September 17, 2010, Dr. Esses performed spinal decompression surgery on Meeks's lower back, noting "profound stenosis" at six levels of the lumbar spine. After the surgery, Dr. Esses reported some improvement, with "no pain with straight-leg raising" on October 4, 2010. However, by November 10, 2010, Meeks began complaining of neck pain. Dr. Esses ordered an ESI on the neck, but Meeks continued to report pain; Dr. Esses prescribed physical therapy and in May 2011 noted that Meeks may be a candidate for surgery.

Meanwhile, Dr. Dent continued to treat Meeks for pain resulting from his lower back and neck. On February 15, 2011, Dr. Dent wrote a "Future Medical Needs Letter," in which Dr. Dent opined it was "probable that [Meeks] will have pain to the low back radiating to the legs for the rest of his life secondary to the fact that there was a lengthy delay between the injury and the lumbar spine surgery." Dr. Dent also found that "Mr. Meeks' low back pain complaints are consistent with his objective findings." He recommended continued pain medication. Dr. Dent found Meeks's "neck pain complaints [to be] consistent with his objective findings" and that Meeks should undergo a second ESI to his neck and possibly cervical spine surgery. Dr. Dent opined [—8—] that Meeks has developed chronic disabling pain and would expect that flare-ups would totally disable Meeks and make it impossible for him to work.

6. Depositions vs. Surveillance: Level of Activity

Salamis had Meeks surveilled without his knowledge on June 9 and 10, 2009, July 13, 14, and 15, 2009, and on September 5 and 6, 2009. The activity on the surveillance videos stands in marked contrast to the pain and limited activity levels Meeks reported to his doctors during this same time frame. The videos revealed Meeks walking around his front lawn and driveway, walking to his truck and bending and leaning over to reach into the truck, driving the truck, often bending at the waist to pull weeds and pick up items, kneeling down and pulling weeds for extended periods of time, doing yard work, climbing steps, standing for extended periods of time, squatting, picking up and carrying around a large baby, and dragging trash to the trash bin.

At his depositions in July 2010 and May 2011 and in reports to his doctors during the period of surveillance, Meeks reported that he was in intense pain, that he could not garden or do yard work, that he did not think he could lift anything heavier than a ten-pound bag of ice, specifically that he did not remember carrying his grandchild, and that he mostly spent time in bed. Of course, the videos show him performing many of these activities without evident pain. After Meeks received the videos from Salamis, he and his attorney submitted an errata sheet, changing some of his answers from his May 2011 deposition. Although he refused to admit that he did yard work even during the hearing before the ALJ, Meeks admitted that he submitted the errata sheet in reality because he saw himself doing things on surveillance that he had denied he could do and realized that he had been caught.

7. Second Opinions

Meeks was also examined by two doctors who were either approved by Salamis or by defendants in a related third-party tort case involving Meeks [—9—] Meeks did not report to Dr. Likover, the doctor approved by Salamis, until seven months after his surgery.[3] Dr. Likover, an orthopedic surgeon, noted fair progress from the lumbar surgery, some pain on straight-leg raises, and opined that continued conservative treatment of Meeks's neck (without surgery) would not be improper.

Dr. Vanderweide is an orthopedic surgeon who examined Meeks before the spinal

---

[3] Before the ALJ, the parties disputed whether this doctor's opinion could be admitted because of a dispute related to Meeks's failure to report for evaluation to Dr. Likover before his surgery. The ALJ appears to have considered the evidence that Petitioners wished to strike, and the parties do not appeal this issue. Therefore, we will not address it. See Hughes v. Johnson, 191 F.3d 607, 613 (5th Cir. 1999).

surgery. He diagnosed Meeks with, among other things, lumbar stenosis, cervical spondylosis, and degenerative disc disease. He opined that "Meeks sustained an injury to the lumbar spine, consistent with the mechanism as described[,] which resulted in acceleration and aggravation of lumbar stenosis caused by advanced degenerative changes which pre-existed the injury event at issue." He also opined that surgical decompression of the lumbar spine was reasonable. This was based on his examination of the MRI and other medical records up to that point, and on Meeks reporting that he had taken the impact of a collision between the personnel basket and the deck of a boat mostly through his legs on April 10, 2009, winding up on the deck of the boat after the basket was thrown to its side and the other occupants were thrown into him. Dr. Vanderweide reported guarding or spasm in Meeks's lumbar spine, lower back pain, and low range of motion. But he found no pain on straight-leg raises. He found no spasm or guarding, problems with range of motion, or need for surgery on Meeks's neck.

Dr. Vanderweide evaluated Meeks again following the lumbar spinal surgery, finding the spinal stenosis had been addressed and that remaining symptoms were related to "significant pre-existing multilevel degen- erative [—10—] disc disease." However, Dr. Vanderweide noted credibility problems: he was "unable to explain the significant change in subjective complaints" regarding Meeks's reported neck pain. He noted significant inconsistencies between the initial evaluation, recent assessments by Dr. Esses, and the latest evaluation, and did not recommend cervical spine surgery. Dr. Vanderweide also stated that Meeks "is now certainly addicted to narcotics," having been regularly using MS Contin since December 2009. Finally, Dr. Vanderweide found it "unreasonable to anticipate that [Meeks] will ever be pain free or 'return to normal,'" an expectation Meeks expressed.[4]

---

[4] Vocational analyses by experts for Meeks and Salamis generally agreed with this impression, finding that Meeks is unlikely to be able to return to the kind of occupations involving heavy labor that he has performed throughout his life. We need not examine this evidence. It would only come into

B. Procedural History

1. The ALJ's First Order

Meeks filed a claim for disability benefits under the LHWCA in May 2009, which was referred to the ALJ. Salamis claimed that Meeks was able to return to regular duty as of April 15, 2009, when Dr. Gidman released him, and that the company provided all the medical care and benefits to which Meeks is entitled. The ALJ held a hearing on June 17, 2011, at which the parties' counsel presented argument and only Meeks testified. After post-trial briefing, the ALJ issued his order and decision ("September 2011 Order").

The September 2011 Order discussed the evidence presented and noted the ALJ's task was to establish whether Meeks had suffered a compensable injury resulting from incidents on the rig, either directly or through aggravation of a preexisting condition. The ALJ noted Meeks's condition would [—11—] be presumed to be a result of his work absent substantial evidence to the contrary. The ALJ found there was "little doubt that something happened on the rig . . . in which employees, including Claimant, were tossed about," and that Meeks suffered dental trauma and his back had "extensive degenerative changes" to its lumbar and cervical spine. The ALJ acknowledged medical opinions in the record that Meeks's symptoms were a result of his work injury, which aggravated a preexisting condition. Yet, he found the medical opinions "were based in large part on the subjective reports and histories provided" by Meeks, and the ALJ found Meeks totally unreliable and not credible.

The ALJ cited Meeks's "demeanor during the hearing" as failing to "create any confidence in the accuracy of his testimony or even his motivation to at least attempt to tell the truth." The ALJ found that the

---

consideration at the third step of the analysis under the LHWCA, and we conclude that Meeks failed to establish a prima facie case of compensable workplace injury at the first step of that analysis. *See Amerada Hess Corp. v. Dir., Office of Worker's Comp. Programs*, 543 F.3d 755, 761 (5th Cir. 2008).

surveillance video contradicted Meeks's previous testimony, that Meeks filed false tax returns, correcting them only to increase his earnings capacity for a lawsuit, and that Meeks frequently misled or withheld information from his doctors and employers. The ALJ credited Meeks's supervisor's statement that Meeks said he had been injured before but never got anything for it and found that "the weight of the objective medical opinion" favored finding the changes to Meeks's back were simply degenerative in nature. Therefore, the ALJ found Meeks had failed to "establish a new injury or aggravation of a preexisting condition," either through his testimony or the medical evidence.

The ALJ likewise found that Meeks's complaints about his teeth were not credible and did not establish an injury, because with broken teeth, there should have been evidence of bruising, swelling, or bleeding. Noting the lack of evidence about such injuries in the reports of the ambulance or the Terrebonne stay, the ALJ rejected this claim. Overall, the ALJ found "the credible evidence of the record insufficient to find that Claimant suffered any new injuries or aggravated any preexisting conditions beyond the transient [—12—] [back] strain that was initially diagnosed, and required only that medical treatment provided by Employer, and resulted in no loss of wages."

2. The Board's First Decision

Meeks appealed to the Board, which reversed the ALJ and remanded for further findings within the LHWCA's framework. The Board found the ALJ's inferences were rational as to Meeks's broken teeth, but remanded for further findings on the work-relatedness of the "loose tooth" Meeks mentioned at the time of the injury, which appeared to have subsequently fallen out. The Board also remanded for further findings regarding Meeks's back and neck injuries, faulting the ALJ for failing to place his findings within the LHWCA's framework or explicitly discuss the presumption in a claimant's favor under Section 920 (a) of the LHWCA, 33 U.S.C. § 920(a) ("the pre-

sumption" or "Section 20(a) presumption"). The Board expressed concern that the ALJ had shifted the burden onto Meeks to prove the work-relatedness of his injuries.

3. ALJ's Second Order, on First Remand

On remand and after further briefing, the ALJ again found that any testimony, findings, or opinions based on Meeks's statements and complaints were entitled to virtually no weight because he found Meeks to be so dishonest and unreliable. The ALJ laid out these findings and his decision in his June 2013 Order. The only facts the ALJ found were established were that Meeks was involved in an incident where he was "tossed about" in a personnel basket, initially reported being fine, but later complained about his back, and commented about never receiving compensation for his injuries before. The only medical information the ALJ found reliable was that Meeks had preexisting spinal conditions and degenerative disk disease, and that as of May 9, 2009, he had two chipped teeth and one missing tooth. The ALJ found no presumption was invoked as to the loose tooth due to Meeks's lack of credibility, and that even if it was invoked, sufficient evidence rebutted it, [—13—] inferring that any intervening trauma that could have caused the chipped teeth could have caused the loose tooth.

Although the ALJ acknowledged that employers are liable for incidents that aggravate preexisting conditions or cause them to become symptomatic, he found Meeks failed to meet even the preliminary, prima facie burden to establish a compensable harm. The only harm the ALJ found "was the lumbar strain for which [Meeks] was treated and from which he was released to full duty." He found the presumption applied as to the strain, that there was no rebuttal evidence, and that Meeks received all reasonable and necessary medical treatment for the strain and sustained no loss of wages. However, he found no presumption was raised as to any greater injuries. The ALJ found that Meeks had not shown he was disabled by the injury, because of his total lack of credibility and how that affected the medical opinions. The ALJ stated:

"[In] more than 15 years as an administrative and criminal law judge, [he] [could]not recall any witness being less credible than Claimant." The ALJ also found that if the presumption *was* raised that Meeks suffered a greater harm to his back and neck, "there was no evidence to rebut it."

4. The Board's Second Decision

After a second appeal, the Board again reversed the ALJ, this time rendering judgment in favor of Meeks, in a July 2014 Decision. The Board concluded that Meeks's back and neck injuries invoked the presumption, that Salamis did not rebut the presumption, and that Meeks had met his burden to show entitlement to temporary total disability. The Board found the ALJ's June 2013 Order was not supported by substantial evidence because objective medical evidence in the record established that Meeks required treatment for his injuries and was prevented from going back to his hard-labor job. The Board also awarded Meeks benefits for his missing tooth, finding it irrational and not supported by substantial evidence to speculate that something else [—14—] may have caused Meeks's tooth to fall out, when there was no record evidence of another incident and Meeks had complained about his tooth on April 10, 2009. Finally, the Board found Meeks had met his preliminary burden to show he could not return to his usual employment as of April 27, 2009, his last day on the job. Therefore, the Board determined that Meeks was entitled to temporary total disability beginning on December 2, 2009, when Dr. Dent began treating Meeks for pain.[5]

5. The ALJ's Third Order and the Board's Final Decision

On second remand, the parties stipulated to Meeks's average weekly wage figure for compensation purposes. The ALJ entered an order awarding temporary total disability compensation from December 2, 2009, to the present and continuing, with provision for

[5] Judge Boggs concurred that Meeks had established the presumption, but dissented from rendering judgment, arguing the ALJ should find the facts in the first instance.

Salamis to pay medical costs for past, present, and future treatment. The Board summarily affirmed the ALJ's January 2015 Order, and Salamis timely appealed the Board's final decision ("February 2015 Decision").

II. Jurisdiction and Standard of Review

We have jurisdiction over the final order of the Board under 33 U.S.C. § 921(c). *See generally Newpark Shipbuilding & Repair, Inc. v. Roundtree*, 723 F.2d 399, 401–02, 403–06 (5th Cir. 1984) (en banc).[6] In reviewing the Board's final decision, we may also review intermediate orders remanding the case to [—15—] the ALJ for further proceedings. *See Mijangos v. Avondale Shipyards, Inc.*, 948 F.2d 941, 943–44 (5th Cir. 1991).

We review the Board's decisions to correct any errors of law and to determine whether the Board "adhered to its proper scope of review." *Ceres Gulf, Inc. v. Dir., Office of Worker's Comp. Programs*, 683 F.3d 225, 228 (5th Cir. 2012) (citation omitted). The Board must uphold the ALJ's findings if those findings are rational, supported by substantial evidence, and consistent with the law. *See id.; Mijangos*, 948 F.2d at 944. "Substantial evidence is 'that relevant evidence—more than a scintilla but less than a preponderance—that would cause a reasonable person to accept the fact finding.'" *Ceres Gulf*, 683 F.3d at 228 (quoting *Coastal Prod. Servs., Inc. v. Hudson*, 555 F.3d 426, 430 (5th Cir. 2009)). Neither we nor the Board may substitute our judgment for that of the ALJ. *See Ortco Contractors, Inc. v. Charpentier*, 332 F.3d 283, 290 (5th Cir. 2003). "The ALJ . . . is

[6] Salamis attempted to appeal the ALJ's decision before the Board had ruled after the second remand. This court dismissed that appeal for lack of jurisdiction because the Board had not issued its final order. *See BIS Salamis, Inc. v. Dir. & Meeks*, No. 14-60681 (Oct. 21, 2014). The Board issued the order from which Salamis now appeals, noting it had only remanded the case for the ALJ to determine Meeks's average weekly wage and that it summarily affirmed the ALJ's last decision "in order to perfect employer's appeal to the Fifth Circuit." The Board's February 2015 Decision is final and appealable. *See generally Mijangos v. Avondale Shipyards, Inc.*, 948 F.2d 941, 943–44 (5th Cir. 1991).

exclusively entitled to assess both the weight of the evidence and the credibility of witnesses," *Ceres Gulf*, 683 F.3d at 228, and this court may vacate the Board's decision if it improperly fails to accept the ALJ's assessments, *see Ortco*, 332 F.3d at 290.

III. Discussion

Salamis argues the Board erred in overturning the ALJ. Salamis asserts that the ALJ's decision to deny benefits was supported by substantial evidence—including the ALJ's determination that Meeks had no credibility—and that the Board exceeded its authority in making its own fact findings from the record. Salamis requests that this court affirm the first two decisions of the ALJ, which denied Meeks's benefits. Meeks argues, among other things, that he established a prima facie case that he suffered a compensable injury during the course and scope of his employment with Salamis, triggering the Section 20(a) presumption in his favor, and that the ALJ's rejection of his claim was not supported by substantial evidence. Meeks contends that the [—16—] assessment of Meeks's credibility does not constitute substantial evidence to support the ALJ's rejection of Meeks's claims, because credibility determinations should not be made in determining whether the presumption has been invoked. Meeks requests affirmance of the final benefits award.

A. *The LHWCA's Framework for Assessing Claims*

The LHWCA provides a three-step framework for adjudicating claims for work-related injuries and is to be liberally construed in favor of injured workers. First, this framework contains a presumption in favor of an employee, the Section 20(a) presumption, which essentially presumes that an employee's "claim comes within the provisions" of the LHWCA. 33 U.S.C. § 920(a). We have held that a claimant may invoke the presumption by establishing a prima facie case, which requires the claimant to "prove" that (1) he suffered harm and (2) conditions of the workplace, or an accident at the workplace, could have caused, aggravated, or

accelerated the harm. *See, e.g., Port Cooper/T. Smith Stevedoring Co. v. Hunter*, 227 F.3d 285, 287 (5th Cir. 2000); *Amerada Hess Corp. v. Dir., Office of Worker's Comp. Programs*, 543 F.3d 755, 761 (5th Cir. 2008).

If a claimant successfully makes such a prima facie case, the ALJ may presume that the work conditions or incident caused the claimant's harm, unless the employer can rebut the presumption at the second step of the analysis "through facts—not mere speculation—that the harm was *not* work-related." *Amerada Hess*, 543 F.3d at 761 (citation omitted). If the employer presents substantial evidence to rebut the Section 20(a) presumption, it falls out of the case and the ALJ determines whether the work condition or incident caused the employee's injury by weighing all of the evidence. *See id.* (citing *Port Cooper*, 227 F.3d at 288). The claimant retains the burden of persuasion at this third and final step of the analysis—if the evidence is evenly balanced, [—17—] the claimant loses. *See Dir., Office of Workers' Comp. Programs, Dep't of Labor v. Greenwich Collieries*, 512 U.S. 267, 280–81 (1994).

Meeks argues that this court has incorrectly imposed on claimants a burden of proving a prima facie case, rather than simply alleging a compensable injury, at the first step of the LHWCA analysis. This argument is unavailing. A claimant for benefits under the LHWCA faces a fairly light burden, but our court and other courts have consistently required prima facie proof of a compensable injury. *See, e.g., Port Cooper*, 227 F.3d at 287 ("In order for [the Section 20(a)] presumption to apply, the claimant must make a *prima facie* showing of causation."); *Conoco*, 194 F.3d at 690–91 (noting the "presumption of causation" may be invoked by "a prima facie case of workplace injury" (citation omitted)).

Additionally, we conclude that an ALJ may make credibility determinations in ascertaining whether a claimant has made a prima facie case. We have approved such credibility determinations in the past. *See, e.g., Ramsay Scarlett & Co. v. Dir., Office of Workers' Comp. Programs*, 806 F.3d 327, 331, 3 Adm. R. 426, 427 (5th Cir. 2015) (upholding an ALJ's finding that a claimant made a prima facie case based partly on the ALJ's credibility determinations).[7]

B. The ALJ's Adjudication of Meeks's Claims and the Board's Review

We review the ALJ's findings to determine whether they were supported by substantial evidence in attempting to determine whether the Board properly reviewed the ALJ or committed legal errors. *Ceres Gulf*, 683 F.3d at [—18—] 228. Consequently, this case turns on whether substantial evidence supported the ALJ's decision to disregard, based on Meeks's lack of credibility, the evidence that might have otherwise established a prima facie case for an aggravation of Meeks's back and neck injuries. *See Mendoza v. Marine Pers. Co.*, 46 F.3d 498, 500 (5th Cir. 1995).

1. Meeks's Back and Neck Claims

Under the LHWCA, Meeks first had to make a prima facie case that (1) he suffered harm, and (2) the personnel-basket incident could have caused, aggravated, or accelerated the harm to his back and neck. *See Port Cooper*, 227 F.3d at 287. The aggravation rule provides that when "an employment injury worsens or combines with a preexisting impairment to produce a disability greater than that which would have resulted from the employment injury alone, the entire resulting disability is compensable." *Ortco*, 332 F.3d at 290 (citation omitted); *see also Louis Dreyfus Corp. v. Dir., Office of Workers' Comp. Programs, U.S. Dep't of Labor*, 125 F.3d 884, 887 (5th Cir. 1997). Multiple doctors opined that the current condition of Meeks's spine,

---

[7] *See also Gold v. Dir., Office of Worker's Comp. Programs*, 424 F. App'x 274, 277–78 (5th Cir. 2011) (rejecting an argument that an ALJ had incorrectly applied the presumption, concluding "[t]he ALJ's determination that [the claimant's] testimony on both prongs of the prima facie case was not credible, and that the credible evidence did not support his allegations, [was] supported by the evidence in the record"); *Turner v. Dir., Office of Worker's Comp. Programs*, 334 F. App'x 693, 696 (5th Cir. 2009) (affirming an ALJ's finding of no back injury and no Section 20(a) presumption because the ALJ discredited the testimony of the claimant and his medical experts).

with its preexisting degenerative disorders, is capable of causing Meeks severe pain and keeping him from working in his previous job. The record does not contain evidence that Meeks's back condition was caused directly by the workplace incident. Accordingly, to prevail, Meeks had to make a prima facie showing that his condition could have been aggravated by the incident with the personnel basket or that the symptoms of his condition may have manifested as a result of that incident. *See Ortco*, 332 F.3d at 290–91.

Dr. Vanderweide and Dr. Dent both opined in general terms that Meeks sustained an injury to his lumbar spine, consistent with or as a result of the incident he described at the oil rig, which aggravated or accelerated his pre-existing degenerative condition. Both doctors credited Meeks's complaints of pain about his back in part based on straight-leg raises and other in-person [—19—] exams they performed, and both doctors diagnosed Meeks with degenerative spinal conditions. The ALJ did not credit this evidence, except to the extent that Meeks had a degenerative, preexisting condition. The ALJ found the doctors' opinions and diagnoses were based on Meeks's own reports of pain and injury, which the ALJ found unreliable based on Meeks's utter lack of credibility. Therefore, the ALJ found Meeks had not shown that the personnel-basket incident could have caused anything more than a strain.

The Board may reject findings that are irrational or unsupported by substantial evidence. *See Ceres Gulf*, 683 F.3d at 228; *Mijangos*, 948 F.2d at 944. In this case, the Board relied on the doctors' findings in concluding that the ALJ's denial of benefits was not supported by substantial evidence. The Board reasoned that even if Meeks was not credible, some of this medical evidence was sufficiently objective that the ALJ should have accounted for it. For example, straight-leg raising, flexion, and extension tests suggested a lack of range of motion and the type of pain consistent with the injuries Meeks claimed. Accounting for this evidence, the Board found Meeks made a prima facie case that the incident with the personnel basket could have aggravated or made symptomatic the preexisting condition of his lumbar spine; therefore, the Board found that Meeks invoked the Section 20(a) presumption.

We disagree. Although this is a difficult case, we conclude that substantial evidence supports the ALJ's determination that Meeks failed to make a prima facie case that the work-related injury could have caused anything more than a transient back strain. An ALJ may accept or reject the conclusions of experts and "is not required to accept the opinion or theory of a medical expert that contradicts the ALJ's findings based on common sense." *Avondale Indus., Inc. v. Dir., Office of Workers' Comp. Programs*, 977 F.2d 186, 189 (5th Cir. 1992). The ALJ may choose between reasonable inferences, and [—20—] the ALJ exclusively determines the weight of the evidence. *Mijangos*, 948 F.2d at 945.

In this case, plentiful evidence demonstrates that Meeks has a degenerative back condition that could reasonably cause the type of pain he alleges. Yet there is no definitive evidence showing Meeks suffered a traumatic injury, and there is no evidence showing a difference in his spine before and after the incident on the personnel basket. The Board determined that it was irrational to disregard the doctors' opinions that the aggravation of Meeks's condition could have been caused by the incident. But these opinions were bare conclusions, unsupported by explanations of how the particular event with the personnel basket might aggravate a preexisting degenerative spinal condition. Apparently, neither Meeks nor Salamis ever deposed the doctors, and they did not testify at the hearing. The record mostly consists of their medical notes and occasionally of short reports containing their conclusions.

Additionally, it is not at all clear that the doctors were assessing the event that actually occurred when they gave conclusory opinions that Meeks's pain was linked to the incident at work. Meeks presented varying descriptions of the incident, testifying at his hearing that the basket "flipped," but telling his doctors that the basket "dropped 10 feet" and hit the deck of the vessel. The ALJ did not have to credit the account Meeks gave to his

doctors. No definitive evidence answers whether the event was a small jostling of the personnel basket or a ten foot fall. In the absence of such evidence, we have the ALJ's finding that Meeks was "such an unreliable witness and dishonest individual that his testimony and the opinions and reports of the doctors who relied on what he told them had virtually no probative value or evidentiary weight." "As a result," regarding what occurred on the boat, the ALJ found that "the only relevant facts that are established as more likely than not" include that Meeks "was involved in an incident where he was tossed about in a personnel basket [—21—] but [initially] reported he was OK when asked." It was not irrational to give the doctors' conclusions little weight, given that they were based on what the ALJ implicitly or explicitly found were non-credible descriptions of the incident and complaints of pain.

Although some of the doctors' findings were based on what they viewed as objective tests, it was not irrational to conclude that Meeks probably faked pain and limited range of motion. *See Mendoza*, 46 F.3d at 500–02. Meeks admitted during the hearing that the surveillance videos accurately reflected his abilities. From June through September of 2009, before his surgery, Meeks was able to walk, bend down to pick weeds and pick up his grandchild, drive, climb steps, squat, kneel to pull weeds for an extended period of time, and drag trash to the trash bin, all without evident pain. This account of his life contrasts with the intense pain he reported to his doctors around that time, and his deposition testimony that he mostly spent time in bed and could not clean, do yard work, or lift anything heavier than ten pounds. Meeks's lack of credibility was bolstered by his dodgy testimony and by his failure to accurately report or pay taxes on his income for years, a discrepancy Meeks corrected only after it would serve his interests to report more income. Additionally, the ALJ noted that "[i]n more than 15 years as an administrative and criminal law judge, [he] [could]not recall any witness being less credible than [Meeks]."

Meeks's treating physicians were influenced by his account of events and their role in attempting to treat the pain he reported to them. There is no indication Meeks's doctors viewed the video surveillance evidence or opined on Meeks's abilities based on such objective evidence. Even so, Dr. Vanderweide found Meeks to lack credibility in his complaints of neck pain after his back surgery, noting "worrisome" inconsistencies and that he could not explain Meeks's subjective complaints of pain in light of the objective medical exams. [—22—]

The Board improperly undervalued the ALJ's credibility determinations, given the lack of completely objective medical evidence supporting Meeks's claim that his degenerative condition suddenly flared up some time after the workplace incident. *Cf. Ortco*, 332 F.3d at 290–91; *Gold v. Dir., Office of Worker's Comp. Programs*, 424 F. App'x 274, 277–78 (5th Cir. 2011). Without further explanation of the doctors' conclusions, it was not irrational to conclude that Meeks probably faked enough of his symptoms and pain to undermine the reliability of his doctors' conclusions.[8] Accordingly, the Board erred in overturning the ALJ. The ALJ's determination that Meeks failed to make a prima facie case of workplace-related, debilitating injury was rational and supported by substantial evidence.[9] *See Ortco*, 332 F.3d at 290–91. As we have said before:

> We are neither doctors nor the original fact finders in this matter, and so, under the appropriate standard of review, we need not assess the plausibility of these

medical accounts, nor do we assess the weight they should be accorded relative to other evidence in the record. . . . Our task is more limited: we ask only whether this evidence was relevant to the ALJ's decision, and whether the ALJ's decision was reasonable based on this evidence.

Operators & Consulting Servs., Inc. v. Dir., Office of Worker's Comp. Programs, 170 F. App'x 931, 937 (5th Cir. 2006) (citation omitted). [—23—]

2. Meeks's Dental Claim

Before the Department of Labor, Meeks's dental claims were reduced to the issue of whether Meeks lost one particular tooth as a result of the work-related incident.[10] No one contests that this claim only involves dental expenses and has not disabled Meeks. We conclude that Meeks should recover the dental expenses associated with the "loose tooth" he reported on April 10, 2009, which had fallen out by the time of his dental appointment with Dr. Um.

The ALJ twice denied this claim after concluding Meeks failed to make a prima facie case because there were no indications that Meeks's mouth was bleeding, that he had any

---

[8] Indeed, it does not seem irrational, as the ALJ suggested, that Meeks had a pre-existing, degenerative condition that caused him chronic pain, and that Meeks very likely seized on a work incident to obtain free medical care and disability.

[9] Because we uphold the ALJ's determination that Meeks failed to prima facie show workplace injury beyond a transient back strain and therefore that Meeks failed to invoke the presumption, we need not reach the rest of the LHWCA analysis. We note that the ALJ found that if Meeks had invoked the presumption, Salamis failed to rebut it, a finding necessary under the second step of the LHWCA framework. *See Ortco*, 332 F.3d at 287, 290. With no rebuttal from Salamis, the analysis would have ended at the second step and resulted in an award of benefits to Meeks. *See id.*

[10] Meeks does not explicitly contest the denial of his claim for the two chipped teeth. Therefore, he has abandoned it before this court. *See Brinkmann v. Dall. Cty. Deputy Sheriff Abner*, 813 F.2d 744, 748 (5th Cir. 1987). To the extent this claim has not been abandoned, the Board did not err in determining that substantial evidence supported the ALJ's rejection of a causal connection between these teeth and the incident. The ALJ inferred that the lack of reports about the chipped teeth or any bruising, bleeding, or mouth injuries on April 10, 2009, belied claims that the two teeth had chipped due to the incident. The Board found this inference rational and upheld it, remanding only for a determination of whether the "loose tooth" Meeks reported on April 10, 2009, could have subsequently fallen out. The ALJ's inference regarding the chipped teeth is rational and supported by substantial evidence. *See Ceres Gulf*, 683 F.3d at 228. Therefore, to the extent we must reach Meeks's claim for dental expenses related to the two chipped teeth, we find no error in the ALJ or Board's rejecting it.

swelling or bruising on his face, or that he reported dental injuries on April 10, 2009. The Board rejected this conclusion, remanding for further findings because the fact that Meeks reported a loose tooth on April 10, 2009, as related to the jarring of his teeth in the incident, might establish a prima facie case that the same tooth later fell out. On remand, the ALJ concluded no prima facie case had been established, or alternatively that Salamis rebutted any such case, because the ALJ inferred that whatever chipped Meeks's teeth before the appointment likely knocked out the other tooth. The Board found this inference irrational, unsupported by the record, and based solely on speculation. The Board reversed, rendering judgment for Meeks on this claim after concluding that Meeks established a [—24—] prima facie case that the incident could have caused his loose and missing tooth and that Salamis did not rebut this claim.

The Board did not exceed its authority in rendering judgment for Meeks on his missing tooth. *Ceres Gulf*, 683 F.3d at 228. Substantial evidence supports the conclusion that Meeks established a prima facie case based on his complaint of a loose tooth on April 10, 2009, plus a subsequently missing tooth. Salamis produced no evidence to rebut this claim or to suggest how else Meeks could have lost his tooth. The ALJ's alternate explanation was not supported by substantial evidence in the record.

IV. Conclusion

"[M]ore than a scintilla" of evidence supports the ALJ's determination that Meeks lacks credibility and that Meeks thus could not prima facie prove that the personnel-basket incident could have aggravated his preexisting condition to the extent he claims. *Id*. We respect the ALJ's prerogative to make these determinations and conclude that the Board erred in reversing the ALJ's rejection of Meeks's back and neck claims. *See, e.g.*, *Gold*, 424 F. App'x at 278–79.

Accordingly, we REVERSE the Board's judgment awarding benefits to Meeks, except as to the Board's conclusion that Meeks was entitled to benefits for his missing tooth, which we AFFIRM. We REINSTATE the ALJ's June 2013 Order, except for that portion which denies Meeks's dental expenses for the missing tooth.[11]

---

[11] We reinstate and affirm the June 2013 Order, rather than the ALJ's September 2011 Order, because it was not an abuse of the Board's authority to remand for more specific findings within the three-step framework of the LHWCA in its first, September 2012 Decision. It is somewhat unclear from the ALJ's September 2011 Order where his findings fell within the burden-shifting framework of an LHWCA claim.

United States Court of Appeals
for the Fifth Circuit

No. 15-30471

NAQUIN

vs.

ELEVATING BOATS, L.L.C.

Appeal from the United States District Court for the
Eastern District of Louisiana

Decided: March 22, 2016

Citation: 817 F.3d 235, 4 Adm. R. 221 (5th Cir. 2016).

Before **DENNIS, ELROD,** and **GRAVES,** Circuit Judges.

[—1—] GRAVES, Circuit Judge:

In this insurance coverage dispute, Elevating Boats, LLC ("EBI") appeals a summary judgment in favor of State National Insurance Company ("SNIC"). For the reasons outlined below, we **AFFIRM** the district court. [—2—]

I.

This appeal flows directly from a previous decision by this court. In that matter, Larry Naquin was using an EBI land-based crane to relocate a test block when the pedestal of the crane snapped, causing the crane to topple over. *Naquin v. Elevating Boats, L.L.C.*, 744 F.3d 927, 931, 2 Adm. R. 200, 200 (5th Cir. 2014). Upon jumping from the crane house, Naquin sustained a broken left foot, a severely broken right foot, and a lower abdominal hernia. *Id.*, 2 Adm. R. at 200. Naquin's cousin's husband, another EBI employee, was crushed by the crane and killed. *Id.*, 2 Adm. R. at 200. Despite reparative surgeries and physical therapy sessions, Naquin was unable to return to physical work. *Id.*, 2 Adm. R. at 201.

Naquin subsequently sued EBI pursuant to the Jones Act, and the suit proceeded to trial. *Id.*, 2 Adm. R. at 201. After a three-day trial, a jury concluded that Naquin was a Jones Act seaman and that EBI's negligence caused his injury. The jury subsequently awarded Naquin $1,000,000 for past and future physical pain and suffering, $1,000,000 for past and future mental pain and suffering, and $400,000 for future lost wages. *Id.*, 2 Adm. R. at 201. EBI appealed, challenging, among other things, the grant of Jones Act seaman status to Naquin and the sufficiency of evidence to establish EBI's negligence. *Id.* at 932, 2 Adm. R. at 201.

Pertinent to this appeal, the *Naquin* majority[1] affirmed the jury's verdict as to liability, concluding that the jury correctly determined that Naquin qualified as a Jones Act seaman; the entire panel, though, agreed that EBI acted negligently in failing to provide a reasonably safe work environment and work equipment. *Naquin*, 744 F.3d at 932–38, 2 Adm. R. at 201–07. Specifically, as to the negligence inquiry, we held: "EBI was the only party responsible for welding the LC-400 [—3—] crane to its base, a weld which was indisputably defective and the direct cause of Naquin's injuries." *Id.* at 937, 2 Adm. R. at 206. We, however, vacated the verdict as it related to damages and remanded the matter to the district court to conduct a new trial on that specific issue. *Id.* at 938–41, 2 Adm. R. at 206–09.

The district court subsequently granted EBI leave to file a third-party complaint against its insurance companies, SNIC and Certain London Insurers ("London Insurers"). In its third-party demand, EBI complained that both SNIC and London Insurers breached their insurance contracts by denying EBI's insurance claims arising from Naquin's accident and by failing to provide EBI with defense and indemnity. EBI, in connection to its claims, also sought statutory bad-faith damages pursuant to Louisiana Civil Code 1997 and Louisiana Recording Statute 22:1973. The district court granted a motion to sever, ordering that EBI's claims against

---

[1] The *Naquin* panel consisted of Circuit Judges Davis and Jones and District Court Judge Milazzo. Judge Jones dissented, "concur[ring] in all of th[e] good opinion except the decision affirming Naquin's status as a seaman." *Naquin*, 744 F.3d at 941, 2 Adm. R. at 210. By her estimation, Naquin was not a Jones Act seaman because he failed both the duration and nature components of the test outlined by the Supreme Court in *Chandris, Inc. v. Latsis*, 515 U.S. 347 (1995).

SNIC and London Insurers be severed from the remaining issue of damages and resolved by a separate trial.

SNIC moved for summary judgment, asserting, chiefly, that EBI was not entitled to coverage under its Protection & Indemnity Policy (the "Policy") because coverage did not extend to Naquin's land-based incident and that EBI failed to comply with the notice requirements imposed by the Policy. EBI responded in opposition, explaining that it was entitled to indemnity under the "any casualty or occurrence" language of the Policy. The remaining opposition to SNIC's summary judgment motion concerned EBI's perceived lack of actual notice. Upon consideration of both parties' arguments, the district court granted summary judgment to SNIC. Thereafter, the district court entered final judgment in favor of SNIC, and later denied EBI's Rule 59(e) Motion to Reconsider.

II.

We consider only whether the district court erred in granting summary judgment to SNIC on the grounds that the Policy did not cover EBI's liability [—4—] for Naquin's incident and that SNIC, therefore, exhibited no bad faith in denying coverage. Summary judgment is proper when "the movant shows that there is no genuine dispute as to any material fact and the movant is entitled to judgment as a matter of law." Fed. R. Civ. P. 56(a). We review the district court's grant of summary judgment de novo, construing all facts and inferences in the light most favorable to the nonmoving party. *See EEOC v. Chevron Phillips Chem. Co.*, 570 F.3d 606, 615 (5th Cir. 2009). Because the proper interpretation of an insurance policy presents a legal question, not a factual one, the district court's interpretations of the Policy are also reviewed de novo. *See Martco Ltd. P'ship v. Wellons, Inc.*, 588 F.3d 864, 878 (5th Cir. 2009).

A. Scope of Coverage

The "Indemnity" provision of the Policy at the heart of this appeal, provides:

Subject to all exclusions and other terms of this Policy, the Underwriters agree to indemnify the Assured for any sums which the Assured, *as owner of the Vessel*, shall have become liable to pay, and shall have paid in respect of *any casualty or occurrence* during the currency of the Policy, but only in consequence of any other matters set forth hereunder . . .

(emphasis added). The district court interpreted this critical language as excluding coverage to EBI due to the circumstances surrounding its liability in *Naquin*. We endorse this interpretation.

In the absence of a specific and controlling federal maritime rule over this dispute, we interpret this maritime insurance contract under Louisiana state law. *See Albany Ins. Co. v. Anh Thi Kieu*, 927 F.2d 882, 886 (5th Cir. 1991). Under Louisiana law, "an insurance policy is a contract between the parties and should be construed using the general rules of contract interpretation set forth in the Louisiana Civil Code." *First Am. Bank v. First [—5—] Am. Transp. Title Ins. Co.*, 585 F.3d 833, 837 (5th Cir. 2009); *see also Cadwallader v. Allstate Ins. Co.*, 848 So. 2d 577, 580 (La. 2003).

Words and phrases used in an insurance policy should be construed using their plain, ordinary and generally prevailing meaning, unless the words have acquired a technical meaning. *Cadwallader*, 848 So. 2d at 580; *Carbon v. Allstate Ins. Co.*, 719 So.2d 437, 439–40 (La. 1998). Thus, when the words of the insurance contract "are unambiguous and the parties' intent is clear, the insurance contract will be enforced as written." *Doerr v. Mobil Oil Corp.*, 774 So. 2d 119, 124 (La. 2004) (citing La. Civ. Code Ann. art. 2046). A contractual "provision susceptible of different meanings must be interpreted with a meaning that renders it effective and not with one that renders it ineffective," so as to avoid rendering any provision in the contract superfluous. La. Civ. Code Ann. art. 2049; *Berk-Cohen Assocs., LLC v. Landmark Am. Ins. Co.*, No. 07-9205, 2009 WL 3738152, at *3–4 (E.D. La. Nov. 5, 2009). The provisions of the contract "must be interpreted in light of the other provisions so that each is given the meaning suggested by the contract as a whole." La. Civ. Code Ann. art. 2050; *First Am. Bank*, 585 F.3d at 837.

As relevant here, SNIC avers that the terms of the subject Policy—specifically, the "as owner of the Vessel" clause—does not provide coverage for the land-based incident due to EBI's negligence as described in *Naquin*. Before the district court, EBI urged a blanket reading of the Policy that would provide coverage for "any casualty or occurrence" for which EBI might become liable.[2] [—6—]

We are persuaded, guided by the law and facts before us, that EBI's strained interpretation of the Policy is unreasonable in this context. *See* La. Civ. Code Ann. art. 2050; *First Am. Bank*, 585 F.3d at 837. We, therefore, follow the district court in holding that there is no genuine issue that the scope of coverage of the Policy does not extend to EBI's liability for the *Naquin* incident. In reaching this conclusion, we decline EBI's invitation to read the provision in the piecemeal fashion that it prefers—a construal that would directly contradict the well-established Louisiana rules regarding contractual interpretation. *See Foret v. La. Farm Bureau Cas. Ins. Co.*, 582 So. 2d 989, 991 (La. App. 1 Cir. 1991) ("An insurance contract must be construed as a whole; one section is not to be construed separately or at the expense of disregarding other sections."). The only way to give meaning to both provisions of the Policy is to construe the Policy as limiting coverage to "any casualty or occurrence" which arises out of EBI's conduct "as owner of the Vessel."

Moreover, our holding is required under our precedent. *See Lanasse v. Travelers Ins.*

---

[2] We note that EBI's arguments on appeal evince a marked departure from those argued in opposition to summary judgment before the trial court. It is the record before the district court that we consider on this appeal. *See Offshore Drilling Co. v. Gulf Copper & Mfg. Corp.*, 604 F.3d 221, 226 (5th Cir. 2010) ("We will not consider an argument asserted for the first time on appeal."); *see also LeMaire v. La. Dep't of Transp. & Dev.*, 480 F.3d 383, 387 (5th Cir. 2007).

Co., 450 F.2d 580 (5th Cir. 1971). In *Lanasse*, the plaintiff was injured when the operator of a platform owned by Chevron allowed a welding machine to swing against the vessel's railing. *Id.* at 582. Chevron claimed, in part, that its liability was covered under the terms of a standard P&I Policy. *Id.* at 583. Chevron, the *Lanasse* court reasoned, "was found at fault for the manner in which the crane was operated. The vessel offered nothing further than a condition or locale for the accident." *Id.* at 584. As we explained:

> *There must be at least some causal operational relation between the vessel and the resulting injury.* The line may be a wavy one between coverage and noncoverage, especially with industrial complications in these ambiguous amphibious operations plus those arising from the personification of the vessel as an actor in a suit in rem. *But where injury is done through nonvessel operations, the vessel must be more than the inert locale of the injury. Nothing more occurred here, for it was Chevron's actions as a platform* [—7—] *operator or as a crane operator that caused the harm, and that does not make it a liability of a shipowner.*

Id. (emphasis added). It follows then that the holding required under this indistinguishable and controlling decision could not be clearer. *Naquin's* incident in no way arose out of EBI's conduct as "owner of the Vessel." *Naquin*, devoid of any indication that EBI was liable due to such conditions, confirms as much; this understanding alone forecloses EBI's arguments to the contrary. *See Naquin*, 744 F.3d at 937, 2 Adm. R. at 206 ("EBI was the only party responsible for welding the LC–400 crane to its base, a weld which was indisputably defective and the direct cause of Naquin's injuries."). Furthermore, the land-based crane did not break on or even in close proximity to a vessel. Thus, EBI's attempts to craft a causal connection to a vessel are discharged, plainly and simply, by the underlying facts and *Naquin's* holding.

Where there is no causal operational relation between the vessel and the resulting injury, there is no extension of coverage for liability. We, therefore, arrive at the identical conclusion as the *Lanasse* court: "it was [EBI's] actions as platform operator or as a crane operator that caused the harm, and that does not make it a liability of a shipowner." 450 F.2d at 584.[3]

B. Bad Faith

Louisiana law instructs that in order for a claim of statutory bad faith to survive, it must be based on a valid underlying claim. *Matthews v. Allstate Ins. Co.*, 731 F. Supp. 2d 552, 566 (E.D. La. 2010). As discussed above, we hold that the Policy does not extend to EBI's liability associated with the defective crane; consequently, EBI has no valid underlying claim on which to stand. [—8—] Accordingly, the district court did not err in dismissing EBI's claim for bad faith.[4]

---

[3] The district court also considered EBI's argument that SNIC was required to provide it with actual notice that the Policy limited coverage to EBI's conduct as owner of a vessel, ultimately finding the Policy's language "sufficiently clear" to give notice regarding the limitation of coverage. We agree that there existed no requirement that SNIC provide EBI with actual notice of the terms of the policy. *See, e.g., Urban Planning and Innovations, Inc. v. Alexander & Sanders Ins. Specialist*, No. 07-7537, 2008 WL 191328, at *1 (E.D. La. Jan. 22, 2008).

[4] Because we affirm the district court's grant of summary judgment to SNIC, we also affirm the district court's denial of EBI's Motion to Reconsider pursuant to Federal Rule of Civil Procedure 59(e). Such motions are not the proper vehicle for rehashing evidence, legal theories, or arguments that could have been offered or raised before entry of judgment. *Templet v. Hydrochem, Inc.*, 367 F.3d 473, 479 (5th Cir. 2004). "Motions for a new trial or to alter or amend a judgment must clearly establish either a manifest error of law or fact or must present newly discovered evidence. These motions cannot be used to raise arguments which could, and should, have been made before the judgment issued. Moreover, they cannot be used to argue a case under a new legal theory." *Simon v. United States*, 891 F.2d 1154, 1159 (5th Cir. 1990) (quoting *Fed. Deposit Ins. Corp. v. Meyer*, 781 F.2d 1260, 1268 (7th Cir.1986)). "Relief under Rule 59(e) is also appropriate when there has been an intervening change in the controlling law." *Schiller v. Physicians Res. Grp. Inc.*, 342 F.3d 563, 567 (5th Cir. 2003) (citing *In re Benjamin Moore & Co.*, 318 F.3d 626, 629 (5th Cir. 2002)). In denying EBI's motion, the district court concluded: "EBI has failed to present evidence to show that this court's previous Order, granting summary judgment on EBI's claims in favor of SNIC, contained manifest errors of fact or law, and that EBI's motion is merely an attempt to rehash arguments which have already been raised before this court." We agree.

III.

We **AFFIRM** the district court's grant of summary judgment in favor of SNIC.

United States Court of Appeals
for the Fifth Circuit

No. 15-30514

SAVOIE
vs.
HUNTINGTON INGALLS, INC.

Appeal from the United States District Court for the
Eastern District of Louisiana

Decided: March 22, 2016

Citation: 817 F.3d 457, 4 Adm. R. 225 (5th Cir. 2016).

Before **CLEMENT, GRAVES,** and **COSTA,** Circuit
Judges.

[—2—] **GRAVES,** Circuit Judge:

From 1952 through 1976, the great majority of ocean-going vessels built at Avondale Shipyard[1] in Louisiana fulfilled contracts from the federal government. The specifications for these Navy and Coast Guard vessels required asbestos insulation through at least 1968. In this lawsuit brought by survivors of a worker who allegedly contracted mesothelioma while working at the shipyard during this time, the question is whether strict liability claims based on the existence of asbestos at the shipyard give rise to federal jurisdiction under the federal officer removal statute.

I.

Joseph Savoie was employed at the shipyard between 1948 and 1996. During his tenure there, Savoie worked both as a clean-up laborer, which involved cleaning up various insulation materials, and as a painter–blaster on vessels the shipyard constructed for the Navy and Coast Guard. The contracts between the shipyard and the government listed numerous specifications, some of which mandated that the shipyard use asbestos in the vessels' thermal insulation. The Navy utilized a quality control system to ensure that the shipyard complied with all contractual requirements, and the shipyard was required to certify compliance for each stage of a particular vessel before the government would release even a single installment payment.

The Plaintiffs contend that although the government supervised the construction of the vessels to ensure that they were in compliance with the contractual requirements, the government did not control the shipyard's safety [—3—] department. The Defendants counter that the Navy inspectors were heavily involved in overseeing the construction process and had final control over any safety issues that arose.

Savoie ultimately contracted mesothelioma, allegedly as a result of asbestos exposure from working on these vessels. Before his death, he filed this suit in state court. He brought numerous negligence claims, such as failure to warn, failure to take reasonable precautions, and failure to use nonasbestos products when permitted by contract. He also brought strict liability claims. He passed away just a month after filing suit. His wife and children substituted as plaintiffs.

The Defendants[2] timely removed the case under the federal officer removal statute, but the Plaintiffs sought remand. The district court construed all of the Plaintiffs' claims as negligence claims. It then found that federal jurisdiction did not exist because the shipyard retained discretion in its safety policies and could have complied with both the government's requirements for the vessels' construction and its state law duties of care.

II.

Orders remanding a case to state court are generally not reviewable. *See* 28 U.S.C. § 1447(d). The statute governing removal

---

[1] At the time Savoie was employed at the shipyard it was owned by Avondale. Avondale has a long history of different titles, but Huntington Ingalls, Inc. is the current successor in interest and one of the Defendants in this action. For clarity, we refer to Avondale and its successors as "the shipyard."

[2] The shipyard and its successors, as well as various insurance company defendants, jointly removed this action. Our analysis focuses on the shipyard because it is the defendant that had the contractual relationship with the government.

procedure provides for only two exceptions: remand orders involving certain civil rights cases, 28 U.S.C. § 1443, and remand orders involving the federal officer removal statute, 28 U.S.C. § 1442. *See* 28 U.S.C. § 1447(d). [—4—]

Our unusual ability to review a remand order in this context reflects the importance Congress placed on providing federal jurisdiction for claims asserted against federal officers and parties acting pursuant to the orders of a federal officer. *See Watson v. Philip Morris Cos.*, 551 U.S. 142, 147 (2007); *Winters v. Diamond Shamrock Chem. Co.*, 149 F.3d 387, 398 (5th Cir. 1998) (both noting that the Supreme Court has long required "liberal" construction of the statute). The reasons for federal jurisdiction in cases against federal officers and their agents borrow from the rationales for both diversity and federal question jurisdiction.[3] *See Watson,* 551 U.S. at 150 (describing the purposes of federal officers' right to remove cases to federal court). As with diversity jurisdiction, there is a historic concern about state court bias. *See id.* ("State-court proceedings may reflect 'local prejudice' against unpopular federal laws or federal officials." (quoting *Maryland v. Soper (No.1)*, 270 U.S. 9, 32 (1926))); *Willingham v. Morgan*, 395 U.S. 402, 405 (1969) ("Obviously, the removal provision was an attempt to protect federal officers from interference by hostile state courts."). As with federal question jurisdiction, there is a desire to have the federal courts decide the federal issues

---

[3] The federal officer removal statute actually has a more venerable lineage than the general federal question jurisdiction statute. The first federal officer removal statute was enacted in 1815 to address state court claims brought by shipowners against federal customs officials in New England states that opposed a trade embargo with England enacted during the War of 1812. *See Watson,* 551 U.S. at 147–48 (citing Customs Act of 1815, ch. 31, § 8, 3 Stat. 198). It has since been amended a number of times. *Id.* 148–49. In contrast, aside from its inclusion in the Judiciary Act of 1801, which was repealed the next year, the general federal question jurisdiction statute has only been on the books since 1875. *See* Richard H. Fallon, Jr., et al., Hart and Wechsler's The Federal Courts and the Federal System 34, 905 (5th ed. 2003).

that often arise in cases involving federal officers. *See Watson,* 551 U.S. at 150 (emphasizing the importance of "federal officials [having] a federal forum in which to assert federal immunity defenses"); *see also* 14C Charles Alan Wright & Arthur R. Miller, Federal Practice and Procedure § 3726 (4th ed. 2015) (noting that [—5—] one of the statute's "basic purposes" is to ensure federal officers have a "federal forum in which to assert federal immunity defenses").

Given these purposes, it is not surprising that the statute speaks in broad language allowing the removal of any state case commenced against:

> The United States or any agency thereof or any officer (or any person acting under that officer) of the United States or of any agency thereof, in an official or individual capacity, for or relating to any act under color of such office or on account of any right, title or authority claimed under any Act of Congress for the apprehension or punishment of criminals or the collection of the revenue.

28 U.S.C. § 1442(a)(1). Recognizing that such "broad language is not limitless," even in a statute that should be afforded a "liberal construction," the Supreme Court has articulated limits based on the statute's "language, context, history, and purposes." *Watson,* 551 U.S. at 147, 157 (holding that a company does not "act[] under" an officer of the United States merely because it is subject to federal regulation). The result is a three-part inquiry for determining whether federal officer removal is proper that aims to ensure that removal occurs when there is a "federal interest in the matter." *Winters,* 149 F.3d at 398 (quoting *Willingham,* 395 U.S. at 406).

The first question is whether the defendant seeking to remove is a "person" within the meaning of the statute. *Id.* At first glance, this may seem like a difficult hurdle, as a private shipyard does not seem like the typical "federal officer" defendant that might face state court hostility. Yet the Supreme Court has long recognized that the removal statute also applies to private persons and corporate entities "'who lawfully assist' the federal officer 'in the performance of his official duty.'" *Watson*, 551 U.S. at 151 (quoting *Davis v. South Carolina*, 107 U.S. 597, 600 (1883)). The current statute reflects this understanding with its "or any person acting under that officer" provision. 28 U.S.C. § 1442(a)(1). Whether the shipyard is a "person" entitled to invoke [—6—] the statute thus turns out to be the easiest inquiry. *See Winters*, 149 F.3d at 398 (holding that a government contractor that supplied Agent Orange was a "person" that could invoke federal officer removal statute). Indeed, the parties agree that the shipyard and its executive officers constitute "persons" under the statute.

The additional two inquiries are the subject of this appeal. First is whether the federal government was directing the defendant's conduct and whether that federally-directed conduct caused the plaintiff's injuries. *See Bartel v. Alcoa S.S. Co.*, 805 F.3d 169, 172–74, 3 Adm. R. 422, 422–25 (5th Cir. 2015) (explaining that mere federal involvement does not satisfy the causal nexus requirement; instead, the defendant must show that its actions taken pursuant to the government's direction or control caused the plaintiff's specific injuries). This "causal nexus" requirement is the one the district court found lacking. As a result, it did not reach the final inquiry, which is whether the defendant asserts a colorable federal defense. *Id.* at 172, 3 Adm. R. at 422.

Before reviewing the district court's finding of no causal nexus, we note another manifestation of the statute's "liberal construction" that impacts our analysis. Although the principle of limited federal court jurisdiction ordinarily compels us to resolve any doubts about removal in favor of remand, *see Acuna v. Brown & Root, Inc.*, 200 F.3d 335, 339 (5th Cir. 2000), courts have not applied that tiebreaker when it comes to the federal officer removal statute in light of its broad reach, *see Watson*, 551 U.S. at 147 (emphasizing the statute's "broad language"). We thus review the district court's decision *de novo*, without a thumb on the remand side of the scale. *See Winters*, 149 F.3d at 398 ("[The] right [of removal] is not to be frustrated by a grudgingly narrow interpretation of the removal statute."); *see also Durham v. Lockheed Martin Corp.*, 445 F.3d 1247, 1252 (9th Cir. 2006) ("We take from [the statute's] history a clear command from both Congress and the Supreme Court that when federal [—7—] officers and their agents are seeking a federal forum, we are to interpret section 1442 broadly in favor of removal."); *City of Cookeville, Tenn. v. Upper Cumberland Elec. Membership Corp.*, 484 F.3d 380, 390 (6th Cir. 2007) (the same) (citing *Durham*).

With respect to the negligence claims, we agree with the district court that the federal government's mandate of asbestos insulation did not cause the shipyard to engage in the challenged conduct. Negligence claims typically involve allegations that the defendant acted unreasonably or failed to act when it would have been reasonable to take some additional measures. Most of the claims in this case are of the latter sort. For example, the Savoies allege that the shipyard is liable for "[f]ailing to provide clean, respirable air and proper ventilation," "[f]ailing to provide necessary showers and special clothing," and "[f]ailing to warn of the dangers of exposure to asbestos."

Just last year, we decided that nearly identical allegations of a failure to warn or take safety precautions concerning asbestos did not challenge actions taken under color of federal authority even though the government was responsible for the existence of the asbestos. *See Bartel*, 805 F.3d at 174, 3 Adm. R. at 424. *Bartel* was brought against the operators of ships owned by the Navy. We explained that although the federal government had installed asbestos in the ships, it had not prevented the operators from warning plaintiffs about the dangers of asbestos or from adopting safety procedures to minimize the workers' asbestos exposure. *Id.* at 173–74, 3 Adm. R. at 423–24. We thus affirmed the remand of the case to state court for lack of a causal nexus. *Id.* at 174–75, 3 Adm. R. at 424–25.

We are not persuaded by the Defendants' attempt to distinguish *Bartel* based on either the nature of the negligence claims alleged here or the degree of the shipyard's discretion. The Savoies' allegations are essentially the same as the ones made in *Bartel* alleging "failure to warn, failure to train, and failure to adopt procedures for the safe installation and removal of asbestos." *Id.* at [—8—] 173, 3 Adm. R. at 423. As in *Bartel*, the shipyard has failed to demonstrate that its contracts with the government prevented it from taking any of these protective measures identified by Plaintiffs. The only evidence it presented to the contrary is the affidavit of Edward Blanchard, the shipyard's supervisor and executive officer, who stated that the Navy inspected and oversaw the vessels for safety. But even he later clarified in a deposition that no federal officer "directed or controlled the [the shipyard's] [s]afety [d]epartment." Other evidence in the record, including testimony from the shipyard's own safety officer, confirms that the government had no control over the shipyard's safety procedures. At most, the Navy may have had the power to shut down projects that failed to comply with federal regulations, but the Navy neither imposed any special safety requirements on the shipyard nor prevented the shipyard from imposing its own safety procedures.

The Savoies' negligence claims thus challenge discretionary acts of the shipyard free of federal interference. As a result, the government's directions to the shipyard via the contract specifications did not cause the alleged negligence, and those claims do not support removal.

This analysis was sufficient to affirm the remand order in *Bartel* because the negligence claims were the only ones we considered. The plaintiffs had also argued that a maritime claim for unseaworthiness, which is essentially a strict liability claim,[4] could

satisfy the causal nexus requirement, but they did so too late having raised the issue only on appeal. *Id.* at 174, 3 Adm. R. at 424–25. We thus had no [—9—] occasion to determine whether federal officer removal was proper for unseaworthiness or other strict liability causes of action. *Id.*, 3 Adm. R. at 424–25.

This case requires us to answer that question as the Savoies assert strict liability causes of action under Louisiana law. LA. CIV. CODE ANN. art. 2317. And removal of the entire case is appropriate so long as a single claim satisfies the federal officer removal statute. Wright & Miller, § 3726.

The district court found that the claims the Savoies labeled as "strict liability" causes of action in actuality alleged negligence. This is true of some of the claims given that label such as the one that alleges that the shipyard "was aware or *should have been aware* of the dangerous condition presented by exposure to asbestos" yet "failed and/or willfully withheld from Mr. Savoie knowledge of the dangers to his health from exposure to asbestos fiber." (emphasis added). But others—"All defendants had care, custody, and control of the asbestos, which asbestos was defective and which presented an unreasonable risk of harm, which asbestos resulted in the injury of Mr. Savoie and for which these defendants are strictly liable under Louisiana law"—are based on the mere use of asbestos on the ships and therefore fit the strict liability label.

As for these claims that sound in strict liability, there is an additional wrinkle. The wrongful death claims cannot be based on strict liability. Those claims are governed by the law in effect at the time the decedent passes away. *See Landry v. Avondale Indus., Inc.*, 877 So. 2d 970, 972 (La. 2004). "Strict liability was abolished in Louisiana in 1996. *See, e.g., Small v. Baloise Ins. Co. of Am.*, 753 So. 2d 234, 240 (La. App. 4 Cir. 1998) ("By requiring knowledge or constructive knowledge under Article 2317.1, the Legislature effectively eliminated strict liability under Article 2317, turning it into a negligence claim. [—10—] This substantive change should not apply retroactively . . . ."" (quoting Frank L. Maraist & Thomas C.

---

[4] *See also McBride v. Estis Well Serv., L.L.C.*, 768 F.3d 382, 394, 2 Adm. R. 320, 329 (5th Cir. 2014) (Clement, J., concurring) (observing that "unseaworthiness was 'an obscure and relatively little used remedy' until it became a strict liability action during the 1940s" (quoting *Miles v. Apex Marine Corp.*, 498 U.S. 19, 25 (1990)).

Galligan, LOUISIANA TORT LAW § 14–1, at 331 (1996))).

But as a survival action allows survivors to bring the claims the decedent could have asserted were he still alive, survival claims based on asbestos exposure are governed by the law in effect when the exposure occurred. *See, e.g., Rando v. Anco Insulations Inc.*, 16 So. 3d 1065, 1072 (La. 2008) (explaining that "law effective on the date of [] significant exposure to asbestos" applies to claim alleging occupational asbestos exposure) (internal quotations omitted). Because Savoie worked at the shipyard for almost half a century prior to Louisiana's abolition of strict liability, that pre-1996 law governs.

So the question becomes: do the survival claims alleging strict liability based on mere use of asbestos at the shipyard give rise to federal jurisdiction? The Savoies argue that even under the old "strict liability" regime, Louisiana law still required a showing that the defendant failed to act with reasonable care, which would bring the claims under *Bartel*. But our best reading of Louisiana law is that a strict liability plaintiff need only prove the following: (1) that the asbestos-containing products that caused his damages were in the "care, custody, and control" of the defendant; (2) that the asbestos-containing products had a "vice, ruin, or defect that presented an unreasonable risk of harm"; and (3) "that the vice, ruin, or defect was the cause-in-fact of the plaintiff's damages." *Dupree v. City of New Orleans*, 765 So. 2d 1002, 1007–08 & n.5 (La. 2000) (stating the elements for a strict liability claim prior to 1996 and recognizing that the exercise of reasonable care was not a defense to strict liability); *see also Wilde v. Huntington Ingalls, Inc.*, 616 F. App'x 710, 715 (5th Cir. 2015) (per curiam); *Watts v. Ga.-Pac. Corp.*, 135 So. 3d 53, 59 (La. App. 1 Cir. 2013) (recognizing that occupational exposure to asbestos can give rise to [—11—] strict liability claims).[5] Of

[5] The Plaintiffs rely heavily on language from *Kent v. Gulf States Utilities Co.*, 418 So. 2d 493 (La. 1982) that suggests that reasonable care is a defense to strict liability, which would make their claims based on strict liability essentially indistinguishable from their negligence claims for

course, strict liability is not automatic liability as the "unreasonable risk of harm" element requires cost-benefit analysis to establish a defect. W. Page Keeton et al., PROSSER AND KEETON ON THE LAW OF TORTS §§ 78, 99, at 555–56, 695 (5th ed. 1984). Yet that defect question is determined at the time of design or manufacture, with downstream users like a shipyard becoming responsible once that defect is proven (thus the "strict liability" label). *Id.* § 99, at 695–96.

This analysis of the elements of strict liability under pre-1996 Louisiana law largely resolves the "causal nexus" inquiry for federal officer removal. The strict liability claims rest on the mere use of asbestos, and that use at the shipyard was pursuant to government directions via contract specifications. Unlike claims based on negligence, those based on strict liability do not turn on discretionary decisions made by the shipyard. *See Bartel*, 805 F.3d at 172–74, 3 Adm. R. at 423–25 (discussing what is required to support a claim for negligence and how a strict liability claim for unseaworthiness might be different).

We have previously recognized that strict liability claims support federal officer removal when the government obligates the defendant to use the allegedly defective product that causes the plaintiff's harm. *See Winters*, 149 [—12—] F.3d at 398–400. In *Winters*, the

the purposes of this case. But that language was merely dicta, and other language in the same opinion suggests that reasonable care would *not* be a defense to a strict liability claim. *See id.* at 497 (*"Under strict liability concepts, the mere fact of the owner's relationship with and responsibility for the damage-causing thing gives rise to an absolute duty to discover the risks presented by the thing in custody."*). Indeed, that case did not even rest on a decision about strict liability, but on negligence because the defendant had actual knowledge of the risk of harm. *See Hebert v. Gulf States Utilities Co.*, 426 So. 2d 111, 114 (La. 1983) (noting that *Kent* was a negligence case). And in any event, the Louisiana Supreme Court's more recent decision almost two decades later in *Dupree* is binding on this court. *See Ford Motor Co. v. Dall. Power & Light Co.*, 499 F.2d 400, 410 n.17 (5th Cir. 1974) (noting that when interpreting state laws, federal courts are "Erie-bound" by the state supreme court's most recent authority).

plaintiff brought strict liability claims against chemical manufacturers for producing Agent Orange, a toxic herbicide that the government used during the Vietnam War to quickly defoliate large areas in order to gain military advantage. *Id.* at 390, 399. The plaintiff claimed that she was exposed to Agent Orange while working as a nurse in Vietnam and that it caused her terminal cancer. *Id.* at 390. In finding federal officer removal proper, we concluded that the government's detailed specifications and supervision over Agent Orange's production, packaging, and delivery, as well as the compulsion under threat of criminal sanctions to meet the government's specifications, established that the defendants had "acted pursuant to federal direction and that a direct causal nexus exist[ed] between the defendants' actions taken under color of federal office and [the plaintiff's] claims." *Id.* at 399–400; *see also Bartel*, 805 F.3d at 173, 3 Adm. R. at 424 (characterizing the causal nexus in *Winters* as resting on these grounds).

That causal relationship also exists here between the government's requirements that the shipyard use asbestos in constructing its Navy and Coast Guard vessels and Savoie's asbestos exposure while working on those same vessels. Like the chemical manufacturers in *Winters*, the shipyard was compelled to meet the government's detailed specifications for what products and materials could be used in the construction of its vessels. And "the only products that [the shipyard] could have used to insulate pipes . . . [as required by contract] on ships it built for the Navy through mid-1969 contained asbestos." As in *Winters*, the government exercised supervision over the shipyard's work to ensure compliance with contractual requirements. And although the shipyard did not face criminal sanctions for failing to meet the government's specifications as the manufacturers in *Winters* did, the shipyard was contractually required to comply and could receive no payments until it certified that all contractual requirements had been met. Thus it is the [—13—] government's detailed specifications, to which the shipyard was contractually obligated to follow, that required the use of asbestos that allegedly caused Savoie's death. This is enough to show

a causal nexus between the Savoies' strict liability claims and the shipyard's actions under the color of federal authority. The district court erred in finding that this requirement was not satisfied.

This does not necessarily mean that removal was proper. Recall a third requirement, whether the defendant possesses a colorable federal defense. The shipyard proposes two: the federal contractor defense, *see Boyle v. United Technologies Corp.*, 487 U.S. 500, 512–13 (1988) (recognizing for the first time the federal contractor defense and setting forth its elements), and a preemption defense under the Longshore and Harbor Workers' Compensation Act, *see* 33 U.S.C. § 905(a) (employer immunity provision), § 933(i) (co-employee immunity provision).

As the district court never had the opportunity to consider whether these defenses are colorable, we will remand to allow it to do so in the first instance. *See, e.g., Humphries v. Elliott Co.*, 760 F.3d 414, 417–18 (5th Cir. 2014) (remanding for consideration of the colorable federal defense requirement when the district court had not reached the issue); *Cf. Robertson v. Exxon Mobil Corp.*, — F.3d —, 2015 WL 9592499, at *3 (5th Cir. Dec. 31, 2015) (remanding to district court to determine whether other exceptions to jurisdiction under CAFA apply where district court had not reached such arguments). As only the survival claims alleging strict liability satisfy the first two requirements of federal officer removal, it is only defenses to those claims—that is, defenses existing under the law that existed when Savoie was exposed to asbestos—that [—14—] should be considered in determining whether the shipyard asserts colorable federal defenses.[6]

---

[6] This means that Defendant's preemption defense is governed by the law at the time Savoie was exposed to asbestos, which occurred before the Louisiana Worker's Compensation Act was amended in 1989 to eliminate any concurrent coverage between that Act and the federal Longshore and Harbor Workers' Compensation Act. *See* La. Rev. Stat. 23:1035.2 (providing that "[n]o compensation shall be payable in respect to the disability or death of any employee covered by . . .

* * *

For these reasons, we VACATE the district court's remand order and REMAND the case for resolution of the remaining jurisdictional requirement.

---

the Longshoremen's and Harbor Worker's Compensation Act, or any of its extensions . . .").

United States Court of Appeals
for the Fifth Circuit

No. 15-40463

MALIN INT'L SHIP REPAIR & DRYDOCK, INC.
vs.
OCEANOGRAFIA, S.A.

Appeal from the United States District Court for the
Southern District of Texas

Decided: March 23, 2016

Citation: 817 F.3d 241, 4 Adm. R. 232 (5th Cir. 2016).

Before **JONES, WIENER,** and **HIGGINSON,** Circuit
Judges.

[—1—] **WIENER,** Circuit Judge:

Defendant-Appellant Oceanografia, S.A. ("OSA") appeals (1) the district court's denial of its motion to vacate attachment under Supplemental Admiralty Rule B and (2) that court's grant of Plaintiff-Appellant Malin International Ship Repair & Drydock, Inc.'s ("Malin") motion for summary judgment. Concluding that both the attachment and the summary judgment were proper, we affirm. [—2—]

I.

FACTS AND PROCEEDINGS

Malin operates a shipyard in Galveston, Texas. In 2008 and 2009, Malin performed work for OSA, a Mexican corporation, and Con-Dive, LLC ("Con-Dive"), a now-defunct Texas company. Not having received payment for its work, Malin sued OSA for the balance of its unpaid invoices for work, services, materials, and supplies that it had provided to OSA at the request of Con-Dive. Malin sought recovery on the alternative theories of breach of contract and quantum meruit.

OSA operated a vessel, the M/V KESTREL, under a bareboat charter agreement. The registered owner of the M/V KESTREL, Cal Dive Offshore Contractors, Inc. ("Cal Dive"), had entered into a charter agreement with Gulf Offshore Construction, Inc. ("GOC"), which in turn bareboat chartered the vessel to

OSA. OSA had taken delivery of the vessel on October 15, 2012. The charter agreement stated that "[a]t the time of delivery[, OSA] shall purchase the bunkers . . . in the said Vessel at the then current market price at the port of delivery." To obtain jurisdiction over OSA pursuant to Supplemental Admiralty Rule B, Malin attached the fuel bunkers[1] aboard the M/V KESTREL on October 29, 2012.

OSA and Cal Dive sought to vacate the attachment, contending that OSA did not hold an attachable interest in the bunkers at the time of Malin's attachment because title to them had not yet passed to OSA. According to OSA [—3—] and Cal Dive, OSA had neither paid for the bunkers nor received an invoice for them and therefore did not own them.

The district court denied their motions, holding that OSA's possessory interest in the bunkers constituted an attachable interest under Rule B. Cal Dive then posted a vessel release bond to substitute for the seized bunkers of the M/V KESTREL and to secure the liability of OSA to Malin.

Malin then sought summary judgment on its breach of contract and quantum meruit claims against OSA. Malin contended that Con-Dive was OSA's agent and had authority to bind OSA to the invoices, or, in the alternative, that OSA had ratified the invoices or is liable to Malin on its claim of quantum meruit. In support, Malin supplied invoices detailing the amounts owed as well as e-mails from OSA indicating that it had received the invoices and agreed to pay them. The invoices also contained provisions for interest and attorneys fees. OSA opposed the motion. It filed only one item of summary judgment evidence: a declaration from an OSA employee stating that Con-Dive did not act as OSA's agent.

---

[1] "Fuel bunkers" is the admiralty term for the fuel used by a vessel. *See Glossary of Marine Insurance and Shipping Terms*, 14 U.S.F. Mar. L. J. 305, 325 (2001–2002) (defining "bunkers" as "[f]uel to be used by the vessel's engines for power during the voyage; but not fuel loaded on board the vessel as cargo").

The magistrate judge recommended granting summary judgment in favor of Malin based on its ratification and quantum meruit theories. The magistrate judge also recommended that Malin be awarded attorneys fees on its ratification claim. The district court accepted and adopted the magistrate judge's Report and Recommendation, then rendered judgment to Malin for the amount of the invoices, plus accrued interest and attorneys fees. This appeal followed.

On appeal, OSA contends that the district court erred in denying its motion to vacate the attachment. It argues that the attachment of the bunkers was improper under Supplemental Rule B because the bunkers were not its [—4—] property. OSA further asserts that the district court erred in granting Malin's motion for summary judgment on its ratification theory.[2]

II.

ANALYSIS

A. Attachment

The propriety of the attachment of the bunkers aboard the M/V KESTREL goes to the district court's jurisdiction over OSA, so we begin there. We review an order denying a motion to vacate an attachment under Rule B for abuse of discretion, and we review issues of law de novo.[3]

Supplemental Rule B provides:

If a defendant is not found within the district when a verified complaint praying for attachment and the affidavit required by Rule B(1)(b) are filed, a verified complaint may contain a prayer

for process to attach the defendant's tangible or intangible personal property—up to the amount sued for—in the hands of garnishees named in the process.[4]

"Rule B allows a district court to take jurisdiction over a defendant in an admiralty or maritime action by attaching property of the defendant."[5] The rule has two purposes: "to secure a respondent's appearance and to assure satisfaction in case the suit is successful."[6] [—5—]

The only issue before us is whether the fuel bunkers constituted OSA's "tangible or intangible personal property" at the time of attachment.[7] Rule B does not define the term "tangible or intangible personal property." Significantly, the rule provides no guidance as to what type of property interest is attachable. OSA urges us to rule that a party must own property for it to be subject to attachment under Rule B, contending that it did not own the bunkers at the time of attachment because it had not yet paid for them. Predictably, Malin counters that an interest in property less than full ownership—here, OSA's agreement to purchase the bunkers coupled with its possession of the bunkers—suffices.

The Supreme Court approved of maritime attachment in *Manro v. Almeida*.[8] Although the Court did not define what constitutes attachable property, it quoted "a book of respectable authority" which states that goods or ships may be attached in the hands of the owner or in the hands of "all others who claim any *right or title* to them . . . ."[9] More than one hundred years later, in *Kingston Dry Dock*

---

[2] OSA's attempt, in its Summary of the Argument, to challenge the district court's award of damages is waived by OSA's failure to brief it adequately. *See United States v. Sealed Appellant 1*, 591 F.3d 812, 823 (5th Cir. 2009).

[3] *Geneve Butane, Inc. v. Nat'l Oil Corp.*, 551 F. App'x 185, 185 (5th Cir. 2014) (unpublished); *see also Shipping Corp. of India Ltd. v. Jaldhi Overseas Pte Ltd.*, 585 F.3d 58, 66 (2d Cir. 2009).

[4] FED. R. CIV. P. SUPP. R. B(1)(a).

[5] *Submersible Sys., Inc. v. Perforadora Cent., S.A. de C.V.*, 249 F.3d 413, 421 (5th Cir. 2001).

[6] *Swift & Co. Packers v. Compania Colombiana Del Caribe, S.A.*, 339 U.S. 684, 693 (1950).

[7] *See Jaldhi*, 585 F.3d at 69 ("As a remedy *quasi in rem*, the validity of a Rule B attachment depends entirely on the determination that the *res* at issue is the property of the defendant at the moment the *res* is attached.").

[8] 23 U.S. (10 Wheat) 473 (1825).

[9] *Id.* at 491–92 (quoting Hall, CLERKE'S PRAXIS part 2, tit. 28) (emphasis added).

Co. v. Lake Champlain Transportation Co.,[10] Judge Learned Hand, writing for the Second Circuit, applied Rule B's precursor and held that a conditional buyer's "conditional right to title" constituted an attachable interest. There, the plaintiff attached two canal boats possessed by the defendant, a conditional buyer. The defendant had contracted for the construction and sale of the boats and had taken possession of them. The contract, however, reserved title to the seller until it received final payment, [—6—] and the defendant had not made payment at the time of attachment. On this basis, the defendant sought to vacate the writ of attachment. Recognizing that possession "is historically the original source of all title," Judge Hand warned that "[i]t would be curious if possession, coupled with a conditional right to title, could now be thought insufficient to support a seizure."[11] Accordingly, that court declined to vacate the attachment.

Later, the Third Circuit in *McGahern v. Koppers Coal Co.* distinguished *Kingston* when considering whether a bareboat charterer possessed an attachable interested in the chartered vessel.[12] The court held that a bareboat charterer holds no attachable interest in the chartered vessel because the charterer has "no title or expectancy or possibility of title, conditional or otherwise."[13] Significantly, under a bareboat charter, "[n]o title passes to the charterer under it, but merely the right to possess and control it for a limited period."[14] The Third Circuit found this result "in entire accord" with *Kingston*: "Clearly the conditional vendee [in *Kingston*], while not the holder of the legal title, did have conditional right to title, . . . which was sufficient to support the seizure. . . . In the present case, on the other hand, respondent . . . had no title or expectancy or possibility of title, conditional or otherwise."[15]

Although these cases recognized the principle that a conditional right to title may

support attachment under Rule B, a more recent unpublished Fourth Circuit opinion adopted a narrower approach. In *Wave Maker Shipping Co., Ltd. v. Hawksphere Shipping Co. Ltd.*,[16] creditors sought to attach a charterer's [—7—] fuel bunkers. Relevantly, the charterer had purchased fuel from a fuel supplier, but had not yet paid for it.[17] Under the contract between the charterer and the fuel supplier, the supplier retained title to the fuel until the charterer paid in full.[18] The charterer contended that the attachment should have been vacated because it did not have title to the fuel; rather, the fuel supplier retained title. Examining whether the Rule B attachment of the fuel bunkers should have been vacated, the Fourth Circuit asked whether the charterer "ever acquired title to the bunkers."[19] In answering this question, the Fourth Circuit relied on principles of English law, which governed the contract at issue.[20] Concluding that the fuel supplier had retained title to the bunkers, the Fourth Circuit vacated the attachment of the fuel in possession of the charterer.[21]

The Second Circuit recently emphasized the importance of ownership in determining whether an interest is attachable under Rule B. In deciding whether electronic fund transfers ("EFTs") are an attachable interest under Rule B, the Second Circuit, relying on New York state law, held that they are not: "Because EFTs in the temporary possession of an intermediary bank are not property of either the originator or the beneficiary under New York law, they cannot be subject to attachment under Rule B."[22] This is because "[f]or maritime attachments under Rule B . . . the question of ownership is critical."[23]

Several district courts have found an attachable property interest under Rule B when the defendant's interest does not rise to

---

[10] 31 F.2d 265, 267 (2d. Cir. 1929).

[11] *Id.* at 266–67.

[12] 108 F.2d 652 (3d Cir. 1940).

[13] *Id.* at 653.

[14] *Id.*

[15] *Id.*

[16] 56 F. App'x 594 (4th Cir. 2003) (unpublished).

[17] *Id.* at 597.

[18] *Id.*

[19] *Id.* at 598.

[20] *Id.* at 598–99.

[21] *Id.* at 599.

[22] *Jaldhi*, 585 F.3d at 71.

[23] *Id.* at 69.

ownership. For example, [—8—] in *World Fuel Services, Inc. v. SE Shipping Lines Pte., Ltd.*,[24] the district court upheld an attachment of fuel bunkers in the possession of the defendant. Although the defendant had not acquired title to the bunkers, the district court upheld the attachment because the defendant had the right to possess the bunkers, use the bunkers, and sell the bunkers.[25] Similarly, the district court in *Alaska Reefer Management LLC v. Network Shipping Ltd.* stated that "Rule B provides for a broad definition of property and does not require actual ownership or title."[26] That district court held that an attachable interest exists under Rule B when the "assets are being held 'for the benefit of' the Defendant or 'in its name.'"[27]

The body of federal maritime jurisprudence presents ambiguity as to whether, as the district court held here, a possessory interest is attachable under Rule B. Neither does federal maritime law categorize the type of interest that OSA held in the fuel bunkers at the time of the attachment. Confronted with such a void, other courts "generally look to state law to determine property rights."[28] Stated differently, "the precedent in federal admiralty law is so thin that we should turn to state law more directly on point."[29] We choose to do so here in the absence of guiding federal maritime law. In doing so, we are in accord with the closest circuit case, *Wave Maker Shipping Co.*, which [—9—] looked to the law governing the contract in determining whether title to fuel bunkers had passed.[30]

At the district court, Cal Dive contended that Texas law governs this issue. The bareboat charter agreement specifies that Texas law applies when federal maritime law is silent. An amendment to the agreement, effective shortly before the instant attachment, specifies that Mexican law applies. Neither party directed us to this amendment or urged us or the district court to apply Mexican law. Under Federal Rule of Civil Procedure 44.1, "[a] party who intends to raise an issue about a foreign country's law must give notice by a pleading or other writing."[31] And "[i]n the absence of sufficient proof to establish with reasonable certainty the substance of the foreign principles of law, the modern view is that the law of the forum should be applied."[32] We therefore look to Texas law.

OSA and GOC executed the bareboat charter agreement on September 12, 2012. The agreement provides that OSA "shall purchase the bunkers" at the time of delivery: "At the time of delivery the Charterers shall purchase the bunkers . . . in the said Vessel at the then current market price at the port of delivery." OSA took delivery of the M/V KESTREL (and consequently its bunkers) on October 15, 2012. Malin attached the fuel bunkers aboard the M/V KESTREL on October 29, 2012. As of October 31, 2012, OSA had neither paid [—10—] for nor received an invoice for the bunkers. Our task is to determine the nature of the property interest OSA held in the fuel bunkers at the time of attachment.

Texas has adopted Article 2 of the Uniform Commercial Code, which governs the sale of goods. Relevant here, Article 2 specifies that

---

[24] No. 10-4605, 2011 WL 446653 (E.D. La. Feb. 4, 2011).

[25] *Id.* at *1–2.

[26] 68 F. Supp. 3d 383, 386–87 (S.D.N.Y. 2014).

[27] *Id.* at 387.

[28] *Jaldhi*, 585 F.3d at 70.

[29] *Reibor Int'l Ltd. v. Cargo Carriers (KACZ-CO.) Ltd.*, 759 F.2d 262, 266 (2d Cir. 1985) ("In short, we agree with the district court that the precedent in federal admiralty law is so thin that we should turn to state law more directly on point. We clearly have this option where we find it appropriate.").

[30] *Wave Maker Shipping Co.*, 56 F. App'x at 598–99 (applying English law in determining whether title to fuel bunkers passed).

[31] FED. R. CIV. P. 44.1.

[32] *Symonette Shipyards, Ltd. v. Clark*, 365 F.2d 464, 468 n.5 (5th Cir. 1966); *see also Karim v. Finch Shipping Co., Ltd.*, 265 F.3d 258, 272 (5th Cir. 2001) ("When the parties have failed to conclusively establish foreign law, a court is entitled to look to its own forum's law in order to fill any gaps." (quoting *Banco de Credito Indus., S.A. v. Tesoreria Gen.*, 990 F.2d 827, 836 (5th Cir. 1993)); *Carey v. Bahama Cruise Lines*, 864 F.2d 201, 206 (1st Cir. 1988) ("By their silence, the litigants[] consent to having their dispute resolved according to the law of the forum.").

"title passes to the buyer at the time and place at which the seller completes his performance with reference to the physical delivery of the goods . . . ."[33] When "the contract requires delivery at destination, title passes on tender there."[34] Were we to apply Article 2, we would conclude that title passed to OSA on delivery of the M/V KESTREL and its fuel bunkers to OSA. Here, however, OSA's obligation to purchase the bunkers did not arise from a contract for the sale of goods, but from the bareboat charter agreement.[35] As Article 2 is thus inapplicable, we apply principles of Texas common law.

Under Texas common law, the instant at which title to personal property passes from seller to buyer depends on the parties' intent.[36] Generally, if the contract does not condition passage of title on payment, a seller passes title to a buyer on delivery of the goods.[37] But, "where the contract of sale of personal property calls for cash on delivery, concurrent payment upon delivery is [—11—] essential to pass the title . . . ."[38] The former is a credit sale; the latter is a cash sale.[39]

The instant agreement specifies that OSA "shall purchase the bunkers" at the time of delivery. Although Cal Dive asserted in the district court that this language indicates that the parties contemplated a cash sale under which OSA would not obtain title until payment, this interpretation goes too far. "Purchase" means "[t]he acquisition of an interest in real or personal property by sale . . . ."[40] And a "sale" may occur based on either an actual payment or a mere promise to make payment.[41] The parties' agreement uses the word "purchase," so it does not necessarily indicate that they intended that OSA make payment before title would pass. Moreover, the agreement is silent as to when payment was due or when title would pass.

In addition, OSA's and Cal Dive's representations throughout this litigation show that Cal Dive did not expect OSA to remit payment for the bunkers at the time of delivery. Both parties have consistently represented that, as of the time of attachment on October 29, 2012, OSA had neither received an invoice for the fuel bunkers nor been asked to pay for them. OSA maintains that this confirms that it never obtained title to the bunkers. We disagree: It shows that OSA was not expected to pay for the bunkers at the time of delivery. Thus, under Texas law, the parties contemplated a credit transaction. Further, there is no evidence in the record indicating that OSA [—12—] and Cal Dive intended to delay the passage of title to the bunkers until OSA remitted full payment.[42] We conclude that, under Texas

---

[33] TEX. BUS. & COM. CODE ANN. § 2.401(b); see also Crocker Nat'l Bank v. Ideco Div. of Dresser Indus., Inc., 839 F.2d 1104, 1107 (5th Cir. 1988) ("Unless otherwise explicitly agreed, title to goods generally passes to the buyer when the seller completes his performance with reference to physical delivery of the goods.").

[34] Id. § 2.401(b)(2).

[35] See Neubros Corp. v. Nw. Nat'l Ins. Co., 359 F. Supp. 310, 319 (E.D.N.Y. 1972) ("For the purposes of the Uniform Commercial Code a bareboat charter for a period of eighteen months is not a sale as defined in sections 2-102, 2-105(1) and 2-106(1) of the Code.").

[36] John E. Morrison & Co. v. Murff, 212 S.W. 212, 214 (Tex. Civ. App.—Galveston 1919, no writ) ("Moreover, the intention of the parties themselves, to be ascertained from their express declaration, or from the circumstances presented, or both, is the dominating consideration in determining whether or not title has passed in the sale of a chattel.").

[37] See, e.g., Luse v. Crispin Co., 344 S.W.2d 926, 930 (Tex. App.—Houston 1961, writ ref'd n.r.e.).

[38] Id. ("A cash sale is one in which the contract calls for payment of the price in cash when the contract is made or the goods are delivered.").

[39] See id.

[40] Purchase, BLACK'S LAW DICTIONARY (10th ed. 2014).

[41] The acquisition of an interest in property "by sale" does not necessarily require payment. See Sale, BLACK'S LAW DICTIONARY (10th ed. 2014) (defining the four elements of a sale as "(1) parties competent to contract, (2) mutual assent, (3) a thing capable of being transferred, and (4) a price in money paid or promised" (emphasis added)).

[42] Compare Luse, 344 S.W. at 929–30 ("Although Williams testified that the sale was a cash sale, the evidence clearly shows that the purchase price was not to be paid by Transcontinental upon delivery of the pipe at Beaumont, but was to be paid upon receipt of Crispin's invoice in Oklahoma. There was no agreement between the parties that payment

law, title to the bunkers passed to OSA on delivery.

Under this analysis, OSA received title to the bunkers on October 15, 2012, the day that it took possession of the M/V KESTREL. Malin attached those bunkers on October 29, 2012. Because OSA held title to the bunkers at the time of Malin's attachment—and title to property unquestionably suffices as an attachable interest under Rule B—we affirm the district court's denial of OSA's motion to vacate the attachment.

B. Summary Judgment

Having confirmed that the district court had personal jurisdiction over OSA by virtue of the attachment of the bunkers on the vessel that it had chartered, we turn to OSA's challenges to the district court's summary judgment in favor of Malin. We review the district court's summary judgment de novo, applying the same standards as the district court.[43]

In his Report and Recommendation on Malin's motion for summary judgment, the magistrate judge found the following facts to be undisputed: (1) [—13—] Con-Dive represented to Malin that it was acting for and with the permission of OSA when it

arranged for the work and services; (2) Malin performed the work and provided the services; (3) through Con-Dive, an OSA employee furnished instructions and directions for Malin's work; (4) Malin periodically invoiced OSA for the work; (5) these invoices contained the terms and conditions of the contracts, including provisions for the collection of service charges and attorney's fees; (6) OSA, through an employee, promised to pay the overdue invoices; (7) OSA did nothing within any reasonably relevant time to disaffirm Con-Dive's authority or Malin's work; and (8) OSA retained all of the benefits of Malin's work. On that record, the magistrate judge recommended finding that OSA ratified Malin's work and invoices and is liable to Malin for payment. The magistrate judge recommended finding in the alternative that OSA is liable for the payment of Malin's invoices on the basis of quantum meruit. The magistrate judge also recommended that Malin be awarded attorneys fees on the basis of its ratification theory, but not on its quantum meruit theory. The district court adopted these findings and entered judgment in favor of Malin.

OSA contends that the district court erred in holding that OSA ratified the contractual obligations of Malin's customer, Con-Dive. Texas law provides that "if a party acts in a manner that recognizes the validity of a contract with full knowledge of the material terms of the contract, the party has ratified the contract and may not later withdraw its ratification and seek to avoid the contract."[44] [—14—]

OSA initially contends that Malin failed to show that its services benefited OSA. Whether Malin's services benefited OSA, however, has no bearing on Malin's ratification theory. Demonstrating that a party accepted benefits under a contract is one way to show ratification, but it is not the only way.[45] Malin

---

should be made before or concurrently with delivery of the pipe at Beaumont. There was no agreement that delivery of the pipe was to be delayed until the purchase price was paid. It was contemplated that delivery should precede the payment of the purchase price."), *and John E. Morrison & Co.*, 212 S.W. at 213 ("There is an utter absence throughout the entire body of evidence of any intimation even that full payment in cash of the balance of the purchase price before removal of the car, or in the alternative the giving of a note therefor, were made or understood to be conditions precedent to completion of the contract of sale, or that they were part and parcel of it."), *with Sinker, Davis & Co. v. Comparet*, 62 Tex. 470, 474 (1884) ("The machinery was sold and delivered to Comparet under an express stipulation that the vendors parted with no title, nor was any acquired by Comparet, until payment was made of the price agreed to be paid as evidenced by the notes given by the purchaser.").

[43] *Ashford v. United States*, 511. F.3d 501, 504 (5th Cir. 2007).

[44] *Advanced Nano Coatings, Inc. v. Hanafin*, 478 F. App'x 838, 843–44 (5th Cir. 2012) (unpublished) (quoting *Verizon Corp. Servs. Corp. v. Kan-Pak Sys., Inc.*, 290 S.W.3d 899, 906 (Tex. App.—Amarillo 2009, no pet.)).

[45] *See United States v. McBride*, 571 F. Supp. 596, 612–13 (S.D. Tex. 1983) ("Ratification may be

proved that its invoices were ratified by OSA when OSA agreed to pay them after receiving them. Even if we were to accept OSA's contention that Malin did not show that OSA benefited from its services, the result would not change.

OSA next contends that the presence of an issue of fact as to whether Con-Dive acted as Malin's agent should have precluded summary judgment on Malin's ratification theory. But an agency relationship is not required to uphold the district court's ruling that OSA ratified Con-Dive's acts.[46]

OSA finally contends that Malin failed to show that OSA ratified the invoices' provisions on interest and attorneys fees. On an undisputed record, the magistrate judge found that Malin invoiced OSA for its services and that "the invoices contained the terms and conditions of the contracts, including the provisions for the collection of service charges and attorney's fees . . . ." Malin [—15—] supplied an affidavit from Gabe Socias, a superintendent at Malin, who testified that "Malin and Oceanografia/Con-Dive agreed to the provision of certain work and services . . . *pursuant to the terms of Malin's invoices.*" Socias further testified that "[t]he invoices

attached are true and correct copies of the originals and accurately reflect the work and services provided by Malin to Oceanografia and Con-Dive." Each invoice includes two parts: (1) a basic invoice, dated at various times in 2008, which reflected the invoice number, date, services rendered, and amount due; and (2) a formal invoice, reflecting, *inter alia*, the original invoice date, the total amount invoiced, the interest due as of February 10, 2009, and the interest and attorneys fees provisions.[47] Socias also attached a June 9, 2009, e-mail from an OSA representative confirming the receipt of Malin's "overdue" invoices.

On appeal, OSA tries to inject ambiguity into the summary judgment record by asserting that there is no evidence that OSA received the formal invoices containing the interest and attorneys fees provisions. It follows, argues OSA, that the evidence does not prove that it ratified the interest and attorneys fees provisions of the invoices.

We note that OSA proffered no summary judgment evidence to show that it did not receive the relevant invoices. By contrast, the unrefuted summary judgment evidence, as established by Socias's affidavit, proves that (1) OSA agreed to Malin's provision of services and work *pursuant to Malin's invoices*, and (2) the attached invoices are the "true and correct copies of the originals . . . ." In addition, the June 9, 2009, e-mail from OSA's representative confirms OSA's receipt of the "overdue" invoice statements and OSA's [—16—] agreement to pay the invoices. We must assume that, if OSA had evidence to create an issue of fact to preclude summary judgment, it would have supplied it.[48] We therefore affirm the district court's deter-

---

manifested in one or more of several ways: a party may ratify, first, by intentionally accepting benefits under the contract; second, by remaining silent or acquiescing in the contract for a period of time after he has the opportunity to avoid it; and third, by recognizing [the] validity of the contract by acting upon it, performing under it, or affirmatively acknowledging it.").

[46] *See McWhorter v. Sheller*, 993 S.W.2d 781, 787 (Tex. App.—Houston [14th Dist.] 1999, pet. denied) ("Most case law interpreting the doctrine of ratification couches its discussion in the context of an existing agency relationship where the agent exceeds the scope of her authority and the principal later accepts the benefits of such act after acquiring full knowledge. Ratification, however, can occur outside this general paradigm. While most cases will fall within the context of an agency relationship, such a relation is not necessary to cause the ratification to be effective. It is true, however, that because ratification is not a form of authorization, the ratification of an act of a stranger will not create an agency relationship, it will only bind the ratifier to the specific transaction that is ratified." (citations omitted)).

[47] The record provides no indication of why all the formal invoices specify the interest accrued as of February 10, 2009. We can only speculate that Malin printed the invoices on this date.

[48] OSA supplied an out-of-time declaration from Gustavo Azcarate—the OSA representative who received Malin's invoices via e-mail. Azcarate's declaration, however, goes only to whether Con-Dive acted as an agent for OSA and says nothing to refute the evidence demonstrating that OSA, through Azcarate, received Malin's invoices.

mination that no material issues of fact exist as to whether OSA received and ratified the invoices, including their interest and attorneys fees provisions. The district court committed no error in granting summary judgment for Malin.

III.

CONCLUSION

We affirm the district court's denial of OSA's and Cal Dive's motions to vacate the attachment, and we affirm the district court's summary judgment in favor of Malin.

AFFIRMED.

United States Court of Appeals
for the Fifth Circuit

No. 15-30239

WORLD FUEL SERVS. SINGAPORE PTE
vs.
BULK JULIANA M/V

Appeal from the United States District Court for the Eastern District of Louisiana

Decided: April 1, 2016

Citation: 822 F.3d 766, 4 Adm. R. 240 (5th Cir. 2016).

Before **JONES** and **JOLLY,** Circuit Judges, and **MILLS,** District Judge.*

   * District Judge of the Northern District of Mississippi, sitting by designation.

[—1—] JONES, Circuit Judge:

"**T**his admiralty and maritime case concerns a Singapore-based marine fuel supplier's attempt to recover a debt arising from the supply of fuel oil bunkers in Singapore to a Panamanian-flag vessel, the M/V BULK JULIANA, which is beneficially owned by a United States company, operated and [—2—] managed by a United States company, and which was chartered by a German company." *World Fuel Servs. Singapore Pte, Ltd. v. Bulk Juliana M/V*, No. 13-5421, 2015 WL 575201, at *1 (E.D. La. Feb. 11, 2015). On summary judgment, the district court applied Singapore law to the formation of the fuel sales contract, enforced the parties' choice of law as the "General Maritime law of the United States," and concluded that the vessel lien under the Federal Maritime Lien Act ("FMLA"), 42 U.S.C. §§ 31341 and 31342, was enforceable. Agreeing with the district court's conclusion and substantially with its reasoning, we **AFFIRM AND REMAND**.

BACKGROUND

World Fuel Services Corp., a Florida corporation, is the parent corporation of the World Fuel Services group of companies. This group of companies, which includes Plaintiff-Appellee WFS Singapore ("WFS Singapore") and WFS Europe, provides fuel to ocean-faring vessels around the world. Bulk Juliana Ltd. is the owner of the vessel M/V BULK JULIANA. On November 7, 2012, Peter Turner ("Turner"), Manager of Commercial Sales at WFS Europe, negotiated on behalf of WFS Singapore with Denmar for the delivery of the bunkers (fuel) to the vessel, which Denmar had recently time-chartered. On November 7, Turner, on behalf of WFS Singapore, confirmed the bunker order via email to Denmar.

The confirmation email outlined the terms of Denmar's bunker order. First, the email described the relative bargaining authorities of WFS Singapore and Denmar:

ALL SALES ARE ON THE CREDIT OF THE VSL [vessel]. BUYER IS PRESUMED TO HAVE AUTHORITY TO BIND THE VSL WITH A MARITIME LIEN. DISCLAIMER STAMPS PLACED BY VSL ON THE BUNKER RECEIPT WILL HAVE NO EFFECT AND DO NOT WAIVE THE SELLER'S LIEN. [—3—]

Next, the email incorporated by reference the "General Terms and Conditions" (the "General Terms") of all such contracts entered into by WFS Singapore:

THIS CONFIRMATION IS GOVERNED BY AND INCORPORATES BY REFERENCE SELLER'S GENERAL TERMS AND CONDITIONS IN EFFECT AS OF THE DATE THAT THIS CONFIRMATION IS ISSUED. THESE INCORPORATED AND REFERENCED TERMS CAN BE FOUND AT WWW.WFSCORP.COM. ALTERNATIVELY, YOU MAY INFORM US IF YOU REQUIRE A COPY AND SAME WILL BE PROVIDED TO YOU.

The "General Terms and Conditions" include three sections relevant to this appeal:

1. <u>INCORPORATION AND MERGER</u>: Each sale of Products shall be confirmed by email, fax or other writing from the Seller to the Buyer ("Confirmation").

The Confirmation shall incorporate the General Terms by reference so that the General Terms thereby supplement and are made part of the particular terms set forth in the Confirmation. The Confirmation and the General Terms shall together constitute the complete and exclusive agreement governing the transaction in question (the "Transaction"). . . .

8. CREDIT AND SECURITY:

(a) Products supplied in each Transaction are sold and effected on the credit of the Receiving Vessel, as well as on the promise of the Buyer to pay, and it is agreed and the Buyer warrants that the Seller will have and may assert a maritime lien against the Receiving Vessel for the amount due for the Products delivered . . . .

(d) All sales made under these terms and conditions are made to the registered owner of the vessel, in addition to any other parties that may be listed as Buyer in the confirmation. Any bunkers ordered by an agent, management company, charterer, broker or any other party are ordered on behalf of the registered owner and the registered owner is liable as a principal for payment of the bunker invoice. . . .

17. LAW AND JURISDICTION: The General Terms and each Transaction shall be governed by the General Maritime Law of the United States . . . The General Maritime Law of the United States [—4—] shall apply with respect to the existence of a maritime lien, regardless of the country in which Seller takes legal action. Any disputes concerning quality or quantity shall only be resolved in a court of competent jurisdiction in Florida. Disputes over payment and collection may be resolved, at Seller's option, in the Florida courts or in the courts of any jurisdiction where either the Receiving Vessel or an asset of the Buyer may be found. Each of the parties hereby irrevocably submits to the jurisdiction of any such court, and irrevocably waives, to the fullest extent it may effectively do so, the defense of an inconvenient forum or its foreign equivalent to the maintenance of any action in any such court. Seller shall be entitled to assert its right of lien or attachment or other rights, whether in law, in equity or otherwise, in any country where it finds the vessel. **BUYER AND SELLER WAIVE ANY RIGHT EITHER OF THEM MIGHT HAVE TO A TRIAL BY JURY IN ANY LEGAL PROCEEDING ARISING FROM OR RELATED TO THE GENERAL TERMS OR ANY TRANSACTION.**

There is no indication in the record that Denmar ever objected to, or inquired about, the contractual terms expressed in the bunker confirmation email.

On November 13, Transocean Oil, a Singapore fuel supplier subcontracted by WFS Singapore, delivered the bunkers to the vessel at the Port of Singapore. R. L. Vicente, Master/Chief Engineer of the vessel, signed the Bunker Delivery Notes and affixed the vessel's stamp to each confirming receipt of the bunkers. On November 15, 2012, WFS Singapore issued an invoice to "MV BULK JULIANA AND/OR HER OWNERS/OPERATORS AND DENMAR . . . ." for the sale.

Because payment was never remitted, WFS Singapore filed a complaint in the Eastern District of Louisiana in August 2013, which sought the arrest of the vessel then docked in the Port of New Orleans and recovery of the sales price. (The complaint also named Denmar as a defendant, but Denmar had become insolvent and was dismissed.) The next day, an arrest warrant was issued by the district court. On September 13, 2013, Bulk Juliana claimed [—5—] ownership of the vessel, posted security to release it, and answered WFS Singapore's complaint. In its answer, Bulk Juliana asserted that: (1) WFS Singapore had no maritime lien under the law of Singapore (where the bunkers were delivered to the vessel); (2) WFS Singapore had no legal basis to assert a maritime lien under 46 U.S.C. § 31342 against the vessel; and (3) the WFS Singapore's arrest of the vessel was wrongful and improper and should be vacated by the district court.

Faced with conflicting motions on the validity and enforceability of the maritime lien, the district court ordered each party to file additional briefing concerning the choice-of-law issue before the court.

WFS Singapore argued that the maritime lien was valid because the contract contained a General Maritime Law of the United States choice-of-law provision that allowed Denmar to bind the vessel through the purchase of necessaries (the bunkers). Alternatively, WFS Singapore argued that even if Singapore law governed the formation of the contract, the parties' United States choice-of-law provision would still be valid, and therefore, the maritime lien would be enforceable. In support, WFS Singapore relied on the uncontroverted affidavit and testimony of Mr. Tan Chaun Bing Kendall ("Mr. Tan"), a Singapore law expert with bunker transaction experience. Mr. Tan opined that the contract's General Terms were valid under Singapore law, that the terms were validly incorporated into the sales agreement, and that the General Maritime Law of the United States choice-of-law provision was enforceable.

Conversely, Bulk Juliana contended that Singapore law controlled the dispute but did not afford WFS Singapore a maritime lien. Further, Bulk Juliana asserted that even if U.S. law controlled, the General Maritime Law of the United States choice-of-law provision in WFS Singapore's General Terms [—6—] only invoked U.S. maritime common law. U.S. general maritime common law, however, is a term of art that, according to Bulk Juliana, is distinct from and does not encompass the federal maritime lien statute. See 46 U.S.C. §31342(a).

The district court held that while Singapore law governed formation of the contract, WFS Singapore's bunker confirmation email validly incorporated by reference the General Terms, which included

the General Maritime Law of the United States choice-of-law provision. Because the General Maritime Law of the United States choice-of-law provision was valid under Singapore law, U.S. law controlled the dispute. Finally, the parties' choice of law provision included by its terms the FMLA, rendering the maritime lien enforceable against the vessel.

Bulk Juliana appeals the district court's denial of its motion for summary judgment and grant of WFS's cross-motion. This court has jurisdiction of the district court's interlocutory ruling based on admiralty law. 28 U.S.C. §1292(a)(3).

STANDARD OF REVIEW

This Court reviews the district court's grant of summary judgment *de novo*, applying the same standards as the district court. *Newman v. Guedry*, 703 F.3d 757, 761 (5th Cir. 2012). Summary judgment is only appropriate if "there is no genuine issue as to any material fact and that the moving party is entitled to a judgment as a matter of law." *Celotex Corp. v. Catrett*, 477 U.S. 317, 322 (1986). "On a motion for summary judgment, [this Court] must view the facts in the light most favorable to the non-moving party and draw all reasonable inferences in its favor." *Deville v. Marcantel*, 567 F.3d 156, 163-64 (5th Cir. 2009). Additionally, this Court reviews questions of law, "including choice of law and contract interpretation, *de novo*." *Waterfowl Liab. Co. v. United States*, 473 F.3d 135, 141 (5th Cir. 2006). [—7—]

DISCUSSION

This appeal presents the following issues: (1) whether, under Singapore law, the contract's General Terms that include a choice of U.S. maritime law were validly incorporated into the agreement and enforceable; (2) whether Denmar, the charterer, had authority to bind the vessel *in rem* even though Bulk Juliana, the owner, was not a party to the contract between WFS Singapore and Denmar; (3) whether the maritime lien was solely created by a contractual term; and (4) whether the choice of law clause using the term "General Maritime Law of the United States" includes the statutory FMLA. We discuss each issue below.

I. Whether the contract's General Terms, which include a U.S. choice of law provision, are valid under Singaporean law and were validly incorporated into the agreement.

In this court, the parties no longer dispute the applicability of Singapore law to the contract's formation; thus, we need not consider whether a preliminary choice of law, based on maritime law principles, must be made as to the contract's formation. *See Lauritzen v. Larsen,* 345 U.S. 571, 582, 73 S. Ct. 921 (1953). Their continued disagreement centers instead on whether the General Terms were validly incorporated into the contract. *See Trans-Tec Asia v. M/V HARMONY CONTAINER,* 518 F.3d 1120, 1124 (9th Cir.), *cert. denied,* 555 U.S. 1062 (2008)(hereafter, "*Trans-Tec*"). The only record evidence on this point consists of undisputed testimony from WFS Singapore's expert witness, Mr. Tan. Mr. Tan testified that "the key guiding principle is that a Singapore court will seek to discern the contractual intention of both parties, which is to be ascertained by reference" to the following factors:

1. Is the incorporating language used sufficiently clear?

2. Does the document to be incorporated expressly state that its contents are to be applicable to the other party sought to be bound? [—8—]

3. Is the document to be incorporated a common source of terms that are implied into such agreements of the same genre as the contract?

4. Did the party sought to be bound by the incorporated terms have access to, and/or was he in fact aware of the document at all material times?

5. Did the party sought to be bound by the incorporated document challenge or object to the applicability of the terms of that document to the contract?

Applying these factors, Mr. Tan opined that due to the "easy availability" of WFS Singapore's General Terms on the internet, as well as the "customary" nature of including such terms in "bunker supply contracts," the General Terms were validly incorporated into the contract, and are enforceable under Singapore law. Mr. Tan also concluded that "[u]nder Singapore law, a contractual provision for governing law where stipulated by parties in their agreement will generally be upheld as valid and enforceable."[1] *See also Trans-Tec,* 518 F.3d at 1126-27 ("That a maritime lien might exist on the vessel under United States law, but would not exist under Malaysian law, was a consequence obviously contemplated by the contracting parties, and . . . results in no fundamental unfairness.").

Bulk Juliana contends that the district court erred in accepting Mr. Tan's conclusions. Under Bulk Juliana's interpretation of the contract, neither the General Terms nor the U.S. choice-of-law provision was incorporated into [—9—] the contract. Specifically, Bulk Juliana argues that that the fourth factor recited by Mr. Tan—"Did the party sought to be bound by the incorporated terms [the vessel] have access to, and/or was he in fact aware of the document at all material times?"—weighs clearly against WFS Singapore because the bunker delivery notes received by the vessel made absolutely no mention of WFS Singapore, the General Terms, or U.S. law. Therefore, the district court misapplied Singapore law in holding that the U.S. choice of law clause was binding on Bulk Juliana and the vessel *in rem*. Absent this clause, Singapore law does not recognize

---

[1] Mr. Tan also cited *Halsbury's Laws of Singapore*, para. 75.344, which states:

Where an express choice has been made of the law of a country, even if the transaction has no connection with the country whose law is chosen, the choice will be given effect unless the choice was illegal or not made bona fide, or if the application of the foreign law will be contrary to the fundamental public policy of the forum.

maritime liens. *See Sembawang Shipyard, Ltd. v. Charger, Inc.*, 955 F.2d 983, 988 (5th Cir. 1992) (holding that, unlike U.S. law, maritime liens are not authorized by Singapore law).

Bulk Juliana has failed to controvert Mr. Tan's testimony. The record is clear that Mr. Tan considered and applied the fourth factor, as well as the other factors, before concluding that the contract was "sufficiently specific to its reference" to the General Terms. Moreover, Mr. Tan opined that in his experience, "it is customary for bunker supply contracts to be concluded on the basis of the supplier's standard terms and conditions that are incorporated by reference in the bunker confirmation." Even assuming *arguendo* that WFS Singapore failed to satisfy the fourth factor described by Mr. Tan, Bulk Juliana offered no authority for the proposition that the failure to establish one out of five factors is fatal to the incorporation of the General Terms under Singaporean law.

Although Mr. Tan's testimony did not address the bunker delivery notes, he affirmed the incorporation of the General Terms by reference to the bunker confirmation email, which provided all the relevant terms and conditions of the contract. We recognize that neither Bulk Juliana nor the vessel was a party to the bunker confirmation email, and therefore did not have access to and/or awareness of the specific document at all material times. Mr. Tan, however, [—10—] testified about the ready availability of the contractual terms via the internet, as well as the prevalence of the practices employed here with respect to sales of necessaries in the shipping industry. Importantly, Mr. Tan pointed out that WFS Singapore's incorporation of the General Terms was "commonplace in the bunkering industry worldwide, and ought to be in the contemplation of ship operators and ship-owners such as [Bulk Juliana]."

Accordingly, the district court did not err in holding that the General Terms, including the U.S. choice-of-law provision, were valid and enforceable under Singapore law and were

validly incorporated into the contract.[2] The remainder of our analysis, contrary to Bulk Juliana's arguments, relies on United States law.

II. Whether Denmar, the charterer, could bind the vessel through a maritime lien even though Bulk Juliana, the owner, was not a party to the contract between WFS Singapore and Denmar

The district court determined that Denmar had presumptive authority to bind the vessel by procuring necessaries even though Bulk Juliana was not a party to the contract with WFS Singapore. Therefore, the maritime lien *in rem* pursuant to the FMLA was valid. *See Triton Marine Fuels, Ltd v. M/V PACIFIC CHUKOTKA*, 575 F.3d 409, 414 (4th Cir. 2009) (quoting *Trans–Tec*, 518 F.3d at 1127-28 (9th Cir.2008)) ("It is a fundamental tenet of maritime law that '[c]harterers and their agents are presumed to have authority to bind the vessel by the ordering of necessaries.'"). This result flows from the application [—11—] of U.S. maritime law, as interpreted by this court and others. Nevertheless, Bulk Juliana challenges the principle that the vessel, a "third party" stranger to the sale, could be bound by the Denmar-WFS Singapore contract for bunkers.

Like the district court, we must follow this court's decision in *QUEEN OF LEMAN*, which unabashedly enforced, against a non-party to the contract, a maritime lien for vessel insurance, which was created under the auspices of a choice of law clause. *Liverpool & London S.S. Protection & Indemnity Ass'n. v. QUEEN OF LEMAN M/V*, 296 F.3d 350, 354-55 (5th Cir. 2002). Bulk Juliana attempts to distinguish this decision on the basis that the

---

[2] Bulk Juliana contends for the first time on appeal that this case presents a recognized exception to the enforcement of a choice-of-law provision—when such a provision is used for the sole purpose of avoiding other applicable law. *See Peh Teck Quee v. Bayerische Landesbank Girozentrale* [1999] 3 SLR (R) 842, 848. On this basis, Bulk Juliana argues that the provision is unenforceable. Bulk Juliana has waived this argument by not raising it in the district court. *See Singleton v. Wulff*, 428 U.S. 106, 120 (1976).

underlying maritime lien in *QUEEN OF LEMAN* was imposed by a contract with one owner of a vessel but enforced against the vessel after its acquisition by another owner. From the standpoint of the third party's lack of knowledge and failure to acquiesce in the creation of the debt, however, we see no principled distinction from this case. Nor have other circuits, which have cited *QUEEN OF LEMAN* with approval in the course of enforcing maritime necessaries liens authorized pursuant to enforcement of choice of law clauses calling for U.S. law. *See Triton Marine Fuels*, 575 F.3d at 414-15; *Trans-Tec*, 518 F.3d at 1126-27.

In fact, each of those cases arises from facts quite similar to those before us. *Triton* upheld a U.S. maritime lien claimed against a vessel and its owner by a foreign company that supplied bunkers in a foreign port. *Trans-Tec* validated a choice of U.S. law, and thus the FMLA lien, where the choice of law was adopted in a contract concerning the sale of fuel to a foreign-flagged vessel in a foreign port. The *Trans-Tec* court quoted *QUEEN OF LEMAN*'s proposition that "there is nothing absurd about applying the law of the jurisdiction into which the ship sails, as the ship's presence in the jurisdiction represents a substantial contact." *Trans-Tec*, 518 F.3d at 1126 (quoting [—12—] *QUEEN OF LEMAN*, 296 F.3d at 354.). The court went on to explain, "*QUEEN OF LEMAN* thus counsels that where foreign parties have specified that they want United States law to determine the existence of a maritime lien in a transaction involving multiple foreign points of contact, and the ship has sailed into the United States, it is reasonable to uphold the choice of American law." *Id.*

It is hard to understand why, but Bulk Juliana acknowledged the holdings of *Triton* and *Trans-Tec* adverse to its position only in a footnote in its brief. Instead, it relies heavily on the Second Circuit's decision in *Rainbow Line, Inc. v. M/V Tequila*, 480 F.2d 1024 (2d Cir. 1973). The Second Circuit alone is arguably contrary to *QUEEN OF LEMAN*. Unlike Bulk Juliana, we do not believe the majority of circuit courts have erred legally or practically when they have found it

appropriate to enforce maritime choice of U.S. law clauses, and the resultant FMLA liens, in these cases. Owners of ocean-going vessels are by their nature internationally oriented, sophisticated, and fully able to protect themselves contractually in their dealings with time charterers from any perceived unfairness by the possible enforcement of maritime necessaries liens in U.S. ports. Further, "recognition of freely negotiated contract terms encourages predictability and certainty in the realm of international maritime transactions." *Trans-Tec*, 518 F.3d at 1131.

As a matter of black-letter law under the FMLA, based on the parties' valid choice of U.S. law and the holdings of this circuit and others, Denmar as time charterer had authority to bind the vessel *in rem* for its purchase of bunkers, and the lien is enforceable in U.S. courts.

III. Whether the maritime lien was created by a contractual term, rather than by an operation of law

Bulk Juliana contends that the U.S. choice-of-law provision in the contract between Denmar and WFS Singapore was an improper attempt to [—13—] create a maritime lien by contract where none can arise except by operation of law. *Rainbow Line*, 480 F.2d at 1026. Citing *QUEEN OF LEMAN*, however, the district court determined that the maritime lien did not arise simply as a matter of contract, but as a matter of law under the FMLA. *World Fuel Servs. Singapore*, 2015 WL 575201, at *6. We agree. The maritime lien on the vessel was not created merely by the terms of the Denmar-WFS Singapore contract. As stated above, the U.S. choice-of-law provision in the contract includes the FMLA. Because the FMLA creates the authority for a charterer to bind the vessel through the procurement of necessaries, a valid maritime lien was created by operation of U.S. law.[3]

---

[3] Bulk Juliana's reliance on *Gulf Trading & Transp. Co. v. The Vessel Hoegh Shield*, 658 F.2d 363 (5th Cir. 1981), is misplaced. In *Hoegh Shield*, as the court noted in *QUEEN OF* LEMAN, the contract at issue did not have a choice-of-law provision governing the existence of a maritime

IV. Whether the term "General Maritime Law of the United States" includes the maritime lien statute, 42 U.S.C. §§ 31341 and 31342.

Bulk Juliana asserts that the contract provision choosing the "General Maritime Law of the United States" incorporates not *all* U.S. maritime law but only judicially crafted maritime common law. *See McBride v. Estis Well Serv., L.L.C.*, 731 F.3d 505, 507-08, 1 Adm. R. 316, 316–17 (5th Cir. 2013). Bulk Juliana essentially contends that the contract relies on "general maritime law," a term of art limited to maritime common law. As such, the term excludes statutory maritime liens, which exist only under the FMLA. Without the express inclusion of the FMLA in the General Terms, WFS Singapore's contract did not recognize Denmar's authority to bind the vessel for purposes of a U.S. maritime lien. [—14—]

Paragraph seventeen of the General Terms provides:

> The General Terms and each Transaction shall be governed by the General Maritime Law of the United States . . . [t]he General Maritime Law of the United States shall apply with respect to the existence of a maritime lien, regardless of the country in which Seller takes legal action. . . . .

Once the validity and enforceability of the choice of law clause were upheld pursuant to Singapore law, the contract's interpretation is controlled by U.S. law. The district court noted that a conclusion that the "General Maritime Law of the United States" term includes the FMLA is supported by the general principles of contract interpretation. *World Fuel Servs. Singapore*, 2015 WL 575201, at *6. The district court stated:

> Clearly WFS chose for its bunker supply contracts the General Maritime Law of the United States because it wanted to secure payments in the form of maritime

lien. *Hoegh Shield*, 658 F.2d at 368. The same distinction pertains to *Arochem Corp. v. Wilomi, Inc.*, 962 F.2d 496 (4th Cir. 1992).

liens. To read the language so narrowly as to conclude that it includes only maritime common law and not maritime statutory law divorces the language from the intended meaning behind it . . . . Only where other tools of contract interpretation do not resolve the dispute does a court deem a term ambiguous and interpret it against its drafter.

Id.; *see also Chembulk Trading LLC v. Chemex Ltd.*, 393 F.3d 550, 555 (5th Cir. 2004) ("A basic principle of contract interpretation in admiralty law is to interpret, to the extent possible, all the terms in a contract without rendering any of them meaningless or superfluous.").

We agree with the district court. Numerous references in the contract refer to maritime liens. The bunker confirmation email specified that the buyer is "presumed" to have authority to bind the vessel with a maritime lien. The contractual language within WFS Singapore's U.S. choice-of-law provision amplifies that: "The General Maritime Law of the United States shall apply with respect to the existence of a maritime lien." This language would make no sense if "General Maritime Law" were construed as a term of art that [—15—] distinguishes between U.S. maritime common law and the FMLA. Paragraph 8(d) of the General Terms provides that: "Any bunkers ordered by an agent, management company, *charterer*, broker or any other party are ordered on behalf of the registered owner and the registered owner is liable as a principal for payment of the bunker invoice." (emphasis added). Because the FMLA provides the exclusive method for a charterer (like Denmar) to bind a vessel through the procurement of necessaries—the maritime lien—without the knowledge of the vessel owner, it is a natural inference that the term "General Maritime Law of the United States" includes the FMLA. Paragraph 8(a) also warrants that the seller will have and may enforce a maritime lien. Bulk Juliana's effort to isolate and artificially constrict the meaning of the choice of law clause in this contract fails in the face of the contract's numerous references to maritime liens.

In addition to using the tools of contract interpretation, the district court relied on another district court decision, *World Fuel Servs. Trading*, 12 F. Supp. 3d at 792, that interpreted an identical U.S. choice-of-law provision. Tracing the history of American maritime lien law in detail, the *World Fuel Servs. Trading* court concluded that the "General Maritime Law of the United States" necessarily included the FMLA because "the 1971 deletion of the duty-of-inquiry 'statutory text' from the Federal Maritime Lien Act clearly evidences Congress's intent to 'speak directly to [the] question,' of whether a supplier of necessaries has a duty to inquire as to the presence and terms of a charter party." *Id.* at 807 (citations omitted). Consequently, "because 'the general maritime law must comply with [Congress's] resolution' of this 'particular issue,'" the *World Fuel Servs. Trading* court held that "'the General Maritime Law of the United States,' includes the Federal Maritime [—16—] Lien Act."[4] *Id.* (citations omitted). The Fourth Circuit affirmed the district court on the more limited basis that Florida law, alternatively applicable to this contract under the General Terms, must apply federal statutes pursuant to the Constitution's Supremacy Clause. Either way, our decision is consistent with the result in the Fourth Circuit's case.

---

[4] On appeal, the Fourth Circuit "assum[ed], without deciding that . . . the FMLA is not part of the "General Maritime Law of the United States." *World Fuel Servs. Trading*, 783 F.3d at 521, 3 Adm. R. 201, 211 (4th Cir. 2015). The Fourth Circuit then proceeded under Florida law—as authorized by the residual language of paragraph 17 of the General Terms—and held that the "Supreme Court has long stated that 'a fundamental principle in our system of complex national policy mandates that the Constitution, laws, and treaties of the United States are as much a part of the law of every state as its own local laws and Constitution.'" *Id.*, 3 Adm. R. at 211 (citations omitted). Therefore, a "choice-of-law provision directing us to the laws of Florida thus encompasses federal statutory law, including the FMLA." *Id.*, 3 Adm. R. at 211.

CONCLUSION

For the foregoing reasons, we **AFFIRM** the order of the district court enforcing the maritime lien and **REMAND** for further proceedings consistent herewith.

United States Court of Appeals
for the Fifth Circuit

No. 15-30597

IN RE DEEPWATER HORIZON

SEACOR HOLDINGS, INC.
vs.
MASON

Appeal from the United States District Court for the
Eastern District of Louisiana

Decided: April 6, 2016

Citation: 819 F.3d 190, 4 Adm. R. 248 (5th Cir. 2016).

Before **KING, SOUTHWICK,** and **HAYNES,** Circuit
Judges.

[—2—] **HAYNES,** Circuit Judge:

Duwayne Mason appeals the district
court's grant of summary judgment in
favor of Seacor Holdings, Inc., Seacor
Offshore, L.L.C., and Seacor Marine, L.L.C.
(collectively, "Seacor"), as well as the denial of
Mason's motion to be recognized as a plaintiff
who opted out of the class action settlement at
issue in this case. For the reasons that follow,
we AFFIRM.

I.

This is one of the many cases to arise from
the Deepwater Horizon oil spill, the facts of
which are well known and need not be recited
at great length. Suffice it to say, Seacor owned
and operated the M/V SEACOR VANGUARD,
a vessel that assisted in putting out the fire
after the explosion in the Gulf of Mexico and
that subsequently took part in the cleanup
efforts. [—3—]

In response to a class action filed against it
relating to damages stemming from the
Deepwater Horizon incident, Seacor filed a
limitation of liability action under 46 U.S.C.
§ 30505 ("Limitation Action"). Duwayne
Mason, an employee of Seacor and a member
of the crew aboard the M/V SEACOR
VANGUARD, filed a claim in the Limitation
Action, alleging that while assisting in the
firefighting efforts aboard the M/V SEACOR

VANGUARD, he was "subjected to intense,
prolonged exposure to chemicals, smoke,
heat[,] and other noxious by-products of the
rig fire resulting in severe and permanent
damage to . . . claimant's lungs and other
parts of his body." In a separate lawsuit
against Seacor, Mason further alleged that
"[w]hile engaged in collecting the oil and
dispersant, plaintiff was exposed to crude oil,
chemical components of the crude oil,
chemical dispersant[,] and other noxious by-
products of the rig fire and oil spill, resulting
in severe and permanent damage to his lungs
and other parts of his body." These two claims
were consolidated with the Deepwater
Horizon multidistrict litigation ("MDL").

"In order to manage this complex litigation,
the district court issued Pretrial Order No. 11
establishing several 'pleading bundles' into
each of which claims of similar nature would
be placed for the purpose of filing a master
complaint, answers, and any Rule 12
motions." *Ctr. for Biological Diversity, Inc. v.
BP Am. Prod. Co.*, 704 F.3d 413, 419, 1 Adm.
R. 193, 194 (5th Cir. 2013). Relevant to this
appeal are bundles: B3, which included claims
related to cleanup efforts and personal injury
or medical monitoring claims for exposure or
other injuries; and B4, which included claims
against owners and operators of response
vessels. After the district court ruled on
motions to dismiss related to pleading bundle
B3, BP American Production Co., BP
Exploration & Production Inc., and BP P.L.C.
(collectively, "BP") negotiated the Medical
Benefits Settlement Agreement (the
"Agreement"), which addresses the claims in
the B3 pleading bundle. The Agreement was
filed with the district court on April 18, 2012,
and [—4—] subsequently amended on May 1,
2012. This Agreement applied to the "Medical
Benefits Settlement Class," which was defined
as natural persons who worked as clean-up
workers between April 20, 2010, and April 16,
2012. The agreement further defined "cleanup workers" as natural persons who
performed response activities, which in turn
was defined as "the clean-up, remediation
efforts, and all other responsive actions
(including the use and handling of
dispersants) relating to the release of oil,
other hydrocarbons, and other substances

from the MC252 WELL and/or the *Deepwater Horizon* and its appurtenances . . . ."

Under the Agreement, all released claims of the class members against all released parties would be dismissed once the Agreement became effective, including those for personal and bodily injuries related to the Deepwater Horizon incident. The Agreement specifically identifies the released parties as including, among others, Seacor. The district court preliminarily approved the Agreement and set forth procedures for individuals to opt out from the Medical Benefits Settlement Class.[1] The initial opt-out deadline was ultimately extended to November 1, 2012. The court granted final approval of the Agreement on January 11, 2013, and the effective date of the Agreement was February 12, 2014.

After the Agreement had been filed with the court, but several months before the opt-out period had expired, Mason moved to sever his claims from [—5—] the MDL. This motion provided that "Mason hereby certifies that he has filed no claim in connection with the BP oil spill nor have any claims been submitted in connection with the [Agreement]." Furthermore, it stated that "[u]ndersigned counsel has thoroughly investigated the nature of the [Agreement] and is satisfied that an adequate remedy is not available for his client within the ambit of that settlement. Undersigned counsel's investigation has been confirmed through detailed discussions with members of the Plaintiffs' Steering Committee handling the MDL."

---

[1] The court ordered that "any Medical Benefits Settlement Class Member wishing to exclude himself or herself from the Medical Benefits Settlement Class must submit a written request stating 'I wish to exclude myself from the Medical Benefits Settlement Class' (or substantially similar clear and unambiguous language), and also containing that Medical Benefits Settlement Class Member's printed name, address, phone number, and date of birth, and enclosing a copy of his or her driver's license or other government-issued identification. The written request to Opt Out must be signed by the Medical Benefits Settlement Class Member seeking to exclude himself or herself from the Medical Benefits Settlement Class . . . ." The Agreement also describes this opt-out procedure.

In its opposition to the motion to sever— filed over a month before the opt-out period expired—Seacor noted that Mason's claims appeared to fall within the ambit of the B3 pleading bundle and the Agreement. Seacor also opposed the motion to sever because it claimed it would "necessarily have to implead others who may have caused" the oil spill at the heart of the class action if "compelled to defend itself in a proceeding that raises the very same issues as those common to the B3 and B4 pleading bundles." On March 5, 2013—after the opt-out deadline—the court denied the motion to sever.[2] Three weeks later, Mason contacted the claims administrator of the Agreement, maintaining that he was not a member of the Medical Benefits Settlement Class, and stating that if he were a member, he wished to be excluded. The [—6—] court denied Mason's subsequent motion to reconsider or in the alternative to extend the opt-out deadline.[3]

---

[2] After the opt-out deadline, in response to the denial of the motion to sever, Mason's counsel filed an affidavit seeking to clarify that he did not view Mason's claims as falling within the Agreement or as relating to the oil spill because they were filed against Seacor, not BP, and because Mason did not personally collect dispersant or participate in recovery and cleanup efforts, except as an engineer in the engine room of the M/V SEACOR VANGUARD while other crew members helped with those efforts. As discussed herein, Mason does not appeal his status as a member of the Medical Benefits Settlement Class. Therefore, we need not and do not address whether the district court properly concluded that Mason is a member of the Medical Benefits Settlement Class whose claims constitute "Released Claims" under the Agreement.

[3] Mason moved for the district court to extend the deadline to opt out, and his appellate briefs include vague language concerning the district court's refusal to extend the opt-out deadline. Yet, Mason does not now appear to challenge the district court's refusal to extend the opt-out deadline. Even if he meant to pursue this issue on appeal, Mason's briefing is vague and entirely unsupported by any citations to authority. We thus do not consider whether the district court should have extended the time for Mason to opt out, as we find any argument on this issue abandoned through inadequate briefing. *See, e.g., Young v. Repine (In re Repine)*, 536 F.3d 512, 518 n.5 (5th Cir. 2008); *see also* FED. R. APP. P. 28(a)(8).

After the Agreement became effective, Seacor moved for summary judgment on Mason's claims against it, citing the release provision of the Agreement. The district court granted the motion and entered final judgment in favor of Seacor, holding that Mason "is a member of the Medical Class" covered by the Agreement and that his claims against Seacor had been released by the Agreement. Additionally, in accordance with its denial of Mason's motion to sever, the district court concluded that Mason's motion to sever was not an effective opt out of the Agreement and that Mason's counsel received sufficient actual notice of that Agreement, and the court declined to extend the opt-out deadline for Mason. Mason timely appealed.

II.

We have jurisdiction over this appeal from an order of final judgment under 28 U.S.C. § 1291. As a preliminary matter, Mason does not appeal his status as a member of the Medical Benefits Settlement Class. Moreover, there is no dispute that Mason did not follow the opt-out procedure set forth by the district court. Rather, Mason's appeal is best understood as raising two issues:

1. Whether the district court abused its discretion in failing to determine that Mason had opted out through informal means; and [—7—]

2. Whether the district court erroneously determined that Mason had received sufficient notice of the Medical Benefits Settlement Agreement.

We address each issue in turn.

A. Informal Opt Out

As a threshold issue, Mason contends it is unclear what standard of review applies to whether a "non-formal" attempt to opt out should be recognized in these circumstances. To the extent we have not spoken on the proper standard of review for a district court's determination of whether a member of a class action proposed for settlement under Rule 23(b)(3) & (c)(2)(B) has opted out of that class,

we hold that review is for an abuse of discretion. *See In re Nissan Motor Corp. Antitrust Litig.*, 552 F.2d 1088, 1096 (5th Cir. 1977) ("In the management of class actions, Federal Rule Civil Procedure 23 necessarily vests the district courts with a broad discretion to enable efficacious administration of the course of the proceedings . . . ."); *see also Sanders v. John Nuveen & Co.*, 524 F.2d 1064, 1075 (7th Cir. 1975), *vacated on other grounds*, 425 U.S. 929 (1976); *cf. Silvercreek Mgmt., Inc. v. Banc of Am. Sec., LLC*, 534 F.3d 469, 473 (5th Cir. 2008) (reviewing a district court's decision whether to extend the opt-out period for an abuse of discretion).

We have consistently applied the abuse of discretion standard in analogous contexts. *Cf. Ayers v. Thompson*, 358 F.3d 356, 368 (5th Cir. 2004) ("[A] district court's denial of a motion to opt out of a class certified under Rule 23(b)(2) is reviewed for abuse of discretion."); *Nichols v. Mobile Bd. of Realtors, Inc.*, 675 F.2d 671, 679 (5th Cir. Unit B 1982) ("A district court's decision on class certification is reviewable only for abuse of discretion."). Other federal courts of appeals have also applied the abuse of discretion standard in similar circumstances. *See, e.g., In re Managed Care Litig.*, 605 F.3d 1146, 1150 (11th Cir. 2010) (reviewing "denials of requests for extensions of time to opt out and denials of assertions of judicial estoppel under the abuse-of-discretion [—8—] standard"); *In re Painewebber Ltd. Partnerships Litig.*, 147 F.3d 132, 135 (2d Cir. 1998) (similar); *cf. In re Vitamins Antitrust Class Actions*, 327 F.3d 1207, 1208–10 (D.C. Cir. 2003) (reviewing for an abuse of discretion the district court's decision to allow an untimely opt out); *Silber v. Mabon*, 18 F.3d 1449, 1453 (9th Cir. 1994) (reviewing the denial of a motion to opt out for an abuse of discretion).

Having established the proper standard of review, we turn to Mason's arguments on the merits. In his first issue on appeal, Mason maintains that his conduct was sufficient to opt out of the Medical Benefits Settlement Agreement by informal means. In so arguing, he points to four actions: (1) the motion to sever; (2) the motion for reconsideration; (3) communication with the claims center; and (4) the request for an extension of the opt-out deadline. The latter three all occurred after the opt-out deadline, so we do not consider them. We consider only Mason's argument that the motion to sever should be deemed an effective "informal" opt out. *Cf. In re Four Seasons Securities Laws Litigation*, 493 F.2d 1288, 1289–91 (10th Cir. 1974) (holding that conduct *prior to the opt-out deadline* was sufficient to constitute an opt out); *Council on Soc. Work Educ., Inc. v. Tex. Instruments Inc.*, 105 F.R.D. 68, 71 (N.D. Tex. 1985) (similar).

We have not directly addressed the degree to which an effort to opt out that does not conform to the designated procedures can be treated as an effective opt out. Case law from other circuits and from the district courts suggests that an opt out request need not perfectly conform to the format chosen by the district court or the proposed settlement agreement to effectively express a desire to opt out of a class action settlement. For example, in *In re Four Seasons Securities Laws Litigation*, the Tenth Circuit concluded that notice of an intent to opt out was communicated by a letter sent to a trustee and the plaintiffs' attorneys from a class-member bank, inquiring whether the [—9—] bank could submit a modified form so that it could remain a member of the class and still pursue a separate suit previously filed in state court. 493 F.2d at 1289–91; *see also Self v. Ill. Cent. R.R.*, No. CIV. A. 96-4141, 1999 WL 262099, at *1–2 (E.D. La. Apr. 29, 1999) (construing a motion to remand a case to state court as sufficiently expressing an intent to opt out when 586 individual plaintiffs "vigorously opposed" removal and inclusion with the class action and following remand, proceeded in state court without notice of the need to opt out of the federal action); *Bonner v. Tex. City Indep. Sch. Dist. of Tex.*, 305 F. Supp. 600, 617 (S.D. Tex. 1969) (declining to certify a class action and relying on the trial testimony of three potential class members that they did not wish to be involved in the action in any way as evincing a desire to opt out of the potential class).

These decisions logically follow from the desire not to require class members "to retain counsel and prepare a formal legal document"

in order to opt out while preventing excessive informal opt outs that "might pose problems of authenticity and ambiguity." 7AA Charles Alan Wright, et al., Federal Practice and Procedure § 1787 (3d ed. 2005). In cases often involving hundreds of unrepresented and potentially unsophisticated parties, some courts have concluded that "considerable flexibility is desirable in determining what constitutes an effective expression of a class member's desire to be excluded." *Id.* Although we have not addressed the precise requirements for allowing class members to informally opt out of class settlements, other courts have concluded that reasonableness is key. *Cf. In re Four Seasons*, 493 F.2d at 1291 ("A *reasonable* indication of a desire to opt out ought to be sufficient." (emphasis added)); *Plummer v. Chem. Bank*, 668 F.2d 654, 657 n.2 (2d Cir. 1982) ("Any *reasonable* indication of a desire to opt out should suffice." (emphasis added)); *Johnson v. Hercules Inc.*, No. CV298-102, 1999 WL 35648160, at *5 (S.D. Ga. Apr. 28, 1999) ("The Court requires nothing more, [—10—] and nothing less, than an unequivocal, explicit, *reasonable*, and timely request for exclusion." (emphasis added)).

We need not decide whether to adopt the approach of these other courts because, even assuming arguendo that we did so, we are presented with vastly different circumstances in this case from those in these other cases. Rather than an informal but unequivocal expression of a desire to opt out or the submission of an imperfect opt out request, the conduct of Mason and his attorneys more closely resembles an after-the-fact attempt to depict completely distinct litigation conduct in another sphere as expressing a desire to opt out.

The district court provided sound reasons for refusing to treat the motion to sever as an opt out. Mason's attorney made clear in an affidavit filed with the district court that he had not discussed the need to opt out with his client before the opt-out date. Additionally, Mason did not sign the motion to sever. These facts show that the motion to sever could not have been interpreted as an informal but effective opt out in this case, to the extent that we would even recognize such an opt out. As the district court noted, the Agreement required that an opt out be signed by the class member, not the attorney, in order to "ensure that the exclusion was with the client's express consent." The district court noted that it "consistently enforced" this "common and practical requirement" throughout the MDL. Since Mason's attorney failed to discuss the need to opt out with his client before the opt-out deadline and Mason did not sign the motion to sever, the district court reasonably concluded the motion to sever could not have been interpreted as an effective opt out of the Agreement. Additional factors supporting the district court's decision include that the motion to sever itself was not "unequivocal" in evincing a desire to opt out, particularly in the event that it was denied. The district court also found relevant that Mason's attorney had actual notice of the settlement and said he [—11—] had "thoroughly investigated" the Agreement,[4] and that Mason's attorney had not followed a court-ordered procedure that would have given him additional information about the Agreement.

Additionally, the district court expressed concern about setting precedent for similar requests in the MDL. That concern has particular relevance in this litigation. Although a concern for encouraging clarity in opt out requests is relevant in many class actions, this case is no ordinary class action. It is particularly complex, even epic, given the number of plaintiffs and defendants, the different types of claims involved (represented by the various pleading bundles), and the thousands of filings before the district court. Indeed, the docket sheet for this case spans over 1,300 pages of the appellate record, representing almost 15,000 docket entries.

The gargantuan size and extraordinary complexity of this litigation therefore supports the district court's decision. This multidistrict litigation "consists of hundreds of cases, with over 100,000 individual claimants . . . ." *Ctr. for Biological Diversity*, 704 F.3d at 419, 1 Adm. R. at 194. When the district court approved the Agreement, it noted the class had potentially 200,000 members and that over 1,700 individuals sent opt-out requests to the claims administrator. Given the size and complexity of this MDL proceeding, the court and parties should not have to intuit an opt out from vague statements made in one of thousands of filings before the court. To hold otherwise would allow class members to make ambiguous statements and motions while waiting to see if the outcome of the class action is favorable. The 1966 amendments to Rule 23 sought to [—12—] prevent exactly this type of gamesmanship. *See In re Nissan Motor*, 552 F.2d at 1104; *Amati v. City of Woodstock*, 176 F.3d 952, 957 (7th Cir. 1999).[5]

The district court has "especially strong and flexible" managerial power in this highly complex MDL. *Ctr. for Biological Diversity*, 704 F.3d at 432, 1 Adm. R. at 205. We will not disturb the eminently reasonable use of that discretion in this circumstance, which does not involve an unrepresented class member, an imperfect opt out request, or an unequivocal but informal expression of an intent to opt out. Accordingly, even assuming arguendo that a reasonable indication of a desire to opt out would suffice, we conclude that the district court did not abuse its discretion in determining that Mason's conduct did not reasonably indicate a desire to

---

[4] As we discuss *infra*, notice to Mason's attorney is imputed to Mason. *See Link v. Wabash R.R. Co.*, 370 U.S. 626, 633–34 & n.10 (1962); *Resendiz v. Dretke*, 452 F.3d 356, 362 (5th Cir. 2006); *Wilson v. Sec'y, Dep't of Veterans Affairs on Behalf of Veterans Canteen Servs.*, 65 F.3d 402, 405 (5th Cir. 1995), *as amended on denial of reh'g* (Nov. 1, 1995); *cf. New York v. Hill*, 528 U.S. 110, 115 (2000).

[5] Mason asserts that the district court erroneously failed to consider the complexity and confusing nature of his claim vis-à-vis the pleading bundles in determining whether he informally opted out. First, Mason has not identified any authority that this consideration is relevant under the law. Second, there is no indication that the district court failed to consider this fact. Third, even assuming this consideration is relevant to the informal opt-out analysis, the remaining facts still overwhelmingly support the district court's decision determining that Mason did not informally opt out, particularly since Mason was represented by counsel to aid him in any complexities.

opt out of the Medical Benefits Settlement Class.

B. Notice of the Medical Benefits Settlement Agreement

In his second issue on appeal, Mason maintains that the notice of the Agreement was constitutionally deficient in both delivery and content. These objections seek to challenge the sufficiency of the notice given regarding the Medical Benefits Settlement Agreement, although this court has already affirmed the district court's order approving the Agreement and the attendant notice procedures. *See In re Deepwater Horizon*, 739 F.3d 790, 819–21, 2 Adm. R. 140, 160–62 (5th Cir. 2014). In fact, BP and others challenged the sufficiency of the notice given to absent class members as part of that appeal, and a panel of this court [—13—] concluded the district court did not abuse its discretion in finding notice of the Agreement was sufficient. *See id.* at 819, 2 Adm. R. at 160–61.

"As a general rule, a judgment in a class action will bind the members of the class." *Kemp v. Birmingham News Co.*, 608 F.2d 1049, 1054 (5th Cir. 1979), *abrogated in part on other grounds by Nilsen v. City of Moss Point, Miss.*, 701 F.2d 556, 560 (5th Cir. 1983). Since Mason does not appeal his status as a member of the Medical Benefits Settlement Class or whether his claims are now "Released Claims" under the Agreement, the judgment affirming approval of the Agreement would typically bar his challenge to notice given about the Agreement.

However, there is an "exception to this rule[,] grounded in due process." *Kemp*, 608 F.2d at 1054. For example, the Eleventh Circuit has held that "[a]bsent class members can collaterally challenge the res judicata effect of a prior class judgment . . . because there was not adequate notice . . . ." *Juris v. Inamed Corp.*, 685 F.3d 1294, 1312–13 (11th Cir. 2012). We held similarly in an unpublished opinion, ultimately concluding that a class member who was not truly absent and who received the required notice was precluded from challenging the prior class action judgment. *See Hunter v. Transamerica*

Life Ins. Co., 498 F. App'x 430, 435 (5th Cir. 2012)[6]; *cf. Gonzales v. Cassidy*, 474 F.2d 67, 74 (5th Cir. 1973).

The facts of this case indicate that Mason may not collaterally attack the class action judgment. Mason argues he was deprived of due process because Mason's attorney did not realize Mason would be considered a member of the Medical Benefits Settlement Class, did not receive any of the electronic filing notifications from the MDL, did not receive the Class Action Settlement [—14—] Notification, and paid no attention to published notifications regarding the Agreement. While *absent* class members may collaterally attack a class action judgment for a lack of notice and due process, Mason was arguably not absent because his counsel had actual notice of the Agreement. *See Hunter*, 498 F. App'x at 435; *Kemp*, 608 F.2d at 1054. Mason's attorney represented to the district court that he discussed the Agreement with the "Plaintiffs' Steering Committee handling the MDL" and that he "thoroughly investigated the nature of the [Agreement]." Even if he elected not to sign up to receive electronic notifications of filings in the MDL, in contravention of the district court's orders, Mason's attorney clearly had notice of the Agreement itself.[7]

These circumstances are inconsistent with the usual context in which we allow collateral attacks by an absent class member who lacked notice and any opportunity to object to a proposed settlement agreement. *Cf. Juris*, 685 F.3d at 1312–14. It is well established that notice to Mason's attorney is imputed to Mason. *See Link v. Wabash R.R. Co.*, 370 U.S. 626, 633–34 & n.10 (1962); *Resendiz v. Dretke*, 452 F.3d 356, 362 (5th Cir. 2006); *Wilson v. Sec'y, Dep't of Veterans Affairs on Behalf of Veterans Canteen Servs.*, 65 F.3d 402, 405 (5th Cir. 1995), *as amended on denial of reh'g* (Nov.

---

[6] Although *Hunter* is not "controlling precedent," it "may be [cited as] persuasive authority." *Ballard v. Burton*, 444 F.3d 391, 401 n.7 (5th Cir. 2006) (citing 5TH CIR. R. 47.5.4).

[7] Because we determine that Mason's counsel received actual notice, we do not address BP and Seacor's arguments that constructive notice given in this case also satisfies due process requirements.

1, 1995). "Thus, this is not a case where an absent class member did not receive notice at all." *Hunter*, 498 F. App'x at 435. Mason had actual notice through his counsel, which satisfies due process.[8] *See United Student Aid Funds, Inc. v. Espinosa*, 559 U.S. 260, [—15—] 272 (2010) (holding that the receipt of actual notice regarding the contents of a Chapter 13 plan satisfied the creditor's due process rights); *Kemp*, 608 F.2d at 1054.[9]

For these reasons, the judgment of the district court is AFFIRMED.

---

[8] Although we conclude Mason is precluded from collaterally attacking the judgment approving the Agreement, even if we assumed arguendo that Mason could attack the notice related to the Agreement, we would find his challenge meritless. Mason claims, inter alia, that the notice was deficient because "nothing in the notice would have alerted Mason that his Jones Act claims against Seacor, his employer, were subsumed in the settlement . . . ." Yet, the notice explicitly stated that "BP and all of the 'Released Parties' (identified in Section II.MMMM of the Medical Benefits Settlement Agreement)" would be released by the [—15—] Agreement for class members who did not opt out. Seacor is identified in the Agreement as a Released Party, an Agreement Mason's counsel claimed to have "thoroughly investigated." Even if Seacor was not specifically named in the notice sent to class members, other courts have found such notice sufficient. *See, e.g., Wal-Mart Stores, Inc. v. Visa U.S.A., Inc.*, 396 F.3d 96, 104–05, 109, 114 (2d Cir. 2005); *Reyn's Pasta Bella, LLC v. Visa USA, Inc.*, 442 F.3d 741, 748 (9th Cir. 2006).

[9] *See also Nunley v. Dep't of Justice*, 425 F.3d 1132, 1139 (8th Cir. 2005) (noting in the context of a forfeiture notice that "a person cannot complain about the constitutionality of the method used to provide notice when he or she has received actual notice (assuming it is timely), for he or she has suffered no harm"); *see, e.g., Diaz v. Romer*, 9 F.3d 116, 1993 WL 425143, at *1 (10th Cir. 1993) (unpublished) ("Because [the class member] had actual notice of the settlement agreement, he was not denied due process.").

United States Court of Appeals
for the Fifth Circuit

No. 15-30980

HEFREN
vs.
MCDERMOTT, INC.

Appeal from the United States District Court for the
Western District of Louisiana

Decided: April 25, 2016
Revised: June 6, 2016

Citation: 820 F.3d 767, 4 Adm. R. 255 (5th Cir. 2016).

Before **KING, CLEMENT,** and **OWEN,** Circuit Judges.

[—1—] PER CURIAM:

Plaintiff–Appellant James Hefren filed suit in state court against Defendant–Appellee McDermott, Inc., alleging personal injuries from McDermott's design and construction of the Front Runner Spar, an offshore drilling and production platform in the Gulf of Mexico. Following removal of the case to federal court, McDermott filed a motion for summary judgment, arguing that Hefren's claims were perempted under Louisiana state law and could no longer be brought. The district court granted the motion for summary judgment, and Hefren now appeals. For the following reasons, we AFFIRM the judgment of the district court. [—2—]

I. FACTUAL AND PROCEDURAL BACKGROUND

The instant case arises out of personal injuries allegedly sustained by Plaintiff–Appellant James Hefren while he was employed by Murphy Exploration & Production Company, USA (Murphy), as a lead operator on the Front Runner Spar. In March 2002, Murphy contracted with Defendant–Appellee McDermott, Inc. (McDermott) to have McDermott design and construct the Front Runner Spar, an offshore facility to be used by Murphy for removing and processing petroleum from the seabed of the Gulf of Mexico.[1] In May 2004, Murphy accepted delivery of the Front Runner Spar and affixed it to the seafloor at the outer continental shelf adjacent to the State of Louisiana where it has remained since, operating as a platform facility with three decks used for crew quarters, drilling, and production.

According to Hefren, he suffered significant injury on or about June 6, 2011, on the Front Runner Spar when a flange of a valve struck him in the face. Following his injury, Hefren filed suit against Murphy and McDermott in the 16th Judicial District Court for the Parish of St. Mary in Louisiana on June 4, 2012.[2] In his complaint, Hefren invoked jurisdiction under the Jones Act and general maritime law and asserted claims for negligence. Hefren alleged that both Murphy and McDermott failed to take precautions for Hefren's safety and specifically alleged that McDermott failed to properly design and construct the Front Runner Spar. Murphy then removed the matter to the United States District Court for the Western District of [—3—] Louisiana on July 12, 2012, asserting diversity jurisdiction under 28 U.S.C. § 1332 and jurisdiction under the Outer Continental Shelf Lands Act (OCSLA). Hefren subsequently filed a motion to remand his case to state court on August 13, 2012, arguing that he was a seaman under the Jones Act and that Jones Act claims could not be removed to federal court on the basis of diversity jurisdiction.[3] However, the motion

---

[1] As previously described by this court, "[a] spar is a nautical structure designed to float with the bulk of the hull below waves—something akin to a giant buoy," and spars have increasingly been used "to exploit oil and gas resources in deeper ocean waters." *Fields v. Pool Offshore, Inc.*, 182 F.3d 353, 355 (5th Cir. 1999).

[2] Hefren's initial complaint improperly named J. Ray McDermott Gulf Contractors, Inc., as a defendant rather than McDermott, Inc. Hefren later supplemented and amended his original complaint, substituting McDermott as a defendant.

[3] Under the Jones Act, "[a] seaman injured in the course of employment . . . may elect to bring a civil action at law, with the right of trial by jury, against the employer." 46 U.S.C. § 30104. Because the Jones Act incorporates "[l]aws of the United States regulating recovery for personal injury . . . of a railway employee," *id.*, it also incorporates those

was denied on October 25, 2012, by a magistrate judge who concluded that Hefren could not maintain a claim under the Jones Act because the Front Runner Spar was not a vessel and therefore Hefren was not a seaman. On May 2, 2013, the district court entered summary judgment for Murphy, dismissing Hefren's tort claims against Murphy as barred by the exclusive remedy provisions of the Longshore & Harbor Workers' Compensation Act.

On February 17, 2014, McDermott filed its own motion for summary judgment, seeking the dismissal of Hefren's claims against it with prejudice. McDermott argued that Hefren's claims were barred or perempted under La. Stat. Ann. § 9:2772, which provides that no action arising out of deficiencies in the design or construction of immovable property can be brought five years after the date on which the property is accepted by the owner.[4]

Because [—4—] Hefren's claims—relating to deficiencies in the Front Runner Spar—were brought in 2013 and Murphy took possession of the Front Runner Spar in 2004, McDermott argued that Hefren's claim was perempted and that McDermott was entitled to judgment as a matter of law. In response, Hefren argued that La. Stat. Ann. § 9:2772 did not apply to his claims against McDermott because the Front Runner Spar was not immovable as only its mooring system was attached to the seabed, allowing it to be unmoored and transported across the ocean. Hefren also argued that he asserted claims outside of the scope of that [—5—] statute when he claimed that McDermott failed to identify safety hazards to Murphy employees.

The district court granted McDermott's motion for summary judgment and dismissed Hefren's claims against McDermott with prejudice on April 9, 2014. Examining the

---

laws' prohibition against removal of actions filed in state court. *See* 28 U.S.C. § 1445(a) ("A civil action in any State court against a railroad or its receivers or trustees, arising under [federal laws applicable to the liability of railroads], may not be removed to any district court of the United States.").

[4] The applicable Louisiana statute provides, in relevant part:

A. Except as otherwise provided in this Subsection, no action, whether ex contractu, ex delicto, or otherwise, including but not limited to an action for failure to warn, to recover on a contract, or to recover damages, or otherwise arising out of an engagement of planning, construction, design, or building immovable or movable property which may include, without limitation, [—4—] consultation, planning, designs, drawings, specification, investigation, evaluation, measuring, or administration related to any building, construction, demolition, or work, shall be brought against any person performing or furnishing land surveying services, as such term is defined in R.S. 37:682, including but not limited to those services preparatory to construction, or against any person performing or furnishing the design, planning, supervision, inspection, or observation of construction or the construction of immovables, or improvement to immovable property, including but not limited to a residential building contractor as defined in R.S. 37:2150.1:

(1)(a) More than five years after the date of registry in the mortgage office of acceptance of the work by owner.

. . .

B. (1) The causes which are perempted within the time described above include any action:
(a) For any deficiency in the performing or furnishing of land surveying services, as such term is defined in R.S. 37:682, including but not limited to those preparatory to construction or in the design, planning, inspection, or observation of construction, or in the construction of any improvement to immovable property, including but not limited to any services provided by a residential building contractor as defined in R.S. 37:2150.1(9).
(b) For damage to property, movable or immovable, arising out of any such deficiency.
(c) For injury to the person or for wrongful death arising out of any such deficiency.
(d) Brought against a person for the action or failure to act of his employees.
(2) Deficiency, as used in this Section, includes failure to warn the owner of any dangerous or hazardous condition, regardless of when knowledge of the danger or hazard is obtained or should have been obtained.

La. Stat. Ann. § 9:2772.

undisputed facts, the court noted that the Front Runner Spar was "a structure permanently affixed to the seabed and not a vessel." The district court then noted that, although Louisiana courts and the Fifth Circuit had never concluded whether spars were immovable property, these courts had held that fixed, offshore platforms permanently affixed to the sea floor were immovable property and that spars were akin to offshore platforms. Based on these cases and certain features of the Front Runner Spar, the court held that the Spar was a "building" and constituted immovable property under La. Stat. Ann. § 9:2772. Among other features, the court noted that the Spar's mooring system was permanently attached to the seabed, the Spar was intended to be at its location for a twenty-year lifetime, it would take months of planning and work to remove the Spar from its anchored position in the Gulf of Mexico, and the Spar had remained fixed in its original location since being attached—even remaining there through several hurricanes. Regarding Hefren's assertion that some of his claims were not within La. Stat. Ann. § 9:2772, the court held that these claims were essentially failure to warn claims and were perempted by the statute. Hefren timely appealed the judgment.

II. STANDARD OF REVIEW

We review a grant of summary judgment *de novo*, applying the same standard as the district court. *Rogers v. Bromac Title Servs., L.L.C.*, 755 F.3d 347, 350 (5th Cir. 2014). Summary judgment is proper "if the movant shows that there is no genuine dispute as to any material fact and the movant is entitled to judgment as a matter of law." Fed. R. Civ. P. 56(a). A genuine dispute of material fact exists "if the evidence is such that a reasonable jury [—6—] could return a verdict for the nonmoving party." *Anderson v. Liberty Lobby, Inc.*, 477 U.S. 242, 248 (1986). However, "[a] mere scintilla of evidence will not preclude granting of a motion for summary judgment." *Schaefer v. Gulf Coast Reg'l Blood Ctr.*, 10 F.3d 327, 330 (5th Cir. 1994) (per curiam). "We construe all facts and inferences in the light most favorable to the nonmoving party

when reviewing grants of motions for summary judgment." *Dillon v. Rogers*, 596 F.3d 260, 266 (5th Cir. 2010) (quoting *Murray v. Earle*, 405 F.3d 278, 284 (5th Cir. 2005)).

III. PEREMPTION UNDER LOUISIANA STATE LAW

In determining whether Hefren's suit is barred, we look to Louisiana law under OCSLA because the Front Runner Spar is located on the outer continental shelf adjacent to the State of Louisiana. *See Fruge ex rel. Fruge v. Parker Drilling Co.*, 337 F.3d 558, 560 (5th Cir. 2003) ("OCSLA adopts the law of the adjacent state . . . as surrogate federal law, to the extent that it is not inconsistent with other federal laws and regulations.").[5] Under the applicable Louisiana law, any action relating to a deficiency "in the design, planning, inspection, or observation of construction, or in the construction of any improvement to immovable property," and alleging personal injury or "failure to warn," is perempted if brought "[m]ore than five years after . . . acceptance of the work by [the] owner." La. Stat. Ann. § 9:2772. Rather than simply [—7—] "barr[ing] the remedy to be enforced" like a statute of limitations, this "peremptive statute . . . totally destroys the previously existing right so that, upon expiration of the statutory period, a cause of action or substantive right no longer exists to be enforced." *KSLA-TV, Inc. v. Radio Corp. of Am.*, 732 F.2d 441, 443 (5th Cir. 1984) (per

---

[5] The applicable provision of OCSLA provides, in relevant part:

To the extent that they are applicable and not inconsistent with this subchapter or with other Federal laws and regulations of the Secretary now in effect or hereafter adopted, the civil and criminal laws of each adjacent State, now in effect or hereafter adopted, amended, or repealed are declared to be the law of the United States for that portion of the subsoil and seabed of the outer Continental Shelf, and artificial islands and fixed structures erected thereon, which would be within the area of the State if its boundaries were extended seaward to the outer margin of the outer Continental Shelf.

43 U.S.C. § 1333(a)(2)(A).

curiam). The parties here disagree over whether the Front Runner Spar is immovable property under Louisiana law. If it is, then Hefren's claims against McDermott fall within the Louisiana statute of peremption and no longer exist because they were brought more than five years after Murphy accepted delivery of the Front Runner Spar.[6]

As the district court properly concluded, the Front Runner Spar is immovable property and Hefren's claims are extinguished under La. Stat. Ann. § 9:2772. In *Olsen v. Shell Oil Co.*, 365 So. 2d 1285, 1290 (La. 1978), the Supreme Court of Louisiana recognized that a fixed offshore drilling platform constituted an immovable "building" within the meaning of a separate Louisiana statute. In particular, the court explained that, in determining whether an object was a building, there was "[a]n inherent requirement . . . that there be a structure of some permanence." *Id.* at 1289. Relying on *Olsen*, a Louisiana appellate court later found that a "fixed drilling platform was a separate immovable," within the meaning of La. Stat. Ann. § 9:2772. *Bruyninckx v. Bratten*, 554 So. 2d 247, 249 (La. Ct. App. 1989). Although spars are not the same as fixed drilling platforms, we have previously noted that a spar can resemble a fixed drilling platform because it "serve[s] as a work platform in a specific, fixed location for the foreseeable future," and is "secured [—8—] to the ocean floor . . . using an elaborate system that guarantees movement will be a difficult and expensive undertaking." *Fields*, 182 F.3d at 358; *see also Mendez v. Anadarko Petroleum Corp.*, 466 F. App'x 316, 317 (5th Cir. 2012) (per curiam) (unpublished) (noting that a spar's "features [we]re . . . consistent with a

fixed structure permanently moored far offshore").

While both *Fields* and *Mendez* were Jones Act cases that ultimately concluded that spars were not vessels for the purpose of the Jones Act, their discussion of spars illustrates the similarity of spars to fixed offshore drilling platforms that are considered immovable property under Louisiana law. This caselaw and the specific facts found by the district court lead us to conclude that the Front Runner Spar is immovable property. Like a "building" under Louisiana law, there is "some permanence" to the Front Runner Spar as it has not moved from its present location, is intended to remain there for its twenty year life, and has a permanent mooring system. *Olsen*, 365 So. 2d at 1289. And while Hefren argues that the Front Runner Spar cannot be immovable because it *could be* moved, he fails to address the district court's finding that it would take planning, work, and deconstruction of the Front Runner Spar in order to move it from its anchored position, a feature that gives the Spar "some permanence."[7] *Id.* [—9—]

IV. CONCLUSION

For the foregoing reasons, the judgment of the district court is AFFIRMED.

---

[6] Hefren argues that his claims against McDermott for failing to instruct Murphy employees on how to operate the equipment are not subject to the statute of peremption because he is alleging a failure to provide adequate instruction rather than a failure to warn. However, under Louisiana law, instructions and warnings are considered part of the design of an object, and both are subject to the statute of peremption as to design defect claims in La. Stat. Ann. § 9:2772. *Smith v. Arcadian Corp.*, 657 So. 2d 464, 469 (La. Ct. App. 1995).

[7] In the alternative, Hefren suggests that the question of whether the Front Runner Spar is immovable property should be certified to the Louisiana Supreme Court. We decline this invitation. Although Louisiana courts do not appear to have answered the question of whether spars are immovable property, we find sufficient guidance in the existing caselaw to decide the instant matter. *See Transcon. Gas Pipeline Corp. v. Transp. Ins. Co.*, 958 F.2d 622, 623 (5th Cir. 1992) (per curiam) ("Certification is not a panacea for resolution of those complex or difficult state law questions which have not been answered by the highest court of the state. Neither is it to be used as a convenient way to duck our responsibility in OCSLA or diversity jurisdiction.").

United States Court of Appeals
for the Fifth Circuit

No. 15-30690

PATTERSON
vs.
AKER SOLUTIONS INC.

Appeal from the United States District Court for the
Eastern District of Louisiana

Decided: June 13, 2016

Citation: 826 F.3d 231, 4 Adm. R. 259 (5th Cir. 2016).

Before HIGGINBOTHAM, DENNIS, and CLEMENT,
Circuit Judges.

[—1—] CLEMENT, Circuit Judge:

In this personal injury suit arising out of events occurring in waters off the coast of Russia, Danny Patterson appeals the district court's dismissal of defendant Aker Subsea AS ("Aker Subsea"), for lack of personal jurisdiction. For the following reasons, we AFFIRM.

I.

Patterson, a U.S. citizen, allegedly sustained a knee injury while working aboard the M/V SIMON STEVIN, a Luxembourg-flagged vessel that was located off the coast of Russia. Patterson was working for Blue Offshore Projects BV ("Blue Offshore") on a project to install subsea production [—2—] equipment in a gas and condensate field. While aboard the M/V SIMON STEVIN, Patterson claims that he was struck by a cable and was injured.

Patterson sued Blue Offshore and two other companies involved in the project, Aker Solutions, Inc. ("Aker Solutions") and FMC Technologies, Inc., in the Eastern District of Louisiana. Patterson alleged that the defendants' negligence caused his injuries. Patterson amended his complaint and added more defendants including Aker Subsea, FMC Kongsberg Subsea AS ("FMC Kongsberg"), and FMC Eurasia, LLC. Aker Subsea and FMC Kongsberg separately moved to dismiss for lack of personal jurisdiction. The district court allowed Patterson additional time to conduct jurisdictional discovery. After completion of the jurisdictional discovery, the district court found that neither specific nor general personal jurisdiction existed over Aker Subsea or FMC Kongsberg. Thus, it granted their motions and dismissed them from the suit.

Patterson sought to certify the district court's dismissal order as a final judgment under Federal Rule of Civil Procedure 54(b). Simultaneously, he appealed the dismissal to this court, arguing that the district court has general personal jurisdiction over both Aker Subsea and FMC Kongsberg. We stayed the appeal pending the district court's determination of the 54(b) motion. The same day, we granted Patterson's unopposed motion to dismiss FMC Kongsberg. After the district court certified its order as final, we lifted the stay. We now consider whether the district court erred in dismissing Aker Subsea under Rule 12(b)(2).[1] [—3—]

II.

We review *de novo* the district court's Rule 12(b)(2) dismissal for lack of personal jurisdiction. *Revell v. Lidov*, 317 F.3d 467, 469 (5th Cir. 2002). "The plaintiff bears the burden of establishing jurisdiction, but need only present *prima facie* evidence." *Id.* We "must accept the plaintiff's uncontroverted allegations, and resolve in [his] favor all conflicts between the facts contained in the parties' affidavits and other documentation." *Id.* (alteration in original) (internal quotation marks omitted).

III.

Patterson argues that the district court erred by dismissing Aker Subsea because, in his view, it has sufficient contacts with the

---

[1] Because the district court certified its dismissal order as a final judgment, this court has jurisdiction over the appeal under 28 U.S.C. § 1291. *See Crowley Mar. Corp. v. Panama Canal Comm'n*, 849 F.2d 951, 953-54 (5th Cir. 1988) (holding that where a premature notice of appeal is filed, a subsequent Rule 54(b) certification is sufficient to validate the notice of appeal).

United States to establish general personal jurisdiction under Federal Rule of Civil Procedure 4(k)(2).[2] Patterson contends that over a three-year period, Aker Subsea entered into eleven secondment agreements[3] whereby it would assign its employees to an American affiliate in Houston, Texas. Under the secondment agreements, the employees sent to the United States remained employees of Aker Subsea. To Patterson, this shows continuous and systematic contacts in the United States sufficient to assert general jurisdiction over Aker Subsea.

Federal Rule of Civil Procedure 4(k)(2)[4] "provides for service of process and personal jurisdiction in any district court for cases arising under federal [—4—] law where the defendant has contacts with the United States as a whole sufficient to satisfy due process concerns and the defendant is not subject to jurisdiction in any particular state." *Adams v. Unione Mediterranea Di Sicurta*, 364 F.3d 646, 650 (5th Cir. 2004). Here, the dispute is whether Aker Subsea has sufficient contacts with the United States to satisfy due process.

"The due process required in federal cases governed by Rule 4(k)(2) is measured with reference to the Fifth Amendment, rather than the Fourteenth Amendment. That is,

---

[2] Patterson does not argue on appeal that specific personal jurisdiction exists over Aker Subsea.

[3] The term secondment means "the detachment of a person . . . from his regular organization for temporary assignment elsewhere." *Webster's Third New Int'l Dictionary* (10th ed. 2014). Here, the secondment agreements sent workers from Aker Subsea in Norway to Aker Solutions, an affiliate, in Houston. Aker Subsea would maintain all of the benefits of the seconded employee in Norway, including Norwegian Social Security, home country pension, and insurance. Aker Solutions was responsible for the day-to-day instruction of the seconded employee.

[4] Rule 4(k)(2) states that "[f]or a claim that arises under federal law, serving a summons or filing a waiver of service establishes personal jurisdiction over a defendant if: [—4—]

(A) the defendant is not subject to jurisdiction in any state's courts of general jurisdiction; and (B) exercising jurisdiction is consistent with the United States Constitution and laws."

Rule 4(k)(2) requires us to consider [Aker Subsea's] contacts with the United States as a whole . . . ." *Submersible Sys., Inc. v. Perforadora Cent., S.A. de C.V.*, 249 F.3d 413, 420 (5th Cir. 2001). Thus, to assert general personal jurisdiction under Rule 4(k)(2), Aker Subsea's contacts with the United States must be so continuous and systematic as to render it essentially at home in the United States. *See id.*; *Daimler AG v. Bauman*, 134 S. Ct. 746, 761 (2014) ("'[T]he inquiry under [*Goodyear Dunlop Tires Operations, S.A. v. Brown*, 564 U.S. 915, 919 (2011)] is not whether a foreign corporation's in-forum contacts can be said to be in some sense 'continuous and systematic,' it is whether that corporation's 'affiliations with the State are so 'continuous and systematic' as to render [it] essentially at home in the forum State.'").

The proper forum for exercising general jurisdiction over a corporation is one in which a corporation is fairly regarded at home. *Goodyear*, 564 U.S. at 924 (citing Brilmayer et al., *A General Look at General Jurisdiction*, 66 Tex. L. Rev. 721, 782 (1988) (identifying place of incorporation and principal place of business as paradigm bases for the exercise of general jurisdiction)). Both Aker Subsea's place of incorporation and principal place of business are in Norway. [—5—] Thus, to exercise general jurisdiction here, these facts must yield what the Supreme Court has described as the "exceptional case."[5]

The record contains no evidence that Aker Subsea had any business contacts with the United States except for eleven secondment agreements. Sending eleven employees to the United States over a brief period does not rise to the level of making Aker Subsea at home in

---

[5] *See Daimler*, 134 S. Ct. at 761 n.19 ("We do not foreclose the possibility that in an exceptional case, see, *e.g.,* [*Perkins v. Benguet Consol. Mining Co.*, 342 U.S. 437 (1952)] . . . a corporation's operations in a forum other than its formal place of incorporation or principal place of business may be so substantial and of such a nature as to render the corporation at home in that State."); *see also Monkton Ins. Servs., Ltd. v. Ritter*, 768 F.3d 429, 432 (5th Cir. 2014) (noting that "[i]t is . . . incredibly difficult to establish general jurisdiction in a forum other than the place of incorporation or principal place of business.").

the United States. The Supreme Court has found a sufficient basis for the exercise of general jurisdiction over a non-resident defendant in only one modern case—*Perkins v. Benguet Consol. Mining Co.*, 342 U.S. 437 (1952)—and Aker Subsea's contacts with the United States do not come close to the level of contacts there.

In *Perkins*, the Court found that the defendant, a Philippine corporation, could be subject to general personal jurisdiction in Ohio based on its extensive contacts within the state. 342 U.S. at 448-49. Due to World War II, the corporation moved certain operations from the Philippines to Ohio. The corporation's contacts with Ohio included: maintaining an office, keeping company files there, corresponding from Ohio about business and employees, paying salaries to the company's president and two secretaries, maintaining company bank accounts, using an Ohio bank as a transfer agent for stock of the company, holding several directors' meetings, managing company policies concerning rehabilitation of company property in the Philippines, and sending funds to pay for projects in the Philippines. *Id.* at 447-48. Here, there is no evidence of contacts with the United States similar to the contacts in *Perkins*. [—6—] There is no evidence that Aker Subsea maintained an office, bank accounts, or conducted any corporate business in the United States. Using *Perkins* as the benchmark of the "exceptional case" where it is appropriate to exercise general jurisdiction over a corporation outside of its principal place of business or place of incorporation, we hold that Aker Subsea's contacts fall well short of effectively operating its business within the United States. At most, Aker Subsea sent eleven of its employees to the United States when it entered into the secondment agreements with its affiliate.[6] These contacts are insufficient to make Aker Subsea essentially at home in the United States.

---

[6] We assume, without deciding, that for purposes of this personal jurisdiction analysis sending an employee to the United States under a secondment agreement is the equivalent of sending an employee to work in the United States.

This court has declined to exercise general personal jurisdiction over a corporation where its most significant and continuous contact with the forum was having employees located there. *See Bowles v. Ranger Land Sys., Inc.*, 527 F. App'x 319, 321-22 (5th Cir. 2013). In *Bowles*, a Texas resident sued an Alabama corporation in Texas for an injury sustained from a car wreck with the corporation's employee in Kuwait. *Id.* at 320. The corporation moved to dismiss for lack of personal jurisdiction. *Id.* The district court examined the corporation's contacts with Texas and reasoned that those contacts were insufficient to subject the corporation to general personal jurisdiction in Texas. *Id.* Thus, it granted the motion. On appeal, this court agreed, finding that the corporation's contacts with Texas were insufficient to exercise general jurisdiction over it. *Id.* The contacts included the following: six employees of the corporation worked at two military bases in Texas; the corporation's employees sometimes worked at or participated in training programs at a British military contractor's facility located in Texas; a small number of employees of the corporation underwent processing at a U.S. military facility [—7—] in Texas before traveling to overseas assignments; the corporation paid unemployment and franchise taxes in Texas; and the corporation's website could be accessed in Texas and contained email addresses for several employees of the corporation. *Id.* at 321. The court noted that the presence of employees was the corporation's most significant and sustained contact with Texas. *Id.* at 322. But this was not enough to establish general jurisdiction: "That a small number of [the corporation's] employees happen to live and work in Texas on projects related to [the corporation's] dealings with the military or with other defense contractors does not indicate a sustained business presence in the state." *Id.* This reasoning applies to the facts here. That a small number of employees of Aker Subsea were seconded to the United States to work for an affiliate does not establish that Aker Subsea has a sustained business presence here.

Additionally, the rare cases where this court has found general jurisdiction over a foreign defendant are distinguishable. In *System Pipe & Supply, Inc. v. M/V Viktor Kurnatovskiy*, 242 F.3d 322, 325 (5th Cir. 2001), the panel concluded that the plaintiff's factual basis for claiming general jurisdiction over the foreign defendant corporation, if established, would be sufficient to show national minimum contacts. Those contacts included the following: (1) the defendant's fleet of vessels regularly called at most major ports in over fifty countries, including the United States; (2) in 1993, the defendant established and began to advertise Azsco America Line to provide service for U.S. Gulf Ports to the Mediterranean and Black Seas; (3) the defendant maintained another line of vessels to carry cargo from the east coast to Israel; (4) at least one of the defendant's vessels had previously been detained in Texas; (5) the defendant's ship, the M/V VIKTOR KURNATOVSKIY, called and discharged the plaintiff's cargo at the Port of Houston; (6) since 1993, the defendant had been a named party in [—8—] approximately fifty actions in United States District Courts; and (7) the defendant had been a defendant in another suit maintained in the Southern District of Texas which was not dismissed for lack of personal jurisdiction. *Id.* Significant here, Aker Subsea has not had the degree of continuous and systematic contacts with the United States that the foreign defendant corporation had with the United States in *System Pipe.* There is no evidence in the record that Aker Subsea has regularly conducted business in the United States, advertised here, maintained assets here, or has been a party to litigation in United States courts.

In *Adams*, this court found that the defendant, a foreign insurer, had sufficient contacts with the United States to assert general jurisdiction over it under Rule 4(k)(2). 364 F.3d at 652. The defendant's contacts included the following: it had paid claims to numerous U.S. companies (155 in all from 1991 to 1994); it had covered numerous other U.S. companies which made no claims; and it had insured hundreds of shipments to the United States. Records showed that the defendant insured approximately 260 shipments to the United States between 1989 and 1995 for one company alone; 138 of these shipments were valued at over $130 million. *Id.* at 651. Even more, the defendant used and paid a number of individuals in the United States as claims adjusters, surveyors, investigators, and other representatives to enable it to conduct business in America. *Id.* Here, there is no evidence that Aker Subsea conducted any business in the United States, let alone the significant level of business conducted by the defendant in *Adams*.[7] [—9—]

Exercising personal jurisdiction over Aker Subsea under Rule 4(k)(2) is appropriate only if its contacts with the United States as a whole are sufficient to satisfy due process concerns. Aker Subsea's limited contacts with the United States—eleven secondment agreements—are insufficient to satisfy due process concerns. Thus, exercising general personal jurisdiction over Aker Subsea would be inappropriate. AFFIRMED.

---

[7] Both *System Pipe* and *Adams* predate *Goodyear* and *Daimler AG*. Scholars have viewed the Court's recent personal jurisdiction decisions as part of an access-restrictive trend. *See, e.g.*, Arthur R. Miller, *Simplified Pleading, Meaningful Days in Court, and Trials on the Merits: Reflections on the Deformation of Federal Procedure*, 88 N.Y.U. L. Rev. 286, 304 (2013).

United States Court of Appeals
for the Fifth Circuit

No. 15-30860

HOLMES MOTORS, INC.
vs.
BP EXPLORATION & PROD., INC.

Appeal from the United States District Court for the
Eastern District of Louisiana

Decided: July 11, 2016

Citation: 829 F.3d 313, 4 Adm. R. 263 (5th Cir. 2016).

Before **HIGGINBOTHAM, DENNIS,** and **CLEMENT,**
Circuit Judges.

[—1—] **HIGGINBOTHAM,** Circuit Judge:

Appellant Holmes Motors, Inc. filed a claim for damages with the Court Supervised Settlement Program. Although Holmes alleged that it qualified as a "Start Up Business," the Claims Administrator reclassified it as a general business claimant. The district court declined to review this decision. Holmes now appeals to this Court, and we AFFIRM.

I.

This case concerns the Deepwater Horizon Economic and Property Damages Settlement Agreement ("Settlement Agreement"). As we have [—2—] explained in several prior opinions,[1] the Court Supervised Settlement Program ("CSSP") is responsible for administering the Settlement Agreement and processing claims related to the Deepwater Horizon oil spill. Appellant Holmes Motors, Inc. ("Holmes") operates a car dealership near Biloxi, Mississippi. In August 2012, Holmes filed a claim with the CSSP. Although Holmes was founded in 1990 and most recently incorporated in 1999, Holmes alleged that it qualified as a "Start Up Business." The Claims Administrator disagreed and "reclassified" Holmes as a general business claimant. After unsuccessfully challenging

this decision through the CSSP's internal appeals process, Holmes filed a request for discretionary review with the district court. The district court denied Holmes's request without opinion. Holmes timely appealed to this Court.

II.

We review the district court's denial of discretionary review for abuse of discretion.[2] In a series of unpublished opinions, our review by the metric of abuse of discretion has asked "whether the decision not reviewed by the district court actually contradicted or misapplied the Settlement Agreement, or had the clear potential to contradict or misapply the Settlement Agreement."[3] Although this formulation is not necessarily exhaustive, we agree that the district court abuses its discretion if either of these circumstances applies. Holmes argues that both apply here.

A.

Holmes's primary argument is that the district court erred by denying discretionary review because the denial left in place an incorrect interpretation [—3—] of the Settlement Agreement. That is, Holmes argues that it qualifies as a "Start Up Business" under the Settlement Agreement. The Settlement Agreement defines a "Start Up Business" as "a business with less than 18 months of operating history at the time of the Deepwater Horizon Incident, as more fully described in Exhibit 7."[4] Holmes claims that the plain meaning of "a business" is a *line of business*, not a business *entity*. As support, Holmes cites several dictionary definitions of "business" that "involve the commercial activity or enterprise, not the actual business entity's formation date, any ownership changes, or any identifying number assigned to it." If this interpretation is accepted, any claimant that changed its line of business within 18 months of the Deepwater Horizon oil spill qualifies as a "Start Up Business."

---

[1] *See In re Deepwater Horizon*, No. 15-30395, 2016 WL 889605, at *1 n.1 (5th Cir. Mar. 8, 2016) (collecting cases).

[2] *See In re Deepwater Horizon*, 785 F.3d 1003, 1011, 3 Adm. R. 325, 329 (5th Cir. 2015).

[3] *See In re Deepwater Horizon*, 2016 WL 889605, at *4 (footnote omitted).

[4] Settlement Agreement § 38.137.

Holmes contends that it made such a change when it switched from selling new and used cars to leasing cars in early 2010.

We reject Holmes's interpretation of the Settlement Agreement. "The Settlement Agreement provides that it 'shall be interpreted in accordance with General Maritime Law.'"[5] "When interpreting maritime contracts, federal admiralty law rather than state law applies."[6] Under admiralty law, a contract "should be read as a whole and its words given their plain meaning unless the provision is ambiguous."[7] At least in the context of a "Start Up Business," the plain meaning of "a business" is a business entity, not a line of business. The Settlement Agreement provides that the term "Start Up Business" is "more [—4—] fully described in Exhibit 7." The introductory paragraph of Exhibit 7, in turn, explains that "[f]or purposes of this Framework, a 'Start-up Business' is considered to be a *claimant* with less than eighteen months of operating history at the time of the DWH Spill." As BP notes, only a business entity can be a "claimant," not a line of business.[8] These interlocking definitions, therefore, resolve the interpretive dispute presented here; a "Start Up Business" is a business entity—not a line of business— with less than 18 months of operating history at the time of the Deepwater Horizon oil spill.

---

[5] *In re Deepwater Horizon*, 785 F.3d 986, 994, 3 Adm. R. 341, 345 (5th Cir. 2015) (quoting Settlement Agreement § 36.1).

[6] *Int'l Marine, L.L.C. v. Delta Towing, L.L.C.*, 704 F.3d 350, 354, 1 Adm. R. 188, 190 (5th Cir. 2013); *see also Norfolk S. Ry. Co. v. Kirby*, 543 U.S. 14, 22-23 (2004) ("When a contract is a maritime one, and the dispute is not inherently local, federal law controls the contract interpretation.").

[7] *Breaux v. Halliburton Energy Servs.*, 562 F.3d 358, 364 (5th Cir. 2009) (quoting *Weathersby v. Conoco Oil Co.*, 752 F.2d 953, 955 (5th Cir. 1984) (per curiam)); *see also Int'l Marine, L.L.C. v. FDT, L.L.C.*, 619 F. App'x 342, 349 (5th Cir. 2015).

[8] *See* Settlement Agreement § 38.15 ("Business Claimant or Business Economic Loss Claimant shall mean an Entity, or a self-employed Natural Person . . . who is an Economic Class Member claiming Economic Damage allegedly arising out of, due to, resulting from, or relating in any way to, directly or indirectly, the Deepwater Horizon Incident.").

But even if Holmes's interpretation of the Settlement Agreement were correct, we would still reject its claim. Holmes urges that it adopted a new "line of business" when it switched from selling new and used cars to leasing cars. Yet Holmes conceded at oral argument that it leased cars before this alleged switch and continued to sell used cars after the switch. The ordinary meaning of a "Start Up Business" also suggests that a claimant must undergo a drastic and fundamental change to enter a new "line of business." We are not persuaded that it is enough for a claimant to switch from selling cars to leasing cars. Although the details of these two business models are different, the basic commercial activity is the same— conveying cars to consumers. Indeed, this is likely why it is common for a company like Holmes to both lease and sell cars. As a result, we conclude that the Claims Administrator's decision did not misapply the Settlement Agreement.

B.

Apart from the merits, Holmes argues that the district court was required to grant discretionary review as part of its duty to "meaningfully [—5—] supervise" the Settlement Agreement. Holmes explains that "[p]ossessing th[e] power [of discretionary review] implies that the MDL court should employ its review power to resolve legitimate issues regarding the meaning of the Settlement Agreement's provisions." Holmes insists that the district court cannot "arbitrarily decide which contract interpretation issues that it wants to address." Drawing on an unpublished opinion of this Court, Holmes contends that review was particularly necessary in this case because its claim implicates an issue that (a) is potentially reoccurring and (b) has divided Appeal Panels.[9]

Holmes is wrong to suggest that the district court must grant review of *all* claims that raise a question about the proper interpretation of the Settlement Agreement.

---

[9] *See In re Deepwater Horizon*, 632 F. App'x 199, 203-04 (5th Cir. 2015).

As this Court has explained, the parties agreed to grant the district court a "discretionary" right of review, "which is not a right for the parties to be granted such review."[10] Any holding that "turn[ed] the district court's discretionary review into a mandatory review . . . would frustrate the clear purpose of the Settlement Agreement to curtail litigation."[11] Holmes's argument that the district court was required to grant review of its particular claim is similarly unpersuasive. In a recent decision, this Court concluded that the district court abused its discretion in denying discretionary review of a claim that raised a question that "ha[s] and will come up repeatedly."[12] Indeed, this Court noted that the question had generated a "split" among the over thirty Appeal Panels that had considered it.[13] Holmes has not made a similar showing. Rather, it has identified two Appeal Panel decisions involving significantly different facts that are—at worst—in tension [—6—] with the decision of the Appeal Panel in this case. "If the discretionary nature of the district court's review is to have any meaning,"[14] the district court cannot be required to exercise its power of discretionary review in these circumstances.

III.

For the reasons stated above, we AFFIRM.

---

[10] *In re Deepwater Horizon*, 785 F.3d at 999, 3 Adm. R. at 349.

[11] *Id.*, 3 Adm. R. at 350; *see also In re Deepwater Horizon*, No. 15-30395, 2016 WL 889605, at *4 (5th Cir. Mar. 8, 2016).

[12] *In re Deepwater Horizon*, 632 F. App'x at 203.

[13] *See id.* at 203-04 & n.3.

[14] *In re Deepwater Horizon*, 2016 WL 889605, at *4.

United States Court of Appeals
for the Fifth Circuit

No. 14-20589

PETROBRAS AM., INC.
VS.
VICINAY CADENAS, S.A.

Appeal from the United States District Court for the
Southern District of Texas

Decided: July 22, 2016
Revised: July 28, 2016

Citation: 829 F.3d 770, 4 Adm. R. 266 (5th Cir. 2016).

Opinion on Rehearing

Before **JOLLY**, **JONES**, and **BENAVIDES**, Circuit Judges.

[—1—] PER CURIAM:

The panel hereby clarifies its previous opinion, *Petrobras Am., Inc. v. Vicinay Cadenas*, 815 F.3d 211, 4 Adm. R. 199 (5th Cir. 2016), as follows.

The holding announced in Part I of the panel's opinion, concluding that the Underwriters did not waive their choice of law argument under the Outer Continental Shelf Lands Act ("OCSLA"), necessarily depended upon the unique statutory scheme created by OCSLA. Through OCSLA, Congress legislated the trichotomy of federal law, state law, and residual maritime law **[—2—]** for disputes arising on the Outer Continental Shelf. *See Rodrigue v. Aetna Cas. & Sur. Co.*, 395 U.S. 352, 355, 89 S. Ct. 1835 (1969) ("the purpose of the [OCSLA] was to define a body of law applicable to the seabed, the subsoil and the fixed structures such as those in question here on the Outer Continental Shelf."). And Section 1333(a) of OCSLA "supersede[s] the normal choice of law rules that the forum would apply." *In re DEEPWATER HORIZON*, 745 F.3d 157, 166, 2 Adm. R. 171, 175 (5th Cir. 2014) (citing *Gulf Offshore Co. v. Mobil Oil Corp.*, 453 U.S. 473, 480–81, 101 S. Ct. 2870 (1981)). Consequently, our holding does not address waiver of a choice of law argument outside of the OCSLA context and does not disturb authorities holding that, in other contexts, a choice of law argument may be waived.

In re HECI Exploration Corp., 862 F.2d 513, 520 (5th Cir. 1988), the case cited by the petition for rehearing en banc for the proposition that the panel's opinion creates an intra-circuit conflict, is emblematic of such non-OCSLA authority. *HECI* is distinguishable for a multitude of reasons: because it is based on ERISA law, involved a preemption defense, and is by its own terms confined to its facts. Indeed, the *HECI* panel emphasized that it "announce[d] no general principle regarding the proper course of conduct for an appellate court confronted with a situation in which the parties fail to argue the applicable federal law in a federally preempted area such as ERISA." *Id.* at 526. Furthermore, the *HECI* holding was "necessarily colored by [the panel's] position" as a "second-level appellate court" reviewing a bankruptcy court decision, *id.*, which is, of course, not the case here.

Finally, this appeal arises in admiralty in an interlocutory posture because the choice of law argument was raised in a motion for leave to amend a complaint, and a claim technically remains pending before the district court. Consequently, the panel opinion does not opine on different scenarios, such as **[—3—]** where a party raises a choice of law argument under OCSLA for the first time after trial and judgment.

United States Court of Appeals
for the Fifth Circuit

No. 16-30003

RICHARD
vs.
DOLPHIN DRILLING LTD.

Appeal from the United States District Court for the
Western District of Louisiana

Decided: August 1, 2016

Citation: 832 F.3d 246, 4 Adm. R. 267 (5th Cir. 2016).

Before **WIENER, HIGGINSON,** and **COSTA,** Circuit
Judges.

[—1—] **HIGGINSON,** Circuit Judge:

This case asks us to resolve a contract dispute between an insurer—Valiant Insurance Company—and the insured—Offshore Energy Services. The [—2—] question is whether Valiant, as an excess insurer on a marine insurance policy, is required to reimburse Offshore for payments in a personal injury settlement. The district court granted summary judgment for Valiant, holding that an exclusion in the insurance policy precludes coverage.

I. Background

This case arises out of personal injuries sustained by Raylin Richard, an Offshore employee, while working on a drillship in the Gulf of Mexico in 2009. Richard sued in January 2011, and Offshore was brought into the suit in August 2011 as a third-party defendant. Offshore brought a cross claim against Liberty Mutual Insurance Company, its primary insurer, in September 2012, and against Valiant, its excess insurer, in January 2014—three years after Richard filed suit. Valiant answered in April 2014, asserting, among other defenses, that under Exclusion 11(d) of its policy with Offshore, which we refer to as the drilling rig exclusion, Valiant did not owe coverage for "any liability for, or any loss, damage, injury or expense caused by, resulting from or incurred by reason of any liability or expense arising out of the ownership, use, or operation of drilling rigs

. . . ." Offshore eventually settled with Richard, but maintained its action for reimbursement against Liberty and Valiant. This appeal involves only Offshore's claim against Valiant.

Valiant moved for summary judgment, arguing that the drilling rig exclusion unambiguously precluded coverage for Richard's accident, which occurred on a drillship, a type of drilling rig. Offshore disagreed, claiming that, among other things, (1) a drillship is not a drilling rig; (2) the drilling rig exclusion does not preclude coverage, and applying it in the manner Valiant suggests would lead to an absurd result because the policy would not cover much; and (3) Valiant waived its right to assert coverage defenses by failing to issue a reservation of rights letter and waiting until April 2014 to raise its [—3—] policy defenses, including the drilling rig exclusion. The district court granted summary judgment for Valiant, rejecting Offshore's affirmative defense of waiver and finding that the "drilling rig exclusion applies to the claims at issue in this case and is a bar to coverage." Offshore timely appealed. After reviewing the briefs and record, we AFFIRM the district court's grant of summary judgment for Valiant.

II. Discussion

A.

We review de novo a grant of summary judgment, applying the same standards as the district court. *Malin Int'l Ship Repair & Drydock, Inc. v. Oceanografia, S.A. de C.V.,* 817 F.3d 241, 249, 4 Adm. R. 232, 237 (5th Cir. 2016). Summary judgment is appropriate when "the movant shows that there is no genuine dispute as to any material fact and the movant is entitled to judgment as a matter of law." Fed. R. Civ. P. 56(a).

B.

The parties agree that Louisiana law applies. "To determine Louisiana law, we look to the final decisions of the Louisiana Supreme Court." *In re Katrina Canal*

Breaches Litig., 495 F.3d 191, 206 (5th Cir. 2007). "In the absence of a final decision by the Louisiana Supreme Court, we must make an *Erie* guess and determine, in our best judgment, how that court would resolve the issue if presented with the same case." *Id.* In the absence of a state supreme court opinion, we look to the state intermediary courts "as the strongest indicator of what a state supreme court would do, absent a compelling reason to believe that the state supreme court would reject the lower courts' reasoning." *Hux v. S. Methodist Univ.*, 819 F.3d 776, 780–81 (5th Cir. 2016). [—4—]

Under Louisiana law, "[a]n insurance policy is a contract between the parties and should be construed by using the general rules of interpretation of contracts set forth in the Louisiana Civil Code." *Cadwallader v. Allstate Ins. Co.*, 848 So. 2d 577, 580 (La. 2003). "This court's role in interpreting insurance contracts is 'to ascertain the common intent of the parties to the contract.'" *Cash v. Liberty Ins. Underwriters, Inc.*, 624 F. App'x 854, 858–59 (5th Cir. 2015) (unpublished) (quoting *Cadwallader*, 848 So. 2d at 580). "The parties' intent, as reflected by the words of the policy, determine[s] the extent of coverage." *Reynolds v. Select Props., Ltd.*, 634 So. 2d 1180, 1183 (La. 1994). Finally, "[w]hen the words of a contract are clear and explicit and lead to no absurd consequences, no further inter-pretation may be made in search of the parties' intent." La. Civ. Code art. 2046.

The drilling rig exclusion states:

III.   Exclusions

  A. This insurance does not apply to:

     . . . .

  11.   Any liability for, or any loss, damage, injury or expense caused by, resulting from or incurred by reason of:

        . . . .

  d. any liability or expense arising out of the ownership, use or operation of drilling rigs, drilling barges, drilling tenders, platforms, flow lines, gathering stations and/or pipelines, but this exclusion shall not apply to craft serving the foregoing such as crew, supply, or utility boats, tenders, barges or tugs. [—5—]

The district court found that the accident giving rise to this litigation occurred on a drilling rig, a term that "clearly encompasses" drillships.[1] The district court then held that the above exclusion precluded coverage for Richard's accident because the accident occurred on a "drilling rig." In reaching its conclusion, the district court looked to this court's unpublished opinion in *Cash*, which held that an identical exclusion precluded coverage under similar circumstances.

In *Cash*, a worker was injured "while being transferred by crane from a platform to a supply vessel." 624 F. App'x at 855. The excess insurance policy in *Cash* contained an identical exclusion to the policy here. Based on that exclusion, we concluded from the plain language of the policy "that the parties intended to exclude platforms from coverage." *Id.* at 860. We reasoned that "[i]f the parties had intended for the use or operation of the platforms to be covered under the policy, they could have drafted the contractual language that way or omitted the term 'platform' from the exclusions section, but they did not." *Id.* We based our decision in *Cash* in large part on a Louisiana Court of Appeals case that reached the same conclusion—*Janex Oil Co. v. Hanover Compressor Co.*, 694 So. 2d 415, 416 (La. App. 4 Cir. 1997). The court in *Janex* faced a nearly identical exclusion, and

---

[1] Offshore argues in passing that the term drilling rig might not encompass drillships, but offers no authority or persuasive reasoning for what it agrees would be a "fine distinction." We are not persuaded by Offshore's argument.

likewise held that "the purpose of this exclusion was to limit coverage to vessels while excluding drilling platforms." *Id.*; *see also Underwriters at Lloyd's London v. OSCA, Inc.*, No. 03-20398, 2006 WL 941794, at *23 (5th Cir. Apr. 12, 2006).

Offshore urges us not to follow our previous holding in *Cash* because, as an unpublished case, it is not binding precedent under Fifth Circuit Rule 47.5.4. While Offshore is correct, we find *Cash*'s reasoning compelling and hold [—6—] that the district court was correct in finding that the drilling rig exclusion in Valiant's policy precluded coverage for Richard's accident. As in *Cash*, we are unpersuaded by Offshore's argument that construing the plain language of the exclusion in this way will lead to "absurd consequences" prohibited by La. Civ. Code art. 2046. Offshore cites two cases in support. While *Clovelly Oil Co., LLC v. Midstates Petroleum Co., LLC*, 112 So. 3d 187, 192 (La. 2013) stands for the general proposition that courts should refrain from construing a contract in a manner that leads to absurd results, the specific facts of that case provide no support to Offshore. The issue in *Clovelly* was whether a lease acquired in 2008 by one of two parties to a 1972 joint operating agreement was covered by the 1972 agreement. In *Ins. Office of Am., L.L.C. ex rel. S R M Props., L.L.C. v. H I Insulation, L.L.C.*, 462 F. App'x 434, 437 (5th Cir. 2012) (unpublished) we held that "interpreting an insurance policy to provide coverage for a non-existent entity" would lead to an absurd consequence under Louisiana law. Here, however, there is no question that Offshore purchased coverage for work its employees actually carried out. The only question is what amount or percentage of this work was not covered due to the exclusion's drilling rig exception. Even accepting Offshore's assertion that it did "99% of its business servicing the offshore oil industry," that would not necessarily mean that the exclusion leads to absurd results, for two reasons. First, the exclusion is clear that it only covers the "ownership, use or operation of drilling rigs, drilling barges, drilling tenders, platforms, flow lines, gathering stations and/or pipelines," and Offshore's claim that it does 99% of its business *servicing* the oil industry

is not the same as a claim that 99% of its business involves the "ownership, use or operation of drilling rigs . . . ." Second, the exclusion does "not apply to craft serving [drilling rigs, drilling barges, drilling tenders, platforms, flow lines, gathering stations and/or pipelines] such as crew, supply, or utility boats, tenders, barges or tugs." It is unclear how much of Offshore's [—7—] business "servicing the offshore oil industry" falls within this exception to the exclusion. Of course, as in *Cash*, to avoid this very situation we reiterate that if parties do not wish for the exclusion to apply to accidents on drilling rigs or on drilling barges or on other listed locations, then they are free to contract accordingly. *See Cash*, 624 F. App'x. at 860.

We are similarly unpersuaded by Offshore's waiver argument: that by waiting until 2014 to raise its policy defenses, including the drilling rig exclusion, and not previously issuing a reservation of right letter, Valiant waived its right to assert coverage defenses. Under Louisiana law, "[w]aiver occurs when there is an existing right, a knowledge of its existence and an actual intention to relinquish it or conduct so inconsistent with the intent to enforce the right as to induce a reasonable belief that it has been relinquished." *Steptore v. Masco Constr. Co.*, 643 So. 2d 1213, 1216 (La. 1994). The district court concluded that Valiant possessed an existing right under the policy and knew of the right,[2] satisfying the first two *Steptore* elements, but did not relinquish its rights based on actual intention or conduct— the third *Steptore* element.

Offshore relies almost exclusively on *Steptore* itself to support its argument that "Valiant's failure to notify [Offshore] of its intent to rely on the drilling rig exclusion . . . for three years . . . resulted in a reasonable belief by [Offshore] that Valiant did not intend to assert coverage defenses." Offshore's primary argument is relinquishment based on conduct.[3] In *Steptore*, the [—8—] Louisiana

---

[2] The district court found that Valiant received notice of the accident in 2011, even though it did not become a party to the lawsuit until 2014.

[3] Offshore also urges this court to find that Valiant had an actual intention to relinquish its

Supreme Court held that "when an insurer, with knowledge of facts indicating noncoverage under the insurance policy, *assumes or continues the insured's defense without obtaining a nonwaiver agreement to reserve its coverage defense*, the insurer waives such policy defense." *Id.* (emphasis added). Here, the district court distinguished *Steptore*, reasoning that because Valiant never assumed the defense of Offshore, "Valiant's failure to issue a reservation of rights letter, without more, does not constitute conduct inducing a reasonable belief in waiver under *Steptore*." We likewise find *Steptore* distinguishable. The plaintiff in *Steptore* filed suit against both the primary and excess insurers, making the excess insurer a full participant in the case from the beginning of the lawsuit. *Id.* at 1214–15. Here, as mentioned, Valiant was not made a party to this case until three years after the initial suit. Thus, as the district court pointed out, "there is no evidence before the court to suggest that Valiant ever assumed the defense of [Offshore]."

Offshore responds by pointing to *Steptore*'s Opinion Denying Rehearing, where the excess insurer for the first time asked the court to draw a distinction between primary and

---

rights based on the testimony of John Moy, a Valiant underwriter. According to Offshore, Moy negotiated with Offshore for its insurance business and was the Valiant employee who received the 2011 notice of Richard's accident. Based on these facts, Offshore concludes that Valiant had "an intent to specifically insure companies like [Offshore] in situations where accidents occurred during their work on . . . drillships." The district court [—8—] rejected this argument, based in part on its conclusion that Moy's testimony was "parol evidence of the policy's meaning." We agree that Moy's testimony on his personal understanding of the Valiant policy does not establish Valiant's actual intention to relinquish its right to assert policy defenses. Valiant did not become a party to the litigation until 2014, and it asserted its policy defenses, including the drilling rig exclusion, in its answer three months later. We do not think that Moy's understanding of the Valiant policy and his receipt of the 2011 notice established an actual intention to relinquish Valiant's right to assert policy defenses when Valiant was not yet a party to the litigation and, thus, had not been required to provide its policy defenses.

excess insurers. *Id.* at 1220. The *Steptore* court declined based on the facts presented in that case. *Id.* We are not persuaded that this rehearing denial aids Offshore here. There is no question that in *Steptore* the excess insurer was involved in the case from the beginning where, as here, Valiant did not become a party to the suit until years later. In sum, we agree [—9—] with the district court that "the facts as alleged by [Offshore] do not show conduct which . . . would induce a reasonable person to conclude that Valiant waived its coverage defenses under the policy at issue in this case."

III. Conclusion

For the foregoing reasons, the judgment of the district court is AFFIRMED. Valiant's opposed motion to strike portions of the record on appeal is DENIED.

United States Court of Appeals
for the Fifth Circuit

No. 15-20490

THOMAS

vs.

CHEVRON U.S.A., INC.

Appeal from the United States District Court for the
Southern District of Texas

Decided: August 11, 2016

Citation: 832 F.3d 586, 4 Adm. R. 271 (5th Cir. 2016).

Before **HIGGINBOTHAM, DENNIS,** and **CLEMENT,**
Circuit Judges.

[—1—] DENNIS, Circuit Judge:

In October 2014, Wren Thomas sued Chevron USA, Inc. (Chevron) and Edison Chouest Offshore, LLC (Edison)[1] in Texas state court. Chevron removed the suit to federal court and filed a motion to dismiss under Rule 12(b)(6). Thomas filed a response to Chevron's motion to dismiss in which he argued that the court should remand the case, deny Chevron's motion to dismiss, or, in the alternative, grant him leave to amend his complaint. After [—2—] the district court converted the motion to dismiss into a motion for summary judgment and allowed the parties to file supplemental briefing, Thomas filed a supplemental brief again requesting, *inter alia*, leave to amend his complaint. In July 2015, the district court issued an opinion granting Chevron's motion for summary judgment and denying Thomas's motion for leave to amend. The court concluded, "Thomas's motion to amend pleadings is denied because the proposed amendment would be futile." Thomas timely appealed. Because the notice Thomas gave of his intent to amend his complaint was sufficient under our circuit's precedent, and because his

amended claims would not have been futile, we VACATE the district court's judgment, REVERSE the court's ruling on Thomas's motion for leave to amend, and REMAND for further proceedings.

I

Thomas was the captain of the *C-Retriever*, a supply vessel supporting Chevron's platform operations in the Agbami Field off the Nigerian coast. In his original petition, Thomas alleged that he told Chevron and Edison, his primary employer, that he feared pirate attacks and worried that the *C-Retriever*'s age, its lack of speed, and the fact that it used easily-accessed VHF radios[2] to communicate its location made the vessel particularly vulnerable. In the spring of 2013 he began receiving threats on the *C-Retriever*'s VHF radio, which he reported to a Chevron area manager and to his Edison supervisors. He asked to be transferred, but Edison did not "effect[] his transfer."

In October 2013, a militant group in Bayelsa, Nigeria, threatened to kidnap Edison crews and burn their vessels if its demands were not met. [—3—] Edison sent a warning to its vessels in the region, including the *C-Retriever*, and encouraged the crews to "stay very vigilant." Four days later, Edison assigned Thomas to make a supply run through what Thomas described as "one of the most pirate-infested areas in West Africa, and directly closer to the source of the recent threats." He objected, but ultimately complied. The *C-Retriever* began the trip on October 22, 2013. In accordance with "usual practice," Edison and Chevron broadcast the vessel's position through VHF radios.

Pirates attacked the *C-Retriever* around 3:00 am on October 23, 2013. Because the vessel did not have a citadel—a fortified safe room designed to protect crewmembers in the event of a pirate boarding—Thomas and his crew hid in the bulk tank room. The pirates breached the room after six hours and began

---

[1] In its motion to dismiss for lack of personal jurisdiction, this defendant stated that it was called Edison Chouest Offshore until June 2006, when it changed its name to Offshore Service Vessels (OSV). It also stated that Edison is no longer a business entity, but that the group of companies OSV is part of sometimes uses "Edison Chouest Offshore" as a trade name.

[2] VHF radios operate in the very high frequency range, transmitting short-range communications on standard, open, international frequencies known as channels.

shooting. Thomas and his engineer surrendered to avoid the loss of life. The pirates held Thomas for 18 days at various "holding camps," where, Thomas states, he was tortured and poorly fed. When he was released, he was malnourished and suffered from posttraumatic stress disorder, sleep disorders, and other medical problems.

Thomas sued Chevron and Edison in Texas state court in October 2014, asserting claims under the Jones Act and for unseaworthiness and maintenance and cure against both defendants. Chevron removed the suit to federal court on November 16, and on November 24 it filed a motion to dismiss under Rule 12(b)(6) on the grounds that Chevron was not Thomas's employer and was not the owner of the vessel on which he was injured.[3] Edison, a [—4—] Louisiana corporation, moved to dismiss for lack of personal jurisdiction. At a hearing on January 23, 2015, the district court allowed the parties to conduct jurisdictional discovery regarding Edison's citizenship, personal jurisdiction over Edison, and Thomas's employment status. On February 5, Thomas filed a response to Chevron's motion to dismiss in which he argued that the court should remand the case, deny Chevron's motion to dismiss, or, in the alternative, grant him leave to amend his complaint "to clarify his general maritime claims and state law claims against Chevron as distinct from employment-related claims against [Edison]." Elsewhere in his response, Thomas specifically noted that his petition "alleges a number of duties and obligations which could be asserted under general maritime law and/or common law against a non-employer, including risk management, providing anti-terrorist security, failure to warn of known risks, and negligence in setting routes and in broadcasting routes in light of the known piracy risks."

On July 6, 2015, the district court converted the motion to dismiss into a motion for summary judgment and allowed the parties to file supplemental briefing. Thomas filed a supplemental brief again requesting, *inter alia*, leave to amend. Specifically, he sought to replace his Jones Act claims with "general maritime law and negligence claims" and argued that "liability theories not dependent on Chevron's status as an employer should survive summary judgment, and those arguments and evidence are incorporated for all purposes herein." Less than a week later, on July 29, the district court issued an opinion granting Chevron's motion for summary judgment and denying Thomas's motion for leave to amend. With respect to Thomas's motion, the court reasoned that "even as amended to remove the Jones Act claims, Thomas's [—5—] claims against Chevron fail as a matter of law. Thomas has not asserted any basis for finding Chevron liable under general maritime law." The court concluded: "Thomas's motion to amend pleadings is denied because the proposed amendment would be futile." Thomas timely appealed.

II

In general, we review the denial of a motion to amend for abuse of discretion. *Fahim v. Marriott Hotel Servs., Inc.*, 551 F.3d 344, 347 (5th Cir. 2008). "A district court abuses its discretion if it: (1) relies on clearly erroneous factual findings; (2) relies on erroneous conclusions of law; or (3) misapplies the law to the facts." *Villarreal v. Wells Fargo Bank, N.A.*, 814 F.3d 763, 767 (5th Cir. 2016) (quoting *Priester v. JP Morgan Chase Bank, N.A.*, 708 F.3d 667, 672 (5th Cir. 2013)). However, where the district court's denial of leave to amend was based solely on futility, this court applies a de novo standard of review "identical, in practice, to the standard used for reviewing a dismissal under Rule 12(b)(6)." *City of Clinton v. Pilgrim's Pride Corp.*, 632 F.3d 148, 152 (5th Cir. 2010). Under that standard, "a complaint must contain sufficient factual matter, accepted as true, to 'state a

---

[3] To state a claim under the Jones Act, a plaintiff must establish that the defendant was his employer. 46 U.S.C. § 30104; *see also Guidry v. S. L Contractors, Inc.*, 614 F.2d 447, 452 (5th Cir. 1980) ("A Jones Act claim also requires proof of an employment relationship either with the owner of the vessel or with some other employer who assigns the worker to a task creating a vessel connection."). Furthermore, "[t]he law is clear that only the Jones Act [—4—] employer/shipowner owes an injured seaman maintenance and cure benefits." *Armstrong v. Trico Marine, Inc.*, 923 F.2d 55, 58 n.2 (5th Cir. 1991).

claim to relief that is plausible on its face.'" *Ashcroft v. Iqbal*, 556 U.S. 662, 678 (2009) (quoting *Bell Atlantic Corp. v. Twombly*, 550 U.S. 544, 570 (2007)). A claim is facially plausible if the complaint "allows the court to draw the reasonable inference that the defendant is liable for the misconduct alleged." *Id.*

III

Rule 15 governs motions to amend made before trial and provides that "[t]he court should freely give leave when justice so requires." FED. R. CIV. P. 15(a)(2). This court has observed that "Rule 15(a) 'evinces a bias in favor of granting leave to amend.'" *Herrmann Holdings Ltd. v. Lucent Techs. Inc.*, 302 F.3d 552, 566 (5th Cir. 2002) (quoting *Dussouy v. Gulf Coast Inv. Corp.*, 660 F.2d 594, 598 (5th Cir. 1981)). A movant is required to give the court some [—6—] notice of the nature of his or her proposed amendments. "[I]n order to take advantage of the liberal amendment rules as outlined in the Federal Rules of Civil Procedure, the party requesting amendment, even absent a formal motion, need only 'set forth with particularity the grounds for the amendment and the relief sought.'" *United States ex rel. Doe v. Dow Chem. Co.*, 343 F.3d 325, 330–31 (5th Cir. 2003) (quoting *United States ex rel. Willard v. Humana Health Plan of Tex. Inc.*, 336 F.3d 375, 386–87 (5th Cir. 2003)).

Although we have not provided strict guidelines as to what constitutes a sufficient request for leave to amend, it is clear that *some* specificity is required. *See, e.g., Doe*, 343 F.3d at 331 (explaining that a "one-page, three-sentence motion" that "offer[ed] no grounds on which an amendment should be permitted" was an insufficient request for leave to amend); *Goldstein v. MCI WorldCom*, 340 F.3d 238, 254–55 (5th Cir. 2003) (affirming denial of motion for leave to amend where the request stated simply: "Should this Court find that the Complaint is insufficient in any way, however, plaintiffs respectfully request leave to amend."); *Willard*, 336 F.3d at 387–88 (determining that a bald statement that a "court should not dismiss a plaintiff's complaint under Rule 9(b) unless the plaintiff

has already been given the opportunity to amend" is an insufficient request of leave to amend); *McKinney v. Irving Indep. Sch. Dist.*, 309 F.3d 308, 315 (5th Cir. 2002) (finding no abuse of discretion in the district court's denial of leave to amend where the plaintiffs failed to file an amended complaint as a matter of right or submit a proposed amended complaint in a request for leave of the court and failed to alert the court as to the substance of any proposed amendment).

Proper notice having been given, permissible reasons for denying a motion for leave to amend include "undue delay, bad faith or dilatory motive on the part of the movant, repeated failure to cure deficiencies by amendments previously allowed, undue prejudice to the opposing party by virtue of [—7—] allowance of the amendment, futility of amendment, etc." *Foman v. Davis*, 371 U.S. 178, 182 (1962). In *Jamieson By & Through Jamieson v. Shaw*, 772 F.2d 1205, 1208 (5th Cir. 1985), we explained that "[w]hen futility is advanced as the reason for denying an amendment to a complaint, the court is usually denying leave because the theory presented in the amendment lacks legal foundation or because the theory has been adequately presented in a prior version of the complaint."

The district court denied Thomas's request for leave to amend on the grounds that amendment would be futile. The court explained:

In his supplemental memorandum submitted after the court converted Chevron's motion to dismiss into one for summary judgment, Thomas objected to the court's apparent decision to rule on Chevron's motion to dismiss and again asked, "subject to and without waiving his motion for remand," that the court permit him to amend his pleadings to "[r]emove Jones Act claims against Chevron and replace those with general maritime law and negligence claims," and to "[r]emove reference to Chevron as Thomas's employer." Thomas stated that his intent in seeking leave to amend was to "conform his pleadings to Chevron and [Edison's] respective positions on employer status" and "allow Thomas to move forward with substantive discovery at trial." But even as amended to remove the Jones Act claims, Thomas's claims against Chevron fail as a matter of law. Thomas has not asserted any basis for finding Chevron liable under general maritime law. The undisputed evidence shows that [Edison] owned the vessel and employed Thomas.

Thomas asserts that the district court misinterpreted or ignored his request to add maritime negligence claims to his complaint, claims which would not depend on an employment or contractual relationship between Thomas and Chevron. Chevron apparently agrees, arguing not that these claims would be futile but rather that they were not stated with sufficient specificity.

Under this court's precedent, Thomas was required only to "set forth with particularity the grounds for the amendment and the relief sought." *Doe*, [—8—] 343 F.3d at 331. Although his motion was not particularly well organized, a review of the pleadings convinces us that Thomas complied with this requirement. He gave notice of the substance of his proposed amendments: he wished to reclassify the claims at ¶ 30 of his complaint as maritime and common law negligence claims. He provided a plausible basis for liability, noting that Chevron owed duties and obligations under maritime and general common law regardless of his employment status. Furthermore, because he requested leave to replace his Jones Act claims with maritime law and negligence claims, the relief he sought was presumably the same as that outlined in his original petition: compensatory damages, punitive damages, interest, reimbursement of costs, and any other general and equitable relief deemed appropriate by the trial court.

Finally, Thomas's proposed amendments would not have been futile. Applying the 12(b)(6) standard, a complaint is futile if it lacks "sufficient factual matter, accepted as true, to 'state a claim to relief that is plausible

on its face.'" *Iqbal*, 556 U.S. at 678. Reading his requests as an attempt to reclassify the claims at ¶ 30 of his complaint as maritime and common law negligence claims, Thomas alleged, *inter alia*, that Chevron: failed to heed official warnings regarding the presence of pirates in waters where the *C-Retriever* sailed; intentionally led the *C-Retriever* into waters where pirates were present and knowingly placed Plaintiffs in harm's way; intentionally broadcast the *C-Retriever*'s route information through VHF airwaves, despite open access to the airwaves; failed to provide adequate security personnel and or security vessel escorts; failed to properly address the specific threats to Thomas's person; and failed to provide appropriate levels of security to protect Thomas. These claims are broadly supported by Thomas's factual allegations.

Further, they are claims upon which relief can be granted. *See* FED. R. CIV. P. 12(b)(b)(6). As we explained in *Withhart v. Otto Candies, L.L.C.*, 431 [—9—] F.3d 840, 842 (5th Cir. 2005), "negligence is an actionable wrong under general maritime law," and the elements of that tort are "essentially the same as land-based negligence under the common law." To state a claim for relief under maritime law, the "plaintiff must 'demonstrate that there was a duty owed by the defendant to the plaintiff, breach of that duty, injury sustained by [the] plaintiff, and a causal connection between the defendant's conduct and the plaintiff's injury.'" *Canal Barge Co. v. Torco Oil Co.*, 220 F.3d 370, 376 (5th Cir. 2000) (quoting *In re Cooper/T. Smith*, 929 F.2d 1073, 1077 (5th Cir. 1991)) (alteration in original). "Under maritime law, a plaintiff is owed a duty of ordinary care under the circumstances." *In re Great Lakes Dredge & Dock Co. LLC*, 624 F.3d 201, 211 (5th Cir. 2010). Significantly, this duty does extend to third parties. *See, e.g., Coats v. Penrod Drilling Corp.*, 61 F.3d 1113, n.27 (5th Cir. 1995 ("The special solicitude for seaman . . . applies under the general maritime law when the Jones Act is inapplicable, such as when a seaman is injured through the fault of a third party.").

The determination of the existence and scope of a duty "involves a number of factors, including most notably the foreseeability of the harm suffered by the complaining party." *Consol. Aluminum Corp. v. C.F. Bean Corp.*, 833 F.2d 65, 67 (5th Cir. 1987). Thomas alleged that Chevron knew about of the real risk of piracy in the region and of the specific threats received by the *C-Retriever*. He alleged that despite its knowledge, Chevron requested that the *C-Retriever* take an unaccompanied support trip that would pass by the source of the recent threats. Finally, he alleged that Chevron broadcast his route information and locations over easily-accessible VHF radios, through which they could be heard by pirates known to be in the area. These allegations are sufficient to suggest that the harm suffered by Thomas was reasonably foreseeable to Chevron and that Chevron consequently owed him a duty not to subject him to the conditions he encountered on his October 22, [—10—] 2013 voyage. *See id*. The allegations are thus "enough to raise a right to relief above the speculative level" and Thomas's claim for relief is plausible on its face, *Twombly*, 550 U.S. at 555; consequently, his amendment would not have been futile, *City of Clinton*, 632 F.3d at 152.

IV

The precise content of Thomas's request for leave to amend was not immediately apparent. However, a review of the pleadings demonstrates that Thomas did in fact give notice of his intent to amend his complaint to include negligence claims under general maritime law. Because these amendments would not have been futile, the district court erred in denying his motion. We therefore VACATE the district court's judgment with respect to claims against Chevron, REVERSE the court's ruling on Thomas's motion for leave to amend, and REMAND for further proceedings.

United States Court of Appeals
for the Fifth Circuit

No. 15-60634

BAKER

VS.

DIRECTOR, OFFICE OF WORKERS' COMPENSATION
PROGRAMS

Petition for Review of an Order of the Benefits
Review Board

Decided: August 19, 2016

Citation: 834 F.3d 542, 4 Adm. R. 276 (5th Cir. 2016).

Before REAVLEY, HAYNES, and HIGGINSON, Circuit Judges.

[—1—] HIGGINSON, Circuit Judge:

Petitioner James Baker appeals the Benefits Review Board's decision affirming the denial of benefits under the Longshore and Harbor Workers' Compensation Act and the Outer Continental Shelf Lands Act. We affirm.

I. Background

James Baker worked as a marine carpenter for eight months at Gulf Island Marine Fabricators, L.L.C.'s waterside marine fabrication yard in [—2—] Houma, Louisiana. He was allegedly injured[1] while building a housing module designed for use on a tension leg offshore oil platform (TLP) named Big Foot. Baker filed a claim for disability benefits under the Longshore and Harbor Workers' Compensation Act (LHWCA), arguing that he is covered by the LHWCA directly as a shipbuilder and, alternatively, is covered under the LHWCA as extended by the Outer Continental Shelf Lands Act (OCSLA).

Big Foot, like other TLPs, is a type of offshore oil platform used for deep water drilling; the parties concede that Big Foot was not built to regularly transport goods or people. Its various parts were constructed in several locations: its base, which is capable of flotation, was built in Korea; its operations modules were built in Aransas Pass, Texas; and its living quarters were built in Houma, Louisiana. All of these components were transported to Ingleside, Texas for assembly—a process that often takes several months, if not years. Although Big Foot can float, it is not capable of self-propulsion, has no steering mechanism, does not have a raked bow, and has no thrusters for positioning once on location. Once completed, Big Foot was scheduled to be towed to a location approximately two hundred miles off the coast of Louisiana and anchored to the sea floor by over sixteen miles of tendons.[2] Anytime it is under tow, Big Foot will be tended to by a crew that is employed to control Big Foot during the voyage. Once anchored, Big Foot will serve as a work platform for the life of the oil field, which is estimated to be twenty years. The U.S. Coast Guard classified Big Foot as a "Floating Outer Continental Shelf [OCS] [—3—] Facility" pursuant to 33 C.F.R. § 143.120, and stated in an email that, as a "non self-propelled vessel," it must be towed to its resting spot on the OCS.

An Administrative Law Judge (ALJ) held a formal hearing on Baker's disability claims; afterwards, he issued a decision and order denying benefits. The ALJ determined that Baker was not covered by the LHWCA because he was not engaged in maritime employment as a shipbuilder, based on his determination that Big Foot is not a "vessel" under the LHWCA. The ALJ next denied Baker's claim for coverage under the OCSLA, concluding that there was no significant causal link between Baker's alleged injury and operations on the OCS. Baker appealed the ALJ's decision to the Benefits Review Board (BRB), which affirmed the ALJ's decision. Baker timely filed with this court a petition for review.

---

[1] The parties stipulated that if Baker suffered an injury, it took place within the scope of his employment for Gulf Island. However, the parties did not stipulate that Baker actually *suffered* an injury.

[2] According to the Office of Workers' Compensation, Big Foot was completed and towed to the Outer Continental Shelf in early 2015. Once on site, however, the tendons designed to secure the rig to the seabed malfunctioned, requiring Big Foot to be towed back to Texas.

II. Discussion

A.

The BRB must uphold the ALJ's factual findings if they are supported by substantial evidence. 33 U.S.C. § 921(b)(3). "Substantial evidence is that relevant evidence—more than a scintilla but less than a preponderance—that would cause a reasonable person to accept the fact finding." *Coastal Prod. Servs. Inc. v. Hudson*, 555 F.3d 426, 430 (5th Cir. 2009). This court reviews the BRB's legal determinations de novo, *id.*, and "afford[s] deference to interpretations of the LHWCA by the Director of the Office of Workers' Compensation Programs," *B & D Contracting v. Pearley*, 548 F.3d 338, 340 (5th Cir. 2008). Where the facts are not in dispute—as in this case—whether LHWCA coverage exists is a question of statutory interpretation and thus is reviewed as a pure question of law. *New Orleans Depot Servs., Inc. v. Dir., Office of Workers' Comp. Programs*, 718 F.3d 384, 387, 1 Adm. R. 228, 229 (5th Cir. 2013) (en banc). [—4—]

B.

Baker first alleges that that he met the requirements for coverage under the LHWCA, which establishes a federal workers' compensation scheme for maritime workers. Prior to 1972, the Act only covered injuries occurring on navigable waters, but Congress has since broadened the LHWCA's coverage to extend to maritime activities occurring on land near the water. *See Chesapeake & Ohio Ry. Co. v. Schwalb*, 493 U.S. 40, 46 (1989). To be eligible for benefits under the LHWCA, a claimant must show that his injury occurred on a maritime situs (the situs requirement), and that he is a maritime employee (the status requirement). *Hudson*, 555 F.3d at 431 (citing 33 U.S.C. §§ 902(3), 903(a)). The parties stipulate that Baker meets the situs requirement—the only question is whether Baker meets the status requirement. To meet the status requirement, Baker must be an "employee" as defined by 33 U.S.C. § 902(3); namely, Baker must be "engaged in maritime employment," which includes "ship repairman, shipbuilder, and ship-breaker." The Supreme Court has added that any other occupation that "entails activities that are an integral or essential part of the loading, unloading, building, or repairing of a vessel" also makes one an employee for purposes of the LHWCA. *Hudson*, 555 F.3d at 439 (emphasis omitted) (citing *Schwalb*, 493 U.S. at 47). Baker was injured while working on modules destined for Big Foot; thus, Baker's entitlement to benefits under the LHWCA turns on whether Big Foot is a vessel as contemplated by the Act. The ALJ and BRB both concluded that Big Foot is not a vessel, and we agree.

The LHWCA does not meaningfully define the term "vessel," so the Supreme Court incorporated the definition provided in the Rules of Construction Act, 1 U.S.C. § 3. *See Stewart v. Dutra Const. Co.*, 543 U.S. 481, 488–90 (2005). "The word 'vessel' includes every description of watercraft or other artificial contrivance used, or capable of being used, as a means of [—5—] transportation on water." 1 U.S.C. § 3. Twice in the last eleven years the Supreme Court has wrestled with whether a particular watercraft qualifies as a vessel as defined by § 3. The first case dealt with a floating dredge known as the *Super Scoop*—"a massive floating platform from which a clamshell bucket [was] suspended beneath the water. The bucket remove[d] silt from the ocean floor and dump[ed] the sediment onto one of two scows that float[ed] alongside the dredge." *Dutra*, 543 U.S. at 484. The *Super Scoop* was used extensively as part of Boston's infamous Big Dig, and had "characteristics common to seagoing vessels, such as a captain and crew, navigational lights, ballast tanks, and a crew dining area." *Id.* However, it only had "limited means of self-propulsion" and was "moved long distances by tugboat." *Id.*

In concluding that the *Super Scoop was* a vessel for the purposes of the LHWCA, the Supreme Court noted that § 3 "requires only that a watercraft be 'used, or capable of being used, as a means of transportation on water' to qualify as a vessel." *Id.* at 495 (quoting 1 U.S.C. § 3). Given that "[§3] does not require that a watercraft be used *primarily* for that purpose," the Court held that the *Super Scoop* met the definition of a vessel because its "function was to move through Boston Harbor, . . . digging the ocean bottom as it moved," which required the *Super Scoop* to "carr[y] machinery, equipment, and a crew over water." *Id.* at 495, 492. The Court concluded that "the *Super Scoop* was not only 'capable of being used' to transport equipment and workers over water—it *was* used to transport those things. Indeed, it could not have dug the Ted Williams Tunnel had it been unable to traverse the Boston Harbor, carrying with it workers like Stewart." *Id.* at 495.

The Supreme Court revisited the question of what qualifies as a vessel eight years later in *Lozman v. City of Riviera Beach*, 133 S. Ct. 735, 1 Adm. R. 2 (2013). In *Lozman*, the Court considered whether a "floating home" was a vessel under [—6—] § 3.[3] The Court once again focused on the language of § 3, but made clear that "[n]ot *every* floating structure is a 'vessel.' . . . even if they are 'artificial contrivance[s]' capable of floating, moving under tow, and incidentally carrying even a fair-sized item or two when they do so." *Id.* at 740, 1 Adm. R. at 3 (second emphasis in original). The Court then concluded that Lozman's house boat was *not* a vessel because, "[b]ut for the fact that it floats, nothing about Lozman's home suggests that it was designed to any practical degree to transport persons or things over water." *Id.* at 741, 1 Adm. R. at 4. This distinguished the house boat from the *Super Scoop*, which the Court noted "was regularly, but not primarily, used (and designed in part to be used) to transport workers and equipment over water." *Id.* at 743, 1 Adm. R. at 5. The house boat, on the other hand, was not regularly used to transport people or goods over water: it "had no rudder or other steering mechanism . . . [i]ts hull was unraked . . . it had a rectangular bottom 10 inches below the water . . . [i]t had no special capacity to generate or store

electricity . . . [and i]ts small rooms looked like ordinary nonmaritime living quarters." *Id.*, 1 Adm. R. at 4. Finally, the Supreme Court noted that while a "lack of self-propulsion is not dispositive, it may be a relevant physical characteristic." *Id.*, 1 Adm. R. at 4 (citation omitted). Lozman's house boat had no self-propulsion—it "was able to travel over water only by being towed. Prior to its arrest, that home's travel by tow over water took place on only four occasions over a period of seven years." *Id.*, 1 Adm. R. at 4.

Returning to our case, we conclude that Big Foot is *not* a vessel. Like the floating home in *Lozman*, Big Foot has no means of self-propulsion, has no steering mechanism or rudder, and has an unraked bow. Big Foot can only be moved by being towed through the water, and when towed to its permanent [—7—] location, Big Foot will not carry "items being transported from place to place (*e.g.*, cargo)," but only "mere appurtenances." *Id.* at 745, 1 Adm. R. at 7. While required to carry a captain and crew when towed, the crew will only be present to ensure Big Foot's transport to its permanent location on the OCS. And unlike the *Super Scoop*, Big Foot will not be used to transport equipment and workers over water in the course of its regular use. *Dutra*, 543 U.S. at 495. In fact, Big Foot is only intended to travel over water once in the next twenty years—the voyage to its operational location on the OCS. Given these undisputed facts, "a reasonable observer, looking to [Big Foot's] physical characteristics and activities, would [not] consider it designed to a practical degree for carrying people or things over water." *Lozman*, 133 S. Ct. at 741, 1 Adm. R. at 3.

Our conclusion that Big Foot is not a vessel under the LHWCA likewise comports with our precedent. In *Bernard v. Binnings Constr. Co., Inc.*, 741 F.2d 824 (5th Cir. 1984), we held that a work punt was not a vessel under the Jones Act[4] because, even though the work

---

[3] Unlike *Dutra*, *Lozman* was not a case brought under the LHWCA. Rather, *Lozman* asked whether the district court had admiralty jurisdiction to consider a suit seeking a federal maritime lien on a floating home under the Federal Maritime Lien Act, 46 U.S.C. § 31342. 133 S. Ct. at 739, 1 Adm. R. at 2. The question of admiralty jurisdiction, however, turned on whether the floating home was a vessel under 1 U.S.C. § 3.

[4] For purposes of the Jones Act, a vessel is defined as a "structure[] designed or utilized for 'transportation of passengers, cargo or equipment from place to place across navigable waters.'" *Binnings*, 741 F.2d at 828–29. While phrased slightly different from 1 U.S.C. § 3's definition of a

punt was frequently moved around a work site, it functioned as a work platform and was not designed for or engaged in the business of navigation. *Id.* at 830. We concluded that "[t]he work punt lacks all indicia of a structure designed for navigation; it has no raked bow, no means of self-propulsion, and no crew quarters or navigational lights." *Id.* at 832. Big Foot likewise was not designed for transportation or navigation—it has no means of self-propulsion, no steering mechanism, and no raked bow; further, Big Foot will not transport objects from place to place, and is intended to remain anchored to the floor of the OCS for twenty years. In *Smith v. Massman Const. Co.*, 607 F.2d 87 (5th Cir. 1979), also a Jones Act case, we likewise concluded that a caisson was [—8—] not a vessel in large part because the caisson's "transportation of men and material, if any occurred, was incidental" to its purpose of "being both a form for concrete in a bridge pier and a part of the pier itself, not for the purpose of being a . . . vessel." *Id.* at 89. The fact that Big Foot will transport a crew and material to the OCS is likewise incidental to its purpose of serving as an oil field work platform. *See also Blanchard v. Engine & Gas Compressor Servs., Inc.*, 575 F.2d 1140, 1141–43 (5th Cir. 1978) (concluding in a Jones Act case that "buildings mounted on virtually permanently sunken barges [were] not Jones Act vessels," and noting that "(m)ere flotation on water does not constitute a structure a 'vessel'" (alteration in original) (quoting *Cook v. Belden Concrete Prods., Inc.*, 472 F.2d 999, 1001 (5th Cir. 1973))); *Warrior Energy Servs. Corp. v. ATP Titan M/V*, 551 F. App'x 749, 752 (5th Cir. 2014) (concluding that a floating oil and gas production facility moored to the floor of the OCS was not a vessel under 1 U.S.C. § 3 because it was "not practically capable of transportation on water").

C.

Baker also challenges the ALJ's determination that his activities as an

---

vessel ("The word 'vessel' includes every description of watercraft or other artificial contrivance used, or capable of being used, as a means of transportation on water."), we are comforted by the fact that our holding today fits well with our Jones Act cases.

employee of Gulf Island did not have a sufficiently substantial nexus to OCS operations such that he is entitled to compensation under the LHWCA as extended by the OCSLA. The OCSLA extends coverage of the LHWCA to "injur[ies] occurring as the result of operations conducted on the outer Continental Shelf for the purpose of exploring for, developing, removing, or transporting by pipeline the natural resources . . . of the outer Continental Shelf." 43 U.S.C. § 1333(3)(b). Baker argues that he was injured "as the result of operations" on the OCS because he was injured while constructing living quarters, which would ultimately be integrated into Big Foot, which would ultimately be placed on the OCS. [—9—]

The Supreme Court recently clarified that a "'claimant must establish a substantial nexus between the injury and extractive operations on the [OCS]' to qualify for workers' compensation benefits under the OCSLA." *Pac. Operators Offshore, LLP v. Valladolid*, 132 S. Ct. 680, 685 (2012) (quoting *Valladolid v. Pac. Operations Offshore, LLP*, 604 F.3d 1126, 1139 (9th Cir. 2010).[5] To meet the substantial nexus test, "the injured employee [must] establish a significant causal link between the injury that he suffered and his employer's on-OCS operations conducted for the purpose of extracting natural resources from the OCS." *Id.* at 691. Baker's injury— incurred on dry land while "building the living and dining quarters for [Big Foot]"—does not satisfy this fact-specific test.

In rejecting the Third Circuit's "but for" test, the Supreme Court was clear in *Valladolid* that the OCSLA was not meant to "cover land-based office employees whose jobs have virtually nothing to do with extractive operations on the OCS." *Id.* at 690. Rather, the Supreme Court acknowledged that "whether an employee injured while performing an off-OCS task qualifies . . . is a question that will depend on the individual circumstances of each case." *Id.* at 691. While not an office employee, Baker's job of constructing living and dining quarters is too

---

[5] In adopting this "substantial nexus" test, the Supreme Court rejected this court's "situs-of-injury" test. *Valladolid*, 132 S. Ct. at 685, 687.

attenuated from Big Foot's future purpose of extracting natural resources from the OCS for the OCSLA to cover his injury. Baker's employment was located solely on land, whereas, for example, the deceased in *Valladolid* spent ninety-eight percent of his time on an offshore drilling platform (even though he was injured while on land). *Id.* at 684. Baker's particular job, to the contrary, did not require him to travel to the OCS *at all*, making his work geographically distant from the OCS. And although Gulf [—10—] Island manufactured the living quarters for Big Foot, the company had no role in moving Big Foot to, installing Big Foot on, or operating Big Foot once placed on the OCS. Based on the specific facts of Baker's employment, we conclude that his injury does not satisfy the substantial nexus test and is not covered under the LHWCA as extended by the OCSLA.

III. Conclusion

For the aforementioned reasons, we AFFIRM.

United States Court of Appeals
for the Fifth Circuit

No. 15-31105

MOENCH
vs.
MARQUETTE TRANSP. CO. GULF-INLAND, L.L.C.

Appeal from the United States District Court for the
Western District of Louisiana

Decided: September 29, 2016
Revised: October 13, 2016

Citation: 838 F.3d 586, 4 Adm. R. 281 (5th Cir. 2016).

Before **KING**, **SMITH**, and **COSTA**, Circuit Judges.

[—1—] **KING,** Circuit Judge:

A towing vessel owned and operated by Defendant–Appellant Marquette Transportation Co. Gulf-Inland, L.L.C., allided with a private vessel, the SES EKWATA, owned by the George T. Moench Irrevocable Trust. Plaintiffs–Appellees, trustees of the George T. Moench Irrevocable Trust, sued Marquette for damages. After a bench trial, the district court awarded damages and attorneys' fees against Marquette. Marquette appeals those awards, as well [—2—] the district court's exclusion of certain expert testimony from trial. For the reasons that follow, we AFFIRM.

I. FACTUAL AND PROCEDURAL BACKGROUND

The SES EKWATA was a 116 foot-long, fiberglass-hulled vessel originally built for military and commercial use, but later converted for private use. In that conversion, the EKWATA was stripped of many components, essentially leaving a bare hull and 8,000 square feet of interior space. In 2005, Plaintiff–Appellee George T. Moench purchased the essentially bare hull of the EKWATA for $200,000.[1] Between 2005 and

2011, he spent $217,000 in materials and equipment to refurbish the vessel. Moench, along with a marine carpenter, also spent thousands of hours laboring on the EKWATA, where Moench lived several months each year.

In late May 2011, Moench moved the EKWATA to a fleeting facility along the Atchafalaya River to keep it safe during expected flooding. On June 10, 2011, the M/V SALVATION, a steel-hulled tug owned and operated by Defendant–Appellant Marquette Transportation Co. Gulf-Inland, L.L.C., which was towing two barges, allided[2] with the EKWATA while it was moored at the fleeting facility. Prior to the allision, the SALVATION's captain knew that the Atchafalaya River was experiencing historic water levels, which created the potential for extreme cross-currents and required him to exercise extreme caution. Yet he proceeded down the river without assistance from another tug, and upon arriving at a holding position in the river, left the controls for a cup of coffee while the on-duty deckhand—who was supposed to [—3—] be on watch—was below deck. By the time the captain returned to the controls, the river's current had taken control of the SALVATION. After unsuccessfully attempting to regain control, the captain decided to allide with the EKWATA to avoid damaging the two barges in tow.

The allision between the steel-hulled SALVATION and fiberglass-hulled EKWATA severely damaged the EKWATA[3] and caused it to take on water. After the allision, Moench attempted to determine the full extent of the damage by dry-docking the EKWATA; however, he was unable to find anyone willing to assume the liability of transporting the

---

[1] The EKWATA's registered owner was the George T. Moench Irrevocable Trust. For ease of reference, we refer to the George T. Moench Irrevocable Trust and George T. Moench interchangeably as "Moench."

[2] An allision is "[t]he contact of a vessel with a stationary object such as an anchored vessel or a pier." *Allision*, BLACK'S LAW DICTIONARY (10th ed. 2014); *see also Apache Corp. v. Global Santa Fe Drilling Co.*, 435 F. App'x 322, 323 n.1 (5th Cir. 2011) (per curiam).

[3] Among other things, the allision resulted in compression damage; an eighteen foot hole on the starboard side of the vessel; another twelve foot by six foot hole on the starboard side of the vessel; various splits and fractures in the hull extending below the water line; and internal damage.

severely damaged vessel for inspection. The EKWATA was subsequently vandalized, which resulted in various materials and equipment Moench purchased being stolen.

Moench filed the instant suit on June 6, 2012, invoking the admiralty and maritime jurisdiction of the district court and asserting general maritime law negligence and unseaworthiness claims against Marquette. Moench claimed the EKWATA was a total (or constructive total) loss as a result of the allision and sought the pre-casualty value of the vessel.[4] Up to and through trial, Marquette contested liability, despite the captain of the SALVATION admitting the facts outlined above. On the issue of damages, Moench testified at trial (without objection from Marquette) to the substantial financial investment he had made in the EKWATA. Moench and Marquette also elicited the testimony of experts at trial to assist the court on the issue of damages. Moench's expert testified that the pre-casualty value of the EKWATA was $850,000–$1.5 million. He also testified that the replacement cost, less [—4—] depreciation, of the EKWATA was $5 million–$7.5 million. Marquette's first expert testified that the EKWATA was a constructive total loss as a result of the allision and that its pre-casualty value was $50,000. Marquette's second expert also testified that the EKWATA was a constructive total loss, concluding that repair costs would be "hundreds of thousands" of dollars while the EKWATA's pre-casualty value was $75,000–$100,000. The third expert presented by Marquette, Larry Strouse, was originally hired and designated by Moench. He testified that repair costs would be $285,000, but admitted this estimate was inconclusive of all damages from the allision because the EKWATA could not be dry-docked to fully assess the damage below the waterline. At trial, Marquette also sought to elicit testimony from Strouse that the pre-casualty value of the EKWATA was $120,000. The district court, however, concluded that he could not

testify to that opinion because it was not expressed in his expert report.

After the bench trial, the district court found Marquette at fault. On the issue of damages, the district court, after considering all of the testimony, found that the EWKATA's pre-casualty value was $417,000 and that the cost of repairing the EKWATA would exceed that value. Based on these findings, the district court concluded that the EKWATA was a constructive total loss and awarded Moench $322,890, representing the pre-casualty value of the EKWATA, less the value of materials and equipment that Moench could have preserved following the allision. The district court also found that Marquette's handling of the case was "an abuse of the process and bad faith" and expressed its "feel[ing]" that an award of reasonable attorneys' fees and costs to Moench was justified under those circumstances. Moench subsequently requested $323,138.90 in fees and costs based on Marquette's handling of the case, submitting detailed declarations and billing records to substantiate its request. Marquette responded that its handling of the case did not warrant [—5—] sanction. Marquette also objected to the amount of fees and costs requested by Moench, principally asserting that it should be reduced as disproportionate to the amount involved and the results obtained. The district court agreed with this latter objection in part and reduced Moench's request by $27,702.81, awarding him $295,436.09. Marquette timely appealed.

II. DISCUSSION

Marquette asserts that the district court erred in (i) making its constructive total loss determination; (ii) refusing to allow Larry Strouse to opine on the EKWATA's pre-casualty value; and (iii) imposing attorneys' fees as a sanction for its handling of the case and awarding the amount of fees it did. We address each assertion in turn.

A. Constructive Total Loss Determination

Marquette asserts that the district court's pre-casualty valuation of the EKWATA and

---

[4] Moench also sought punitive damages and lost business revenue from Marquette. The district court dismissed these claims, and they are not directly at issue in this appeal.

its finding that the costs of repair would exceed that valuation are not supported by the record, particularly the expert testimony introduced at trial. Thus, Marquette argues, the district court erred in concluding that the EKWATA was a constructive total loss and in awarding Moench damages on that basis.

We review the district court's constructive total loss determination for clear error. *See Ryan Walsh Stevedoring Co. v. James Marine Servs., Inc.*, 792 F.2d 489, 491 (5th Cir. 1986). A vessel is a total (or constructive total) loss when repair is not physically or economically feasible, such as when the cost of repairs exceeds the vessel's pre-casualty value. *See Gaines Towing & Transp., Inc. v. Atlantia Tanker Corp.*, 191 F.3d 633, 635 (5th Cir. 1999); *see also Pillsbury Co. v. Midland Enters., Inc.*, 715 F. Supp. 738, 763 (E.D. La. 1989). In the case of total (or constructive total) loss, the owner is entitled to recover the pre-casualty value of the vessel (i.e., the price which would result from the hypothetical fair negotiations between an owner willing to sell and a purchaser [—6—] desiring to buy). *See Standard Oil Co. of N.J. v. S. Pac. Co.*, 268 U.S. 146, 155–56 (1925); *see also Gaines Towing & Transp.*, 191 F.3d at 635. When a vessel's pre-casualty value cannot be established by recent comparable sales, there is no precise rule or formula for valuation. *See Standard Oil*, 268 U.S. at 155–56. Instead, the district court "should consider any and all evidence before it" that bears on value. *Greer v. United States*, 505 F.2d 90, 93 (5th Cir. 1974). This includes evidence of the vessel's purchase price and the cost of any improvements to the vessel. *Id.* "[O]ther evidence such as replacement cost, depreciation, expert opinion and the amount of insurance" should also be considered to determine pre-casualty value. *King Fisher Marine Servs., Inc. v. NP Sunbonnet*, 724 F.2d 1181, 1185 (5th Cir. 1984); *see also Carl Sawyer, Inc. v. Poor*, 180 F.2d 962, 963 (5th Cir. 1950). The court must then make an "informed judgment." *Bloomfied S.S. Co. v. Brownsville Shrimp Exch.*, 243 F.2d 869, 873 (5th Cir. 1957). In doing so, the court is not bound by any single piece of evidence, including the opinions or formulas elicited by

the parties' experts.[5] *See Bloomfield*, 243 F.2d at 873 (rejecting argument that district court was bound by vessel's purchase price, book value, or similar values reached by expert surveyor); *see also Lukens v. Comm'r*, 945 F.2d 92, 96 (5th [—7—] Cir. 1991). If the district court's valuation "is within the range of figures that may properly be deduced from the evidence," it is not clearly erroneous, even if the valuation is not "a figure as to which there is specific testimony." *Lukens*, 945 F.2d at 96 (quoting *Anderson v. Comm'r*, 250 F.2d 242, 249 (5th Cir. 1957)).

The district court had the benefit of witnessing the testimony at trial and was in the best position to resolve the conflicting testimony concerning value and repair cost. *See Ryan*, 792 F.2d at 491. With regard to value, the district court found that the EKWATA was an uncommon vessel which could not be valued based on comparable sales and that much of the evidence on valuation was unreliable. It credited the vessel's purchase price ($200,000) and the cost of materials and equipment spent improving it ($217,000) as the most reliable of the recognized indicia of value. *See Greer*, 402

---

[5] Marquette seems to argue that, even after it presented evidence, the district court was (and consequently this court is) bound by the evidence presented in Moench's case-in-chief. However, this court made clear in *Greer* that the district court "should consider any and all evidence before it." 505 F.2d at 93. This necessarily included the evidence Marquette elected to present. Our conclusion in *Greer* is consistent with the general rule that, where both parties have offered evidence, "the party supported by the weight of the evidence will prevail regardless of which party bore the burden of persuasion, proof, or preponderance." *Whitehouse Hotel Ltd. P'ship v. Comm'r*, 615 F.3d 321, 332 (5th Cir. 2010) (quoting *Blodgett v. Comm'r*, 394 F.3d 1030, 1039 (8th Cir. 2005)); *see also Belk v. Charlotte-Mecklenburg Bd. of Educ.*, 269 F.3d 305, 328–29 (4th Cir. 2001). It is also consistent with our general practice of testing the sufficiency of the evidence on appeal by viewing the entire record. *See Wealden Corp. v. Schwey*, 482 F.2d 550, 551 (5th Cir. 1973) (rejecting request "for a review of the evidence as it stood when plaintiff closed the presentation of his evidence"); *see also Fed. Ins. Co. v. HPSC, Inc.*, 480 F.3d 26, 32 (1st Cir. 2007); *Gaffney v. Riverboat Servs. of Indiana*, 451 F.3d 424, 451 n.29 (7th Cir. 2006).

F.2d at 93. The district court's $417,000 valuation was near the middle of the experts' opinions ($50,000–$1.5 million) and well below replacement cost, less depreciation ($5–7.5 million)—both of which are recognized indicia of value. *See King Fisher Marine Servs.*, 724 F.2d at 1185. The district court's valuation was "within the range of figures that may properly be deduced from the evidence" and thus not clearly erroneous. *Lukens*, 945 F.2d at 96 (quoting *Anderson*, 250 F.2d at 249); *see also Greer*, 505 F.2d at 93; *Bloomfield*, 243 F.2d at 874.

With regard to repair cost, the district court heard the undisputed testimony at trial that the steel-hulled SALVATION's allision with the fiberglass-hulled EKWATA caused severe damage to the EKWATA. The damage was severe enough that all of the expert witnesses agreed (in spite of their differing opinions on value and repair cost) that the EKWATA was a total loss, either real or constructive. The district court credited the expert testimony that repair costs would total "hundreds of thousands" of dollars. It also noted Strouse's testimony "that repairs would be in the range of $285,000 was, admittedly, incomplete and inconclusive" because Strouse could not fully [—8—] assess the damage below the waterline without having the EKWATA dry-docked. Although Strouse's estimate nominally included damage below the waterline, we cannot say, given the other testimony and Strouse's uncertainty about damage below the waterline, that the district court clearly erred in finding that the cost of repairing the severely damaged EKWATA exceeded its pre-casualty value and, therefore, the EKWATA was a constructive total loss.

B. Exclusion of Expert Testimony

Marquette next asserts that the district court erred in refusing to allow Larry Strouse to opine on the EKWATA's pre-casualty value, even though he did not express an opinion on that in his expert report. According to Marquette, Strouse was a non-retained expert witness and thus was not required to provide any report under Federal Rule of Civil Procedure 26(a)(2)(B). Therefore, argues Marquette, Strouse should have been allowed

to testify on any "facts or data obtained or observed in the course of the sequence of events giving rise to the litigation," whether included in his report or not. *See* Fed. R. Civ. P. 26(a)(2)(C).

This court reviews a district court's exclusion of expert testimony for abuse of discretion. *See Brown v. Ill. Cent. R. R. Co.*, 705 F.3d 531, 535 (5th Cir. 2013). But even when this court finds an abuse of discretion, it will not reverse the district court's ruling unless it affected the party's "substantial rights." 28 U.S.C. § 2111; *see also* Fed. R. Evid. 103(a). The party claiming the error bears the burden of demonstrating its substantial rights were prejudiced. *See McClain v. Lufkin Indus., Inc.*, 519 F.3d 264, 282 (5th Cir. 2008). "A ruling has affected the substantial rights of the party if, when considering the evidence presented at trial, the ruling had a substantial effect on the outcome of the trial." *U.S. Bank Nat'l Ass'n v. Verizon Commc'ns, Inc.*, 761 F.3d 409, 430 (5th Cir. 2014). The exclusion of cumulative evidence does not affect a [—9—] party's substantial rights. *See Sanford v. Johns–Manville Sales Corp.*, 923 F.2d 1142, 1148 (5th Cir. 1991).

Assuming *arguendo* that the district court abused its discretion in refusing to allow Strouse to opine on the EKWATA's pre-casualty value, Marquette has failed to demonstrate that this refusal substantially affected the outcome of the trial. Strouse's proffered testimony would have been merely cumulative of other testimony on pre-casualty value offered at trial. Marquette repeatedly emphasized that the EKWATA's pre-casualty value was substantially less than the amount testified to by Moench's expert (and what the district court ultimately found). Marquette elicited testimony from two experts that the pre-casualty value of the EKWATA was less than $100,000 because the EWKATA was "cosmetically and mechanically deficient." As Marquette itself recognizes on appeal, Strouse's testimony would have simply "confirmed each of these opinions." Because Strouse's testimony was admittedly cumulative, the district court's error, if any, did not affect Marquette's substantial rights. *See Sanford*, 923 F.2d at 1148.

C. Attorneys' Fee Award

Marquette finally argues that it had a good faith basis for questioning Moench's pre-casualty valuation; thus, the district court was not justified in awarding attorneys' fees as a sanction for its handling of the case.[6] Moreover, Marquette argues, the award was excessive.

We review a district court's determination of an attorneys' fee award under an abuse of discretion standard and the findings of fact supporting the [—10—] award under a clearly erroneous standard. *See Black v. SettlePou, P.C.*, 732 F.3d 492, 496 (5th Cir. 2013). The general rule in federal court, the so-called "American Rule," is that litigants are responsible for their own fees. *Alyeksa Pipeline Serv. Co. v. Wilderness Soc'y*, 421 U.S. 240, 247, 257 (1975). Federal courts, however, possess "inherent power" to assess fees as sanctions when the losing party has "acted in bad faith, vexatiously, wantonly, or for oppressive reasons."[7] *Chambers v.*

---

[6] On appeal, Marquette also argues, as it did in the district court, that the parties' settlement negotiations were improperly considered in making the fee award. In ruling on this argument, the district court stated that the parties' settlement negotiations were not the basis for its fee award, rather they were "simply additional evidence of Marquette's actions which the Court found throughout the case to be an abuse of the process and bad faith." With respect to the district court's statement that the parties' settlement negotiations were not the [—10—] basis for its fee award, "[w]e have no choice but to believe [the district court]." *Gulf States Utils. Co. v. Ecodyne Corp.*, 635 F.2d 517, 519 (5th Cir. Unit A 1981).

[7] When "invoking its inherent power" to sanction, a district court "must comply with the mandates of due process." *Chambers*, 501 U.S. at 50; *see also Roadway Express, Inc. v. Piper*, 447 U.S. 752, 767 (1980). Although Marquette asserts, in passing, that the district court's award was made *sua sponte*, it does not offer any supporting argument or citation to authority indicating that the district court failed to comply with due process. Accordingly, any due process argument Marquette could have made was inadequately briefed and therefore waived. *See* Fed. R. App. P. 28(a)(8)(A);

NASCO, Inc., 501 U.S. 32, 45–46 (1991) (quoting *Alyeksa Pipeline Serv.*, 421 U.S. at 258–59). Under this test, sanctions are warranted when a party "knowingly or recklessly raises a[n objectively] frivolous argument, or argues a meritorious claim for the purpose of harassing an opponent." *Gate Guard Servs., L.P. v. Perez*, 792 F.3d 554, 561 & n.4 (5th Cir. 2015) (quoting *Rodriguez v. United States*, 542 F.3d 704, 709 (9th Cir. 2008)). Thus, even when a party is pursuing a meritorious claim or defense, sanctions may be assessed when the party "abuse[s] . . . the judicial process in the method of prosecution" of that claim or defense. *Batson v. Neal Spelce Assocs. Inc.*, 805 F.2d 546, 550 (5th Cir. 1986). Pursuing "an aggressive litigation posture" is not an abuse of the judicial process, "[b]ut advocacy [—11—] simply for the sake of burdening an opponent with unnecessary expenditures of time and effort clearly [is]." *Id.*

Here, the district court detailed the factual findings underpinning its conclusion that Marquette abused the judicial process and acted in bad faith during the course of the litigation. Specifically, the district court found that Marquette contested liability up to and through trial even though it "clearly knew the extent of its liability based on the circumstances of the case and the actions of its captain . . . [and] was fully aware of the fact that [Moench] had no liability whatsoever for this allision." The district court further found that Marquette "presented two experts who were so lacking they could not even properly name the vessel [at issue]."

---

see also Willis v. Cleo Corp., 749 F.3d 314, 319 (5th Cir. 2014). But even if it was not, we could not conclude that the district court abused its discretion by failing to give Marquette the opportunity to be heard at a meaningful time and in a meaningful manner—the fundamental requirement of due process, *Armstrong v. Manzo*, 380 U.S. 545, 552 (1965)—because it considered and responded to all of Marquette's various written submissions. *See Merriman v. Sec. Ins. Co. of Hartford*, 100 F.3d 1187, 1191–92 (5th Cir. 1996) ("[T]he opportunity to respond through written submissions usually constitutes sufficient opportunity to be heard." (citing *Spiller v. Ella Smithers Geriatric Ctr.*, 919 F.2d 339, 347 (5th Cir. 1990))).

On appeal, Marquette does not specifically challenge any of these findings. Instead, Marquette asserts that the fee award was unwarranted because Marquette had a good faith basis to challenge the quantum of damages and thus in proceeding through a trial. But even if true, this fact did not justify Marquette's intransigence on liability or the means by which Marquette defended Moench's damages claim—namely, one expert who, according to the district court's findings, opined on value "without including any comparables, without considering the equipment on the vessel, without an accurate description of the vessel, and without reliable underlying information" and a second expert who, according to the district court's findings, "not only failed to correct the *glaringly* incorrect information set forth in [the first expert's] report, but incorporated it into his own." *See Gate Guard Servs.*, 792 F.3d at 562–63; *Batson*, 805 F.2d at 550–51. We cannot say that the district court's findings on bad faith were clearly erroneous or that the court abused its discretion in awarding Moench fees as a sanction based on those findings.

Having concluded that the district court did not abuse its discretion in awarding attorneys' fees as a sanction, we must address the amount of fees [—12—] awarded by the district court. The parties agree that the two-step lodestar method applies to the calculation of the fee award. Under this method, a court must first calculate the "lodestar" amount "by multiplying the reasonable number of hours expended on the case by the reasonable hourly rates for the participating lawyers." *Migis v. Pearle Vision, Inc.*, 135 F.3d 1041, 1047 (5th Cir. 1998). "There is a strong presumption of the reasonableness of the lodestar amount." *Black*, 732 F.3d at 502. But the district court may increase or decrease the lodestar amount "based on 'the relative weights of the twelve factors set forth in *Johnson* [*v. Georgia Highway Express, Inc.*, 488 F.2d 714 (5th Cir. 1974)].'" *Id.* (quoting *Saizan v. Delta Concrete Prods. Co.*, 448 F.3d 795, 800 (5th Cir. 2006)).[8]

In reviewing lodestar adjustments, this court reviews the district court's analysis "only to determine if the court sufficiently *considered* the appropriate criteria." *Id.* (quoting *La. Power & Light Co. v. Kellstrom*, 50 F.3d 319, 329 (5th Cir. 1995)). A district court must provide "a reasonably specific explanation for all aspects of a fee determination." *Perdue v. Kenny A.*, 559 U.S. 542, 558 (2010). This does not, however, require a district court to recite or even mention the *Johnson* factors, so long as "the record clearly indicates that the district court has utilized the *Johnson* framework as the basis for its analysis." *Union Asset Mgmt. Holding A.G. v. Dell, Inc.*, 669 F.3d 632, 642 (5th Cir. 2012) (internal quotation marks and citation omitted); *see also EEOC v. Agro Distribution, LLC*, 555 F.3d 462, 473 (5th Cir. 2009). [—13—]

Marquette does not challenge the district court's determination of the lodestar amount itself. Rather, it challenges the district court's decision not to reduce (or further reduce) that amount based on the *Johnson* framework, namely the degree of success obtained by Moench. According to Marquette, the district court's factual findings do not indicate that the court even considered the *Johnson* framework. We disagree. Although the district court did not explicitly recite the *Johnson* factors, its findings clearly evince that the *Johnson* framework was the basis for its analysis. Specifically, they demonstrate that the district court considered Marquette's objection to the fee request, namely that the fees sought were disproportionate to the amount involved and the results obtained (*Johnson* factor 8); carefully reviewed the detailed declarations and billing records submitted by Moench to determine which fees could be reduced or eliminated based on

---

[8] The twelve *Johnson* factors are as follows: (1) the time and labor required; (2) the novelty and difficulty of the questions; (3) the skill requisite to perform the legal services properly; (4) the preclusion of other employment by the attorney due

to acceptance of the case; (5) the customary fee for similar work in the relevant community; (6) whether the fee is fixed or contingent; (7) time limitations imposed by the client or the circumstances; (8) the amount involved and the results obtained; (9) the experience, reputation, and ability of the attorneys; (10) the undesirability of the case; (11) the nature and length of the professional relationship with the client; and (12) awards in similar cases. *See Johnson*, 488 F.2d at 717–19.

Marquette's objection; and did, in fact, reduce or eliminate certain fees based on Marquette's objection. The district court's findings, like others we have reviewed, certainly "could have used more details," *Forbush v. J.C. Penny Co.*, 98 F.3d 817, 823 (5th Cir. 1996), but nonetheless they make sufficiently clear that the district court did "consider the relationship between the extent of success and the amount of the fee award," *Combs v. City of Huntington*, 829 F.3d 388, 395 (5th Cir. 2016) (alteration omitted) (quoting *Farrar v. Hobby*, 506 U.S. 103, 115–16 (1992)). Marquette's arguments with respect to the *Johnson* framework do not persuade us that the district court abused its discretion by declining to make further downward adjustment to the fee award.

III. CONCLUSION

For the foregoing reasons, we AFFIRM the judgment of the district court.

United States Court of Appeals
for the Fifth Circuit

No. 16-60073

SIMMS
vs.
LOCAL 1752, INT'L LONGSHOREMEN ASS'N

Appeal from the United States District Court for the
Southern District of Mississippi

Decided: September 29, 2016
Revised: October 13, 2016

Citation: 838 F.3d 613, 4 Adm. R. 288 (5th Cir. 2016).

Before **KING, SMITH,** and **COSTA,** Circuit Judges.

[—1—] **KING,** Circuit Judge:

Patrick Simms, who is not a union member, was denied referral for employment because he refused to pay a fee to use the union's hiring hall. The district court dismissed his suit asserting that the fee was unlawful. We find no error and AFFIRM.

I. FACTUAL AND PROCEDURAL BACKGROUND

As alleged in the complaint, CSA Equipment Company, LLC ("CSA") and Defendant–Appellee International Longshoremen Association Local 1752 ("Local 1752") are parties to a collective bargaining agreement, and as part of [—2—] this agreement, CSA must hire all of its clerks and other employees through the hiring hall operated by Local 1752. "[A]s a condition of obtaining employment through [Local 1752's] hiring hall," an individual must either be a union member or pay a "service fee." CSA assists in the collection of this fee by deducting the amount due from the employee's paycheck if the employee signs a checkoff authorization card.

Plaintiff–Appellant Patrick Simms works for CSA primarily as a clerk in charge and, therefore, is required to use Local 1752's hiring hall. Simms is not a member of Local 1752 and did not make the required payments to Local 1752 for use of its hiring hall. Local 1752 sent Simms a letter stating, in part, that

"to be in good standing [Simms] must either pay Hiring Hall fees or be a dues paying member of one of the Locals," and since Simms was not a union member, he "must make some arrangement with the Hiring Hall and the Locals to pay the Hiring Hall fees related to being referred for work." If Simms failed to pay the fees, the letter stated that he would "no longer be able to be referred for hire through the Hiring Hall."

Simms did not make the required payments, and on May 1, 2015, according to Simms's complaint, "Local 1752 caused CSA to not employ Simms." In other words, Simms would no longer be referred for employment with CSA through the hiring hall. Ten days later, however, Simms "sign[ed] under protest" an agreement with Local 1752 to pay in installments the delinquent fees, allowing him to be referred through the hiring hall once again.

On October 8, 2015, Simms filed suit against Local 1752 asserting that it breached its duty of fair representation; its assessment of mandatory fees to Simms, a non-union member, for using the hiring hall was prohibited by Mississippi's right to work law; and the payment agreement was void as against public policy for those reasons. On January 8, 2016, the district court granted Local 1752's motion to dismiss. The court held that Simms's [—3—] allegations were insufficient to state a claim for breach of the duty of fair representation, and that Mississippi's right to work law was preempted by federal law "with respect to the issue of requiring non-members to pay hiring hall fees." The court further held that Simms's claim that the payment agreement he had reached with the union was void as against public policy was not cognizable because the relevant Mississippi law was preempted by federal law. Simms timely appealed.

II. STANDARD OF REVIEW

This court reviews "a district court's order on a motion to dismiss for failure to state a claim under Rule 12(b)(6) de novo" and "accept[s] 'all well-pleaded facts as true, viewing them in the light most favorable to the plaintiff.'" *New Orleans City v. Ambac Assurance Corp.*, 815 F.3d 196, 199–200 (5th Cir. 2016) (quoting *In re Katrina Canal Breaches Litig.*, 495 F.3d 191, 205 (5th Cir. 2007)). "Dismissal is appropriate when the plaintiff has not alleged 'enough facts to state a claim to relief that is plausible on its face' and has failed to 'raise a right to relief above the speculative level.'" *True v. Robles*, 571 F.3d 412, 417 (5th Cir. 2009) (quoting *Bell Atl. Corp. v. Twombly*, 550 U.S. 544, 555, 570 (2007)).

III. MISSISSIPPI'S RIGHT TO WORK LAW

We first turn to Simms's primary argument that section 14(b) of the National Labor Relations Act ("NLRA"), 29 U.S.C. § 164(b), allows enforcement of Mississippi's right to work law, Miss. Code Ann. § 71-1-47,[1] thereby

---

[1] While Local 1752 argued in the district court that Mississippi's right to work law did not apply to hiring hall fees regardless of federal preemption, Local 1752 does not make this argument on appeal. Section 71-1-47 states, *inter alia*, the following:

(a) Any agreement or combination between any employer and any labor union or labor organization whereby any person not a member of such union or organization shall be denied the right to work for an employer, or whereby such membership is made a condition of employment or continuation of employment by such employer, or whereby any such union or organization acquires an [—4—] employment monopoly in any enterprise, is hereby declared to be an illegal combination or conspiracy and against public policy.

(b) No person shall be required by an employer to become or remain a member of any labor union or labor organization as a condition of employment or continuation of employment by such employer.

. . .

(d) No employer shall require any person, as a condition of employment or continuation of employment, to pay any dues, fees, or other charges of any kind to any labor union or labor organization.

(e) Any person who may be denied employment or be deprived of continuation of his employment in violation of any paragraph of this section shall be entitled to recover from such employer and from any other person, firm, corporation, or association acting in concert with him, by

[—4—] precluding the assessment of hiring hall fees to Simms. "[I]n passing the NLRA Congress largely displaced state regulation of industrial relations," and thus, states "may not regulate activity that the NLRA protects, prohibits, or arguably protects or prohibits." *Wis. Dep't of Indus., Labor & Human Relations v. Gould Inc.*, 475 U.S. 282, 286 (1986) (citing *San Diego Bldg. Trades Council, Millmen's Union, Local 2020 v. Garmon*, 359 U.S. 236 (1959)). Section 14(b), however, provides a limited exception:

> Nothing in this subchapter shall be construed as authorizing the execution or application of agreements requiring membership in a labor organization as a condition of employment in any State or Territory in which such execution or application is prohibited by State or Territorial law.

29 U.S.C. § 164(b). According to Simms, Local 1752's requirement that he pay fees for obtaining referrals through the hiring hall amounts to compulsory union "membership" under section 14(b), and therefore, Mississippi can prohibit those fees via its right to work law. Local 1752, however, contends that section 14(b) does not apply, and Mississippi's right to work law is therefore preempted under these circumstances. [—5—]

At the outset, it is important to describe clearly the scope of several allegations in the complaint. First, the only fees at issue are fees assessed to Simms, a non-union member, for obtaining referrals through Local 1752's exclusive hiring hall. Second, Simms does not allege that these fees were unreasonable or excessive relative to the costs of operating the hiring hall. Instead, Simms's argument is that, regardless of the amount, all hiring hall fees can be prohibited by a state right to work law because payment of those fees amounts to union "membership" under section 14(b).

---

appropriate action in the courts of this state, such actual damages as he may have sustained by reason of such denial or deprivation of employment.
Miss. Code Ann. § 71-1-47.

This argument hinges on Simms's interpretation of how the hiring hall fees at issue here fit within two provisions of the NLRA, sections 8(a)(3) and 14(b), which were first added to the NLRA by the Taft-Hartley Act in 1947.[2] It is instructive first to review the historical context of the relevant aspects of the Taft-Hartley Act. *See Commc'ns Workers v. Beck*, 487 U.S. 735, 747 (1988) ("[T]he structure and purpose of § 8(a)(3) are best understood in light of the statute's historical origins."). Prior to the Taft-Hartley Act, section 8(a)(3) of the NLRA permitted closed shop, union shop, and agency shop agreements. *Oil, Chem. & Atomic Workers Int'l Union v. Mobil Oil Corp.*, 426 U.S. 407, 414 (1976). Generally speaking, a closed shop is a type of union-security agreement that requires prospective employees to become union members before commencing employment. *Id.* at 409 n.1. In contrast, a union shop, which requires employees to join the union after being hired, and an agency shop, which requires employees to make payments to the union after being hired but not to join the union, are less stringent types of union-security agreements. *See id.* "By 1947, [closed shops] had come under increasing attack," and Congress determined that they should be banned. *Beck*, 487 U.S. at 748. That [—6—] being said, Congress also recognized that prohibiting closed shops could create a free rider problem—*i.e.*, employees choosing not to contribute financially to the union but still benefiting from the union's actions. *See id.*

Against this historical backdrop, section 8(a)(3) of the Taft-Hartley Act attempted to accomplish the "twin purposes" of eliminating "the most serious abuses of compulsory unionism . . . by abolishing the closed shop" but still allowing certain union-security agreements to counter the free rider problem. *NLRB v. Gen. Motors Corp.*, 373 U.S. 734, 740–41 (1963). Specifically, section 8(a)(3) "makes it an unfair labor practice for an employer 'by discrimination in regard to hire or tenure of employment . . . to encourage or

discourage membership in any labor organization.'" *Beck*, 487 U.S. at 744 (quoting 29 U.S.C. § 158(a)(3)). While this would appear to bar any union-security agreement, section 8(a)(3) also contains a proviso that allows unions to require "membership" as a condition of employment thirty days after the beginning of employment so long as the following safeguards are met:

> [N]o employer shall justify any discrimination against an employee for nonmembership in a labor organization (A) if he has reasonable grounds for believing that such membership was not available to the employee on the same terms and conditions generally applicable to other members, or (B) if he has reasonable grounds for believing that membership was denied or terminated for reasons other than the failure of the employee to tender the periodic dues and the initiation fees uniformly required as a condition of acquiring or retaining membership . . . .

29 U.S.C. § 158(a)(3); *see also Beck*, 487 U.S. at 744–45. "Taken as a whole, § 8(a)(3) permits an employer and union to enter into an agreement requiring all employees to become union members as a condition of continued employment, but the 'membership' that may be so required has been 'whittled down to its financial core.'" *Beck*, 487 U.S. at 744–45 (footnote omitted) (quoting *Gen. Motors*, 373 U.S. at 742). [—7—]

"While § 8(a)(3) articulates a national policy that certain union-security agreements are valid as a matter of federal law, § 14(b) reflects Congress' decision that any State or Territory that wishes to may exempt itself from that policy." *Oil, Chem. & Atomic Workers*, 426 U.S. at 416–17. As explained by the Supreme Court, section 14(b) "was designed to prevent other sections of the Act from completely extinguishing state power over certain union-security arrangements. And it was the proviso to § 8(a)(3), expressly permitting agreements conditioning employment upon membership in a labor union, which Congress feared might have this result." *Retail Clerks Int'l Ass'n, Local 1625 v.*

---

[2] Labor Management Relations (Taft-Hartley) Act, ch. 120, sec. 101, §§ 8(a)(3), 14(b), 61 Stat. 136, 140–41, 151 (1947) (codified at 29 U.S.C. §§ 158(a)(3), 164(b)).

Schermerhorn, 373 U.S. 746, 751 (1963) (footnote omitted); *see also Laborers' Int'l Union, Local No. 107 v. Kunco, Inc.*, 472 F.2d 456, 458 (8th Cir. 1973) ("This statute can best be described as an exception to the general rule that the federal government has preempted the field of labor relations regulation."). However, "[s]ince § 8(a)(3) already prohibits the closed shop, the more restrictive policies that § 14(b) allows the States to enact relate not to the hiring process but rather to conditions that would come into effect only *after* an individual is hired." *Oil, Chem. & Atomic Workers*, 426 U.S. at 417.

With this statutory framework in mind, we turn to the primary issue in this case and conclude that section 14(b) does not allow Mississippi to prohibit unions from requiring non-union members to pay a hiring hall fee. Therefore, Mississippi's right to work law, Miss. Code Ann. § 71-1-47, is preempted by federal law to the extent that it prohibits non-union members from being required to pay hiring hall fees. We further agree with the district court that this ruling does not invalidate Mississippi's right to work law in its entirety, but rather only insofar as it could be interpreted as prohibiting unions from requiring non-union members to pay a hiring hall fee.

For nearly 70 years after the NLRA was amended by the Taft-Hartley Act, courts have consistently treated hiring halls as being distinct from union- [—8—] security agreements generally. An exclusive hiring hall is not per se illegal under the NLRA, and it only becomes illegal if it operates in a discriminatory manner. *See Local 357, Int'l Bhd. of Teamsters v. NLRB*, 365 U.S. 667, 673–74 (1961). While the existence of an exclusive hiring hall may encourage union membership, section 8(a)(3) "does not outlaw all encouragement or discouragement of membership in labor organizations; only such as is accomplished by discrimination is prohibited." *Id.* at 674–76 (quoting *Radio Officers' Union of Commercial Telegraphers Union v. NLRB*, 347 U.S. 17, 42–43 (1954)).

Moreover, it is settled law that hiring halls can require non-union members to pay a

reasonable fee related to the costs of operating the hiring hall. *See, e.g., Pittsburgh Press Co. v. NLRB*, 977 F.2d 652, 657 (D.C. Cir. 1992) ("Congress, the Supreme Court, and the NLRB thus agreed on the basic principles of a legitimate hiring hall for which nonunion workers could be charged a fee by the union . . . ."); *NLRB v. Hous. Maritime Ass'n*, 337 F.2d 333, 336 (5th Cir. 1964) ("Reasonable and nondiscriminatory charges for the union's referral services were legal.").[3] This stands in contrast to union-security agreements, which constitute illegal discrimination under the NLRA unless they satisfy section 8(a)(3)'s proviso. *See Beck*, 487 U.S. at 744 ("[Section 8(a)(3)] contains two provisos without which all union-security clauses would fall within this otherwise broad condemnation . . . .").

And this distinction makes sense. Hiring halls serve a unique purpose, one in which the union can act as an employment agency or referral system for the employer, benefiting all of the parties involved. *See Pittsburgh Press*, 977 F.2d at 657 (comparing the original hiring hall with its modern day attributes); [—9—] *Local 357*, 365 U.S. at 673–74 ("Senator Taft made clear his views that hiring halls are useful, that they are not illegal per se, that unions should be able to operate them so long as they are not used to create a closed shop . . . ."). For example, as part of a hiring hall, "[a] union may . . . employ its facilities, its phone lines, its network for identifying and recruiting workers, its judgment and expertise in matching a worker's skills with a particular job, or its members' time and effort in building and maintaining a job referral system." *Pittsburgh Press*, 977 F.2d at 661. This distinction is why, unlike a union-security agreement, no court that we are aware of, and Simms has pointed to none, has held that referral fees assessed to non-union members for use of a hiring hall can be prohibited under a state right to work law. Put another way, while a union-security agreement can amount to union "membership" under section 14(b),

---

[3] Conversely, an unreasonable or excessive hiring hall fee assessed to non-union members can constitute an unfair labor practice. *See, e.g., NLRB v. Local 138, Int'l Union of Operating Eng'rs*, 385 F.2d 874, 877–78 (2d Cir. 1967).

requiring a non-union member to pay a reasonable referral fee for the use of an exclusive hiring hall does not.

Indeed, more than fifty years ago this court held that section 14(b) does not apply to hiring halls. *NLRB v. Hous. Chapter, Associated Gen. Contractors, Inc.*, 349 F.2d 449, 453 (5th Cir. 1965) ("[T]he long and short of the matter is that § 14(b) contemplates only those forms of union security which are the practical equivalent of compulsory unionism."); *see also Kunco*, 472 F.2d at 458–59; *NLRB v. Tom Joyce Floors, Inc.*, 353 F.2d 768, 771 (9th Cir. 1965). Contrary to Simms's position, assessing a fee to non-union members for use of a hiring hall does not distinguish the instant case from this precedent. It is settled law that, under the NLRA, exclusive hiring halls can assess non-union members a reasonable fee for the costs of operating the hiring hall. Such a fee does not constitute union "membership" under section 14(b), and this conclusion is reinforced by the fact that this fee relates to pre-hire rather than post-hire conduct. *See Oil, Chem., & Atomic Workers*, 426 U.S. at 417 ("It is evident, then, that § 14(b)'s primary concern is with state regulation of the [—**10**—] post-hiring employer-employee-union relationship."); *see also Int'l Union of the United Ass'n of Journeymen & Apprentices of the Plumbing and Pipefitting Indus. v. NLRB*, 675 F.2d 1257, 1262 (D.C. Cir. 1982) ("Use of a hiring hall precedes hiring, and therefore does not constitute 'membership' under § 14(b)."). We reject Simms's contention that the fact that the fees here were supposed to be collected at a later date via deductions from Simms's paycheck (rather than prior to the referral) transforms this into post-hire conduct.

Simms points to *Beck* in support of his argument that the mandatory payment of any fee to a union constitutes "membership" for the purposes of sections 8(a)(3) and 14(b). By this reasoning, Simms concludes that the hiring hall fee assessed in the instant case is either illegal under the NLRA or allowed under section 8(a)(3)'s proviso and, therefore, can be banned under Mississippi's right to work law. But *Beck* does not support this

argument.[4] *Beck* concerned a union-security agreement—not a hiring hall—and these are treated distinctly under the NLRA.[5] As discussed above, unions may require non-union members to pay a reasonable fee for the use of an exclusive hiring hall without violating the NLRA. Simply put, *Beck* does not dictate that the hiring hall fees assessed to Simms amount to union "membership" under section 14(b). [—**11**—]

IV. THE DUTY OF FAIR REPRESENTATION

Simms also fails to allege sufficient facts to state a cognizable claim for breach of the duty of fair representation. Under the NLRA, unions have a duty of fair representation "to serve the interests of all members without hostility or discrimination toward any, to exercise its discretion with complete good faith and honesty, and to avoid arbitrary conduct." *Breininger v. Sheet Metal Workers Int'l Ass'n Local Union No. 6*, 493 U.S. 67, 73 (1989) (quoting *Vaca v. Sipes*, 386 U.S. 171, 177 (1967)). This duty extends to exclusive hiring halls and is violated when a union's actions are "arbitrary, discriminatory, or taken in bad faith." *Fowlkes v. Ironworkers Local 40*, 790 F.3d 378, 388 (2d Cir. 2015) (citing *Air Line Pilots Ass'n v. O'Neill*, 499 U.S. 65, 67 (1991)); *see also Milright & Mach. Erectors, Local Union 720 v. NLRB*, 798 F.2d 781, 784 (5th Cir. 1986) ("We have interpreted the duty of fair representation to mean that a union operating an exclusive hiring hall 'may not apply arbitrary or invidious criteria in referring employees to jobs.'" (quoting *Int'l*

---

[4] Taking Simms's argument to its logical conclusion, if a hiring hall fee were required to satisfy section 8(a)(3)'s proviso to be lawful, then a hiring hall fee assessed at the time of referral would not be lawful under the NLRA. Part of the proviso mandates that union "membership" must not be required until at least 30 days after employment, which would be violated by a hiring hall fee that is assessed when the employee is first referred. In other words, Simms's argument would in effect treat hiring halls that charge non-union members a reasonable fee the same as closed shops, which is not the case under the NLRA.

[5] For similar reasons, Simms's reliance on *Sweeney v. Pence*, 767 F.3d 654 (7th Cir. 2014), is misplaced.

Union of Operating Eng'rs Local 406 v. NLRB,
701 F.2d 504, 508 (5th Cir. 1983))).[6]

Simms, however, does not allege any conduct by Local 1752 that was arbitrary, discriminatory, or done in bad faith. Simms's only allegation on this point can be summarized as the following: he has to pay fees to Local 1752 for use of its hiring hall, and if he does not pay those fees, the hiring hall will stop referring him and he will not be able to obtain employment with CSA. This allegation, however, is insufficient to state a claim for breach of the duty of fair [—12—] representation. As discussed above, an exclusive hiring hall can legally require non-union members to pay a reasonable fee, *see, e.g., Pittsburgh Press,* 977 F.2d at 657. Simms does not allege that the amount of the fee was unreasonable, relying instead only on the fact that a fee was assessed at all. Nor does Simms make any other relevant allegations about the hiring hall's criteria or procedures. Simms's argument that any hiring hall fee assessed to non-union members breaches the duty of fair representation is contrary to settled law, and once again, his reliance on *Beck* is unavailing given that *Beck* did not concern a hiring hall.[7]

V. CONCLUSION

For the foregoing reasons, the judgment of the district court is AFFIRMED.

---

[6] Because Simms has only alleged that the mere fact that a fee was assessed to non-union members was a breach of the duty of fair representation, we need not address whether exclusive hiring halls require a heightened duty of fair representation. *See Bowerman v. Int'l Union, United Auto., Aerospace & Agric. Implement Workers of Am., Local No. 12,* 646 F.3d 360, 368–69 (6th Cir. 2011) (discussing how the Ninth and D.C. Circuits have applied a heightened standard to hiring halls but that a previous panel on the Sixth Circuit had not). Simms would also fail to allege a cognizable claim under a heightened standard.

[7] Simms does not otherwise advance an argument on appeal that the payment agreement he reached with Local 1752 was void as against public policy. Even if he did, we agree with the district court that this claim is not cognizable given that Simms cannot state a claim under Mississippi law based on the required fees at issue here.

United States Court of Appeals
for the Fifth Circuit

No. 15-30827

EDWARDS
VS.
CONTINENTAL CAS. CO.

Appeal from the United States District Court for the
Western District of Louisiana

Decided: November 2, 2016
Revised: November 3, 2016

Citation: 841 F.3d 360, 4 Adm. R. 294 (5th Cir. 2016).

Before **WIENER, CLEMENT,** and **COSTA,** Circuit Judges.

[—1—] **WIENER,** Circuit Judge:

Plaintiff-Appellee, Thomas R. Edwards, sued Defendant-Appellant, Continental Casualty Company ("Continental"), seeking a declaratory judgment that Continental was required to defend him, pursuant to a professional liability insurance policy, in an action brought against Edwards by Cal Dive International, Incorporated ("Cal Dive"). Edwards filed a motion for partial summary judgment seeking a declaration that Continental had a duty to defend him in the suit filed by Cal Dive and Continental filed a motion for summary judgment seeking dismissal of Edwards's claims. The district [—2—] court granted Edwards's motion, holding that Continental had a duty to defend Edwards in the action brought by Cal Dive. We reverse and render judgment rejecting Edwards's claims against Continental.

I. FACTS AND PROCEEDINGS

Edwards represented Andrew Schmidt, a commercial diver, in a personal injury suit, *Schmidt v. Cal Dive Int'l, Inc. (Cal Dive I)*, against Schmidt's employer, Cal Dive, for a brain injury sustained during a work-related dive.[1] The parties entered into a multi-million dollar settlement agreement before trial under which Cal Dive and its insurer paid a lump sum to Schmidt and funded an additional payment through annuity contracts. As a part of the settlement, Cal Dive paid attorney's fees to Edwards through an annuity contract for his representation of Schmidt.

One year after the settlement, Cal Dive and its insurer filed suit against Schmidt and Edwards in *Cal Dive Int'l, Inc. v. Schmidt (Cal Dive II)*, alleging that Schmidt exaggerated or fabricated the extent of his injuries in *Cal Dive I*.[2] Claiming that it was fraudulently induced to settle, Cal Dive sought reimbursement of its lump sum payment to Schmidt and its cost of funding the annuity contracts to Schmidt and to Edwards. It asserted claims for unjust enrichment and restitution against Edwards. Cal Dive alleged that it incurred significant expenses defending itself in Cal Dive I, including, among other costs, attorney's fees, court costs, and other litigation expenses. Cal Dive claimed that it was entitled to restitution from Edwards of all funds that he unjustly received under the invalid settlement agreement. The district court [—3—] dismissed Cal Dive's complaint for failure to state a claim, and this court affirmed.[3]

Edwards's law firm maintained a professional liability policy with Continental Casualty Company that named Edwards as an insured. Edwards timely notified Continental of the claims brought against him in *Cal Dive II* and sought defense and coverage, but Continental declined to provide either.

Edwards filed a declaratory judgment action against Continental in district court, seeking a declaration that his firm's professional liability policy required Continental to defend him in *Cal Dive II*. Edwards filed a motion for partial summary judgment and Continental filed a motion for summary judgment. The district court granted partial summary judgment in favor of Edwards, holding that Continental had a duty to defend him and Continental appealed.[4]

---

[1] No. 12-cv-00930 (W.D. La. filed Apr. 19, 2012).

[2] No. 14-cv-03033 (W.D. La. filed Oct. 15, 2014).

[3] *Cal Dive Int'l, Inc. v. Schmidt*, 639 F. App'x 214 (5th Cir. 2016) (per curiam) (unpublished).

[4] *Edwards v. Continental Cas. Co.*, No. 15-cv-00168, 2015 WL 5009015 (W.D. La. Aug. 19, 2015).

The sole issue on appeal is whether the district court erred in holding that Continental had a duty to defend Edwards in *Cal Dive II*. Continental argues that: (1) Cal Dive did not assert covered claims against Edwards because the claims did not arise from an "act or omission" in the rendering of legal services by Edwards, and (2) the "damages" sought by Cal Dive were not covered under the policy.

II. ANALYSIS

A. Summary Judgment

"We review a grant of summary judgment *de novo* under the same standard applied by the district court."[5] Summary judgment is appropriate [—4—] when "there is no genuine dispute as to any material fact and the movant is entitled to judgment as a matter of law."[6] We consider the evidence in the light most favorable to the nonmoving party and draw all reasonable inferences in its favor.[7]

"Once a movant who does not have the burden of proof at trial makes a properly supported motion" for summary judgment, "the burden shifts to the nonmovant to show that [the motion] should not be granted."[8] To do so, the nonmovant must "identify specific evidence in the record and . . . articulate the precise manner in which that evidence supports his or her claim."[9] Neither we nor the district court have a duty to "sift through the record in search of evidence to support" the nonmovant's opposition to summary judgment.[10]

B. Insurance Coverage

Continental contends that it had no duty to defend Edwards in the underlying action because Cal Dive's claims against Edwards are not the kind that are covered by the insurance policy. The policy provides that Continental "shall have the right and duty to defend in the **Insured's** name and on the **Insured's** behalf a **claim** covered by this Policy even if any of the allegations of the claim are groundless, false or fraudulent."[11] The operative policy language specifies that a "claim" is one "arising out of an act or omission, including **personal injury**, in the rendering of or failure to render **legal [—5—] services**."[12] "Legal services" are defined as "services . . . performed by an **Insured** for others as a lawyer."[13]

The parties do not dispute that Louisiana law applies to this diversity action. Under Louisiana law, "[t]he duty to defend is determined by examining the allegations of the injured plaintiff's petition . . . and the insurer is obligated to tender a defense unless the petition unambiguously excludes coverage."[14] Continental's duty to defend is activated by a claim covered by the policy.

The claims filed against Edwards in this action are not the type of claims that are covered by his firm's insurance policy with Continental, so Edwards is not seeking defense against a "covered" claim. This is so because Cal Dive's claims against Edwards do not "arise out of an act or omission . . . in [Edwards's] rendering of or failure to render legal services." Even though Cal Dive's unjust enrichment and restitution claims against Edwards have some general and remote relation to his *representation of Schmidt*, Cal Dive does not allege a single professional act or omission by Edwards that gives rise to such claims. Instead, Cal Dive named Edwards in the underlying action only because Edwards received settlement funds from Cal Dive for

---

[5] *Boone v. Citigroup, Inc.*, 416 F.3d 382, 392–93 (5th Cir. 2005).

[6] FED. R. CIV. P. 56(a).

[7] *See Lawyers Title Ins. Corp. v. Doubletree Partners, L.P.*, 739 F.3d 848, 856 (5th Cir. 2014).

[8] *Ragas v. Tenn. Gas Pipeline Co.*, 136 F.3d 455, 458 (5th Cir. 1998).

[9] *Id.; accord RSR Corp. v. Int'l Ins. Co.*, 612 F.3d 851, 857 (5th Cir. 2010).

[10] *Forsyth v. Barr*, 19 F.3d 1527, 1537 (5th Cir. 1994) (quoting *Skotak v. Tenneco Resins, Inc.*, 953 F.2d 909, 915 n.7 (5th Cir. 1992)).

[11] **Emphasis in original.**

[12] **Emphasis in original.**

[13] **Emphasis in original.**

[14] *Hardy v. Hartford Ins. Co.*, 236 F.3d 287, 290 (5th Cir. 2001) (citing *Yount v. Maisano*, 627 So. 2d 148, 153 (La. 1993)).

his representation of *Schmidt*. Cal Dive did not allege that Edwards did or failed to do anything to warrant its claims. In fact, Cal Dive specifically alleged that it does "not believe that Edwards . . . [was] aware of Schmidt's fraud." Cal Dive's complaint, for which Edwards seeks defense from Continental, contains no allegations against Edwards, save for his receipt of settlement funds in the nature of attorney's fees as a result of his client's alleged fraud. Acts or omissions in the rendering of legal services by Edwards to his client, Schmidt, [—6—] are simply not at issue. Thus, Continental's insurance policy does not provide coverage to Edwards in *Cal Dive II*.

Edwards nevertheless insists that the "arising out of" language of the policy should be applied broadly to provide coverage for Cal Dive's claims. It is true that (1) Louisiana courts read the words "arising out of" expansively, requiring nothing more than "but for" causation, and (2) ambiguous provisions in insurance policies are strictly construed against the insurer and in favor of FINA insurance policy does not provide coverage in this case because Cal Dive's claims did not "arise out of" an act or omission by Edwards in the rendering of legal services to Cal Dive. Applied to these facts, the discrete language in Edwards's policy is not ambiguous.

Edwards also contends that this reading of the insurance policy would result in professional liability policies only covering claims for malpractice and other attorney misdeeds. This argument fails to recognize that the insurance policy at issue does not provide coverage in this particular situation for this particular conduct. Alone, Edwards's representation of Schmidt cannot serve as an act or omission in Edwards's rendering of legal services. Such an interpretation would effectively read the words "act or omission" out of the policy's definition of a claim. In other situations with other insurance policies, a professional liability policy might cover the conduct at issue here. In this case, however, the language of the policy does not provide coverage to Edwards for Cal Dive's claims.

III. CONCLUSION

For the foregoing reasons, we REVERSE the district court's order granting Edwards's motion for summary judgment and RENDER judgment rejecting Edwards's claims against Continental.

(Reporter's Note: Dissenting opinion follows on p. 297).

[—7—] CLEMENT, Circuit Judge, dissenting:

I would affirm the district court's holding that Continental's duty to defend—which is much broader than its duty to provide coverage—was triggered by Cal Dive's complaint against Edwards. We have construed the words "arising out of" used in the policy as "broad, general, and comprehensive terms effecting broad coverage." *Red Ball Motor Freight, Inc. v. Emps. Mut. Liab. Ins. Co. of Wis.*, 189 F.2d 374, 378 (5th Cir. 1951). They simply require that a claim flow from, be incident to, or have a connection with an act or omission in rendering legal services. *See id.*; *see also Perkins v. Rubicon, Inc.*, 563 So. 2d 258, 259 (La. 1990) (reading "arising out of" as only "requiring a connexity similar to" but-for causation). Edwards successfully represented Schmidt in a suit against Cal Dive through litigation and settlement. Cal Dive's claims for unjust enrichment and restitution against Edwards at least have an incidental relationship to his legal representation of Schmidt. Because we must "liberally interpret[]" the allegations of the complaint and hold that the insurer is obligated to tender a defense unless the allegations "unambiguously exclude coverage," I would affirm. *Yount v. Maisano*, 627 So. 2d 148, 153 (La. 1993).

United States Court of Appeals
for the Fifth Circuit

No. 16-60008

IN RE C.F. BEAN L.L.C.

Appeals from the United States District Court for the
Southern District of Mississippi

Decided: November 4, 2016

Citation: 841 F.3d 365, 4 Adm. R. 298 (5th Cir. 2016).

Before JONES, DENNIS, and PRADO, Circuit Judges.

[—2—] PRADO, Circuit Judge:

This appeal involves a third-party complaint alleging maritime products liability. In 2012, Mark Barhanovich was killed in coastal waters south of Biloxi, Mississippi, when the Suzuki outboard engine on his fishing boat struck an underwater dredge pipe, flipped into his boat, and struck him. Barhanovich's estate filed claims in federal district court against C.F. Bean, LLC, Bean Meridian, LLC, and Archer Western Contractors, LLC (collectively, "Bean"), which were responsible for dredging operations in the area. Bean ultimately settled Barhanovich's claims, and C.F. Bean, LLC pled guilty to one count of misconduct or neglect of ship officers in a criminal proceeding related to the same accident.

While Barhanovich's claims were pending, Bean filed a third-party complaint against Suzuki Motor Corporation ("SMC"), among others. After Barhanovich's claims were settled, the district court excluded expert testimony put forth by Bean, and granted SMC's motion for summary judgment against Bean. On appeal, Bean argues that the district court erred in: (1) excluding Bean's original expert report; (2) excluding Bean's second expert report; (3) [—3—] relying upon Bean's criminal proceeding to decide civil liability issues; (4) denying Bean's motion to conduct certain testing on the motor involved in the accident; (5) failing to apply the superseding cause doctrine; and (6) holding that Bean cannot meet its summary judgment burden without expert testimony. We

AFFIRM in part, REVERSE in part, and REMAND for further proceedings.

I. FACTUAL AND PROCEDURAL BACKGROUND

On September 16, 2012, Barhanovich was operating a recreational fishing boat in the waters south of Biloxi, Mississippi, when his boat's SMC-made outboard motor struck a submerged dredge pipe. This dredge pipe was owned by Bean Meridian, LLC and operated by C.F. Bean, LLC pursuant to a subcontract with Archer Western Contractors, LLC. The swivel bracket on the motor broke as a result of this collision, causing the motor to rotate up into the boat, where it struck and fatally injured Barhanovich. In 2013, Bean filed a maritime limitation action under 46 U.S.C. § 30511, seeking to limit its liability for Barhanovich's death. Shortly thereafter, Barhanovich's estate sued Bean for wrongful death. These cases were subsequently consolidated.

In May 2014, Bean filed a third-party complaint against SMC and other third-party defendants, including Suzuki Motor America Inc. ("SMAI"). Bean's claims against the Suzuki entities sought indemnity or contribution based on products liability, sounding in both negligence and strict liability theories. Bean subsequently amended this complaint, most recently in October 2014. SMC was properly served in December 2014, and filed its answer in January 2015. The district court dismissed Bean's claims against the other third-party defendants, leaving SMC the only remaining third-party defendant in this case.

The district court issued a series of case management orders setting out discovery deadlines. The final deadline for Bean's initial designation of experts [—4—] was October 20, 2014. SMC then had until November 21, 2014, to designate its experts, and Bean had until December 5, 2014, to designate rebuttal experts. Bean timely designated Edward Fritsch as its mechanical engineering expert in October 2014, but did not designate a rebuttal expert. SMC itself never formally designated an expert; instead, it adopted

SMAI's timely expert designation when it served its initial disclosures in January 2015.

Third-party discovery continued until August 1, 2015. On July 9, 2015, SMC moved for summary judgment, and moved to strike Fritsch's expert report and exclude his testimony. In its response to SMC's motion to strike, Bean included a "supplemental" report by Fritsch dated July 15, 2015. In its reply, SMC asked that the court also exclude this second report as untimely. In September 2015, Bean settled with Barhanovich's estate. That same month, C.F. Bean, LLC pled guilty to one count of misconduct or neglect of ship officers under 18 U.S.C. § 1115 in a criminal proceeding related to the Barhanovich accident. *United States v. C.F. Bean, LLC*, No. 1:15-cr-71 (S.D. Miss. Nov. 3, 2015). On November 5, 2015, Bean filed a "motion in limine" seeking to conduct additional testing on the SMC motor involved in the accident. The district court understood Bean's motion as a request to reopen discovery.

On November 16, 2015, the district court granted SMC's motion to strike both of Fritsch's expert reports and exclude his testimony at trial. The court also denied Bean's motion for additional testing. Bean moved for reconsideration of these decisions, but the district court denied that motion. The court then granted summary judgment against Bean, concluding that Bean could not establish a genuine issue of material fact regarding its claims against SMC without expert testimony. This appeal followed.

II. STANDARD OF REVIEW

This case arose in admiralty. Therefore, the district court had jurisdiction under 28 U.S.C. § 1333. We have jurisdiction to review the district [—5—] court's final judgment under 28 U.S.C. § 1291. This final judgment incorporated the district court's exclusion of Bean's expert reports and testimony, denial of Bean's motion for additional testing of the motor, and grant of summary judgment against Bean.

We review a district court's exclusion of expert testimony for abuse of discretion.

Sierra Club, Lone Star Chapter v. Cedar Point Oil Co., 73 F.3d 546, 569 (5th Cir. 1996). We give the district court "wide latitude in determining the admissibility of expert testimony" under Federal Rule of Evidence 702, and its "decision will not be disturbed on appeal unless 'manifestly erroneous.'" *Watkins v. Telsmith, Inc.*, 121 F.3d 984, 988 (5th Cir. 1997) (quoting *Eiland v. Westinghouse Elec. Corp.*, 58 F.3d 176, 180 (5th Cir. 1995)). Additionally, we consider four factors to determine whether a district court abused its discretion by excluding expert testimony as untimely: "(1) the explanation for the failure to identify the witness; (2) the importance of the testimony; (3) potential prejudice in allowing the testimony; and (4) the availability of a continuance to cure such prejudice." *Geiserman v. MacDonald*, 893 F.2d 787, 791 (5th Cir. 1990).

We review de novo a district court's grant of summary judgment. *Juino v. Livingston Parish Fire Dist. No. 5*, 717 F.3d 431, 433 (5th Cir. 2013). Just as the district court must, we view "all facts and evidence in the light most favorable to the non-moving party." *Id.* Summary judgment is appropriate "if the movant shows that there is no genuine dispute as to any material fact and the movant is entitled to judgment as a matter of law." Fed. R. Civ. P. 56(a). A genuine dispute of material fact exists when the "evidence is such that a reasonable jury could return a verdict for the nonmoving party." *Royal v. CCC & R Tres Arboles, L.L.C.*, 736 F.3d 396, 400 (5th Cir. 2013) (quoting *Anderson v. Liberty Lobby, Inc.*, 477 U.S. 242, 248 (1986)). [—6—]

Finally, we review a district court's decision not to reopen discovery for abuse of discretion. *Marathon Fin. Ins., RRG v. Ford Motor Co.*, 591 F.3d 458, 469 (5th Cir. 2009). Our standard of review in these cases "poses a high bar; a district court's discretion in discovery matters will not be disturbed ordinarily unless there are unusual circumstances showing a clear abuse." *Id.* (quoting *Seiferth v. Helicopteros Atuneros, Inc.*, 472 F.3d 266, 276 (5th Cir. 2006)).

III. DISCUSSION

We affirm the district court's exclusion of Fritsch's first expert report. However, we reverse the district court's exclusion of Fritsch's second expert report, notwithstanding its untimeliness. Because the district court ruled that Bean could not defeat summary judgment without expert testimony, the district court's grant of summary judgment is also reversed. Finally, we affirm the district court's denial of Bean's motion to conduct additional testing on the motor. On remand, however, we encourage the district court to consider whether to reopen discovery to allow (1) SMC to adequately respond to Fritsch's second expert report and (2) Bean to test the motor. The district court should also consider lesser sanctions for Bean's untimeliness, such as costs and attorneys' fees for SMC's additional discovery.

A. Bean's First Expert Report

The district court excluded Bean's first expert report because it found the report insufficient to support Bean's products liability claims against SMC. Specifically, the district court found that Fritsch's opinions in his initial report "ma[d]e no substantive reference to the design or warnings associated with the Suzuki motor." *See Daubert v. Merrell Dow Pharm., Inc.*, 509 U.S. 579, 591 (1993) (explaining that Federal Rule of Civil Procedure 702 requires expert reports to be relevant to facts at issue). Bean argues that the first report did address the defective nature of SCM's motor, and points to where the original report stated: "But for a structural failure of the swivel bracket of the Suzuki [—7—] outboard motor on Mr. Barhanovich's boat, the motor and its spinning propeller would not have moved into the boat's occupant space and would not have injured or killed Barhanovich." This opinion merely stated the obvious: that the swivel bracket broke and Barhanovich died as a result. Moreover, the first report—the purpose of which was "to estimate the boat impact speed that would have been required to produce the type of motor damage which occurred in the mishap"—did not relate the motor's defective nature to the data discussed

therein. At best, Bean's defect claim was "connected to existing data only by the *ipse dixit* of the expert." *Gen. Elec. Co. v. Joiner*, 522 U.S. 136, 146 (1997). A district court does not abuse its discretion by excluding this kind of conclusory opinion. *See, e.g., Boyd v. State Farm Ins.*, 158 F.3d 326, 331 (5th Cir. 1998) (excluding an expert's opinion that "offers nothing more than [an] unsupported conclusion"). Therefore, we affirm the district court's exclusion of Bean's first expert report.

B. Bean's Second Expert Report

The district court excluded Bean's second expert report as untimely. This second report, also prepared by Fritsch, is dated July 15, 2015. It was attached as an exhibit to Bean's opposition to SMC's motion to strike the first expert report. At the earliest, Bean submitted this report over seven months after the deadline for designating rebuttal experts, and just two weeks before the close of discovery for third-party claims. Bean raises two arguments for admitting this second report. First, Bean argues that the report was merely supplementary, and therefore timely under Federal Rule of Civil Procedure 26(e). Second, Bean argues that even if the report was not supplementary, the district court abused its discretion by excluding it. We address both arguments in turn.

The district court correctly held that Bean's second expert report did not merely supplement the first. Federal Rule of Civil Procedure 26(e) requires [—8—] parties to supplement previous disclosures if they learn that such disclosures are incorrect or incomplete. This duty extends to information included in expert reports and given during expert depositions. Fed. R. Civ. P. 26(e)(2). Parties must make these supplemental expert disclosures by the time Rule 26(a)(3) pretrial disclosures are due. *Id.* However, supplemental "disclosures are not intended to provide an extension of the deadline by which a party must deliver the lion's share of its expert information." *Sierra Club*, 73 F.3d at 571. Initial expert disclosures must be "full and complete." S.D. Miss. Civ. R. 26(a)(2).

Bean argues that Fritsch's opinions in the second report "merely expanded on" his earlier opinion that the motor spun up into the boat due to a structural failure of the swivel bracket. If so, the first report was far from "full and complete": it did not even mention whether the motor suffered from any kind of defect.[1] The second report, by contrast, clearly stated that SCM "knew or should have known" of the motor's "potential hazard" and "fail[ed] to provide adequate warnings"; that the motor was "an unreasonably dangerous product"; and that "a design change was both technologically and economically feasible." These opinions clearly relate to Bean's negligence, failure to warn, and design defect theories.

Fritsch based the conclusions in his second report primarily on documents and deposition testimony provided by SMC. These materials described "driftwood tests" conducted by SMC in 2003. In these tests, an SMC [—9—] motor would hit a stationary object (driftwood) at various speeds up to fifty kilometers per hour (thirty-one miles per hour). At lower speeds, a shock-absorbing mechanism blunted the force of impact. This mechanism (involving rods, cylinders, and a piston) allowed the motor to safely rotate backwards to a certain degree, without breaking the swivel bracket. Under some conditions, however, the swivel bracket did break or crack at higher speeds. These tests, as well as other technical reports produced by SMC, suggested that the swivel bracket could break at speeds above thirty-one miles per hour. Beyond this point, the shock-absorbing mechanism could be exhausted, meaning that the motor had rotated backwards to its maximum safe extent. SMC's

deposition also revealed another accident in which a Suzuki motor hit a stationary object, rotated up into the boat, and killed an occupant. Fritsch stated that there was an economically feasible alternative that would lessen this hazard: to thicken the swivel bracket, which SMC did for later models that featured greater horsepower. Fritsch also revised his estimate of how fast Barhanovich's boat had to be travelling in order to produce the catastrophic break, from twenty-eight miles per hour (determined experimentally as described in the first report) to thirty-five miles per hour (determined using SMC's data as well as his own experimental results). Apart from this revision to the boat's speed, the analysis and opinions in the second report were largely new rather than supplementary. For this reason, the district court did not err in finding that the second report was not supplementary under Federal Rule of Civil Procedure 26(e). Thus, Bean's second expert report was in fact untimely.

The district court's choice of sanction, however, constituted an abuse of discretion. When a party fails to disclose information required by Federal Rule of Civil Procedure 26(a), "the party is not allowed to use that information . . . to supply evidence on a motion . . . or at a trial, unless the failure was substantially justified or is harmless." Fed. R. Civ. P. 37(c)(1). The district [—10—] court may order alternative sanctions as well, such as awarding costs and attorneys' fees to the other parties. Fed. R. Civ. P. 37(c)(1)(A)–(C). We consider four factors to determine whether a district court abused its discretion by excluding testimony as a sanction for violation of a discovery order: "(1) the explanation for the failure to identify the witness; (2) the importance of the testimony; (3) potential prejudice in allowing the testimony; and (4) the availability of a continuance to cure such prejudice." *Geiserman*, 893 F.2d at 791. Under the particular circumstances of this case, these factors suggest that the district court abused its discretion by excluding Bean's second expert report for untimeliness.

Under the first factor, Bean provides a reasonable explanation for failing to disclose Fritsch's opinions by the expert disclosure

---

[1] This is not to suggest that Fritsch could have provided a defect opinion in the first report. At the time, he knew little more than the mere fact of the accident, and his experiment failed to replicate the kind of catastrophic break that occurred in Barhanovich's swivel bracket. Fritsch had not been able to test the subject motor and did not yet have access to SCM's "driftwood tests" (discussed below). Under these evidentiary constraints, it would have been difficult for Fritsch to establish either negligence or an unreasonably dangerous defect—of design, manufacturing, or failure to warn. *See generally* Restatement (Second) of Torts § 402A (Am. Law Inst. 1975).

deadline. The district court, and SMC on appeal, focused on why Bean failed to request an extension of the expert disclosure deadline. Bean presents no answer to this question. Instead, Bean focuses on why it could not have submitted the second report by the expert disclosure deadline. Bean explains that it could not obtain discovery from SMC until SMC answered the third-party complaint in January 2015, well beyond the deadline for expert disclosures. The driftwood tests, technical reports, and deposition testimony—on which Fritsch based his second report—were all unavailable in October 2014, when Bean's initial expert disclosures were due.

Bean's explanation for its delay in disclosing Fritsch's defect opinions is reasonable. Parties are not generally expected to disclose expert opinions before discovery commences. Indeed, Fritsch based his second report in part on information—particularly the driftwood tests—that was not available to him before discovery. So we cannot say that Fritsch acted unreasonably by waiting to form opinions about the defective nature of SMC's motor until receiving discovery from SMC. In addition, the district court made no finding of bad faith [—11—] on Bean's part. *Cf. Verzwyvelt v. St. Paul Fire & Marine Ins.*, 204 F.R.D. 309, 311 (W.D. La. 2001) (holding that exclusion was inappropriate in part because defendants showed "a lack of organization" but "no bad faith" in failure to timely disclose expert report). Neither has Bean repeatedly caused delay in this litigation. *Cf. Barrett v. Atl. Richfield Co.*, 95 F.3d 375, 380–81 (5th Cir. 1996) (dilatory tactics weighed against relief on appeal for proponent of excluded evidence).

To be sure, Bean's failure to request an extension of the expert disclosure deadline does injure its argument. *See, e.g., Metro Ford Truck Sales, Inc. v. Ford Motor Co.*, 145 F.3d 320, 324 (5th Cir. 1998) (failure to request an extension of expert disclosure deadline in trial court weighed against proponent of excluded evidence on appeal); *Barrett*, 95 F.3d at 381 (same). In Bean's defense, however, it did timely designate Fritsch as an expert; the first report was simply incomplete. *Cf. Geiserman*, 893 F.2d at 789 (appellant did not designate

any expert witness until after deadline). On balance, Bean's explanation weighs in favor of reversing the district court.

Under the second factor, Bean's second expert report and Fritsch's testimony were important to Bean's case. In fact, from the district court's perspective, expert testimony in this case was critical: the court granted summary judgment because Bean lacked admissible expert testimony. We have reversed the district court in several other cases where the excluded testimony is similarly essential. *See, e.g., Betzel v. State Farm Lloyds*, 480 F.3d 704, 707–08 (5th Cir. 2007); *EEOC v. Gen. Dynamics Corp.*, 999 F.2d 113, 116 (5th Cir. 1993); *Murphy v. Magnolia Elec. Power Ass'n*, 639 F.2d 232, 235 (5th Cir. 1981). *But see Geiserman*, 893 F.2d at 791 (noting that the significance of the excluded testimony was "so much the more reason to be sure its introduction was properly grounded"). [—12—]

This case differs from others where we upheld exclusion of a party's expert in part because that party could call other experts to testify on a particular issue. For example, in *Metro Ford Truck Sales*, we noted that only one of the appellant's expert witnesses was excluded, and the appellant in that case did not even claim that exclusion "impacted its summary judgment positions." 145 F.3d at 324 n.6. Likewise, in *1488, Inc. v. Philsec Investment Corp.*, 939 F.2d 1281 (5th Cir. 1991), we observed that "[e]nforcement of the district court's [scheduling] order did not leave the defendants without an expert witness on the issue of valuation." *Id.* at 1288. Here, by contrast, Fritsch was Bean's only expert who could testify about a defect, and his testimony was crucial to Bean's case. The importance of Fritsch's report and testimony weigh in favor of reversing the district court.

Under the third factor, admitting Bean's second expert report and allowing Fritsch to testify would prejudice SMC. Bean submitted this report near the end of the discovery period, leaving SMC little opportunity to examine and rebut Fritsch's new opinions. To properly rebut and re-depose Fritsch would cost substantial time and expense to SMC. On the other hand, Bean submitted its second expert report before the discovery deadline, and several months before trial was scheduled. This was not a case of one party ambushing the other with undisclosed expert opinions at trial. *Cf. Miksis v. Howard*, 106 F.3d 754, 760 (7th Cir. 1997) (striking expert disclosures submitted three days before trial). Nevertheless, the prejudice to SMC weighs against reversing the district court.

Under the fourth factor, a continuance would have sufficed to cure prejudice to SMC. This Court has repeatedly stated that "a continuance is the 'preferred means of dealing with a party's attempt to designate a witness out of time.'" *Campbell v. Keystone Aerial Surveys, Inc.*, 138 F.3d 996, 1001 (5th Cir. 1998) (quoting *Bradley v. United States*, 866 F.2d 120, 127 n.11 (5th Cir. [—13—] 1989)). SMC itself requested a continuance as an alternative to excluding Bean's second expert report. A continuance would allow SMC to produce a rebuttal report and re-depose Fritsch. The suitability of a continuance to cure prejudice to SMC weighs in favor of reversing the district court.

Notwithstanding the wide latitude we give district courts in deciding discovery matters, excluding Fritsch's second report and his testimony was not the appropriate sanction in this case. Bean's explanation for not submitting a complete expert report by the disclosure deadline is reasonable. Although Bean cannot explain why it did not move to extend the deadline, there is no indication of bad faith on Bean's part. The expert report and testimony were essential to Bean's case. And a continuance would cure much of the prejudice to SMC from Bean's late disclosure. On these facts, excluding critical expert testimony was disproportionately harsh for what amounts to failure to request an extension of the expert disclosure deadline. More appropriate sanctions include allowing SMC to re-depose and rebut Fritsch, and awarding SMC costs and attorneys' fees for this additional discovery.

C. Summary Judgment

The district court granted summary judgment against Bean after excluding Fritsch's expert reports and testimony. In fact, Bean's lack of admissible expert testimony was the ground on which the court granted summary judgment. Specifically, the court found that "the nature of Bean's claim against Suzuki . . . implicates scientific, technical, or other specialized knowledge, and that no reasonable trier of fact could find for Bean and Archer Western on their products liability claim against Suzuki in the absence of such expert testimony." Because we reverse the district court's exclusion of Fritsch's second expert report and testimony, we must also reverse the court's summary judgment against Bean. We need not address Bean's other arguments for reversal of summary judgment. [—14—]

D. Bean's Motion for Additional Testing of the Motor

Finally, the district court denied Bean's "motion in limine" for additional testing of Barhanovich's motor. The district court understood Bean's request as a motion to reopen discovery. Bean filed this motion on November 5, 2015, at which time the motor was in the custody of the U.S. Coast Guard. The Coast Guard had taken control of Barhanovich's boat shortly after the accident. Bean argues that it repeatedly requested access to test the motor, which the Coast Guard repeatedly denied due to the parallel criminal investigation. That investigation ended on November 3, 2015, when judgment was entered following C.F. Bean, LLC's guilty plea. Judgment in a Criminal Case, *C.F. Bean, LLC* (No. 1:15-cr-71). Bean seeks to test the strength of the subject swivel bracket to help determine whether it suffered from a design or manufacturing defect.

Bean did not make this request until several months after the close of discovery, and only a few weeks before the trial was scheduled to begin. Although it may have been futile for Bean to make this request while the criminal investigation was ongoing, Bean could have requested a stay of its civil case instead. Under these circumstances, the district court did not abuse its discretion by denying Bean's eleventh-hour motion. *See, e.g., Pustejovsky v. Pliva, Inc.*, 623 F.3d 271, 278 (5th Cir. 2010) (affirming district court's denial of request to re-depose a witness where the request was made after the court granted summary judgment). On remand, however, the district court should consider whether to reopen discovery for the limited purpose of allowing (1) SMC to rebut and re-depose Fritsch and (2) Bean to test the motor. The district court should also consider awarding costs and attorneys' fees to SMC for its additional discovery. [—15—]

IV. CONCLUSION

For the foregoing reasons, we AFFIRM in part, REVERSE in part, and REMAND for further proceedings.

(Reporter's Note: Dissenting opinion follows on p. 305).

[—16—] **JONES,** Circuit Judge, dissenting:

I respectfully dissent from the panel majority's holding (and only this holding) that the district court abused its discretion by excluding Bean's untimely second expert report. The panel majority states the correct legal standards but, in my opinion, misapplies them to the case at hand. The upshot of the majority's reasoning is to revise and extend the district court's already generous pretrial discovery order.

Placing the court's exclusion order in the litigation timeline is critical. On September 16, 2012, Mark Barhanovich died after his boat struck a dredge pipe operated by Bean and the boat's Suzuki motor catapulted into the boat and hit him. Six months later, Bean filed a limitation-of-liability action, and Barhanovich's estate sued Bean. After consolidating the cases, the district court granted Bean leave on April 23, 2014, to file a third-party complaint against Suzuki Motor Corporation (SMC). Later in 2014, Bean filed an amended third-party complaint against SMC. Bean's complaint demanded indemnification from SMC based on a theory of products liability. On January 2, 2015, SMC filed its answer.

The case was initially set for trial in August 2015, but the district court granted the parties' requests for extension of discovery-related deadlines six different times, which delayed both the general discovery deadline and the trial date. The court entered its initial case management order on October 16, 2013, scheduling the case for trial on August 3, 2015. On the parties' requests, it then amended the order on July 17, 2014; August 25, 2014; December 11, 2014; February 4, 2015; March 18, 2015; and July 10, 2015—each time extending discovery-related deadlines. As a result, the overall discovery deadline was August 1, 2015, and the trial was set to occur during a three-week term of court [—17—] beginning November 30, 2015. Bean did not settle with the Barhanovich family until September 2015.

In the meantime, Bean needed experts to prove up its products-liability claims against SMC. After the district court granted the parties' requests for extensions of the expert-designation deadlines, Bean's initial expert-designation deadline was October 20, 2014, and its rebuttal expert-designation deadline was December 5, 2014. Bean timely designated Edward Fritsch as its expert; his report largely took to task Barhanovich for piloting his boat at an excessive speed. As the panel majority note, Fritsch's initial report "was far from 'full and complete'" and "did not even mention whether the motor suffered from any kind of defect"—the core of a products-liability case. Despite the inadequacy of Fritsch's initial report, and despite the district court's demonstrated willingness to extend expert-designation deadlines, Bean sought no extension of the October and December deadlines.

Then, between July 15 and 30, 2015—two and a half years after Bean initiated this suit, nine months after Bean's expert-designation deadlines passed, and mere days before the August 1 discovery deadline—Bean made its move. On July 30, Bean filed a second report by Fritsch dated July 15 in opposition to SMC's motion for summary judgment. As the panel majority agree, Fritsch's second report contained "largely new" opinions that "clearly relate to Bean's negligence, failure to warn, and design defect theories." The district court struck this report because it was not filed by Bean's expert-designation deadlines, "and despite seeking and receiving numerous extensions of other deadlines in this case, Bean has never requested an extension of the deadline for submission of rebuttal experts." The district court emphasized that "Bean was well aware of the nature of its claims against Suzuki long before these deadlines expired," and yet, "Bean has proffered no [—18—] good explanation for why it failed to timely request that its expert disclosure deadline be continued, or that the deadline for submitting rebuttal experts be extended." In light of Bean's failure to explain its errors, the district court declined to permit Bean's "ambush" of SMC and struck the report.

The question presented here is whether the district court's exclusion of Fritsch's untimely second report was "a clear abuse of discretion." *Geiserman v. MacDonald,* 893

F.2d 787, 790 (5th Cir. 1990). The answer to this question turns in large part on Bean's explanation for its failure timely to disclose Fritsch's second report. *See id.* at 791. In my view, neither Bean's proffered explanation nor the record can support the holding that the district court clearly abused its discretion.

Bean's sole excuse for its untimely submission is a red herring. Bean asserts that it did not obtain the discovery documents that undergird Fritsch's second report until several months after the expert-designation deadlines passed, and without those documents, it was impossible to offer an expert report concerning the Suzuki motor. That conclusion does not follow from Bean's premise. At most, its premise shows only that at the time of its initial deadlines, Bean could not offer Fritsch's second report. The documents' initial unavailability, however, says nothing about Bean's subsequent delay in disclosing a report based on later-acquired documents or Bean's failure to request deadline extensions. Bean thus ignores the central issue in this case, which is whether the district court abused its discretion by excluding Fritsch's second report, not at the time of Bean's initial expert-designation deadlines but instead after a subsequent nine-month delay.

On this question, three reasons can be elicited from the record in support of the district court's discretionary decision to exclude the second report. To begin, even viewed in its most favorable light, Bean's argument concerning the [—19—] unavailability of SMC's documents seems disingenuous. Bean had obtained the SMC documents on which Fritsch's second report was based nearly four months before it produced the report to SMC and the court. Bean's opening brief admits that "Suzuki . . . provide[d] full responses [to Bean's discovery requests] . . . [on] April 6, 2015." Bean did not file Fritsch's second report until July 30, 2015. The four-month time gap speaks for itself.

Moreover, the relationship between the documents disclosed on April 6 and the report filed on July 30 is unmistakable. Fritsch's report emphasizes that "[t]he principal purpose of this report is to comment on the

Suzuki documents that have been produced in the discovery process since October 2014." He compared his current analysis to his analysis "[p]rior to Suzuki's production of its design and test documents." Fritsch highlighted at least six documents that he found particularly important to his analysis:

- Limited Warranty for 2001 and Later Four Stroke Models, which "specifically lists striking submerged objects as one of the situations not covered by the warranty."

- Test Standard for Running on Driftwood, which "describes a test protocol by which a Suzuki motor, mounted on a test boat, is subjected to an impact with a moored, floating wooden log of a specified standard length and diameter."

- Test report SES T 8561, which "describes a series of driftwood tests conducted on the DF225/250 outboard motor during the period from July 1 to August 1, 2003."

- A "technical reporting memo," which "indicates that the shock blow setting was 515.4 kgf/cm² (7,330 psi)."

- Engineering Change Notice 93J-069, which Fritsch described as "[a] document of significant utility."

- Engineering Change Notice 93J-0668, which Fritsch described as "[a]nother document of interest" and "notable." [—20—]

Finally, after surveying the documents, the report transitions to a heading entitled "Calculations Using Information from Suzuki's Documents." That section emphasizes the importance of these documents:

The documents produced by Suzuki provide a wealth of dimensional information on the DF225 motor as well as data on the performance of that motor in the driftwood impact tests conducted by Suzuki in 2003. That dimensional information and test data have provided me with inputs for a variety of calculations that are relevant to quantify general performance characteristics of the middle unit of the DF225 motor and the probable behavior of that unit in the subject accident. On the pages to follow, a series of seven figures (Figures 6 through 12) are presented to summarize the results of those calculations.

In short, Fritsch's second report was based on documents that Bean acquired nearly four months before it filed Fritsch's report with the district court.

It is thus hard to take seriously Bean's argument that it could not disclose a report without the necessary supporting documents, when even after receiving the crucial documents, Bean waited nearly four months, up to the eve of the close of discovery, to file the report with the court.

Second, Bean never sought to extend its expert-designation deadlines and, as the panel majority concede, Bean "presents no answer to [the] question" why it failed to do so. Bean's failure to request deadline extensions is curious; Bean clearly knew before the expiration of the deadlines that Fritsch's initial expert report did not tackle defects in the Suzuki motor or mounting. If for no other reason, Bean knew this because about a month before Bean's deadline for identifying a rebuttal expert, SMC's expert's report stated: "I find no engineering opinions in Fritsch's report which are critical of the design or construction of the Suzuki outboard motor." In light of Bean's obvious failure initially to produce expert evidence against SMC, the district court explained that "Bean has proffered no good explanation for why it failed to timely request [—21—] that its expert disclosure deadline be continued, or that the deadline for submitting rebuttal experts be extended." Even in its briefing to this court, Bean provides no such explanation. Its failure to do so surely does not weigh in favor of finding that the district court clearly abused its discretion.

And third, that the district court had accommodated the parties and granted numerous extensions of discovery deadlines makes an abuse-of-discretion finding all the more unsupportable. This court treats as paramount "a trial court's need to control its docket." *Hamburger v. State Farm Mut. Auto. Ins.*, 361 F.3d 875, 884 (5th Cir. 2004). Indeed, "[a]dherence to . . . scheduling orders [is] critical in maintaining the integrity of judicial proceedings," and "we are loath to interfere with the court's enforcement of that order" where the court has not abused its discretion. *1488, Inc. v. Philsec Inv. Corp.*, 939 F.2d 1281, 1289 (5th Cir. 1991). This case should be no exception. As the district court recounted, it had granted at least six prior motions to extend various deadlines, and it had been "liberal in granting the parties' prior requests for extensions of deadlines." Under these circumstances, we should hardly fault the district court for putting its foot down "less than one month before trial" and "declin[ing] to again amend the Case Management Order and reopen expert testimony." The district court made a quintessential discretionary decision to control its docket to which this court must defer.

In light of Bean's flimsy excuse and a holistic review of the record, I cannot agree that "Bean's explanation weighs in favor of reversing the district court." Bean's proffered explanation goes only to the state of affairs at the time its disclosure deadlines passed, but it does not explain Bean's failure to seek deadline extensions and otherwise timely disclose Fritsch's second report. A district court that has accommodated litigants at every turn and declines to do so at the eleventh hour when a litigant has not sought a similar accommodation [—22—] or disclosed an expert report within a reasonable period of time cannot be said to have clearly abused its discretion. I respectfully dissent.

United States Court of Appeals
for the Fifth Circuit

No. 16-30009

DEPERRODIL
vs.
BOZOVIC MARINE, INC.

Appeal from the United States District Court for the
Western District of Louisiana

Decided: November 17, 2016
Revised: November 21, 2016

Citation: 842 F.3d 352, 4 Adm. R. 308 (5th Cir. 2016).

Before **JOLLY, BARKSDALE,** and **SOUTHWICK,**
Circuit Judges.

[—1—] BARKSDALE, Circuit Judge:

In this maritime-tort action for injuries arising out of plaintiff's being taken to a work site on a vessel operated by defendant, a third-party tortfeasor, primarily at issue is whether the collateral-source rule allows plaintiff to recover the unpaid, written-off portion of his billed medical expenses, when the remaining, paid portion of the billed expenses was through workers'-compensation insurance provided by his non-tortfeasor employer, pursuant to the Longshore and Harbor Workers' Compensation Act (LHWCA). Also at issue are: whether liability can be imposed on the vessel's owner for injuries **[—2—]** suffered in rough seas when the passenger knew the weather conditions and risks; and whether a district court may use an above-average work-life expectancy to calculate future lost wages. AFFIRMED in part; VACATED in part; REMANDED.

I.

Robert dePerrodil was injured while aboard the M/V THUNDERSTAR, a 65-foot crewboat owned and operated by Bozovic Marine, Inc. DePerrodil, a 70-year-old oilfield consultant with more than four decades of oilfield experience, worked for Petroleum Engineers, Inc. (PEI). PEI chartered the vessel, operated by Captain Bozovic, to take dePerrodil from Venice, Louisiana, to his work site on an offshore platform.

When dePerrodil and Captain Bozovic realized dePerrodil would not be able to board the platform because the liftboat was not present, dePerrodil asked Captain Bozovic to return to port. Facing rough seas while returning, Captain Bozovic steered the vessel over an eight-to-ten-foot wave at full throttle; but, he did not decelerate upon reaching the crest. The vessel fell into the wave's trough, causing dePerrodil (who was standing in the wheelhouse) to fall to the floor. He suffered, *inter alia*, injuries to his back.

Pursuant to the LHWCA, PEI carried workers'-compensation insurance for dePerrodil. *See* 33 U.S.C. § 932(a)(1). That insurer for PEI paid $57,385.50 for dePerrodil's medical expenses.

Following a bench trial for this action based on admiralty jurisdiction, the court concluded Bozovic Marine was negligent for: failure to "request that dePerrodil go to the passenger area of the vessel"; failure to stay apprised of the weather conditions; and "erratic operation" of the vessel. *DePerrodil v. Bozovic Marine, Inc.*, No. 6:13-cv-849, 2015 WL 8542829, at *3 (W.D. La. 10 Dec. 2015). As a result of the court's concluding dePerrodil was comparatively negligent for staying in the wheelhouse, instead of moving independently to **[—3—]** the passenger compartment, dePerrodil received 10% liability; Bozovic Marine, 90%. *Id.* at *4.

In awarding dePerrodil $984,395.52, *id.* at *7, the court held, *inter alia*, the collateral-source rule barred any discount of the medical expenses PEI and its insurer were billed, but not required to pay. *Id.* at *4–5. Accordingly, the court awarded the full amount of those expenses billed for dePerrodil's treatment, $186,080.30, even though only approximately one-third of them were paid. *Id.* at *7. And, in calculating future lost wages, the court used an above-average work-life expectancy of 75 years, as recommended by an expert vocational-rehabilitation counselor. *Id.* at *6–7.

II.

Maritime law governs this action. *See Exec. Jet Aviation, Inc. v. City of Cleveland, Ohio*, 409 U.S. 249, 253 (1972). Courts exercising maritime jurisdiction apply general principles of negligence law to tort actions. *See, e.g., Canal Barge Co. v. Torco Oil Co.*, 220 F.3d 370, 376 (5th Cir. 2000); *Daigle v. Point Landing, Inc.*, 616 F.2d 825, 827 (5th Cir. 1980).

A.

Regarding Bozovic Marine's maintaining the court erred in finding it liable for 90% of dePerrodil's injuries, the determination of a legal duty is reviewed *de novo*. *Theriot v. United States*, 245 F.3d 388, 394–95 (5th Cir. 1998). On the other hand, findings of negligence, including causation, are reviewed for clear error. *See Trico Marine Assets, Inc. v. Diamond B Marine Servs., Inc.*, 332 F.3d 779, 786 (5th Cir. 2003). Accordingly, the conclusion that Bozovic Marine owed a duty of reasonable care is reviewed *de novo*; the findings of fact, pursuant to the proper legal standard, for clear error.

In a bench trial, the court must make separate findings of fact and conclusions of law. Fed. R. Civ. P. 52(a)(1). "Findings of fact, whether based on oral or other evidence, must not be set aside unless clearly erroneous, and [—4—] the reviewing court must give due regard to the trial court's opportunity to judge the witnesses' credibility." Fed. R. Civ. P. 52(a)(6). "A finding is clearly erroneous when the appellate court, viewing the evidence in its entirety, is left with the definite and firm conviction that a mistake has been made." *Bertucci Contracting Corp. v. M/V ANTWERPEN*, 465 F.3d 254, 258–59 (5th Cir. 2006) (internal quotation marks omitted).

1.

For the following reasons, the proper legal duty was applied. *See DePerrodil*, 2015 WL 8542829, at *2–3. As the court stated, vessel owners owe their passengers a duty of reasonable care under the circumstances. *See Kermarec v. Compagnie Generale Trans-*

atlantique, 358 U.S. 625, 630 (1959). Our court has held "shipowners, relatively speaking, are held to a high degree of care for the safety of their passengers". *Smith v. Southern Gulf Marine Co. No. 2*, 791 F.2d 416, 420 (5th Cir. 1986). Among the relevant factors are the type of carrier, the crew's experience, the risk involved, defendant's degree of control over passengers, and defendant's ability to take precaution against the risk. *See id.* at 421. Because the court properly identified Bozovic Marine's legal duty before evaluating liability, its negligence finding is reviewed for clear error.

As discussed, the court found Captain Bozovic breached his duty by: (1) failing to tell dePerrodil to move to the passenger area (failure to warn); (2) failing to stay apprised of the relevant weather conditions; and (3) operating the vessel erratically. *DePerrodil*, 2015 WL 8542829, at *3. Bozovic Marine contends it did not breach its duty of reasonable care because the risks were open and obvious to dePerrodil: he was a longshoreman with four decades of experience in the Gulf; knew the seas were rough; and had a clear view of the weather conditions from the wheelhouse. Therefore, Bozovic Marine [—5—] maintains, the captain did not have a duty to protect dePerrodil from the open-and-obvious risk of losing his balance in rough seas.

A vessel owner does not need to warn passengers or make special arrangements for open-and-obvious risks. *See Massey v. Williams-McWilliams, Inc.*, 414 F.2d 675, 678–79 (5th Cir. 1969); *Superior Oil Co. v. Trahan*, 322 F.2d 234, 237 (5th Cir. 1963); *see also Counts v. Lafayette Crewboats, Inc.*, 622 F. Supp. 299, 301 (W.D. La. 1983). For example, in *Superior Oil*, our court found a seaman comparatively negligent when he attempted to board a vessel by jumping from another deck. 322 F.2d at 235. Critical to the seaman's negligence was "that [he] was an experienced seaman and should have been fully cognizant of the danger involved". *Id.* at 237. Thus, failure to avoid an obvious risk led to the finding of comparative negligence. *See id.*

The case at hand is distinguishable because the court found Captain Bozovic liable based, in part, on his specific operation of the vessel, rather than his failure to warm dePerrodil of the risk. Captain Bozovic testified he watched the prior evening's weather report on television, but did not continue to monitor weather conditions on the date he ferried dePerrodil. DePerrodil testified: Captain Bozovic made him aware of the 25 mile-per-hour winds; dePerrodil could see it "was choppy"; he had been on a vessel before when the Gulf was rough; and he was unconcerned about the weather conditions.

Once underway, dePerrodil was standing in the wheelhouse, helping Captain Bozovic look for the liftboat. When they realized dePerrodil would not be able to accomplish his job, he asked the captain to return to port. Captain Bozovic turned the vessel around, heading back into the wind and rougher seas, telling dePerrodil to "hold on". Confronted with four-to-six-foot waves, Captain Bozovic began accelerating up the swells and decelerating down. [—6—] DePerrodil's expert testified this was the proper method for operating the vessel in high seas.

Soon thereafter, however, an eight-to-ten-foot wave approached the vessel. Captain Bozovic accelerated to full throttle up the swell, but did not decelerate after cresting the wave. The vessel dropped into the resulting trough, and dePerrodil and a deckhand "went weightless". DePerrodil fell to the floor, injuring, *inter alia*, his back. Captain Bozovic then decreased speed and idled back to port without further incident.

The court did not clearly err in concluding, *inter alia*, that Captain Bozovic breached his duty to dePerrodil by cresting the eight-foot wave at full throttle. The failure to decelerate was the proximate cause of dePerrodil's injuries. This operational error is underscored by Captain Bozovic's ability to idle the vessel back to port after the accident. That is to say, but for Captain Bozovic's operation of the vessel, dePerrodil would not have suffered his injuries.

The accident would have occurred regardless of whether dePerrodil knew the risks of rough seas. Notwithstanding dePerrodil's being aware of the weather, Captain Bozovic's operation of the vessel cannot be considered an "open and obvious" risk to dePerrodil. As the court stated, "inclement weather does not absolve a captain from operating his vessel in a reasonably prudent manner". *DePerrodil*, 2015 WL 8542829, at *3. Therefore, as noted, it was not clear error to find Bozovic Marine breached its duty of reasonable care under these circumstances. Because the operational negligence is sufficient to sustain Bozovic Marine's liability, it is unnecessary to consider the court's other bases for liability: failure to warn; and failure to monitor the weather.

2.

The court's apportionment of liability is also reviewed for clear error. *Barto v. Shore Constr., L.L.C.*, 801 F.3d 465, 471, 3 Adm. R. 415, 417 (5th Cir. 2015). It found [—7—] dePerrodil negligent for remaining in the wheelhouse, instead of moving independently to the passenger area, and assigned him 10% liability. *DePerrodil*, 2015 WL 8542829, at *4. DePerrodil does not dispute this finding. Bozovic Marine, on the other hand, maintains the parties should, at least, be equally liable.

The evidence showed dePerrodil was in the wheelhouse to look for his work site and did not intend to go below once they were in rough seas (nor was he told to leave the wheelhouse). At trial, the parties did not present evidence about whether the injury would have occurred had dePerrodil been in the passenger area. Based on the trial record, including Captain Bozovic's control over the vessel, it was not clear error to assign 90% of the liability to Bozovic Marine.

B.

Bozovic Marine maintains the court erred in applying the collateral-source rule and awarding dePerrodil medical expenses as billed, rather than paid. The application of the rule is reviewed *de novo*. *Johnson v. Cenac*

Towing, Inc., 544 F.3d 296, 304 (5th Cir. 2000).

The collateral-source rule bars a tortfeasor from reducing his liability by the amount plaintiff recovers from independent sources. *Davis v. Odeco, Inc.*, 18 F.3d 1237, 1243 (5th Cir. 1994). It is a substantive rule of law, as well as an evidentiary rule (disallowing evidence of insurance or other collateral payments that may influence a fact finder). *Id.*

In its simplest form, the rule asks whether the tortfeasor contributed to, or was otherwise responsible for, a particular income source. *See Bourque v. Diamond M. Drilling Co.*, 623 F.2d 351, 354 (5th Cir. 1980). If not, the income is considered "independent of (or collateral to) the tortfeasor", and the tortfeasor may not reduce its damages by that amount. *Davis*, 18 F.3d at 1243. In practice, the rule allows plaintiffs to recover expenses they did not [—8—] personally have to pay. *See id.* Without the rule, however, a third-party income source would create a windfall for the tortfeasor. *Id.* at 1244. Thus, the rule reflects a policy determination: better a potential windfall for the injured plaintiff than the liable tortfeasor. *See* Restatement (Second) of Torts § 920A cmt. b. (Am. Law Inst. 1979) ("[I]t is the position of the law that a benefit that is directed to the injured party should not be shifted so as to become a windfall for the tortfeasor".).

The analysis is complicated when a tortfeasor contributes to a portion of the collateral source. *See, e.g., Davis*, 18 F.3d at 1244. For instance, an employer-tortfeasor may pay part of an employee's health-insurance plan. *See Johnson*, 544 F.3d at 305. In that situation, courts ask whether the collateral source is a bargained-for fringe benefit. *See id.* If so, the fringe benefit is compensation to which the employee is already entitled; as a result, an employer cannot reduce its liability by paying employment compensation. *Davis*, 18 F.3d at 1244. Thus, bargained-for fringe benefits are considered collateral to an employer's liability. *Id.* On the other hand, when an employer obtains a liability-insurance plan, it is providing pre-accident insurance to protect

itself from post-accident expenses. *See Phillips v. Western Co.*, 953 F.2d 923, 932 (5th Cir. 1992) (citing *Allen v. Exxon Shipping Co.*, 639 F. Supp. 1545, 1547–48 (D. Me. 1986)). There, the collateral-source rule does not apply. *See id.*

Courts, therefore, must determine whether a payment stems from a fringe benefit or a prophylactic protection against liability. As our court stated, the "[c]urrent application of the collateral source rule thus turns on the *character* of the benefits received, as well as the *source* of those benefits". *Davis*, 18 F.3d at 1244 (emphasis in original).

Here, the parties rely on a five-factor test from *Phillips* to determine whether the collateral-source rule applies to workers'-compensation insurance. [—9—] *Phillips*, 953 F.2d at 932. *Phillips* and its progeny, however, arise in the employer-tortfeasor context. *See, e.g., Johnson*, 544 F.3d at 305–07; *Davis*, 18 F.3d at 1244–45; *Phillips*, 953 F.2d at 927, 932. The *Phillips* factors are applicable only when the tortfeasor contributes to the benefit. *See Johnson*, 544 F.3d at 304–05. PEI was neither negligent, nor responsible for, dePerrodil's injuries; rather, Bozovic Marine is a third-party tortfeasor. Accordingly, the *Phillips* analysis is inapposite, and the standard collateral-source rule asks whether the payment source was independent of the liable party. *See Davis*, 18 F.3d at 1243.

PEI's LHWCA insurer paid dePerrodil's medical expenses. Bozovic Marine played no role in securing that insurance coverage. Thus, the collateral-source rule applies, and Bozovic Marine is liable for the medical expenses the insurer paid on dePerrodil's behalf. (33 U.S.C. § 933 entitles insurers to subrogation for LHWCA payments.)

The question remains, however, whether the maritime collateral-source rule allows plaintiffs to recover the amount billed, or only the amount paid. As noted, dePerrodil was billed $186,080.30, but the insurer was only required to pay $57,385.50; the balance was written-off. Neither dePerrodil, PEI, nor its insurer were ever liable for the $128,694.80 write-off. (Along that line, citing Louisiana and California law, the court stated: "A plaintiff cannot recover economic damages for medical fees that the provider is precluded, either by agreement or by law, from collecting from the employer". *DePerrodil*, 2015 WL 8542829, at *5. But, notwithstanding its just-stated rule, and without further analysis, it awarded dePerrodil the amount initially billed, $186,080.30. *Id.* at *7.)

There is no direct authority regarding the treatment of written-off LHWCA medical expenses in the maritime-tort context. Consequently, we must look to persuasive authority, namely state and analogous maritime [—10—] authority. *See Manderson v. Chet Morrison Contractors, Inc.*, 666 F.3d 373, 381 (5th Cir. 2012) (reviewing prior state-law and maritime decisions). State laws differ as to their approach to written-off expenses in tort cases; within our circuit alone, three different rules prevail. In Mississippi, the collateral-source rule allows plaintiffs to recover write-offs. *See Wal-Mart Stores, Inc. v. Frierson*, 818 So. 2d 1135, 1139–40 (Miss. 2002) (allowing plaintiff to submit evidence of written-off Medicaid expenses). Texas, on the other hand, does not "allow recovery as damages of medical expenses a health care provider is not entitled to charge". *Haygood v. De Escabedo*, 356 S.W. 3d 390, 396 (Tex. 2012) (considering amounts charged in excess of Medicaid limits). In contrast to the rules in each of these two States, Louisiana allows write-off recovery if plaintiff provided consideration for the benefit or suffered a diminution in patrimony. *See Bozeman v. State*, 879 So. 2d 692, 705–06 (La. 2004).

In the maritime context, our court considered a similar issue in *Manderson*, 666 F.3d at 382. There, the question was, *inter alia*, whether the collateral-source rule allows recovery of written-off medical expenses when an employer paid the expenses as part of its maritime cure obligation. The *Manderson* court stated:

> [O]ur court has repeatedly held an injured seaman may recover maintenance and cure only for those expenses "actually incurred". *E.g., Davis*, 18 F.3d at 1246; *Boudreaux v.*

United States, 280 F.3d 461, 468 (5th Cir. 2002). Accordingly, the relevant amount is that needed to satisfy the seaman's medical charges. This applies whether the charges are incurred by a seaman's insurer on his behalf and then paid at a written-down rate, or incurred and then paid by the seaman himself, including at a non-discounted rate.

666 F.3d at 382. Based on this discussion, our court held it was error to award the amount charged, rather than paid. *Id.* [—11—]

Although *Manderson* is not binding—it involved maritime cure, not a maritime tort or LHWCA insurance—it is the most applicable of the various approaches to write-offs. Moreover, its rationale is very persuasive because maritime cure and LHWCA insurance create similar obligations for employers.

Cure is a vessel-owner's long-established duty to pay medical expenses for seamen injured at sea. *Id.* at 380. It compels an employer to pay work-related medical expenses, regardless of "fault or negligence of the shipowner". *Bertram v. Freeport McMoran, Inc.*, 35 F.3d 1008, 1013 (5th Cir. 1994).

The LHWCA was enacted in part based on shortcomings of maritime cure. *See generally P.C. Pfeiffer Co. v. Ford*, 444 U.S. 69, 75, 78 (1979) (discussing Congressional intent behind the LHWCA). Longshoremen and harbor workers do not necessarily qualify for maritime maintenance and cure because a significant portion of their work is done on shore. *Id.* To cover these workers, Congress enacted the LHWCA, which incorporates and replaces several aspects of maritime common law. *See* 33 U.S.C. § 905 ("Exclusiveness of liability"); *P.C. Pheiffer*, 444 U.S. at 75 ("Congress intended that a worker's eligibility for federal benefits would not depend on whether he was injured while walking down a gangway or while taking his first step onto the land.").

The LHWCA requires employers to carry workers'-compensation insurance to pay for work-related injuries. 33 U.S.C. § 932. Like maritime cure, LHWCA creates a no-fault basis for paying a longshoreman's medical expenses. 33 U.S.C. § 904(b) ("Compensation shall be payable irrespective of fault as a cause for the injury."). When a third-party tortfeasor is responsible for the employee's injury, cure and LHWCA insurance function in the same manner: the employer (or its insurer) has an immediate duty to pay medical expenses even though it is not at fault. These similarities counsel that *Manderson*—prohibiting write-off recovery—provides the correct rule for both maritime cure and LHWCA maritime-tort cases. [—12—]

In sum, LHWCA medical-expense payments are collateral to a third-party tortfeasor only to the extent paid; in other words, under those circumstances, plaintiff may not recover for expenses billed, but not paid. Therefore, the district court erred in awarding the full amount billed. Instead, the proper measure of those damages is the far lesser amount the insurer paid to cover dePerrodil's medical expenses: $57,385.50.

C.

Finally, Bozovic Marine asserts the court miscalculated dePerrodil's future lost earnings because it did not use the Bureau of Labor Statistics (BLS) work-life expectancy average. Damages calculations are findings of fact, reviewed for clear error. *Comar Marine, Corp. v. Raider Marine Logistics, L.L.C.*, 792 F.3d 564, 574, 3 Adm. R. 371, 376 (5th Cir. 2015).

Courts use work-life expectancy data to calculate future earnings, unless there is evidence supporting a variation from the average. *E.g., Madore v. Ingram Tank Ships, Inc.*, 732 F.2d 475, 478 (5th Cir. 1984). "Such an average is not conclusive. It may be shown by evidence that a particular person, by virtue of his health or occupation or other factors, is likely to live and work a longer, or shorter, period than the average." *Id.* (emphasis omitted).

According to BLS data, dePerrodil had a work-life expectancy of 72 years. At trial, however, dePerrodil presented a vocational-rehabilitation counselor as an expert witness. She interviewed dePerrodil on two occasions and reviewed his medical history. She concluded it was "very reasonable" dePerrodil would work until age 75; this conclusion was based on: dePerrodil's testimony that he and his wife had an agreement he would work until age 75; his work history; his earnings records; and his healthcare providers' recommendations for future treatment. DePerrodil's expert economist then provided the court with two calculations, one using BLS' age-72 work-life expectancy; the other, the vocational counselor's age-75 expectancy. With both [—13—] calculations before it, the court awarded future lost wages based on an age-75 retirement. *See DePerrodil*, 2015 WL 8542829, at *5–6.

Bozovic Marine points to two cases in which a court erred by using the plaintiff's stated retirement goal, rather than the BLS average. In *Madore*, the parties each presented expert testimony supporting a 25.8-year work-life expectancy for the injured seaman. 732 F.2d at 478. The calculations were based on the BLS average, and the parties presented no other evidence on the matter. *Id.* Nonetheless, the district court awarded lost-wage damages based on a work-life expectancy of 30 years (until the plaintiff turned 65). *Id.* Our court held this was error because the parties presented no evidence to justify a departure from the BLS average. *Id.*

Another district court chose an above-average calculation "in the middle" of the BLS projection and the Social Security retirement age of 67. *See Barto*, 801 F.3d at 475, 3 Adm. R. at 420. There, the only relevant evidence was plaintiff's testimony he planned to work until he could retire, "[w]hatever the retirement age is". *Id.*, 3 Adm. R. at 420. Our court stated: "even if the district court believed [plaintiff] wanted to work until age 67, *wanting* to work until age 67 is not the only or even the most significant factor in determining whether someone actually *will* work until age 67". *Id.*, 3 Adm. R. at 420 (emphasis in original). Citing *Madore*, our court held this vague testimony was insufficient to support an above-average work-life expectancy. *Id.* at 475–76, 3 Adm. R. at 420.

Here, the court's use of age 75 to calculate damages was not clearly erroneous. DePerrodil fully developed the evidentiary basis for such a departure from the BLS average. Unlike in *Madore*, dePerrodil presented an expert (vocational-rehabilitation counselor) and the medical history upon which the expert based her opinion. As was the case in *Barto*, dePerrodil's stated retirement goal was a critical piece of information. Unlike *Barto*, however, dePerrodil's goal was specific and corroborated by an agreement with [—14—] his wife to work until age 75. Furthermore, the vocational counselor agreed it was a "very reasonable" goal, considering his medical history, work history, and future medical prognosis. Neither of the plaintiffs in *Madore* or *Barto* presented a vocational expert to justify a departure from the BLS statistics. For these reasons, it was not clear error for the court to credit the vocational counselor's expert testimony and award lost-wage damages until age 75.

III.

For the foregoing reasons, the judgment is AFFIRMED, except for the award of medical expenses; that award is VACATED. This matter is REMANDED for entry of an amended judgment consistent with this opinion.

United States Court of Appeals for the Sixth Circuit

United States Court of Appeals
for the Sixth Circuit

No. 15-5385

EDWARDS
VS.
CSX TRANSP. INC.

Appeal from the United States District Court for the Eastern District of Tennessee at Greeneville

Decided: May 6, 2016

Citation: 821 F.3d 758, 4 Adm. R. 316 (6th Cir. 2016).

Before **SUTTON** and **GRIFFIN**, Circuit Judges, and **OLIVER**, Chief District Judge.*

*The Honorable Solomon Oliver, Jr., Chief Judge, United States District Court for the Northern District of Ohio, sitting by designation.

[—2—] SUTTON, Circuit Judge:

Federal law regulates the bathrooms of trains. Invoking the relevant statutes and regulations, Ricky Edwards, a train engineer, claims that CSX Transportation owes him damages because an unsanitary locomotive toilet led to a career-ending injury. The engineer overreads the relevant provisions. While they require CSX to have such toilets and to clean them once a day, they do not require railroad companies to ensure that the toilets are clean at any given moment between inspections. Because CSX met the relevant requirements and because Edwards has abandoned any claim that CSX was otherwise negligent in caring for this bathroom, we affirm the district court's rejection of this claim as a matter of law.

I.

Edwards worked as a train engineer for CSX for thirty-one years. When he arrived at work on May 28, 2012, ready to move a train from Bostic, North Carolina, to Erwin, Tennessee, he had an upset stomach. What he found on board did not improve matters. The bathroom in the lead locomotive was "nasty," Edwards saw and smelled. R. 29-1 at 16. "[U]rine, human waste, . . . [and] blue chemical" were "splattered" all over the toilet. *Id.* There were "[f]eces . . . [i]n the bowl" and

dirt on the floor. *Id.* Edwards sprayed disinfectant in the lavatory, closed its door, and started the trip.

During a stop that occurred about eighty miles and six hours later, Edwards' nausea escalated. He felt an urge to vomit. Unwilling to use a foul bathroom, he sprinted to a catwalk that ran along the outside of the locomotive. He threw up over the side. Then he vomited a second time and in the process fell over the handrail onto the ground below. The fall broke two of his vertebrae and cracked a rib—and ended his career with CSX.

Edwards sought damages under the Federal Employers' Liability Act. *See* 45 U.S.C. §§ 51–60. He argued that the pertinent regulations required CSX to keep its locomotive bathroom sanitary. *See* 49 C.F.R. pt. 229; *see also* 49 U.S.C. § 20701. Had the toilet not been so **[—3—]** dirty, he claimed, he would have gone there to vomit instead of heading outside to the catwalk and thus never would have fallen.

CSX sought summary judgment, arguing that the link between the dirty toilet and Edwards' injury was too tenuous to establish causation. The district court agreed. Our court reversed, holding that "the determination whether the unsanitary toilet played any part in producing Edwards's injuries [is] for the factfinder." *Edwards v. CSX Transp., Inc.*, 574 F. App'x 614, 620 (6th Cir. 2014).

On remand, CSX sought summary judgment again, arguing that (1) Edwards failed to show that the railroad violated the toilet-cleanliness regulations (a negligence per se theory of liability, 45 U.S.C. § 51; 49 U.S.C. § 20701) and (2) Edwards had abandoned his negligence claim (a general negligence theory of liability, 45 U.S.C. § 51). CSX complied with the rules, it argued, by performing a daily inspection the day before Edwards' injury, when it inspected and cleaned the bathroom. *See* 49 C.F.R. § 229.21. The district court held that CSX complied with the regulations as a matter of law, precluding liability for Edwards' injuries.

II.

A.

The Federal Employers' Liability Act provides the exclusive right of action to "any person," such as Edwards, "suffering injury while he is employed by [an interstate railroad]," such as CSX. 45 U.S.C. § 51; *see N.Y. Cent. R.R. Co. v. Winfield*, 244 U.S. 147, 153–54 (1917). One path of establishing a claim under the Act is negligence—a lack of reasonable care in cleaning the bathroom. *See Urie v. Thompson*, 337 U.S. 163, 173–74, 178 (1949). Edwards has abandoned that route. The other path for establishing a claim under the Act is negligence per se. If Edwards establishes a violation of another federal law, in this instance the Locomotive Inspection Act, 49 U.S.C. § 20701, which regulates the safety of locomotives, he is eligible for relief so long as he can establish causation and damages, 45 U.S.C. § 51; *see Urie*, 337 U.S. at 188–91; *Gowins v. Penn. R.R. Co.*, 299 F.2d 431, 433 (6th Cir. 1962). All that matters at this stage of the case, then, is whether Edwards can show a violation of the Locomotive Inspection Act or its regulations. [—4—]

In relevant part, the Locomotive Inspection Act says that a railroad company "may use . . . a locomotive . . . only when the locomotive . . . and its parts and appurtenances—(1) are in proper condition and safe to operate without unnecessary danger of personal injury; [and] (2) have been inspected as required under this chapter and regulations prescribed by the Secretary of Transportation under this chapter." 49 U.S.C. § 20701.

Under the regulations promulgated under the Act, railroads have several relevant duties. They must inspect locomotives that are in use at least once a day. 49 C.F.R. § 229.21. During this daily inspection, the railroad surveys the locomotive, makes repairs, and identifies any safety issues. *Id.* § 229.21(a)–(b). Separate regulations govern inspections of bathrooms in "lead locomotives"—those at the front of a train. *Id.* § 229.5. "The sanitation compartment of each lead locomotive in use," they begin, "shall be

sanitary." *Id.* § 229.139(a). "All components required . . . shall be present . . . [and] operate as intended." *Id.* § 229.139(b). "Water shall be present in sufficient quantity to permit flushing." *Id.* § 229.139(b)(2). "No blockage [shall be] present that prevents waste from evacuating the bowl." *Id.* § 229.139(b)(4). The railroad may delay fixing some problems, but it must write them down when it first notices the issue. *Id.* § 229.139(d). Cleaning each bathroom, checking that things work, and noting continuing problems thus are all things that happen when a railroad conducts its daily inspection.

A separate section, § 229.137(c), tells railroads what to do if, after a daily inspection, a lead locomotive still has a dirty bathroom. "[I]f the railroad determines during the daily inspection . . . that a locomotive toilet facility is . . . unsanitary," it says, "the railroad shall not use the locomotive in the lead position." *Id.* § 229.137(c). This rule comes with some qualifications. If, for example, the daily inspection takes place where the railroad cannot clean the bathroom, it may use the locomotive until it can solve the problem or until the next daily inspection, "whichever occurs first." *Id.* § 229.137(c)(5).

The Federal Railroad Administration's interpretation of these regulations is consistent with this language. "[T]he duty to remedy an unsanitary condition," the agency explained in the preamble to these rules, "arises only at the daily inspection." 67 Fed. Reg. 16,032, 16,037 (Apr. 4, 2002). "En route failures that occur after the daily inspection impose no burden on the railroad, until the next daily inspection is due." *Id.* at 16,043. A compliance manual makes the [—5—] same point, confirming that a railroad meets its duty by cleaning the toilet at the required inspection. *See* Fed. R.R. Admin., Office of R.R. Safety, Motive Power and Equipment Compliance Manual 8-79 (2012). These interpretations by the agency are consistent with the regulations, have not changed, and have no markings of litigation gamesmanship. "When an agency interprets its own regulation," the Supreme Court has told us, we must "defer[] . . . unless that interpretation is plainly erroneous or inconsistent with the regulation" or we see an "indication that [the agency's] current view is a change from prior practice or a *post hoc* justification adopted in response to litigation." *Decker v. Nw. Envtl. Def. Ctr.*, 133 S. Ct. 1326, 1337 (2013) (quotation omitted); *see Bowles v. Seminole Rock & Sand Co.*, 325 U.S. 410, 413–14 (1945).

Taken together, CSX's regulatory obligations come to this in today's case. It used engine 823 as a lead locomotive at the front of a train. At the daily inspection before Edwards' injury, CSX thus had to make the bathroom on engine 823 "sanitary." 49 C.F.R. § 229.139(a); *see id.* § 229.21. CSX performed this inspection on May 27, sanitized the bathroom, and reported no issues. That allowed CSX to use engine 823 as a lead locomotive until the next daily inspection became due. *See id.* § 229.137(c). Because CSX had to perform this daily inspection once a "calendar day," the May 28 inspection had not become due when Edwards fell at 6:15 p.m. *Id.* § 229.21. CSX as a result complied with the regulations, even if the toilet was as dirty as Edwards described it and even if the toilet caused his injuries.

In reaching this conclusion, we note that Edwards does not challenge the validity of the regulations. And he does not challenge the validity of the agency's interpretation of them. Whether *Seminole Rock* deference is or is not "long for this world" thus makes no difference to this case. *Bryana Bible v. United Student Aid Funds, Inc.*, 807 F.3d 839, 841 (7th Cir. 2015) (Easterbrook, J., concurring in the denial of rehearing en banc); *see Perez v. Mortg. Bankers Ass'n*, 135 S. Ct. 1199, 1213–25 (2015) (Thomas, J., concurring in the judgment); *Decker*, 133 S. Ct. at 1338–39 (Roberts, C.J., concurring); *id.* at 1339–42 (Scalia, J., concurring in part and dissenting in part). [—6—]

B.

Attempting to fend off this conclusion, Edwards emphasizes that the key regulation says that the "sanitation compartment of each lead locomotive in use shall be sanitary." 49 C.F.R. § 229.139(a). To his mind, that means bathrooms in lead locomotives must be "sanitary" at each moment that the locomotive is "in use." Bolstering this reading, he adds, is the expansive meaning given to the word "use" in the Locomotive Inspection Act. "A railroad carrier," the Act says, "may use or allow to be used a locomotive" only if it meets the Act's requirements. 49 U.S.C. § 20701. And a locomotive is "in use" almost any time it is not stopped for repair. *See, e.g., Wright v. Ark. & Mo. R.R. Co.*, 574 F.3d 612, 620–22 (8th Cir. 2009); *Angell v. Chesapeake & Ohio Ry. Co.*, 618 F.2d 260, 261–62 (4th Cir. 1980); *see also Brady v. Terminal R.R. Ass'n of St. Louis*, 303 U.S. 10, 13 (1938). All of this, says Edwards, means that if engine 823 was "in use" when he fell, its bathroom had to be sanitary.

But this reads too much into § 229.139(a) and too little into the context in which it appears. Yes, bathrooms of in-use lead locomotives must be "sanitary." But that does not tell us how and when railroads meet that obligation. The rest of the regulations answer that question. A railroad meets the obligation of sanitary bathrooms by making daily inspections of them, just as CSX did. The regulations do not create a violation—negligence per se—any time someone finds a bathroom in an unsanitary condition, no matter the cause, no matter the time of the last inspection. The regulations require a daily inspection, 49 C.F.R. § 229.21, and the section that contains § 229.139(a) speaks only to "servicing requirements," *id.* § 229.139. Otherwise, the regulations would create a 24/7 strict liability duty—one that, as the district court pointed out, would require a full-time bathroom supervisor. Nothing in the regulations suggests such a strict requirement.

Edwards' interpretation also sells other provisions short. We must interpret regulations, no less than other legal texts, "in a way that renders them compatible, not contradictory." *Maracich v. Spears*, 133 S. Ct. 2191, 2205 (2013) (quotation omitted). Section 229.137(c), to repeat, generally prohibits railroads from putting locomotives that have dirty bathrooms after the last daily inspection at the front of a train, but it allows this to happen in specified circumstances.

Section 229.139(a), interpreted as Edwards suggests, would prohibit railroads from ever using a [—7—] lead locomotive with a dirty bathroom, no exceptions. That interpretation cannot be squared with § 229.137(c), which authorizes some exceptions.

Nor does it help him that a railroad's duties under the Act are "absolute and continuing" and that negligence per se liability may arise without regard to whether the railroad acted reasonably. *Lilly v. Grand Trunk W. R.R. Co.*, 317 U.S. 481, 485 (1943) (quotation omitted); *see also Kernan v. Am. Dredging Co.*, 355 U.S. 426, 430–31 (1958). All these authorities do is take us back to the threshold question: Did CSX violate the regulations? As shown, it did not.

It bears adding that, for employees in Edwards' situation, their only recourse is not negligence per se—establishing a violation of the regulations. They also may establish that the railroad did not use "reasonable care in furnishing its employees with a safe place to work." *Atchison, Topeka & Santa Fe Ry. Co. v. Buell*, 480 U.S. 557, 558 (1987). Edwards, however, has abandoned that alternative path to liability here.

Another part of the locomotive regulations, one that does not deal with bathrooms, also fails to support Edwards' argument. Section 229.119(c) requires railroads to keep "[f]loors of cabs, passageways, and compartments . . . free from oil, water, waste, or any obstruction that creates a slipping, tripping or fire hazard." Courts have held under this provision that "[t]he presence" of oil residue on the floor may "violate[] the Locomotive Inspection Act on its face." *Kehdi v. BNSF Ry. Co.*, Civil No. 06-6242-AA, 2007 WL 2994600, at *4 (D. Or. Oct. 11, 2007); *see Reed v. Norfolk S. Ry. Co.*, 312 F. Supp. 2d 924, 928–29 (N.D. Ohio 2004). If a tripping hazard suffices to violate the regulations, reasons Edwards, a dirty bathroom suffices as well. The key problem is that the § 229.119(c) regulations do not parallel the bathroom ones. And above all, they do not come with this guidance: "En route failures that occur after the daily inspection impose no burden on the railroad, until the next daily inspection is due." 67 Fed. Reg. at 16,043.

Edwards also claims that CSX is liable based on prior holdings of this court and of the district court. This court, in the prior appeal in this case and in unrelated litigation, has (correctly) noted that federal regulations require railroads to provide their employees with sanitary locomotive toilets in order to avoid liability. *See Edwards*, 574 F. App'x at 619; [—8—] *Szekeres v. CSX Transp., Inc.*, 731 F.3d 592, 599 (6th Cir. 2013); *Szekeres v. CSX Transp., Inc.*, 617 F.3d 424, 427–28 (6th Cir. 2010). The district court made a similar point. None of these statements, however, addressed *when* a railroad satisfies that obligation. That is the question presented today and nothing stands in our way of answering it. *See, e.g., John B. v. Emkes*, 710 F.3d 394, 403 (6th Cir. 2013); *Yeschick v. Mineta*, 675 F.3d 622, 633 (6th Cir. 2012); *Asplundh Tree Expert Co. v. Bates*, 71 F.3d 592, 597 (6th Cir. 1995).

For these reasons, we affirm.

United States Court of Appeals
for the Sixth Circuit

No. 14-4231

WILLIAMSON
VS.
RECOVERY LTD. PARTNERSHIP

Appeal from the United States District Court for the
Southern District of Ohio at Columbus

Decided: June 10, 2016

Citation: 826 F.3d 297, 4 Adm. R. 320 (6th Cir. 2016).

Before **BOGGS** and **SUHRHEINRICH**, Circuit Judges,
and **MURPHY**, District Judge.*

*The Honorable Stephen J. Murphy, III, United
States District Judge for the Eastern District of Michigan,
sitting by designation.

[—2—] BOGGS, Circuit Judge:

This appeal involves yet another skirmish in the legal battle over the treasure from the *S.S. Central America*, the history of which was recounted in an earlier decision by this panel in *Williamson v. Recovery Ltd. Partnership (Williamson II)*, 731 F.3d 608, 1 Adm. R. 348 (6th Cir. 2013). In this case, we review the district court's imposition of sanctions against the defendants' attorney, Richard Robol, for hampering the enforcement of a court order in bad faith. For the reasons discussed below, we affirm.

I. Background

On July 20, 2006, the United States District Court for the Southern District of Ohio adopted a consent order intended to resolve a suit by Dispatch Printing Company (Dispatch) against Recovery Limited Partnership (RLP) and Columbus Exploration, LLC (CX) for an accounting of the gold from the *S.S. Central America* shipwreck. Paragraph 3 of the consent order provided that: "Within sixty (60) days after entry of this Order, Defendants shall provide Plaintiffs' accountant . . . with full access and opportunity to review the documents and materials regarding the period from January 1, 2000 through the date of entry of this Order, identified in the July 11, 2006 list by

Accountant, for the purpose of preparing a report . . . of the financial affairs and condition of CX and RLP."

On December 5, 2006, the district court issued a contempt order against the defendants based on a number of grounds, one of which was their failure to turn over "an inventory of the gold recovered and sold." Without an inventory of the gold that the defendants recovered and sold, it was "inconceivable that any degree of thorough auditing could commence." The district court went on to remark:

> The Court is troubled by the Defendants' position regarding documents relating to the sale of gold. While counsel for the Defendants represented to the Court that the documents could not be located, no testimony was presented in support of such contention. Further, the Court is deeply skeptical of the Defendants' claim that such critically important documents could not be located. Moreover, following the hearing conducted in this case, and prior to the issuance of this [—3—] Order, the Defendants have filed a Motion asking the Court to review *in camera* records relating to the sale of the gold. Such documents were required to be turned over by the Defendants to Plaintiffs' accountant within sixty days of the Order issued by this Court on July 20, 2006. The Defendants presented no evidence regarding any efforts made to locate such documents, or explaining how such documents were not in the possession of the Defendants. The recent Motion [filed by the defendants] asks for an *in camera* inspection of documents originally claimed to be lost, leading this Court to find a total lack of good faith of at least CX and RLP in compliance with the July 20, 2006 Order.

Paragraph 2 of the contempt order, as later amended, provided that the "Defendants shall tender to the Plaintiffs' accountant an inventory of the gold." The court also stated that the "record in this case shall be kept open regarding this violation," and that the "Court reserves for a later date sanctions or other remedies with regard to such violations."

In response to the contempt order, the defendants turned over an inventory of the gold that they sold to the California Gold Marketing Group from February 15 to September 1, 2000. They did not, however, turn over any prior inventories, which would have provided a complete accounting of the treasure recovered from the ship. Unsatisfied with the defendants' efforts to comply with numerous provisions of the consent order, even after the contempt order, Dispatch filed another motion to hold the defendants in contempt on March 9, 2007.

At the contempt hearing on April 24, 2007, Dispatch's attorney, Steven Tigges, and the defendants' attorney, Richard Robol, argued about whether the defendants possessed any inventories that predated the sale to California Gold:

> Mr. Tigges: Secondly, Your Honor, your order from July 20 of 2006 was very clear. They are to produce documents regarding the period from January 1, 2000. A document may be [produced] prior to that date regarding [treasure sold during] that period.
>
> The Court: I am familiar with the dispute.
>
> Mr. Tigges: An inventory of assets clearly is that. . . . Your Honor will recall prior to the agreement with California Gold, these [defendant] entities had an agreement to sell the gold through Christie's. And it's inconceivable that Christie's would undertake that agreement of an advance of upwards of $30 million to these entities and not have an inventory of what they were buying. So those documents plainly exist, Your Honor. [—4—]
>
> Mr. Robol: May I clarify one thing? This is not for purposes of argument. This is for purposes of Mr. Tigges's understanding. We have produced the inventories, even if they are pre-2000

inventories. I don't want there to be any ambiguity in his mind about that. We have produced all the inventories.

Thus, Robol clearly represented to the court that the defendants were not in possession of any pre-California-Gold-sale inventories. At the close of the contempt hearing, the district court clarified the scope of its contempt order from December 2006:

> [T]he defendants shall tender to the accounting firm anything that could be construed as an inventory of any kind regarding assets recovered from the shipwreck that would have been sold during the relevant time of this audit or review. So, in other words, if there are assets recovered in 1980 that were sold in 2001, and there is an inventory that goes with them [sic] assets, then that is to be turned over.

Although the court did not hold the defendants in contempt at that time, it issued a second contempt order against them in September 2009 for causing "significant delay and expense." The court concluded: "The accounting was sandbagged by the Defendants through a variety of means. What should have taken several months has taken several years. . . . The Court finds the Defendants have willfully violated the prior Orders of this Court." This court affirmed that decision in *Williamson v. Recovery Ltd. Partnership (Williamson I)*, 467 F. App'x 382 (6th Cir. 2012).

Throughout the years of litigation, Robol represented on multiple occasions that the California-Gold-sale inventory was the only inventory in the defendants' possession:

- At a hearing on September 7, 2007, Robol said: "Now let me address the specifics of the inventory. What you have been told is false, false, false. The company has no inventories of the gold sold other than what has been provided." Robol also stated: "We provided the inventory that the company had. We provided the inventory of that asset, the treasure that was sold to the California Gold Marketing Group."

- In a trial brief filed on December 3, 2008, Robol stated that the defendants "produced the only inventory in their possession in late 2006, which was the inventory of the gold items sold to the California Gold Marketing Group."

- At a hearing on December 8, 2008, Robol said: "We produced the one and only inventory that the company had, which was the inventory relating to the sale to the party that we had spoken about, the California Gold Marketing Group." [—5—]

- In an appellate brief filed with this court on March 19, 2010, in *Williamson I*, Robol stated: "The first inventory—the only inventory that Columbus Exploration had in its possession, custody or control—was provided to KPMG shortly after the December 5, 2006 Order. . . . [That] inventory listed every item of gold treasure sold to the California Gold Marketing Group." Robol reiterated that claim in a reply brief filed on June 1, 2010.

In 2013, Dispatch obtained the appointment of a receiver that it had first sought in 2008 in order "to take control of RLP and CX, dissolve them and liquidate their assets, and wind up their affairs." The receiver recovered thirty-six file cabinets containing RLP and CX records that were stored in the basement of a duplex that Robol owned and partially leased to the defendants. Within those cabinets, the receiver found numerous treasure inventories created prior to the California Gold sale that were never turned over to Dispatch. Among the inventories was a master inventory, printed on hundreds of sheets of printer paper bound in a hard cover labeled "89 & 90 COIN AND BAR MASTER COPY." That inventory was one of many inventories found in the cabinets, which in total span thousands of pages and comprise most of the seventeen-volume appendix to Dispatch's brief.

On October 16, 2013, Dispatch filed a motion asking the district court to exercise its inherent powers to sanction Robol for engaging in bad-faith conduct during the litigation. The district court conducted a three-day sanctions hearing, with testimony from numerous witnesses, and concluded that Robol engaged in sanctionable bad-faith conduct when he concealed the existence of the pre-California-Gold-sale inventories. In calculating the sanctions, the district court rejected Dispatch's initial request for $1,717,388—the entirety of its litigation expenses—and limited the sanctions to "the amount equal to the cost of pursuing this Motion for Sanctions, as well as the amount expended . . . to uncover this fraud and locate the inventories uncovered by the Receiver." Dispatch submitted bills for $249,359.85, which the district court reduced to $224,580. After the district court entered its sanctions order, Robol appealed.

II. Standard of Review

We review the district court's exercise of its inherent power to sanction for abuse of discretion. *First Bank of Marietta v. Hartford Underwriters Ins. Co.*, 307 F.3d 501, 510 (6th Cir. 2002). "An abuse of discretion exists if the district court based its ruling on an erroneous view [—6—] of the law or a clearly erroneous assessment of the evidence." *Ibid.* (quoting *Apostolic Pentecostal Church v. Colbert*, 169 F.3d 409, 417 (6th Cir. 1999)).

III. Bad Faith

A. Applicable Law

The district court sanctioned Robol under its inherent powers for acting in bad faith. *See Chambers v. NASCO, Inc.*, 501 U.S. 32, 45–46 (1991). In coming to that conclusion, the court purported to apply Sixth Circuit precedent stating that a plaintiff can be sanctioned for advancing claims in bad faith if the court finds "[1] that the claims advanced were meritless, [2] that counsel knew or should have known this, and [3] that the motive for filing the suit was for an improper purpose." *First Bank of Marietta*, 307 F.3d at 524 (quoting *Big Yank Corp. v. Liberty Mut. Fire Ins. Co.*, 125 F.3d 308, 313 (6th Cir. 1997)). Although we have previously described the *Big Yank* test as "a three-prong test to determine whether a district court may properly impose sanctions," *BDT Prods., Inc. v. Lexmark Int'l, Inc.*, 602 F.3d 742, 752 (6th Cir. 2010), that test clearly contemplates a situation in which a plaintiff has filed a frivolous lawsuit. That test is not applicable to this case, which involves a motion for sanctions against a stonewalling attorney.

The district court also purported to apply Sixth Circuit precedent stating that a party seeking to show a fraud on the court must present clear and convincing evidence of the following elements: "1) [conduct] on the part of an officer of the court; that 2) is directed to the judicial machinery itself; 3) is intentionally false, willfully blind to the truth, or is in reckless disregard of the truth; 4) is a positive averment or a concealment when one is under a duty to disclose; and 5) deceives the court." *Johnson v. Bell*, 605 F.3d 333, 339 (6th Cir. 2010) (quoting *Carter v. Anderson*, 585 F.3d 1007, 1011 (6th Cir. 2009)). Dispatch urges on appeal that we also apply this test. The problem with applying this test is that the fraud-on-the-court doctrine deals with courts' inherent power to vacate their judgments, whereas this case involves a court's inherent power to sanction for misconduct in litigation.

The confusion seems to have arisen from Dispatch's argument to the district court that proving fraud on the court—as opposed to bad faith—would allow it to recover the entirety of its [—7—] litigation expenses in the case—$1,717,388. That argument was based on *Universal Oil Products Co. v. Root Refining Co.*, 328 U.S. 575 (1946), a case in which the Supreme Court said in dicta that, when a court properly exercises its inherent power to *vacate its judgment due to fraud*, "the entire costs of the proceedings could justly be assessed against the guilty parties." *Id.* at 580. *Universal Oil* was quoted in *Chambers* for the proposition that fraud on the court can constitute sanctionable bad-faith conduct. 501 U.S. at 43–44, 46. Based on *Chambers*'s

citation to *Universal Oil*, Dispatch imported the fraud-on-the-court test—used to decide whether a judgment should be vacated—into this case involving sanctions, and the district court applied that test. Although the Supreme Court's decision in *Chambers* mentioned fraud on the court as an example of bad faith, the fraud-on-the-court doctrine is not applicable in this case because this case involves a court's inherent power to sanction.

Despite the district court's erroneous application of these legal tests, we may affirm the court's order on any ground that is supported by the record. *See Moore v. Lafayette Life Ins. Co.*, 458 F.3d 416, 446 (6th Cir. 2006). In our view, the proper question is whether Robol showed "bad faith by . . . hampering [the] enforcement of a court order." *Chambers*, 501 U.S. at 46 (quoting *Hutto v. Finney*, 437 U.S. 678, 689 n.14 (1978)). That inquiry requires us to ask two questions: Did the party or attorney engage in conduct that hampered the enforcement of a court order? If so, did that party or attorney act in bad faith? Having clarified the appropriate legal test, we now turn to the question of whether Robol hampered the enforcement of a court order in bad faith.

B. Analysis

In 2006, the district court entered a consent order requiring the defendants to turn over documents regarding the period from January 1, 2000, to July 20, 2006. The purpose of the consent order was to allow Dispatch's accountant, KPMG, to perform a complete accounting of the treasure and determine whether any treasure was missing. Essential to KPMG's ability to perform that accounting were the defendants' inventories of the treasure that they recovered from the *S.S. Central America*. As the district court observed in its contempt order dated December 5, 2006: "It is inconceivable that any degree of thorough auditing could commence without such documents." [—8—]

By refusing to notify the court of the existence of inventories created prior to the California-Gold-sale inventory and falsely claiming that the California-Gold-sale inventory was the only inventory in the defendants' possession, Robol hampered the enforcement of the 2006 consent order. If Robol had disclosed the existence and location of the pre-California-Gold-sale inventories, Dispatch would not have been forced to wait until 2013, after years of costly litigation, to obtain the inventories. As the district court stated in its order sanctioning Robol, by "representing to this Court and the Court of Appeals, on multiple occasions, that his clients had no other inventories, or indeed that such inventories ever existed," Robol "hamper[ed] the enforcement of a court order."

The parties do not dispute that Robol's inaccurate statements hampered the enforcement of the district court's order. Instead, they focus on the question of whether Robol acted in bad faith. There is a dearth of case law explicating the meaning of bad faith in this context. For our purposes, it suffices to say that bad faith includes conduct undertaken with the intention of hampering the enforcement of a court order. In this case, the bad-faith inquiry requires us to examine whether Robol knew that the defendants possessed the undisclosed inventories or was willfully blind to their existence when he made his misrepresentations to the court. If Robol knew about the inventories or was willfully blind to their existence, then his repeated misrepresentations would not be innocent, and there would be a strong inference that Robol intentionally hampered the enforcement of the district court's order.

Dispatch points to a number of facts as evidence that Robol knew of the existence of the pre-California-Gold-sale inventories, the most important of which include:

1991 Letter. On October 28, 1991, while trying to obtain a loan from Bank One, Robol sent a letter to the CEO of Bank One enclosing a forty-three-page inventory of the treasure recovered from the *S.S. Central America.* Dispatch cites this letter as evidence that Robol knew about the existence of, and indeed at one point possessed, an earlier inventory of the treasure, which he did not disclose to the court.

Virginia Admiralty Litigation. Robol served as the attorney for a business entity related to RLP, Columbus-America Discovery Group, Inc., in the 1990s in a Virginia admiralty case that [—9—] dealt with the subrogation claims of insurance companies who had paid insurance claims when the *S.S. Central America* sank. *See Columbus-Am. Discovery Grp., Inc. v. Atl. Mut. Ins. Co.,* 974 F.2d 450 (4th Cir. 1992); *Columbus-Am. Discovery Grp., Inc. v. Unidentified, Wrecked & Abandoned Sailing Vessel,* 742 F. Supp. 1327 (E.D. Va. 1990). Dispatch argues that Robol must have known of his clients' inventories through this litigation because they were an important subject of that litigation. Robol's cocounsel in the admiralty case, Rex Elliott, testified to this effect at Robol's sanctions hearing.

Bob Evans. Bob Evans was the employee at RLP who created and maintained its inventories. He testified at the sanctions hearing that Robol was aware that Evans's job was to create and maintain the inventories in the 1980s and 1990s. Dispatch argues that Evans's testimony shows that Robol must have known of the existence of inventories that were created prior to the creation of the California-Gold-sale inventory.

Jim Henson. Jim Henson is the financial advisor for the receiver who was appointed in 2013. On September 17, 2013, he attended a meeting at which Robol was present and talked to Robol about the undisclosed inventories. Henson recounted the conversation in his testimony at the sanctions hearing:

Q: Now, shifting gears with you again, sir. After you and your team found these various inventory documents that we've been looking at, did you ever have occasion to speak to Mr. Robol about them?

A: I did.

Q: What were the circumstances?

A: We were at a meeting at Gil Kirk's office.

Q: Who is Gil Kirk?

A: I'm sorry. Mr. Kirk was a former member of the board at Columbus Exploration, CX. We were at a meeting at his office on the 17th of September and the issue of the inventories came up.

Q: How did it come up?

A: I believe it was brought up because we reported that we had Mr. Evans trying to reconcile the inventories to make sure there was no missing gold. Mr. Kirk [—10—] was particularly interested in that because he said that it reflected badly on him if there was missing gold.

Q: Did Mr. Robol say anything?

A: Mr. Robol really said so you found these inventories. We [sic] said, yes, we found them. And he referenced that the inventories were part of the materials that Mr. Thompson, who had been the CEO of Columbus Exploration, had not wanted turned over to the court as part of a court proceeding.

Q: Did he say why?

A: Yes. He said that Thompson was a secrecy [sic] -- had great concerns about secrecy and confidentiality and therefore didn't want to share materials unless he was absolutely forced to.

Dispatch argues that Henson's testimony conclusively shows that Robol knew about the existence of other inventories and intentionally misled the court when he said that the California-Gold-sale inventory was the only inventory in the defendants' possession.

We find Dispatch's arguments to be highly persuasive. The aforementioned facts provide powerful evidence that Robol knew of, or was willfully blind to, the existence of undisclosed inventories. As a result, there is a strong inference that Robol intentionally misled the district court for the purpose of hampering the enforcement of the 2006 consent order.

Robol's response to Dispatch's compilation of evidence is weak. He argues that, although he knew that undisclosed inventories existed at certain points in time, he did not know that they existed in the defendants' possession—in the basement of his duplex—during the times that he stated that the California-Gold-sale inventory was the only inventory in the defendants' possession. Robol suggests that "[n]obody knows where the recovered inventories resided" before their discovery in 2013, and "the documents could have been *anywhere* between 2006 and 2009."

Furthermore, Robol notes that the undisclosed inventories were discovered in the side of the duplex that he leased to the defendants—431 West Sixth Avenue—rather than the side in which his law office was located—433 West Sixth Avenue. According to Robol the "two areas had separate entrances and were sealed off from one another." Robol argues that he could not [—11—] legally have gone into the defendants' side of the building to search their files without their authorization; therefore he had no choice but to rely on the statements of his clients, which he believed to be true at the time of his misrepresentations.

The fatal flaw in both of these arguments is that, even if we assume that Robol did not know the specific fact that the inventories were located in his duplex during his misrepresentations—a claim of which Robol has not convinced us—Robol surely had enough knowledge about the inventories that when his clients told him that the California-Gold-sale inventory was all they had, he could not have believed that statement. Given Robol's composition of the 1991 letter to Bank One, representation in the Virginia admiralty litigation, interactions with Bob Evans, and conversation with Jim Henson, not even believing in "six impossible things before breakfast" could lead to the conclusion that Robol reasonably believed that his clients did not possess additional inventories. Lewis Carroll, *Through the Looking-Glass, and What*

Alice Found There 100 (1872). Jim Henson's testimony regarding his conversation with Robol is particularly incriminating, as Henson testified that Robol admitted that he knew about the existence of additional inventories in the defendants' possession and purposely hid them from the court. By making misrepresentations about those inventories, Robol hampered the enforcement of the district court's 2006 consent order in bad faith. For that reason, we hold that the district court did not abuse its discretion when it concluded that Robol engaged in sanctionable bad-faith conduct.

IV. Calculation of Sanctions

The district court imposed $224,580 in sanctions on Robol, which was its calculation of "the amount equal to the cost of pursuing this Motion for Sanctions, as well as the amount expended . . . to uncover this fraud and locate the inventories uncovered by the Receiver." Robol raises two arguments for why this calculation was an abuse of discretion. First, he argues that the $224,580 in fees incurred by Dispatch is not entirely attributable to his individual conduct in the litigation. Second, he argues that, because Dispatch already received a $700,000 settlement from a codefendant, Gilman Kirk, Dispatch has already been fully compensated and would be receiving a windfall. [—12—]

Neither of these arguments is persuasive because they are premised on the idea that sanctions are meant to be solely restitutive. It is well established under Supreme Court and Sixth Circuit precedents that a court's inherent power to sanction serves a punitive purpose, based on the need to deter misconduct and vindicate the court's authority. In *Chambers*, the Supreme Court stated that courts' inherent power to sanction serves the "dual purpose" of "vindicate[ing] judicial authority" and "mak[ing] the prevailing party whole for expenses caused by his opponent's obstinacy." 501 U.S. at 46 (quoting *Hutto*, 437 U.S. at 689 n.14). In that case, Chambers had argued that the district court "failed to tailor the sanction to the particular wrong." *Id.* at 56. The Supreme Court disagreed, holding that because the

district court needed "to ensure that such abuses were not repeated," it was "within the court's discretion to vindicate itself and compensate NASCO by requiring Chambers to pay for all attorney's fees." *Id.* at 57.

In *Stalley ex rel. United States v. Mountain States Health Alliance*, Stalley challenged the district court's exercise of its inherent power to sanction on the ground that the court did not explain why it had to award the defendants all of their fees and expenses ($276,589.69) in order to assure the desired deterrence. 644 F.3d 349, 351–52 (6th Cir. 2011). We noted that "sanctions imposed . . . pursuant to a court's inherent authority" are "punitive." *Id.* at 352 (quoting *Red Carpet Studios Div. of Source Advantage, Ltd. v. Sater*, 465 F.3d 642, 647 (6th Cir. 2006)). Therefore, "even assuming that the award was greater than necessary to deter future violations—a contention of which Stalley has failed to convince us—another valid basis exists for the award that Stalley has not challenged." *Ibid.* In *Red Carpet Studios*, the case quoted in *Stalley*, we held that a district court can award sanctions that are less than the harm that was suffered by the opposing party. 465 F.3d at 647. In that context we stated that "sanctions imposed . . . pursuant to a court's inherent authority are punitive." *Ibid.*

Chambers, Stalley, and *Red Carpet Studios* establish that courts have broad discretion under their inherent powers to fashion punitive sanctions. Although sanctions cannot be so unreasonable that they constitute an abuse of discretion, there is no requirement of a perfect causal connection between the sanctioned conduct and the attorney's fees awarded, due to the punitive nature of the sanctions. In this case, the sanctions imposed by the district court—"equal to the cost of pursuing this Motion for Sanctions, as well as the amount expended . . . to uncover [—13—] this fraud and locate the inventories uncovered by the Receiver"—are reasonably punitive and within the district court's discretion.

Dispatch's $700,000 settlement with Gilman Kirk does not change our assessment.

Dispatch originally moved for sanctions against four individuals: Robol, plus three executives from the defendant businesses, Gilman Kirk, Tommy Thompson, and Michael Ford. That motion sought $1,717,388, the entire cost of the litigation. Awarding Dispatch $224,580 from Robol would still leave it with much less than the entire cost of the litigation. As such, it does not strike us as a windfall for Dispatch, although it does strike us as a reasonable punishment for Robol. We hold that the district court did not abuse its discretion when it sanctioned Robol for the cost of uncovering his fraud and pursuing the motion for sanctions.

V. Conclusion

The district court's order is AFFIRMED.

This page intentionally left blank

United States Court of Appeals for the Seventh Circuit

United States Court of Appeals
for the Seventh Circuit

No. 15-2646

ABDUWALI ABDUKHADIR MUSE
VS.
DANIELS, WARDEN, FCI TERRE HAUTE

Appeal from the United States District Court for the
Southern District of Indiana, Terre Haute Division

Decided: February 24, 2016*

*The appeal was decided by non-precedential order on
February 24, 2016. The court reissued the decision as an
opinion on March 4, 2016.

Citation: 815 F.3d 265, 4 Adm. R. 330 (7th Cir. 2016).

Before **EASTERBROOK, KANNE,** and **SYKES,** Circuit
Judges.

[—1—] **EASTERBROOK,** Circuit Judge:

Abduwali Muse pleaded guilty to piracy, 18 U.S.C. §2280, among other crimes, for his role in boarding the *MV Maersk Alabama* in 2009 in international waters off the coast of Somalia and taking its captain hostage. [—2—]

Muse initially told federal agents that he was 16 at the time of his capture, which created a potential for prosecution under the special rules applicable to juveniles. See 18 U.S.C. §§ 5031–42. The day before a hearing set to determine his age, Muse told an FBI agent that he was between 18 and 19. At the hearing Muse refused to testify. Magistrate Judge Peck, of the Southern District of New York, concluded that Muse was at least 18 when the crime occurred, which led to his prosecution as an adult. He pleaded guilty and was sentenced to 405 months' imprisonment. The plea agreement contains a clause promising "not to seek to withdraw his guilty plea or file a direct appeal or any kind of collateral attack challenging his guilty plea or conviction based on his age either at the time of the charged conduct or at the time of the guilty plea."

Notwithstanding the waiver, Muse filed a proceeding under 28 U.S.C. §2255 asking the Southern District of New York to set aside his conviction on the grounds that a magistrate judge lacked authority to decide whether he was an adult in 2009 and that his lawyer furnished ineffective assistance by not pursuing that question vigorously. Chief District Judge Preska denied that motion, relying on the waiver in the plea agreement. Muse appealed, but the Second Circuit declined to issue a certificate of appealability. Turning to the Southern District of Indiana, where he is imprisoned, Muse filed a petition for a writ of habeas corpus under 28 U.S.C. §2241. Again he lost, this time because the district court concluded that §2255(e) applies.

Section 2255(e) provides: "An application for a writ of habeas corpus in behalf of a prisoner who is authorized to apply for relief by motion pursuant to this section, shall not [—3—] be entertained if it appears that the applicant has failed to apply for relief, by motion, to the court which sentenced him, or that such court has denied him relief, unless it also appears that the remedy by motion is inadequate or ineffective to test the legality of his detention." *Webster v. Daniels*, 784 F.3d 1123 (7th Cir. 2015) (en banc), discusses when §2255 as a whole is "inadequate or ineffective to test the legality of" federal detention. The district court properly concluded that Muse has not identified any deficiency or inadequacy in §2255. The reason he could not contest the magistrate judge's decision has nothing to do with §2255. It is, instead, the consequence of his own decision to waive any entitlement to raise the age issue on collateral attack. That waiver would apply equally in a proceeding under §2241, had not §2255(e) taken precedence, for §2241 is a form of collateral attack.

Muse's brief in this court ignores his waiver and §2255(e) alike. Instead he presents an argument about the extent to which 28 U.S.C. §636(b)(1)(A) permits magistrate judges to resolve contests about criminal defendants' ages. The brief thus gives us no reason to question the district court's decision.

AFFIRMED

United States Court of Appeals
for the Seventh Circuit

No. 15-3174

CALUMET RIVER FLEETING, INC.
VS.
INTERNATIONAL UNION OF OPERATING ENG'RS,
LOCAL 150, AFL-CIO

Appeal from the United States District Court for the
Northern District of Illinois, Eastern Division

Decided: May 31, 2016

Citation: 824 F.3d 645, 4 Adm. R. 331 (7th Cir. 2016).

Before **WOOD**, Chief Judge, and **SYKES** and
HAMILTON, Circuit Judges.

[—1—] **HAMILTON**, Circuit Judge:

In July 2013, plaintiff Calumet River Fleeting, Inc. fired a boat operator, and defendant International Union of Operating Engineers, Local 150, AFL-CIO ("the Union") filed a grievance with Calumet over the termination. Calumet refused to participate in the arbitration, saying that although it was once a party to a collective bargaining [—2—] agreement with the Union, Calumet had terminated its participation in that agreement before the dispute arose over the firing. When the Union took steps to start the arbitration, Calumet filed this suit to stop it. The Union counterclaimed for an order compelling arbitration. The district court granted summary judgment to Calumet, holding that it was no longer a party to any agreement with the Union that might have required arbitration.

The Union has appealed, arguing that an earlier arbitration award in an unrelated proceeding had found that Calumet was an alter ego of Selvick Marine Construction, LLC, a company that was a party to the collective bargaining agreement. By virtue of the alter ego relationship, the Union contends that Calumet had to submit to arbitration.

We affirm. We first find that we have appellate jurisdiction over this matter despite the lack of a separate judgment. On the merits, the arbitration award on which the Union relies does not show that Calumet was still a party to the collective bargaining agreement. Calumet is entitled to judgment as a matter of law.

I. *Factual Background and Procedural History*

We review *de novo* a district court's decision on cross-motions for summary judgment. *Exelon Generation Co. v. Local 15, International Brotherhood of Electrical Workers*, 540 F.3d 640, 643 (7th Cir. 2008). The general standards for summary judgment do not change: with "cross summary judgment motions, we construe all facts and inferences therefrom 'in favor of the party against whom the motion under consideration is made.'" *In re United Air Lines, Inc.*, 453 F.3d 463, 468 (7th Cir. 2006), quoting *Kort v. Diversified Collection Services, Inc.*, 394 [—3—] F.3d 530, 536 (7th Cir. 2005). Because we need consider only Calumet's motion for summary judgment, we resolve all factual disputes and draw all reasonable inferences in the Union's favor.

A. *Background of the Companies and Their Relationship with the Union*

Plaintiff Calumet River Fleeting, Inc. is a Wisconsin corporation engaged in marine towing. It was formed by John Selvick in 1999. The International Union of Operating Engineers, Local 150, AFL-CIO is a labor organization that represents heavy equipment operators, mechanics, and other employees in parts of Illinois, Indiana, and Iowa.

In 2006, Calumet and the Union signed a memorandum of agreement binding Calumet to the terms of the Great Lakes Floating Agreement. The Floating Agreement is a collective bargaining agreement that covers marine construction. The memorandum of agreement contained an "evergreen clause" requiring the employer to adhere to the terms of each successive edition of the agreement unless and until the agreement was properly terminated.

In September 2008, Calumet terminated its participation in the Floating Agreement. This meant that contractors who were themselves signatories to the Floating Agreement could no longer hire Calumet without violating the agreement's subcontracting provision. Less than two years later, in April 2010, John Selvick organized a new company called Selvick Marine Construction, LLC. Selvick Marine signed a memorandum of agreement with the Union on June 2, 2010 adopting the terms of the Floating Agreement. Mr. Selvick also signed a towing addendum on Selvick Marine's behalf. The [—4—] towing addendum covers non-construction towing work. Like the Floating Agreement, it contains an evergreen clause.

B. *The 2012 Arbitration*

In September 2011, the Union filed three grievances against Selvick Marine, initiating the three-step grievance procedure prescribed by the Floating Agreement. The Union alleged that Selvick Marine had violated the Floating Agreement when it performed certain work without following the agreement's procedures. It was actually Calumet, not Selvick Marine, that had performed the work in question, but the Union sought to hold Selvick Marine accountable. Under the Union's theory, the two companies were alter egos, so Calumet's actions—and its failure to comply with the Floating Agreement—were attributable to Selvick Marine, which was a party to the Floating Agreement.

The parties could not agree on the grievances, so the Union submitted them to arbitration. Selvick Marine appeared to participate. Calumet did not, although it had been served with a subpoena *duces tecum* that identified the date and time of the arbitration. In between hearing dates, the Union filed suit to enforce the subpoena. In that suit, Calumet argued that it was not Selvick Marine's alter ego, but it never made the same argument in front of the arbitrator.

On July 24, 2012, the arbitrator issued his decision and award. He found that John Selvick had formed Selvick Marine to recapture work that Calumet had lost when it terminated its agreement with the Union. The arbitrator concluded that Selvick Marine and Calumet were alter ego companies, pointing out: Mr. Selvick supplied capital to Selvick Marine; employees of both companies reported to the same location for [—5—] work; Selvick Marine used only Calumet boats in its work; and the companies shared stationery, employees, forms, logs, worksheets, fueling vendors, and insurance policies. Although Selvick Marine maintained it was a separate company, the arbitrator disagreed. He expressly declined to pass judgment on the legality of the arrangement between Calumet and Selvick Marine, but he found that when Calumet performed work using union employees in the Union's territory, that work was subject to the Floating Agreement by virtue of Selvick Marine's signatory status. He then sustained the Union's grievances.

Turning to the question of a remedy, the arbitrator found that the work that had violated the Floating Agreement could not be undone, nor could Selvick Marine retroactively comply with the relevant provisions of the agreement. He ordered back pay and benefits to make whole the Union workers who had not been compensated in conformity with the Floating Agreement. He did not order any prospective relief, however, noting that the 2009–2011 Floating Agreement had expired on December 31, 2011 and that it was unclear whether any continuing relationship existed between the Union, Selvick Marine, and Calumet since the agreement's expiration. Thus, he concluded, he was "without authority to issue such a prospective remedy."

Neither Selvick Marine nor Calumet ever sought to vacate or modify the arbitration award. Selvick Marine simply complied with it. Sometime in 2011 or 2012, though, Selvick Marine dissolved and liquidated operations. [—6—]

C. *The Present Dispute*

In July 2013, Calumet fired one of its boat operators, Angelo Zuccolo. The Union grieved the firing and eventually demanded arbitration. Calumet refused to participate in the arbitration on the ground that it was not a party to any collective bargaining agreement with the Union. The Union notified the American Arbitration Association of the dispute and requested an arbitration panel. Calumet then filed this suit seeking both a declaration that it was not a party to any collective bargaining agreements with the Union and an injunction preventing the Union from continuing with the arbitration. The Union counterclaimed, seeking, among other things, to enforce the July 2012 arbitration decision finding that Selvick Marine and Calumet were alter egos and an order compelling Calumet to submit to arbitration pursuant to the Floating Agreement. The Union agreed to postpone the arbitration pending the outcome of this suit.

Both parties moved for summary judgment. The district court rejected the Union's argument that the 90-day statute of limitations to challenge an arbitration award applied to Calumet's claims. The court also rejected the Union's attempt to rely on the arbitrator's alter ego finding to show that Calumet had been a party through Selvick Marine. The Union had offered no basis apart from the arbitrator's conclusion to support an alter ego finding, so the court concluded that it had no basis to enforce against Calumet in this action the arbitrator's finding that Calumet and Selvick Marine were alter egos. Finally, the district court rejected the Union's argument that the Norris-LaGuardia Act, 29 U.S.C. § 101 et seq., prohibited injunctive relief in the case. [—7—]

For these reasons, the court granted Calumet's motion, denied the Union's motion, and dismissed the Union's counterclaims. The court did not, however, enter a separate judgment pursuant to Federal Rule of Civil Procedure 58. On September 30, 2015, the Union filed a notice of appeal.

II. *Appellate Jurisdiction*

Before addressing the merits of the appeal, we must be sure we have appellate jurisdiction. The Union contends it has appealed a final decision under 28 U.S.C. § 1291. Generally, an order is final for appeal purposes under § 1291 "if it ends the litigation and leaves nothing to be decided in the district court." *United States v. Ettrick Wood Products, Inc.*, 916 F.2d 1211, 1216 (7th Cir. 1990).

The question of appellate jurisdiction arose because the district court issued a memorandum opinion on the motions but did not enter a separate judgment under Federal Rule of Civil Procedure 58(a), which requires that a judgment be "set out in a separate document." "The grant of a motion for summary judgment is not one of the exceptions to the separate document requirement listed in Rule 58(a), so a separate document was required in this case to have a proper Rule 58 judgment." *Perry v. Sheet Metal Workers' Local No. 73 Pension Fund*, 585 F.3d 358, 361 (7th Cir. 2009); see also *Alpine State Bank v. Ohio Casualty Insurance Co.*, 941 F.2d 554, 558 (7th Cir. 1991) ("In satisfying the requirement of Rule 58, neither the memorandum opinion explaining the ruling on summary judgment, nor the minute order announcing the summary judgment can be substituted for a declaratory judgment."). And although Calumet had sought injunctive as well as declaratory relief, the court issued no separate injunction or declaration of rights following the memorandum opinion. [—8—]

At oral argument, we asked for supplemental briefs on appellate jurisdiction. The responses satisfy us that we have jurisdiction over this appeal. First, the district court's failure to enter a separate Rule 58 judgment is not always decisive. Compliance with Rule 58 makes appellate jurisdiction simpler for the parties and the courts, but we may still have jurisdiction if we "know from other sources" that there has been a final judgment. *First Nat'l Bank of Chicago v. Comptroller of the Currency*, 956 F.2d 1360, 1363 (7th Cir. 1992); see also Fed. R. App. P. 4(a)(7)(B) ("A failure to set forth a judgment or order on a separate document when required by Federal Rule of Civil Procedure 58(a) does not affect the validity of an appeal from that judgment or order."). The federal rules deal with such oversights by district courts. When a judgment is not set forth on a separate document but Rule 58(a) requires it, we treat judgment as entered 150 days after the entry of the judgment or order on the civil docket. Fed. R. Civ. P. 58(c)(2)(B); Fed. R. App. P. 4(a)(7)(A)(ii); see also *Perry*, 585 F.3d at 362. In this case, the district court entered its memorandum opinion and order on September

4, 2015. The 150-day period thus lapsed on February 1, 2016, at which point judgment was effectively entered for appeal purposes, and the Union's earlier notice of appeal "is treated as filed on the date of and after the entry." Fed. R. App. P. 4(a)(2).

So the district court's failure to enter a Rule 58 judgment does not require dismissal. We still must ask whether the district court was finished with the case, even though it did not enter a separate injunction or declaration of the parties' rights. We take the question of the injunction first. Both the Federal Rules of Civil Procedure and the Norris-LaGuardia Act, which governs the issuance of injunctions in labor disputes, require the court to make any injunction specific. *See* Fed. R. [—9—] Civ. P. 65(d)(1) (order granting injunction must "state the reasons why it issued," "state its terms specifically," and "describe in reasonable detail … the act or acts restrained or required"); 29 U.S.C. § 109 (requiring that findings of fact be "made and filed by the court" and that injunction be limited to a prohibition of a "specific act or acts"). The absence of a separate and specific injunction could be a serious problem, but the parties' supplemental briefs told us that they have reached a compromise on the issue of injunctive relief. We see no need to remand to the district court for entry of an injunction that Calumet no longer seeks or needs.[1]

As for the request for declaratory judgment, we have said that "in declaratory judgment actions, district courts must declare specifically and separately the respective rights of the parties, not simply state in a memorandum opinion, minute order, or a form prescribed for judgment in a civil case that a motion has been granted or denied." *Alpine State Bank*, 941 F.2d at 558. No such declaration appears in the record. Still, we may nevertheless have jurisdiction if "'the

practicalities weigh heavily' toward a common sense conclusion that the district court intended to enter a final judgment." *Id.* at 559 (internal citation omitted), quoting *Newman-Green, Inc. v. Alfonzo-Larrain*, 490 U.S. 826, 837 (1989).

Calumet's motion for summary judgment asked the district court to "enter a declaration that Calumet is not subject to the terms of any collective bargaining agreement with" the [—10—] Union. The court concluded "that based on the undisputed facts Calumet is not a signatory to the 2012–2014 [Floating Agreement] or any collective bargaining agreement with the Union. Calumet thus cannot be compelled to arbitrate the Zuccolo grievance or submit to an audit." It then granted Calumet's motion for summary judgment, which addressed all of Calumet's claims, and dismissed the Union's counterclaims. Despite the absence of a separate Rule 58 judgment, the district court's memorandum and the absence of any other claims or later actions by the court make sufficiently plain both what the court declared and that the district court was finished with the case. We thus have jurisdiction over this appeal. *Metzl v. Leininger*, 57 F.3d 618, 620 (7th Cir. 1995); *see also Buck v. U.S. Digital Communications, Inc.*, 141 F.3d 710, 711 (7th Cir. 1998) ("If the terms of declaratory relief appeared in the court's opinion and it were plain that the case is finished, we would not stand on ceremony—at least not as far as the need for a 'final decision' is concerned, although the lack of specificity might make the decision hard to enforce."). We proceed to the merits, where we can be brief.

III. *Analysis*

The district court correctly concluded that the arbitration award did not bind Calumet to the 2012–2014 Floating Agreement. We briefly address two preliminary matters that simplify our approach to the appeal. First, as noted above, the Union initially contended that the Norris-LaGuardia Act prohibited an injunction in this case. Since the parties have reached an agreement that eliminates the request and/or need for injunctive relief, we need not decide whether the district court

---

[1] We also need not decide whether or not Federal Rule of Civil Procedure 65 applies to cases otherwise covered by the Norris-LaGuardia Act. See Fed. R. Civ. P. 65(e)(1) (Rule 65 provisions "do not modify … any federal statute relating to temporary restraining orders or preliminary injunctions in actions affecting employer and employee[.]").

correctly decided the Norris-LaGuardia issue. Second, because the Union agreed to postpone the arbitration pending [—11—] the outcome of this suit, it waived any argument that Calumet was required to allow the arbitration to reach a conclusion before proceeding with this case in court. *Cf. AT&T Broadband, LLC v. International Brotherhood of Electrical Workers*, 317 F.3d 758 (7th Cir. 2003) (discussing timing of litigation regarding arbitrability of a dispute and concluding company seeking anti-arbitration injunction was not entitled to pre-arbitration judicial review).

On the merits, the Union's argument begins and ends with the finding of alter ego in the 2012 arbitration award. The Union asks us to treat that finding as binding Calumet to the Floating Agreement for purposes of the dispute over Mr. Zuccolo's firing based on Selvick Marine's previous status as a party to the Floating Agreement. In support, the Union relies on the rule that failure to challenge an arbitration award within the applicable limitations period renders the award final. *See International Union of Operating Engineers, Local 150 v. Rabine*, 161 F.3d 427, 433–34 (7th Cir. 1998) ("The rule is a simple one: If you receive notice of an adverse decision in a federal labor arbitration, challenge it within 90 days or expect to pay up."). The Union also relies on the great deference courts give to arbitrators' awards, enforcing them as long as the arbitrator has arguably interpreted the collective bargaining agreement between the parties even if the courts believe the arbitrator seriously erred. *E.g., Prate Installations, Inc. v. Chicago Regional Council of Carpenters*, 607 F.3d 467, 471 (7th Cir. 2010), quoting *Clear Channel Outdoor, Inc. v. International Unions of Painters & Allied Trades, Local 770*, 558 F.3d 670, 677 (7th Cir. 2009).

These general rules are correct, but they do not address this situation. When the arbitrator entered the 2012 award, he [—12—] made clear that it should have no prospective effect. Not only did he refuse to order prospective compliance with the terms of the Floating Agreement, he did so expressly because the precise point on which the Union's current argument depends—the existence of a continuing relationship between Calumet and the Union—had not been established:

> Moreover, it is unclear on the record before the Arbitrator whether there is any continuing relationship, contractual or otherwise, between either IUOE Local 139 and/or IUOE Local 150 and [Selvick Marine] and/or [Calumet] since the expiration of the [Floating Agreement] on December 31, 2011.

Selvick Marine chose not to fight the alter ego determination or the award of back pay and benefits. It just paid the award. At that point, the alter ego determination had served its purpose, holding that Calumet had violated the agreement in the past and that Selvick Marine was liable for those violations. As a purely retrospective determination, the award could have no additional impact on Calumet's relationship with the Union going forward. In other words, once Selvick Marine paid the award, nothing remained for Calumet to challenge.

It therefore makes no difference here that an arbitration award cannot be challenged after the limitations period runs, *Rabine*, 161 F.3d at 433–34, or that judicial review of an award is so limited, *Prate Installations*, 607 F.3d at 471. The Union made a strategic decision to rely entirely on the award's alter ego finding as a basis to compel arbitration, but the award simply does not serve that function. It provided no prospective relief and had no prospective effect. It did not establish that Calumet was a party to the Floating Agreement when it [—13—] fired Zuccolo. It did not establish that Calumet was then the alter ego of Selvick Marine, which had dissolved sometime in 2011 or 2012.

Arbitration "is a matter of contract and a party cannot be required to submit to arbitration any dispute which he has not agreed so to submit." *AT & T Technologies, Inc. v. Communications Workers of America*, 475 U.S. 643, 648 (1986) (internal quotation marks omitted), quoting *United Steelworkers of America v. Warrior & Gulf Navigation Co.*, 363 U.S. 574, 582 (1960). The Union has failed to pose a genuine dispute of fact as to whether Calumet agreed to submit the termination of Zuccolo to arbitration. Its alter ego argument failed as discussed above, and the undisputed facts of record show that Calumet terminated its participation in the Floating Agreement in 2008. Nor has the Union presented any evidence that Calumet itself signed on to later versions of the agreement. On this record, Calumet was entitled to judgment as a matter of law.

We DISMISS the portion of the Union's appeal related to injunctive relief. The judgment of the district court is otherwise AFFIRMED.

United States Court of Appeals
for the Seventh Circuit

No. 14-2484

DEB
vs.
SIRVA, INC.

Appeal from the United States District Court for the
Southern District of Indiana, Indianapolis Division

Decided: August 11, 2016

Citation: 832 F.3d 800, 4 Adm. R. 337 (7th Cir. 2016).

Before **FLAUM, MANION,** and **ROVNER,** Circuit Judges.

[—1—] **ROVNER,** Circuit Judge:

Ashoke Deb contracted with an Indian moving company, Allied Lemuir, to move his belongings from Calcutta, India to St. John's, Canada, but his belongings never left India. He now seeks to hold the defendants, two United States companies, SIRVA, Inc. and Allied Van Lines, Inc., responsible for the improper disposal and loss of his personal property in connection with his move. SIRVA and Allied moved to dismiss the complaint, arguing that Deb [—2—] had failed to state a claim for which the court could grant relief, that he had failed to join a necessary party, and that the United States federal courts were not the proper venue for his claim. The district court agreed with the latter argument and dismissed on the grounds of forum non conveniens. Deb appeals. Because we have determined that the district court did not hold the defendants to their burden of demonstrating that India was an available and adequate forum for this litigation, we vacate and remand the case to the district court to do so.

I.

Because the defendants, SIRVA and Allied Van Lines, moved to dismiss, we will construe the facts in the plaintiff's favor for now, but will discuss the nuances of our assumptions below. *Jackson v. Payday Fin.*, LLC, 764 F.3d 765, 773, n.19 (7th Cir. 2014), *cert. denied*, 135 S. Ct. 1894 (2015).

In August, 2009, in preparation for his move from Calcutta, India to his current home in St. John's in the Province of Newfoundland and Labradour, Canada, Deb, a citizen and resident of Canada, contracted with an Indian company, Allied Lemuir, to move his personal belongings from Calcutta to St. John's. Deb's belongings, however, never left India. On September 5, 2009, Allied Lemuir e-mailed Deb and informed him that sea freight charges had risen substantially, and consequently, Deb would need to pay an additional amount of money to have the items shipped. Deb refused to pay the additional amount and demanded that Allied Lemuir fulfill its obligations under the contract as written. At the same time that Deb was attempting to settle matters with Allied Lemuir in India, he also contacted the defendants, the United States companies of SIRVA and Allied Van Lines, in an effort to obtain his personal goods. Furthermore, from December 2010 [—3—] until May 2011, Deb's Canadian counsel attempted to resolve the issue with an attorney for Allied Van Lines Canada ("Allied Canada").

Allied Lemuir sent Deb a letter dated January 30, 2010, demanding additional charges that had accrued for demurrage, fumigation, renewal of customs clearance, and sea freight. The letter stated that if Deb failed to remit payment within seven days, it would assume he was no longer interested in the shipment. Deb did not respond to the letter directly, but rather relied on his Canadian lawyer to pursue a resolution by other means, including by contacting the defendants in this case and corresponding with them over the course of several months. On August 11, 2010, SIRVA's claim services department responded to Deb's inquiries, stating that they were unable to identify any record of Deb's shipment in SIRVA's system, but stated that if the move was through Allied or North American, the claims service representative would forward the message to the proper party if Deb provided a registration number. According to a letter dated August 26, 2010, which Deb says he did not receive until it was sent to his counsel on April 12, 2013, Allied Lemuir eventually sold Deb's property to pay the additional amounts it had demanded from Deb.

Deb filed a legal action against Allied Canada in the Supreme Court of Newfoundland and Labrador, Canada, in the Trial Division on November 5, 2010. And, a few years later, on July 12, 2013, while the Canadian case was still pending, he filed his complaint in this case in the Indiana State Superior Court against SIRVA and Allied Van Lines, both of which are Delaware corporations with their principal place of business [—4—] in Illinois and corporate offices in Indiana.[1] On August 5, 2013, the defendants jointly filed a successful notice of removal in the district court in the southern district of Indiana. Deb seeks to hold SIRVA and Allied Van Lines responsible for the damages from the improper disposal and ultimate loss of his personal property, which he alleges include original works of intellectual property that, together with his other personal belongings, exceed a value of $75,000. His amended complaint alleges that SIRVA and Allied Van Lines are liable to Deb as "joint venturers." (R. 27, pp. 3-4, Page ID 286-287) (Plaintiff's Supp. App. B003-B004).

The district court granted the defendants' motion to dismiss on June 6, 2014, based on the ground of forum non conveniens, noting that both India and Canada offered appropriate alternative forums for the action. Deb appeals.

II.

A.

The defendants filed their motion to dismiss pursuant to Federal Rule of Civil Procedure 12(b)(6) (failure to state a claim upon which relief can be granted), 12(b)(7) (failure to join a party), and 12(b)(3) (improper

venue). Subsumed within this last category were the common law principles of forum non conveniens and abstention. The district court dismissed the case on the ground of forum non conveniens. [—5—]

As the Latin name suggests, the doctrine of forum non conveniens addresses the matter of convenience to the parties. As the Supreme Court explained,

> A federal court has discretion to dismiss a case on the ground of forum non conveniens when an alternative forum has jurisdiction to hear the case, and trial in the chosen forum would establish oppressiveness and vexation to a defendant out of all proportion to plaintiff's convenience, or the chosen forum [is] inappropriate because of considerations affecting the court's own administrative and legal problems.

Sinochem Int'l Co. v. Malaysia Int'l Shipping Corp., 549 U.S. 422, 429 (2007) (citing a long line of Supreme Court precedent) (internal citations omitted). Today, the doctrine applies in the federal courts only when the other jurisdiction is a foreign one.[2] Stated more simply, a district court may dismiss a case on forum non conveniens grounds when it determines that there are "strong reasons for believing it should be litigated in the courts of another, normally a foreign, jurisdiction." *Fischer v. Magyar Allamvasutak Zrt.*, 777 F.3d 847, 866, *cert. denied*, 135 S. Ct. 2817 (2015) (*citing Sinochem*, 549 U.S. at 429-30). A dismissal for forum non conveniens is "committed to the sound discretion of the trial court" and "may be reversed only [—6—] when there has been a clear abuse of discretion." *Piper Aircraft Co. v. Reyno*, 454 U.S. 235, 257

---

[1] The district court stated that SIRVA has its principal place of business in Indiana. *Deb v. SIRVA Inc.*, No. 1:13-CV-01245-TWP, 2014 WL 2573465, at *1 (S.D. Ind. June 6, 2014) (R. 55 at p.2, Page ID 740), but this appears to be incorrect. *See* Declaration of Abigail M. Jones, Memorandum in Support of Defendant's Motion to Dismiss Plaintiff's Amended Complaint, Exhibit 1, ¶ 6.

[2] The common law doctrine of forum non conveniens has continuing application in federal courts only in cases where the alternative forum is a foreign one. Otherwise, if the issue is one of convenience within the United States federal court system, the Federal Rules of Civil Procedure allow for transfer, rather than dismissal, when a sister federal court is the more convenient forum. *See* 28 U.S.C. §§ 1404(a), 1406(a); *Sinochem*, 549 U.S. 422, 430.

(1981); *Abad v. Bayer Corp.*, 563 F.3d 663, 665 (7th Cir. 2009).

The doctrine of forum non conveniens, however, is an exceptional one that a court must use sparingly. *Gulf Oil Corp. v. Gilbert*, 330 U.S. 501, 504, 509 (the doctrine should be applied only in "exceptional circumstances," and "rather rare cases.") *See also Carijano v. Occidental Petroleum Corp.*, 643 F.3d 1216, 1224 (9th Cir. 2011) ("The doctrine of forum non conveniens is a drastic exercise of the court's inherent power ... . Therefore, we have treated forum non conveniens as an exceptional tool to be employed sparingly.") "[U]nless the balance is strongly in favor of the defendant, the plaintiff's choice of forum should rarely be disturbed. *Gulf Oil*, 330 U.S. at 504.

The exceptional nature of a dismissal for forum non conveniens means that a defendant invoking it ordinarily bears a heavy burden in opposing the plaintiff's chosen forum. *Sinochem*, 549 U.S. at 430; *Gulf Oil*, 330 U.S. at 508; *In re Hudson*, 710 F.3d 716, 718 (7th Cir. 2013); *In re Factor VIII or IX Concentrate Blood Products Litigation*, 484 F.3d 951, 956 (7th Cir. 2007). A heavy burden is appropriate, because if the doctrine is success-fully invoked, the result is not a transfer to another court but a dismissal, and the plaintiff will not be able to refile his case in any other court if the statute of limitations has run. *In re Hudson*, 710 F.3d at 718.

When a plaintiff's choice is not his home forum, however, the presumption in the plaintiff's favor "applies with less force," for the assumption that the chosen forum is appropriate is in such cases "less reasonable." *Sinochem*, 549 U.S. at 430 (*citing Piper Aircraft*, 454 U.S. at 255–56). In *U.S.O. Corp. v. Mizuho Holding Co.*, 547 F.3d 749, 752 (7th Cir. 2008), we noted [—7—] that "[I]f the plaintiff is suing far from home, it is less reasonable to assume that the forum is a convenient one. ... [and T]he risk that the chosen forum really has little connection to the litigation is greater.") (citing *In re Factor VIII or IX Concentrate Blood Products Litigation*, 484 F.3d at 956.) It is true that Deb lives in Newfoundland, Canada and not

the United States, but although the citizenship of the plaintiff defending against a forum non conveniens claim is relevant to the issue of convenience, it is not dispositive of the issue. *See, e.g., Scottish Air Int'l, Inc. v. British Caledonian Grp., PLC*, 81 F.3d 1224, 1232 (2d Cir. 1996). As we noted in the blood products litigation, the issue is not so much about the foreign citizenship of the plaintiff, but rather what that foreign nationality might indicate about the convenience to the plaintiff. *In re Factor VIII or IX Concentrate Blood Products Litig.*, 484 F.3d at 956. In other words, when a plaintiff is suing far from home

the risk that the chosen forum really has little connection to the litigation is greater. We do not understand this as any kind of bias against foreign plaintiffs. That would be inconsistent with many treaties the United States has signed as well as with the general principle that our courts are open to all who seek legitimately to use them. It is instead a practical observation about convenience. A citizen of Texas who decided to sue in the federal court in Alaska might face an equally skeptical court, which might conclude that convenience requires a change in venue under the federal statutory counterpart to forum non conveniens. [—8—]

Id. at 956. Nonetheless, it is undoubtedly true that although Deb is not a citizen or resident of the United States, litigation in Indiana would be far more convenient from a geographical perspective than one in India. And in any case, even if we apply the presumption in favor of Deb with less force, it is still the defendants' burden to oppose the chosen forum.

In short, as we consider whether the district court exerted permissible discretion to dismiss the case on forum non conveniens grounds, we consider whether it properly placed the burden on the defendants to demonstrate that a finding of forum non conveniens was within the realm of appropriate conclusions.

To determine whether a dismissal for forum non conveniens is appropriate, a court first must determine if an alternative and adequate forum is available and then go on to balance the interests of the various participants. We start with the availability of the forum because, "[a[s a practical matter, it makes little sense to broach the subject of forum non conveniens unless an adequate alternative forum is available to hear the case. Therefore, the first step in any forum non conveniens inquiry is to decide whether such a place exists." *Kamel v. Hill-Rom Co.*, 108 F.3d 799, 802 (7th Cir. 1997) (citing *Piper Aircraft*, 454 U.S. at 254 n.22). The availability of the forum is really a two-part inquiry involving availability and adequacy. *In re Factor VIII or IX Concentrate Blood Products Litig.*, 484 F.3d at 957. "An alternative forum is available if all parties are amenable to process and are within the forum's jurisdiction. An alternative forum is adequate when the parties will not be deprived of all remedies or treated unfairly." *Id.* (*citing Kamel*, 108 F.3d at 803). Adequacy only comes into play to the [—9—] extent that the remedy would be so inadequate that for all intents and purposes the forum is not available. *Piper Aircraft*, 454 U.S. at 255, n.22. A forum is not inadequate merely because the law in the foreign jurisdiction is less favorable to the party opposing dismissal. *Id.* at 247, 250; *Stroitelstvo Bulgaria Ltd. v. Bulgarian-Am. Enter. Fund*, 589 F.3d 417, 421 (7th Cir. 2009).

We begin, therefore, by looking to the defendants to see if they have met their burden of establishing that an alternative forum is available and adequate. *Fischer*, 777 F.3d at 867. After demonstrating that India offered an adequate forum, we would go on to balance the interests by focusing on the (1) relative ease of access to sources of proof; (2) availability of compulsory process and costs for attendance of witnesses; (3) possibility of viewing the premises, if appropriate; and (4) other practical issues, including the ease of enforcement of any ultimate judgment. *See Gulf Oil*, 330 U.S. at 508. As we will describe, however, we need not go on to balance the interests, because we conclude that the defendants have failed to show there

was an available and adequate forum available elsewhere.

B.

The district court concluded that there were "two possible forums that satisfy this requirement" of an alternate available forum—Canada and India. *Deb v. SIRVA Inc.*, No. 1:13-CV-01245-TWP, 2014 WL 2573465, at *3 (S.D. Ind. June 6, 2014) (R. 55 at 5, Page ID 744). We begin first with the analysis of India as an alternate forum. The defendants argued that India was an appropriate forum because the Indian courts could exercise jurisdiction over Allied Lemuir, and "assuming, *arguendo*, [—10—] that Deb's joint venture theory is correct, and SIRVA and [Allied Van Lines] were doing business in India as Allied Lemuir, and, therefore, responsible for the joint venture's actions, the Indian courts would be able to exercise jurisdiction over SIRVA and [Allied Van Lines]." Defendants' brief at 19-20.

It is worth stopping for a moment to unpack the defendants' argument further. Recall that Deb contracted with Allied Lemuir to move his belongings. The failed contract was with Allied Lemuir. Deb never sued Allied Lemuir, but instead sued two United States companies, the defendants here, SIRVA and Allied Van Lines. As we just explained, in order for a district court to dismiss this case for forum non conveniens, the defendants have the burden of demonstrating that an alternate forum is available—in other words, that Deb could sue these defendants, SIRVA and Allied Van Lines, in India. And the only way that Deb can sue SIRVA and Allied Van Lines in India is if the defendants had something to do with the wrongdoing that occurred in India—either that they broke the contract and sold the goods (which we know they did not do) or they have some legally sufficient affiliation with Allied Lemuir that would allow the Indian courts to exert jurisdiction over them.

Oddly, in order to support dismissal for forum non conveniens then, the defendants end up trying to thread a small-eyed needle by claiming, on the one hand, that they could be subject to jurisdiction in India, while simultaneously refusing to acknowledge an actual legal affiliation with Allied Lemuir. To do this, the brief on appeal dances around these issues by making naked assertions such as, "the District Court also properly found that the Indian courts would be able to exercise jurisdiction over SIRVA and [Allied Van Lines], even [—11—] without their consent," or by trying to connect Allied Lemuir with the defendants without really connecting them:

> Here, as the District Court correctly found, the Indian Courts may exercise jurisdiction over Allied Lemuir as a resident of India that conducted business in India. Further, as the District Court determined, assuming *arguendo*, that Deb's joint venture theory is correct, and that SIRVA and [Allied Van Lines] were doing business in India as Allied Lemuir, and, therefore, responsible for the joint venture's actions, the Indian courts would be able to exercise jurisdiction over SIRVA and [Allied Van Lines] because: (1) Allied Lemuir is an Indian corporation and resident; and (2) SIRVA and [Allied Van Lines] would have been doing business in India and responsible for the joint venture's actions.

Defendants' brief at 16, 19. All of these assertions depend on the notion that SIRVA and Allied Van Lines were somehow connected with Allied Lemuir. But it is the defendant's burden to demonstrate that forum non conveniens is appropriate, and the only evidence to support this contention comes from the bald assertions in the *plaintiff's* compliant that SIRVA and Allied Van Lines were doing business in India as a joint venture with Allied Lemuir.

The plaintiff's assertion, to which the defendants' point to support a dismissal, is that Allied Lemuir is a member of the SIRVA Group and is part of a joint venture with SIRVA and Allied Van Lines. (R. 27, pp. 2-3, Page ID 285-286) (Plaintiff's [—12—] Supp. App. B002-B003). To support that assertion, Deb attached to the complaint some

marketing materials that Allied Lemuir posted on the internet boasting of its affiliation with SIRVA and Allied Van Lines. *Id.* at Ex. C. Of course, at this point, in the current posture of a motion to dismiss, the defendants' affiliation with SIRVA and Allied Van Lines has never been questioned, tested or explored. All we have is some pages printed out from the internet in which a foreign company with the word "Allied" in its name is asserting in marketing material that it is reliable because it is affiliated with two international companies, one of which also has the name "Allied" in its name. The material has not been authenticated or verified, no court has ever made a determination about any connection between Allied Lemuir and the defendants in this case, and the defendants have never admitted any connection to Allied Lemuir. This is so because this case comes before us on a motion to dismiss in which a court cannot determine the truth of factual assertions. When considering a motion to dismiss, the district court ordinarily assumes the truth of all well-pleaded allegations in the plaintiff's complaint. *Firestone Fin. Corp. v. Meyer*, 796 F.3d 822, 826 (7th Cir. 2015). But this rule is less absolute when considering a motion to dismiss under Federal Rule 12(b)(3) than under Rule 12(b)(6). Under Rule 12(b)(3), which allows for dismissal for improper venue, the district court assumes the truth of the allegations in the plaintiff's complaint, *unless* contradicted by the defendant's affidavits. 5B Charles Alan Wright & Arthur R. Miller, Federal Practice and Procedure § 1352 (2004). Rule 12(b)(3) is a somewhat unique context of dismissal in that a court may look beyond the mere allegations of a complaint, [—13—] and need not view the allegations of the complaint as the exclusive basis for its decision. *Estate of Myhra v. Royal Caribbean Cruises, Ltd.*, 695 F.3d 1233, 1239 (11th Cir. 2012).

This Circuit has not had the opportunity to discuss the intricacies of the assumptions a court should make when a defendant contradicts the plaintiff's bald assertion of venue in a motion to dismiss for improper venue under Rule 12(b)(3), but we have before concluded that, when considering a motion to dismiss in general, a court may consider matters outside of the pleadings to resolve factual questions pertaining to jurisdiction, process, or indispensable parties. *English v. Cowell*, 10 F.3d 434, 437 (7th Cir. 1993). Moreover, other circuits to have considered the question agree that it is appropriate for a district court to look outside the complaint, or particularly at a defendant's contradictory statements, when considering a motion to dismiss under Rule 12(b)(3). For example, the Second Circuit has noted:

> If the defendant presents evidence that venue is improper and the plaintiff responds with contrary evidence, "it may be appropriate for the district court to hold a Rule 12(b)(3) motion in abeyance until the district court holds an evidentiary hearing on the disputed facts." *Murphy*, 362 F.3d at 1139. … "Alternatively, the district court may deny the Rule 12(b)(3) motion while granting leave to refile it if further development of the record eliminates any genuine factual issue." *Id.*

Hancock v. Am. Tel. & Tel. Co., 701 F.3d 1248, 1261 (10th Cir. 2012). And the Ninth Circuit has noted that when the outcome of a 12(b)(3) motion might have a "dramatic effect on the [—14—] plaintiff's forum choice … no disputed fact should be resolved against that party until it has had an opportunity to be heard." *Murphy v. Schneider Nat'l, Inc.*, 362 F.3d 1133, 1139 (9th Cir. 2004); *Pierce v. Shorty Small's of Branson Inc.*, 137 F.3d 1190, 1192 (10th Cir. 1998) ("Plaintiff contends that in responding to a motion to dismiss for improper venue, he was entitled to rely upon the well pled facts of his complaint. This is true, however, only to the extent that such facts are uncontroverted by defendant's affidavit."); *Home Ins. Co. v. Thomas Indus., Inc.*, 896 F.2d 1352, 1355 (11th Cir. 1990) ("When a complaint is dismissed on the basis of improper venue without an evidentiary hearing, the plaintiff must present only a prima facie showing of venue. … Further, [t]he facts as alleged in the complaint are taken as true to the extent they are uncontroverted by defendants' affidavits.") (internal citations omitted).

Ordinarily these cases speak of the ability of a court to view evidence of the party moving to dismiss (the defendant) in order to rebut the allegations of the non-movant's (the plaintiff's) complaint asserting facts supporting its chosen venue. This case is unique in that, in an unusual course of events, the *defendants* cite to the *plaintiff's* bare allegation of a joint venture in the complaint in order to support their contention that the case should be dismissed under Rule 12(b)(3). But the general premise is the same. Where one party makes a bald claim of venue and the other party contradicts it, a district court may look beyond the pleadings to determine whether the chosen venue is appropriate.

It is worth noting that the plaintiff's burden in defending a motion to dismiss is low. Other than the exceptions discussed, a court generally accepts the plaintiff's allegations as [—15—] true for purposes of the motion to dismiss, as long as the complaint contains sufficient factual allegations to state a claim for relief that is legally sound and plausible on its face. *Ashcroft v. Iqbal*, 556 U.S. 662, 678 (2009). The defendants' burden in alleging forum non conveniens, however, is heavy. *Sinochem*, 549 U.S. at 430. Defendants must submit evidence of an adequate and alternative forum. Combining the principles we discussed above—that the district court may look beyond the bare allegations of the complaint where the defendants dispute facts related to venue, and that defendants bear the heavy burden of showing an alternate forum— we look to see whether the district court placed the burden on the defendants to demonstrate that an alternate forum was available, and whether the defendants met that burden. We conclude that the district court did not hold the defendants to the burden, nor did the defendants meet it. To the contrary, to the extent the defendants offered any evidence or argument at all, it was evidence that they would not, in fact, be subject to jurisdiction in India.

Much of the language of the Defendants' Memorandum in Support of its Motion to Dismiss argues that they had nothing to do with Allied Lemuir's actions and thus could not be associated with the Indian company.

The defendants do not even offer any evidence that they were doing business in India. If, in fact, the defendants had nothing to do with Deb's loss and have no connection to Allied Lamuir, an Indian court would have no business asserting jurisdiction over them. In short, rather than supporting their burden of demonstrating that there is an available and alternative forum in India, they instead offer allegations that they would not be subject to jurisdiction in India. For example, in their briefing below on the motion to dismiss, the defendants state the following: [—16—]

Deb's assertion that Defendants had an agency, joint venture, or any other kind of relationship among themselves, with Allied Lemuir, or anyone else that could impute liability on Defendants for breach of contract or conversion is equally unavailing. Deb has failed to offer any evidence of a joint venture or even alleged an association of two or more persons to carry out a single business enterprise for profit.

Memorandum in Support of Defendants' Motion to Dismiss Plaintiff's Amended Complaint at 10. (R. 30, p.10, Page ID 414). The memorandum is replete with similar allegations which, if true, would seem to lead to the conclusion that a court in India could not assert jurisdiction over the defendants. For example, the defendants state:

• "While Deb makes much ado about a self-serving, unauthenticated Allied Lemuir document (Amended Complaint Ex. C) purporting to demonstrate that Allied Lemuir was created as a joint venture between Lemuir, [Allied Van Lines] and several other Allied companies, merely calling a relationship a 'joint venture' does not mean that a joint venture exists." *Id.* (internal citation omitted);

• "Deb added allegations in an attempt to bolster his assertion that SIRVA and [Allied Van Lines] are liable to Deb for the acts of Allied Lemuir as 'joint venturers' (which they are not). *Id.* at 2, (R. 30, p.2, Page ID 406);

• "Defendants are Delaware Corporations that are not in privity with Deb, and have never conducted any business with him. Further, Deb has failed to establish any 'joint venture' or agency relationship between or among Defendants [—17—] and Allied Lemuir (and in particular, at the time of the shipment) or any reason to believe that Deb had transacted with anyone other than Allied Lemuir to transport his belongings." *Id.;*

• "Defendants have never conducted business or entered into any agreements with Deb ... Instead Plaintiff's dealings in transporting his household belongings have been exclusively with Allied Lemuir, *a legally separate entity.*" *Id.* at 3, (R. 30, p.3, Page ID 407) (emphasis ours);

• "Defendants are not liable to Deb under common agency principles when Defendants never agreed to act as principal creating any sort of agency relationship between Defendants and Allied Lemuir as to this shipment." *Id.* at 10, (R. 30, p.10, Page ID 414);

• "Defendants cannot be held liable to Deb for Allied Lemuir or anyone else's actions under a joint venture, agency, apparent authority, or any other theory, and Deb's Amended Complaint must be dismissed for his failure to state a claim upon which relief can be granted." *Id.* at 12, (R. 30, p.12, Page ID 416)

• Allied Lemuir, a separate and distinct Indian company, not a party to this lawsuit, arranged with Deb to transport Deb's belongings from India to Canada. *Id.* at 15, (R. 30, p.15, Page ID 419);

• "Even assuming the veracity of these facts (which Defendants dispute) Deb has failed to assert cognizable or viable claims. There was no mistaking that Deb was dealing exclusively with Allied Lemuir for this shipment. Not one docu- [—18—] ment memorializing the transaction governing the transportation of Deb's personal belongings mentions SIRVA or AVL." *Id.* at 11, (R. 30, p.11, Page ID 415).

Having spent so much time asserting that they had no relationship with Allied Lemuir, it is no wonder that the defendants were left to make broad conclusory allegations about India as an available forum. In its memorandum in support of the motion to dismiss, under the section labeled "India is an Available Forum" the defendants correctly note that the case law requires that "all parties must be subject to the jurisdiction of the foreign court and amenable to process." *Id.* at 20 (R. 30, p.2, Page ID 424). They then baldly assert that "India meet[s] the requirements of an adequate alternative forum." *Id.* at 20. That is the whole of the defendants' claim that India is an available forum.[3] They do not offer any evidence that they would be subject to jurisdiction in India, but rather simply conclude without reasoning, law, or concessions that India is an adequate alternative. The defendants cannot have it both ways. They cannot vehemently deny any connection with the underlying actions giving rise to this litigation or any connection to Allied Lemuir, and simultaneously assert that the plaintiff could sue them in an Indian court. If there is an [—19—] independent basis on which an Indian court might assert jurisdiction over the defendants, unconnected to the facts of this case, the defendants have not noted it.

Without any evidence or a concession to the jurisdiction of the Indian courts, whatever the burden defendants had to show an adequate and alternative forum in India, there can be no doubt that the defendants did not meet it. And their appellate brief is no more illuminating. The defendants' argument on the adequacy of India as a forum in this court is simply that "the District Court correctly determined that Canada and India were

---

[3] In their brief before this court, the defendants argue that Deb only challenged the adequacy of India as a forum but not the availability. It was, however, the defendants' burden to meet in the first instance. *Sinochem*, 549 U.S. at 430. And in any event, Deb explicitly argued below and in his brief on appeal that the "Defendants fail to provide evidence that they are subject to jurisdiction in India." Plaintiff's Brief at 13, Plaintiff's Response in Opposition to Defendant's Motion to Dismiss at 20 (Plaintiff's Supp. Appendix B060).

available alternative forums." Defendants' brief at 11-12. And because the defendants have no evidence, they rely upon a 1978 case from the Second Circuit for the proposition that the district court need "nothing more than a belief" that the Indian courts would be able to exercise jurisdiction. Defendants' brief at 15 (citing *Schertenlieb v. Traum*, 589 F.2d 1156, 1163 (2d Cir. 1978). The defendants deduce this principle from language of the *Schertenlieb* case which states "that a district court should not dismiss unless it justifiably *believes* that the alternative forum will take jurisdiction, if the defendant consents." *Id.* (emphasis ours). In addition to being an almost 40 year old case from a different circuit, the *Schertenlieb* case not only does not help the defendants, it undermines their argument entirely. To begin, the language of the case requires a "justifiable belief"— presumably one supported by evidence. *Id.* We can assume this is so because in *Schertenleib*, the Second Circuit affirmed the lower court's dismissal on forum non conveniens grounds based on three strong factors that demonstrated that an alternate forum was available: first, the court had expert testimony that the defendant could be subject to jurisdiction in the foreign forum if the defendant conceded to jurisdiction there; second, it had [—20—] the defendant's actual concession to jurisdiction in the foreign forum; and third, the court also secured the defendant's agreement to waive the statute of limitations should the case need to return to the district court in the United States. *Id.* at 1160, 1166. In this case, on the other hand, the defendants' only argument is that the district court "properly found that the Indian courts would be able to exercise jurisdiction over SIRVA and AVL, even without their consent." Defendants' brief at 16. The defendants do not tell us why that finding was proper, particularly when it was based on the district court's naked belief—without evidence, without expert testimony, and without a concession to jurisdiction. Nothing in the *Schertenleib* case stands for the proposition that a district court's unsupported belief that a defendant would be subject to jurisdiction in a foreign court, without more, is enough to grant a motion to dismiss for forum non conveniens. In fact, the cases clearly refute the idea that a district court's mere belief is enough and instead place in the hands of the defendant the burden (and generally a heavy one) of demonstrating the availability and adequacy of the foreign forum. *Atl. Marine Const. Co. v. U.S. Dist. Court for W. Dist. of Texas*, 134 S. Ct. 568, 583 n.8 (2013); *Sinochem*, 549 U.S. at 430; *Gulf Oil*, 330 U.S. at 508; *Fischer*, 777 F.3d at 867; *In re Hudson*, 710 F.3d at 718; *In re Factor VIII or IX Concentrate Blood Products Litigation*, 484 F.3d at 956; *U.S.O. Corp. v. Mizuho Holding Co.*, 547 F.3d 749, 749–50 (7th Cir. 2008); *In re Ford Motor Co., Bridgestone/Firestone N. Am. Tire, LLC*, 344 F.3d 648, 652 (7th Cir. 2003).

The defendants also argue that the district court was not required to condition the dismissal of Deb's complaint on the defendants' concession to jurisdiction in India. Defendant's brief at 16-17 (citing *Leetsch v. Freedman*, 260 F.3d 1100, 1104 (9th Cir. 2001)). This may be so, but a concession is merely one [—21—] form of evidence that a defendant can present to meet her burden of demonstrating that a foreign jurisdiction will be available and adequate. This is precisely what the *Leetsch* court explains: there is no "inflexible test requiring conditional dismissal" but rather, "a district court can be required to impose conditions if there is a justifiable reason to doubt that a party will cooperate with the foreign forum." *Leetsch*, 260 F.3d at 1104. The defendants' many arguments disavowing any connection to Allied Lemuir and the events giving rise to this litigation give this court more than fair pause about whether they will cooperate with the Indian forum. The defendants in this case have not consented to jurisdiction in India and have offered not one shred of evidence that they would be subject to jurisdiction in India.

In contrast to the matter before us, in the cases in which one party successfully moved to dismiss a case for forum non conveniens, that party presented evidence of an available and adequate alternate forum or made a concession that it would accept service and jurisdiction there in order to guarantee availability of the alternate forum. For example, in *Fischer*, the district court had before it a list of the available remedies, plaintiffs' concerns with bringing suit in the foreign forum, and expert testimony from both sides as to whether those concerns were enough to render the forum inadequate. *Fischer*, 777 F.3d at 867. In the blood products litigation, the court heard expert testimony from experienced British lawyers, some of whom supported the plaintiffs and others who supported the drug companies, and eventually accepted the defendants' claim of an available alternative forum, but only after the defendants agreed to accept service in the United Kingdom. *In re Factor VIII or IX Concentrate Blood Products Litig.*, 484 F.3d at 956-57. And in *Kamel*, 108 F.3d at 803, the defendant [—22—] expressly consented to Saudi Arabia's jurisdiction and then submitted the affidavit of an expert in Saudi Arabian law to assure the court that Saudi law would recognize the defendant's consent to jurisdiction or have jurisdiction even without consent. *Id.* Once again we note that the defendants here offered no evidence, no experts, and no concession. The district court abused its discretion by finding that the Indian courts "should be able to exercise jurisdiction over the Defendants" without placing the burden on the defendants to demonstrate that this was so. *See Deb*, 2015 WL 2372465, at *3 (R. 55 at 6, Page ID 745).

To the extent that the defendant offers any information in support of its burden, it is the generalized conclusion that in other cases, involving other facts and other parties, courts have determined that India is an adequate forum. Memorandum in Support of Defendants' Motion to Dismiss Plaintiff's Amended Complaint at 21 (R. 30, p.21, Page ID 425). The defendants cite cases to argue that India's legal system, like ours, was inherited from the British, and that its remedies for breach of contract and conversion are similar to ours. *Id.* Such generalized information does not meet the burden that the defendants must satisfy to demonstrate that Deb realistically could sue SIRVA and Allied Van Lines in India.

The defendants' newly introduced references to Indian law fail for the same reason. In this court, the defendants have attached documents purporting to be from the Indian Code of Civil Procedure and case law from a jurisdiction in India. These documents are not in the record and were never presented to the district court. A party appealing a Rule 12(b)(6) dismissal may elaborate on his factual allegations so long as the new elaborations are consistent with the pleadings, [—23—] *Geinosky v. City of Chicago*, 675 F.3d 743, 745, n.1 (7th Cir. 2012), and we assume that the same would be true for a Rule 12(b)(3) dismissal. But SIRVA and Allied are not the parties opposing dismissal here. They had their shot at bearing the burden of demonstrating that the United States was an inconvenient forum. The question we face in this appeal is whether the district court properly dismissed this case under the doctrine of forum non conveniens without holding the defendants to their burden of demonstrating that there was an available and adequate remedy elsewhere. It did not.

Deb argues in his reply brief that the new documents do not even address the power of the Indian courts to exercise personal jurisdiction. We do not know what they do or do not assert. The relevant point is that they were not made part of the record below and have never been authenticated nor subject to an adversarial process in which the parties had an opportunity to argue about their meaning and import.

We can conclude that the district court failed to hold the defendants to any burden—whether heavy or not—of demonstrating that there is an alternate available and adequate forum for this litigation.

C.

The district court also ostensibly based its forum non conveniens dismissal on the basis that Canada offered a second possible forum. Its only discussion of the matter, however, was to say:

> In this case, there are two possible forums that satisfy this requirement. Mr. Deb has already filed a claim in the Canadian courts arising out of the same course of conduct that gave rise to [—24—] the instant case, and he does not argue that the Canadian court forum is somehow improper.

Deb, 2014 WL 2573465, at *3 (R. 55, p.5, Page ID 744).

The parties never briefed the issue of the Canadian court as an alternative forum, however. The discussion about Canada in the briefing below centered on whether the United States courts ought to abstain from hearing this matter under the *Colorado River* doctrine. *See Colo. River Water Conservation Dist. v. United States*, 424 U.S. 800, 817 (1976).[4] That doctrine allows courts to conserve judicial resources by abstaining from accepting jurisdiction when there is a parallel proceeding elsewhere. *Id.* It has sometimes been applied when identical concurrent litigation is, as in this case, pending abroad. *See U.S.O. Corp.*, 547 F.3d at 750. Abstention under the *Colorado River* doctrine may only be used in "exceptional" circumstances if it would promote "wise judicial administration." *Freed v. J.P. Morgan Chase Bank, N.A.*, 756 F.3d 1013, 1018 (7th Cir. 2014).

The determinations under the *Colorado River* doctrine for abstention are not the same as those made when deciding whether a case should be dismissed for forum non conveniens. Our decision in *Adkins v. VIM Recycling, Inc.*, 644 F.3d 483, 498-99 (7th Cir. 2011) provides a concise description of [—25—] the process for determining whether *Colorado River* abstention is appropriate:

> First, the court must determine whether the concurrent state and federal actions are actually parallel. If so, the court must consider second whether exceptional circumstances justify

---

[4] In their Memorandum in Support of Defendants' Motion to Dismiss Plaintiff's Amended Complaint, the defendants merely state that Canada would also be an appropriate alternate forum for the reasons indicated in their argument about *Colorado River* abstention. But such undeveloped arguments are waived. *Rahn v. Bd. of Trs. of N. Ill. Univ.*, 803 F.3d 285, 295 (7th Cir. 2015), *cert. denied*, 136 S. Ct. 1685 (2016).

abstention. ... Two suits are parallel for *Colorado River* purposes when substantially the same parties are contemporaneously litigating substantially the same issues. Precisely formal symmetry is unnecessary. A court should examine whether the suits involve the same parties, arise out of the same facts, and raise similar factual and legal issues. In essence, the question is whether there is a substantial likelihood that the [foreign] litigation will dispose of all claims presented in the federal case. Any doubt regarding the parallel nature of the [state] suit should be resolved in favor of exercising jurisdiction.

Id.

The district court did not engage in a *Colorado River* abstention analysis. Nor did it ever engage in a forum non conveniens analysis about Canada similar to the one we described above for India. Other than its first assertion that Canada was a possible forum, all of its discussion pertained to India as a forum. It is true that Deb sued Allied Canada in a Canadian court, but again, we have no idea whether Allied Canada has any connection to the defendants in this case, let alone whether they are "substantially the same party" (*see Adkins*, 644 F.3d at 498) and the defendants did not offer any evidence that they would be subject to jurisdiction in Canada. [—26—]

In sum, although it is within a district court's sound discretion to dismiss a suit for forum non conveniens (*Piper Aircraft*, 454 U.S. at 257), it can only do so after placing the burden on the defendant to demonstrate availability and adequacy of an alternative forum. The district court erred by failing to properly place the burden. It may be that after conducting a proper look into the adequacy of the forum along with a balancing of the interests, the court may determine that a dismissal for forum non conveniens is indeed appropriate. Based on the bare claims before the district court, however, such a determination was in error. The defendants may refile their motion in an attempt to meet

their burden. For that reason we VACATE the decision of the district court and REMAND for further proceedings consistent with this opinion.

United States Court of Appeals
for the Seventh Circuit

No. 16-1544

KELHAM
VS.
CSX TRANSP., INC.

Appeal from the United States District Court for the Northern District of Indiana, Hammond Division

Decided: October 27, 2016

Citation: 840 F.3d 469, 4 Adm. R. 348 (7th Cir. 2016).

Before **BAUER**, **POSNER**, and **MANION**, Circuit Judges.

[—1—] POSNER, Circuit Judge:

The plaintiff, Chance Kelham, a railroad engineer, sued the railroad that employed him, accusing it of having negligently caused him to be injured, for which he seeks compensation under the Federal Employers' Liability Act, 45 U.S.C. §§ 51 *et seq.* The case was tried to a jury, which exonerated the railroad, precipitating this appeal. [—2—]

On the day of the accident that Kelham claims caused his injury, he was driving a mile-long freight train comprised of two locomotives and 69 empty cars. Ordered to halt the train briefly on a parallel track to enable a train with a higher priority to pass it, Kelham duly halted his train. Unfortunately another train, which was also supposed to wait on the parallel track, failed to stop at a red stop signal and collided with Kelham's train from behind. Because of the length of his train and the weight of its locomotive (212 tons), the collision caused the locomotive to lurch forward slightly. A mechanical engineer testifying for the railroad compared what a forward-facing video camera attached to the front of Kelham's locomotive showed to what was shown by a video camera attached to another locomotive of the same make and model. That locomotive was placed in the same location on the tracks as the locomotive of Kelham's train when it had begun its lurch, and was then moved slowly forward so that the video from its camera could be compared with the video from the camera attached to the front of Kelham's locomotive. The comparison indicated that the lurch forward could not have exceeded seven or eight inches, or lasted more than a third of a second—numbers that the engineer testified indicated that the train had accelerated as a result of the collision at an average of 13.5 feet per second squared.

Kelham complains that the engineer compared the two videos by eye rather than by mathematical calculations, didn't measure the height of the camera on the comparison locomotive, and didn't account for the "bounce and shudder" movement of the train. But the trial judge correctly ruled that these objections could be adequately explored on cross-examination. [—3—]

Kelham's claim that the locomotive "bounced" vertically is implausible given the locomotive's weight and the slightness of the lurch, and while he points to testimony from Knipp, the other conductor in the cab at the time of the accident, that the locomotive "bounced ... back and forth," that isn't the same as bouncing up and down. Kelham also claims that the "bounce and shudder" are visible in the video of the accident, but CSX's expert, who watched the video, disagreed, and the jurors were shown the video at trial and could decide for themselves. The jury rejected Kelham's challenges to the railroad's testimony, awarding judgment to the railroad.

The railroad concedes that the accident was caused by the negligence of its employees—the crew of the second train who ran the red light; the issue is whether the lurch resulting from the impact of the second train when it collided with Kelham's train caused the injuries of which he complains. He testified that when the lurch occurred he'd just risen from his seat in the locomotive cab and begun to walk down the three stairs to the locomotive's bathroom. The stairwell faced forward, so someone walking down the stairs would be facing the front of the train. Kelham claims that as he began to walk down, the lurch from the impact caused him to fall forward—almost indeed to somersault—down the stairs, causing a serious injury to his back which aggravated a condition that he had called "spondylitic spondylolisthesis"—the forward slippage of a vertebra—which had been asymptomatic before the accident but afterward required surgery.

A biomechanical engineer testified for the railroad that the forward lurch of the locomotive should have pushed [—4—] Kelham backward rather than forward, since he was facing the front of the train at the time of the accident. If you're sitting in the back seat of a taxi stopped for a traffic light, then when the light changes and the cab surges ahead you'll feel yourself pushed against the back of your seat, while if the taxi was moving and then slowed or stopped you would feel yourself pushed forward, toward the divider between the front and rear seats. The engineer further testified that if the lurch had pushed Kelham backward without causing him to hit the back wall of the locomotive cab, it would have been too weak to injure him. In addition the train conductor sitting next to Kelham in the locomotive cab did not see him fall when the locomotive lurched. And for days after the accident he told no one that he'd fallen, even though he spent a good deal of that time with coworkers, supervisors, and medical personnel. Nor had he any bruises or any other visible injuries from the fall, even though he testified that at the end of the somersault his back and neck were against a bulkhead door and his feet were over his head. He argued that the biomechanical engineer had ignored the "bounce and shudder" and assumed he'd been positioned upright at the time of the accident, while he claims that he was learning forward, that the studies cited by the engineer of how people who are standing on a platform react when the platform moves don't apply to someone who is walking down stairs, as Kelham claims he was, and that the engineer did not cite studies on the aggravation of spondylitic spondylolisthesis specifically—but again the trial judge correctly ruled that Kelham's objections could be explored on cross-examination, and the jury didn't have to believe him.

There is no question that Kelham has serious back pain, but the railroad presented evidence that the pain preexisted [—5—] the forward lurch of his train. Indeed he'd begun complaining of back pain in 2007, four and a half years before the collision, and the pain had worsened over time. An MRI on October 5, 2009 revealed a herniated disc and a bulging disc, along with the spondylitic spondylolisthesis. On the recommendation of an orthopedic surgeon he was given a "nerve root block" (a strong anesthetic) a week later and in the following months received epidural steroid injections from a pain management specialist. A few weeks after the nerve root block he complained of pain and obtained prescriptions for morphine and Vicodin—opioid pain medications—and had continued to receive and fill prescriptions for the drugs up until the time of the accident, including five times in the five months immediately preceding it.

His back pain persisted after the accident, eventually leading him to have surgery; we say "persisted" because by his own admission it was similar to the pain that he had experienced and taken opioids to alleviate before the accident. Indeed he told medical staff—repeatedly—that he was seeking treatment for symptoms that he'd been experiencing for years. And indeed the surgery he had was for the same back pain for which he'd taken opioids before the accident. His post-accident surgeon conceded in a deposition that "surgery was an option for [Kelham]" before the accident, and that he would defer to CSX's expert on whether the lurch could have caused Kelham's post-accident symptoms. And Kelham's pre-accident doctor conceded in a deposition that the spondylitic spondylolisthesis, which Kelham claims became symptomatic only after the accident, could have been responsible for some of his pre-accident symptoms. Indeed it would be a miracle had those symptoms vanished right before the lurch (they couldn't have vanished a significant time [—6—] before it as otherwise he would have stopped taking the opioids, which are dangerous medicines), only to recur—the identical symptoms—as a consequence of the lurch. And the trial judge correctly rejected Kelham's objections to admitting the evidence about his history of back problems and the unfavorable statements from the depositions of his pre- and post-accident doctors.

After the surgery he was advised to undergo physical therapy, which his medical records indicate that he did but only intermittently, and though he has only modest functional limitations, which would not prevent him from working in some capacity for a railroad, he has declined to seek reemployment in the railroad industry. It was not unreasonable for a jury to find that Kelham had fabricated the claim that he was injured by the lurch, as unless the railroad bought his story it would not be required by the Federal Employers' Liability Act to compensate Kelham for the cost of the surgery that he needed to repair the consequences of pre-accident ailments for which the railroad was not responsible. The jury was entitled to conclude that the negligence of the railroad that resulted in the collision and ensuing lurch had no causal relation to his injuries— that, to repeat, the injuries were the product of ailments that preceded the lurch.

AFFIRMED

United States Court of Appeals
for the Seventh Circuit

No. 15-2477

UNITED STATES
vs.
EGAN MARINE CORP.

Appeals from the United States District Court for the
Northern District of Illinois, Eastern Division

Decided: December 12, 2016

Citation: 843 F.3d 674, 4 Adm. R. 351 (7th Cir. 2016).

Before **EASTERBROOK** and **ROVNER**, Circuit Judges,
and **SHADID**, District Judge.*

* Of the Central District of Illinois, sitting by
designation.

[—1—] **EASTERBROOK**, Circuit Judge:

Barge EMC-423 exploded on January 19, 2005, while under way between Joliet and Chicago with a cargo of clarified slurry oil. The blast threw deckhand Alex Oliva into the water; he did not survive. Contend- [—2—] ing that Dennis Egan, master of the tug Lisa E that had been pushing the barge, had told Oliva to warm a pump using a propane torch, the United States obtained an indictment charging Egan and the tug's owner (Egan Marine Corp.) with violating 18 U.S.C. §1115, which penalizes maritime negligence that results in death, plus other statutes that penalize the negligent discharge of oil into navigable waters.

After a bench trial, Judge Zagel found that the prosecution had established, beyond a reasonable doubt, that Egan gave the order to Oliva, that the torch caused the explosion, that Oliva died as a result, and that the barge released oil as a further result. That such an order, if given, was negligence (or worse) no one doubted; open flames on oil carriers are forbidden by Coast Guard regulations and normal prudence. The court sentenced Egan to six months' imprisonment, a year's supervised release, and restitution of almost $6.75 million. Egan Marine was placed on probation for three years and ordered to pay the same restitution, for which it and Egan are jointly and severally liable.

The criminal prosecution was the second trial of these allegations. Two years before the grand jury returned its indictment, the United States had filed a civil suit against Egan Marine seeking damages on the same theory: that Egan directed Oliva to warm the pump using a torch, whose flame caused an explosion, a death, and an oil spill. That case, too, went to a bench trial. And Judge Leinenweber, who heard the evidence, determined that the United States had not proved its claim. 2011 U.S. Dist. LEXIS 138087 (N.D. Ill. Oct. 13, 2011) at *11 ("the Government did not prove, by a preponderance of the evidence, that Alex Oliva was using a propane torch on the cargo pump of the EMC 423 at the time [—3—] of the incident"). The United States did not appeal from that adverse decision but instead pressed forward with this criminal prosecution.

Egan and Egan Marine sought the benefit of issue preclusion (collateral estoppel), arguing that the United States should not be allowed to contend that they are guilty beyond a reasonable doubt after Judge Leinenweber found that the proof did not show culpability even by a preponderance of the evidence. But Judge Zagel rejected this contention.

The Supreme Court has said that the outcome of a civil case has preclusive force in a criminal prosecution. See *Yates v. United States*, 354 U.S. 298, 335–36 (1957). (*Burks v. United States*, 437 U.S. 1 (1978), overruled a different portion of *Yates* relating to double jeopardy; *Burks* did not question the portion of *Yates* dealing with preclusion.) If the United States cannot prove a factual claim on the preponderance standard, it cannot logically show the same thing beyond a reasonable doubt. The prosecutor maintains that this statement in *Yates* was dictum, but we do not think that characterization appropriate. It was integral to the Court's rationale—for although the Justices proceeded to conclude that the civil suit did not block the Yates prosecution under ordinary principles of preclusion, it would not have undertaken that exercise had the Court believed issue preclusion categorically inapplicable to the civil–criminal sequence.

United States v. Weems, 49 F.3d 528 (9th Cir. 1995), and *United States v. Rogers*, 960 F.2d 1501 (10th Cir. 1992), both took *Yates* at face value and held that a criminal prosecution can be blocked by the preclusive effect of a decision in a civil case. No court of appeals has held otherwise. But the United States maintains, and Judge Zagel concluded, that our deci- [—4—] sion in *United States v. Alexander*, 743 F.2d 472 (7th Cir. 1984), means that preclusion is unavailable notwithstanding *Yates*.

Alexander held that the outcome of an *administrative* proceeding cannot be invoked to block the resolution of a criminal indictment. The opinion observed that many administrative systems are designed to be informal and expeditious, and that when the agency loses an administrative adjudication it may not be entitled to judicial review. 743 F.2d at 477. Making the administrative process reliable enough to justify preclusive effect in a criminal prosecution might require a substantial investment of prosecutorial resources—if that were even possible under the statute in question. The United States' alternative might be to forego the administrative proceeding, which could have bad consequences of its own.

When using these considerations of public policy to decide whether to give preclusive effect to administrative adjudications, *Alexander* drew on *Standefer v. United States*, 447 U.S. 10 (1980), which had concluded that it would be unwise to apply nonmutual preclusion from one criminal prosecution to another. Standefer and Niederberger had been charged with joint criminal activity. Niederberger was tried first and acquitted; Standefer maintained that he was entitled to the benefit of that adjudication, because it takes two to tango. The Court held not, observing (447 U.S. at 21–23) that nonmutual preclusion (that is, using the result in A's case to determine the result in B's) is designed largely to reduce litigation costs in civil suits, while the criminal process has different and more important goals. The Justices added that acquittals in criminal prosecutions are unreasoned and cannot be reviewed (given the Double Jeopardy Clause); they may reflect compromise or misunderstanding rather [—5—] than a determination of contested facts. That's why inconsistent verdicts within a single criminal prosecution do not work in a defendant's favor. See, e.g., *Bravo-Fernandez v. United States*, No. 15–537 (U.S. Nov. 29, 2016).

Standefer did not cast doubt on *Yates*. The considerations that led the Court to abjure nonmutual preclusion in the criminal–criminal sequence do not pertain to mutual preclusion in the civil–criminal sequence. Many a civil decision is fully explained (as Judge Leinenweber's was), and all are reviewable on appeal. The Supreme Court understands mutual preclusion not just as a judicial work-saving device but as a matter of right for the litigants involved. See, e.g., *Federated Department Stores, Inc. v. Moitie*, 452 U.S. 394 (1981).

This is so even when one of the litigants is the United States. See, e.g., *Montana v. United States*, 440 U.S. 147 (1979); *United States v. Stauffer Chemical Co.*, 464 U.S. 165 (1984). The prosecutor's brief in our case tells us that allowing Judge Leinenweber's decision to foreclose the criminal charges would cause the United States either to pour extra resources into civil suits, disrupting its litigation strategy, or to forego or postpone such suits pending the outcome of criminal cases. Similar arguments were made by the Solicitor General in *Montana* and *Stauffer Chemical*, where the United States maintained that the outcome of a poorly litigated civil case (perhaps pursued by a single Assistant United States Attorney in some remote outpost) should not be allowed to block a new suit that has the Department of Justice's full attention and may be designed to serve a vital public goal. But the Justices had none of this. They concluded that ordinary rules of preclusion apply to the United States and that the Department of Justice must navigate around established legal rules, [—6—] rather than the rules giving way to bureaucratic convenience. (The Court made an exception for offensive nonmutual issue preclusion in *United States v. Mendoza*, 464 U.S. 154 (1984), again reflecting *Standefer*'s conclusion that nonmutual preclusion is a matter of wise policy rather than of litigants' entitlements.)

There is of course a potential for nonmutuality in the civil–criminal sequence—but it is the United States that prefers a situation in which it can win but not lose. The United States filed the civil suit seeking damages and hoped to enjoy the fruits of victory. But it tells us that a loss meant little, because after losing it could pursue the criminal prosecution and ask a different judge or jury to reach a different outcome. The principal stakes in both the civil and criminal cases are money. Six months in prison are not to be sneezed at, but the main contest has been about recompense for Oliva's death and the oil released from the barge. What would have been labeled "damages" in the civil case is called "restitution" in the criminal case, but the money covers the same losses either way. And had the criminal case gone to trial first and defendants been acquitted, the United States doubtless would be arguing that it could still pursue civil remedies because of the different burdens of persuasion. See, e.g., *One Lot Emerald Cut Stones v. United States*, 409 U.S. 232, 234–35 (1972); *Helvering v. Mitchell*, 303 U.S. 391, 397–98 (1938).

Every litigant would like multiple chances to win; that's what the United States is claiming, while it contends that for Egan and Egan Marine any one loss would be dispositive (at least for financial issues). And, by bringing the civil case first, the United States received the benefit of civil discovery, which is more extensive than that allowed in criminal prose- [—7—] cutions by Fed. R. Crim. P. 16—discovery that it could put to use in the criminal case as well as the civil one. We understand why the United States seeks these advantages but do not think it entitled to them, without the detriment of being bound by the civil judgment if it loses. If it fails to show some fact in the civil suit by a preponderance of the evidence, it is precluded from trying to show the same thing beyond a reasonable doubt.

Judge Zagel stated that, even if issue preclusion applies in the civil–criminal sequence (as we have concluded it does), he would exercise discretion not to use that doctrine in this prosecution. He did not say where that discretion comes from or address the significance of decisions such as *Federated Department Stores* that reject judicial efforts to treat rules of preclusion as dispensable whenever judges prefer another outcome. See 452 U.S. at 399–402.

Normal rules of preclusion have some flex. For example, "[a] new determination of the issue [may be] warranted by differences in the quality or extensiveness of the procedures followed in the two courts". *Restatement (Second) of Judgments* §28(3). In other words, if the first forum's procedures do not conduce to sufficiently reliable decisions, the second forum may decide that it is best to determine the issue anew. This is what *Alexander* said about the difference between administrative adjudication and criminal litigation. But Judge Zagel did not conclude that Judge Leinenweber had conducted the civil trial unreliably or that any of the other exceptions in *Restatement* §28 had been established; he simply announced that he would disregard the civil judgment because that course seemed best to him. That's not an appropriate way to treat the outcome of a properly conducted federal civil trial. [—8—]

Egan Marine was the only defendant in the civil suit. The United States maintains that Egan therefore cannot receive the benefit of the judgment, which it sees as the sort of nonmutual issue preclusion forbidden by *Standefer*. (The United States also contends that Egan forfeited his entitlement to the benefit of issue preclusion, but he preserved his position by telling the district court that he was adopting Egan Marine's arguments on issue preclusion.)

Standefer used the word "nonmutual" to refer to the use of preclusion across different persons, so that A's victory over C in one case would imply B's victory over C in another. But the law of preclusion has long recognized that if A and B are in a contractual relation ("in privity" as judges often say) then they are entitled to the same treatment under normal principles of mutual preclusion. Egan and Egan Marine were in such a relation. Indeed, in the civil suit the United States contended that Egan Marine was vicariously liable for Egan's acts precisely because of their employment relation. The civil suit was about Egan's conduct, which was attributed to his employer, and Judge Leinenweber's core finding (which we quoted earlier) was that the United States had not shown that Oliva was using a propane torch at all, let alone that in using a torch he was following Egan's directive. When a court rejects a claim of vicarious liability based on a worker's conduct, the worker is as much entitled to the benefit of that judgment as is the employer. *Muhammad v. Oliver*, 547 F.3d 874 (7th Cir. 2008); *Restatement* §51. Cf. *Taylor v. Sturgell*, 553 U.S. 880, 893–95 (2008) (canvassing situations in which a nonparty gets the benefit of a judgment). Having argued in the civil suit that Egan Marine was liable for Egan's conduct, the United States cannot now treat Egan and the corporation as strangers to each other. **[—9—]**

Another way to see this is to recall that *Standefer* dealt with considerations unique to nonmutual preclusion in criminal litigation: acquittals are unexplained and unreviewable on appeal. Judge Leinenweber's decision, by contrast, was accompanied by an opinion and reviewable in this court—though the United States chose not to appeal. It is much easier to see why a reviewable civil finding that X has not been shown by a preponderance of the evidence should foreclose a contention that X is true beyond a reasonable doubt than it is to carry one criminal acquittal over to a different case.

Because both Egan and Egan Marine are entitled to the benefit of the civil judgment, we need not discuss any of the remaining issues. The convictions are reversed, and the case is remanded for the entry of judgments of acquittal.

United States Court of Appeals for the Eighth Circuit

United States Court of Appeals
for the Eighth Circuit

No. 15-3115

BLAKE MARINE GROUP
VS.
CARVAL INVESTORS LLC

Appeal from the United States District Court for the
District of Minnesota-Minneapolis

Decided: July 13, 2016

Citation: 829 F.3d 592, 4 Adm. R. 356 (8th Cir. 2016).

Before **MURPHY,** and **SHEPHERD,** Circuit Judges, and
PERRY,[1] District Judge.

[—1—] **MURPHY,** Circuit Judge:

Blake Marine Group, Inc. (Blake) brought this action against CarVal Investors LLC (CarVal) and CVI GVF (Lux) Master S.A.R.L. (CVI Lux), alleging tortious interference with Blake's contract to lease a barge and crane to a third party. The [—2—] district court[2] dismissed Blake's complaint as time barred after applying Alabama's two year statute of limitations. Blake appeals, and we affirm.

I.

Blake is an Alabama corporation which was based in Alabama at all times relevant to this case.[3] CarVal is a Delaware LLC based in Minnesota, and CVI Lux is a related entity organized under Luxembourg law. CVI Lux is also a shareholder of Oceanografia, S.A. de CV (Oceanografia), a Mexican company which provides offshore support services to oil companies.

On January 23, 2009 Blake entered into a charter agreement to lease a barge to Oceanografia for $40,000 per day. The barge was equipped with a crane to be installed on one of Oceanografia's offshore vessels for use in performing its contract with an oil company. On January 29 CarVal emailed Oceanografia from its Minnesota offices and directed it to terminate the charter agreement, asserting that CVI Lux had not consented to that charter as required by its shareholder agreement. Oceanografia terminated the charter later that day.

In January 2013 Blake sued CarVal in New York state court for tortious interference with the charter agreement after learning that CarVal had leased its own vessel to Oceanografia. Blake later voluntarily dismissed that suit and brought this action in the federal district court in Minnesota in January 2015, asserting a similar tortious interference claim against both CarVal and CVI Lux. CarVal and CVI Lux then filed a motion to dismiss which the district court granted after concluding that Alabama's two year statute of limitations barred Blake's claim. The court explained [—3—] that it had applied the Alabama statute rather than Minnesota's six year statute of limitations because Alabama's interest in protecting its resident Blake outweighed Minnesota's interest in compensating nonresident plaintiffs. Blake appeals.

II.

A.

We review de novo the district court's dismissal of Blake's complaint, including its choice of law analysis. *Whitney v. The Guys, Inc.,* 700 F.3d 1118, 1123 (8th Cir. 2012). To determine the applicable limitations period we look to the choice of law rules of the forum state, which in this case is Minnesota. *Id.* Under its "borrowing statute," Minnesota applies the limitations period of the state whose substantive law governs a claim. *See* Minn. Stat. § 541.31.

To determine the state law governing Blake's claim, we apply Minnesota's three step choice of law analysis. *Whitney,* 700 F.3d at 1123–24. The first two steps inquire whether differing state laws present an "outcome-determinative" conflict and whether each law

---

[1] The Honorable Catherine D. Perry, United States District Judge for the Eastern District of Missouri, sitting by designation.

[2] The Honorable Joan N. Ericksen, United States District Judge for the District of Minnesota.

[3] In 2012 Blake moved its principal place of business to Louisiana.

"constitutionally may be applied to the case at hand." *Id.* at 1123. The third step then requires a multifactored test to consider the "(1) predictability of result; (2) maintenance of interstate and international order; (3) simplification of the judicial task; (4) advancement of the forum's governmental interest; and (5) application of the better rule of law." *Id.* at 1124.

Here, the parties agree that the choice between Alabama's two year limitations period and Minnesota's six year limitations period is outcome determinative and that either state's law may constitutionally be applied. They also agree that the first, third, [—4—] and fifth factors under step three are irrelevant to this case.⁴ Their arguments thus focus on the remaining two factors— maintenance of interstate order and advancement of the forum's governmental interest.

The Minnesota Supreme Court has explained that the primary concern regarding the maintenance of interstate order is "whether the application of Minnesota law would manifest disrespect for [another state's] sovereignty or impede the interstate movement of people and goods." *Jepson v. Gen. Cas. Co. of Wisconsin*, 513 N.W.2d 467, 471 (Minn. 1994). This factor is relevant in tort suits where there is evidence of forum shopping and Minnesota has only a "remot[e] connection" to the claim. *Nesladek v. Ford Motor Co.*, 46 F.3d 734, 739 (8th Cir. 1995). In this case appellees argue that Blake has engaged in forum shopping by dismissing its New York action and refiling in Minnesota, seeking a longer limitations period. Since Minnesota is the state where the alleged

tortious interference occurred and it also is where CarVal is based, we conclude that Minnesota "has sufficient contacts with and interest in the facts and issues being litigated" to mitigate concerns about the disruption of interstate order. *Id.* The second factor is therefore neutral. *See, e.g., Hague v. Allstate Ins. Co.*, 289 N.W.2d 43, 48–49 (Minn. 1978).

The fourth factor, advancement of the forum's governmental interest, "requires analysis not only of Minnesota's governmental interests, but also of [Alabama's] public policy." *Nesladek*, 46 F.3d at 739. Blake first argues that Minnesota has an interest in compensating tort victims which favors the application of Minnesota law. [—5—] *See Jepson*, 513 N.W.2d at 472. Our court has previously explained, however, that a state's "interest in protecting nonresidents from tortious acts committed within the state . . . is only slight and does not support application of its law to the litigation." *Hughes v. Wal-Mart Stores, Inc.*, 250 F.3d 618, 621 (8th Cir. 2001). In contrast, "[c]ompensation of an injured plaintiff is primarily a concern of the state in which [the] plaintiff is domiciled."⁵ *Kenna v. So-Fro Fabrics, Inc.*, 18 F.3d 623, 627 (8th Cir. 1994) (quoting *Bryant v. Silverman*, 703 P.2d 1190, 1194 (Ariz. 1985)). Here, Alabama's interest in compensating Blake, a resident of that state, outweighs Minnesota's interest and favors the application of Alabama law. *See Nesladek*, 46 F.3d at 740 ("balance of interests" favored application of nonforum state's law where plaintiff was resident of that state at time of injury).

Blake contends that the application of Minnesota's six year limitations period would better serve Alabama's interest in compensating tort victims since it would allow more time for its claim to proceed. Blake has however not provided any authority to show that Minnesota would apply its own law in order to promote another state's policy interests (particularly where, as here, that state's own laws do not further such

---

⁴ While the predictability of result factor is irrelevant "when an action arises out of an accident," *Hughes v. Wal-Mart Stores, Inc.*, 250 F.3d 618, 620 (8th Cir. 2001), the alleged tortious conduct in this case was intentional. Thus, the predictability factor is not necessarily immaterial. *See, e.g., Nw. Airlines, Inc. v. Astraea Aviation Servs., Inc.*, 111 F.3d 1386, 1394 (8th Cir. 1997) (discussing predictability of result in defamation action). We conclude on balance that this factor does not favor application of either Minnesota or Alabama law in this case.

⁵ Notably, the cases on which Blake relies to demonstrate Minnesota's interest in compensating tort victims all had Minnesota plaintiffs. *See Jepson*, 513 N.W.2d at 470; *Danielson v. Nat'l Supply Co.*, 670 N.W.2d 1, 3 (Minn. Ct. App. 2003).

interests). We conclude that Blake's argument misconstrues Minnesota's choice of law rules. When analyzing the fourth choice of law factor, we determine which state's law to apply based on "the relative policy interests of the two states." *Nesladek*, 46 F.3d at 739. We do not, as Blake suggests, apply whatever law we believe best advances the interests of the state with the most significant interests at stake.

According to Blake, Minnesota also has an interest in holding its own residents (one of which is CarVal) accountable for any torts they commit within the state. Our court rejected a similar argument in *Hughes*, however, when we concluded that a forum state's "interest in having its product liability laws enforced against its own [—6—] corporate residents" did not support application of its law in that case, in which the plaintiff was a nonresident. *Hughes*, 250 F.3d at 621. While Blake emphasizes that the alleged interference here originated from CarVal's Minnesota offices, the resulting injury occurred outside of Minnesota, and "we fail to see how any important [Minnesota] governmental interest is significantly furthered by ensuring that nonresidents are compensated for injuries that occur in *another state*." *Id*. (emphasis in original). We conclude that the fourth choice of law factor favors the application of Alabama law. Since this is the only factor which favors either state's law, the district court did not err by applying Alabama law and dismissing Blake's claim as time barred.

Blake also asserts that even if the choice of law factors favor Alabama law, the district court should have applied the "fairness exception" to Minnesota's borrowing statute. That exception requires the application of Minnesota's statute of limitations if the conflicting statute is "substantially different" from Minnesota's and "has not afforded a fair opportunity to sue." Minn. Stat. § 541.33. Since Blake did not raise this argument below, however, it is waived. *See, e.g., Corn Plus Co-op. v. Cont'l Cas. Co.*, 516 F.3d 674, 680 (8th Cir. 2008).

B.

Blake next contends that the district court should have applied the doctrine of laches under its admiralty jurisdiction when assessing timeliness, but we conclude that such jurisdiction is lacking in this case. A party invoking a district court's admiralty jurisdiction must satisfy two requirements. First, the party must show that "the tort occurred on navigable water or [that] injury suffered on land was caused by a vessel on navigable water." *Jerome B. Grubart, Inc. v. Great Lakes Dredge & Dock Co.*, 513 U.S. 527, 534 (1995). They must also show that the tort had a "potentially disruptive impact on maritime commerce" and that the conduct resulting in the tort had a "substantial relationship to traditional maritime activity." *Id*. [—7—]

In this case, Blake has not shown that the alleged tort occurred on navigable waters. For purposes of admiralty jurisdiction, a tort arises where the injury occurs. *See J. Lauritzen A/S v. Dashwood Shipping, Ltd.*, 65 F.3d 139, 142 (9th Cir. 1995). Blake argues that its damages occurred at sea since appellees prevented the installation of its crane on Oceanografia's vessel, thus interfering with Oceanografia's maritime operations. Neither of these interests represents the financial injury Blake has alleged in this case, however. Blake's alleged damages consist of lost future income from the charter, but any such damages were not sustained at sea. *See, e.g., Great Plains Trust Co. v. Union Pac. R. Co.*, 492 F.3d 986, 993 (8th Cir. 2007) ("purely economic" damages from breach of contract at corporate headquarters). Moreover, Blake also seeks to recover costs it incurred in obtaining the barge, and "this portion of the claimed damages arose solely on land at the time of [Oceanografia's] breach." *J. Lauritzen*, 65 F.3d at 143. We therefore conclude that Blake has not satisfied the first requirement for invoking federal admiralty jurisdiction and that laches does not apply.

C.

Blake finally contends that even if Alabama's limitations period applies, the statute should have been tolled based on appellees' fraudulent concealment of the facts underlying its claim. We disagree.

Federal plaintiffs must plead "allegations of fraud, including fraudulent concealment for tolling purposes . . . with particularity." *Great Plains*, 492 F.3d at 995. In this case, Blake has not alleged "facts which show that the [appellees] fraudulently prevented discovery of the wrongful act on which the action is based." *Sellers v. A.H. Robins Co.*, 715 F.2d 1559, 1561 (11th Cir. 1983) (applying Alabama law). To the contrary, Blake alleged that by 2010 it had learned of facts underlying its tortious interference claim—specifically, that appellees had "intentionally and maliciously cause[d] Oceanografia to breach the [charter agreement] and that such facts supported" its claim. Blake thus was aware of the alleged interference for more [—8—] than two years before this suit was filed, and "a limitation period is tolled only until the plaintiff discovers . . . his cause of action." *Id.*; *see also Serra Chevrolet, Inc. v. Edwards Chevrolet, Inc.*, 850 So.2d 259, 265 (Ala. 2002) (elements of tortious interference claim under Alabama law). Accordingly, there was no basis to toll the two year limitations period.

III.

For these reasons we affirm the judgment of the district court dismissing the complaint of Blake Marine Group, Inc.

United States Court of Appeals
for the Eighth Circuit

No. 15-2106

BURCKHARD
vs.
BNSF RY. CO.

Appeal from the United States District Court for the District of North Dakota-Bismarck

Decided: September 14, 2016

Citation: 837 F.3d 848, 4 Adm. R. 360 (8th Cir. 2016).

Before **SMITH**, and **COLLOTON**, Circuit Judges, and **GRITZNER**,[1] District Judge.

[—1—] PER CURIAM: [—2—]

Plaintiffs, personal representatives of the decedents, sued BNSF Railway Company (BNSF) for the deaths of two BNSF employees, Todd Burckhard and Blaine Mack. After rejecting BNSF's motions for judgment as a matter of law (JMOL), the district court[2] submitted the case to a jury. The jury found in favor of plaintiffs. After the verdict, BNSF moved the district court to alter or amend the judgment based on an agreement that plaintiffs had entered with BNSF prior to trial. The district court denied BNSF's motion. On appeal, BNSF argues that the district court (1) improperly denied its JMOL motions, (2) made several erroneous evidentiary rulings, and (3) improperly denied its motion to alter or amend the judgment. We affirm.

I. *Background*

Under federal law, railway employees can work a maximum of 12 consecutive hours. When their hours of service expire, railway employees need to be relieved midroute. BNSF contracted with Coach America to provide transportation for some of its crews.

After Burckhard and Mack were relieved by an incoming crew, Coach America dispatched a driver, Timothy Rennick, to transport them from Oswego, Montana, to Glasgow, Montana. Rennick collected Burckhard and Mack and began the approximately 40-mile trip. While en route, a pickup truck driven by a drunk driver, Ron Keiser, struck their vehicle. The collision killed Burckhard and Mack.

Plaintiffs presented three theories of BNSF's liability at trial: (1) BNSF, through its agent Rennick, negligently operated the vehicle used to transport Burckhard and Mack; (2) BNSF and its agent, Coach America, negligently failed to properly train Rennick; and (3) BNSF, through its agent Rennick, negligently failed to follow appropriate defensive driving rules. The evidence at trial concerning the [—3—] crash included Rennick's statement taken the day after the crash by a BNSF claims representative,[3] the testimony of the Montana State Trooper that investigated the accident, and data from Coach America's vehicle's video camera and "black box." Additional evidence described the training that Coach America provided its drivers and a BNSF curfew policy.

Rennick told the claims representative that he saw Keiser's truck veer into his lane about "a minute, maybe two minutes at the most" before the collision. Rennick responded by pulling into Keiser's lane. Keiser steered his truck back into his lane of travel and collided with Rennick's vehicle before Rennick could react. The investigating Montana State Trooper, Sergeant Jeffrey Kent, testified that he found no signs that Keiser's truck left the paved road or 15-foot shoulder. The video camera captured the eight seconds before the collision in quarter-second snapshots. The camera's footage shows that Rennick attempted to avoid Keiser's vehicle by entering Keiser's lane. According to the "black box," Rennick did not apply braking until approximately 2.75 seconds before the collision. The "black box" also showed that the speed of Rennick's vehicle was 51 miles per hour 2.5 seconds before the collision.

---

[1] The Honorable James E. Gritzner, United States District Judge for the Southern District of Iowa, sitting by designation.

[2] The Honorable Daniel L. Hovland, United States District Judge for the District of North Dakota.

[3] Rennick passed away before he could be deposed.

Over BNSF's objection, the district court allowed plaintiffs to submit evidence of a BNSF curfew policy that applied to "deadheading."[4] The curfew policy forbids transportation of railway employees on public roads between 10:00 p.m. and 4:00 a.m. when "deadheading." According to BNSF, one of the reasons for the curfew was "a commonsense, good-judgment decision of daylight versus night." BNSF explained [—4—] that transportation during the night presents additional risks, such as drunk and sleepy drivers.

BNSF sought to introduce evidence that Burckhard and Mack were given a choice between transportation by vehicle or train once they were relieved from service. The district court excluded the evidence to avoid confusing the jury and because the evidence could potentially inject irrelevant defenses into the trial.

BNSF also sought to have Sergeant Kent testify that he believed that Rennick did not act negligently and chose the safest course of action given the circumstances. Plaintiffs objected to the testimony as cumulative. The district court agreed and also held that it was inappropriate to allow Sergeant Kent to testify as a lay witness on the ultimate factual issue. The district court allowed Sergeant Kent to testify about factual information obtained as part of his investigation but prohibited Sergeant Kent from testifying that Rennick acted reasonably.

At the close of plaintiffs' case, BNSF moved for JMOL pursuant to Federal Rule of Civil Procedure 50(a). BNSF argued that plaintiffs' first theory of liability failed because they did not offer sufficient evidence that the risk was reasonably foreseeable. Likewise, BNSF argued that plaintiffs' third theory of liability

---

[4] BNSF describes "deadheading" as a process that involves transporting train crews over a long distance in order to staff terminals sufficiently. BNSF explains that this process is planned in advance and is different than the transportation required to relieve railway employees when their hours of service have expired. Burckhard and Mack were not transported pursuant to a "deadheading" process but were relieved as part of a combined service crew.

failed because they did not offer expert testimony establishing that BNSF had a duty to implement a curfew policy covering employees, such as Burckhard and Mack. BNSF did not renew these motions under Rule 50(b) after the jury verdict.

Following the verdict, BNSF moved the district court to alter or amend the judgment. Plaintiffs received $600,000 before trial in "Off Track Vehicle Accident Benefits" as part of BNSF's Collective Bargaining Agreement. BNSF claimed that the agreement required plaintiffs to apply the $600,000 as an offset to any recovery. The district court denied the motion because it considered the agreement to be collateral to the merits of the case. BNSF now appeals. [—5—]

II. *Discussion*

Plaintiffs suit arises under the Federal Employers' Liability Act (FELA), 45 U.S.C. § 51 *et seq.* FELA renders railroads liable for injuries or deaths of its employees "resulting in whole or in part from the negligence of [the railroad]." 45 U.S.C. § 51.

A. *JMOL Motions*

In preverdict motions, BNSF moved the district court to enter JMOL on two bases: (1) "Plaintiffs failed to offer any evidence that [BNSF] should have or could have foreseen the conduct of Keiser that cause[d] the harm at issue"; and (2) "Plaintiffs failed to offer *any* expert testimony to establish the standard of care applicable to BNSF for crew calls and train movements." BNSF argues that the district court erred in denying these JMOL motions. Plaintiffs contend that BNSF waived these arguments by failing to renew them in a Rule 50(b) motion. BNSF counters that its arguments involve legal questions and therefore did not need to be raised in a renewed JMOL.

Typically, we review de novo a district court's denial of a JMOL motion, viewing the evidence in the light most favorable to the verdict. *Hyundai Motor Fin. Co. v. McKay Motors I, LLC*, 574 F.3d 637, 640 (8th Cir. 2009). But we have no basis to review a party's JMOL motion challenging the sufficiency of the evidence where the party does not renew its Rule 50(a) motion in a postverdict Rule 50(b) motion. *Ludlow v. BNSF Ry. Co.*, 788 F.3d 794, 800 (8th Cir. 2015). BNSF argues that legal questions, on the other hand, are appealable after final judgment even if not renewed in a postverdict motion. Assuming for the sake of analysis that a purely legal issue may be raised on appeal without a Rule 50(b) motion, neither of BNSF's two disputed issues on appeal falls in that category. [—6—]

1. *Foreseeability*

BNSF casts its foreseeability argument as a legal question. It argues that a drunk driver's actions are not reasonably foreseeable. Therefore, BNSF contends, as a matter of law, that it did not breach its duty to Burckhard and Mack by failing to take measures to protect against Keiser's driving.

Although FELA does not incorporate common law "proximate causation," reasonable foreseeability of harm is an essential ingredient of FELA negligence. *CSX Transp., Inc. v. McBride*, 564 U.S. 685, 702–03 (2011). Reasonable foreseeability circumscribes the duties a railroad owes its employees. *Id.* Where a railroad "has no reasonable ground to anticipate that a particular condition . . . would or might result in a mishap and injury, then the [railroad] is not required to do anything to correct [the] condition." *Id.* at 703 (first and third alteration in original) (quotation and citation omitted). Provided that negligence is proved, no matter how insignificant its role in producing the injury, "the manner in which [the injury] occurred" need not be foreseeable. *Id.* at 703–04.

At oral argument, BNSF argued that plaintiffs needed to prove certain things—"a pattern of accidents," "frequent death, injury, disability," and a "dangerous road"—for the accident to be reasonably foreseeable. Its brief likewise argues that "there must be *evidence* of foreseeability of injury to the railroad for a plaintiff to prevail in an FELA case." (Emphasis added.) Nevertheless, when

confronted with its failure to renew its argument in a postverdict JMOL motion, BNSF urged that foreseeability is a legal question and not something to be proved. Our case law addressing reasonable foreseeability of harm, however, reveals that the question is factual and not legal. *See, e.g., Lager v. Chicago Nw. Transp. Co.*, 122 F.3d 523, 525 (8th Cir. 1997) (affirming grant of summary judgment to railroad because "[t]he evidence in the record . . . [was] insufficient to support [plaintiff's] claim"); *Vidlak v. Burlington N. R.R.*, 16 F.3d 1229 (8th Cir. 1993) (unpublished per curiam) (affirming grant of summary judgment to railroad because plaintiff "failed to offer any evidence [—7—] of foreseeability"); *Ackley v. Chicago & N. W. Transp. Co.*, 820 F.2d 263, 267 (8th Cir. 1987) (noting that "[t]he Supreme Court has emphasized the jury's role in determining whether an employer has breached its duties under the FELA"); *Richardson v. Missouri Pac. R. Co.*, 677 F.2d 663, 666 (8th Cir. 1982) (reversing judgment of the district court because plaintiff "failed to adduce sufficient evidence" of reasonably foreseeability). The Supreme Court's decision in *McBride* confirms this route. Whether a railroad has reasonable grounds to foresee that a particular condition might result in an injury depends on the evidence of each particular case. *See McBride*, 564 U.S. at 702–03. We have no basis to review BNSF's foreseeability argument because it challenges the sufficiency of the evidence and was not renewed in a Rule 50(b) motion.

2. *Expert Testimony*

BNSF also contends that whether expert testimony concerning the applicable standard of care was required to support the jury's finding of negligence is a legal issue that need not be renewed in a Rule 50(b) motion. We reject this suggestion and conclude that BNSF failed to preserve its challenge on this point.

According to BNSF, the disputed issue at trial was whether it breached its standard of care by allowing employees to choose between transportation by van or by train. The company contends that the plaintiffs should have been required to present expert testimony on BNSF's standard of care in transporting employees. Without such evidence, BNSF asserts, the district court should have dismissed the claim alleging negligence for allowing the decedents to be transported by van at night.

Assuming for the sake of analysis that "purely legal issues" need not be raised in a Rule 50(b) motion to preserve those issues for appeal, BNSF's argument on expert testimony is not such an issue. Whether expert testimony is necessary depends on the facts of the case. Here, the question is whether there was sufficient evidence [—8—] to establish a standard of care without expert testimony. The district court said that lay testimony was enough to support a finding of negligence; BNSF agues that the lay testimony was insufficient and that an expert was needed. Our cases show that this is a dispute over the sufficiency of the evidence. *S&A Farms, Inc. v. Farm.com*, 678 F.3d 949, 954–55 (8th Cir. 2012) (concluding that where plaintiff presented no expert testimony on the relevant standard of care, a reasonable jury would have no way of knowing whether Farms.com acted within the standard of care, so summary judgment was appropriate); *Hall v. Arthur*, 141 F.3d 844, 847 (8th Cir. 1998) (concluding that because expert testimony concerning surgeon's standard of care could be applicable to his assistant, "we reject Dr. Gocio's assertion that there was insufficient evidence that he violated the standard of care"); *see also Olivier v. Robert L. Yeager Mental Health Ctr.*, 398 F.3d 183, 190-91 (2d Cir. 2005) ("Because Olivier did not introduce expert testimony as to medical standards, there was no legally sufficient evidentiary basis for a reasonable jury to find for Olivier.") (internal quotation and brackets omitted).

BNSF was required to renew in a Rule 50(b) motion its contention that lay testimony was insufficient to establish a standard of care and that expert testimony was required. *See Rosenberg v. DVI Receivables XIV, LLC*, 818 F.3d 1283, 1292 (11th Cir. 2016). Because BNSF failed to do so, the issue is waived.

B. *Evidentiary Rulings*

BNSF next argues that the district court erred in the following three evidentiary rulings: (1) the district court excluded evidence that Burckhard and Mack had the option to be transported by train or car, (2) the district court admitted evidence of BNSF's curfew policy, and (3) the district court limited Sergeant Kent's testimony. We review a district court's evidentiary rulings "for clear abuse of discretion, reversing only when an improper evidentiary ruling affected the defendant's substantial rights or had more than a slight influence on the verdict." *Chism v. CNH Am. LLC*, 638 F.3d 637, 640 (8th Cir. 2011) (quotation and citation omitted). [—9—]

1. *Choice of Means of Transportation*

BNSF sought to introduce evidence that Burckhard and Mack were given a choice of train or car transportation upon expiration of their hours of service. BNSF argues that it was prejudiced by the district court's refusal to allow the proffered evidence because plaintiffs were able to leave the jury with the impression that BNSF forced Burckhard and Mack into a less-safe mode of transportation.

The defenses of contributory negligence and assumption of the risk were not present in the case. The district court excluded evidence relating to choice of transportation under Federal Rule of Evidence 403 to avoid potentially injecting those defenses into the trial. Rule 403 permits a court to "exclude relevant evidence if its probative value is substantially outweighed by a danger of one or more of the following: unfair prejudice, confusing the issues, misleading the jury, undue delay, wasting time, or needlessly presenting cumulative evidence." Fed. R. Evid. 403.

The district court did not abuse its discretion in excluding the evidence. A district court's Rule 403 ruling "depends on factors that are uniquely accessible to the trial judge who is present in the courtroom and uniquely inaccessible to an appellate judge who must take the case on a cold record." *Olson v. Ford*

Motor Co., 481 F.3d 619, 623 (8th Cir. 2007). BNSF contends that the probative value of the evidence was high because it helped establish that the risk of a drunk driver was not foreseeable. Assuming that the evidence had some probative value, the district court, nonetheless, had to weigh its probative value against its potential prejudice. Offering evidence that the decedents could have chosen a different mode of transportation proves little where the gravamen of the negligence claim is not the mode of transportation but the negligence of the transport operator. Despite the exclusion of its preferred evidence, BNSF was able to offer evidence that federal law permitted transportation at night on public roadways. BNSF was also allowed to argue in closing that transportation at night on public roadways is not negligent. The district court ultimately determined that the evidence's probative value was substantially outweighed by the potential of [—10—] confusing the issues caused by injecting irrelevant defenses. This was not an abuse of discretion.

2. *Curfew Policy*

BNSF also argues that the district court erred when it admitted evidence of BNSF's curfew policy. Plaintiffs were allowed to introduce evidence that BNSF prohibited deadheading train crews from public-roadway transportation between 10:00 p.m. and 4:00 a.m. BNSF argues that the evidence had "no bearing on this action" because Burckhard and Mack were not deadheading and that it "proved to be extremely prejudicial."

Rule 401 defines relevant evidence as evidence that "has any tendency to make a [consequential] fact more or less probable than it would be without the evidence." Fed. R. Evid. 401. Here, the district court found that the evidence was relevant because it showed that BNSF had some concerns about the transportation of its employees at night on the public roadways. BNSF's knowledge of the risks associated with nighttime driving was a consequential fact in plaintiffs' negligence action. This evidence had some tendency to make that fact more probable. The admission of the evidence also did not unfairly prejudice BNSF. The district court permitted BNSF to offer evidence addressing the differences between deadheading crews and the combined service crews. The district court did not abuse its discretion in admitting the evidence relating to BNSF's deadheading policy.

3. *Sergeant Kent's Opinion Testimony*

BNSF sought to have Sergeant Kent testify that in his opinion Rennick did not react negligently to Keiser's driving. BNSF argues that the district court improperly excluded a portion of Sergeant Kent's trial testimony for two reasons. First, it claims that the district court improperly treated Sergeant Kent's testimony as lay opinion rather than expert testimony. Second, even if it were lay opinion, BNSF argues that the testimony was improperly excluded under Rule 403. [—11—]

The district court determined that Sergeant Kent's proffered testimony characterizing Keiser's driving went beyond the scope of inquiry of an investigating officer. The district court ruled that a qualified expert should provide analysis of Rennick's reaction to Keiser's driving instead. The district court also considered the testimony inadmissible under Rule 403 on the grounds that its probative value was far outweighed by the dangers of unfair prejudice and cumulative evidence. The district court permitted two other BNSF witnesses—Aubrey Hutchins, Coach America's safety director, and Clancy King, BNSF's defensive driving expert—to comment on Rennick's driving. Sergeant Kent's testimony was cumulative of the testimony of these witnesses, and it was not an abuse of discretion for the district court to exclude it on that ground. *See* Fed. R. Evid. 403; *see also Van Dyke v. Coburn Enters., Inc.*, 873 F.2d 1094, 1101–02 (8th Cir. 1989) (explaining that a district court may exclude evidence that has been "rehashed and rehashed").

C. *Rule 59(e) Motion*

Lastly, BNSF argues that the district court erred in denying its motion to alter or amend the judgment pursuant to Federal Rule of Civil Procedure 59(e). After the jury returned its verdict and the district court entered judgment, BNSF moved the district court to offset the judgment based on the "Off Track Vehicle Accident Benefits" agreement entered into by plaintiffs and BNSF. The agreement stated that the amounts received by plaintiffs "*may* be applied as an offset by the railroad against recovery that is obtained." (Emphasis added.) We accord a district court broad discretion in determining whether to grant a motion to alter or amend judgment, and we will not reverse absent a clear abuse of discretion. *United States v. Metro. St. Louis Sewer Dist.*, 440 F.3d 930, 933 (8th Cir. 2006).

One of the main purposes of Rule 59(e) is to allow a district court to "rectify its own mistakes in the period immediately following the entry of judgment." *White v. N.H. Dept. of Emp't Sec.*, 455 U.S. 445, 450 (1982) (footnote omitted). "Federal Rule of Civil Procedure 59(e) was adopted to clarify a district court's power to correct [—12—] its own mistakes in the time period immediately following entry of judgment." *Innovative Home Health Care, Inc. v. P.T.-O.T. Assocs. of the Black Hills*, 141 F.3d 1284, 1286 (8th Cir. 1998) (citation omitted). Thus, Rule 59(e) generally may be invoked "only to support reconsideration of matters properly encompassed in a decision of the merits." *White*, 455 U.S. at 451 (citation omitted).

The district court denied BNSF's motion because the agreement that was the basis for BNSF's claimed setoff was collateral to the merits of plaintiffs' FELA action. BNSF's motion to alter or amend the judgment is based upon payments it made to plaintiffs pursuant to an agreement that was not an issue resolved at trial. The action before the district court, and tried to the jury, encompassed only claims under FELA and negligence under Montana common law. The agreement was not encompassed within the decision on the merits of plaintiffs FELA case. Moreover, the agreement had the potential to spawn additional litigation over the use of the word "may." The district court did not abuse its discretion in denying BNSF's Rule 59(e) motion.

III. *Conclusion*

Accordingly, we affirm the judgment of the district court.

(Reporter's Note: Concurring opinion follows on p. 366).

[—12—] SMITH, Circuit Judge, concurring:

I concur in the court's opinion. I write separately because I conclude that whether expert testimony concerning the applicable standard of care was required to support the jury's negligence finding is a legal question that BNSF need not have renewed in a Rule 50(b) motion. *See supra* Part.II.A.2. Nonetheless, I find that the district court did not err in refusing to require plaintiffs to offer expert testimony.

Subject matter requiring specialized knowledge and training such as medicine, engineering, and architecture generally requires expert testimony to aid the factfinder. But, where the claim is basic negligence and no specialized knowledge is needed, the **[—13—]** jury can render a decision without expert testimony. Deciding whether expert testimony is needed to establish a claim turns on the specific facts of the case. *See Bartak v. Bell-Galyardt & Wells, Inc.*, 629 F.2d 523, 530 (8th Cir. 1980). While the determination is fact dependent, it also rests upon a legal standard. The question is neither purely legal nor purely factual; it is a mixed question of law and fact. *See Pullman-Standard v. Swint*, 456 U.S. 273, 290 n.19 (1982) (noting that mixed questions of law and fact are "questions in which the historical facts are admitted or established, the rule of law is undisputed, and the issue is whether the facts satisfy the statutory standard, or to put it another way, whether the rule of law as applied to the established facts is or is not violated"). We have committed the determination of whether expert testimony is admitted to the sound discretion of trial courts, and we will not reverse a trial court's decision unless it is clearly erroneous. *Bartak*, 629 F.2d at 530.

Here, BNSF's argument is that the case presented questions that simply could not be determined by a factfinder without expert input of the standard of proper or reasonable care in the railroad industry. This is a legal question, and like all legal questions, it cannot be resolved in the abstract but must be analyzed in conjunction with the facts of the particular case. Doing so does not convert it into a sufficiency-of-the-evidence argument; it

remains a legal question. *Cf. Rosemann v. Sigillito*, 785 F.3d 1175, 1181 (8th Cir. 2015) (agreeing with the district court that expert testimony was required to establish the proper standard of care and, without it, the plaintiff's claim of professional negligence was not submissible); *Brooks v. Union Pac. R.R.*, 620 F.3d 896, 900 (8th Cir. 2010) (affirming grant of summary judgment to defendant because plaintiff failed to offer expert testimony). For that reason, I conclude that BNSF's argument challenges a determination committed to the district court, not the jury, and, therefore, is not an argument that must be renewed in a Rule 50(b) motion. *See Linden v. CNH Am., LLC*, 673 F.3d 829, 833 (8th Cir. 2012) (limiting the requirement to renew a Rule 50(a) motion to sufficiency-of-the-evidence challenges). We require an argument to be renewed in a Rule 50(b) motion "because it allows the **[—14—]** district court, which has first-hand knowledge of witnesses, testimony, and issues, an opportunity after the verdict to review the legal sufficiency of the evidence." *Ludlow*, 788 F.3d at 800 (quotations and citations omitted). The trial court thus is able to review the decision of the factfinder, be it a jury or the court itself. Whether expert testimony is necessary, though, is not entrusted to the factfinder; rather, it is a determination made by the court to assist the factfinder in weighing the evidence. Here, BNSF's expert-testimony argument, directed at the trial court, is preserved for appellate review.[5]

---

[5] The per curiam opinion cites *Hall v. Arthur*, 141 F.3d 844 (8th Cir. 1998), in support of its conclusion that BNSF's argument that expert testimony was required is a sufficiency-of-the-evidence argument. Specifically, the opinion relies on the following statement: "[W]e reject Dr. Gocio's assertion that there was insufficient evidence that he violated the applicable standard of care." *Id.* at 847. This statement does not bear the load placed upon it, as it simply does not state that the determination of whether expert testimony is required is a sufficiency-of-the-evidence question. *Hall* dealt with a doctor arguing "that since he acted only as an assistant in Mr. Hall's surgery, the Halls had to produce expert testimony as to the standard of care applicable to an assistant in order to allow the jury to reach the question of his potential negligence." *Id.* As the court noted, the applicable law required that the violation of the

The ultimate determination of whether expert testimony is required, however, remains committed to the trial court's sound discretion; here, the district court did not err in refusing to require plaintiffs to offer expert testimony on crew calls and train movements. Plaintiffs' theory of liability did not rely on BNSF's negligence in the mode of transportation. In its final jury instructions, the district court told the jury to disregard any evidence or argument "suggesting that BNSF should have scheduled [—15—] its trains and crews to make sure that Todd Burckhard and Blaine Mack reached Glasgow before their 12-hours in service expired." The district court permitted plaintiffs to reference BNSF's curfew policy in arguing that BNSF knew that nighttime transportation by public roadways presented additional risks. The district court considered these additional risks a "matter of common sense." Plaintiffs' argument went to the narrow issue of the foreseeability of drunk drivers; contrary to BNSF's contention, it did not introduce the additional theory of liability that BNSF was negligent for permitting nighttime transportation on public roadways. Thus, BNSF's standard of care for crew calls and train movements was not at issue. Accordingly, I conclude that expert testimony was not necessary on this subject.

---

standard of care be established by expert testimony when the asserted negligence does not lie within the jury's comprehension as a matter of common knowledge. *Id.* The court merely rejected the doctor's argument that a *separate* expert was required to establish the standard applicable to him as an assistant and that the plaintiffs could not rely on the expert to establish the standard of care for the lead doctor. *Id.*

This page intentionally left blank

United States Court of Appeals for the Ninth Circuit

United States Court of Appeals
for the Ninth Circuit

No. 14-50154

UNITED STATES
vs.
CRUZ-MENDEZ

Appeal from the United States District Court for the
Southern District of California

Decided: January 27, 2016*

Citation: 811 F.3d 1172, 4 Adm. R. 370 (9th Cir. 2016).

Before **RAWLINSON** and **NGUYEN**, Circuit Judges, and
PONSOR, Senior District Judge.**

* The panel unanimously concluded this case is
suitable for decision without oral argument. *See* Fed. R.
App. P. 34(a)(2).

** The Honorable Michael A. Ponsor, Senior District
Judge for the U.S. District Court for Massachusetts,
sitting by designation.

[—3—] **PONSOR**, Senior District Judge:

Defendant Raul Cruz-Mendez received an eighty-month sentence after pleading guilty to possessing one-hundred kilograms or more of marijuana on a vessel. In the same sentencing proceeding, he received a consecutive twelve-month sentence for violation of the terms of supervised release imposed in a prior case. On appeal, he raises two issues. First, Cruz-Mendez challenges the district court's imposition of a two-level enhancement to his offense level for the marijuana conviction, as contemplated under U.S.S.G. § 2D1.1(b)(3)(C) (the "pilot/captain" enhancement). Second, he contends that the combined sentence of ninety-two months was substantively unreasonable.

We have jurisdiction under 28 U.S.C. § 1291 and 18 U.S.C. § 3742(a). We affirm.

BACKGROUND

The underlying facts are not significantly disputed. On October 5, 2013, Customs and Border Protection agents [—4—] aerially observed two men operating a so-called "panga" vessel[1] off the coast of Ensenada, Mexico, heading northwest toward the United States. They also spotted several bales of suspected narcotics visible in the open hull. Shortly afterwards, a U.S. Coast Guard vessel initiated an interception of the panga, during which the helicopter crew observed defendant and another man dumping bales overboard. Warning shots from the Coast Guard vessel, and finally disabling gunfire directed at the engine, ultimately succeeded in bringing the panga to a stop, whereupon law enforcement agents recovered thirty-one bales of marijuana totaling over 568 kilograms. Cruz-Mendez and a co-defendant were arrested for possession of marijuana with intent to distribute, on a vessel, in violation of 46 U.S.C. §§ 70503 and 70506. At the time of his arrest, Cruz-Mendez was on supervised release for a 2008 conviction for transporting undocumented aliens in a vessel, in violation of 8 U.S.C. § 1324.[2]

On December 5, 2013, Cruz-Mendez pled guilty to the marijuana charge, and on January 6, 2014, he admitted to a violation of the terms of supervised release imposed in connection with his 2008 conviction. A consolidated sentencing hearing took place on April 1, 2014.

The presentence report filed by the probation department included application of the two-level "pilot/captain" enhancement for the specific offense characteristic of acting [—5—] "as a pilot, copilot, captain, navigator, flight officer, or any other operation officer aboard any craft or vessel carrying a controlled substance[.]" U.S.S.G. § 2D1.1(b)(3)(C). With the enhancement, the probation department calculated Cruz-Mendez's guideline range to be seventy to eighty-seven months. After Cruz-Mendez objected to the two-level increase, the probation department filed an addendum asserting that, because Cruz-Mendez and his co-defendant possessed the skill of being able to pilot a vessel and

---

[1] A panga boat is "an open-bow vessel commonly used for smuggling." *United States v. Ramos-Atondo*, 732 F.3d 1113, 1117 (9th Cir. 2013).

[2] Cruz-Mendez had one additional earlier conviction in 2007 for possession with intent to sell marijuana.

exercised that skill in furtherance of their crime, the two-level increase was warranted. The government recommended a sentence of sixty months, based on a sentencing guidelines range of sixty to seventy-one months, which did not include the two-level upward adjustment.

At the hearing, the district court overruled Cruz-Mendez's objection to the application of the "pilot/captain" enhancement. Specifically, Cruz-Mendez argued that he and his co-defendant had equal responsibility on the boat, with each piloting the boat at different points of the voyage. The court determined that, by the Coast Guard's observation and by his own admission, Cruz-Mendez was operating the panga and was therefore the pilot of the vessel under the plain text of the enhancement. After recognizing the parties' agreement that the starting offense level was twenty-eight, the district court increased the level by two with the application of the "pilot/captain" enhancement.

With a three-level reduction for acceptance of responsibility and a four-level reduction based on the district's "fast track" program, the offense level was twenty-three, with a criminal history category of IV, generating a sentencing guideline range of seventy to eighty-seven months. The court imposed upon Cruz-Mendez a sentence in [—6—] the middle of this range: eighty months. With regard to the violation of supervised release the district court found, without objection, that the sentencing guideline range was fifteen to twenty-one months, but varied to a below-guideline sentence of twelve months, consecutive to the eighty-month sentence on the marijuana charge, resulting in a total of ninety-two months.

Cruz-Mendez filed a timely notice of appeal contesting both the application of the "pilot/captain" enhancement and the substantive reasonableness of the total sentence.

STANDARD OF REVIEW

We review the district court's interpretation of the Sentencing Guidelines *de novo* and its application of the Guidelines to the facts of the case for abuse of discretion. *United States v. Garcia-Guerrero*, 635 F.3d 435, 438 (9th Cir. 2011). We review the substantive reasonableness of a sentence for abuse of discretion. *United States v. Autery*, 555 F.3d 864, 871 (9th Cir. 2009).

DISCUSSION

A. Interpretation and Application of the Enhancement

Cruz-Mendez contends that the district court's use of the "pilot/captain" enhancement to increase his offense level was legal error because the plain meaning of the terms "pilot," "captain," "navigator," and "officer," as well as the Guidelines commentary, structure, and legislative history, all support a narrow reading of the enhancement such that it applies only to individuals either who occupied a position of authority on the vessel or who possessed "special skills" [—7—] aboard the ship. Cruz-Mendez asserts that, because he simply operated a panga by standing at the tiller of the outboard motor, he lacked the requisite special skills or authority on the vessel to support the imposition of the enhancement.

The proper application of a "pilot/captain" enhancement is an issue of first impression in this circuit. We agree with every other circuit court to consider this issue—the First, Fifth, Seventh, and Eleventh—and hold that the proper reading of the "pilot/captain" enhancement is not as constrained as Cruz-Mendez suggests. *See United States v. Bautista-Montelongo*, 618 F.3d 464, 466–67 (5th Cir. 2010) (adopting the holdings of the First, Seventh, and Eleventh Circuit Courts of Appeals that the enhancement applied to a defendant who "drove a boat containing contraband"); *United States v. Rendon*, 354 F.3d 1320, 1329 (11th Cir. 2003) (declining to adopt a technical definition of "captain" and applying it to a defendant who operated a boat); *United States v. Senn*, 129 F.3d 886, 896–97 (7th Cir. 1997) (stating that "the plain language of the statute carries the day" and declining to find that a pilot or captain must have special skills), *abrogated on other* grounds, *United States v. Vizcarra*, 668 F.3d 516, 523 n.2 (7th Cir. 2012); *United States v. Guerrero*, 114 F.3d 332, 346 (1st Cir. 1997) (finding that the term "pilot" did not require proof of any special skill or authority, only evidence that the person steered the vessel).

The plain language of § 2D1.1(b)(3)(C), which calls for a two-level enhancement where "the defendant *acted* as a pilot, copilot, captain, navigator, flight officer, or any other operation officer aboard *any craft or vessel* carrying a controlled substance" (emphasis added), is strongly indicative of a broad scope, not dependent on a finding of any particular formal training or type of boat. *See United States v. Shill*, [—8—] 740 F.3d 1347, 1351 (9th Cir. 2014) (stating that "analysis begins and ends with the ordinary meaning of the statutory language"). The fact that the Guidelines commentary acknowledges that pilots and boat captains may use "special skills" also subject to a two-level adjustment under § 3B1.3 and dictates that the two sections may not *both* apply to the same conduct does not mean, as Cruz-Mendez would have it, that § 2D1.1(b)(3)(C) can *only* apply where such special skills are demonstrated by a pilot or captain. Such a reading would lead to complete overlap between the two sections, and would also ignore situations where an individual obviously assumed the role of pilot or captain but demonstrated little skill in doing so. *See Senn*, 129 F.3d at 890 (upholding application of the enhancement where defendant was listed as captain on customs documents and directed boat operations, but journey involved several stops for repairs, a stop for fuel, and a stop to ask directions from a passing freighter, followed by difficulty locating Jamaica). As with our sister circuits, we decline to apply "rigid requirements of professionalism" to the "pilot/captain" enhancement and instead opt for a "common sense approach." *Bautista-Montelongo*, 618 F.3d at 467.

We find no error in the application of the "pilot/captain" enhancement on the facts of this case. By Cruz-Mendez's own account, he was a lifelong fisherman hired to transport marijuana bales, and in so doing he operated a boat laden with substantial cargo in open water by controlling both its speed and direction.[3] Such conduct fully justifies the [—9—] imposition of the two-point enhancement. *Cf. United States v. Cartwright*, 413 F.3d 1295, 1299 (11th Cir. 2005) (upholding application of the enhancement where defendant was a lifelong fisherman who was one of several men who drove the boat).

B. Reasonableness of the Sentence

The district court's imposition of the twelve-month sentence for violation of supervised release consecutive to the eighty-month sentence for possession of marijuana on a vessel, resulting in a global sentence of ninety-two months, was not an abuse of discretion. *See Autery*, 555 F.3d at 871. In fact, the district court exercised its discretion in departing downward from the Guidelines range, "just not by as many months as [the defendant] requested." *United States v. Ayala-Nicanor*, 659 F.3d 744, 752 (9th Cir. 2011). Under these circumstances, we cannot say that the below-Guidelines sentence was substantively unreasonable.

CONCLUSION

For the foregoing reasons, the judgment of the district court is **AFFIRMED**.

---

[3] While Cruz-Mendez highlights that he had no authority over his co-defendant, he does not argue that his co-defendant had any authority over him while they were on the panga. *See Bautista-Montelongo*, 618 F.3d at 466–67 (upholding application of enhancement to career fisherman who, [—9—] *inter alia*, did not use navigational tools and had no crew other than co-conspirator).

United States Court of Appeals
for the Ninth Circuit

No. 13-17358

MARILLEY
vs.
BONHAM

Decided: February 26, 2016

Citation: 815 F.3d 1178, 4 Adm. R. 373 (9th Cir. 2016).

[—1—] THOMAS, Chief Judge:

Upon the vote of a majority of nonrecused active judges, it is ordered that this case be reheard en banc pursuant to Federal Rule of Appellate Procedure 35(a) and Circuit Rule 35-3. The three-judge panel opinion shall not be cited as precedent by or to any court of the Ninth Circuit.

United States Court of Appeals
for the Ninth Circuit

No. 15-35392

SHELL OFFSHORE INC.
vs.
GREENPEACE, INC.

Appeal from the United States District Court for the District of Alaska

Decided: March 4, 2016

Citation: 815 F.3d 623, 4 Adm. R. 374 (9th Cir. 2016).

Before **KOZINSKI, TASHIMA,** and **SMITH, JR.,** Circuit Judges.

[—3—] TASHIMA, Circuit Judge:

Plaintiffs Shell Offshore Inc. and Shell Gulf of Mexico Inc. (together, "Shell"), subsidiaries of Royal Dutch Shell plc, and Defendant Greenpeace, Inc. ("Greenpeace"), a non-profit environmental organization, are long-term foes in this Court. Shell has invested significant amounts of time and money in its search for oil in the Chukchi Sea, a stretch of ocean off the northwest coast of Alaska. Greenpeace regards Shell's efforts as dangerous and environmentally irresponsible. As a result, it has engaged in several direct-action protests in an effort to impede Shell's exploration activities.

In this appeal, the parties once again clash over the propriety of a preliminary injunction entered by the district court to protect Shell from certain more vigorous and more intrusive aspects of Greenpeace's activism.

On appeal, Greenpeace challenges the injunction on several jurisdictional bases, as well as on the merits. We do not reach any of these issues, however, because we conclude that the appeal is moot. Accordingly, we dismiss the appeal and remand for further proceedings. [—4—]

I. BACKGROUND

A. The 2012 Litigation

In 2012, Greenpeace launched a campaign to "Stop Shell" from drilling for oil in the Chukchi Sea, as part of its greater efforts to "Save the Arctic." Opposed to a project they considered to be a critical threat to the environment, Greenpeace activists unlawfully boarded several ships employed by Shell in its offshore drilling operations. In response, Shell filed suit in the District of Alaska. It sought a preliminary injunction to prevent Greenpeace from interfering with its vessels during the Arctic drilling season. *See Shell Offshore Inc. v. Greenpeace, Inc. ("Greenpeace I")*, 864 F. Supp. 2d 839, 841–42 (D. Alaska 2012). The district court granted Shell's request. The resulting injunction established safety zones around each of the vessels in Shell's Arctic drilling fleet, which Greenpeace was prohibited from entering. *Id.* at 854–56. The injunction also barred Greenpeace from committing various torts and acts of trespass against Shell's vessels. *Id.* at 855.

Greenpeace appealed the preliminary injunction, and we affirmed. *Shell Offshore Inc. v. Greenpeace, Inc. ("Greenpeace II")*, 709 F.3d 1281, 1292, 1 Adm. R. 388, 395 (9th Cir. 2013). While the appeal was pending, the Arctic drilling season ended and the preliminary injunction expired. *Id.* at 1287, 1 Adm. R. at 391. We concluded that the case was nevertheless not moot because the mootness exception for cases "capable of repetition, yet evading review" applied. *Id.*, 1 Adm. R. at 391. We reasoned that Shell held multi-year drilling rights in the Chukchi Sea and "[a] preliminary injunction limited to a single Arctic Ocean open water season . . . will never last long enough to allow full litigation" of the merits. *Id.*, 1 Adm. R. at 391. Following our decision in [—5—] *Greenpeace II*, Shell voluntarily dismissed the action without prejudice.

B. The 2015 Litigation

In January 2015, Shell announced renewed plans to drill in the Chukchi Sea during the summer drilling season. In response,

Greenpeace resurrected its "Stop Shell" campaign. On April 6, 2015, six activists boarded and secured themselves to the *Polar Pioneer*, a drilling vessel under contract with Shell. The activists—one of whom was a Greenpeace employee—remained on board the *Polar Pioneer* for six days. One day after the activists commenced their protest, Shell filed a new suit—the instant action—against Greenpeace in the District of Alaska, asserting claims for both injunctive relief and monetary damages.

After an evidentiary hearing, the district court granted Shell a preliminary injunction against Greenpeace. *Shell Offshore, Inc. v. Greenpeace, Inc.*, 2015 WL 2185111 (D. Alaska 2015). As in 2012, the preliminary injunction established safety zones around each of Shell's contracted vessels. The injunction also established aerial safety zones around all helideck-equipped ships; banned Greenpeace from engaging in specified actions affecting Shell's systems and facilities; and prohibited Greenpeace from operating "any drones anywhere within the Burger Prospect in the Chukchi Sea" during the drilling season. *Id.* at *6–8. Greenpeace timely appealed the preliminary injunction, challenging the district court's jurisdiction to issue the injunction, in addition to contesting the injunction on the merits. We have jurisdiction over this interlocutory appeal under 28 U.S.C. § 1292(a)(1). [—6—]

1. The St. John's Bridge Protest

In July 2015, while this appeal was pending and the preliminary injunction remained in effect, Greenpeace activists suspended themselves from St. John's Bridge over the Willamette River in Portland, Oregon. As stated in an email to supporters, the activists' purpose was to block one of Shell's contracted vessels, the *Fennica*, from leaving the Portland harbor. The *Fennica* fell within the preliminary injunction's safety zones, so Shell moved the district court to enforce the injunction.

After an emergency hearing, the district court entered a preliminary order of civil

contempt (the "Contempt Order"). The Contempt Order imposed sanctions "so long as [Greenpeace] activists continue to hang from the St. John's Bridge in Portland." The sanctions were structured as a progressively increasing schedule of fines against Greenpeace: $2,500 for each hour in contempt during the first day; $5,000 per hour during the second day; $7,500 per hour during the third day; and $10,000 per hour thereafter. Shell contends that Greenpeace activists remained suspended from the bridge for seven hours in violation of the Contempt Order.[1] The district court has yet to enter a final order sanctioning Greenpeace.[2] [—7—]

2. Shell Abandons Its Drilling Efforts

In September 2015, Shell announced that it would cease exploration in offshore Alaska for the foreseeable future. We issued an order to show cause why this appeal, and the underlying action, should not be dismissed as moot. In response, Shell argued that although the underlying litigation continued to present a case or controversy to the district court, this appeal would become moot upon the expiration of the preliminary injunction. Greenpeace disagreed and argued the inverse: that the pending preliminary Contempt Order rescued the appeal from mootness, but that Shell's actions had rendered the underlying litigation moot. The preliminary injunction expired on its own terms on November 1, 2015, and Shell did not seek to renew it.

II. DISCUSSION

"We have an independent obligation to consider mootness *sua sponte*." *Greenpeace II*, 709 F.3d at 1286, 1 Adm. R. at 390 (quoting *NASD Dispute Resolution, Inc. v. Judicial Council*, 488 F.3d 1065, 1068 (9th Cir. 2007)). "A case is moot when the issues presented are no longer 'live' or the parties lack a legally

---

[1] The Contempt Order was expressly denominated as "preliminary" because it was "entered without a full evidentiary hearing in light of the emergency, expedited nature of the situation in Portland." It contemplated an evidentiary hearing at a later date.

[2] District court proceedings have been stayed pending this appeal.

SHELL OFFSHORE INC. V. GREENPEACE, INC., 4 Adm. R. 374 (9th Cir. 2016)

cognizable interest in the outcome." *City of Erie v. Pap's A.M.*, 529 U.S. 277, 287 (2000) (quoting *Cty. of L.A. v. Davis*, 440 U.S. 625, 631 (1979)). When events change such that the appellate court can no longer grant "any effectual relief whatever to the prevailing party," any resulting opinion would be merely advisory. *Id.* (quoting *Church of Scientology of Cal. v. United States*, 506 U.S. 9, 12 (1992)). In such a case, the appellate court lacks jurisdiction and must dismiss the appeal. *SEIU v. Nat'l Union of Healthcare Workers*, 598 F.3d 1061, 1068 (9th Cir. 2010). We first address, as we must, the question of mootness before we can [—8—] consider the substance of the parties' contentions. *Greenpeace II*, 709 F.3d at 1286, 1 Adm. R. at 390.

A. The Preliminary Injunction

All of the issues on appeal derive from the district court's May 8 order granting Shell a preliminary injunction. Thus, our jurisdiction to hear this appeal hinges on whether the parties have a continued, legally cognizable interest in the validity of the injunction. The injunction expired on November 1, 2015, and Shell has not sought to renew it. As a result, the injunction no longer constrains Greenpeace, and it can no longer be enforced by Shell's motion. Because the only order on appeal has now expired, we are unable to grant any effectual relief to either party. This appeal is moot.[3]

---

[3] Unlike our decision in *Greenpeace II*, 709 F.3d at 1287, 1 Adm. R. at 391, the mootness exception for disputes "capable of repetition, yet evading review" does not apply to this appeal. In 2012, even after the preliminary injunction expired, Shell continued to hold oil and gas leases in the Chukchi Sea. As we stated then, there was no reason to believe that Greenpeace would not renew its protest actions upon Shell's return to the Arctic. *Id.* at 1288, 1 Adm. R. at 391. Indeed, that is exactly what occurred. By contrast, in 2015, Shell called a halt to all Arctic exploration "for the foreseeable future." Moreover, the U.S. Department of the Interior has cancelled further lease sales for the region through 2017. Thus, at this point, any assertion that Greenpeace is likely to resume its Arctic protests against Shell would be purely speculative.

Even though the preliminary injunction has expired and Shell has pulled out of the Arctic, Greenpeace argues that the still-pending contempt proceeding rescues its appeal from mootness. This argument is unavailing. Only compensatory contempt proceedings survive the termination of an underlying injunction. Here, as we explain below, the district [—9—] court imposed only a coercive civil contempt sanction. Because the contempt proceeding at issue here is coercive, it cannot rescue the appeal from mootness.

1. The District Court Issued a Coercive Civil Contempt Order

A court's contempt powers are broadly divided into two categories: civil contempt and criminal contempt. "The difference between criminal and civil contempt is not always clear. The same conduct may result in citations for both civil and criminal contempt." *United States v. Rylander*, 714 F.2d 996, 1001 (9th Cir. 1983) (citing *United States v. UMWA*, 330 U.S. 258 (1946)). In distinguishing between criminal and civil contempt, we must look to the sanction's "character and purpose." *Int'l Union, UMWA v. Bagwell*, 512 U.S. 821, 827 (1994). "The purpose of civil contempt is coercive or compensatory, whereas the purpose of criminal contempt is punitive." *Koninklijke Philips Elecs. N.V. v. KXD Tech., Inc.*, 539 F.3d 1039, 1042 (9th Cir. 2008) (quoting *United States v. Armstrong*, 781 F.2d 700, 703 (9th Cir. 1986)). The civil contemnor is said to "carr[y] the keys of his prison in his own pocket," whereas the criminal contemnor "is furnished no key, and he cannot shorten the term by promising not to repeat the offense." *Bagwell*, 512 U.S. at 828–29.

A court may wield its civil contempt powers for two separate and independent purposes: (1) "to coerce the defendant into compliance with the court's order"; and (2) "to compensate the complainant for losses sustained." *UMWA*, 330 U.S. at 303–04; *see also Ohr ex rel. NLRB v. Latino Express, Inc.*, 776 F.3d 469, 479–80 (7th Cir. 2015) ("A civil contempt order can serve to coerce a party to obey a court order, or it can be intended to compensate a party who has [—10—] suffered unnecessary injuries or costs because of contemptuous conduct." (collecting cases)); *Lasar v. Ford Motor Co.*, 399 F.3d 1101, 1110–11 (9th Cir. 2005); *Coleman v. Espy*, 986 F.2d 1184, 1190 (8th Cir. 1993); *Whittaker Corp. v. Execuair Corp.*, 953 F.2d 510, 517 (9th Cir. 1992). "The test . . . is 'what does the court primarily seek to accomplish by imposing the sanction?'" *Falstaff Brewing Corp. v. Miller Brewing Co.*, 702 F.2d 770, 778 (9th Cir. 1983) (quoting *Shillitani v. United States*, 384 U.S. 364, 370 (1966)). Because civil compensatory sanctions are remedial, they typically take the form of unconditional monetary sanctions; whereas coercive civil sanctions, intended to deter, generally take the form of conditional fines.[4] *See id.* at 780 (citing *Gompers v. Buck's Stove & Range Co.*, 221 U.S. 418, 444 (1911)). Thus, the ability to purge is perhaps the most definitive characteristic of coercive civil contempt. *Bagwell*, 512 U.S. at 829 ("Where a fine is not compensatory, it is civil only if the contemnor is afforded an opportunity to purge."); *see also Lasar*, 399 F.3d at 1110.

Further complicating matters, it is possible for sanctions that were initially imposed for a civil, coercive purpose to change over time; indeed, civil coercive contempt may eventually evolve into criminal contempt. *Richmark Corp. v. Timber Falling Consultants*, 959 F.2d 1468, 1481 (9th Cir. [—11—] 1992) (noting that "the propriety and even the nature of the contempt sanction can change over time"); *see also United States v. Rylander*, 460 U.S. 752, 757 (1983) (stating that the test for civil contempt on appeal is whether contemnor has the *present* ability to comply, not whether it could have complied in the past); *SEC v. Elmas Trading Corp.*, 824 F.2d 732, 732–33 (9th Cir. 1987) (noting that civil contempt may

become criminal over time). This is because, in order to categorize the contempt properly, a court must look to the purpose of the contempt at the time it is *enforced*, rather than at the time it is *imposed*. "A court's power to impose coercive civil contempt depends upon the ability of the contemnor to comply with the court's coercive order," something which may change over time. *Falstaff Brewing Corp.*, 702 F.2d at 778 (citing *Shillitani*, 384 U.S. at 371).

Here, the district court's Contempt Order imposes sanctions "so long as [Greenpeace] activists continue to hang from the St. John's Bridge in Portland." As described above, the Contempt Order fined Greenpeace $2,500 per hour for the first 24-hour period it violated the injunction, then incrementally increased the hourly fine per 24-hour period until it reached a cap of $10,000 per hour. The sanctions were thus imposed primarily to coerce Greenpeace into compliance with the preliminary injunction. Further accrual of the conditional fines could have been avoided by Greenpeace at any time, should it have choosen to recall the activists and comply with the injunction. The district court's civil sanctions are therefore properly understood to be coercive. *See also Consol. Rail Corp. v. Yashinsky*, 170 F.3d 591, 596 (6th Cir. 1999) ("[T]he Supreme Court has recognized that per diem fines like this one are generally coercive." (citing *Bagwell*, 512 U.S. at 826)). [—12—]

2. A Coercive Civil Contempt Order Is Moot When the Underlying Preliminary Injunction Terminates

As described by our sister circuits, the "general rule" requires that "[i]f a civil contempt order is coercive in nature . . . it is mooted when the proceeding out of which it arises terminates." *Ohr*, 776 F.3d at 479–80; *see also Travelhost, Inc. v. Blandford*, 68 F.3d 958, 961–62 (5th Cir. 1995); *Klett v. Pim*, 965 F.2d 587, 590 (8th Cir. 1992) ("A court cannot impose a coercive civil contempt sanction if the underlying injunction is no longer in effect." (citing *Shillitani*, 384 U.S. at 370)).

While our own caselaw has never clearly expressed this principle, it is implicit in the logic of our previous decisions. In *Frankl v.*

---

[4] Whether fines are payable to the opposing party or to the court may also be a factor in deciding whether they are coercive or compensatory. This factor alone, however, is not determinative. *Cf. Lasar*, 399 F.3d at 1111 (not determinative as between civil and criminal contempts); *F.J. Hanshaw Enters., Inc. v. Emerald River Dev., Inc.*, 244 F.3d 1128, 1138 n.7 (9th Cir. 2001) ("Whether a fine is payable to the court . . . as opposed to the complainant is a relevant, although not necessarily determinative, factor in determining whether a sanction is punitive." (citing, *inter alia*, *Hicks v. Feiock*, 485 U.S. 624, 631–32 (1988))).

HTH Corp., for example, we held that an otherwise-moot preliminary injunction continued to raise a "live" controversy "because its resolution [was] crucial to a pending claim for *retrospective* monetary relief . . . ." 650 F.3d 1334, 1342 (9th Cir. 2011) (emphasis added). While we did not discuss the distinction between compensatory and coercive civil contempt, our holding was explicitly premised on the compensatory nature of the pending contempt proceeding. *See also Lasar*, 399 F.3d at 1108–09 (finding litigation not moot where compensatory contempt sanctions still pending); *cf. Falstaff Brewing Corp.*, 702 F.2d at 780 (recognizing that, in the discovery context, coercive contempt is unenforceable when compliance with underlying order becomes "impossible" or "futile").

The justification for this bright-line distinction between compensatory and coercive contempts arises out of their disparate purposes. Once an injunction has been terminated, [—13—] a court may still award compensation to the plaintiff as a result of injuries caused by its opponent's contumacy. But a coercive sanction would no longer serve any purpose: Once the injunction has expired, there is no longer anything left to coerce. Instead, enforcing the sanctions could only serve to punish the contemnor. *See Bagwell*, 512 U.S. at 829 ("When a contempt involves the prior conduct of an isolated, prohibited act, the resulting sanction has no coercive effect."). Thus, once the underlying injunction has been terminated and the contemnor can no longer purge its contempt through compliance, the contempt becomes criminal.

"Criminal contempt is a crime in the ordinary sense, and criminal penalties may not be imposed on someone who has not been afforded the protections that the Constitution requires of such criminal proceedings." *Bagwell*, 512 U.S. at 826 (citations and internal quotation marks omitted). Thus, in cases where the underlying proceeding has been rendered moot, the coercive contempt proceeding must be vacated in order to avoid a due-process violation. *See FTC v. Verity Int'l, Ltd.*, 443 F.3d 48, 70 (2nd Cir. 2006);

Yashinsky, 170 F.3d at 596 (explaining that the contemnor "need not pay the [accumulated] fines . . . because those fines no longer serve the purpose of coercing his compliance . . . and requiring [him] to pay the accumulated fines now would only serve to punish him for his intransigence").

Here, the preliminary injunction has expired and will not be renewed. Thus, there is no longer anything left for the district court to coerce Greenpeace to do. Enforcing the fee-schedule monetary sanction would only serve to punish Greenpeace for its past contumacious actions. Accordingly, the pending contempt proceedings must be vacated. With no [—14—] surviving contempt proceedings, the appeal has lost any legally significant, present effects; it is therefore moot.[5]

B. The Underlying Proceeding

Even where one issue in a case has been rendered moot, others may remain. *See, e.g., Camenisch*, 451 U.S. at 394; *Powell v. McCormack*, 395 U.S. 486, 497 (1969). As discussed above, Greenpeace's appeal of the preliminary injunction is moot. Shell's complaint, however, also seeks damages for injuries allegedly arising out of Greenpeace's 2015 "Stop Shell" campaign.[6] These issues

---

[5] Greenpeace also argues that the appeal is not moot because the preliminary injunction order raised issues on the merits that "could affect the future of litigation in the district court." This argument ignores the rule that "the findings of fact and conclusions of law made by a court granting a preliminary injunction are not binding at trial on the merits." *Univ. of Tex. v. Camenisch*, 451 U.S. 390, 395 (1981). The validity of the preliminary injunction may become an issue in future district court proceedings—but at this point, that is only speculation. We thus leave it to the district court to address the remaining merits issues in the first instance.

[6] For example, in Paragraph 4 of the Complaint's Requests for Relief, Shell prays for "[a]n award of damages including incidental damages for all economic harm resulting from the tortious actions of Greenpeace Inc. and the individual defendants, and economic harm to Shell as a result of tortious actions by others with whom Greenpeace Inc. is acting in concert."

were not settled—or mooted—either by the expiration of the preliminary injunction or by Shell's announcement that it has cancelled further exploration in the Arctic. Whether and to what extent Greenpeace injured Shell in the course of its 2015 "Stop Shell" campaign remains a live controversy as to which the district court retains the jurisdiction to award appropriate [—15—] relief, if a finding of liability is made. We leave it to the district court to consider Shell's remaining claims in the first instance on remand.

III. CONCLUSION

This appeal is moot, and therefore must be dismissed. Accordingly, we also vacate the district court's July 30, 2015, Contempt Order. The case is remanded for further proceedings consistent with this opinion. Each side shall bear its own costs on appeal.

DISMISSED and REMANDED.

United States Court of Appeals
for the Ninth Circuit

No. 13-56762

MCINDOE
VS.
BATH IRON WORKS CORP.

Appeal from the United States District Court for the
Central District of California

Decided: March 31, 2016

Citation: 817 F.3d 1170, 4 Adm. R. 380 (9th Cir. 2016).

Before **KOZINSKI**, **O'SCANNLAIN**, and **BYBEE**, Circuit Judges.

[—4—] O'SCANNLAIN, Circuit Judge:

We must decide whether two naval warships are "products" for the purposes of strict products liability and whether a genuine issue of fact exists as to whether asbestos-containing materials originally installed upon such ships caused a decedent's injuries.

I

In the 1960s, James McIndoe served aboard two U.S. Naval ships which contained pipe insulation made from asbestos. From 1961–1963, he served aboard the *USS Coral Sea*, an aircraft carrier built by a predecessor in interest to [—5—] Huntington Ingalls Inc. (Huntington) and commissioned in 1947. From 1966–1967, he served aboard the *USS Worden*, a guided missile cruiser built by Bath Iron Works Corporation (Bath) and commissioned in 1963. Aboard each ship, McIndoe was allegedly present during maintenance work involving the removal of pipe insulation that caused asbestos fibers to float in the air he breathed.

On September 27, 2011, McIndoe died from complications related to mesothelioma, a form of cancer closely associated with asbestos exposure. Plaintiffs-Appellants are McIndoe's legal heirs, who filed suit in California state court against Bath and Huntington,[1] arguing that McIndoe's exposure to asbestos-containing materials aboard their ships contributed to his death. McIndoe's heirs raised design, manufacture, and failure-to-warn claims based on theories of both strict products liability and general negligence. The case was removed to federal district court under 28 U.S.C. § 1442(a)(1), where Bath and Huntington each moved for summary judgment. The district court granted both motions on the grounds that the ships were not products for purposes of strict liability and that the heirs could not establish a genuine issue of material fact regarding whether the shipbuilders were responsible for installing any asbestos-containing insulation that caused McIndoe's injuries. McIndoe's heirs timely appealed, and these cases have been consolidated before our court. [—6—]

II

We review de novo a district court's grant of summary judgment, and, "viewing the evidence in the light most favorable to the nonmoving party, [determine] whether there are any genuine issues of material fact and whether the district court correctly applied the relevant substantive law." *Colwell v. Bannister*, 763 F.3d 1060, 1065 (9th Cir. 2014) (internal quotation marks omitted). "[T]here is no issue for trial unless there is sufficient evidence favoring the nonmoving party for a jury to return a verdict for that party. If the evidence is merely colorable, or is not significantly probative, summary judgment may be granted." *R.W. Beck & Assocs. v. City & Borough of Sitka*, 27 F.3d 1475, 1480 n.4 (9th Cir. 1994) (internal quotation marks omitted). "Arguments based on conjecture or speculation are insufficient . . . ." *Id.*

Federal maritime law—"an amalgam of traditional common-law rules, modifications of those rules, and newly created rules"— governs this case. *E. River S.S. Corp. v. Transamerica Delaval Inc.*, 476 U.S. 858, 865 (1986); *see Wallis v. Princess Cruises, Inc.*, 306 F.3d 827, 840 (9th Cir. 2002) (federal

---

[1] The lawsuit also named a number of other defendants who are not parties to this appeal.

maritime law applies to torts that occur on navigable water and bear a substantial relationship to traditional maritime activity).

III

McIndoe's heirs first argue that Bath and Huntington should be held strictly liable for defects in materials originally installed on the ships they built. The Supreme Court has recognized that federal maritime law incorporates actions for products liability, including those that sound in [—7—] strict liability. *E. River S.S. Corp.*, 476 U.S. at 865. The question whether a naval warship is to be considered a "product" in this context, however, appears to be one of first impression for the federal courts of appeals.

When analyzing products-liability claims under maritime law, we look to the Restatement of Torts (the "Restatement")—particularly the most recent Third Restatement—for guidance. *Oswalt v. Resolute Indus., Inc.*, 642 F.3d 856, 860 (9th Cir. 2011); *see also Saratoga Fishing Co. v. J.M. Martinac & Co.*, 520 U.S. 875, 879 (1997) (citing both Second and Third Restatements in evaluating maritime products-liability action). The Third Restatement defines a "product" subject to strict liability as "tangible personal property *distributed commercially* for use or consumption." Restatement (Third) of Torts: Prods. Liab. § 19(a) (Am. Law Inst. 1998) (emphasis added). "[O]nly when the complained of injury was allegedly caused by a defect in something within this . . . definition of 'product' should the defendant manufacturer or seller be strictly liable for the harm caused." *Id.* § 19 reporter's note, cmt. a. Injuries caused by other items are actionable only "under negligence, misrepresentation, or some other liability theory." *Id.*

By these terms, the Restatement would exclude warships that were never "distributed commercially" from the realm of strict products liability. This makes sense. The general aim of strict liability is to "plac[e] responsibility on the . . . party most able to prevent harm" caused by dangerous products and thus to incentivize proper "design and quality control" of such products. *All Alaskan*

Seafoods, Inc. v. Raychem Corp., 197 F.3d 992, 995 (9th Cir. 1999) (citing Third Restatement). Therefore, "strict liability should be imposed on the party best able to protect persons from hazardous equipment." *E.* [—8—] *River S.S. Corp.*, 476 U.S. at 866. These goals would be advanced little by imposing liability on the builder of a custom-ordered naval ship. As evidence submitted in this case suggests, a ship built under government contract[2] may not even be designed by the builder but instead by the government itself or another outside professional. Further, the shipbuilder does not manufacture—and has little ability to control the quality of—the many thousands of component parts installed on each ship, let alone to account in its pricing for the virtually unlimited liability that would flow from a rule holding it strictly liable for their dangers. We do not believe that federal maritime law—the primary goal of which is to protect and to promote the "smooth flow of maritime commerce," *Foremost Ins. Co. v. Richardson*, 457 U.S. 668, 674–76 (1982)—would countenance such a sweeping grant of liability. *See generally Mack v. Gen. Elec. Co.*, 896 F. Supp. 2d 333, 344–46 (E.D. Pa. 2012) (discussing principles of strict liability and maritime law).

We therefore agree with the district court that McIndoe's heirs cannot sustain an action for strict products liability premised upon the notion that the warships in question are [—9—] themselves "products" under maritime law.[3] Accordingly, the heirs may prevail only under a theory of negligence.

---

[2] McIndoe's heirs do not dispute that Bath and Huntington built the relevant ships pursuant to government contract.

[3] We express no opinion on the circumstances under which a commercially distributed or mass-produced vessel would qualify as a "product" under maritime law. McIndoe's heirs cite cases in which the manufacturers of such vessels have been held strictly liable for their flaws. But such vessels enter the general stream of commerce in a way custom-built vessels do not, and thus the cases cited say little for the standards that should govern liability for the naval shipbuilders at issue here. *See generally* Restatement (Third) of Torts: Prods. Liab. § 19 cmt. e. (Am. Law Inst. 1998) (distinguishing pre-fabricated or mass-produced homes from those

IV

We turn to the heirs' general negligence claims. To prevail on such claims, they must demonstrate, among other things, that McIndoe's injuries were caused by exposure to asbestos that was attributable to the shipbuilders' conduct. To do so, McIndoe's heirs must be able to show both that he was actually exposed to asbestos-containing materials that were installed by the shipbuilders and that such exposure was a substantial contributing factor in causing his injuries. *Lindstrom v. A-C Prod. Liab. Tr.*, 424 F.3d 488, 492 (6th Cir. 2005). We examine each requirement in turn.

A

First, McIndoe's heirs must show that he was exposed to asbestos from materials that Bath or Huntington installed aboard the *Coral Sea* and *Worden*. The heirs do not claim [—10—] that the shipbuilders were responsible for replacing or maintaining such insulation after the ships were commissioned. Therefore, they must show exposure to asbestos from materials that were *originally* installed aboard the ships. The heirs seek to demonstrate McIndoe's asbestos exposure through the first-hand observations of two lay witnesses and, based on these observations, the opinion of one purported expert.

Regarding the *USS Coral Sea* (built by Huntington and commissioned in 1947), McIndoe's heirs offered a declaration of Brian Tench, who boarded the ship as an ensign in 1961 and spent significant time with McIndoe in engineering spaces of the ship. Tench testified that there were insulated steam pipes throughout the engineering spaces in which he worked with McIndoe; that "[b]ased on his training and experience," he knew such insulation contained asbestos;[4] that, he saw

McIndoe in the area of others removing asbestos-containing insulation on 20–30 different occasions; and that the removal of the insulation created "large amounts of visible dust" in the air McIndoe breathed. Tench states that he knows some of the removed pipe insulation was original to the ship because he could tell from the thickness of the paint on the insulation that it had been painted 6–8 times, indicating to him that it must have been aboard the ship for some time. [—11—]

Regarding the *USS Worden* (built by Bath and commissioned in 1963), McIndoe's heirs offered a declaration of Thomas Sappington, who boarded the ship in 1964 and worked for two years in one of the ship's fire rooms. Sappington declared that there were thousands of feet of insulated pipe in the fire rooms; that McIndoe was "often" present when maintenance was performed, which involved the removal of pipe insulation; and that the process of removing the insulation created visible dust in the air McIndoe breathed. Much like Tench, Sappington declared that he could distinguish the ship's original pipe insulation from later-installed replacement insulation based on visible seams between new and old insulation and on variances in the thickness of their paint,[5] and that he believes much of the insulation removed in McIndoe's presence was original to the ship.

McIndoe's heirs built upon these accounts through the declaration of Charles Ay, a professional asbestos consultant who worked aboard hundreds of naval ships as a pipe insulator in the 1960s–1980s. Ay stated that, based on his experience, he knew that insulation used on high-pressure pipelines in Naval ships built in the 1940s–1960s always contained asbestos; that nearly half of all originally installed insulation aboard such

---

which are built and sold "one house at a time"); *see also Stark v. Armstrong World Indus., Inc.*, 21 F. App'x 371, 378 n.6 (6th Cir. Oct. 3, 2001) ("[Custom-built] vessels resemble custom-designed houses, which are also not likely to be considered 'products' under the Restatement.").

[4] It is not clear from Tench's declaration how he obtained this knowledge, other than his conclusory

statements that he came to learn it. And there is some reason to doubt that Tench's knowledge could be established at trial, given his statement that he relied at least partly on statements of others who said that the insulation contained asbestos.

[5] Like Tench, Sappington also refers to statements of others who told him which sections of insulation had been replaced and which were original.

vessels was not removed during the life of the ship; that during McIndoe's time aboard the *Coral Sea*, at least 70 percent of the original asbestos-containing insulation would have remained; that during McIndoe's time aboard the *Worden*, "virtually all" of the original insulation would have remained; and that he personally saw thousands [—12—] of lineal feet of asbestos-containing pipe insulation while working as an insulator aboard each ship (in the mid-1960s on the *Worden* and the 1970s on the *Coral Sea*). Based on his experience and the statements of Tench and Sappington, Ay concluded that it is "virtually impossible" that McIndoe would have avoided being exposed to asbestos dust from original insulation during his time aboard each ship.

We agree with the district court that the evidence that McIndoe was exposed to asbestos originally installed by the shipbuilders is not especially strong. The only direct evidence presented to support the claim that such insulation was removed in McIndoe's presence is the rather implausible testimony of Tench and Sappington that, nearly 50 years later, they recall the thickness of the paint on the removed insulation to such a degree that they can surmise the age of the insulation. To these direct accounts, Ay can add only his speculation as to what materials a person in McIndoe's position would have encountered, with no actual knowledge of McIndoe's activities aboard the ships. Nevertheless, viewing these statements in the light most favorable to the plaintiffs, *Colwell*, 763 F.3d at 1065, we conclude that a jury *could* determine that McIndoe was exposed to originally installed asbestos, even if it seems unlikely that a jury *would* do so. Such evidence therefore creates a genuine issue of fact regarding whether McIndoe was at least exposed to asbestos from the shipbuilders' materials.

B

But even if the evidence may establish that McIndoe was actually exposed to asbestos installed by the shipbuilders, his heirs still must show that any such exposure was a *substantial* [—13—] *contributing factor* to his injuries.[6] *Lindstrom*, 424 F.3d at 492.

1

Absent direct evidence of causation, a party may satisfy the substantial-factor test by demonstrating that the injured person had substantial exposure to the relevant asbestos for a substantial period of time. *See id.; see also Menne v. Celotex Corp.*, 861 F.2d 1453, 1462 (10th Cir. 1988) ("More significant under traditional causation tests than the question of mere exposure to [asbestos-containing] products is whether the exposure was sufficiently sustained (or frequent) and intense to constitute a proximate cause of [the plaintiff's] mesothelioma."). Evidence of only minimal exposure to asbestos is insufficient; there must be "a high enough level of exposure that an inference that the asbestos was a substantial factor in the injury is more than conjectural." *Lindstrom*, 424 F.3d at 492 (internal quotation marks omitted).

McIndoe's heirs failed to put forward such evidence here. Even crediting the assertions of their two first-hand [—14—] witnesses, at most the heirs have provided evidence that McIndoe was "frequently" present during the removal of insulation aboard the *Worden* and was present 20–30 times during such removal aboard the *Coral Sea*. But, as the district court found, even if McIndoe was around asbestos dust several times, his heirs presented no evidence regarding the *amount*

---

[6] *Lindstrom*, from the Sixth Circuit, appears to be the only federal Court of Appeals decision to consider squarely the causation standard applicable to asbestos claims under maritime law. But the Sixth Circuit's analysis comports with the general approach taken by other federal courts in asbestos cases, and we agree with the district court and the parties that such standard governs our analysis. *See also Benefiel v. Exxon Corp.*, 959 F.2d 805, 807 (9th Cir. 1992) (applying "substantial factor" requirement to maritime tort); *Curtis v. ABB Inc.*, 622 F. App'x 661 (9th Cir. Nov. 13, 2015) (mem.) (applying *Lindstrom* to asbestos claim); Restatement (Third) of Torts: Liab. for Physical & Emotional Harm § 36, reporter's note, cmt. b (Am. Law Inst. 2010) (citing numerous jurisdictions that employ the substantial-factor standard to limit scope of liability in asbestos cases).

of exposure to dust from originally installed asbestos, or critically, the *duration* of such exposure during any of these incidents. Without such facts, McIndoe's heirs can only speculate as to the actual extent of his exposure to asbestos from the shipbuilder's materials. At this stage, more is needed. *See Cafasso v. Gen. Dynamics C4 Sys., Inc.*, 637 F.3d 1047, 1061 (9th Cir. 2011); *R.W. Beck & Assocs.*, 27 F.3d at 1480 n.4.

2

The heirs do not seriously contend that they provided evidence demonstrating that McIndoe suffered substantial exposure to originally installed asbestos for a substantial period of time. Instead, they argue that evidence of prolonged exposure is not needed, because they presented the opinion of Dr. Allen Raybin—a medical expert who asserted that *every* exposure to asbestos above a threshold level is necessarily a substantial factor in the contraction of asbestos-related diseases.

The district court properly rejected this argument. McIndoe's heirs appear to have introduced Dr. Raybin's testimony and his "every exposure" theory of asbestos causation to reject the substantial-factor test as a whole. Dr. Raybin did not speak to the severity of McIndoe's own asbestos exposure beyond the basic assertion that such exposure was significantly above ambient asbestos levels. [—15—] More critically, Dr. Raybin did not speak to the severity of McIndoe's exposure to *originally installed* asbestos—and generally did not make distinctions between the overall dose of asbestos McIndoe breathed aboard the ships and that portion of such exposure which could be attributed to the shipbuilders' materials.[7] Likewise, Dr. Raybin did not

opine on the *effect* of McIndoe's actual exposure to the shipbuilders' asbestos-containing materials, except in the broadest sense. Namely, while Dr. Raybin concluded that the exposures described by Sappington and Tench would have substantially contributed to McIndoe's injuries, he explicitly and directly based such conclusion on his "each and every exposure" theory of causation. Taken together, Dr. Raybin's testimony aims more to establish a legal conclusion—what general level of asbestos exposure is required to show disease causation—than to establish the facts of McIndoe's own injuries.

McIndoe's heirs cite no case approving the use of such a sweeping opinion to satisfy causation under maritime law. Indeed, in *Lindstrom*, the Sixth Circuit explicitly rejected an argument similar to the heirs', concluding that such a theory of liability would render the substantial-factor test essentially meaningless. *See* 424 F.3d at 493. Allowing causation to be established through testimony like Dr. Raybin's would "permit imposition of liability on the manufacturer of any [—16—] [asbestos-containing] product with which a worker had the briefest of encounters on a single occasion." *Id.* This is precisely the sort of unbounded liability that the substantial factor test was developed to limit. *See* Restatement (Third) of Torts: Liab. for Physical & Emotional Harm § 36 reporter's note, cmt. b (Am. Law Inst. 2010). Because the heirs' argument would undermine the substantial factor standard and, in turn, significantly broaden asbestos liability based on fleeting or insignificant encounters with a defendant's product, we, too, reject it.[8]

---

[7] To the extent that Dr. Raybin attempted to assert that the encounters described by Tench and Sappington "are high level exposures that occurred for a prolonged period of time," he had no basis on which to do so. As described above, Tench and Sappington failed to provide information regarding the intensity or duration of McIndoe's alleged exposures to originally installed asbestos aboard the *Worden* and *Coral Sea*; McIndoe's heirs cannot

rely on a third-party expert to fill in those percipient gaps for them.

[8] As the Sixth Circuit acknowledged, rejection of this argument still allows a plaintiff to satisfy causation through expert testimony that the plaintiff's actual exposure to certain materials substantially contributed to the development of his injuries. It simply prevents the type of sweeping testimony offered here—that *all* exposures to asbestos above background levels necessarily and substantially contribute to development of diseases like mesothelioma. *See Lindstrom*, 424 F.3d at 493.

Notwithstanding the declaration of Dr. Raybin, McIndoe's heirs failed to put forward evidence demonstrating that McIndoe was substantially exposed to asbestos from the shipbuilders' materials for a substantial period of time. The heirs have established no genuine issue of fact regarding whether any such exposure was a substantial factor in McIndoe's injuries, and thus they cannot prevail on their general negligence claims.[9] *See Lindstrom*, 424 F.3d at 492–93. [—17—]

V

The judgment of the district court is **AFFIRMED**.

---

[9] Because we conclude that McIndoe's heirs cannot establish a prima facie case for their claims, we do not consider the shipbuilders' asserted affirmative defenses.

United States Court of Appeals
for the Ninth Circuit

No. 13-72929

SSA TERMINALS
vs.
CARRION

On Petition for Review of an Order of the Benefits
Review Board

Decided: May 11, 2016

Citation: 821 F.3d 1168, 4 Adm. R. 386 (9th Cir. 2016).

Before **MCKEOWN, RAWLINSON,** and **DAVIS,** * Circuit
Judges.

* The Honorable Andre M. Davis, Senior Circuit
Judge for the U.S. Court of Appeals for the Fourth
Circuit, sitting by designation.

[—4—] MCKEOWN, Circuit Judge:

In 1987, Robert Carrion sustained a severe knee injury while working as a chassis mechanic. Although Carrion returned to his physically demanding job and worked for the next fifteen years, his knee continued to deteriorate. He took early retirement in 2002, when his pain became so great that he could walk only with difficulty. After Carrion's former employer ceased paying for treatment, he filed for disability under the Longshore and Harbor Workers' Compensation Act ("LHWCA" or "the Longshore Act"), 33 U.S.C. § 901 *et seq.*

By the time he filed his claims in 2008, Carrion had endured decades of persistent pain without any actual or [—5—] expected improvement. Without doubt, he was disabled, and his doctors unanimously concluded that he eventually would require total knee replacement surgery. Even though no surgery was on the horizon, his employer classified the injury as a temporary disability. The question we address is whether, after such a protracted period of disability, the prospect of a hypothetical future surgery and its anticipated benefits can transform an otherwise permanent disability into a temporary one for purposes of the Longshore Act. We hold that it cannot.

BACKGROUND

Carrion tore his right medial meniscus and right anterior cruciate ligament in January 1987 while working for Matson Terminals, Inc. ("Matson"). Although Carrion returned to work, his knee continued to deteriorate and he has endured persistent pain ever since. After Carrion's injury, SSA Marine Terminals ("SSA") took over Matson. Carrion became an SSA employee, but Matson continued paying for his knee treatments. Carrion took early retirement in 2002. At that point, the medial joint space in his knee was "completely gone." His treating physician, Dr. Caldwell, advised him that he would eventually require a total knee replacement, but recommended that Carrion forgo the surgery until his symptoms worsened.

Four years later, Matson stopped authorizing payments for Carrion's knee treatments. In the spring of 2008, Carrion filed claims against both Matson and SSA seeking benefits under the LHWCA. He listed the date of his cumulative knee injury as February 28, 2002—his retirement date. [—6—]

Dr. Stark, an expert hired by Matson, examined Carrion in September of 2008. Like Dr. Caldwell, Dr. Stark concluded that Carrion required total knee replacement surgery. Dr. Stark also diagnosed Carrion's knee condition as the result of both a "natural progression of [his] degenerative arthritis and also [the] cumulative trauma" he experienced in his physically demanding work. One year later, SSA hired Dr. von Rogov, who similarly concluded, after examination, that Carrion would need total knee replacement surgery. In Dr. von Rogov's view, Carrion's condition was solely the result of the "natural progression of the January [8] 1987 injury," since he would have required a total knee replacement after that trauma even if he had only undertaken sedentary activities since that time. At the time of the administrative hearing in 2009, Carrion was in pain "all day and all night," but had not yet received a knee replacement.

The Administrative Law Judge ("ALJ") determined that Carrion did not learn of the causal connection between his work for SSA and his cumulative trauma injury until he received Dr. Stark's 2008 report. Carrion thus filed his claim against SSA within the one-year statute of limitations governing claims under the LHWCA. Noting that "[a]t first blush, it seems [Carrion's] injury is permanent," and acknowledging that Carrion's "condition has lasted for a long period of time," the ALJ nevertheless concluded that Carrion's disability was temporary. The ALJ reasoned that Carrion was contemplating knee replacement surgery, which his doctors agreed would likely alleviate his symptoms, and thus "medical improvement through the knee replacement was available" once "his pain became too much." The ALJ noted, however, that if Carrion decided against surgery and [—7—] opted to "live with the knee pain indefinitely, he would be found permanently disabled."

SSA appealed the ALJ's timeliness determination to the Benefits Review Board ("BRB" or "the Board"), and Carrion cross-appealed the ALJ's finding that his disability was temporary. The BRB affirmed the ALJ on both issues. We review the Board's decisions "for errors of law and for adherence to the substantial evidence standard. . . . On questions of law, including interpretations of the LHWCA, we exercise de novo review." *Gen. Constr. Co. v. Castro*, 401 F.3d 963, 965 (9th Cir. 2005) (internal quotations and citations omitted).

ANALYSIS

The threshold inquiry is whether Carrion timely filed his claim. The Longshore Act imposes a one-year statute of limitations on disability claims, which begins to run once the employee is, or should be, aware "of the relationship between the injury . . . and the employment." 33 U.S.C. § 913(a). We have explained that § 913(a) contemplates an impairment of earning power, and thus an employee only becomes aware of an injury for statutory purposes when he becomes "aware of the full character, extent, and impact of the harm done to him." *Todd Shipyards Corp. v. Allan*, 666 F.2d 399, 401–02 (9th Cir. 1982) (quotations omitted).

Both the ALJ and the BRB correctly applied this standard by looking to the date when Carrion became aware that his work for SSA caused a second, cumulative traumatic injury resulting in an impairment of his earning power. Substantial evidence supports the conclusion that Carrion did not "become aware of the full character, extent, and impact of the [—8—] harm done to him" until he received Dr. Stark's report, several months after Carrion filed his claim against SSA.

Before seeing Dr. Stark's evaluation, Carrion had no understanding of the medical principle of cumulative trauma. Carrion's treating physician, Dr. Caldwell, testified that he never explained the concept of cumulative trauma to Carrion, and as the ALJ noted, a layperson would not understand that "the incremental erosion or worsening of a knee condition can be the basis for a cumulative trauma claim." Even after Carrion became an SSA employee in 1999, Matson continued paying for Carrion's knee treatments, thus reinforcing Carrion's reasonable belief that his disability was solely the result of the trauma he sustained in 1987. Indeed, SSA's own expert, Dr. von Rogov, initially concluded that Carrion's disability was solely attributable to the 1987 injury. Although Carrion experienced ongoing pain and required ongoing medical treatment, those circumstances alone are insufficient to establish knowledge of a cumulative trauma. *See, e.g., Abel v. Dir., Office of Workers' Comp. Programs*, 932 F.2d 819, 823 (9th Cir. 1991) (claimant's recurring pain and persistent symptoms insufficient to establish awareness of injury for purposes of § 913(a)); *J.M. Martinac Shipbuilding v. Dir., Office of Workers' Comp. Programs (Grage)*, 900 F.2d 180, 184 (9th Cir. 1990) (claimant's pain and other symptoms did not establish awareness of a compensable injury). We thus affirm the BRB's decision upholding the ALJ's conclusion that Carrion timely filed his claim against SSA.

With this issue resolved, we turn to the crux of this appeal: whether Carrion's knee injury was a temporary or permanent disability. The Longshore Act creates "two independent areas of analysis," one assessing the nature, or [—9—] duration, (temporary versus permanent) and the other the degree of the disability (partial versus total). *Pac. Ship Repair & Fabrication, Inc. v. Dir., Office of Workers' Comp. Programs (Benge)*, 687 F.3d 1182, 1185 (9th Cir. 2012) (quoting *Stevens v. Dir., Office of Workers' Comp. Programs*, 909 F.2d 1256, 1259 (9th Cir. 1990)). Four separate disability categories stem from this framework: permanent total disability; temporary total disability; permanent partial disability; and temporary partial disability. 33 U.S.C. § 908(a)–(c), (e). Two of these qualifiers, permanent and temporary, "go to the nature of the disability." *Benge*, 687 F.3d at 1185 (quoting *Stevens*, 909 F.2d at 1259). Only the nature of Carrion's disability is at issue here.

Curiously, the Longshore Act does not define "temporary" or "permanent," although the classification issue arises on a continuing basis. We have held that "[a] disability is temporary 'so long as there [is] a possibility or likelihood of improvement through normal and natural healing.'" *Castro*, 401 F.3d at 968 (quoting *Stevens*, 909 F.2d at 1259) (second alteration in original). A disability may become permanent if (1) a claimant reaches "maximum medical improvement"—the point at which "the injury has healed to the full extent possible" and normal and natural healing is no longer likely, *Stevens*, 909 F.2d at 1257 (citing *Watson v. Gulf Stevedore Corp.*, 400 F.2d 649, 654 (5th Cir. 1968)); or (2) the condition has "continued for a lengthy period, and it appears to be of lasting or indefinite duration, as distinguished from one in which recovery merely awaits a normal healing period." *Watson*, 400 F.2d at 654.

The *Watson* test clarifies that "permanent" is not tantamount to "eternal" or "everlasting" and "does not foreclose the possibility that [the] condition may change." *Id.* [—10—] at 654–55. In accordance with this rationale, a disability may be categorized as permanent even if it is not medically incurable. *Pittsburgh & Conneaut Dock Co. v. Dir., Office of Workers' Comp. Programs*, 473 F.3d 253, 259–60 (6th Cir. 2007) (upholding determination that disability was permanent under *Watson* where cognitive limitations had lasted more than a year and a half longer than

typical recovery period, despite evidence of potential for improvement with psychotherapy). Under either test, the question is whether the disability will resolve after a normal and natural healing period. If the answer is yes, the disability is temporary. If the answer is no, the disability is permanent.

Neither the permanent nor the temporary classification is necessarily static. In *Benge*, we considered whether a disability classified as permanent could be reclassified as temporary. Despite the "common-sense and linguistic appeal" of "[t]he notion that a 'permanent' disability is immutable," we held that "[a] disability initially deemed permanent is not immutably so." 687 F.3d at 1185–86. Thus, we reasoned, "healing related to a flare up, relapse, surgery, or other major treatment could" transform a permanent disability into a temporary one, as the "vicissitudes of the individual's responsiveness to medical treatment" lead to a "new and unknown maximum medical improvement point." *Id.* at 1186–87. As a practical matter, the start of a new "healing period functions as a 'reset' button for a disability previously-determined to be permanent." *Id.* at 1186.

Benge's logic dictates our answer to the question of whether the prospect of future surgery rendered Carrion's disability temporary. Absent the contingency of future surgery, Carrion's disability would unequivocally be permanent. From the time of his injury until his hearing, [—11—] Carrion lived with constant, debilitating pain. He had no hope of normal or natural healing, only an expectation of further deterioration and the theoretical possibility of improvement through a still-distant surgery. Even the ALJ acknowledged that if Carrion "decided to forgo the surgical option and live with the knee pain indefinitely, he would be found permanently disabled."

Nevertheless, the ALJ concluded that Carrion's "condition is not one of lasting or indefinite duration because the symptoms will likely be diminished through surgery," and found that Carrion "is temporarily disabled because he is seeking surgery to improve his condition."[1] Evaluating an individual's condition based on the presumed effect of a theoretical future treatment makes scant sense—particularly in light of the "vicissitudes of the individual's responsiveness to medical treatment." *Id.* at 1186–87. For example, an anticipated surgery or course of treatment may never come to pass if an individual develops a heart condition, becomes immuno-compromised, or simply concludes that the risks of the procedure outweigh the benefits. Worse yet, a claimant might die without ever having the surgery. Alternatively, advances in medical therapies and technologies could lead to more successful medical interventions for chronic conditions, which in turn could lead to new periods of healing and "a new [—12—] and unknown maximum medical improvement point" for the patient. *Id.* at 1186. Accordingly, the appropriate question to ask is not whether a future surgery would ameliorate Carrion's knee condition, but whether there was actual or expected improvement to his knee after a normal and natural healing period.

The impact of a future knee replacement should be assessed after the surgery, not in anticipation of such a contingency. Importantly, the Longshore Act permits modifications of disability awards to account for just such changed circumstances. *See* 33 U.S.C. § 922 ("[O]n the ground of a change in conditions . . . the deputy commissioner may . . . issue a new compensation order which may terminate, continue, reinstate, increase, or decrease" compensation, within certain time limits).

SSA additionally claims that Carrion waived his argument that his disability is permanent because he did not raise it until his post-hearing brief before the ALJ and then only as an alternative argument. This argument need not detain us long.

"The administrative waiver doctrine, commonly referred to as issue exhaustion, provides that it is inappropriate for courts reviewing agency decisions to consider arguments not raised before the administrative agency involved." *Coal. for Gov't Procurement v. Fed. Prison Indus., Inc.*, 365 F.3d 435, 461–62 (6th Cir. 2004) (citing *United States v. L.A. Tucker Truck Lines, Inc.*, 344 U.S. 33, 37 (1952)). But, the doctrines of exhaustion and waiver "are not designed to extinguish claims which, although not comprehensively or artfully presented in the early stages of the administrative process, are presented fully before the process ends." *Getty Oil Co. v. Andrus*, 607 F.2d 253, 256 (9th Cir. 1979). [—13—]

The question of whether Carrion was permanently disabled did not spring up on appeal. Rather, in his post-hearing brief before the ALJ, Carrion argued that he was permanently disabled. The ALJ devoted nearly two-and-a-half pages to this argument. The issue was squarely presented to the BRB, which reviewed the ALJ's rejection of permanent disability. If the agency "actually addressed [the] issue, the policies underlying the exhaustion doctrine . . . are satisfied." *W. Radio Servs., Co. v. Qwest Corp.*, 530 F.3d 1186, 1203 (9th Cir. 2008); *see also Abebe v. Gonzales*, 432 F.3d 1037, 1041 (9th Cir. 2005) (en banc) (holding that an issue is exhausted when an agency considers and decides it, even if petitioner failed to raise the issue before the agency). Because Carrion presented his claim of permanent disability well before the conclusion of the administrative process and neither SSA nor the agency were blindsided by the argument, we conclude that the doctrines of exhaustion and waiver are inapplicable. *See Abel*, 932 F.2d at 821.

Costs on appeal shall be awarded to Respondents.

---

[1] Both the ALJ and the Board cited several BRB decisions categorizing disabilities as temporary where surgery was anticipated. In these cases, however, surgery was either imminent or the claimants' disabilities had not persisted for prolonged periods without actual or expected improvement. In relying on these cases, the ALJ and the Board neglected to consider that Carrion's disability persisted for years without any expectation of "normal or natural healing." Under such circumstances, the mere prospect of eventual surgery cannot transform an otherwise undeniably permanent disability into a temporary one.

PETITION DENIED AND CROSS-PETITION GRANTED.

United States Court of Appeals for the Ninth Circuit

No. 14-71512

FENSKE

vs.

SERVICE EMPLOYEES INT'L, INC.

On Petition for Review of an Order of the Benefits Review Board

Decided: August 26, 2016*

Citation: 835 F.3d 978, 4 Adm. R. 391 (9th Cir. 2016).

Before **NOONAN, WARDLAW,** and **PAEZ,** Circuit Judges.

* The panel unanimously concludes this case is suitable for decision without oral argument. *See* Fed. R. App. 34(a)(2).

[—4—] NOONAN, Circuit Judge:

James Fenske petitions for review of a decision of the Benefits Review Board of the Department of Labor (the "Board") holding that Fenske could not receive concurrent payments for total disability and permanent partial disability under the Longshore and Harbor Workers' Compensation Act (the "Act"), 33 U.S.C. §§ 901–50. While we generally disallow concurrent awards, Fenske seeks relief under our holding in *Stevedoring Servs. of Am. v. Price*, 382 F.3d 878 (9th Cir. 2004) (as amended) ("*Price*"), which allows concurrent awards for certain time-delayed injuries. We deny Fenske's petition for review of the Board's decision.

FACTS AND PROCEEDINGS

James Fenske was a truck driver for a United States government contractor in Iraq during the Iraq War. On October 9, 2005, a suicide bomber in a vehicle collided head-on with the truck Fenske was driving. The bomb did not explode, but Fenske suffered severe injuries to his lower back from the collision. This accident ended Fenske's tour in Iraq.

Fenske sought compensation under the Act for his injuries. An Administrative Law Judge ("ALJ") awarded Fenske temporary total disability benefits from October 9, 2005 until July 27, 2008, followed by permanent partial disability benefits. The ALJ later granted Fenske's petition to modify the award, granting him permanent total disability benefits, rather than partial disability benefits, from July 28, 2008 onwards. [—5—]

During the proceedings, Fenske also presented an audiogram from June 4, 2009, which showed hearing loss in both ears. The parties stipulated to a 9.7% permanent loss of hearing and the ALJ found that the hearing loss was caused by Fenske's work in Iraq. The ALJ held that under the Board's precedent, concurrent payments for the hearing loss were unavailable because Fenske was already receiving compensation for total disability. *See B.S. (Stinson) v. Bath Iron Works Corp.*, 41 BRBS 97 (2007); *Johnson v. Del Monte Tropical Fruit Co.*, 45 BRBS 27 (2011).

Fenske appealed to the Board, which upheld the ALJ's decision denying concurrent payments. Fenske now petitions for review of the Board's decision.

STANDARD OF REVIEW

We review the Board's decisions on questions of law de novo. *Price*, 382 F.3d at 883. The Board reviews the ALJ's factual findings for substantial evidence and we review the Board to ensure it applied that standard. *Todd Shipyards Corp. v. Dir., OWCP*, 792 F.2d 1489, 1491 (9th Cir. 1986).

We review the litigation position of the Director of the Office of Workers' Compensation Programs with some deference under *Skidmore v. Swift & Co.*, 323 U.S. 134 (1944), and *United States v. Mead Corp.*, 533 U.S. 218 (2001). *Price v. Stevedoring Servs. of Am.*, 697 F.3d 820, 824–33 (9th Cir. 2012) (en banc) ("*Price II*"). The degree of deference we provide the government depends on "the thoroughness evident in its consideration, the validity of its reasoning, its consistency with earlier and later pronouncements, and all those factors which give it power to [—6—] persuade, if lacking power to control." *Skidmore*, 323 U.S. at 140.

DISCUSSION

I

Fenske seeks concurrent compensation for a "scheduled" injury (hearing loss) under 33 U.S.C. § 908(c)(13) and total disability caused by his back injury. Under the Act, a worker suffering permanent or temporary total disability is entitled to two-thirds of his or her weekly wage during the continuance of the disability. *Id.* § 908(a), (b). Similarly, a worker suffering a permanent partial disability under 33 U.S.C. § 908(c)(21) is entitled to two-thirds of his or her lost wage-earning capacity for the continuance of the disability.

"Scheduled" losses, in contrast, are a set of common statutorily-enumerated permanent partial disabilities, such as hearing loss, that are compensated at two-thirds of a worker's weekly wages for a number of weeks prescribed by statute. *See id.* § 908(c)(1)–(20); *see, e.g., id.* § 908(c)(13)(B) ("Compensation for loss of hearing in both ears, two-hundred weeks."). The length of compensation is proportionally shorter if the loss is not complete: a 25% loss of hearing requires only fifty rather than two-hundred weeks of payment. *See id.* § 908(c)(19).

We have generally denied concurrent payments involving total disability because the Act "invokes wage-compensation principles rather than tort principles." *Rupert v. Todd Shipyards Corp.*, 239 F.2d 273, 274–77 (9th Cir. 1956) (per curiam) (denying concurrent payments for permanent total [—7—] disability and facial disfigurement, a scheduled loss under § 908(c)(20)). While tort principles seek to compensate a plaintiff for every injury wrongfully suffered, *see Memphis Cmty. Sch. Dist. v. Stachura*, 477 U.S. 299, 306–07 (1986); Dan B. Dobbs, et al., *The Law of Torts* § 10 (2d ed. 2016), wage-compensation principles repay workers for lost earning capacity, not the injury itself. Once a worker has lost all earning capacity through total disability, an additional award would constitute "double dipping," that is, the worker would be compensated "for a loss of

earning capacity that is accounted for in another award." *Price*, 382 F.3d at 885.[1]

These principles and the rule against double dipping apply to scheduled losses. *Rupert*, 239 F.2d at 275–76. The D.C. Circuit has held that scheduled losses are "based upon a damages concept rather than loss of wage-earning capacity" because they are paid regardless of an actual loss in earning capacity. *See Henry v. George Hyman Constr. Co.*, 749 F.2d 65, 73 (D.C. Cir. 1984). However, a scheduled loss disability only exists under the Act if there is an "incapacity . . . to earn the wages which the employee was [previously] receiving." 33 U.S.C. § 902(10). Rather than changing the Act's underlying wage-compensation principles, scheduled losses exist to "ameliorate an otherwise intolerable administrative burden by providing a certain and easily applied method of determining the effect on wage earning capacity of typical and classifiable injuries." *Rupert*, 239 F.2d at 275–76; *see* [—8—] *also Korineck v. Gen. Dynamics Corp. Elec. Boat Div.*, 835 F.2d 42, 43–44 (2d Cir. 1987).

II

While accepting the above principles, Fenske argues that he should be paid a concurrent award based on our holding in *Price*. There, the petitioner suffered a permanent partial disability under § 908(c)(21) and was awarded two-thirds of his lost earning potential. *Price*, 382 F.3d at 882. Years later, Price suffered a second injury causing permanent total disability. *Id.* We held that under those circumstances, concurrent payments were warranted because the later total disability award was based on a wage that had already been decreased by the earlier partial disability. *Id.* at 889; *see also Hastings v. Earth Satellite Corp.*, 628 F.2d 85,

---

[1] We have never directly held that the double dipping prohibition applies to temporary total disability under § 908(b). Because Fenske's argument is premised entirely on our holding in *Price*, described below, we need not reach the issue here. *See Cruz v. Int'l Collection Corp.*, 673 F.3d 991, 998 (9th Cir. 2012) ("'We review only issues which are argued specifically and distinctly in a party's opening brief.'" (citation omitted)).

91 (D.C. Cir. 1980) (allowing concurrent payments under similar circumstances).

Fenske seeks to extend *Price*'s holding beyond permanent partial disabilities under § 908(c)(21) to scheduled losses. We need not address this issue: a prerequisite for applying the *Price* theory is that the partial disability preceded the total disability. Because Fenske's hearing loss did not precede his back injury, *Price* does not apply.

While Fenske was exposed to excessive noise throughout his employment in Iraq, the only evidence of his hearing loss was an audiogram obtained on June 4, 2009, four years after his employment ended. In *Bath Iron Works Corp. v. Director, Office of Workers' Compensation Programs*, the Supreme Court held that hearing loss is not a latent disease involving a delayed onset of disability. 506 U.S. 153, 162, 165 (1993) ("*Bath Iron Works*"); *see also* 33 U.S.C. § 910(i). [—9—] Instead, hearing loss "occurs simultaneously with the exposure to excessive noise" and "the injury is complete when the exposure ceases." *Bath Iron Works*, 506 U.S. at 165. As a result, the Court held that when a post-retirement audiogram shows hearing loss, "the date of last exposure—the date upon which the injury is complete—is the relevant time of injury for calculating a retiree's benefits for occupational hearing loss." *Id.* Under this rule, Fenske's date of last exposure was the same day Fenske suffered his back injury and was forced to leave Iraq.

Fenske argues that we should formulate an alternate rule based on the Supreme Court's statement in *Bath Iron Works* that a hearing loss injury "occurs simultaneously with the exposure to excessive noise." *Id.* Although not addressed by *Bath Iron Works* directly, Fenske's argument is simply inconsistent with the bright-line date-of-last-exposure rule adopted by the Court. That rule "aids in the goal of avoiding unnecessary administrative difficulties and delays" by not setting the date of disability on the exact date of injury. *Ramey v. Stevedoring Servs. of Am.*, 134 F.3d 954, 962 (9th Cir. 1998) (citations and internal quotation marks omitted). As an injury that progresses with exposure over time,

determining the date and extent of hearing loss before the date of last exposure would likely delay proceedings and require more speculation than fact.

Additionally, we have previously rejected attempts to set the date of hearing loss disability earlier than the date of last exposure when the proof of earlier hearing loss was anything less than a reliable audiogram. In *Ramey*, a worker obtained an audiogram during his employment and two other audiograms after he retired, all of which showed hearing loss. *Id.* at 960–62. The ALJ found one of the post-retirement [—10—] audiograms to be the most reliable and therefore "determinative." *Id.* We held that "the date of last exposure prior to the determinative [post-retirement] audiogram" was the relevant date for disability benefits and rejected the date set by the less-reliable audiogram obtained during employment. *Id.*; *see also Stevedoring Servs. of Am. v. Dir., OWCP*, 297 F.3d 797, 803–05 (9th Cir. 2002) (holding that a reliable audiogram obtained during employment can be one of multiple determinative audiograms). Here, Fenske does not even provide unreliable evidence of hearing loss before his date of last exposure to excessive noise.

In a case where the only evidence of hearing loss is a post-retirement audiogram, we hold that the *Bath Iron Works* rule applies when determining the timing of disabilities under *Price*. Fenske's last day of exposure to excessive noise was the same day as his back injury and *Price* does not apply.

III

Fenske requests that if the full measure of concurrent payments are not available, he should at least be provided a decreased award capped at two-thirds of his wage under *ITO Corp. of Baltimore v. Green*, 185 F.3d 239 (4th Cir. 1999). There, the Fourth Circuit held that the total of multiple awards should have a ceiling of two-thirds of a worker's average weekly wage—the amount awarded to a worker with total disability. *Id.* at 242–43. This relief would benefit Fenske because his total disability award was capped by § 906(b) at 200 times the national average weekly wage, an amount that was less than two-thirds of his average weekly wage for multiple years. The § 906(b) cap does not limit the total amount paid for multiple awards. *Price*, 382 F.3d at 889–92. [—11—]

This argument provides no additional rationale for allowing concurrent payments. We decline to provide the requested relief.

CONCLUSION

Under wage-compensation principles, concurrent payments for total disability and scheduled permanent partial disability are generally unavailable. The *Price* exception does not apply because Fenske's hearing loss did not precede his back injury. We **DENY** Fenske's petition for review.

United States Court of Appeals
for the Ninth Circuit

No. 13-17358

MARILLEY
VS.
BONHAM

Appeal from the United States District Court for the
Northern District of California

Decided: December 21, 2016

Citation: 844 F.3d 841, 4 Adm. R. 395 (9th Cir. 2016).

Before **THOMAS**, Chief Judge, and **REINHARDT, WARDLAW, FLETCHER, BERZON, SMITH, JR., MURGUIA, NGUYEN, HURWITZ, OWENS,** and **FRIEDLAND,** Circuit Judges.

[—4—] **FLETCHER,** Circuit Judge:

California charges nonresident commercial fishers higher fees for vessel registrations, licenses, and permits than it charges resident commercial fishers. A certified class of nonresident commercial fishers challenges the fee differentials under the Privileges and Immunities Clause and the Equal Protection Clause. We hold that California's fee differentials do not violate either clause.

I. Background

California requires both resident and nonresident commercial fishers to register their vessels and to purchase licenses and permits in order to engage in commercial fishing in the waters of the state. *See* Cal. Fish & Game Code §§ 7852, 7881 (2013). For many years, California has [—5—] managed its commercial fishery at a substantial loss. *See* Cal. Fish & Game Code §§ 710.5(a), 710.7(a)(1) (2007). In Fiscal Year (FY) 2010–11, the year for which we have the most extensive documentation in the record, California's Department of Fish and Game spent approximately $20 million managing its commercial fishery. In the same year, California received approximately $5.8 million in fees—including registration, license, and permit fees paid by residents and nonresidents—from participants in its

commercial fishing industry. The approximately $14 million shortfall was covered by California's general tax revenues.

California has statutorily mandated fees for commercial fishing vessel registrations, licenses, and permits. *See* Cal. Fish & Game Code §§ 713, 7852, 7881, 8280.6, 8550.5. Fees are adjusted annually based on inflation. Beginning in 1986, California charged nonresidents more than residents for certain commercial fishing registrations, licenses, and permits. In 1986, California for the first time charged nonresidents more than residents for herring gill net permits. In 1993, California for the first time charged nonresidents more for commercial fishing vessel registrations and commercial fishing licenses. In 1995, California for the first time charged nonresidents more for Dungeness crab permits.

In license year 2010, the fees for resident and nonresident commercial fishers were as follows:

Commercial fishing vessel registration:
 Resident: $317.00
 Nonresident: $951.50 [—6—]

Commercial fishing license:
 Resident: $120.75
 Nonresident: $361.75

Dungeness crab vessel permits:
 Resident: $254.00
 Nonresident: $507.50

Herring gill net permits:
 Resident: $336.00
 Nonresident: $1,269.00

Cal. Dep't Fish & Game, *Digest of California Commercial Fishing Laws and Licensing Requirements* (2010). Dungeness crab and herring were (and are) limited entry fisheries for which a limited number of permits was (and is) available.

Depending on the activity in question, a commercial fisher in California could be required to pay several fees. For example, a fishing vessel owner who personally engaged in fishing for herring was required to pay a vessel registration fee, a commercial fishing license fee, and a herring gill net permit fee. For a California resident holding a single permit, the total cost in 2010 would have been $773.75. For a nonresident, the total cost would have been $2,582.25, or 3.3 times as much as for a resident. A vessel owner who personally engaged in fishing for Dungeness crab was required to pay a vessel registration fee, a commercial fishing license fee, and a Dungeness crab permit fee. For a California resident, the total cost in 2010 would have been $691.75; for a nonresident, the total cost would have been $1,820.75, or 2.6 times as much as for a resident. Of the approximately $5.8 million in fees paid to California in FY [—7—] 2010–11 by the commercial fishing industry, approximately $435,000 came from fee differentials paid by nonresidents.

Plaintiffs, a class of nonresident commercial fishers, challenge the four nonresident fee differentials—for commercial fishing vessel registrations, commercial fishing licenses, Dungeness crab permits, and herring gill net permits. Plaintiffs brought a class action in district court against California's Director of the Department of Fish and Game (for convenience, "California"), challenging the fee differentials as violating the dormant Commerce Clause, the Privileges and Immunities Clause, and the Equal Protection Clause. Plaintiffs voluntarily dismissed their dormant commerce clause claim. The parties filed cross-motions for summary judgment on the remaining two claims. The district court ruled for the plaintiff class on its privileges and immunities claim, did not reach its equal protection claim, and entered judgment under Federal Rule of Civil Procedure 54(b). California appealed the grant of Plaintiffs' motion for summary judgment and the denial of its own motion for summary judgment. A divided three-judge panel of this court affirmed. *Marilley v. Bonham*, 802 F.3d 958, 3 Adm. R. 601 (9th Cir. 2015). We granted rehearing en banc. *Marilley v. Bonham*, 815 F.3d 1178, 4 Adm. R. 373 (9th Cir. 2016).

For the reasons that follow, we reverse the grant of summary judgment to Plaintiffs. We remand with directions to grant summary judgment to California.

II. Standard of Review

We review de novo a district court's decision granting or denying a motion for summary judgment. *Rocky Mountain* [—8—] *Farmers Union v. Corey*, 730 F.3d 1070, 1086 (9th Cir. 2013).

III. Discussion

A. Privileges and Immunities

Article IV, Section 2, clause 1, of the Constitution provides that "[t]he Citizens of each State shall be entitled to all Privileges and Immunities of Citizens in the several States." The Clause's "primary purpose . . . was to help fuse into one Nation a collection of independent, sovereign States." *Toomer v. Witsell*, 334 U.S. 385, 395 (1948). The Clause "establishes a norm of comity" between citizens of separate states. *Austin v. New Hampshire*, 420 U.S. 656, 660 (1975).

A challenge under the Privileges and Immunities Clause entails "a two-step inquiry." *Sup. Ct. of Va. v. Friedman*, 487 U.S. 59, 64 (1988); *United Bldg. and Constr. Trades Council v. Camden*, 465 U.S. 208, 218 (1984); *see also Council of Ins. Agents & Brokers v. Molasky-Arman*, 522 F.3d 925, 934 (9th Cir. 2008). At step one, the plaintiff bears the burden of showing that the challenged law "fall[s] within the purview of the Privileges and Immunities Clause." *Friedman*, 487 U.S. at 64 (quoting *Camden*, 465 U.S. at 221–22); *see also Schoenefeld v. Schneiderman*, 821 F.3d 273, 279 (2d Cir. 2016) (quoting *Friedman*, 487 U.S. at 64). If the plaintiff makes the required step-one showing, at step two the burden shifts to the state to show that the challenged law is "closely related to the advancement of a substantial state interest." *Friedman*, 487 U.S. at 65 (citing *Sup. Ct. of N.H. v. Piper*, 470 U.S. 274, 284 (1985)); *see also* [—9—] *Schoenefeld*, 821 F.3d at 279 (quoting *Friedman*, 487 U.S. at 67).

We address these two steps in turn.

1. Purview of the Clause

The "threshold matter" in any Privileges and Immunities Clause case is whether a challenged law "fall[s] within the purview" of the Clause. *Camden*, 465 U.S. at 218 (quoting *Baldwin v. Mont. Fish & Game Comm'n*, 436 U.S. 371, 388 (1978)). A plaintiff must show that the challenged law treats nonresidents differently from residents and impinges upon a "fundamental" privilege or immunity protected by the Clause. *Camden*, 465 U.S. at 218. Because California charges higher fees to nonresident commercial fishers, *see* Cal. Fish & Game Code §§ 7852, 7881, 8280.6, 8550.5, we easily conclude that Plaintiffs' interests are "facially burdened." *McBurney v. Young*, 133 S. Ct. 1709, 1715 (2013); *see also Hillside Dairy Inc. v. Lyons*, 539 U.S. 59, 66–67 (2003); *Carlson v. State*, 798 P.2d 1269, 1274 (Alaska 1990) ("[L]icense fees which discriminate against nonresidents are *prima facie* a violation of [the Privileges and Immunities Clause]."). Further, an unbroken line of authority characterizes commercial fishing as a "common calling" that is protected by the Privileges and Immunities Clause. *See Mullaney v. Anderson*, 342 U.S. 415, 417–19 (1952) (striking down Alaska's differentials for commercial fishing licenses as violating the Privileges and Immunities Clause); *Toomer*, 334 U.S. at 403 ("[C]ommercial shrimping in the marginal sea, like other common callings, is within the purview of the privileges and immunities clause."); *Connecticut ex rel. Blumenthal v. Crotty*, 346 F.3d 84, 96 (2d Cir. 2003) (holding that "commercial lobstering" falls within the purview of the Privileges and Immunities Clause); [—10—] *Tangier Sound Waterman's Ass'n v. Pruitt*, 4 F.3d 264, 266 (4th Cir. 1993) (explaining that commercial fishing is a "protected privilege" because it implicates "'the right to earn a living'" (quoting *Toomer*, 344 U.S. at 403)); *Carlson*, 798 P.2d at 1274 ("Commercial fishing is a sufficiently important activity to come within the purview of the Privileges and Immunities Clause.").

We therefore conclude that California's challenged fee differentials fall within the purview of the Privileges and Immunities Clause.

2. Closely Related to the Advancement of a Substantial State Interest

a. Commercial Fishing Fees and State Subsidy

California's differential fees for nonresident fishers have not reduced the percentage of nonresidents obtaining permits. In license year 1986, the year differential fees were introduced for herring gill net permits, nonresidents held 17.5% of these permits in California. In license year 2012, the most recent year for which we have information in the record, nonresidents held 19% of these permits. In license year 1993, the year differential fees were introduced for commercial fishing vessel registrations and commercial fishing licenses, nonresident commercial fishers held 7.2% of all commercial fishing vessel registrations and 6.6% of all commercial fishing licenses in California. In license year 2012, nonresident commercial fishers registered 9.4% of all commercial fishing vessel registrations and 12.9% of all commercial fishing licenses in California. In license year 1995, the year differential fees were charged for Dungeness [—11—] crab permits, nonresidents held 9.8% of these permits. In license year 2012, nonresidents held 13.9% of these permits.

According to a declaration of Tony Warrington, Assistant Chief of the Law Enforcement Division of California's Department of Fish and Game ("DFG") (now the Department of Fish and Wildlife), a "reasonable and conservative estimate" of commercial fishing enforcement expenditures by the Law Enforcement Division in FY 2010–11 is $10,320,963. According to a declaration of Helen Carriker, Deputy Director of Administration of DFG, additional FY 2010–11 expenditures by the License and Revenue Branch of DFG and by the Marine Region of DFG were $9,499,000. Carriker states, however, that these numbers do "not capture all of DFG's commercial fishing costs," and that "all DFG programs benefit commercial fishermen in some way." These numbers also do not include fishing-related conservation expenditures by other California agencies, such as the California Coastal Commission.

Based on the numbers provided by Warrington and Carriker, a conservative estimate is that California spent approximately $20,000,000 in FY 2010–11 on enforcement, management, and conservation activities benefitting commercial fishers.

Warrington estimated the FY 2010–11 expenditures by the Law Enforcement Division of DFG attributable to the Dungeness crab fishery as $921,394, and attributable to the herring gill net fishery as $75,094. He noted, however, that these numbers "likely underestimate the enforcement costs for these two fisheries" because not all personnel costs (in terms of both numbers of people and numbers of overtime hours) were included, and because some equipment expenses were not included. Carriker estimated the FY 2010–11 expenditures by the License and Revenue Branch of DFG [—12—] attributable to the Dungeness crab fishery as $83,921, and attributable to the herring gill net fishery as $97,431. According to a declaration by Marci Yaremko, Environmental Program Manager for DFG, FY 2010–11 expenditures by the Marine Region of DFG attributable to the Dungeness crab fishery were "at least" $109,797, and attributable to the herring gill net fishery were "at least" $285,981. Combining the expenditures by the Law Enforcement Division, the License and Revenue Branch, and the Marine Region, in FY 2010–11 California's DFG spent at least $1,115,112 attributable to the Dungeness crab fishery and at least $458,506 attributable to the herring gill net fishery.

During FY 2010–11, California residents registered 2,812 commercial fishing vessels; nonresidents registered 304 vessels. Nonresidents' vessels thus accounted for approximately 10% of the total registrations in that year. California residents purchased 5,618 commercial fishing licenses; nonresidents purchased 775 licenses. Nonresidents accounted for approximately 12% of the total licenses. California residents paid the yearly fee for 500 Dungeness crab permits; nonresidents paid the fee for 76 permits. Nonresidents accounted for approximately 13% of the total Dungeness crab permits. California residents paid the yearly fee for 180

herring gill net permits; nonresidents paid the fee for 39 permits. Nonresidents accounted for approximately 18% of the total herring gill net permits.

During FY 2010–11, California received, from residents and nonresidents, a total of approximately $2,415,000 for commercial vessel registrations, commercial fishing licenses, Dungeness crab permits, and herring gill net permits. Of that amount, approximately $435,000 was due to fee differentials [—13—] paid by nonresident fishers. Broken down by category, the fee differentials were approximately $193,000 for commercial fishing boat registrations; approximately $187,000 for commercial fishing licenses; approximately $19,000 for Dungeness crab permits; and approximately $36,000 for herring gill net permits.

Overall, during FY 2010–11 California received approximately $5,800,000 in commercial fishing revenues, including revenues from resident and nonresident fishing vessel registrations, fishing licenses, Dungeness crab permits, and herring gill net permits. Using $20,000,000 as the conservative estimate of California's overall commercial fishery expenditures, the FY 2010–11 shortfall was slightly over $14,000,000. If we exclude from the calculation fee differentials paid by nonresidents, the shortfall in FY 2010–11 was approximately $14,435,000. The shortfall was covered by California's general tax revenues. This shortfall was a subsidy, or benefit, provided by California taxpayers to the commercial fishing industry in California. The question before us is whether, or to what degree, nonresident commercial fishers may be required to pay differential fees to account for their proportionate share of that subsidy, or benefit.

b. Advancement of a Substantive State Interest

i. State Expenditures and Compensation by Nonresidents

(a) State Expenditures

The Supreme Court has decided two cases in which differential fees were charged to nonresident commercial fishers. First, in *Toomer v. Witsell*, 334 U.S. 385 (1948), [—14—] South Carolina charged a license fee of $25 for commercial shrimp boats owned by state residents. It charged a license fee of $2,500—one hundred times greater—to commercial shrimp boats owned by nonresidents. *Id.* at 389. The Court wrote that "South Carolina plainly and frankly discriminates against non-residents, and the record leaves little doubt but what the discrimination is so great that its practical effect is virtually exclusionary." *Id.* at 396–97; *see also id.* at 398 (noting "a near equivalent of total exclusion"). The Court struck down the fee differential as a violation of the Privileges and Immunities Clause. *Id.* at 403. The Court was careful, however, to endorse differential fees that were compensation or reimbursement for state-provided benefits as to which nonresidents would otherwise be free riders. The Court wrote that the Clause allows a state "to charge non-residents a differential which would merely compensate the State for any added enforcement burden they may impose or for any conservation expenditures from taxes which only residents pay." *Id.* at 399.

Second, in *Mullaney v. Anderson*, 342 U.S. 415 (1952), the Tax Commissioner of Alaska charged a commercial fishing license fee of $5 to residents and a $50 fee—a ten times greater fee—to nonresidents. Alaska sought to justify the fee differential based on enforcement costs attributable to nonresident commercial fishers, but the record did not support its attempted justification. Indeed, wrote the Court, the Tax Commissioner and his Deputy "specifically disclaimed any knowledge of the dollar cost of enforcement." *Id.* at 418. Applying the Privileges and Immunities Clause to a Territory (as Alaska then was), the Court struck down the fee differential. The Court quoted the language from *Toomer* endorsing differential fees that prevent nonresidents from free riding on state-provided enforcement and conservation [—15—] efforts, *id.* at 417, and the Court was careful to say that precise cost and reimbursement figures were not required in order to justify differential fees, *id.* at 418 ("Constitutional issues affecting taxation do not turn on even approximate mathematical determinations.").

To justify the fee differentials challenged in this case, California points to the approximately $14 million yearly shortfall in its expenditures in managing its commercial fishery. As noted above, without the revenue produced by the fee differentials, the yearly shortfall would be an additional $435,000. California contends that the fee differentials charged to nonresident commercial fishers appropriately compensate it for costs incurred in enforcement and conservation efforts attributable to nonresidents as their proportionate share, and that the fee differentials reduce (though do not entirely eliminate) the free-rider problem that would otherwise exist.

On several occasions, the Supreme Court has stated that a state's expenditures may justify discrimination against nonresidents that would otherwise be impermissible under the Privileges and Immunities Clause. As just noted, the Court stated in *Toomer* and *Mullaney* that a state may charge differential fees to nonresident commercial fishers in order to recover the state's expenditures in enforcement and conservation measures that are attributable to the nonresidents. In *Camden*, a municipal ordinance required that at least forty percent of workers employed on city construction projects be residents of Camden, New Jersey. The Court wrote, "The fact that Camden is expending its own funds or funds it administers in . . . terms of a grant is certainly a factor—perhaps the crucial factor—to be considered in evaluating whether the statute's discrimination [—16—] violates the Privileges and Immunities Clause." *Camden*, 465 U.S. at 221.

The Court's decisions under the Commerce Clause make much the same point about state expenditures. Commerce Clause decisions are relevant to the Privileges and Immunities Clause because the two clauses share the same underlying concerns. *See, e.g., Hicklin v. Orbeck*, 437 U.S. 518, 531–32 (1978) ("[T]he mutually reinforcing relationship between the Privileges and Immunities Clause . . . and the Commerce Clause—a relationship that stems from their common origin in the Fourth Article of the Articles of Confederation and their shared vision of federalism . . .—renders several Commerce Clause decisions appropriate support for our conclusion [under the Privileges and Immunities Clause]." (internal citation omitted)). In *Reeves, Inc. v. Stake*, 447 U.S. 429 (1980), South Dakota built and owned its own cement plant. When demand for cement exceeded supply, South Dakota instituted a policy of satisfying all orders from South Dakota customers first, relegating out-of-state customers to the end of the line. The Court sustained the policy against a dormant Commerce Clause challenge, writing:

> The State's refusal to sell to buyers other than South Dakotans is "protectionist" only in the sense that it limits benefits generated by a state program to those who fund the state treasury and whom the State was created to serve . . . . Such policies, while perhaps "protectionist" in a loose sense, reflect the essential and patently unobjectionable purpose of state government—to serve the citizens of the State. [—17—]

Id. at 442. Similarly, in *McBurney v. Young*, 133 S.Ct. 1709 (2013), the Supreme Court rejected a dormant Commerce Clause challenge to a Virginia Freedom of Information Act provision under which only Virginia residents were allowed to compel production of state government documents. Citing *Reeves*, the Court wrote, "Insofar as there is a 'market' for public documents in Virginia, it is a market for a product that the Commonwealth has created and of which the Commonwealth is the sole manufacturer." *Id.* at 1720. The Court therefore held that

Virginia could reserve for its citizens the benefits of the product it had created through the expenditure of state funds.

(b) Compensation by Nonresidents for State-provided Benefits

The core principle of the foregoing cases is that when a state makes an expenditure from a fund to which nonresidents do not contribute, and when the state provides a benefit through that expenditure to both residents and nonresidents, the state may exclude nonresidents from the benefit either in whole or in part, or it may seek compensation from nonresidents for the benefit conferred. When the benefit at issue is access to a natural resource, the state may not exclude nonresidents, but it may seek reimbursement for money spent to manage and preserve the resource. In such cases, as the Court wrote in *Toomer*, the Privileges and Immunities Clause allows a state "to charge non-residents a differential which would merely compensate the State for any added enforcement burden they may impose or for any conservation expenditures from taxes which only residents pay." *Toomer*, 334 U.S. at 399. [—18—]

Several related principles come from these same cases. First, the benefit provided to a nonresident, and the appropriate amount of compensation from the nonresident, need not be determined with mathematical precision. The constitutional question "do[es] not turn on even approximate mathematical determinations." *Mullaney*, 342 U.S. at 418. Second, we accord states deference in determining the benefit provided and the appropriate amount of compensation. A privileges and immunities inquiry "must . . . be conducted with due regard for the princip[le] that the States should have considerable leeway in analyzing local evils and in prescribing appropriate cures." *Toomer*, 334 U.S. at 396. Third, in seeking compensation from nonresidents, a state must treat nonresidents and residents with "substantial equality." *Id.* at 396 ("[I]t was long ago decided that one of the privileges which the [Privileges and Immunities Clause] guarantees to citizens of State A is that of doing business in State B on terms of substantial equality with the citizens of that State.").

Consistent with these principles, we may calculate at a general level the benefit provided by California and the appropriate compensation from nonresident fishers. California spent approximately $20,000,000 managing its commercial fishing industry in FY 2010–11. Not including the fee differentials paid by nonresident fishers, California received a total amount of approximately $5,365,000 in fees from the commercial fishing industry. This amount includes all fees, not limited to commercial fishing license fees, commercial fishing vessel registration fees, Dungeness crab permits, and herring gill net permits. Of that total amount (again excluding the amount paid in fee differentials), approximately $1,980,000 came from registration, license, and permit fees paid by commercial fishers. The remaining [—19—] approximately $3,385,000 came from fish landing taxes and from licensing fees paid by fish buyers, sellers, and importers. The shortfall in revenues (excluding nonresident differentials) in FY 2010–11 was approximately $14,635,000, or approximately 73% of the entire amount spent by California in managing its commercial fishery. The shortfall was a subsidy, or benefit, provided by California to its commercial fishing industry, paid by California taxpayers. All commercial fishers in California—residents and non-residents alike—benefited from this subsidy.

We will assume, as a rough estimate, that commercial fishers as a whole benefited from the states' subsidy in proportion to the amount they paid in fees. Excluding fee differentials, the amount paid to California by commercial fishers ($1,980,000) was 37% of the total amount paid to California by the entire commercial fishing industry ($5,365,000). Thirty-seven percent of the state's $14,635,000 subsidy is approximately $5,341,000. That amount went to commercial fishers as their proportionate share of the subsidy in FY 2010–11. Nonresident commercial fishers in California were 12% of all commercial fishers in FY 2010–11. Twelve percent of the $5,341,000 subsidy that went to all commercial fishers is approximately $641,000. California could have charged up to that amount to nonresident fishers in FY 2010–11, as their proportionate share of the subsidy, or benefit, provided to them by California out of its general fund. In actual fact, nonresident fishers paid a total of $435,000 in fee differentials in FY 2010–11, substantially less than the amount of their proportionate share of the subsidy, or benefit, provided to them by California. [—20—]

We may also calculate the subsidies provided to the two specific fisheries for which California charges fee differentials—Dungeness crab and herring. As described above, in FY 2010–11 California's DFG spent approximately $1,115,000 attributable to the Dungeness crab fishery and approximately $460,000 attributable to the herring fishery. As noted above, the overall subsidy provided by California to its commercial fishery is 73% of California's total expenditures for managing its commercial fishery. We will assume, as a rough estimate, that 73% of the amount spent on the Dungeness crab and herring fisheries is the amount by which those specific fisheries were subsidized in FY 2010–11.

Seventy-three percent of the subsidy provided to the Dungeness crab fishery is approximately $814,000. Nonresidents were 13% of the Dungeness crab permit holders in FY 2010–11. Thirteen percent of $814,000 is approximately $106,000, which is the proportionate share of the subsidy provided to nonresident Dungeness crab fishers in FY 2010–11. The differential fee charged to nonresident Dungeness crab fishers in FY 2010–11 was approximately $19,000, substantially less than the $106,000 subsidy, or benefit, provided to them.

Seventy-three percent of the subsidy provided to the herring fishery is approximately $335,000. Nonresidents were 18% of the herring gill net permit holders in FY 2010–11. Eighteen percent of $335,000 is approximately $60,000. The differential fee charged to nonresident herring gill net fishers in FY 2010–11 was $36,000, substantially less than the $60,000 subsidy, or benefit, provided to them. [—21—]

Thus, whether the calculation is made at the general level of all nonresident commercial fishers, or at the specific level of nonresident commercial fishers for Dungeness crab and herring, the fee differentials charged by California are less than the amount by which California subsidizes the management of the nonresidents' portions of its commercial fishery.

In contrast to the fee differential charged in *Toomer*, California commercial fishing differentials are not "virtually exclusionary." *Toomer*, 334 U.S. at 397. Indeed, quite the contrary. As the numbers given above demonstrate, the percentages of nonresident fishing vessel registrations, nonresident commercial fishing licenses, nonresident Dungeness crab permits, and nonresident herring gill net permits have all increased since the institution of differential fees for nonresidents. Further, in contrast to the fee differentials in *Toomer* and *Mullaney*, the multiples of the fees charged to residents are relatively modest. In *Toomer*, South Carolina charged nonresident shrimpers one hundred times what it charged residents. In *Mullaney*, Alaska charged nonresident fishers ten times what it charged residents. In California, the multiples ranged from about two to slightly less than four.

We therefore conclude that the fee differentials charged by California are permitted under the Privileges and Immunities Clause.

ii. California Taxes Paid by Nonresident Fishers

The above analysis is premised on the nonresident fishers in this case not having paid "taxes which only [California] residents pay." *Toomer*, 334 U.S. at 399. Plaintiffs did not [—22—] argue in the district court or in their briefs to us that they have paid California income tax on their earnings from commercial fishing in California, and that they are therefore protected by the Privileges and Immunities Clause from having to pay fee differentials. Plaintiffs made this argument for the first time during oral argument before our en banc panel. Our dissenting colleagues

use Plaintiffs' late-raised argument as the central rationale of their dissent. We could hold Plaintiffs' argument waived for failure to raise it in the district court and for failure to raise it in their briefs to us. However, we address it on the merits, for there is enough uncontested information in the record to allow us to consider and reject it. Because we reject the argument, there is no unfairness to California resulting from Plaintiffs' failure to raise it until oral argument before our en banc panel.

If Plaintiffs paid more than *de minimus* income tax to California, such that they should be assimilated, either entirely or in part, to California resident taxpayers for purposes of the Privileges and Immunities Clause, we would have to modify our analysis. However, we do not need to do so because the three named plaintiffs have paid either no or minimal California income tax. One of the named plaintiffs has fished commercially in California for many years and has never paid California income tax. The other two named plaintiffs have fished commercially in California for many years; each has paid income taxes in California for only three of those years.

Named plaintiff Savior Papetti lives in McKinney, Texas. He owns two commercial fishing boats. He uses one of them to fish in Alaska. He has kept the other boat in San Francisco since 2000. He does not own any herring gill net permits, but has fished regularly for herring in California, missing only a [—23—] few years, by leasing permits from others. He has fished for Dungeness crab regularly since 2006 except for a "couple [of] years." He stated in his deposition that he has filed California tax returns "every year." He specifically stated that he has not paid California income tax since 1992. There is nothing in the record to indicate that he paid California income taxes before 1992.

Named plaintiff Salvatore Papetti, Savior's father, lives in Bellingham, Washington. He states in his deposition that he has worked as a commercial fisherman since 1963. He owns two commercial fishing boats. He keeps one of them in Alaska. He now uses it to fish for salmon, but in the past has used it to fish for Dungeness crab and herring in California. At the time of his deposition, his other boat was in Washington for repairs. He uses that boat to fish for herring in Alaska and in California, and for salmon in Washington. He fished for Dungeness crab in California as late as 2007. About five or six years ago, he sold his crab permit to his son Savior. He has never missed a herring season in California except the year the season was closed due to an oil spill in San Francisco Bay. He has filed California income tax returns "every year," but has paid income taxes to California in only three of those years. He paid $331 in 2004, $652 in 2009, and $2,273 in 2010.

Finally, named plaintiff Kevin Marilley lives in Lynden, Washington. He has worked as a commercial fisherman since 1974. He owns three commercial fishing boats. He keeps two in Alaska and uses them to fish there. He keeps the third boat in Bellingham, Washington, and uses it to fish for salmon in Alaska and herring in California. He fished for squid and herring in California between 1989 and 2005, and fished for squid in California in 2009. He regularly fished for [—24—] herring in California through 2007. He stated in his deposition that he intended to fish for herring in California in 2013. He stated in his deposition that he "believe[d]" he filed a California tax return for every year he fished in California up through 2003. The last time he filed a tax return in California was 2003. He paid income tax in California in only three years. He paid $153 in 1994, $3,161 in 1995, and $845 in 1996. He last paid California income tax twenty years ago.

Our dissenting colleagues do not ask to alter our analysis based on the non-existent or minimal California income taxes paid by the three named plaintiffs. Rather, they ask us to do so based on an unsupported assumption that unnamed class members paid substantially more in California income taxes than did the named plaintiffs.

The record contains no evidence of California income taxes paid by any of the unnamed class members. Attorneys for the plaintiff class had an opportunity in the district court to present evidence of California income taxes paid by unnamed class members, but they failed to present any such evidence. Nor did they make any argument in the district court based on payment of California income taxes by any class member, named or unnamed. An assumption that unnamed class members paid substantially more than the named plaintiffs is inconsistent with the basic premises of class certification. Federal Rule of Civil Procedure 23(a)(3) requires that the "claims . . . of the representative parties [be] typical of the claims . . . of the class." That is, a claim by an unnamed member of the class must match a "typical" claim by a named plaintiff. In this case, there is no such "typical" claim in the complaint because the named plaintiffs made no claim whatsoever based on their payment of California [—25—] income taxes. Rule 23(a)(2) also requires that there be "questions of law or fact common to the class." If a claim based on the payment of California income taxes had been made in the district court (which it was not), that claim was required to have been based on law or fact "common to the class." To the extent there were facts common to such a claim, if it had been made, the only facts in evidence were those recounted above.

In short, our dissenting colleagues ask us to make an assumption, based on sheer speculation, that unnamed class members paid substantially more in California income taxes than did the named plaintiffs. We respectfully decline to make that assumption.

B. Equal Protection

Plaintiffs also challenged California's commercial fishing fee differentials under the Equal Protection Clause. The district court struck down the fee differentials as a violation of the Privileges and Immunities Clause and did not reach the equal protection question. We could remand to the district court to address that question in the first instance, but in the interest of judicial efficiency we decide the question ourselves.

Because California's commercial fishing fee differentials do not "classify persons based on protected characteristics, such as race, alienage, national origin, or sex" or "affect the exercise of fundamental rights," rational basis review applies. *Fields v. Legacy Health Sys.*, 413 F.3d 943, 955 (9th Cir. 2005); *see also Country Classic Dairies, Inc. v. State of Mont., Dep't of Commerce Milk Control Bureau*, 847 F.2d 593, 596 (9th Cir. 1988) ("[T]he right to pursue a calling is [—26—] not a fundamental right for purposes of the Equal Protection Clause." (citing *New Orleans v. Dukes*, 427 U.S. 297, 303–05 (1976) (per curiam))); *see also Medeiros v. Vincent*, 431 F.3d 25, 32 (1st Cir. 2005) ("The right to 'make a living' is not a 'fundamental right,' for either equal protection or substantive due process purposes."). Therefore, in order to succeed Plaintiffs must "negat[e] every conceivable basis which might support the legislative classification" between residents and nonresidents. *Fields*, 413 F.3d at 955. As explained above, California has a "substantial reason" for charging nonresident differentials. It has an obvious interest in recovering from nonresident commercial fishers their share of the benefit provided to them by its management of its commercial fishery. Congress has recognized this interest as legitimate. *See* Pub. L. No. 109-13, § 6036(b)(1), 119 Stat. 231. But even absent such congressional endorsement, California's interest in receiving compensation for the benefit its management confers provides a "rational basis" for its fee differentials.

Conclusion

We reverse the district court's grant of summary judgment to Plaintiffs. California's fee differentials for commercial fishing vessel registrations, fishing licenses, Dungeness crab permits, and herring gill net permits survive the Privileges and Immunities Clause challenge because the differentials are justified by a substantial reason that is closely related to the differential fees. The fees survive the Equal Protection Clause challenge because California has a rational basis for charging the differential fees. California is [—27—] therefore entitled to summary judgment on both of Plaintiffs' claims. We remand with directions to the district court to enter summary judgment for California.

REVERSED and **REMANDED**.

(Reporter's Note: Dissenting opinion follows on p. 405).

[—27—] **M. SMITH,** Circuit Judge, with whom **HURWITZ** and **OWENS,** Circuit Judges, join in full, and **REINHARDT** and **BERZON,** Circuit Judges, join as to Part III, dissenting:

The majority assumes away the major defect in its analysis: the fact that nonresident fishermen pay multiple California taxes too, yet nonetheless commence each fishing season thousands of dollars in the hole by virtue of California's discriminatory differentials. To avoid dealing with this problem, the majority employs the analytical head fake of fixating on the named plaintiffs and ignoring the rest of the class. It then opines that the named plaintiffs' tax liability is *de minimus*, assumes that finding is representative, and concludes that its analysis need go no further.

That approach is deeply flawed. Our analysis cannot properly ignore the bevy of taxes nonresident fishermen pay collectively to the State. Moreover, the majority improperly transposes the evidentiary burden: it is California that must demonstrate that the differentials recoup a subsidy funded only by its residents. Hence, any purported lack of evidence on the tax liability of nonresident fishermen *counts against* the State, not the other way around. The majority shrugs this off, and thereby fails to require California to bear the burden the Privileges and Immunities Clause demands. [—28—]

California, like the majority, overlooks how nonresident taxes defray the costs of any subsidy for conservation, and thereby fails to meet its burden to show its discrimination is "closely drawn" to the achievement of a substantial state objective. *Sup. Ct. of Va. v. Friedman,* 487 U.S. 59, 68 (1988). For that reason, I would affirm the district court's judgment in favor of the plaintiffs, and I respectfully dissent.

I.

Salvatore Papetti and his wife Nancy fish for herring together in a two person team. They make the trip to San Francisco from Bellingham, Washington, to fish on their boat, the "Pacman." It is tough work—"being on the ocean day and night, your body wears out" because "when there's fish, you just got to go go go go . . . they're here today and they're gone tomorrow. . . . You got to catch as much as you can when you can." They fish "five days a week, 24 hours a day, Sunday sundown till Friday noon." They land their catch every day while the fish are still fresh to ensure the bounty does not spoil.

They hold two commercial fishing licenses, three herring gill net permits, and one commercial fishing vessel registration. This would cost them $1566.50 in license fees if they were California residents, using the majority's numbers from 2010. California, however, extracts $5482.00 from the Papettis, based simply on their status as nonresidents. So, Salvatore and Nancy start the season with a $3915.50 deficit, relative to their in-state competitors. Adding insult to injury, every year it gets worse because commercial fishing fees are automatically indexed for inflation. Cal. Fish & Game Code § 713 (2013). The effect [—29—] of the indexing is to widen the gap between resident and nonresident fishing license fees each season.

Savior Papetti—Nancy and Salvatore's son—must endure the same built-in headwinds. He registers a boat in California, obtains a fishing license, and secures permits to fish for herring and crab. But since he hails from McKinney, Texas, he starts each season $2062.00 behind his California resident competitors. Kevin Marilley is no different. He sets sail on the "Sundance Kid" near San Francisco to fish for herring. He registers his boat, obtains a fishing license, and has three herring gill net permits, so he starts $3674.50 in the red, unlike his California resident competitors. Frustrated by the disadvantage, Marilley and the Papettis challenge four of California's differential fees under the Privileges and Immunities Clause of the U.S. Constitution.

A.

The Privileges and Immunities Clause is one of the cornerstones upon which our nation was built. Its origins add an important perspective on the State's burden in this dispute.

After the revolution, "[t]he strong sympathies . . . which bound the States together during a common war, dissolved on the return of peace." *Gibbons v. Ogden*, 22 U.S. 1, 223 (1824) (Johnson, J. concurring). For the first time, the states found themselves "in the unlimited possession of those powers over their own commerce, which they had so long been deprived of, and so earnestly coveted." *Id.* at 224. State parochialism "began to show itself in iniquitous laws and impolitic measures, from which grew up a conflict of commercial regulations, destructive to the harmony of the States." *Id.* [—30—]

New York, for instance, obtained firewood from Connecticut and goods from the farms of New Jersey, but because such trade harmed domestic industry, the State required "every Yankee sloop" and "Jersey market boat" to pay an entrance fee and a duty. JOHN FISKE, THE CRITICAL PERIOD OF AMERICAN HISTORY, 1783–1789 150–52 (1897). New Jersey retaliated by laying a tax on property New York had acquired in Sandy Hook. *Id.* at 152. Connecticut's merchants refused "to send any goods whatever into the hated state for a period of twelve months." *Id.* Yet, as three other New England states "closed their ports to British shipping," Connecticut saw fit to "thr[ow] hers wide open, an act which she followed up by laying duties upon imports from Massachusetts." *Id.* at 148–49. Connecticut's practice of "denying to outlanders the treatment that its citizens demanded for themselves was widespread." *Austin v. New Hampshire*, 420 U.S. 656, 660 (1975). "This came to threaten at once the peace and safety of the union." *H. P. Hood & Sons, Inc. v. Du Mond*, 336 U.S. 525, 533 (1949) (internal quotation marks omitted).

The new country initially tried to solve the problem with the toothless Articles of Confederation, which provided:

The better to secure and perpetuate mutual friendship and intercourse among the people of the different States in this Union, the free inhabitants of each of these States . . . shall be entitled to all privileges and immunities of free citizens in the several States; and the people of each State shall have free ingress and regress to and from any other State, and shall enjoy therein all the privileges of trade and commerce, subject to the same duties, [—31—] impositions, and restrictions as the inhabitants thereof . . . .

Art. IV. Since no state could unilaterally enforce this provision, the economic interaction of the several states became more and more fraught. Ultimately, this internecine, economic fratricide became "the immediate cause[] that led to the forming of a [constitutional] convention." *Gibbons*, 22 U.S. at 224; *see also* KATHLEEN M. SULLIVAN & GERALD GUNTHER, CONSTITUTIONAL LAW 82 (17th ed. 2010) ("The poor condition of American commerce and the proliferating trade rivalries among the states were the immediate provocations for the calling of the Constitutional Convention.")

The Privileges and Immunities Clause was primarily aimed at "creat[ing] a national economic union," *Sup. Ct. of N.H. v. Piper*, 470 U.S. 274, 279–80 (1985), and was taken from the Articles of Confederation "with no change of substance or intent, unless it was to strengthen the force of the clause in fashioning a single nation," *Austin*, 420 U.S. at 661. It affirms "[t]he Citizens of each State shall be entitled to all Privileges and Immunities of Citizens in the several States." U.S. Const. art. IV, § 2, cl. 1. Alexander Hamilton referred to the Clause quite simply as "the basis of the Union." The Federalist No. 80, at 502 (B. Wright ed., 1961). It "place[d] the citizens of each State upon the same footing with citizens of other States, so far as the advantages resulting from citizenship in those States are concerned." *Paul v. Virginia*, 75 U.S. 168, 180 (1868). The Court found it gave outsiders "an exemption from higher taxes or impositions than are paid by the other citizens of the state." *Corfield v. Coryell*, 6 F.Cas. 546, 552 (No. 3,230) (Cir. Ct. E.D. Pa. 1823). "It has been justly said that no [other] provision in the [—32—] Constitution has tended so strongly to constitute the citizens of the United States one people . . . ." *Paul*, 75 U.S. at 180.

B.

In light of this background, when states erect barriers that impair our national economic unity, they bear a significant burden of justification: laws implicating the Clause must serve a "substantial state interest" and be "closely related" to the advancement of that interest to be valid. *Friedman*, 487 U.S. at 65. A substantial interest does not exist "unless there is something to indicate that non-citizens constitute a peculiar source of the evil at which the [discriminatory] statute is aimed." *Hicklin v. Orbeck*, 437 U.S. 518, 525–26 (1978) (quotation marks omitted, brackets in original). States of course do have some flexibility in prescribing appropriate cures for local ills and, when levying fees, need not demonstrate mathematical precision. *See Toomer v. Witsell*, 334 U.S. 385, 396 (1948). But citizens of State A must be allowed to do business in State B "on terms of *substantial equality* with the citizens of that State." *Id.* (emphasis added).

C.

The "evil" the fee differentials target in this case is the potential for nonresidents to "free ride" on California's investment in its fisheries.[1] The State's valid interest thus lies [—33—] in seeking reimbursement for a benefit funded exclusively by California residents. In this situation, California may exact only "a differential which would merely compensate the State for [1] any added enforcement burden [nonresidents] may impose or [2] for any conservation expenditures from taxes *which only residents pay*." *Toomer*, 334 U.S. at 399 (emphasis added).[2] [—34—]

California elected to put all of its eggs in the second basket, as it never asserted, much less provided any evidence, that nonresident commercial fishermen impose any added enforcement or management burden on the State.[3] In conducting our analysis, we thus look to the aggregate benefits nonresident fishermen receive at the expense of California's taxpayers. To calculate that benefit, I will leverage, but do not endorse, the majority's handiwork.

The majority assumes the $20 million spent on licensing and enforcement is akin to

---

[1] The California legislature never articulated this aim, but the State insists the fee differentials were passed to close a budget gap. It is undisputed that nonresident fishermen were never actually identified as a unique source of any problem that would justify charging them a differential. Additionally, as "the Clause forbids a State from intentionally [—33—] giving its own citizens a competitive advantage in business or employment," it is appropriate to examine whether the differentials were enacted for a protectionist purpose. *McBurney v. Young*, 133 S. Ct. 1709, 1716 (2013). Here, California's enactment of the Dungeness crab fee differential bears the hallmarks of economic protectionism. As the district court observed, the California Assembly Committee on Water, Parks, and Wildlife opposed an early version of the bill, noting it "provided[d] an unfair advantage to the sponsors of the bill—the Pacific Coast Federation of Fisherman [sic] [a resident fishermen advocacy group]—by making it very difficult for any new crab fishers to obtain permits and enter the market." The Department of Fish and Game ("DFG") later commented "[t]his bill

is an attempt to . . . control competition to California fishermen and processors from out of state." DFG's enrolled bill report described the legislation as "an industry sponsored bill to prevent out-of-state commercial fishermen from moving into California and getting an undue share of the California Dungeness crab resource." When the fee was renewed in 2006, Senate Republican analysis of the bill observed "where resource management crosses the line into economic protectionism it should be opposed . . . DFG should explore other management options that focus on maintaining the crab population instead of the industry population."

[2] The majority suggests that "a state's expenditures may justify discrimination against nonresidents." Maj. Op. at 15. But the cases it cites involve the Commerce Clause, not the Privileges and Immunities Clause, and assume that nonresidents do not "fund the state treasury." *Reeves, Inc. v. Stake*, 447 U.S. 429, 224 (1980); *McBurney v. Young*, 133 S. Ct. 1709, 1712–13 (2013) (quoting *Reeves*, 447 U.S. at 224).

[3] The State concedes it did not analyze the impact of nonresident commercial fishermen on its fisheries generally, nor identify any savings it would realize if nonresidents were excluded from participating in its fisheries. As such, there is no evidence in the record that the differentials compensate for any added burden or expense nonresidents impose on commercial fisheries.

conservation. Maj. Op. at 18–19. It then finds a $14,635,000 shortfall, after accounting for $5,365,000 received in fees, not including differentials. *Id.* Next, the majority assumes commercial fishermen benefitted from the subsidy in proportion to the amount they paid in fees ($1,980,000 / $5,365,000).[4] *Id.* That equals thirty-seven (37) percent of the $14,635,000 shortfall, meaning fishermen were subsidized to the tune of $5,341,000. *Id.* at 19. Since nonresidents account for twelve percent of commercial fishermen, the majority tags them with twelve percent of that amount. *Id.* at 19. In other words, according to the majority, nonresident fishermen received a $641,000 "subsidy." *Id.*

This analysis fails because it assumes that the State's subsidy derives from "taxes which only residents pay," *Toomer*, 334 U.S. at 399, notwithstanding the fact that the [—35—] record shows that nonresident commercial fisherman pay California taxes as well. Nonresident fishermen, in other words, must "be assimilated, either entirely or in part, to California resident taxpayers for purposes of the Privileges and Immunities Clause," Maj. Op. at 22, because—like Golden State residents—they too pay taxes to fund the State's conservation expenditures.

II.

A.

The State's expert, Dr. Carriker, says commercial fishermen in California earned $150 million in 2009, $179 million in 2010, and $204 million in 2011. The State also consistently represented it could charge fees to nonresident fishermen in relation to their percentage of overall fishermen. Thus, taking the majority's number, we can attribute twelve percent of those earnings to the efforts of out-of-state fishermen. By that account, nonresident fishermen paid personal income taxes to the State on earnings approximating $18–$24 million.[5]

We can also consider it in another way. Using the landings data submitted both for residents and nonresidents, Dr. Carriker submits that the "average per-fisherman income" [—36—] in California was $91,293.03 in 2009, $105,858.00 in 2010, and $105,070.28 in 2011. If we assume nonresident fishermen are comparable to their in-state counterparts, nonresidents would be liable for at least 9.3 percent in personal income taxes on roughly those amounts. *See* Franchise Tax Board, 2014 ANNUAL REPORT tbl.A1-B (2014), *available at* https://www.ftb.ca.gov/Archive/ AboutFTB/Tax_Statistics/Reports/2014/ Annual_Report.shtml#Tax_Rates (showing personal income tax rates for each income level from 1935 to 2014) [hereinafter 2014 FTB Report].

Alternatively, if we divide the aggregate earnings (approximately $24 million) by the number of nonresident fishermen (775), nonresidents would be paying California taxes on $31,000 per year on average. This estimate, however, assumes income is distributed evenly, notwithstanding the fish will bite for some fishermen more than others. Accordingly, $31,000 might be construed as the median income, meaning half of nonresident fishermen would make more each year, and the other half less. In that scenario, it would not be surprising for the named plaintiffs to have made modest in-state tax payments, even where nonresident fisherman collectively contribute substantially.

California never contemplated, much less accounted for, the contributions nonresident fishermen make in personal income taxes.[6]

---

[4] The State never advanced, let alone justified, this assumption.

[5] To be clear, California taxes the income of nonresidents "derived from sources within this state," Cal. Rev. & Tax. Code § 17041(i)(1)(B),

"including income from a business, trade, or profession carried on within this State." Cal. Code Regs. tit. 18, § 17951-2. California also imposes a property tax on boats, including those registered in California but located outside of it. *See* California State Board of Equalization, Frequently Asked Questions — Personal Property, https://www.boe.ca.gov/proptaxes/faqs/ personal.htm.

[6] Regardless of when the issue was raised, the above evidence has always been in the record, and we review a district court's decision granting a motion for summary judgment de novo. *Rocky Mountain Farmers Union v. Corey*, 730 F.3d 1070, 1086 (9th Cir. 2013).

Based on the evidence in the record, however, we can reasonably infer nonresident fishermen's incomes [—37—] contribute meaningfully in the aggregate to the State's conservation expenditures. *See, e.g.*, SER 20 ("[A] substantial portion of General Fund revenue comes from nonresident sources, including personal income tax paid by nonresidents, including nonresident commercial fishermen.").

Consider also the fact that California derives close to thirty percent of the General Fund from sales and use tax revenue. Nonresident fishermen like the Papettis pay those taxes just as California residents do—to purchase food, fuel, and other necessary materials in California. I assume that nonresident fishermen are also a salty bunch, and likely pay excise taxes too, on cigarettes, beer, wine, and alcohol, thereby adding further to the State's general revenue. Yet California makes no effort to account for any of these nonresident funds in justifying its fee differentials, or to explain how nonresidents remain on the "same footing" as residents in spite of them. That simply is unjustifiable; under the Privileges and Immunities Clause California is required to do more. *See Mullaney v. Anderson*, 342 U.S. 415, 418 (1952) ("[S]omething more is required than bald assertion to establish a reasonable relation between the higher fees and the higher cost[s] to the [State]."); *Tangier Sound Waterman's Ass'n v. Pruitt*, 4 F.3d 264, 267 (4th Cir. 1993) (finding differential not "closely related" to asserted interest because, among other things, State gave "no recognition" to sales and use taxes paid by nonresident fishermen); *Carlson v. State*, 798 P.2d 1269, 1278 (Alaska 1990) (reading *Toomer* "to mean that if nonresident fishermen paid the same taxes as Alaskans and these taxes were substantially the sole revenue source for the state out of which conservation expenditures were made, then differential fees would not be permissible"). [—38—]

The majority concedes its analysis would have to be "modif[ied]" if nonresident fisherman "paid more than *de minimus*" taxes to California, Maj. Op. at 22, but it shrugs off the few thousands of dollars the named plaintiffs paid to California as being insufficient to meet its novel standard. By itself, this is error—the State must demonstrate "a reasonable relationship between the danger represented by non-citizens, *as a class*, and the severe discrimination practiced upon them." *Toomer*, 334 U.S. at 399 (emphasis added). In this case, California has failed to make any such showing.

Apparently unable to respond more adequately to our argument, the majority steps purposefully to the plate, swings as hard as it can, and whiffs, by fixating on Rule 23's class certification standards. Emphatically, those standards do not require that class members be carbon copies of each other. They therefore cannot excuse the majority's failure to grapple with the hole in its argument. For instance, the majority invokes "commonality," but "[t]he existence of shared legal issues with *divergent factual predicates* is sufficient" to meet that "permissive" standard. *Hanlon v. Chrysler Corp.*, 150 F.3d 1011, 1019 (9th Cir. 1988) (emphasis added). Likewise, "typicality" requires "only that [the named plaintiffs'] claims be 'typical' of the class, not that [the named plaintiffs] be identically positioned to each other or to every class member." *Parsons v. Ryan*, 754 F.3d 657, 686 (9th Cir. 2014); *see also Ellis v. Costco Wholesale Corp.*, 657 F.3d 970, 985 n.9 (9th Cir. 2011) ("Differing factual scenarios resulting in a claim of the same nature as other class members does not defeat typicality.").

Here, the district court found both elements satisfied because the plaintiffs "articulated a common constitutional issue at the heart of each proposed class member's claim for [—39—] relief," and resolution of that issue "would inform similar claims by other proposed class members regardless of factual differences among class members." This finding by no means warrants the majority's factual assumption that every class member paid the same amount as the named plaintiffs in state taxes to California. Maj. Op. at 25. Indeed, Rule 23 requires only that each class member here pay fees higher than those charged to in-state residents. And, though the extent of nonresident tax liability might be a common question, Rule 23 permits certification even where the answer varies based on the unique factual circumstances of each nonresident fisherman. In short, neither "commonality" nor "typicality" mean the majority must assume every nonresident fisherman, across all species, location, and circumstance, earned the same income as the named plaintiffs and owed the same taxes to the state of California. Maj. Op. at 24–25. In fact, the opposite conclusion is more reasonable given some nonresidents fish for herring, others for crab, and still others for both, to say nothing of the fishermen who add outings for crayfish or lobster, amongst many other commodities. Were it not evident enough that the majority is seeking to avoid the elephant in the room, it bemoans the absence of any information about the income taxes nonresident fishermen pay to California, *id.* at 24, without even considering the aggregate statistics cited above, and the reasonable inferences drawn from those data.[7] [—40—]

---

[7] The majority asserts our inferences are unsupported, but that is incorrect. Our assessment derives from the aggregate earnings statistics California placed into the record, which were taken from landings data submitted both for resident and nonresident commercial fishermen. *See supra* II.A. We do *not* claim, as the majority states, that every unnamed class member makes "substantially more" than the named plaintiffs. Maj. Op. at 24. Our argument is that the record reasonably reflects that nonresident fishermen—taken collectively, across the full range of their [—40—] income distribution—pay taxes that contribute materially to the State's conservation expenditures (a fact California completely ignores). Unlike the majority's hypothesis, under which unnamed class members are clones of the named plaintiffs, our assessment comports with common sense. We appreciate that 775 fisherman—some of whom fish the whole year in California, others of whom fish part-time—will earn incomes that fall along a distribution, such that some will owe California income taxes, and others will not. Given that point, the majority has no basis, under Rule 23 or otherwise, to assume the California tax liability of the three named plaintiffs is broadly representative. More importantly, it is California's burden to demonstrate our understanding is untrue in order to justify its discriminatory differentials. It has made no such showing in this case.

Even if we accept the majority's framing, the named plaintiffs can *still* "be assimilated . . . to California resident taxpayers." Maj. Op. at 22. We have no reason to believe that fishermen are any different from resident and nonresident tax-filers in the State more generally. And whereas fifty-eight (58) percent of resident filers owe personal income taxes to California, *sixty* (60) percent of nonresident filers owe them.[8] *Compare* 2014 FTB Report tbl.B-4A (showing 58.4 percent of residents returns were taxable in 2013), *with id.* tbl.B-4G (showing 60.2 percent nonresident returns were taxable in 2013). So, like ordinary Californians, some nonresident fishermen pay the State more in personal income [—41—] taxes than others, but like Californians generally, nonresident fishermen contribute meaningfully to the State's coffers collectively. All told, the majority improperly focuses on a few fishermen whose contributions it deems insignificant on the overall tax liability spectrum, but the record reflects, and common sense dictates, nonresident fishermen's taxes contribute materially to conservation expenditures.

B.

By chalking up to a rounding error the taxes nonresidents pay, the majority effectively shifts the applicable burden. Yet, any purported lack of evidence on the tax liability of nonresident fishermen is a strike against California, not against the plaintiffs. It is California that shoulders the burden to demonstrate that its discrimination "bears a close relation to the achievement of

---

Next, while it is true that "[i]f a claim based on the payment of California income taxes had been made in the district court, that claim was required to have been based on law or fact 'common to the class,'" Maj. Op. at 25, that observation affords the majority no help. The law common to the class is the constitutional issue under the Privileges and Immunities Clause, and Rule 23(a)(2), stated in the disjunctive, requires nothing more. In other words, the only common "claim" that is required by Rule 23 to appear in the complaint is the one the plaintiffs advanced—that each class member pays fees higher than those charged to California residents.

[8] The Franchise Tax Board's 2014 Annual Report is the most recent available data.

substantial state objectives." *Friedman*, 487 U.S. at 70. Moreover, it is California that must demonstrate its differentials "merely compensate" for expenditures that derive from taxes "which only residents pay." *Toomer*, 334 U.S. at 399. Finally, it is California that must demonstrate it permits nonresident fishermen to do business "on terms of substantial equality" with citizens of the State. *Id.* at 396. Unfortunately, the majority lets California off the hook, for while the State is owed some deference, it made no effort to account for nonresident taxes whatsoever. California simply fails to meet its burden. The upshot is that nonresident fishermen stand on different footing than residents, whether fisherman or not. They alone pay differentials but must also pay the same taxes on income earned within the State.

To illustrate, the 775 nonresident fishermen can be charged for a $641,000 "subsidy," even though they pay state [—42—] taxes to cover this conservation expenditure. In-state fishermen, by contrast, receive a $4,700,080 subsidy, but California's 15,000,000 taxpayers collectively foot the bill. Accordingly, using the majority's numbers, California residents, whether fisherman or not, pay about thirty cents on average towards the subsidy to in-state fishermen, whereas nonresident fishermen are charged over $800 each on average for the "subsidy" they receive.[9]

---

[9] Notably, *Carlson* rejected the "proposition that the state may subsidize its own residents in the pursuit of their business activities and not similarly situated nonresidents, even though this results in substantial inequality of treatment." 798 P.2d at 1278. The court found such a system "economically indistinguishable from imposing a facially equal tax on residents and nonresidents while making it effectively unequal by a system of credits and exemptions." *Id.* It declined to strike down the differential imposed by Alaska on this basis because state taxes were not "substantially the sole revenue source" for conservation expenditures. *Id.* (noting 86 percent of state revenues derived from petroleum production). The opposite is true here—personal income tax and sales tax made up 86 percent of General Fund revenues for the year ending June 30, 2015. *See* California State Controller's Office, COMPRE-HENSIVE ANNUAL FINANCIAL REPORT FOR THE FISCAL

It bears repeating: California shoulders the burden of showing the additional fees charged to nonresidents are closely related to the "taxes which only residents pay," *Toomer*, 334 U.S. at 399, and California must permit nonresident fishermen to do business on terms of substantial equality with citizens of the State. By overlooking how the taxes nonresident fishermen pay the State defray the costs of any subsidy for conservation, California fails to meet its burden. The fee differentials must accordingly be struck down. [—43—]

C.

If left to stand on this showing, we have no reason to think interstate fee differentials will not proliferate. Indeed, California could, for example, charge nonresident truckers and commercial airline pilots fees for earning a living off state-subsidized highways and airports. And why wouldn't states seek to recoup from those professions conservation expenditures aimed at maintaining air quality? As in this case, they need only intend to close a budget gap and need not identify any relationship between the shortfall and nonresident truckers or pilots. Further, they need not determine what burdens nonresidents impose, if any, on the state's air, roads, and other infrastructure. Nor would they need to identify any savings the state would realize if nonresident truckers and pilots were excluded. Finally, they could, like California, ignore nonresident taxes in setting the fee, so long as a few of the truckers or pilots earned incomes that led to modest in-state tax payments. The Privileges and Immunities Clause should preclude such barriers because they disrupt interstate economic harmony unjustifiably. The majority unfortunately holds otherwise, and thereby subverts one of the most important economic compacts that initially bound us together.

III.

This country is more than a league of confederated states—it is a nation. Yet the

---

YEAR ENDED JUNE 30, 2015 42 (2016), *available at* http://www.sco.ca.gov/Files-ARD-Local/LocRep/cafr15web.pdf.

enactment of discriminatory fee differentials promotes our economic balkanization. We must be mindful of competing interests when evaluating such measures, but they require ample justification. California's showing in this case does not come close to meeting its [—44—] burden, so the fee differentials are illegal under the Privileges and Immunities Clause. I respectfully dissent.

(Reporter's Note: Dissenting opinion follows on p. 413).

[—44—] **REINHARDT,** Circuit Judge, dissenting, in which **BERZON,** Circuit Judge, joins:

I concur in Part III of Judge M. Smith's dissent and agree that California failed to carry its burden of demonstrating that the differential fees it charges to nonresidents are "closely drawn" to the achievement of a "substantial state objective." *Supreme Court of Virginia v. Friedman,* 487 U.S. 59, 68 (1988). Permissible state objectives include "compensat[ing] the State for any added enforcement burden they may impose or for any conservation expenditures from taxes which only residents pay." *Toomer v. Witsell,* 334 U.S. 385, 399 (1948). Here, California does not contend that nonresident fishermen impose any sort of added enforcement burden. Nor does the state provide persuasive evidence that its fee differentials bear a "reasonable relationship" to its legitimate interest in receiving compensation from nonresidents for its "conservation expenditures from taxes which only residents pay." *Toomer,* 334 U.S. at 399 (1948). Therefore, I agree with Judge M. Smith that the state has failed to make the requisite showing to justify *any* differential. That conclusion does not embrace either of the views expressed by the original panel as to how a differential should be calculated when it is in fact justified. *See Marilley v. Bonham,* 802 F.3d 958, 966–68, 3 Adm. R. 601, 606–08 (9th Cir. 2015), *reh'g en banc granted,* 815 F.3d 1178, 4 Adm. R. 373 (9th Cir. 2016) (Graber., J., dissenting) (comparing the "per capita" and "fair share" approaches to calculating a justified fee differential).

This page intentionally left blank

United States Court of Appeals for the Tenth Circuit

United States Court of Appeals
for the Tenth Circuit

No. 14-4118

IN RE ARAMARK SPORTS AND ENTERTAINMENT
SERVS., LLC

Appeal from the United States District Court for the
District of Utah

Decided: August 1, 2016

Citation: 831 F.3d 1264, 4 Adm. R. 416 (10th Cir. 2016).

Before **HARTZ**, **PHILLIPS**, and **MORITZ**, Circuit
Judges.

[—1—] **HARTZ**, Circuit Judge:

This suit arose out of a recreational boating accident on Lake Powell that claimed the lives of four adults. The boat had been rented from Aramark Sports and Entertainment Services, LLC. Because the accident occurred on navigable waters, the case falls within federal admiralty jurisdiction. *See Foremost Ins. Co. v. Richardson*, 457 [—2—] U.S. 668 (1982). Anticipating that it would be sued for damages, Aramark filed in the United States District Court for the District of Utah a petition under the Limitation of Liability Act, 46 U.S.C. §§ 30501–12, which permits a boat owner to obtain a ruling exonerating it or limiting its liability based on the capacity or value of the boat and freight. The district court denied the petition, leaving for further proceedings the issues of gross negligence, comparative fault, and the amount of damages. Aramark appeals the denial. After determining that we have appellate jurisdiction, we hold that the district court erred in its application of admiralty principles of duty and remand for further proceedings.

I. BACKGROUND

A. The Accident

Aramark rents boats out of the Wahweap Marina on Lake Powell, near the Utah-Arizona border. In April 2009 three married couples—the Bradys, the Prescotts, and the Tarantos—went on vacation to Lake Powell.

On Friday, April 24 the Bradys and Prescotts went to Aramark's boat rental office at Wahweap to procure a boat for the next day. Mr. Prescott signed a contract to rent a Baja 202 Islander, which is classified in the owner's manual as a Design Category C boat based on its limited "ability to withstand wind and sea or water conditions." Aplee. Supp. App., Vol. 4 at 417. For Category C boats the manual lists a "Maximum wind speed" of 27 knots (31 miles per hour). The manual further states:

> The wind speed and wave height specified as the upper limit for your category of boat does not mean that you or your passengers can survive if [—3—] your boat is exposed to these conditions. It is only the most experienced operators and crew that may be able to operate a boat safely under these conditions. You must always be aware of weather conditions and head for port or protected waters in sufficient time to avoid being caught in high winds and rough water. Do not take chances!

Id. The boaters were never informed of the Baja's Category-C classification.

When the contract was signed, the National Weather Service (NWS) forecast for the next day on Lake Powell called for breezes from 15–23 miles per hour and gusts up to 37 miles per hour. That forecast was based on data collected at 3:44 a.m. that morning. Before the boaters left, Aramark rental agent Phyllis Coon gave that forecast to Mr. Prescott and told him that he would be given an updated forecast the next morning when they picked up the boat.

Early Saturday morning the NWS updated its Lake Powell forecast for noon to 6 p.m. on Saturday to call for sustained winds of 25 to 35 miles per hour and gusts as high as 55 miles per hour. When the three couples arrived on Saturday morning to begin their trip, Aramark's boat-rental instructor, who told the boaters about the weather channel on the boat's radio, did not inform them of the updated forecast, nor did they request it. He asked Mr. Brady if he knew how to use the radio and Mr. Brady said he did.

The group left Wahweap at about 8 a.m. and safely arrived at their planned destination, Rainbow Bridge. On their return trip to Wahweap, they stopped to refuel at Dangling Rope Marina, also operated by Aramark. Aramark employee Scott Bergantz spoke with some of them during the stop. He testified by deposition that because the water was rough he invited the couples to stay at Dangling Rope if they were [—4—] uncomfortable. This testimony is disputed, and the district court made no findings concerning any offer of hospitality.

Mr. Brady testified that after his group left Dangling Rope the water was "bumpy" and then "got rough" as they entered a small bay. Aplt. App. at 103. The boat proceeded through a "small opening" and then into "a larger bay, which turned out to be Padre Bay," at which point "the wind came up like unbelievable. It was ruthless." *Id.* at 104. At one point Mrs. Brady noticed water at her feet inside the boat and then heard her husband issue a mayday call. The boat sank shortly thereafter. The Bradys were able to reach a rock pile from which they were later rescued. The Prescotts and Tarantos lost their lives.

B. Governing Law

Admiralty law is not a commonplace in the Tenth Circuit, so a brief introduction to some relevant law may be useful.

1. Admiralty and Maritime Jurisdiction

The United States Constitution extends the "judicial power to . . . all Cases of admiralty and maritime Jurisdiction." U.S. Const. art. III, § 2. The first Congress enacted a statute under that authority, stating: "[T]he district courts shall have . . . exclusive original cognizance of all civil causes of admiralty and maritime jurisdiction; saving to suitors, in all cases, the right of a common law remedy, where the common law is competent to give it." Judiciary Act of 1789, ch. 20, § 9, 1 Stat. 73, 76–77. The second clause is often referred to as the saving-to-suitors clause. The original statute has [—5—] been amended several times and now reads: "The district courts shall have original jurisdiction, exclusive of the courts of the States, of: (1) Any civil case of admiralty or maritime jurisdiction, saving to suitors in all cases all other remedies to which they are otherwise entitled."[1] 28 U.S.C. § 1333. The Supreme Court has said that despite the change in language, the "substance [of the saving-to-suitors clause] has remained largely unchanged." *Lewis v. Lewis & Clark Marine, Inc.,* 531 U.S. 438, 443–44 (2001).

That substance is quite broad. For the most part, the saving-to-suitors clause has been construed to permit in personam claims within federal admiralty and maritime jurisdiction to be brought in state court as well as in federal court. *See Lewis,* 531 U.S. at 445 ("[T]he saving to suitors clause [is] a grant to state courts of *in personam* jurisdiction, concurrent with admiralty courts."); Grant Gilmore & Charles L. Black, Jr., *The Law of Admiralty* § 1–13, at 40 (2d ed. 1975) ("Where the suit is in personam, it may be brought *either* in federal court under the admiralty jurisdiction . . . *or,* under the saving clause, in an appropriate non-maritime court, by ordinary civil action."). "The right of a common law remedy, so saved to suitors, ... includes remedies *in pais,* as well as proceedings in court; judicial remedies conferred by statute, as well as those existing at the common law; remedies in equity, as well as those enforceable in a court of law." *Lewis,* 531 U.S. at 445 (internal quotation marks omitted).

But note that the saving-to-suitors clause preserves "remedies" not "rights." *See* 28 U.S.C. § 1333(1) ("saving to suitors in all cases all other remedies to which they are [—6—] otherwise entitled"). Federal maritime and admiralty law still controls the applicable substantive law. The clause's scope "does not . . . include attempted changes by the States in the substantive admiralty law, but it does include all means other than proceedings in admiralty which may be employed to enforce the right or to redress the injury involved." *Lewis,* 531 U.S. at 445 (ellipsis and internal quotation marks omitted). One particular

---

[1] 28 U.S.C. § 1333(2) relates to prizes under admiralty and maritime law.

attraction of proceeding under the saving-to-suitors clause is that there is generally a right to trial by jury in state-court proceedings but, absent some limited statutory exceptions, there is no right to a jury in an action brought under admiralty or maritime jurisdiction. *See Romero v. Int'l Terminal Operating Co.*, 358 U.S. 354, 363, 368–69 (1959); 2 Thomas J. Schoenbaum, *Admiralty and Maritime Law* § 21-10, at 571–74 (5th ed. 2011); Fed. R. Civ. P. 38(e) ("These rules do not create a right to a jury trial on issues in a claim that is an admiralty or maritime claim under Rule 9(h).").

Thus, the *exclusive* federal jurisdiction expressed at the outset of 28 U.S.C. § 1333 does not live up to its apparent promise. That is not to say, however, that the promise is empty. There is exclusive federal jurisdiction to hear an in rem action against a vessel or other maritime property, "[a] procedure unique to American admiralty practice" in which the "action is brought against the vessel itself as defendant." 2 Schoenbaum, *supra*, § 21-3, at 535; *see Lewis*, 531 U.S. at 444 ("[P]roceedings *in rem* were deemed outside the scope of the [saving-to-suitors] clause because an *in rem* action was not a common law remedy, but instead a proceeding under civil law"). And state-court proceedings are [—7—] restricted by the statute employed by Aramark here—the Limitation of Liability Act. We now turn to that statute.

2. The Limitation of Liability Act

Congress enacted the Limitation of Liability Act in 1851 "to encourage shipbuilding and to induce capitalists to invest money in this branch of industry." *Lewis*, 531 U.S. at 446 (internal quotation marks omitted). It was following the lead of other nations. *See Norwich & N.Y. Transp. Co. v. Wright*, 80 U.S. 104, 120 (1871). In the seventeenth century the Dutch scholar Hugo Grotius had written that "men would be deterred from investing in ships if they thereby incurred the apprehension of being rendered liable to an indefinite amount by the acts of the master." *Id.* at 116. Various European nations had therefore adopted laws limiting the owner's liability to the value of the ship and freight. *See id.* at 116–17. In England, for example, once a ship owner confessed liability and paid the value of the ship and freight into court, his exposure would be limited to that sum and he would have the right to stay any suit against him for damages. *See id.* at 118.

The current version of the Limitation of Liability Act was codified in 2006 at 46 U.S.C. § 30501 *et seq.*[2] Its key provision limits the boat owner's liability to the limitation fund—"the value of the vessel and pending freight," *id.* at § 30505(a)—provided that the acts giving rise to the damage occurred "without the privity or knowledge of the owner," [—8—] *see id.* at § 30505(b).[3] The vessel's value is measured "*after* the voyage on which the incident occurred. Thus if the ship is lost, the value is zero." *Pickle v. Char Lee Seafood, Inc.*, 174 F.3d 444, 449 (4th Cir. 1999) (citation omitted) (internal quotation mark omitted). *Pending freight* is "the total earnings for the voyage, both prepaid and uncollected." *In re Caribbean Sea Transp., Ltd.*, 748 F.2d 622, 626 (11th Cir. 1984). If the limitation fund is

---

[2] Many pre-2006 cases reference the Act at its then-locus, 46 U.S.C. App. § 181 *et seq. See, e.g., Lewis*, 531 U.S. at 441.

[3] 46 U.S.C. § 30505 states:

(a) In general. Except as provided in section 30506 of this title [relating to claims for personal injury or death], the liability of the owner of a vessel for any claim, debt, or liability described in subsection (b) shall not exceed the value of the vessel and pending freight. If the vessel has more than one owner, the proportionate share of the liability of any one owner shall not exceed that owner's proportionate interest in the vessel and pending freight.

(b) Claims subject to limitation. Unless otherwise excluded by law, claims, debts, and liabilities subject to limitation under subsection (a) are those arising from any embezzlement, loss, or destruction of any property, goods, or merchandise shipped or put on board the vessel, any loss, damage, or injury by collision, or any act, matter, or thing, loss, damage, or forfeiture, done, occasioned, or incurred, without the privity or knowledge of the owner.

(c) Wages. Subsection (a) does not apply to a claim for wages.

insufficient to pay all claims, it is divided by claimants "in proportion to their respective losses." 46 U.S.C. § 30507. For personal-injury or death claims the cap on liability may be increased to $420 times the tonnage of the vessel; but this applies only to a "seagoing" vessel, *id.* at § 30506—that is, one that "does, or is intended to, navigate in the seas beyond the Boundary Line in the regular course of [their] operations," *In re Talbott Big Foot, Inc.*, 854 F.2d 758, 761 (5th Cir. 1988); *see id.* ("The Boundary Line is that line which divides the high seas from rivers, harbors, and inland waters."). **[—9—]**

"[F]ederal courts have exclusive jurisdiction to determine whether a vessel owner is entitled to limited liability." *Lewis*, 531 U.S. at 442. To govern procedures under the Limitation Act, the Supreme Court promulgated rules a century and a half ago. The current version of those rules is found in Rule F (entitled "Limitation of Liability") of the Supplemental Rules for Admiralty or Maritime Claims and Asset Forfeiture Actions. Under Rule F a ship owner seeking limitation must file a complaint "set[ting] forth the facts on the basis of which the right to limit liability is asserted and all facts necessary to enable the court to determine the amount to which the owner's liability shall be limited." Fed. R. Civ. P. Supp. Admiralty Rule F(2). Necessary facts include a description of the voyage, the amount of any pending demands against the owner, and the present value of the vessel. *See id.* Once the owner files the complaint and deposits with the court or a trustee an amount equal to the limitation fund (or security therefor), plus security for costs and interest, "all claims and proceedings against the owner or the owner's property with respect to the matter in question shall cease"; and if moved to do so by the ship owner, "the court shall enjoin the further prosecution of any action or proceeding . . . subject to limitation in the action." *Id.* at F(3). If the court grants limitation, it then distributes the limitation fund "pro rata, subject to all relevant provisions of law, among the several claimants in proportion to the amounts of their respective claims, duly proved." *Id.* at F(8).

Rule F echoes much of the procedure under prior English law. *See generally Norwich*, 80 U.S. at 117–20. But it is not identical. One innovation has been in the rule **[—10—]** since first promulgated in 1871. Although English practice required the owner to admit his liability at the outset, the Supreme Court thought that such an admission "is, perhaps, not necessary in an admiralty court." *Id.* at 124. Under Rule F, "[i]n the process of seeking limited liability, the owner [is] permitted to contest the fact of liability," *Lewis*, 531 U.S. at 447; *see* Rule F(2) (the complaint may "demand exoneration from as well as limitation of liability").

"The determination of whether a shipowner is entitled to limitation employs a two-step process." *Farrell Lines Inc. v. Jones*, 530 F.2d 7, 10 (5th Cir. 1976). "First, the court must determine what acts of negligence or conditions of unseaworthiness caused the accident." *Id.* "Second, the court must determine whether the shipowner had knowledge or privity of those same acts of negligence or conditions of unseaworthiness." *Id.* There are three possible outcomes to a limitation petition: exoneration, limitation, or no limitation. If no negligence is shown, the inquiry ends and the district court will typically issue an order exonerating the owner from liability. *See In re Trawler Snoopy, Inc.*, 268 F. Supp. 951, 953 (D. Me. 1967) ("If no liability is found to exist, the petitioner is entitled to a decree of exoneration, and there is no need to consider the claim to limitation."). If claimants demonstrate negligence, the burden shifts to the owner to show lack of privity or knowledge. *See Farrell Lines*, 530 F.2d at 10. If the owner meets this burden, the court caps the owner's liability at the value of the vessel and pending freight, resolves the claims, and apportions the fund. *See* Rule F(8). But if the owner fails to establish lack of privity or knowledge, the court denies the limitation petition and the **[—11—]** owner is as fully liable as it would have been absent the Limitation Act. *See* 46 U.S.C. § 30505. The claimant then may pursue relief in any suitable forum. *See Pickle*, 174 F.3d at 449 ("If the shipowner fails to establish its right under the Limitation Act and limitation is therefore denied, the claimants are released to pursue their original claims in full."); *Wheeler v. Marine Navigation Sulphur Carriers, Inc.*, 764 F.2d 1008, 1011 (4th Cir. 1985) ("Each circuit that has considered this question has ruled that once limitation is denied, plaintiffs should be permitted to elect whether to remain in the limitation proceeding or to revive their original claims in their original fora."). *See generally* Gilmore & Black, *supra*, § 10–41, at 935 (when limitation is denied, "[t]he lower courts have on the whole found that . . . plaintiffs, by virtue of the saving to suitors clause, should be allowed to choose the forum of litigation").

Although a limitation-of-liability proceeding may fully dispose of a maritime claim against a ship owner, that is not always the case. As noted in the previous paragraph, if the limitation court does not exonerate or limit the liability of the defendant, the claim can proceed in another court. And even if the vessel's owner succeeds in limiting liability, proceedings may then move to another venue as long as the owner's right to limitation is protected. *See Lewis*, 531 U.S. at 454–55. For example, when the sum of all claims is less than the limitation fund, and thus does not threaten the owner with liability exceeding the fund, the federal court hearing the limitation-of-liability proceeding may lift the injunction against other proceedings and allow litigation of the claims in state court. *See id.* at 450–51. Similarly, when a single claimant agrees not to [—12—] seek a recovery greater than the limitation fund, the federal court should permit the claim to proceed elsewhere. *See id.* at 448–50. The owner may even plead the defense of limitation in state court rather than file a limitation action in federal district court. *See Langnes v. Green*, 282 U.S. 531, 541–43 (1931); *Cody v. Phil's Towing Co.*, 247 F. Supp. 2d 688, 691 (W.D. Pa. 2002) ("Although a limitation proceeding commonly is commenced as a separate action by the filing of a petition, invocation of the statutory rights created by the Act also can be accomplished through a plea of limited liability asserted in the answer to a plaintiff's complaint."); 2 Schoenbaum, *supra*, § 15-5, at 181 ("Limitation may be invoked either as a defense to an action seeking damages or as an independent complaint in admiralty."); Gilmore & Black, *supra*, § 10–14, at 853 n.52. In such instances the state court can resolve certain limitation-related issues, such as the limitation amount. *See Langnes*, 282 U.S. at 543. But the state court lacks jurisdiction to consider the owner's entitlement to limitation; if a plaintiff wishes to challenge that entitlement, the federal district court, not the state court, "has exclusive cognizance of such a question." *Id.*; *see Lewis*, 531 U.S. at 442. The federal court may therefore retain jurisdiction over a limitation action while the litigation proceeds in state court, just in case the state-court litigation threatens the owner's limitation rights. *See Lewis*, 531 U.S. at 448–50, 453–55.

C. Procedural History

Aramark filed a limitation complaint in federal court before any claim against it had been brought. The estates and heirs of the Prescotts and Tarantos (Claimants) filed [—13—] answers and counterclaims seeking damages for wrongful death. The Bradys, who are not parties to this appeal, filed an answer and counterclaim that did not seek damages but sought indemnification from Aramark in case they were held liable for the deaths of the Tarantos or the Prescotts. Claimants then successfully moved to bifurcate the limitations issues from those raised by their counterclaims for wrongful death, for which they claimed the right to a jury trial. The court left for later resolution whether, if Aramark failed on its limitation complaint, to grant Claimants' request to proceed in state court on their wrongful-death claims. Phase one was a bench trial on the limitation issue, leaving nonlimitation issues such as gross negligence, damages, and apportionment of fault for a phase-two jury trial. The court found that negligence had "at least in part" caused the accident and that such negligence was within Aramark's privity or knowledge. It therefore could not exonerate Aramark from liability and denied Aramark's petition for limitation.

II. APPELLATE JURISDICTION

Before addressing the merits, we must assure ourselves of our appellate jurisdiction. Aramark asserts that jurisdiction lies under 28 U.S.C. § 1292(a)(3), which states that "courts of appeals shall have jurisdiction of appeals from . . . [i]nterlocutory decrees of . . . district courts or the judges thereof determining the rights and liabilities of the parties to admiralty cases in which appeals from final decrees are allowed."

Claimants argue that § 1292(a)(3) does not grant us jurisdiction because "the district court did not fully or ultimately determine the rights and liabilities of the parties [—14—] or the merits of the controversy between them." Aplee. Br. at 2. In particular, they point out that the court "did not pass upon various issues pertaining to liability and the merits of the controversy," such as their "allegations of gross negligence, request for punitive damages, and allocation of degrees of fault as well as compensatory damages." *Id.*

This argument would be convincing if jurisdiction under 28 U.S.C. § 1291 were being invoked. That section restricts appellate jurisdiction to "final decisions" of the district courts, and the unresolved issues pointed out by Claimants would prevent the court's decision below from being final. *See, e.g., Liberty Mut. Ins. Co. v. Wetzel*, 424 U.S. 737, 744 (1976) ("[J]udgments [limited to the issue of liability] are by their terms interlocutory, and where assessment of damages or awarding of other relief remains to be resolved have never been considered to be 'final' within the meaning of 28 U.S.C. § 1291." (citation and internal quotation marks omitted)); *Roska ex rel. Roska v. Sneddon*, 437 F.3d 964, 970 (10th Cir. 2006) ("Because further proceedings are necessary to determine causation and the amount of damages, if any, the district court's order is not final and the grant of Plaintiffs' motion is not immediately appealable [under § 1291].")"; *Albright v. UNUM Life Ins. Co. of Am.*, 59 F.3d 1089, 1092 (10th Cir. 1995) (noting "the general and well-established rule that an order that determines liability but leaves damages to be calculated is not final" (internal quotation marks omitted)).

But the bailiwick of § 1292(a)(3) is not final decisions. It is "interlocutory decrees" in admiralty "cases in which appeals from final decrees are allowed." Since the statute was enacted in 1925, *see Schoenamsgruber v. Hamburg Am. Line*, 294 U.S. 454, [—15—] 457 (1935), federal courts have been consistent in giving the statutory language its plain meaning: all that is required is that a right or liability of a party have been determined. As stated in one of the earlier appellate decisions on the statute:

It is obvious that [the statutory language] does not mean *all* the rights and liabilities of the parties for, if so, the only appeal allowable is from the final decree denying any limitation and determining the amount of the claims and their share of the fund. The question is, Is *any* right of [the appellant] finally determined by the decree fixing the limit of liability?

Rice Growers Ass'n of Cal. v. Rederiaktiebolaget Frode, 171 F.2d 662, 663 (9th Cir. 1948) (emphasis added).

The decision in *In re S.S. Tropic Breeze*, 456 F.2d 137 (1st Cir. 1972), illustrates how far appellate courts have gone in hearing appeals under § 1292(a)(3) when liability is at issue. The ship had been libeled to pay crew wages. *See id.* at 138. Tropical Commerce Corporation had chartered the vessel and installed cement equipment. *See id.* A party with a mortgage on the vessel had argued in district court that Tropical could claim an interest in the cement equipment only out of the proceeds of the ship's sale, but the court had ruled that the mortgagee was bound by a stipulation to pay Tropical the value of the equipment, provided that Tropical actually owned the equipment. *See id.* The court referred to a master the issues of whether Tropical owned the equipment and its value. *See id.* The mortgagee appealed the ruling that it could itself be liable to Tropical for the equipment's value, rather than Tropical being limited to collecting out of the proceeds of the ship's sale. *See id.* Tropical moved to dismiss the appeal because the [—16—] issues of ownership and value were still to be determined. The First Circuit denied the motion, relying on § 1292(a)(3). It wrote:

> It is true that the usual interlocutory appeal under section 1292(a)(3) is from an order finally determining that one party is liable to another and referring the cause to an assessor for the determination of damages. The statute is not limited to such situations, however, but, rather, applies to any decree finally determining the liability of one of the parties, even if it leaves open an issue which may, ultimately preclude recovery by a particular plaintiff.

Id. at 139 (citations omitted). "The fact that this question [of Tropical's title] was left open," wrote the court, "does not mean that the court did not adequately determine rights within the meaning of 28 U.S.C. § 1292(a)(3), which broadly permits admiralty appeals." *Id.*

Section 1292(a)(3) was designed to allow ship owners to seek an appeal to halt litigation at an early stage, in the hope of eliminating the need for further proceedings. "Congress intended 28 U.S.C. § 1292(a)(3) to permit parties to appeal the finding of liability on the merits, before undergoing the long, burdensome, and perhaps unnecessary damages proceeding." *Evergreen Int'l (USA) Corp. v. Standard Warehouse*, 33 F.3d 420, 424 (4th Cir. 1994); *see also United States v. The Lake George*, 224 F.2d 117, 118 (3d Cir. 1955) ("[T]he classic example of [§ 1292(a)(3)'s] day-to-day operation is presented when there is a determination of liability as distinguished from amount."). To be sure, not every district-court ruling on a potentially dispositive issue in an admiralty suit is appealable under § 1292(a)(3). *See Schoenamsgruber*, 294 U.S. at 458 (denying right to appeal order to arbitrate maritime claims); *In re Ingram Towing Co.*, 59 F.3d 513, 517 [—17—] (5th Cir. 1995) ("Orders which do not determine parties' substantive rights or liabilities . . . are not appealable under section 1292(a)(3) even if those orders have important procedural consequences." (internal quotation marks omitted)). The decision to be reviewed must have involved substantive "rights and liabilities." But that is the case here. There has been a determination of liability, the express concern of the jurisdictional statute— Aramark was not exonerated and would have to pay *some* damages, with the amount depending on how much at fault others were, whether Aramark was grossly negligent, and how much in damages was suffered by Claimants.

There is particular reason to permit appeals of denials of limitation or exoneration, because the dispute is then likely to go to another court. If the ship owner files a limitation claim after suit has been brought against it in a different forum (say, a state court), the earlier suit would be stayed during the limitation proceeding, but the stay would be lifted if limitation and exoneration are denied. And even if the limitation action is filed before suit is brought against the owner, the claimants may wish to proceed elsewhere once the limitation issue has been resolved. For example, in *Lewis* the Supreme Court approved the district court's order permitting a suit to proceed in state court even though the vessel owner filed for limitation in federal court before the plaintiff had sued in state court and the plaintiff had counterclaimed for personal-injury damages in the federal suit. *See* 531 U.S. at 441. (The district court had ruled that it was not necessary to resolve the limitation issue because the plaintiff's claim was less than the limitation fund conceded by the owner (although the court retained jurisdiction to protect [—18—] the owner's limitation rights in case the state-court judgment exceeded the limitation amount). *See In re Lewis & Clark Marine, Inc.*, 31 F. Supp. 2d 1164, 1169–70 (E.D. Mo. 1998).) Indeed, Claimants have sought to continue this litigation in state court. *See* Motion to Bifurcate at 2, *In re Aramark*, No. 2:09-cv-00637-TC-PMW, Doc. No. 173 (D. Utah Oct. 30, 2012). Why wait (even if federal appellate practice permitted that course) till state-court litigation has concluded before taking an appeal of the limitation ruling? Such delay could be particularly problematic because the federal district court's rejection of Aramark's limitation complaint "is res judicata on the issue of liability." *Republic of France v. United States*, 290 F.2d 395, 397 (5th Cir. 1961). It makes sense to resolve finally (through appellate review) those limitation rulings to which the state court must defer during its proceedings, rather than conducting a federal appeal after a state-court judgment and thereby risking the need for a state retrial if the federal appeal leads to reversal. The value of comity between jurisdictions suggests avoiding such offense to state proceedings.

It is therefore not surprising that appellate courts have regularly exercised jurisdiction over denials of petitions for limitation of liability. *See, e.g., In re Bankers Trust Co.*, 651 F.2d 160, 163–64 (3d Cir. 1981) (reversing denial of limitation); *Waterman S. S. Corp. v. Gay Cottons*, 414 F.2d 724, 727 (9th Cir. 1969) (affirming denial); *Coleman v. Jahncke Serv., Inc.*, 341 F.2d 956, 957 (5th Cir. 1965) (affirming denial); *Republic of France*, 290 F.2d at 401 (reversing denial). [—19—]

Republic of France is illustrative. The United States sued France following a horrendous explosion (the Texas City Disaster) started on a French ship loaded with fertilizer-grade ammonium nitrate manufactured by the United States. *See* 290 F.2d at 396. It sued in two capacities: first, as the assignee of hundreds of individual claims for deaths, personal injuries, and property damages, for which the United States had paid the claimants an aggregate sum of $16 million; second, as successor to the Reconstruction Finance Corporation, which had lost $350,000 in goods. *See id.* France filed a limitation action, *see id.*, but the district court found France negligent and declined to exonerate it or limit its liability, *see id.* at 398. Admiralty law at that time permitted damages to be reduced for a claimant's own negligence, *see Pope & Talbot v. Hawn*, 346 U.S. 406, 409 (1953) (contributory negligence can be considered "in mitigation of damages as justice requires"), and the United States conceded that the court had not yet adjudicated France's claim that the United States was negligent, *see Republic of France*, 290 F.2d at 397 n.4. In addition, the United States still had to prove liability on its asserted claims (presumably by establishing causation for the alleged damages to property and for the personal injury or death of the hundreds of persons whose claims had been assigned to it). *See id.* Yet after acknowledging that "[t]he only ultimate issue so far determined by the district court is that the petitioners are not entitled to exoneration from or limitation of liability," the court of appeals still found jurisdiction under § 1292(a)(3) on the ground that the district court "finally determined the rights and liabilities of the parties by denying the petition for exoneration from or limitation of liability." *Id.* at 397. Similarly, [—20—] here the district court denied limitation and exoneration. That suffices to establish our jurisdiction under § 1292(a)(3), even though the district court declined to rule on nonlimitation issues.

Citing *Becker v. Poling Transportation Corp.*, 356 F.3d 381, 387–88 (2d Cir. 2004), and other cases, Claimants assert that "[s]ection 1292(a)(3) is construed narrowly." Aplee. Br. at 1. But these cases stand for nothing more than that the statute will not be stretched to include matters beyond its purview, which is rulings determining "the rights and liabilities of the parties to admiralty cases." 28 U.S.C. § 1292(a)(3). Two of the cited cases actually held that the appellate court had jurisdiction. *Becker*, which expressly stated that the statute confers appellate jurisdiction even when the district court "has left unsettled the assessment of damages or other details required to be determined prior to entry of a final decree," 356 F.3d at 387, decided that it had jurisdiction to hear an appeal from an interlocutory ruling that held the appellant liable for a fire but left open some claims for indemnity and contribution, *see id.* at 386–88. And in *Deering v. National Maintenance & Repair, Inc.*, 627 F.3d 1039, 1041–43 (7th Cir. 2010), the court exercised jurisdiction over an appeal from an order dismissing a counterclaim. Also, in two cited cases denying appellate jurisdiction the appealed decision had not addressed liability. *See Evergreen*, 33 F.3d at 422–25 (declining to exercise jurisdiction over appeal of order granting summary judgment to defendants because claims should have been brought in arbitration); *Astarte Shipping Co. v. Allied Steel & Exp. Serv.*, 767 F.2d 86, 88 (5th Cir.

1985) (order confirming an attachment in admiralty is not appealable under [—21—] § 1292(a)(3) because it does not determine the rights and liabilities of the parties). As for the two remaining cited cases, the courts held that they lacked appellate jurisdiction to resolve an *issue* concerning liability because there remained other issues to be resolved before it could be known whether the party had any liability. In *Francis ex rel. Francis v. Forest Oil Corp.*, 798 F.2d 147, 149–50 (5th Cir. 1986) (per curiam), the Fifth Circuit ruled that it had no jurisdiction to hear an appeal of the district court's order denying a summary-judgment motion that had asserted that the wrongful-death claims had been contractually released, thereby leaving liability for trial. And in *The Lake George*, the Third Circuit ruled that it lacked jurisdiction to hear the appeal of a district-court order dismissing one of four causes of action seeking forfeiture, 224 F.2d at 118–19; because three other causes of action remained live, it said, "[t]he liability of the vessel to forfeiture has yet to be determined," *id.* at 119. We need not decide whether we agree with those two decisions because in our case the district court definitively resolved that Aramark would bear liability for the accident. In any event, whatever the precise implications of these two opinions, we can be confident that they do not cast doubt on our jurisdiction in this case. Both the Third and Fifth Circuits have held that the denial of limitation and exoneration is appealable. *See In re Bankers Trust*, 651 F.2d at 163–64 (3d Cir.); *Republic of France*, 290 F.2d at 401 (5th Cir.).

Claimants have not cited, nor are we aware of, any decision rejecting appellate jurisdiction over a denial of limitation and exoneration. We hold that we have jurisdiction over this appeal. We therefore turn to the merits. [—22—]

III. EXONERATION

A two-step process governs whether a ship owner is entitled to limitation or exoneration. "First, the court must determine what acts of negligence or conditions of unseaworthiness caused the accident. Second, the court must determine whether the shipowner had knowledge or privity of those same acts of negligence or conditions of unseaworthiness." *Farrell Lines*, 530 F.2d at 10. Because Claimants do not assert unseaworthiness and Aramark does not claim lack of privity or knowledge, the two-step inquiry in this case boils down to whether negligence by Aramark caused the accident.

The question of negligence is governed by federal maritime law. "With admiralty jurisdiction comes the application of substantive admiralty law." *East River S.S. Corp. v. Transamerica Delaval, Inc.*, 476 U.S. 858, 864 (1986); *see* 1 Schoenbaum, *supra*, § 5-2, at 251 ("[O]nce admiralty jurisdiction is established . . . a plaintiff's case will be determined under principles of maritime negligence rather than common law negligence."). "Absent a relevant statute, the general maritime law [is] developed by the judiciary." *East River*, 476 U.S. at 864. "Drawn from state and federal sources, the general maritime law is an amalgam of traditional common-law rules, modifications of those rules, and newly created rules." *Id.* at 864–65; *see* 1 Schoenbaum, *supra*, § 4-1, at 220 ("The general maritime law is a body of concepts, principles and rules, originally customary and international in origin, that have been adopted and expounded over time by the federal courts."). In developing maritime law, "courts sitting in admiralty may draw guidance from, *inter alia,* the extensive body of state law . . . and from treatises and [—23—] other scholarly sources." *Exxon Co., U.S.A. v. Sofec, Inc.*, 517 U.S. 830, 839 (1996). In particular, maritime courts have regularly looked to the current Restatement of Torts for guidance. *See Oswalt v. Resolute Indus., Inc.*, 642 F.3d 856, 860 (9th Cir. 2011) (following Restatement (Third) of Torts: Products Liability (1998)); *St. Paul Fire & Marine Ins. Co. v. Lago Canyon, Inc.*, 561 F.3d 1181, 1190 n.18 (11th Cir. 2009) (same); *Krummel v. Bombardier Corp.*, 206 F.3d 548, 552 (5th Cir. 2000) (same); *All Alaskan Seafoods, Inc. v. Raychem Corp.*, 197 F.3d 992, 995 (9th Cir. 1999) (same); *Lobegeiger v. Celebrity Cruises, Inc.*, No. 11-21620-CIV, 2011 WL 3703329, at *16–17 (S.D. Fla. Aug. 23, 2011) (following Restatement (Third) of Torts: Physical and Emotional Harm (2010)).

A. General Tort Principles

The district court found that Aramark "had a duty to be advised of the current weather forecasts and wind advisories before allowing any party to leave" and "breached its duty of reasonable care when it allowed the Prescott Party to leave the morning of April 25, 2009." Order at 14. The court found that because the forecast called for high winds and the boat's owner's manual stated that the boat was unsafe in winds exceeding 31 miles per hour, Aramark could have foreseen that the boat would sink, leading to the injury or death of its passengers. And because the accident was foreseeable, the court reasoned, Aramark had a duty to prevent the boaters from venturing onto Lake Powell. Aramark responds that it had no duty to be advised of and warn of weather conditions [—24—] and that to require concessionaires to close down whenever a danger is foreseeable would unduly impede access to national parks.

Before we determine what, if any, duty Aramark owed the boaters, we express our disagreement with the district court's methodology. Even if we accept that the accident was foreseeable, foreseeability does not equate to duty. In a maritime products-liability case, the Supreme Court expressly rejected the notion that a manufacturer's duty is coextensive with foreseeability: "In products-liability law, where there is a duty to the public generally, foreseeability is an inadequate brake. Permitting recovery for all foreseeable claims for purely economic loss could make a manufacturer liable for vast sums. . . . The law does not spread its protection so far." *East River*, 476 U.S. at 874 (citations omitted) (internal quotation marks omitted).

Instead, in a negligence case, such as the one before us, the role of foreseeability should be in assessing whether a person acted with reasonable care—that is, without negligence, *see* Restatement (Third) of Torts: Physical and Emotional Harm (Restatement (Third)) § 3, at 29 ("A person acts negligently if the person does not exercise reasonable care under all the circumstances.")—*after* the court has determined that there is a duty. In his classic formulation Judge Learned Hand wrote that whether a person is negligent "is a function of three variables: (1) The probability [of injury]; (2) the gravity of the resulting injury, if [it occurs]; (3) the burden of adequate precautions." *United States v. Carroll Towing Co.*, 159 F.2d 169, 173 (2d Cir. 1947). To exercise reasonable care one must take a precaution if the cost of doing so is less than the [—25—] probability of injury times the magnitude of the potential injury. *See id.* The Restatement (Third) has refined this formula: "To establish the actor's negligence, it is not enough that there be a likelihood of harm; the likelihood must be *foreseeable* to the actor at the time of conduct." Restatement (Third) § 3 cmt. g, at 33 (emphasis added). Thus, the Restatement states: "Primary factors to consider in ascertaining whether the person's conduct lacks reasonable care are the *foreseeable* likelihood that the person's conduct will result in harm, the *foreseeable* severity of any harm that may ensue, and the burden of precautions to eliminate or reduce the risk of harm." *Id.* § 3, at 29 (emphasis added). Under the Restatement, lack of foreseeability can still be a basis for judgment in favor of the defendant. But it "is not a no-duty determination. Rather, it is a determination that no reasonable person could find that the defendant has breached the duty of reasonable care." *Id.* § 7 cmt. j, at 83.

Of course, it makes no practical difference whether we say that a defense judgment based on nonforeseeability is a no-duty determination or a no-breach determination. But when the potential for injury *is* foreseeable, it can make a decisive difference whether or not the court equates duty and foreseeability. The district court, not without some support in caselaw, ruled that Aramark had a duty simply because the danger was foreseeable. We think the better view, however, is that the determination of duty is a policy matter, not based on the foreseeability of danger in the particular case. The Restatement (Third) reflects this approach in the black letter of § 7:

(a) An actor ordinarily has a duty to exercise reasonable care when the actor's conduct creates a risk of physical harm. [—26—]

(b) In exceptional cases, when an articulated countervailing principle or policy warrants denying or limiting liability in a particular class of cases, a court may decide that the defendant has no duty or that the ordinary duty of reasonable care requires modification.

Id. at 77. That is, "in some categories of cases, reasons of principle or policy dictate that liability should not be imposed. In these cases, courts use the rubric of duty to apply general categorical rules withholding liability." *Id.* cmt. a, at 77.

Such limitations on duty are widely accepted for a variety of reasons. One reason is "general social norms of responsibility." *Id.* cmt. c, at 79. As an example, the Restatement notes:

[M]any courts have held that commercial establishments that serve alcoholic beverages have a duty to use reasonable care to avoid injury to others who might be injured by an intoxicated customer, but that social hosts do not have a similar duty to those who might be injured by their guests. Courts often justify this distinction by referring to commonly held social norms about responsibility.

Id. Similarly, the joy and benefits of sports, and respect for individual autonomy, have caused courts to limit liability for injuries in athletic competition. *See id.* at 78. Sometimes factors that go beyond the specific case may cause courts to adopt a no-duty rule even when "reasonable minds could differ about the application of the negligence standard to a particular category of recurring facts." *Id.* cmt. i, at 81. "In conducting its analysis, the court may take into account factors that might escape the jury's attention in a particular case, such as the overall social impact of imposing a significant precautionary obligation on a class of actors. These cases are properly decided as duty or no-duty cases." *Id.* For example, courts have held that because

treating physicians are in the best position to inform patients of the risks and benefits of prescription drugs, drug [—27—] manufacturers must provide warnings to physicians but ordinarily have no duty to warn individual patients. *See id.* cmt. i, at 82. In sum:

A no-duty ruling represents a determination, a purely legal question, that no liability should be imposed on actors in a category of cases. Such a ruling should be explained and justified based on articulated policies or principles that justify exempting these actors from liability or modifying the ordinary duty of reasonable care. These reasons of policy and principle do not depend on the foreseeability of harm based on the specific facts of a case. They should be articulated directly without obscuring references to foreseeability.

Id. cmt. j, at 82.

For the sake of completeness, we note that two additional conditions must be met to establish liability even if it has been determined that the defendant had a duty and breached the standard of care. First, the defendant's action must have factually caused the harm, meaning "the harm would not have occurred absent the conduct." *Id.* § 26, at 346. Second, the injury must have "result[ed] from the risks that made the actor's conduct tortious." *Id.* § 29, at 493. The confusing term *proximate cause* is sometimes used to describe this second condition, *see id.* cmt. b, at 494, but the better term is *scope of liability*. The central idea is that "an actor should be held liable only for harm that was among the potential harms—the risks—that made the actor's conduct tortious." *Id.* cmt. d, at 495–96. For example, a man who hands a loaded gun to a child negligently creates the risk that the child will shoot someone; if the child drops the gun on her toe, breaking it, the man is not liable because dropping the gun onto the foot is not within the scope of risks that rendered the man's action negligent. *See id.* illus. 3, at 496–97. [—28—]

B. Aramark's Duty

We now turn to Aramark's duty in this case. As we understand Claimants' argument, Aramark had a duty not to rent the boat because of the dangers apparent from the weather forecast and the limited capacity of the boat to withstand high winds. Implicit in this argument is the argument that Aramark had a duty to warn the boaters about the weather forecast and the boat's limited capacity. It is useful to discuss separately the alleged duties to warn of the weather and to warn of the boat's capacity because different considerations apply to each. We first address whether Aramark had a duty to warn of the weather; then whether Aramark had a duty not to rent the boat because of the weather; and then whether Aramark had a duty to warn of the boat's limited capacity.

In our view, Aramark had no duty to obtain a weather forecast and provide it to the boaters. As we noted above in the general discussion of duty, notions of personal responsibility regularly underlie no-duty determinations. The question here is whether the defendant must protect the plaintiff against a danger not created by the defendant when the plaintiff could take the same protective steps at least equally easily and well. The rented boat was equipped with a radio for obtaining weather reports. The boaters could obtain the forecast with the same minimal effort that the Aramark representative at the marina could. Also, forecasts are notoriously iffy. The forecasts available on the boat radio during the trip would be more timely than the forecast that could be provided by the representative before the trip began. With all this in mind, it is unsurprising that [—29—] every reported decision (cited to or found by us) to consider the point has held that there is no duty to acquire a weather forecast and provide it to customers.

Of particular note is *Leach v. Mountain Lake*, 120 F.3d 871, 872–73 (8th Cir. 1997), also involving a fatal boating accident after the renting marina neither obtained weather information nor passed it on to its customers. *See id.* at 872. As here, the weather was calm when the boat was rented, but the NWS had issued an advisory warning of strong afternoon gusts. The Eighth Circuit held that as a matter of law "the marina had no . . . duty to acquire and pass on weather information," affirming the district court's reasoning "that weather information is readily available to those who rent boats (should they choose to seek it), that boaters can themselves observe weather and sea changes and ascertain water temperature, and that the ability of boaters to do this is not in any way dependent upon what marinas do or do not tell them." *Id.* at 873; *see also, e.g., Grant v. Wakeda Campground, LLC*, 631 F. Supp. 2d 120, 128 (D.N.H. 2009) ("Both the inherent unreliability of weather forecasts and the fact that weather changes constantly justify not imposing on defendant a greater duty to monitor the weather than can be expected of plaintiffs. . . . [T]here is no basis to impose a duty to monitor the weather as part of the duty to keep the [campground] safe."); *Petition of Binstock*, 213 F. Supp. 909, 915 (S.D.N.Y. 1963) (prospective boat purchaser died in a storm while testing the boat; the court ruled that the seller had no duty to warn of weather conditions when "such perils as may have existed were equally apparent to and cognizable by [purchaser and seller]"); *West v. City of St. Paul*, 936 P.2d 136, 139 (Alaska 1997) ("Because most [—30—] weather conditions are open and obvious, and can be discovered with reasonable diligence, a wharfinger does not have a duty to warn of such dangers."); *cf. Black v. United States*, 441 F.2d 741, 744 (5th Cir. 1971) (ruling in a plane-crash case that any negligence of flight controller was superseded by pilot's negligence because "[i]t was the pilot's responsibility to obtain a weather briefing" and the pilot could have obtained weather updates "merely by monitoring the stations along his route"); *Croce v. Hall*, 657 A.2d 307, 312 (D.C. 1995) (landlord had no duty to monitor weather reports so that he could be prepared to immediately clear sidewalk of snow; "weather predictions are often wrong").

Similar considerations undoubtedly underlie, at least in part, limitations on liability for negligent failure to warn set forth in § 18 of the Restatement (Third). The black letter states:

(a) A defendant whose conduct creates a risk of physical or emotional harm can fail to exercise reasonable care by failing to warn of the danger if:
(1) the defendant knows or has reason to know: (a) of that risk; and *(b) that those encountering the risk will be unaware of it; and*
(2) *a warning might be effective in reducing the risk of harm.*

Restatement (Third) § 18 (emphasis added); *see* Scope Note to §§ 17–19 at 183 ("To some extent these rules . . . involve matters with public-policy significance that courts have deemed to be duty issues under § 7, to be decided by courts rather than by juries."). Thus, under § 18 a defendant is not liable for failing to warn of a danger to another person when the defendant would expect the other person to be aware of the danger or if the warning would not be effective in reducing the risk, even if the defendant created the [—31—] risk. Here, the defendant did not create the danger and had no greater capacity to learn of the danger than the injured persons did, particularly when one considers the advisability of getting periodic updates of the forecast. We conclude that Aramark had no duty to monitor the weather and provide a forecast to the boaters.[4]

---

[4] Claimants suggest that Aramark "assumed the responsibility of providing weather information to [the boaters] yet failed to provide accurate and up-to-date such information." Aplee. Br. at 43; *see id.* at 37 ("Aramark exacerbated the situation by telling [the boaters] that they would receive an updated forecast and the rental prospects would be reevaluated the following morning, but then failed to do so."); *id.* at 35 ("Aramark . . . undertook the responsibility of providing weather forecast information to [the boaters]."). A duty may arise where a party voluntarily undertakes to warn others of weather conditions, and those others rely on that party for those warnings. *See* Restatement (Second) of Torts § 323 (1965); *Sall v. T's, Inc.*, 136 P.3d 471, 473–74, 484 (Kan. 2006) (golf course assumed the duty to use a horn to warn its patrons of dangerous thunderstorms, which lightning-strike victim relied on to his detriment). We question whether Claimants adequately raised on appeal an

It would be even more problematic to impose upon Aramark a duty to shut down boat rentals based on the forecasts it receives. If Aramark has no duty to customers to monitor and report the weather forecast, we see no basis for requiring it to monitor the weather and then make the decision for customers about whether it is advisable to venture onto the lake. *See Grant*, 631 F. Supp. 2d at 129 (no duty to close campground). Such decisions are sometimes made by governmental authorities (for example, the NPS could close Lake Powell to boating, although it did not restrict access on the day of the accident). *But see Johnson v. U.S., Dep't of Interior*, 949 F.2d 332, 337 (10th Cir. 1991) [—32—] (although rock climbers in Grand Teton National Park are required to obtain a permit, park rangers have no authority to stop them from attempting dangerous climbs). Claimants, however, have pointed us to no comparable duties under tort law. Imposing a duty that so limits personal choice in the context of recreation would be particularly inappropriate. We have already noted that the duty of ordinary care—imposed on those who created the danger—has generally been relaxed in the context of athletic competition. Similarly, nearly every state has encouraged landowners to freely open their property for outdoor recreation by relaxing the traditional standard of care for landowners to keep their property safe. *See Klepper v. City of Milford, Kansas*, 825 F.2d 1440, 1444 (10th Cir. 1987). "[T]hese statutes promote casual recreational use of open space by relieving landowners of the concern that they will be sued for injuries to strangers who hunt, trek, fish, and otherwise recreate on their land or water free of charge." *Id.* Absent such statutes, landowners would "simply close their lands to public use and many recreational oppor-

---

assumed-undertaking theory of duty. But in any event they failed to raise an assumed-duty theory below, as illustrated by the district court's discussion of duty, which contains no reference to an assumed undertaking. (That was a reasonable course for Claimants because it would be hard for them to prove reliance when the boaters never requested the weather information on the day they took the boat.) The issue was therefore forfeited. *See Tele-Communications, Inc. v. C.I.R.*, 104 F.3d 1229, 1232 (10th Cir. 1997).

tunities thereby would be lost to the public."
Id. Requiring marinas to stop renting boats
because of forecasted bad weather would
without doubt unnecessarily limit oppor-
tunities for adventure that many seek. *See*
Aplt. App. at 99–100 (Trial Tr.) (according to
Aramark's agent, although she suggested to
the rental party that rather than renting their
own boat they book passage on a "warm" and
"comfortable" tour boat piloted by Aramark,
they declined because "they wanted the
adventure. They wanted to go by themselves
rather than a tour boat group of people." *Id.*).
The weather may turn out to be calm, or the
boaters may take precautions that minimize
risk. We therefore [—33—] reject Claimants'
contention that Aramark could be liable for
negligence in allowing the boaters to rent the
boat.

We need not decide whether a marina could
be liable for gross negligence or recklessness
in renting a boat during inclement weather.
The evidence of record here, particularly the
fact that the forecasted bad weather was not
supposed to arrive for several hours, would
not support such a claim.

Our discussion thus far has addressed only
the claims of duty that depend on information
regarding the weather. We have assumed that
the boating party was fully informed in all
other respects. But Claimants have not
contended that the weather in itself was the
sole source of risk when the boat was rented.
They claim that what made the forecasted
weather particularly dangerous was that the
boat was not designed for such weather
conditions. As we stated above, we think that
implicit in their claim is the contention that
Aramark had a duty to warn the boaters of
this design limitation. Such a duty to warn is
quite different from a duty to warn about the
weather when the boaters had at least as good
access to information as Aramark. We can
think of no reason of policy or principle to
excuse Aramark from negligence for failure to
warn a renter of a boat's limitations.
Therefore, Restatement (Third) § 7(a) applies
and Aramark had a duty to exercise
reasonable care. But we express no view on
whether Aramark failed to exercise such care.
Because the relevant facts have not been
resolved by the district court, we must remand
for further proceedings on the issue. [—34—]

Finally, we consider Aramark's contention
that even if it had been negligent, the boaters'
own negligence was the superseding cause of
the accident. The alleged acts of superseding
negligence are failure to obtain a weather
forecast before departing or to monitor
weather updates during the journey; failure to
wear life vests; failure to monitor
deteriorating conditions or to take action to
safeguard against them; and declining to seek
safe harbor, including declining an offer to
stay at Dangling Rope. We cannot say as a
matter of law that these were superseding
causes. The contention that the boaters failed
to monitor or safeguard against worsening
conditions is factually disputed, as is the
availability of a safe harbor and the nature of
the conversation at Dangling Rope. In any
event, Aramark's claimed negligence was its
failure to warn of the boat's wind limitation,
and we decline to declare as a matter of law
that the boaters would have acted the same if
they had been so warned.

IV. CONCLUSION

We VACATE the judgment below and
REMAND to the district court for further
proceedings to determine whether Aramark
negligently failed to warn the boaters of the
information contained in the Baja owner's
manual.

This page intentionally left blank

United States Court of Appeals for the Eleventh Circuit

United States Court of Appeals
for the Eleventh Circuit

No. 14-12482

HOEFLING
VS.
CITY OF MIAMI

Appeal from the United States District Court for the
Southern District of Florida

Decided: January 25, 2016

Citation: 811 F.3d 1271, 4 Adm. R. 432 (11th Cir. 2016).

Before **JORDAN** and **CARNES**, Circuit Judges, and
GOLDBERG,* Judge.

* Honorable Richard W. Goldberg, Judge of the United
States Court of International Trade, sitting by
designation.

[—2—] JORDAN, Circuit Judge:

For about eight years, James Edward
Hoefling, Jr. lived on his 29-foot
sailboat in state waters off the South
Florida coast. In August of 2010, however,
City of Miami marine patrol officers seized the
sailboat and had it destroyed. According to
Mr. Hoefling—who sued the City and its
officers under 42 U.S.C. § 1983, federal
maritime law, and state law—they did so
unlawfully, without justification and without
notice.

Mr. Hoefling appeals from the district
court's dismissal of his second amended
complaint in its entirety. After a review of the
record, and with the benefit of oral argument,
we conclude that the district court got some
things right and some things wrong. We
therefore affirm in part, reverse in part, and
remand for further proceedings.

I

The second amended complaint, which is
the operative pleading, alleges the following
facts, which we accept as true. *See Timson v.
Sampson*, 518 F.3d 870, 872 (11th Cir. 2008).
[—3—]

A

In late May of 2010, while Mr. Hoefling
was aboard his sailboat in Dinner Key, several
City marine patrol officers pulled alongside in
their own vessel. At the time, the sailboat was
seaworthy and had an intact hull, a mast, an
engine, a rudder, working sails (which were
stored in the cabin), and an anchor light. Mr.
Hoefling told the officers that he was the
owner of the sailboat, produced U.S. Coast
Guard documentation of his ownership, and
provided his driver's license and cell phone
number. Officer Alejandro Macias incorrectly
opined to Mr. Hoefling that the sailboat was
derelict or at risk of being derelict. Contrary
to what Officer Macias said, the sailboat was
not derelict under Florida law, as it was not
"left, stored, or abandoned" in a "wrecked,
junked, or substantially dismantled condition." Fla. Stat. § 823.11.

None of the officers advised Mr. Hoefling
that he was at risk of having his sailboat
taken away or destroyed. One of the officers,
however, cited Mr. Hoefling for not having a
marine sanitary device and told him that he
should get a better anchor light. The officers
also told Mr. Hoefling that he needed to take
care of these issues "or move his vessel."

Before leaving, one of the officers placed a
City of Miami code enforcement notice on the
side of the vessel. The notice contained five
boxes with possible code violations (lost or
abandoned property, goods stored on private
property, [—4—] property unlawfully parked
in a residential district, vessel obstructing an
established City channel, and unlawful
anchoring, mooring, or docking). None of the
five boxes on the notice, however, were
checked off.

Within days of his interaction with the
officers, Mr. Hoefling purchased a marine
sanitary device and installed a better anchor
light. He continued to live in the sailboat for
the next three months. During that time, he
received no further communication from the
City indicating that he had to do more to bring
his sailboat into legal compliance.

On August 20, 2010, while he was on a short trip for work-related reasons, Mr. Hoefling received a call from a friend who told him that the police had taken his sailboat. Mr. Hoefling later found out that this was part of the City's systematic roundup and destruction of ugly boats—what the City calls a "cleanup" program.

When he returned from his trip, he learned that the City and two of its marine patrol officers—Officer Ricardo Roque and Sergeant Jose Gonzalez—had seized and destroyed his sailboat and everything contained inside. He eventually located the remains of his sailboat and personal possessions in a trash dumpster. In the years since the destruction of his sailboat, Mr. Hoefling has been forced to live a transient lifestyle, requiring the assistance of others for shelter and other necessities. [—5—]

According to the second amended complaint, the City and its officers did not have the legal authority to seize and destroy the sailboat, as it was not abandoned or derelict, had an identifiable owner, and did not pose a hazard to navigation or the environment. Even if the sailboat was deemed to be abandoned or derelict, Mr. Hoefling alleged, the City and its officers were required to provide him adequate notice (such as placing a notice of dereliction on the vessel and informing him of the notice) and consider alternatives to immediate destruction, such as taking the sailboat to a compound or marking it off with reflective tape and broadcasting a notice to mariners.[1]

B

The second amended complaint—which named the City, Officer Roque, and Sgt. Gonzalez as defendants—contained five claims. Each of the claims was asserted against all of the defendants.

---

[1] Unlike the initial complaint, which attached the May code enforcement notice, and the first amended complaint, which attached several incident reports written by City marine patrol officers, the second amended complaint did not have any exhibits.

Count I, pursuant to § 1983, alleged substantive and procedural due process violations under the Fourteenth Amendment; Count II, also pursuant to § 1983, alleged an unreasonable search and seizure under the Fourth Amendment; Counts III and IV, sounding in admiralty, respectively alleged the intentional and negligent destruction of property; and Count V alleged an unconstitutional taking in violation [—6—] of the Florida and United States Constitutions. Mr. Hoefling sought compensatory and punitive damages for the seizure and destruction of his sailboat.

The district court granted the defendants' Rule 12(b)(6) motion to dismiss the second amended complaint, *see Hoefling v. City of Miami*, 17 F.Supp.3d 1227 (S.D. Fla. 2014) (*Hoefling II*), and its order of dismissal is the subject of this appeal. Our review, unless otherwise noted, is plenary. *See Hill v. White*, 321 F.3d 1334, 1335 (11th Cir. 2003).

II

The district court dismissed the complaint on some general grounds and some claim-specific grounds. We discuss the general grounds first.

A

The district court, quoting one of our decisions, applied a "heightened pleading" standard to Mr. Hoefling's § 1983 claims. *See Hoefling II*, 17 F.Supp.3d at 1232 (quoting *Keating v. City of Miami*, 598 F.3d 753, 762–63 (11th Cir. 2010)). As the defendants conceded at oral argument, this was incorrect.

We used to apply a heightened pleading standard in § 1983 cases in an effort to "eliminate nonmeritorious claims." *Arnold v. Bd. of Educ. of Escambia Cnty.*, 880 F.2d 305, 309 (11th Cir. 1989). In 1993, however, the Supreme Court held, in a municipal liability case under § 1983, that "it is impossible to square a 'heightened pleading standard' . . . with the liberal system of 'notice pleading' set [—7—] up by the Federal Rules." *Leatherman v. Tarrant Cnty. Narcotics Intelligence & Coordination Unit*, 507 U.S. 163, 168 (1993).

After *Leatherman*, we eliminated the heightened pleading standard in § 1983 cases not involving qualified immunity. *See, e.g., Swann v. S. Health Partners, Inc.*, 388 F.3d 834, 837–38 (11th Cir. 2000).

Following the Supreme Court's decisions in *Bell Atlantic Corp. v. Twombly*, 550 U.S. 544 (2007), and *Ashcroft v. Iqbal*, 556 U.S. 662 (2009), we got rid of heightened pleading altogether in § 1983 cases. We held that "it is clear that there is no 'heightened pleading standard' as it relates to cases governed by Rule 8(a)(2), including civil rights complaints." *Randall v. Scott*, 610 F.3d 701, 710 (11th Cir. 2010). It is true that *Keating*—the case cited by the district court—equated our former heightened pleading standard with the newer *Iqbal* standard, but we later ruled in *Randall* that this language in *Keating* was dicta. *See id.*at 707 n.2.

We expressly held in *Randall*, and reaffirm today, that "whatever requirements our heightened pleading standard once imposed have since been replaced by those of the *Twombly-Iqbal* plausibility standard . . . . [which] applies to *all* civil actions . . . ." *Id. See also Saunders v. Duke*, 766 F.3d 1262, 1266 (11th Cir. 2014) ("After . . . *Iqbal* . . . , which applied the *Twombly* pleading standard in a civil rights/qualified immunity context, there is no longer a 'heightened pleading' standard in 'cases governed by Rule 8(a)(2), including civil [—8—] rights [cases]' under § 1983.") (quoting *Randall*, 610 F.3d at 710) (alterations in original). Accordingly, the district court should not have placed a "heightened pleading" burden on Mr. Hoefling for his § 1983 claims.[2]

---

[2] The district court did not have the benefit of *Saunders* when it dismissed Mr. Hoefling's second amended complaint. But *Randall*, which eliminated heightened pleading in all § 1983 cases, had already been decided. In any event, we cite to *Saunders* because we "appl[y] the law as it exists at the time of its review, not as it existed at the time the district court rendered its decision." *Bradford v. Bruno's, Inc.*, 94 F.3d 621, 623 (11th Cir. 1996) (citing *Gibson v. Berryhill*, 411 U.S. 564, 580–81 (1973)).

B

When he filed his initial complaint, Mr. Hoefling attached as an exhibit the code enforcement notice left on his sailboat on May 27, 2010. And in his first amended complaint, Mr. Hoefling attached as exhibits three City of Miami incident reports (one for May 27, 2010, one for August 20, 2010, and one for September 20, 2010). Accepting as true the assertions of City marine patrol officers contained in those reports, the district court had previously found that Mr. Hoefling had notice of the derelict state of his sailboat. *See Hoefling v. City of Miami*, 876 F.Supp.2d 1321, 1328–31 (S.D. Fla. 2012) (*Hoefling I*).

Although Mr. Hoefling did not attach the code enforcement notice or the incident reports as exhibits to his second amended complaint, the district court—at the defendants' urging—considered the contents of those reports in ruling on the motion to dismiss that complaint. Based in part on what the City marine patrol officers wrote in those reports, the district court again found that Mr. Hoefling was [—9—] told that his sailboat was derelict prior to its removal, and accordingly dismissed the due process claims in Count I. The district court also relied on what the reports said to conclude that the sailboat was in fact derelict. Given that conclusion, the district court dismissed the Fourth Amendment claim in Count II and the takings claim in Count V. And, relying in part on the reports to establish that the officers were acting within their lawful authority, the district court dismissed the maritime destruction of property claims in Counts III and IV. *See Hoefling II*, 17 F.Supp.3d at 1237–38, 1243–44. This, too, was error. Before we explain why, we take a moment to describe the incident reports relied upon by the district court.

The May 27 report, written by Officer Macias, indicated that Mr. Hoefling's sailboat "[was] derelict, in that it [was] left stored and abandoned in a substantially dismantled condition upon public state waters. [It] ha[d] no motor, sails, helm or rudder for propulsion or steering." D.E. 33 at 14. In that same report, Officer Macias stated that he told Mr.

Hoefling about the problems and advised him that the sailboat was subject to removal under Fla. Stat. § 823.11 if it was not brought into compliance with Florida law. *Id.*

The August 20 report, written by Officer Roque, stated that Mr. Hoefling's sailboat, which was scheduled for "derelict vessel cleanup," was found "covered with garbage." It also indicated that a "red inverter" was found onboard and "turned into [the] property [department] under the owner[']s name." *Id.* at 10–11. **[—10—]**

The September 20 report (which identifies Sgt. Gonzalez as the supervising officer and was written by Officer Macias) contained the following narrative: "On Friday[,] August 20, 2010[,] Officer Ricardo Roque #27435 observed vessel to still be in its derelict condition and had it removed from state waters and destroyed by a city contractor." *Id.* at 17.

The district court "summarily" rejected Mr. Hoefling's argument that it should not consider the reports which had been attached to the first amended complaint but omitted from the second amended complaint. *See Hoefling II*, 17 F.Supp.3d at 1232 n.6. Accepting as true the narrative in the May 27 report, the district court again found that Mr. Hoefling had "notice of the derelict condition of the vessel." *Id.* at 1230. *See also id.* at 1234, 1237–38. The district court thought Mr. Hoefling was "attempt[ing] to pull the wool over the [c]ourt's eyes by disavowing those exhibits" and "declining to attach them" to the second amended complaint, something the court considered "a transparent attempt to overcome [its] prior adverse finding." *Id.* at 1235 n.11.

A district court can generally consider exhibits attached to a complaint in ruling on a motion to dismiss, and if the allegations of the complaint about a particular exhibit conflict with the contents of the exhibit itself, the exhibit controls. *See, e.g., Crenshaw v. Lister,* 556 F.3d 1283, 1292 (11th Cir. 2009) (citing cases). The classic example is when a plaintiff attaches a document to his **[—11—]** complaint but his allegations about what the document is or says contradict the document itself. *See,*

e.g., Simmons v. Peavy-Welsh Lumber Co., 113 F.2d 812, 813 (5th Cir. 1940) (letter in breach of contract action). But that general principle does not govern here.

As a matter of law, the second amended complaint filed by Mr. Hoefling "supersede[d] the former pleading[s]; the original pleading[s] [were] abandoned by the amendment, and [were] no longer a part of [Mr. Hoefling's] averments against his adversar[ies]." *Dresdner Bank AG v. M/V Olympia Voyager,* 463 F.3d 1210, 1215 (11th Cir. 2006). So when Mr. Hoefling filed the second amended complaint, the first amended complaint (and its attached exhibits) became a legal nullity.

As *Dresdner Bank* explains, our cases do not permit a district court to consider, on a motion to dismiss, exhibits attached to an earlier complaint that a plaintiff has expressly disavowed or rejected as untrue in a subsequent amended complaint. In *Dresdner Bank,* for example, we held that, when a plaintiff amends its original complaint to make clear "it had rejected" a certain contract provision, it will not be bound by the terms of the contract simply because it had attached the contract to the original complaint. *Id.* And "[e]ven if [the] original complaint could be construed to affirm the proposed contract," the result would be the same because the original complaint "was wholly superseded by the amended complaint which proceeded under a different theory." *Id.* **[—12—]**

Dresden Bank governs here. In his second amended complaint, Mr. Hoefling expressly alleged that his sailboat was seaworthy and not derelict, as it had an intact hull, a mast, an engine, a rudder, working sails (which were stored in the cabin), and an anchor light. Those allegations directly conflict with the assertions in Officer Macia's May 27 and September 20 reports that the sailboat did not have a motor, sails, or rudder. Mr. Hoefling also specifically denied in the second amended complaint that he was given notice on May 27 that his vessel was derelict and/or at risk of being removed and destroyed. According to the second amended complaint, Mr. Hoefling was cited that day only for not having a marine sanitary device and was told to get a better anchor light. And, as the second amended complaint alleges, the code enforcement notice placed on the side of the sailboat did not have any violations checked off.

Mr. Hoefling did allege in his second amended complaint that Officer Macias gave him an "incorrect opinion" that the sailboat was derelict or at risk of being derelict, but viewing the allegations as a whole, and drawing reasonable inferences in Mr. Hoefling's favor, *see, e.g., Urquilla-Diaz v. Kaplan Univ.*, 780 F.3d 1039, 1054 (11th Cir. 2015), that opinion did not amount to adequate notice of a violation which made the sailboat subject to removal and destruction under Florida law. At the very least, the allegations in the second amended complaint dispute Officer Macias' May 27 report that the sailboat was in a derelict state. [—13—] Moreover, that complaint does not admit (or give any credence to) the statement in the August 20 report that the sailboat was found covered with garbage.

Four months after the district court dismissed Mr. Hoefling's second amended complaint, we reviewed a case where a civil rights plaintiff attached police reports to his complaint in support of one claim, but expressly alleged that the reports were substantively false with regard to another claim. *See Saunders*, 766 F.3d at 1270. We held that when a "plaintiff attaches a police report to his complaint and alleges that it is false, . . . the contents of the report cannot be considered as true for purposes of ruling on a motion to dismiss." *Id.* "Otherwise officers sued under § 1983 could just attach police reports referenced in a civil rights complaint to their motions to dismiss and ask courts to consider the contents of those reports, even if they contradicted the allegations of the complaint." *Id.* We recognize, as we noted earlier, that the district court did not have the benefit of *Saunders* when it ruled. But under *Dresdner Bank* it should not have accepted as true the contents of the incident reports to find, when ruling on the motion to dismiss the second amended complaint, that Mr. Hoefling had notice that his sailboat was derelict or that the vessel was in fact derelict.

We also reject the defendants' argument that the doctrine of "judicial estoppel" prevents Mr. Hoefling from filing a second amended complaint that rejected the information contained in the reports he attached as exhibits to the [—14—] earlier complaints. At a minimum, judicial estoppel requires a party's later position to be contradictory or "clearly inconsistent" from an earlier one. *See New Hampshire v. Maine*, 532 U.S. 742, 750 (2001); *Burnes v. Pemco Aeroplex, Inc.*, 291 F.3d 1282, 1285 (11th Cir. 2002). From his initial complaint forward, Mr. Hoefling has always alleged that his sailboat was not abandoned or derelict, and that the City's marine patrol officers failed to give him adequate notice prior to its seizure and destruction. He has never adopted the contents of the incident reports as true, and therefore it is wrong for the defendants to argue that the second amended complaint "expressly and implicitly adopted" as true the statements in the incident reports. *See* Br. for Appellees at 23. The doctrine of judicial estoppel just does not apply.

So, to the extent that the district court dismissed the federal constitutional claims in Counts I, II, and V, and the maritime claims in Counts III and IV, based on the contents of the incident reports, it erred. On remand the district court should assess the sufficiency of the procedural due process, search and seizure, and takings claims without reliance on the disputed portions of the incident reports. It should assume, as Mr. Hoefling has alleged, that the sailboat was not derelict, and that he was never given adequate notice that it was derelict and subject to removal and destruction. [—15—]

III

We now turn to some of the district court's claim-specific grounds for dismissal.

A

As a municipality, the City cannot be held vicariously liable under § 1983 for constitutional violations committed by its officers. *See Monell v. Dep't of Social Servs.*, 436 U.S. 658, 693–94 (1978). Mr. Hoefling must ultimately prove that the City had a policy, custom, or practice that caused the deprivation. *See e.g., City of Canton v. Harris*, 489 U.S. 378, 385 (1989); *Weiland v. Palm Beach County Sheriff's Office*, 792 F.3d 1313, 1328 (11th Cir. 2015); *McDowell v. Brown*, 392 F.3d 1283, 1289 (11th Cir. 2004).

With respect to the procedural due process claim in Count I and the Fourth Amendment claim in Count II, the district court concluded that the second amended complaint was insufficient as to municipal liability because Mr. Hoefling failed to identify the City official who acted as the final policymaker. *See Hoefling II*, 17 F.Supp.3d at 1239. In our view, the district court was mistaken.

Monell, the Supreme Court has explained, is a "case about responsibility," and is meant to limit § 1983 liability to "acts which the municipality has officially sanctioned or ordered." *Pembaur v. City of Cincinnatti*, 475 U.S. 469, 478, 480 (1986). There are, however, several different ways of establishing municipal [—16—] liability under § 1983. A municipality can be liable for an official policy enacted by its legislative body (e.g., an ordinance or resolution passed by a city council). *See Monell*, 436 U.S. at 661, 694–95; *McCusik v. City of Melbourne*, 96 F.3d 478, 483 (11th Cir. 1996). Municipal liability may also attach if final policymakers have acquiesced in a longstanding practice that constitutes the entity's standard operating procedure. *See Bd. of Cty. Commissioners v. Brown*, 520 U.S. 397, 403–04 (1997); *Brown v. City of Ft. Lauderdale*, 923 F.2d 1474, 1481 n. 11 (11th Cir. 1991). And a municipality can be held liable "on the basis of ratification when a subordinate public official makes an unconstitutional decision and when that decision is then adopted by someone who does have final policymaking authority." *Matthews v. Columbia County*, 294 F.3d 1294, 1297 (11th Cir. 2002). So not all theories of municipal liability under § 1983 require (or depend on) a single final policymaker.

The Supreme Court has spoken of establishing a municipality's final policy-maker in evidentiary terms. For example, it has said that *"proof* that a municipality's legislative body or authorized decisionmaker has intentionally deprived a plaintiff of a federal protected right necessarily establishes the municipality acted culpably." *Brown*, 520 U.S. 397 at 405 (emphasis added). We too have discussed the "evidence" concerning the decision of a final policymaker. *See, e.g., Carter v. City of Melbourne*, 731 F.3d 1161, 1167 (11th Cir. 2013); [—17—] *Campbell v. Rainbow City*, 434 F.3d 1306, 1313 (11th Cir. 2006). *Cf. Mandel v. Doe*, 888 F.2d 783, 792–93 (11th Cir. 1989) ("identification of the policymaker may often involve fact-sensitive inquiries"). We therefore believe that identifying and proving that a final policymaker acted on behalf of a municipality is "an evidentiary standard, and not a pleading requirement." *Swierkiewicz v. Sorema, N.A.*, 534 U.S. 506, 510 (2002). *See Twombly*, 550 U.S. at 570 (distinguishing but not overruling *Swierkiewicz* on this point). Although Mr. Hoefling may ultimately have to identify (and provide proof concerning) a single final policymaker in order to survive summary judgment or prevail at trial, *see, e.g., Grech v. Clayton County*, 335 F.3d 1326, 1329 (11th Cir. 2003), we do not think that he had to name that person in his complaint in order to survive a Rule 12(b)(6) motion. All he needed to do was allege a policy, practice, or custom of the City which caused the seizure and destruction of his sailboat. And that, as we detail below, he did.

B

The "touchstone of [a] § 1983 action against a government body is an allegation that official policy is responsible for a deprivation of civil rights protected by the Constitution." *Monell*, 436 U.S. at 690. Given that a complaint need only state enough facts to "state a claim for relief that is plausible on its face," *Twombly*, 550 U.S. at 570, we conclude that the second amended complaint [—18—] sufficiently pled a municipal liability claim for the alleged procedural due process and Fourth Amendment violations.

In addition to what he pled concerning the seizure and destruction of his own sailboat, Mr. Hoefling also alleged the following. First, on August 20, 2010, while out of town, Mr.

Hoefling received a call from a friend "notifying him that the police were taking boats." And, in fact, on his return, he discovered that his own sailboat had been "unlawfully seized." Second, Mr. Hoefling alleged that "local mariners" told him, and that he was "independently aware, that others have fallen victim to similar conduct as a result of the City['s] and [the marine patrol officers'] failure to adhere to law and appropriate procedures regarding the investigation and destruction of potentially derelict vessels." Third, Mr. Hoefling alleged that the City refers to this "systematic roundup and destruction of ugly boats in its waters" as a "cleanup" program. Based on these allegations, Mr. Hoefling alleged that the City had a "policy, custom, and/or practice" of "failing to abide by" the state laws, regulations, and procedures governing the "investigation and . . . removal of derelict vessels located in state waters." Furthermore, he alleged that the defendants did "not follow established law and procedures intended to safeguard against the unlawful destruction of private property[,] . . . instead choosing to remove and destroy [his] property without due process. In sum, the City and its [—19—] marine patrol officers, "as a matter of policy, custom, and/or practice, ignored [his] fundamental rights, as well as the fundamental rights of other vessel owners."

These are not the sort of "naked allegations" we found wanting in *Weiland*, 792 F.3d at 1329–30 (brackets and quotation marks deleted). Under *Leatherman*, *Twombly*, and *Iqbal*, Mr. Hoefling's allegations were sufficient to state a facially plausible municipal liability claim because they permit "the reasonable inference that [the City] is liable for the misconduct alleged." *Iqbal*, 556 U.S. at 678. *See Hailey v. City of Boston*, 657 F.3d 39, 51–52 (1st Cir. 2011) (applying *Twombly* and *Iqbal* and holding that municipal liability claim was sufficiently pled).

The case cited by the district court, *Grech*, 335 F.3d at 1329, does not call for a contrary result, as it was in a summary judgment posture, and at that stage of a case the plaintiff cannot merely rely on the allegations in his complaint. Significantly, the defendants cannot point to any post-*Leatherman* Supreme Court or circuit cases—and we have not been able to locate any ourselves—holding that a complaint asserting a § 1983 municipal liability claim must, as a Rule 8(a) pleading matter, always specifically identify the municipality's final policymaker by name.

C

In our view, Mr. Hoefling also sufficiently stated a claim for an unconstitutional seizure under the Fourth Amendment. In *Soldal v. Cook County*, [—20—] 506 U.S. 56, 60–61 (1992), the Supreme Court unanimously held that a landlord's removal and towing of a mobile home, in violation of state law and with the assistance of sheriff's deputies, constituted a seizure under the Fourth Amendment: "As a result of the state action in this case, the Soldals' domicile was not only seized, it was literally carried away, giving new meaning to the term 'mobile home.' We fail to see how being unceremoniously dispossessed of one's home in the manner alleged to have occurred here can be viewed as anything but a seizure involving the protection of the Fourth Amendment." *Id.* at 61. In so ruling, the Supreme Court rejected the notion that "the Fourth Amendment protects against unreasonable seizures of property only when privacy or liberty is also implicated." *Id.* at 65. Here the defendants' alleged removal and destruction of Mr. Hoefling's sailboat, under the circumstances described in the second amended complaint, similarly constitutes a seizure under the Fourth Amendment. Mr. Hoefling alleged that his sailboat was not derelict, that he was not given adequate notice by the City that it was derelict and therefore subject to removal, and that the vessel was removed and destroyed by the City pursuant to a systematic "cleanup" program to get rid of ugly boats.

The next question, of course, is whether the seizure was constitutionally reasonable, and that question requires a "careful balancing of governmental and private interests." *Soldal*, 506 U.S. at 71 (internal quotation marks and citation [—21—] omitted). The district court, again relying on the contents of the incident reports, concluded that Officer Roque and Sgt. Gonzalez were entitled to qualified immunity on the seizure claim because the sailboat was derelict and because Mr. Hoefling had been given notice of its derelict state and told to remove the vessel or bring it into compliance. *See Hoefling II*, 17 F.Supp.3d at 1230–31, 1233–34. But, as we have already explained, it was not appropriate to consider the reports for the truth of the statements contained in them in assessing the sufficiency of Mr. Hoefling's second amended complaint.

The Supreme Court has instructed that, in assessing the two prongs of the qualified immunity standard at the summary judgment stage, the evidence must be viewed in the light most favorable to the plaintiff. *See Tolan v. Cotton*, 134 S.Ct. 1861, 1866 (2014) (reversing grant of qualified immunity because court resolved factual disputes and inferences against the plaintiff: "Our qualified immunity cases illustrate the importance of drawing inferences in favor the non-movant, even when, as here, the court decides only the clearly-established prong of the standard."). The same general principle, of course, applies when qualified immunity is raised at the motion to dismiss stage. *See St. George v. Pinellas Cnty.*, 285 F.3d 1334, 1338 (11th Cir. 2002) (explaining that, when "reviewing [a] grant of qualified immunity by the district court . . . on a Rule 12(b)(6) motion to dismiss, we must construct our own firewall between the facts pleaded in the [—22—] complaint and any evidence, construing the complaint in favor of the plaintiff[ ]"). On remand, the district court should address qualified immunity anew, crediting the factual allegations in the second amended complaint and without reference to the disputed contents of the incident reports.

D

We agree with the district court that Mr. Hoefling did not state a substantive due process claim in his second amended complaint. That claim, therefore, was properly dismissed.

The substantive component of the Due Process Clause "protects individual liberty against certain government actions regardless of the fairness of the procedures used to implement them." *Collins v. City of Harker Heights, Tex.*, 503 U.S. 115, 125 (1992) (internal quotation marks and citation omitted). It is "state conduct [which] can properly be characterized as arbitrary, or conscience shocking, in a constitutional sense." *Neal ex rel. Neal v. Fulton Cnty. Bd. of Educ.*, 229 F.3d 1069, 1074 (11th Cir. 2000) (brackets, internal quotation marks, and citation omitted). To state a substantive due process claim, a plaintiff must allege (1) a deprivation of a constitutionally protected interest, and (2) that "the deprivation was the result of an abuse of governmental power sufficient to raise an ordinary tort to the stature of a constitutional violation." *Executive 100, Inc. v. Martin Cnty.*, 922 F.2d 1536, 1541 (11th Cir. 1991). "A deprivation is of [—23—] constitutional stature if it is undertaken for improper motive and by means that were pretextual, arbitrary and capricious, and without rational basis." *Id. See also Reserve, Ltd. v. Town of Longboat Key*, 17 F.3d 1374, 1379 (11th Cir. 1994) (same).

Mr. Hoefling alleges that the City violated his substantive due process rights because it has a marine patrol "cleanup program" that identifies boats it considers ugly, and then seizes and destroys those boats without giving their owners notice or an opportunity to contest their removal or destruction. Although the Supreme Court in *Sodal* did not address whether the removal and towing of the mobile home could give rise to both a Fourth Amendment seizure claim and a Fourteenth Amendment substantive due process claim, *see* 560 U.S. at 70, we have since held that where law enforcement officials unlawfully seize a person's home, any constitutional protection that its owner may have comes from the Fourth, and not the Fourteenth, Amendment. *See Tinney v. Shores*, 77 F.3d 378, 381 (11th Cir. 1996) (holding that the Supreme Court, in *Sodal* and other cases, "foreclosed" substantive due process claims under such circumstances). We are bound by *Tinney*, and therefore hold that Mr. Hoefling—who has a Fourth Amendment seizure claim available to him—cannot also claim a violation of substantive due process. [—24—]

IV

We think it is best to allow the district court to re-examine the remaining claims and the qualified immunity issues without a heightened pleading standard and without accepting as true the contents of the incident reports. Having said that, we have some suggestions for the district court on remand.

With respect to the procedural due process claim, the district court should analyze whether this is one of those situations where the existence of a post-deprivation remedy is sufficient, as in *Tinney*, 77 F.3d at 380, or whether Mr. Hoefling has sufficiently alleged that the destruction of his sailboat was pursuant to a policy or practice of the City (i.e., the alleged "cleanup" program) such that pre-deprivation notice was feasible and required under cases like *Hudson v. Palmer*, 468 U.S. 517, 532 (1984) (explaining that, "where the property deprivation is effected pursuant to an established state procedure," a post-deprivation state remedy cannot satisfy due process), and *Rittenhouse v. DeKalb Cnty.*, 764 F.2d 1451, 1455 (11th Cir. 1985) (holding that the focus on the adequacy of post-deprivation remedies—due to the random, unauthorized act of an employee—does not apply "where a deprivation occurs pursuant to an established state procedure," because in those circumstances, a "predeprivation process is ordinarily feasible"). The district court should also consider the impact, if any, of *Grayden v. Rhodes*, 345 F.3d 1225, 1237–44 (11th Cir. 2003), on the notice issue. [—25—]

As for the federal and state takings claims, the district court should take into account the Supreme Court's recent decision in *Horne v. Dep't of Agric.*, 135 S. Ct. 2419, 2426 (2015) ("The Government has a categorical duty to pay just compensation when it takes your car, just as when it takes your home."). The district court may also need to address whether the ripeness principle set forth in *Williamson Cnty. Reg'l Planning Com'n v. Hamilton Bank of Johnson City*, 473 U.S. 172, 194 (1985), a regulatory takings case, applies to a case involving a physical taking. A number of circuits have held that a plaintiff alleging a physical taking must seek compensation through available state remedies before filing suit under § 1983. *See, e.g., Kurtz v. Verizon N.Y., Inc.*, 758 F.3d 506, 513–14 (2d Cir. 2014); *Greenfield Mills, Inc. v. Macklin*, 361 F.3d 934, 958 (7th Cir. 2004).

In sum, we affirm the district court's dismissal of Mr. Hoefling's substantive due process claim. We reverse the district court's dismissal of the other claims and remand for further proceedings consistent with this opinion.

AFFIRMED IN PART, REVERSED IN PART, AND REMANDED FOR FURTHER PROCEEDINGS.

United States Court of Appeals
for the Eleventh Circuit

No. 15-10784

REGANIT

vs.

SECRETARY, DEP'T OF HOMELAND SEC.

Appeal from the United States District Court for the
Southern District of Florida

Decided: February 25, 2016

Citation: 814 F.3d 1253, 4 Adm. R. 441 (11th Cir. 2016).

Before **PRYOR**, **CARNES**, and **FAY**, Circuit Judges.

[—2—] PER CURIAM:

Defendants, who are the Department of Homeland Security and related entities, denied Plaintiff Edwin Rosete Reganit's application for naturalization. Plaintiff sought review of this denial in district court, pursuant to 8 U.S.C. § 1421(c).[1] The district court granted summary judgment to Defendants. Plaintiff now appeals, arguing that the district court erred by characterizing him as an alien crewman, which thereby rendered him statutorily ineligible to become a United States citizen because it meant that he had not been lawfully admitted for permanent residence. After careful review, we affirm.

I. BACKGROUND

A. Factual Background

The parties stipulated to the following facts. Plaintiff, a native and citizen of the Philippines, entered the United States on May 27, 2001, with a C-1/D[2] visa to work on board a ship owned by Discovery Cruise Lines. Plaintiff worked as a [—3—] butcher on the ship for approximately two weeks before becoming ill. Approximately one more week passed, and because Plaintiff was still sick, Discovery Cruise Lines began the process of arranging for him to de-board the ship to receive medical assistance in the United States. On June 29, 2001, Plaintiff was granted a temporary medical parole into the United States, valid only until July 28, 2001, pursuant to 8 U.S.C. § 1182(d)(5).

When Plaintiff de-boarded the ship, employees of Discovery Cruise Lines escorted him to a doctor in Miami and remained with him at a hotel until he returned to the ship. After returning to the ship, Plaintiff worked for approximately one more week. However, because he was still ill, Discovery Cruise Lines once again arranged for him to see a doctor in Miami. But while in Miami, Plaintiff resigned from his position on the ship and Discovery Cruise Lines then arranged his travel back to the Philippines.

Plaintiff, however, did not return to the Philippines, as he should have done. Instead, he remained in the United States, and later he married his current wife, Aileen, in 2002. In 2005, Aileen filed an I-130 petition for alien relative on behalf of Plaintiff and Plaintiff filed an I-485 application for adjustment of status to that of a lawful permanent resident based on his marriage to a United States citizen. On his adjustment of status application, Plaintiff stated that his last entry into the United States was on May 27, 2001, and that his status upon entering was C-1. [—4—]

On June 13, 2006, United States Citizenship and Immigration Services ("CIS") granted Plaintiff's application and his status was adjusted to that of a lawful permanent

---

[1] Section 1421(c) of Title 8 of the United States Code states that, "A person whose application for naturalization . . . is denied, after a hearing before an immigration officer . . . may seek review of such denial before the United States district court for the district in which such person resides." 8 U.S.C. § 1421(c).

[2] A C-1/D visa is a dual visa. A "C-1" visa is given to a nonimmigrant alien who is in "immediate and continuous transit through the United States." 8 U.S.C. § 1101(a)(15)(C). A "D" visa is given to a nonimmigrant alien serving aboard a vessel or aircraft "who intends to land temporarily and solely in pursuit of his calling as a crewman and to depart from the United States with the vessel or aircraft on which he arrived or some other vessel or aircraft." *Id.* § 1101(a)(15)(D)(i); *see also Matter of G-D-M-*, 25 I. & N. Dec. 82, 83 (BIA 2009).

resident. Upon becoming a lawful permanent resident, Plaintiff traveled outside of the United States multiple times between 2007 and 2012. He showed his lawful permanent resident card to immigration authorities each time he re-entered the United States.

On March 4, 2011, Plaintiff applied to become a United States citizen. Discovering that Plaintiff had been admitted to the United States as a crewman, CIS determined that its approval of his adjustment of status application in 2005 had been in error and that, as a result, Plaintiff was not statutorily eligible to adjust status to that of a lawful permanent resident. Stated another way, because Plaintiff could not show that he had been lawfully admitted for permanent residence, he did not meet all of the requirements necessary to become a naturalized citizen. Accordingly, CIS denied his application for citizenship and after Plaintiff appealed, it affirmed its denial of Plaintiff's application.

B. Procedural History

In February 2014, Plaintiff filed this action pursuant to 8 U.S.C. § 1421(c) against the Secretary of the Department of Homeland Security; the Acting Director of the CIS; the District Director of the Miami District of CIS; the Director of the Kendall Field Office of CIS; and the Attorney General of the United States, in their [—5—] official capacities. In his amended complaint, Plaintiff alleged that Defendants violated his rights under the Immigration and Nationality Act ("INA") and the Administrative Procedures Act by denying his application for naturalization.

Plaintiff later moved for summary judgment. He argued that notwithstanding his initial entry into the United States as only a crewman, he was eligible for adjustment of status based on his temporary medical parole into the United States on June 29, 2001. From that premise, he further contended that he was thereafter properly granted lawful permanent resident status, meaning that he met this requirement for becoming a United

States citizen.[3] Defendants also moved for summary judgment, arguing that Plaintiff's admission to the United States on a crewmen visa precluded any adjustment of status to that of a lawful permanent resident, thereby rendering him statutorily ineligible for naturalization.

The district court granted summary judgment in favor of Defendants. The district court concluded that the plain language of 8 U.S.C. § 1255(c), which bars alien crewmen from adjusting status, in conjunction with the federal regulation governing the parole of alien crewmen, 8 C.F.R. § 253.1, mean that Plaintiff's temporary medical parole did not alter his status as a crewman. Because Plaintiff could not establish that he was lawfully admitted for permanent residence based on [—6—] this medical parole, he failed to meet the statutory requirements for naturalization. This appeal followed.

II. DISCUSSION

A. Standard of Review

We review the district court's grant of summary judgment *de novo. United States v. Jean-Baptiste*, 395 F.3d 1190, 1192 (11th Cir. 2005). The burden is on the party moving for summary judgment to establish that no genuine issue of material fact exists. *Liese v. Indian River Cty. Hosp. Dist.*, 701 F.3d 334, 341–42 (11th Cir. 2012). We view all evidence and draw all reasonable inferences in favor of the non-moving party. *Id.*

B. Applicable Law

"American citizenship is a precious right." *Costello v. United States*, 365 U.S. 265, 269 (1961). An individual who seeks to obtain naturalized United States citizenship must

---

[3] Alternatively, Plaintiff also argued that even if he was not lawfully admitted for permanent residence based on his medical parole, he was subsequently admitted for permanent residence when he later traveled outside of the United State and gained re-entry as a lawful permanent resident. The district court rejected this argument, and Plaintiff does not challenge this ruling on appeal.

comply with the statutory requirements for naturalization. *See Fedorenko v. United States*, 449 U.S. 490, 505–06 (1981). These requirements require, among other things, that the alien show he was lawfully admitted for permanent residence in the United States. 8 U.S.C. § 1427(a).

The term "lawfully admitted for permanent residence" is defined as "the status of having been lawfully accorded the privilege of residing permanently in the United States as an immigrant in accordance with the immigration laws." 8 [—7—] U.S.C. § 1101(a)(20). To be "lawfully admitted for permanent residence," an alien's adjustment to lawful permanent resident status must be "in compliance with the substantive requirements of the law." *Savoury v. U.S. Att'y Gen.*, 449 F.3d 1307, 1313–18 (11th Cir. 2006). For that reason, we have held that an alien whose status was mistakenly adjusted to that of a lawful permanent resident was not an alien lawfully admitted for that purpose. *See id.* (concluding that an alien was not eligible for a waiver of inadmissibility based on a mistaken adjustment of status done in violation of the substantive requirements of the law).

In order for an alien to adjust status to that of a lawful permanent resident, the alien must: (1) have been "inspected and admitted or paroled into the United States"; (2) apply for adjustment of status; (3) be eligible to receive an immigrant visa and be admissible to the United States; and (4) have an immigrant visa immediately available to him at the time of filing. 8 U.S.C. § 1255(a).

Alien crewmen, however, are explicitly barred from adjusting to lawful permanent resident status. *Id.* § 1255(c). An alien crewman is defined as "a person serving in any capacity on board a vessel or aircraft." *Id.* § 1101(a)(10). Moreover, the definition of immigrant excludes "an alien crewman serving in good faith as such in a capacity required for normal operation and service on board a vessel . . . who intends to land temporarily and solely in pursuit of his calling as a crewman." *Id.* § 1101(a)(15)(D)(i). [—8—]

The INA provides that the Attorney General may, in his discretion and on a case-by-case basis, parole an alien into the United States temporarily for humanitarian reasons or significant public benefit. 8 U.S.C. § 1182(d)(5)(A).

C. Plaintiff was not Statutorily Eligible for Naturalization

In order for Plaintiff to have been statutorily eligible for naturalization, he must show that he was lawfully admitted for permanent residence. *See* 8 U.S.C. § 1427(a). But alien crewmen are barred from adjusting to lawful permanent resident status. 8 U.S.C. §§ 1101(a)(20), 1255(c); *see also Savoury*, 449 F.3d at 1313–18. And there is no dispute that Plaintiff was an alien crewman on board a cruise ship who was issued only a crewmen visa for purposes of entry into this country. There is also no dispute that after his arrival, Plaintiff was granted a temporary medical parole into the United States under § 1182(d)(5) to obtain treatment for an illness that had arisen while he was working on the ship. Consequently, this case turns on a matter of first impression in our Court: whether Plaintiff's grant of medical parole under § 1182(d)(5) altered his crewman status. We conclude that it did not.

We first address Plaintiff's argument that he shed his "alien crewman" status under the INA once he became ill on board the ship and was allowed to temporarily de-board for purposes of receiving medical treatment. Plaintiff concedes that his initial entry in May 2001 was as a crewman, but he contends that [—9—] by de-boarding temporarily in June 2001 to receive medical treatment, he ceased "pursuit of his calling as a seaman." Yet, in determining whether an alien should be classified as a crewman, we have stated that "the focal issue is whether [the alien] entered the United States in pursuit of his calling as a seaman." *Parzagonis v. I.N.S.*, 747 F.2d 1389, 1390 (11th Cir. 1984). The Board of Immigration Appeals ("BIA") has further explained that it "examine[s] an alien's visa and the circumstances surrounding his entry into the United States to determine if he entered as a crewman." *Matter of G-D-M-*, 25 I. & N. Dec. 82, 85 (BIA 2009).

For the sake of this discussion, we will assume that a non-crewman alien who was medically paroled into the United States under § 1182(d)(5)(A) might later be eligible to adjust status. But the applicable statutes and regulations do not permit an alien crewman to bypass the statutory bar on his adjustment of status merely by the fortuity of a subsequent medical parole to treat an illness arising while serving as a crew member. Section 253.1(e) of Title 8 of the Code of Federal Regulations governs the parole of alien crewmen. That provision states that an alien crewman without a conditional landing permit and in need of medical treatment or observation may be paroled into the United States pursuant to § 1182(d)(5). 8 C.F.R. § 253.1(e). But an alien granted such parole is to remain in the custody of the agent of the vessel, and the vessel is to cover the expenses of the medical treatment. *Id.* [—10—]

Reading this regulation together with § 1255(c)—which clearly bars alien crewmen from adjusting to lawful permanent resident status—we conclude that an alien crewman granted medical parole pursuant to 8 C.F.R. § 253.1(e) does not cease being a crewman and thereby rid himself of the statutory bar on adjustment of status. *See* 8 U.S.C. § 1255(c); 8 C.F.R. § 253.1(e). In fact, the BIA has stated that Congress intended "to bar all occupational seamen . . . who have relatively easy access to the United States [and] have used the seaman route to enter the United States for permanent residence." *Matter of Goncalves*, 10 I. & N. Dec. 277, 279 (BIA 1963). Nothing in the applicable statutes imply that an alien crewman who has been admitted as such, but who subsequently receives a medical parole while working on board a ship, thereby becomes eligible for adjustment of status.

Indeed, in the present case, it is clear that Plaintiff's medical parole was obtained in pursuit of his calling as a seaman. *See Parzagonis*, 747 F.2d at 1390; *Matter of G-D-M-*, 25 I. & N. Dec. at 85. Having received only a crewmen visa, Plaintiff fell ill while working

on board the Discovery Cruise Lines ship. Consistent with the federal regulation governing the parole of alien crewmen, Discovery Cruise Lines arranged for Plaintiff's medical parole and his subsequent doctor's visits, and stayed with him at a hotel in Miami. *See* 8 C.F.R. § 253.1(e). Notably, Plaintiff did in fact return to the ship after his first doctor's visit. And once he decided to quit his position as a crewman, Discovery Cruise Lines [—11—] arranged for Plaintiff's travel home to the Philippines. In short, Plaintiff's visa and the circumstances surrounding his entry into the United States establish that he was a crewman throughout the applicable period of time.

Plaintiff also argues that the district court erroneously interpreted 8 C.F.R. § 253.1(e) to mean that an alien paroled into the United States will remain an alien crewman forever. The district court, however, did not make such a pronouncement. Instead, it considered all of the circumstances surrounding Plaintiff's entry in 2001 in reaching its conclusion that his entry was in pursuit of his calling as a seaman.[4] *See Matter of G-D-M-*, 25 I. & N. Dec. at 85.

We are also not persuaded by Plaintiff's argument that the policy reasons for barring alien crewmen from adjustment of status ceased to exist once he was allowed to seek temporary medical care while serving on board the ship. Given their "relatively easy access to the United States," alien crewmen who have been admitted for the limited purpose of pursuing their occupation are prohibited from taking advantage of this access to later adjust status. *See Matter of Goncalves*, 10 I. & N. Dec. at 279; 8 C.F.R. § 253.1(e). Again, Plaintiff was able to obtain a temporary medical parole, which expired on

---

[4] The BIA has determined that an occupational crewman is not barred from adjustment of status if the alien's most recent admission into the United States was not in pursuit of his calling as a seaman. *See Matter of Rebelo*, 13 I. & N. Dec. 84, 85–86 (BIA 1968) (concluding that an alien was not barred from adjustment of status because, although he was occupationally a crewman, his most recent entry into the United States was as a visitor for pleasure).

July 28, 2001, only because he had first been granted entry as an alien crewman. [—12—]

In summary, because Plaintiff was a crewman when he entered this country, he cannot establish that he was lawfully admitted for permanent residence. *See* 8 U.S.C. §§ 1101(a)(20), 1255(c). As a result, Plaintiff does not meet the statutory requirements for naturalization. *See* 8 U.S.C. § 1427(a). Accordingly, the district court did not err by granting summary judgment in favor of the Defendants.

III. CONCLUSION

For the reasons stated above, we **AFFIRM** the judgment of the district court.

United States Court of Appeals
for the Eleventh Circuit

No. 14-15351

SUAZO
VS.
NCL (BAHAMAS), LTD.

Appeal from the United States District Court for the
Southern District of Florida

Decided: May 10, 2016

Citation: 822 F.3d 543, 4 Adm. R. 446 (11th Cir. 2016).

Before **MARCUS, JORDAN,** and **WALKER,*** Circuit
Judges.

* Honorable John Walker, Jr., United States Circuit
Judge for the Second Circuit, sitting by designation.

[—2—] **MARCUS,** Circuit Judge:

In this appeal, we address a question of first impression in the Circuit: whether a cruise ship employee who is injured on the job, and whose employment contract contains an arbitration agreement governed by the New York Convention and Chapter 2 of the Federal Arbitration Act, can bar arbitration by showing that high costs may prevent him from effectively vindicating his federal statutory rights in the arbitral forum. Our New York Convention precedent suggests (but does not hold) that a party may only raise this type of public-policy defense in opposition to a motion to enforce an arbitral award *after* arbitration has taken place, and not in order to defeat a motion to compel arbitration. However, we need not definitively answer this question today because, even if we were to assume that the plaintiff-appellant Willman Suazo could raise a cost-based (public policy) defense in response to defendant-appellee NCL's motion to compel arbitration, on this record he has plainly failed to establish that the costs of arbitration would preclude him from arbitrating his federal statutory claims. Thus, we affirm the district court's order compelling the parties to arbitrate. We deny, however, the defendant's motion for sanctions.

I.

In 1958, the United Nations Economic and Social Council adopted the Convention on the Recognition and Enforcement of Foreign Arbitral Awards. [—3—] *Convention Done at New York June 10, 1958*, T.I.A.S. No. 6997, 21 U.S.T. 2517 (Dec. 29, 1970) (the "New York Convention"). The New York Convention requires signatory states to recognize written arbitration agreements "concerning a subject matter capable of settlement by arbitration." New York Convention, art. II(1). The United States became a signatory to the Convention in 1970. Chapter 2 of the Federal Arbitration Act, the "Convention Act," implements the New York Convention: "The Convention on the Recognition and Enforcement of Foreign Arbitral Awards of June 10, 1958, shall be enforced in the United States in accordance with this chapter." 9 U.S.C. § 201. The Supreme Court has explained that "the principal purpose" behind the adoption of the Convention "was to encourage the recognition and enforcement of commercial arbitration agreements in international contracts and to unify the standards by which agreements to arbitrate are observed and arbitral awards are enforced in the signatory countries." *Scherk v. Alberto-Culver Co.*, 417 U.S. 506, 520 n.15 (1974).

We have elaborated on this theme:

The purpose of the New York Convention, and of the United States' accession to the convention, is to "encourage the recognition and enforcement of international arbitral awards," *Bergesen v. Joseph Muller Corp.*, 710 F.2d 928, 932 (2d Cir. 1983), to "relieve congestion in the courts and to provide parties with an alternative method for dispute resolution that [is] speedier and less costly than litigation." *Ultracashmere House, Ltd. v. Meyer*, 664 F.2d 1176, 1179 (11th Cir. 1981). . . . The Convention, and American enforcement of it through the FAA, "provide[ ] businesses with a widely used system through which to obtain domestic enforcement of international commercial [—4—] arbitration awards resolving contract and other transactional disputes, subject only to minimal standards of domestic judicial review for basic fairness and consistency with national public policy." G. Richard Shell, "Trade Legalism and International Relations Theory: An Analysis of the World Trade Organization," 44 *Duke L.J.* 829, 888 (1995).

Indus. Risk Insurers v. M.A.N. Gutehoffnungshutte GmbH, 141 F.3d 1434, 1440 (11th Cir. 1998).

Basically, the Convention Act creates two causes of action in federal court for a party seeking to enforce an arbitration agreement that falls under the New York Convention: a motion to *compel* arbitration "in accordance with the agreement," 9 U.S.C. § 206; and a motion to *"confirm"* an arbitral award, *id.* § 207 (emphasis added). The Convention provides that certain defenses may be raised in response to each cause of action. Article II of the Convention, like 9 U.S.C. § 206, applies at the "initial arbitration-enforcement stage." *Escobar v. Celebration Cruise Operator, Inc.*, 805 F.3d 1279, 1286 (11th Cir. 2015). Article II carefully prescribes a limited set of defenses that may be considered at the *arbitration-enforcement* stage:

> The court of a Contracting State, when seized of an action in a matter in respect of which the parties have made an agreement within the meaning of this article, shall, at the request of one of the parties, refer the parties to arbitration, unless it finds that the said agreement is *null and void, inoperative or incapable of being performed.*

New York Convention, art. II(3) (emphasis added). "Importantly, Article II contains no explicit or implicit public-policy defense at the initial arbitration- [—5—] enforcement stage." *Escobar*, 805 F.3d at 1287. We have held that the Convention *requires* that a motion to compel arbitration must be granted "so long as (1) the four jurisdictional prerequisites are met and (2) no available affirmative defense under the Convention applies." *Lindo v. NCL*

(Bahamas), Ltd., 652 F.3d 1257, 1276 (11th Cir. 2011) (footnote omitted) (citing *Bautista v. Star Cruises*, 396 F.3d 1289, 1294-95 (11th Cir. 2005)); *see also Escobar*, 805 F.3d at 1285-86. An arbitration agreement falls within the jurisdiction of the New York Convention if: (1) the agreement is "in writing within the meaning of the [New York] Convention"; (2) "the agreement provides for arbitration in the territory of a signatory of the [New York] Convention"; (3) "the agreement arises out of a legal relationship, whether contractual or not, which is considered commercial"; and (4) a party to the agreement is not an American citizen or the commercial relationship has some reasonable relation with one or more foreign states. *Bautista*, 396 F.3d at 1294 n.7.

Article V of the Convention, like 9 U.S.C. § 207, governs only the *"award-enforcement"* stage, and provides for a substantially broader set of defenses that may be raised in response to a motion to confirm an arbitral award. *See* New York Convention, art. V(1)-(2). One of Article V's seven permitted defenses is a "public policy" defense: [—6—]

> Recognition and enforcement of an arbitral award may also be refused if the competent authority in the country where recognition and enforcement is sought finds that:
>
> . . .
>
> (b) The recognition or enforcement of the award would be contrary to the public policy of that country.

Id., art. V(2). Notably, this public-policy defense, like the other Article V defenses, "applies only at the award-enforcement stage." *Lindo*, 652 F.3d at 1263. Therefore, parties must "wait until the award-enforcement stage to assert an Article V public-policy claim." *Escobar*, 805 F.3d at 1287.

Chapter 1 of the FAA governs domestic arbitration, and provides a broad array of defenses to the enforcement of arbitration agreements in the cases that it governs. *See* 9 U.S.C. § 2 (Courts shall enforce agreements governed by Chapter 1 of the FAA "save upon such grounds as exist at law or in equity for the revocation of any contract."). However, the broad defenses applicable in the context of domestic arbitration are not generally available in cases governed by the New York Convention:

> Domestic defenses to arbitration are transferrable to a Convention Act case only if they fit within the limited scope of defenses [contained in Articles II and V of the Convention]. Such an approach is required by the unique circumstances of foreign arbitration[, where]
>
>> concerns of international comity, respect for the capacities of foreign and transnational tribunals, and sensitivity to the need of the international commercial system for predictability in the resolution of disputes require that we enforce the parties' agreement, even [—7—] assuming that a contrary result would be forthcoming in a domestic context.

Mitsubishi Motors Corp. v. Soler Chrysler–Plymouth, Inc., 473 U.S. 614, 629 (1985).

Bautista, 396 F.3d at 1302.

The "effective vindication doctrine" is one defense that the federal courts have recognized in the context of domestic arbitration. As the Supreme Court has explained:

> The "effective vindication" exception . . . originated as dictum in *Mitsubishi Motors,* where we expressed a willingness to invalidate, on "public policy" grounds, arbitration agreements that "operat[e] ... as a prospective waiver of a *party's right to pursue* statutory remedies." 473 U.S., at 637, n. 19 (emphasis added). Dismissing concerns that the arbitral forum was inadequate, we said that "so long as the prospective litigant effectively may vindicate its statutory cause of action in the arbitral forum, the statute will

continue to serve both its remedial and deterrent function." *Id.,* at 637. Subsequent cases have similarly asserted the existence of an "effective vindication" exception, *see, e.g., 14 Penn Plaza LLC v. Pyett,* 556 U.S. 247, 273–274 (2009); *Gilmer v. Interstate/Johnson Lane Corp.,* 500 U.S. 20, 28 (1991), but have similarly declined to apply it to invalidate the arbitration agreement at issue.

> . . . . As we have described, the exception finds its origin in the desire to prevent "prospective waiver of a party's *right to pursue* statutory remedies," *Mitsubishi Motors, supra,* at 637, n. 19 (emphasis added). That would certainly cover a provision in an arbitration agreement forbidding the assertion of certain statutory rights. And it would perhaps cover filing and administrative fees attached to arbitration that are so high as to make access to the forum impracticable. *See Green Tree Financial Corp.–Ala. v. Randolph,* 531 U.S. 79, 90 (2000) ("It may well be that the existence of large arbitration costs could preclude a litigant ... from effectively vindicating her federal statutory rights"). But the fact that it is not worth the expense involved in [—8—] *proving* a statutory remedy does not constitute the elimination of the *right to pursue* that remedy.

Am. Exp. Co. v. Italian Colors Rest., 133 S. Ct. 2304, 2310-11 (2013) (footnote omitted). The Supreme Court has never invoked the effective vindication doctrine to justify the refusal to *enforce* an arbitration clause in either the domestic or foreign arbitration context. *Id.* at 2310. Moreover, we are aware of no court that has even applied the effective vindication doctrine to invalidate an arbitration agreement in the context of a New York Convention case. *See Escobar,* 805 F.3d at 1291.

II.

A.

The basic facts essential to the resolution of this appeal are undisputed. Suazo, a Nicaraguan citizen, signed an employment contract (the "Employment Agreement") with NCL to work aboard one of its cruise ships. The Employment Agreement plainly requires arbitration of any dispute arising out of his employment with NCL:

> ARBITRATION – Seaman agrees, on his own behalf and on behalf of his heirs, executors, and assigns, that any and all claims, grievances, and disputes of any kind whatsoever relating to or in any way connected with the Seaman's shipboard employment with Company . . . shall be referred to and resolved exclusively by binding arbitration pursuant to the United Nations Convention on Recognition and Enforcement of Foreign Arbitral Awards [(the "New York Convention")], except as otherwise provided in any government mandated contract . . . . [—9—]

> The place of the arbitration shall be the Seaman's country of citizenship, unless arbitration is unavailable under The Convention in that country, in which case, and only in that case, said arbitration shall take place in Nassau, Bahamas. The substantive law to be applied to the arbitration shall be the law of the flag state of the vessel. . . .

> The arbitration referred to in this Article is exclusive and mandatory. Lawsuits or other proceedings between the Seaman and the Company may not be brought except to enforce the arbitration provision of this Agreement or to enforce a decision of the Arbitrator.

The Agreement is silent as to who must bear the costs of arbitration. However, it says that "the employment relationship established hereunder shall at all times be subject to and governed by the [Collective Bargaining Agreement ("CBA")]."

The CBA in turn provides:[1]

7. Arbitration

. . . .

e. In the event a dispute between the [Norwegian Seafarers' Union ("NSU")] and NCL, or between NCL and a Seafarer represented by the NSU, cannot be resolved through good faith negotiations and either party commences an arbitration proceeding, NCL shall bear the reasonable costs related to the arbitration process from beginning to end including, but not limited to fees charged and expenses incurred by arbitrators, and any costs related to proceedings brought by the NSU necessary to enforce a decision. The NSU and NCL shall each bear the costs of their own attorney fees and legal representation. [—10—]

f. If the Seafarer rejects the representation appointed by the NSU at arbitration or thereafter, or if he or she initiates arbitration independently, then he or she will cover the cost of his or her own legal representation, if any. Where the Seafarer is not represented by the NSU, the arbitrator shall seek the NSU's opinion as to the interpretation of this Agreement before making a decision.

Thus, the CBA provides that, if the Seafarer is represented by the Norwegian Seafarers' Union in arbitration, NCL will bear the "reasonable costs related to the arbitration process from beginning to end." However, the CBA is silent as to who bears the cost of arbitration if the "Seafarer rejects the

---

[1] The CBA was not provided to the district court. However, it was referenced in the Employment Agreement, which was presented to the district court. Moreover, NCL quoted from the CBA at length in its filings in the district court and offered to submit it upon request. Suazo did not object to NCL's references to the CBA in the district court or request that the full CBA be submitted. Accordingly, we consider the pertinent portions of the CBA on appeal.

representation appointed by the NSU." In this situation—which the parties agree is applicable here—both NCL and the International Center for Dispute Resolution, which performs the arbitrations between NCL and its employees, have taken the position that the employee and NSU must each bear one-half of the costs until the arbitrator decides who will pay the costs.

Suazo worked for NCL aboard the Bahamian vessel *Norwegian Epic*, where his duties consisted of frequent heavy lifting. In April 2011, he was injured while lifting heavy garbage bins as part of his duties onboard the ship. He went to the ship's doctor complaining of back pain, was prescribed pain medications, and was sent back to work. His pain continued to worsen until he could no longer work. On August 24, 2011, Suazo was flown home to Nicaragua on medical leave. NCL did not make arrangements for his medical care in Nicaragua until after Suazo [—11—] contacted the local hiring agency requesting medical attention. On August 31, 2011, NCL referred Suazo to an orthopedic surgeon, who diagnosed him with a herniated disc that was compressing a nerve in his spine and prescribed physical therapy and epidural steroid injections. Suazo received treatment throughout 2012, but his medical care was terminated in December 2012 before he was healed. NCL ignored requests to reinstate his medical care.

B.

On December 20, 2013, Suazo, represented by private counsel, brought suit against NCL in Florida circuit court in Miami-Dade County. The four-count complaint asserted claims for negligence under the Jones Act, 46 U.S.C. § 30104, and under general maritime law. NCL timely removed the case to the United States District Court for the Southern District of Florida pursuant to 9 U.S.C. § 205, which allows for the removal of state court actions relating to an arbitration agreement that falls under the New York Convention "at any time before the trial thereof." After removing the case to federal court, NCL filed a motion to dismiss and compel arbitration.

Suazo opposed NCL's motion to compel arbitration. He noted that, although the employment agreement was silent as to who would bear the costs of arbitration for individuals who forego representation by the Norwegian Seafarers' Union, NCL had said that it would require him to pay half of the costs of arbitration. He [—12—] claimed that he was too poor to bear that cost and, therefore, that the district court should refuse to compel arbitration in the first place. Suazo submitted an affidavit in support of his opposition, which stated, in pertinent part only this:

> 5. I am from a poor rural community in Nicaragua. It is not easy to find work in my home country.
>
> 6. I am the main source of income in my family. I financially support my family.
>
> 7. I do not have any money to pay for an arbitration, much less for an arbitrator's salary.
>
> 8. I do not have the means to pay for thousands of dollars to an arbitrator. To do so would mean to deprive my family of support.

On November 4, 2014, the district court granted NCL's motion and compelled the parties to arbitrate, retaining jurisdiction of the case in order to enforce the arbitration award "if appropriate." The court reasoned that Suazo's argument that he could not afford to pay the costs of arbitration invoked the "effective vindication doctrine," which was a "public policy" defense that could not be considered at the arbitration-enforcement stage under the New York Convention.[2] This timely appeal ensued.

Suazo raises a single question on appeal: whether he may defeat NCL's motion to compel arbitration by showing that he is too

---

[2] The district court also rejected Suazo's claims that the FAA precludes enforcement of arbitration agreements in seaman's employment contracts, and that the arbitration agreement's choice of foreign law rendered the agreement unenforceable. Suazo has not raised those arguments on appeal.

poor to afford the costs of [—13—] arbitration. On May 6, 2015, NCL moved to dismiss the appeal for want of jurisdiction, suggesting that the district court's order compelling arbitration was a non-final, non-appealable order under 9 U.S.C. § 16(b). While that motion was pending in our Court, NCL moved for sanctions, arguing that Suazo's appeal was frivolous and that the Court should award it double costs and reasonable attorneys' fees.

On June 23, 2015, we denied NCL's motion to dismiss, concluding that the order compelling arbitration was a final, appealable order. *See* 9 U.S.C. § 16(a)(3); *Martinez v. Carnival Corp.*, 744 F.3d 1240, 1243-45, 2 Adm. R. 551, 552–53 (11th Cir. 2014) (holding that an order compelling arbitration was final and appealable where the order denied all pending motions as moot, administratively closed the case, and neither expressly stayed nor expressly dismissed the case); *Bautista*, 396 F.3d at 1294 (holding that a district court's retention of jurisdiction to enforce or confirm a resulting arbitral award does not destroy finality). NCL's motion for sanctions is still pending in this Court.

III.

We review *de novo* a district court order granting a motion to compel arbitration. *In re Checking Account Overdraft Litig.*, 754 F.3d 1290, 1293 (11th Cir. 2014). The district court was required to compel arbitration if the arbitration agreement satisfied the four jurisdictional prerequisites found in the New York [—14—] Convention and none of Article II's arbitration-enforcement stage defenses applied. *Lindo*, 652 F.3d at 1276. It is undisputed that the four jurisdictional prerequisites have been met. The parties agree that: the employment agreement is in writing; the agreement provides for arbitration in Nicaragua, which has signed the Convention; Suazo's employment with NCL was a commercial relationship; and Suazo is not an American citizen. *See Bautista*, 396 F.3d at 1295 n.7 (listing jurisdictional requirements). Suazo argues, nevertheless, that the district court erred in compelling him to arbitrate because he cannot afford the costs of arbitration that he will be required to pay and, therefore, he will be unable to effectively vindicate his federal statutory rights in the arbitral forum.

A.

We have not squarely decided whether a party can raise a cost-based effective vindication defense at the arbitration-enforcement stage under the New York Convention, and we are aware of no other federal circuit court that has done so. Nevertheless, three of our decisions provide substantial guidance.

In *Bautista v. Star Cruises*, 396 F.3d 1289 (11th Cir. 2005), several cruise ship employees who were injured at work brought suit in federal district court against their employers, asserting claims under the Jones Act, 46 U.S.C. § 688, and under the general maritime law of the United States. *Id.* at 1292. The district court found that the employment relationship was governed by an arbitration clause and [—15—] compelled the parties to arbitrate the dispute under the New York Convention. *Id.* at 1294. The plaintiffs appealed the order compelling arbitration, arguing, among other things, that the arbitration provision was unconscionable. *Id.* at 1301-02.

We affirmed the order compelling arbitration. We began by explaining that the New York Convention "requires that courts enforce an agreement to arbitrate unless the agreement is 'null and void, inoperative or incapable of being performed.'" *Id.* at 1301 (quoting New York Convention, art. II(3)). We adopted the First Circuit's view that Article II's "'null and void' clause . . . limits the bases upon which an international arbitration agreement may be challenged to standard breach-of-contract defenses," and that the clause "must be interpreted to encompass only those situations—such as fraud, mistake, duress, and waiver—that can be applied neutrally on an international scale." *Id.* at 1302 (internal quotation marks omitted) (quoting *DiMercurio v. Sphere Drake Ins. PLC*, 202 F.3d 71, 79-80 (1st Cir. 2000)). We observed that unconscionability could provide a defense to arbitration enforcement in the domestic context, but that "[d]omestic defenses to arbitration are transferrable to a Convention Act case *only if* they fit within the limited scope of defenses" contained in the Convention. *Id.* (emphasis added). Because we "doubt[ed] that there exists a precise, universal definition of [unconscionability] that may be applied effectively across the range of countries **[—16—]** that are parties to the Convention," we refused to consider the plaintiffs' unconscionability defense and affirmed the order compelling arbitration. *Id.*

After *Bautista*, some confusion arose in this Circuit about which defenses could properly be raised at the arbitration-enforcement stage under the New York Convention. In *Thomas v. Carnival Corp.*, 573 F.3d 1113 (11th Cir. 2009), a panel of our Court reversed a district court's order compelling arbitration because the arbitration agreement required the application of Panamanian law and would, therefore, deprive the plaintiff of his ability to assert his United States statutory claims. *Id.* at 1124. Citing Article V—which, unlike Article II, contains an explicit public policy defense—the panel reasoned that the New York Convention allowed a party to defeat a motion to compel arbitration by establishing that an arbitration clause "is null and void as a matter of public policy." *Id.* at 1120-24 & n.17.

We addressed the apparent conflict between *Bautista* and *Thomas* in *Lindo v. NCL (Bahamas), Ltd.*, 652 F.3d 1257 (11th Cir. 2011). In *Lindo*, a Bahamian cruise ship employee sued his employer, NCL, in Florida circuit court in Miami-Dade County, alleging that he had injured his back while lifting trash bags at work, bringing a claim under the Jones Act. *Id.* at 1260-61. The employment agreement between NCL and the employee required all such claims to be arbitrated in the employee's country of citizenship, which was Nicaragua, and that the law of the **[—17—]** vessel, which was the Bahamas, would apply. *Id.* NCL removed the case to federal court and moved to compel arbitration; the district court granted the motion. *Id.* at 1261-62. Lindo appealed and, relying heavily on *Thomas*, argued that the application of Bahamian law in the arbitral forum would prevent him from effectively vindicating his United States statutory rights under the Jones Act. He also asserted that the arbitration agreement was unconscionable and, therefore, unenforceable. *Id.* at 1276.

We affirmed the district court's order compelling arbitration. First, we explained, we were required to "start our analysis with a strong presumption in favor of the arbitration agreement in Lindo's Contract," and that presumption was unaffected by the fact that Lindo was seeking to litigate federal statutory claims. *Id.* at 1275-76. Because Lindo conceded that the four jurisdictional prerequisites to the New York Convention were met, *id.* at 1276 & n.17, we needed only to decide whether Lindo's effective vindication argument constituted an available affirmative defense under the Convention. Citing *Bautista*, 396 F.3d at 1302, we held that Lindo had not made any "claim—much less any showing—of fraud, mistake, duress, or waiver," and he therefore could not avoid arbitration under Article II. *Id.* at 1276.

We explained that *Thomas* could not help Lindo avoid arbitration because, "to the extent *Thomas* allowed the plaintiff seaman to prevail on a new public **[—18—]** policy defense under Article II, *Thomas* violate[d] *Bautista* and our prior panel precedent rule." *Id.* at 1278. Furthermore, Lindo could not raise any public policy defense under Article V because "Article V applies only at the arbitral award-enforcement stage and not at the arbitration-enforcement stage." *Id.* at 1280. Moreover, we noted that it was likely Bahamian law would permit Lindo to pursue the same types of claims as American law. Thus, Lindo's "public policy" defense was "premature" at the *arbitration-enforcement* stage, since Lindo could challenge the manner in which the arbitration was conducted under Article V at the *arbitral award-enforcement* stage, when "the arbitrator . . . will have ruled and the record will show what legal principles were applied and what Lindo recovered, or did not recover, and why." *Id.* at 1284. To allow Lindo to raise his choice-of-law effective vindication argument at the arbitration-enforcement stage, we concluded, "would effectively eviscerate the mutually binding nature of the

Convention" because it would enable all signatory nations to refuse to enforce arbitration agreements that selected any law but their own. *Id.*

Most recently, in *Escobar v. Celebration Cruise Operator*, 805 F.3d 1279 (11th Cir. 2015), we confronted the precise question presented in this case: whether a cost-based effective vindication defense could be raised at the arbitration-enforcement stage under the New York Convention. In *Escobar*, the plaintiff—a cruise ship employee who had been injured on the job—brought suit [—19—] in state court against his employer, who removed the case to federal court and moved to compel arbitration. *Id.* at 1282-83. The plaintiff had signed an employment agreement that contained an arbitration clause, which stated: "[a]lthough [the employer] shall bear the initial cost of the arbitration, each [party] shall be responsible for one half of the cost of arbitration." *Id.* at 1282. Escobar argued that his arbitration fees would be $20,000 for even a short, three-day arbitration, and he submitted an affidavit stating that he had no money to pay the fees. *Id.* at 1283. Nevertheless, the district court granted the motion to compel arbitration. *Id.* Escobar appealed, arguing under the effective vindication doctrine that the cost-splitting provision in the arbitration agreement "effectively denie[d] him access to the forum because he is indigent." *Id.* at 1291.

We affirmed. We began by observing that we had found no court that had ever applied the effective vindication doctrine to a New York Convention case. *Id.* at 1291. Yet we found it unnecessary to decide whether Escobar's cost-based effective vindication defense could be raised at the arbitration-enforcement stage, in as much as Escobar's effective vindication claim failed for three other reasons. "First, to the extent Escobar could make [an effective vindication] claim in a New York Convention case," it was "premature for Escobar to do so at this arbitration-enforcement stage." *Id.* at 1292. We reached this conclusion because the cost-splitting clause in the arbitration agreement required the employer to pay the initial [—20—] fee to "open the doors to begin the

arbitration and begin the proceedings," *id.* at 1292 & n.16, meaning that "Escobar has access to the forum," *id.* at 1292.

Second, we determined that the "most reasonable reading" of the cost-splitting clause was that the employer would "initially pay for the cost of the arbitration itself," and that Escobar "ultimately [would] be responsible for his one-half share." *Id.* Recognizing that "the precise application of the cost-splitting clause [was] an issue properly for the arbitrator to consider," we found that Escobar had failed to show that he was likely to incur "any costs *due prior to the arbitrator's decision.*" *Id.* (emphasis added). Third, we determined that Escobar had not provided any evidence of how much arbitration actually would cost him, and, therefore, had failed to carry his burden to prove that he would be denied access to the forum. *Id.* Thus, we observed that based on the arbitration clause language and his own filings, Escobar had "wholly failed to establish that he would be denied access to the forum." *Id.* We indicated that "the appropriate time for Escobar to raise any argument relating to the payment of fees would be at the award-enforcement stage, if and when [his employer] attempt[ed] to collect arbitral costs from him." *Id.*

B.

Because Suazo is attempting to defeat a motion to compel arbitration, he can only raise his cost-based effective vindication defense if it falls within the defenses [—21—] enumerated in Article II of the New York Convention. *See Lindo*, 652 F.3d at 1263. Again, Article II requires that a court enforce an agreement to arbitrate "unless it finds that the said agreement is [1] null and void, [2] inoperative or [3] incapable of being performed." New York Convention, art. II(3). The Supreme Court has never applied the effective vindication doctrine and "no court [] has applied it in the context of a New York Convention case." *Escobar*, 805 F.3d at 1291. We have never determined whether a cost-based effective vindication defense can be raised under the "incapable of being performed" clause of Article II, and we need not resolve that question today because Suazo has fallen far short of establishing that enforcing the arbitration agreement in this case will effectively deny him access to the arbitral forum.

In order to prevail on a cost-based effective vindication defense in a domestic arbitration case—assuming such a defense can be raised under Article II—a party seeking to avoid arbitration must "demonstrate that he faces such 'high costs' if compelled to arbitrate his claim . . . that he is effectively precluded from vindicating his [federal statutory] rights in the arbitral forum." *Musnick v. King Motor Co. of Fort Lauderdale*, 325 F.3d 1255, 1259 (11th Cir. 2003) (quoting *Green Tree*, 531 U.S. at 90). Recently in *Escobar*, we explained:

The "party seek[ing] to invalidate an arbitration agreement on the ground that arbitration would be prohibitively expensive . . . bears the burden of showing the likelihood of incurring such costs." *Green Tree*, 531 U.S. at 92. The mere existence of a cost-splitting clause in [—22—] an arbitration agreement does not satisfy a plaintiff's burden to prove the likelihood of prohibitive costs. *See Musnick v. King Motor Co. of Fort Lauderdale*, 325 F.3d 1255, 1259 (11th Cir. 2003). Rather, a party invoking the effective-vindication doctrine because the cost of arbitration is prohibitively expensive must present evidence of two things: (1) "the amount of the fees he is likely to incur;" and (2) "his inability to pay those fees." *Id.* at 1260. Speculative fear of high fees is insufficient. *Id.*

Escobar, 805 F.3d at 1291.

In *Escobar*, the arbitration agreement at issue required the employer to bear the initial cost of arbitration, but then required the parties to evenly split the remaining costs of arbitration. *Id.* at 1282. Escobar presented affidavit evidence that he "was unemployed, had $0 in his bank account, and did not have any money to pay for arbitration." *Id.* at 1283. In addition, his counsel opined that Escobar's share of the arbitration fees could amount to $20,000. *Id.*

We rejected Escobar's effective vindication defense for three reasons. First, Escobar would have been able to bring his claims in the arbitral forum because the arbitration agreement at issue required the employer to "pay the initial cost of arbitration." *Id.* at 1292 (internal quotation marks omitted). Second, we understood the arbitration agreement to require the employer to pay for all of the costs of arbitration and then to seek reimbursement from Escobar, so Escobar had not "shown that he is likely to incur any costs *due prior to the arbitrator's decision.*" *Id.* (internal quotation marks omitted and emphasis added). And third, [—23—] Escobar had not provided any evidence (apart from counsel's speculation) to show how much arbitration would cost him. *Id.*

In this case, Suazo's evidential foundation offered in support of his effective vindication argument falls short of even the paltry showing that we found insufficient in *Escobar*. In the district court, Suazo submitted no evidence concerning "the amount of the fees he is likely to incur." *Escobar*, 805 F.3d at 1291 (internal quotation mark omitted). His counsel simply opined that arbitration costs could exceed $20,000, but he cited no evidence in support of that claim. Suazo also submitted an email exchange with NCL's counsel, which stated that Suazo would be billed for half of the costs of arbitration "until a decision is made by the arbitrator once appointed." In a later email, NCL's counsel clarified this to mean that "the costs are to be equally divided among the parties until such time as the arbitrator addresses the issue." Finally, in his appellate brief, Suazo cited to additional evidence outside the record regarding the costs of arbitration, which suggests that Suazo would have to pay up to $2,000 to initiate arbitration and $1,750 as a final arbitration fee, assuming that the arbitrator required the parties to continue splitting costs until the end of arbitration.[3] Even if we could consider

---

[3] In his reply brief on appeal, Suazo cited to the website of the International Center for Dispute Resolution ("ICDR"), the arbitration body that would hear his claim. That website shows that the "Initial Filing Fee" for a claim of Suazo's value is $4,000, and the "Final Fee" is $3,500. *See ICDR, International Dispute Resolution Procedures,*

the [—24—] evidence submitted for the first time on appeal, which we generally would not do, *see Sammons v. Taylor*, 967 F.2d 1533, 1544 (11th Cir. 1992), Suazo still could not prevail.

Suazo's factual foundation for regarding his "inability to pay [the arbitration] fees," *Escobar*, 805 F.3d at 1291, is insufficient. The only record evidence offered is Suazo's affidavit, which states, in sum, that he lives in a poor community where it is "not easy to find work," that he "do[es] not have money to pay for an arbitration, much less for an arbitrator's salary," and that he "do[es] not have the means to pay for thousands of dollars to an arbitrator." These conclusory statements do not establish that Suazo could not afford to pay even $3,750, a figure he claims he *might* incur in arbitration. Indeed, Suazo's affidavit is less specific than the affidavit offered by the plaintiff in *Escobar*, which said that he was unemployed and had $0 in his bank account. *Escobar*, 805 F.3d at 1283.

We recognize that the arbitration agreement in this case is distinguishable from the agreement at issue in *Escobar*. While "application of the cost-splitting clause is an issue properly for the arbitrator to consider," *id.* at 1292, it seems likely that Suazo will be required to bear half of the cost of initiating arbitration and "may" also become responsible for some other costs prior to the arbitrator's decision. Even so, on this almost barren record, Suazo has not carried his burden [—25—] of proving that it is likely that unaffordable costs will deny him "access to the forum." *Id.*

We hold that Suazo cannot prevail on his effective vindication defense for a second and independent reason. The CBA between Suazo and NCL provided that, as long as Suazo was represented by the Norwegian Seafarers' Union, NCL "shall bear the reasonable costs related to the arbitration process from beginning to end." However, if Suazo chose to initiate arbitration "independently" of the

Amended and Effective July 1, 2015, http://info.adr.org/ICDRfeeschedule/. He contends that he would have to pay half of that fee, or $2,000.

NSU, the CBA is silent as to who must bear the costs of arbitration. On this record, it appears that the only reason Suazo would be required to bear any cost in arbitrating his dispute with NCL is because he opted to retain private counsel instead of proceeding to arbitrate with union-appointed counsel. The agreement gave him a choice: arbitrate for free with your union-chosen representation, or pay your own way with counsel of your choice. Having chosen the latter course of action, we will not second-guess the bargain struck in the contract and let Suazo eat his cake and have it too. Because the arbitration agreement and the CBA gave him the ability to arbitrate for free and thereby "vindicate[e] his [federal statutory] rights in the arbitral forum," *Musnick*, 325 F.3d at 1259, his effective vindication defense is unmeritorious.[4] [—26—]

Thus, since Suazo has not established any basis on which to deny NCL's motion to compel arbitration, we affirm the district court's order compelling the parties to arbitrate the dispute.

IV.

After Suazo filed his opening appellate brief, NCL moved for sanctions pursuant to Fed. R. App. P. 38 and 28 U.S.C. § 1927, arguing that Suazo's appeal is frivolous because his "public policy defense has been repeatedly and expressly rejected by binding Eleventh Circuit precedent following *Lindo*," and seeking an award of double costs and reasonable attorneys' fees from Suazo or his counsel.

Fed. R. App. P. 38 provides:

If a court of appeals determines that an appeal is frivolous, it may, after a separately filed motion or notice from the court and reasonable opportunity to

---

[4] At oral argument, Suazo's counsel suggested that NSU would not actually represent a seafarer in a dispute with NCL and, therefore, the CBA does not provide an alternative means of [—26—] effectively vindicating his rights. However, there is no evidence in this record that the CBA does not operate as its text suggests or that Suazo sought and was refused NSU representation.

respond, award just damages and single or double costs to the appellee.

"Rule 38 sanctions have been imposed against appellants who raise 'clearly frivolous claims' in the face of established law and clear facts." *Farese v. Scherer*, 342 F.3d 1223, 1232 (11th Cir. 2003). Where an appeal requires a court to decide an issue of first impression in a circuit court, it is not frivolous. *See Albra v. Advan, Inc.*, 490 F.3d 826, 835 (11th Cir. 2007). Title 28 U.S.C. § 1927, in turn, provides: [—27—]

> Any attorney or other person admitted to conduct cases in any court of the United States or any Territory thereof who so multiplies the proceedings in any case unreasonably and vexatiously may be required by the court to satisfy personally the excess costs, expenses, and attorneys' fees reasonably incurred because of such conduct.

We have "consistently held that an attorney multiplies proceedings unreasonably and vexatiously within the meaning of the statute only when the attorney's conduct is so egregious that it is tantamount to bad faith." *Amlong & Amlong, P.A. v. Denny's, Inc.*, 500 F.3d 1230, 1239 (11th Cir. 2006) (internal quotation marks omitted).

Sanctions are not appropriate in this case. To the extent that NCL's motion was based on its claim that we did not have jurisdiction to consider this appeal, we already decided that NCL was incorrect when we denied NCL's motion to dismiss. Moreover, Suazo's appeal was not frivolous. He raised a single argument on appeal relating to the effective vindication doctrine, which involved a question of first impression in our Court. Finally, Suazo's appeal did not unnecessarily multiply the proceedings in this case, since he raised only a single issue, and a narrow one at that. Accordingly, we deny NCL's motion for sanctions.

ORDER TO COMPEL ARBITRATION AFFIRMED AND MOTION FOR SANCTIONS DENIED.

United States Court of Appeals
for the Eleventh Circuit

No. 15-13659

UNITED STATES
vs.
IGUARAN

Appeal from the United States District Court for the Southern District of Florida

Decided: May 12, 2016

Citation: 821 F.3d 1335, 4 Adm. R. 457 (11th Cir. 2016).

Before **CARNES**, Chief Judge, **MARTIN** and **ANDERSON**, Circuit Judges.

[—1—] PER CURIAM:

Danfi Gonzalez Iguaran pleaded guilty to one count of conspiring to distribute cocaine while on board a vessel subject to the jurisdiction of the United [—2—] States, in violation of the Maritime Drug Law Enforcement Act (MDLEA), 46 U.S.C. §§ 70503(a)(1), 70506(b). On appeal, he contends for the first time that the district court did not have subject matter jurisdiction because the record does not establish that the vessel in which he was apprehended was subject to the jurisdiction of the United States.

As an initial matter, the government contends that we should review only for plain error because Iguaran did not raise his jurisdictional objection in the district court.[1] The government is wrong. *See McCoy v. United States*, 266 F.3d 1245, 1249 (11th Cir. 2001) ("[J]urisdictional errors are not subject to plain- or harmless-error analysis."). The district court's subject matter jurisdiction is a question of law that we review *de novo* even when it is raised for the first time on appeal. *See United States v. Giraldo-Prado*, 150 F.3d 1328, 1329 (11th Cir. 1998); *see also Henderson ex rel. Henderson v. Shinseki*, 562 U.S. 428, 434, 131 S. Ct. 1197, 1202 (2011) (noting that "[o]bjections to subject-matter jurisdiction . . . may be raised at any time"); *United States v. Cotton*, 535 U.S. 625, 630, 122 S. Ct. 1781, 1785 (2002) ("[D]efects in subject-matter jurisdiction require correction regardless of whether the error was raised in district court."). We review for clear error the [—3—] district court's factfindings relevant to jurisdiction. *United States v. Tinoco*, 304 F.3d 1088, 1114 (11th Cir. 2002).

The MDLEA makes it a crime to conspire to distribute a controlled substance while on board "a vessel subject to the jurisdiction of the United States." 46 U.S.C. §§ 70503(a)(1), 70506(b). The Act also states that "[j]urisdiction of the United States with respect to a vessel subject to this chapter is not an element of an offense" and that "[j]urisdictional issues arising under this chapter are preliminary questions of law to be determined solely by the trial judge." 46 U.S.C. § 70504(a). Based on that language, this Court has "interpreted the 'on board a vessel subject to the jurisdiction of the United States' portion of the MDLEA as a congressionally imposed limit on courts' subject matter jurisdiction, akin to the amount-in-controversy requirement contained in 28 U.S.C. § 1332." *United States v. De La Garza*, 516 F.3d 1266, 1271 (11th Cir. 2008); *see also United States v. Betancourth*, 554 F.3d 1329, 1332–33 (11th Cir. 2009). Thus, "for a district court to have adjudicatory authority over a charge that a defendant conspired to violate the substantive crime defined in [the MDLEA], the Government must preliminarily show that the conspiracy's vessel was, when apprehended, subject to the jurisdiction of the United States." *De La Garza*, 516 F.3d at 1272 (quotation marks omitted). [—4—]

The MDLEA identifies various circumstances that would render a vessel subject to the jurisdiction of the United States. For example, "a vessel without nationality" counts as a "vessel subject to the

---

[1] In support of its argument that plain error review applies, the government relies on our unpublished decisions in *United States v. Estrada-Obregon*, 270 F. App'x 978 (11th Cir. 2008), and *United States v. Madera-Lopez*, 190 F. App'x 832 (11th Cir. 2006). Neither decision constitutes binding precedent. *See* 11th Cir. R. 36-2 ("Unpublished opinions are not considered binding precedent."); *United States v. Irey*, 612 F.3d 1160, 1215 n.34 (11th Cir. 2010) ("Unpublished opinions are not precedential . . . .").

jurisdiction of the United States" for purposes of the MDLEA. 46 U.S.C. § 70502(c)(1)(A). In turn, the term "vessel without nationality" includes "a vessel aboard which the master or individual in charge fails, on request of an officer of the United States authorized to enforce applicable provisions of United States law, to make a claim of nationality or registry for that vessel." *Id.* § 70502(d)(1)(B). Under those definitions, if Iguaran and his coconspirators failed, on request of the United States officials who apprehended them, to "make a claim of nationality," their vessel was "without nationality" and "subject to the jurisdiction of the United States."

In this case, the district court did not expressly make any factual findings with respect to its jurisdiction. The government contends, however, that Iguaran's plea agreement, which was consistent with his factual proffer and presentence investigation report, establishes the district court's jurisdiction. In the plea agreement, Iguaran agreed to plead guilty to conspiring to possess with intent to distribute cocaine "with individuals who were on board a vessel that was subject to the jurisdiction of the United States." That statement, the government appears to argue, constitutes an admission of jurisdiction. [—5—]

The government's argument fails because, as we have repeatedly held, "[p]arties may not stipulate jurisdiction." *W. Peninsular Title Co. v. Palm Beach Cty.*, 41 F.3d 1490, 1492 n.4 (11th Cir. 1995); *see also Travaglio v. Am. Express Co.*, 735 F.3d 1266, 1269–70 (11th Cir. 2013) ("[I]t is fundamental that parties may not stipulate to federal jurisdiction."); *Bush v. United States*, 703 F.2d 491, 494 (11th Cir. 1983) ("The mere fact that the parties stipulated to jurisdiction does not automatically vest authority in the district court to adjudicate all the issues presented, for subject matter jurisdiction cannot be assumed by the court nor can it be waived by the parties."). Parties may, however, "stipulate to *facts* that bear on our jurisdictional inquiry." *Eng'g Contractors Ass'n of S. Fla. v. Metro. Dade Cty.*, 122 F.3d 895, 905 (11th Cir. 1997); *see also Ry. Co. v. Ramsey*, 89 U.S. (22 Wall.) 322, 327 (1874). A

court's task is to determine whether "the stipulated facts give rise to jurisdiction." *W. Peninsular Title Co.*, 41 F.3d at 1492 n.4 (emphasis omitted).

In the plea agreement, Iguaran does not admit to facts that give rise to jurisdiction. The agreement does not state, for example, that Iguaran and his coconspirators failed to "make a claim of nationality" upon request when United States officials apprehended them. Instead, it asserts that Iguaran was on a vessel subject to the United States' jurisdiction. That is a question of law and one which, as we have already explained, parties may not stipulate or admit to. *See Travaglio*, [—6—] 735 F.3d at 1269–70; *W. Peninsular Title Co.*, 41 F.3d at 1492 n.4; *Bush*, 703 F.2d at 494. Iguaran's factual proffer, his presentence investigation report, and the transcript from his change of plea hearing also fail to supply facts which establish that Iguaran's vessel was subject to the jurisdiction of the United States. And the record is devoid of any other facts that would provide a basis for federal subject matter jurisdiction. As a result, we are unable to determine whether the district court had jurisdiction over Iguaran's case.

The government points out that one of Iguaran's coconspirators, in a separate proceeding against him, admitted to facts that would establish jurisdiction in his case. For example, that coconspirator admitted in his plea agreement that when they were apprehended "none of the defendants claimed to be the master of the vessel," "none made a claim of nationality," and the vessel "was, therefore, a stateless vessel subject to the jurisdiction of the United States." His admission is irrelevant here because the question is whether the record in Iguaran's case, not some other case, establishes jurisdiction. It does not.

When a party's failure to challenge the district court's jurisdiction is at least partially responsible for the lack of a developed record, we have said that "the proper course of action . . . is to remand the case to the district court for factual findings" as to jurisdiction. *Williams v. Best Buy Co.*, 269 F.3d 1316, 1320

(11th Cir. 2001); *see also Belleri v. United States*, 712 F.3d 543, 548 (11th Cir. 2013) [—7—] (stating that when we discover "a serious question regarding the factual predicate for subject-matter jurisdiction, we should remand for a finding to resolve the jurisdictional question") (quotation marks and alteration omitted); *Rolling Greens MHP, LP v. Comcast SCH Holdings LLC*, 374 F.3d 1020, 1020–21 (11th Cir. 2004) (remanding to the district court "for limited purpose of determining whether diversity jurisdiction exists"). Although neither side requests it, a limited remand is the proper course of action in this case.

We therefore remand the case to the district court for the limited purpose of determining whether subject matter jurisdiction exists. On limited remand, the government "should be afforded an opportunity to submit evidence in support of its assertion" that Iguaran's vessel was subject to the jurisdiction of the United States, and Iguaran should be afforded an opportunity to present evidence that it was not. *Williams*, 269 F.3d at 1321. The district court should then determine whether the government has carried its burden of establishing that the vessel in which Iguaran was apprehended was subject to the jurisdiction of the United States. If the court determines that the government has proven that, it should reinstate Iguaran's conviction; if the court determines that the government has not proven that, it should enter a judgment dismissing for lack of jurisdiction the charge against Iguaran. [—8—]

The judgment is **VACATED** and the case is **REMANDED** for further proceedings consistent with this opinion.

United States Court of Appeals
for the Eleventh Circuit

No. 15-12597

TUNDIDOR
vs.
MIAMI-DADE COUNTY

Appeal from the United States District Court for the
Southern District of Florida

Decided: August 3, 2016

Citation: 831 F.3d 1328, 4 Adm. R. 460 (11th Cir. 2016).

Before **W. PRYOR** and **J. PRYOR**, Circuit Judges, and
VOORHEES, * District Judge.

* Honorable Richard L. Voorhees, United States
District Judge for the Western District of North Carolina,
sitting by designation.

[—1—] W. PRYOR, Circuit Judge: **[—2—]**

The appeal requires us to decide whether
a canal is navigable for purposes of
admiralty jurisdiction, 28 U.S.C. § 1333,
if an artificial obstruction prevents vessels
from using the canal to conduct interstate
commerce. Youry Tundidor suffered injuries
while aboard a vessel traveling in the Coral
Park Canal, a drainage canal in Miami-Dade
County. Tundidor sued the County for
negligence, but the district court dismissed his
complaint for lack of subject-matter
jurisdiction. Admiralty jurisdiction extends
only to waters that are navigable in interstate
commerce. Because an artificial obstruction
prevents vessels from traveling from the Coral
Park Canal to places outside of Florida, we
agree with the district court that Tundidor's
injuries did not occur on navigable waters for
purposes of admiralty jurisdiction. We affirm.

I. BACKGROUND

In July 2013, Tundidor suffered serious
injuries while he was a passenger on a
pleasure boat traveling south on the Coral
Park Canal. As the boat approached the Coral
Park Canal Bridge, near SW 94th Avenue and
SW 12th Street, the four passengers lowered
their heads, and the vessel passed under the
bridge. As the boat emerged on the south side
of the bridge, Tundidor raised his head and hit
a water pipe. The force of the impact ejected
Tundidor from the boat and into the canal.

The Coral Park Canal is a drainage canal
located in southwest Miami-Dade County. It
joins the Tamiami (or C-4) Canal at the
intersection of SW 94th Avenue [—3—] and
SW 8th Street, which forms a low-lying bridge
over the canal at the intersection. The
Tamiami Canal extends eastward past the
Miami International Airport and connects to
the Miami River. The Miami River leads to
the Biscayne Bay and the Atlantic Ocean.

Along the Tamiami Canal, between the
Coral Park Canal and the Miami River, a
series of low-lying bridges, water pipes, and
railroad tracks partially obstruct the
waterway. None of the bridges are bascule
bridges, which can open to allow vessels to
pass. Many of these bridges are supported by
submerged structural columns, narrowing the
area a vessel has to pass.

After this series of obstructions, toward the
eastern end of the Tamiami Canal sits a water
control structure labeled S-25B, which
prevents overdrainage and saltwater
intrusion. The structure has mechanical gates
that open only underwater. The structure
prevents navigation from the western side of
the water control structure to the Miami
River. A sign next to the structure states,
"DANGER—NO BOATING BEYOND THIS
POINT."

Tundidor sued Miami-Dade County, the
owner and operator of the main water line, in
the district court for negligence. He invoked
federal admiralty jurisdiction on the ground
that the accident occurred on a navigable
waterway. The County moved to dismiss the
suit for lack of subject-matter jurisdiction. The
County raised a factual challenge to
jurisdiction; that is, the County argued that
the [—4—] Coral Park Canal does not have a
navigable connection to the Miami River, the
Biscayne Bay, or the Atlantic Ocean. The
district court granted the motion to dismiss.

II. STANDARD OF REVIEW

On a motion to dismiss for lack of subject-matter jurisdiction, "[w]e review the district court's legal conclusions *de novo* and its factual findings for clear error." *Carmichael v. Kellogg, Brown & Root Servs., Inc.*, 572 F.3d 1271, 1279 (11th Cir. 2009).

III. DISCUSSION

Federal district courts have "original jurisdiction, exclusive of the courts of the States, of . . . [a]ny civil case of admiralty or maritime jurisdiction." 28 U.S.C. § 1333(1). In a tort case, a complaint must satisfy two elements to invoke admiralty jurisdiction: "(1) there must be a significant relationship between the alleged wrong and traditional maritime activity (the nexus requirement) and (2) the tort must have occurred on navigable waters (the location requirement)." *Aqua Log, Inc. v. Lost & Abandoned Pre-Cut Logs & Rafts of Logs*, 709 F.3d 1055, 1059, 1 Adm. R. 448, 450 (11th Cir. 2013). The County contends that Tundidor's complaint fails to satisfy the location requirement. [—5—]

The Supreme Court of the United States long ago defined "navigable waters" in *The Daniel Ball*, 77 U.S. (10 Wall.) 557 (1870), as waters that are capable for use in commerce:

Those rivers must be regarded as public navigable rivers in law which are navigable in fact. And they are navigable in fact when they are used, or are susceptible of being used, in their ordinary condition, as highways for commerce, over which trade and travel are or may be conducted in the customary modes of trade and travel on water. And they constitute navigable waters of the United States within the meaning of the acts of Congress, in contradistinction from the navigable waters of the States, when they form in their ordinary condition by themselves, or by uniting with other waters, a continued highway over which commerce is or may be carried on with other States or foreign countries in the customary modes in which such commerce is conducted by water.

Id. at 563. As a leading treatise explains, the test of navigability for purposes of admiralty jurisdiction has two requirements: the waters must be navigable in fact and have an "interstate nexus." *See* 1 Thomas J. Schoenbaum, *Admiralty and Maritime Law* § 3-3 (5th ed. 2015).

In *Aqua Log*, we rejected the proposition that "admiralty jurisdiction should extend only to those waterways with present or planned commercial activity." 709 F.3d at 1059, 1 Adm. R. at 450. We held that "a waterway is navigable for admiralty-jurisdiction purposes if, in its present state, it is capable of supporting commercial activity." *Id.* at 1056, 1 Adm. R. at 448. But we did not decide whether a waterway with artificial obstructions that prevent commerce can satisfy this test. [—6—]

Although the Miami River is a navigable waterway, *see Sea Vessel, Inc. v. Reyes*, 23 F.3d 345, 346 n.1 (11th Cir. 1994), the Coral Park Canal is not navigable because the S-25B water control structure prevents vessels on the canal from traveling outside the State of Florida. The Supreme Court has stated that "[i]n determining the boundaries of admiralty jurisdiction, we look to the purpose of the grant." *Exxon Corp. v. Cent. Gulf Lines, Inc.*, 500 U.S. 603, 608 (1991). "A body of water that is confined within a state and does not form part of an interstate waterway is not an admiralty concern." *Alford v. Appalachian Power Co.*, 951 F.2d 30, 32 (4th Cir. 1991) (citing *The Robert W. Parsons*, 191 U.S. 17, 26 (1903)). The S-25B water control structure obstructs the commercial highway. Because the Coral Park Canal cannot support interstate commerce, it cannot satisfy the location requirement of admiralty jurisdiction.

Every circuit court to consider the issue has ruled that when artificial obstructions on a waterway block interstate commercial travel, the waterway cannot support admiralty jurisdiction. *See LeBlanc v. Cleveland*, 198 F.3d 353, 359 (2d Cir. 1999); *Alford*, 951 F.2d at 33–34 (4th Cir.);

Livingston v. United States, 627 F.2d 165, 169–70 (8th Cir. 1980); *Chapman v. United States*, 575 F.2d 147, 149–51 (7th Cir. 1978); *Adams v. Montana Power Co.*, 528 F.2d 437, 440–41 (9th Cir. 1975). For example, in *Adams*, the Ninth Circuit held that a 25-mile stretch of the Missouri River in Montana enclosed on both sides by dams was not a navigable [—7—] water. 528 F.2d at 439. The Ninth Circuit reasoned that "if the damming of a water-way has the practical effect of eliminating commercial maritime activity, no federal interest is served by the exercise of admiralty jurisdiction over the events transpiring on that body of water, whether or not it was originally navigable." *Id.* at 440. We agree with that reasoning.

Tundidor argues that the test for navigable waters is one of historical navigability. He argues that the Coral Park Canal is navigable because it has a navigable connection to the Tamiami Canal, which historically served as a navigable waterway supporting commercial activity. Tundidor misunderstands the controlling precedents.

Tundidor argues that the use of the term "ordinary condition" in *The Daniel Ball*, 77 U.S. (10 Wall.) at 563, establishes a test of historical navigability, but the Supreme Court later explained that "'[n]atural or ordinary conditions' refers to volume of water, the gradients and the regularity of the flow," *United States v. Appalachian Elec. Power Co.*, 311 U.S. 377, 407 (1940) (footnote omitted) (quoting *United States v. Oregon*, 295 U.S. 1 (1935)). As the Second Circuit has explained, "[U]nder the *Daniel Ball* test, an otherwise unnavigable river may not be rendered navigable simply because, in extraordinary conditions, its waters rise high enough to support forms of transportation normally impossible." *LeBlanc*, 198 F.3d at 357. *The Daniel Ball* did not address whether a body of water "remains [—8—] navigable for admiralty jurisdiction purposes when it is made impassable by an artificial obstruction." *Id.*

Tundidor also argues that we adopted a test of historical navigability in *Aqua Log* because we noted that "[h]istorically,

commercial vessels used both the Flint River and Spring Creek for transportation," 709 F.3d at 1057, 1 Adm. R. at 448, but the parties in *Aqua Log* agreed that the Flint River and Spring Creek were, at the time of our decision, capable of transporting commercial vessels. *Id.*, 1 Adm. R. at 448. Based on the parties' concession, we had no opportunity to adopt a test of historical navigability.

Tundidor cites several other decisions that purportedly apply or endorse a test of historical navigability, but these decisions do not involve admiralty jurisdiction. Tundidor cites decisions about the power of Congress under the Commerce Clause, *see The Montello*, 87 U.S. 430 (1874); the statutory authority of the Army Corps of Engineers, *see Miami Valley Conservancy Dist. v. Alexander*, 692 F.2d 447 (6th Cir. 1982); the statutory authority of the Federal Energy Regulatory Commission, *see Consol. Hydro, Inc. v. FERC*, 968 F.2d 1258 (D.C. Cir. 1992); and the public ownership of submerged lands, *see United States v. Holt State Bank*, 270 U.S. 49 (1926). To be sure, the term "navigable waters" is relevant in several different areas of the law: it is used to define the scope of the power of Congress under the Interstate Commerce Clause, *see South Carolina v. Georgia*, 93 U.S. 4 (1876); to define regulatory jurisdiction under several federal statutes, [—9—] *see, e.g., United States v. Republic Steel Corp.*, 362 U.S. 482 (1960); to circumscribe state ownership of submerged lands, *see Utah v. United States*, 403 U.S. 9 (1971); and to identify a navigational servitude, *see Kaiser Aetna v. United States*, 444 U.S. 164 (1979). But "the test for navigability is not applied in the same way in these distinct types of cases." *PPL Mont., LLC v. Montana*, 132 S. Ct. 1215, 1228 (2012). Specifically, "the expansive definitions of navigability developed in commerce clause cases are not really appropriate in other contexts where the actual capability of a stream to support navigation is critical." *Livingston*, 627 F.2d at 169; *see also Kaiser Aetna*, 444 U.S. at 173 ("Reference to the navigability of a waterway adds little if anything to the breadth of Congress' regulatory power over interstate commerce."). The Supreme Court has explained that "any reliance upon judicial precedent must be predicated upon careful appraisal of the *purpose* for which the concept of 'navigability' was invoked in a particular case." *Kaiser Aetna*, 444 U.S. at 171 (quoting *United States v. Kaiser Aetna*, 408 F. Supp. 42, 49 (D. Haw. 1976)).

The "indelible navigability" doctrine—the principle that once a waterway becomes a navigable water of the United States, it remains a navigable water of the United States—makes sense in other contexts. For instance, "Congress' commerce power is designed in part to preserve and protect the nation's waterways which, in their natural condition, are navigable in interstate commerce." *Adams*, 528 F.2d at [—10—] 440. "The damming of a previously navigable waterway by a state cannot divest Congress of its control over a potentially useful artery of commerce, since such obstructions may always be removed." *Id.* And a test of historical navigability promotes the purpose of the doctrine of navigational servitude: "[U]nder a contemporary navigability standard, the present-day owner of riparian rights could defeat a public easement merely by erecting an impassable obstacle in the waterway." *LeBlanc*, 198 F.3d at 359.

In contrast with those other areas of the law, extending jurisdiction to waters incapable of commercial activity serves no purpose of admiralty jurisdiction. "The purpose behind the grant of admiralty jurisdiction was the protection and the promotion of the maritime shipping industry through the development and application, by neutral federal courts, of a uniform and specialized body of federal law." *Adams*, 528 F.2d at 439; *accord* Preble Stolz, *Pleasure Boating and Admiralty: Erie at Sea*, 51 Calif. L. Rev. 661, 670 (1963) ("The civil jurisdiction of the admiralty courts was only occasionally adverted to in the debates in the Constitutional Convention and the state ratifying conventions. . . . [B]ut those who have reviewed the history seem generally agreed that much of the justification for federal civil jurisdiction in admiralty was the protection of merchants, notably foreign traders . . . ."). We explained in *Aqua Log* that admiralty jurisdiction extends to waterways

where there is no current commerce but the waterway is [—11—] capable of supporting commerce because it "creates a climate conducive to commercial maritime activity" and because "a test . . . that requires actual commercial activity is unpredictable." 709 F.3d at 1061, 1 Adm. R. at 452. But "in the absence of commercial activity, present or potential, there is no ascertainable federal interest justifying the frustration of legitimate state interests." *Adams*, 528 F.2d at 439; *accord Chapman*, 575 F.2d at 149–50 ("No purpose is served by application of a uniform body of federal law, on waters devoid of trade and commerce, to regulate the activities and resolve the disputes of pleasure boaters." (quoting *Adams*, 528 F.2d at 440)).

Tundidor also argues that, even without a historical analysis, the Coral Park Canal has a navigable connection to the Miami River with minor portage around the water control structure. Alejandro Suarez, an experienced boater, stated in an affidavit that he had traveled in a two-person canoe from the Coral Park Canal to the S-25B water control structure. From there, Suarez landed the canoe on a grass embankment south of the structure, got out of the canoe, carried the canoe a few hundred feet around the structure, and then launched the canoe back into the water on the other side. Tundidor argues that a waterway can be navigable regardless of the type or size of vessels presently navigating the waterway and despite occasional portages. But again, Tundidor cites decisions that consider the power of Congress and federal agencies, not admiralty jurisdiction. *See Econ. Light & [—12—] Power Co. v. United States*, 256 U.S. 113 (1921); *Consol. Hydro*, 968 F.2d 1258; *Miami Valley Conservancy Dist.*, 692 F.2d 447.

Portage does not allow the Coral Park Canal to satisfy the location requirement of admiralty jurisdiction because portage is neither a "customary," *The Daniel Ball*, 77 U.S. (10 Wall.) at 563, nor a practical means of carrying on interstate commerce. In *LeBlanc*, the Second Circuit rejected the argument that an area of the Hudson River cut off by a dam was navigable for purposes of admiralty jurisdiction because "kayakers can portage around the dams." 198 F.3d at 360. "Navigability requires that the body of water be capable of supporting *commercial* maritime activity," and "the possibility of recreational use assisted by multiple portages" is insufficient. *Id.*

Tundidor also cites descriptions of the Tamiami Canal by a federal agency and a state agency, but neither are evidence that the Tamiami Canal is navigable for the purposes of admiralty jurisdiction. The Environmental Protection Agency has stated that the Tamiami Canal is a "navigable water of the United States" under the Clean Water Act, but the Supreme Court has explained that "the meaning of 'navigable waters' in the Act is broader than the traditional understanding of that term," *Rapanos v. United States*, 547 U.S. 715, 731 (2006) (plurality opinion); *accord id.* at 768 (Kennedy, J., concurring in the judgment). The Miami-Dade Expressway Authority has also described the Tamiami Canal as an "important [—13—] water management system, transportation corridor, and recreational facility," but the Expressway Authority made no legal determination. And a "transportation corridor" is not the same as a highway supporting interstate commerce.

IV. CONCLUSION

We **AFFIRM** the dismissal of Tundidor's complaint.

United States Court of Appeals
for the Eleventh Circuit

No. 15-11891

GOWDY

vs.

MITCHELL

Appeal from the United States District Court for the Southern District of Florida

Decided: August 26, 2016

Citation: 835 F.3d 1310, 4 Adm. R. 465 (11th Cir. 2016).

Before **MARCUS, DUBINA,** and **MELLOY,** * Circuit Judges.

* Honorable Michael J. Melloy, United States Circuit Judge for the Eighth Circuit, sitting by designation.

[—2—] MELLOY, Circuit Judge:

This appeal arises from an order by the United States District Court for the Southern District of Florida, dated March 31, 2015. In that order, the district court affirmed eight rulings of the United States Bankruptcy Court for the Southern District of Florida. The bankruptcy court found, in part, that Appellant James Gowdy was liable for civil contempt. The bankruptcy court also imposed compensatory sanctions against Gowdy. Gowdy raises five issues on appeal. We affirm in most respects but reverse and remand for redetermination of the amount of the Trustee fee award.

I.

In June 1989, Appellee Mitchell, a commercial fisherman, sued two Florida corporations, Ocean Warrior, Inc. ("Ocean Warrior"), and Warrior Fleet, Inc., in the United States District Court for the Western District of Washington. He alleged the corporations failed to provide "basic maritime remedies of maintenance, cure and unearned wages" after he was injured while working aboard the corporations' commercial shrimping vessel, the F/V Janice. Mitchell also filed an *in rem* maritime claim against the F/V Janice, naming as its owner Ocean [—3—] Warrior. The United States District Court for the Western District of Washington had the F/V Janice arrested in admiralty. On August 28, 1990, the district court in Washington ordered the *in rem* sale of the F/V Janice and the sale took place on the same day.

On the same day as the sale, Ocean Warrior filed a Chapter 11 Petition in the United States Bankruptcy Court for the Southern District of Florida. The sale of the F/V Janice was voided. The bankruptcy court determined there was substantial equity in the boat, over and above the amount claimed in Mitchell's lawsuit. As a result, on May 9, 1991, the bankruptcy court ordered that Gowdy, the president of Ocean Warrior, be allowed to continue to operate the F/V Janice. The bankruptcy court ordered that Gowdy maintain insurance on the boat. The bankruptcy court also ordered the boat to remain in U.S. waters off the state of Washington pending the determination of Mitchell's maritime claim. In April of 1992, the district court in Washington awarded Mitchell a judgment for his maritime claim.

Based on the Washington district court's judgment, the bankruptcy court in Florida ordered Ocean Warrior to deposit $38,000.00 into the court's registry as security for Mitchell.[1] No money was deposited, insurance was not maintained on the F/V Janice, and the F/V Janice disappeared in August 1992. When the boat [—4—] disappeared, Gowdy also disappeared. The bankruptcy court in Florida and the district court in Washington each issued warrants for Gowdy's arrest. The Washington warrant was for criminal contempt in connection with the suspected theft of the F/V Janice.

On February 10, 1993, with Ocean Warrior's only valuable asset missing and a bankruptcy reorganization no longer possible, the bankruptcy court converted Ocean Warrior's Chapter 11 case to a Chapter 7 case and appointed a Trustee. The case was closed and reopened several times over the years. Then, on December 2, 1999, the bankruptcy

---

[1] It is undisputed that the F/V Janice was worth far in excess of $38,000.00. In fact, it was represented to the bankruptcy court that the boat was worth over $250,000.00, and an examiner later valued the boat at $225,000.00.

court closed the case with the condition that "[t]he court shall retain jurisdiction to reopen this case in the event the Vessel F/V Janice and/or Mr. James Gowdy are located. All existing Orders shall remain in full force and effect."

In June 2011, nearly twenty years after the F/V Janice and Gowdy disappeared, United States Marshals arrested Gowdy in Texas. At that time, he alleged that the F/V Janice had been stolen by a group of Colombians and that he had nothing to do with the theft. He also alleged that he came back into possession of the boat but subsequently lost it to creditors for liens. Gowdy was brought before the United States District Court for the Western District of Washington on the arrest warrant issued by that court. In September 2011, the Washington district [—5—] court released Gowdy on his own recognizance and deferred to the civil contempt proceedings in the United States Bankruptcy Court for the Southern District of Florida. On October 17, 2011, the bankruptcy court reopened the bankruptcy proceedings and entered an Order to Show Cause as to why Gowdy should not be held in civil contempt.

The bankruptcy court held a hearing on December 8, 2011, regarding its show cause order. Gowdy appeared *pro se* at the hearing. Gowdy initially indicated he thought he was being brought before the court on criminal contempt. However, the bankruptcy judge made it clear to Gowdy that the December 2011 hearing was for civil contempt only. According to the bankruptcy judge, Gowdy was not in danger of being incarcerated as a result of the hearing and the only issue was the location of the boat and damages owed to Mitchell if it could not be located. Gowdy refused to disclose the location of the F/V Janice or answer any questions about what had happened to the boat.

The court found Gowdy in civil contempt and ordered him to produce the F/V Janice or pay the amount due on Mitchell's judgment. On May 4, 2012, the bankruptcy court entered a written order finding Gowdy in civil contempt for violating "numerous" prior orders of the court, including provisions in

orders dated February 9, 1991, and August 7, 1992. The May 4, 2012 order allowed Gowdy to [—6—] purge the civil contempt by either returning the F/V Janice or depositing funds into the court's registry to compensate Mitchell for damages caused by Gowdy's contempt. The court gave Gowdy 90 days to purge his contempt before other sanctions would be considered, such as incarceration until the contempt was purged.

On June 19, 2012, Gowdy filed an affidavit alleging he had no assets, seeking to avoid paying filing fees to appeal the bankruptcy court's civil contempt order. However, Gowdy's representations about his finances excluded reference to his interest in a pending maritime personal injury lawsuit in Texas. Gowdy's Texas lawsuit later settled for $449,637.22. Gowdy also excluded reference to his interest in a Texas home. Gowdy opined that the home was valued at $75,000.00 whereas Mitchell asserts on appeal that the home's publicly assessed value is approximately $120,000.00. On September 7, 2012, the Trustee commenced an adversary proceeding against Gowdy, seeking recovery for the conversion of the F/V Janice, turnover of the F/V Janice, and injunctive relief relating to the settlement funds due to Gowdy. Following interpleader proceedings, on May 29, 2013, the Trustee received $224,818.63 from the Texas court registry.

On July 17, 2013, the bankruptcy court entered an order awarding interim attorneys' fees and costs to the Trustee. On December 11, 2013, the bankruptcy [—7—] court entered an order temporarily staying the disbursement of funds to Mitchell pending the adversary proceeding's conclusion or final conclusion of any appeal of the July 17, 2013 order. On March 7, 2014, the bankruptcy court ordered sanctions against Gowdy for failing to purge his civil contempt. In that order, the bankruptcy court also approved the disbursement of funds to Mitchell and authorized the entry of a final judgment against Gowdy and in favor of the Trustee. On April 8, 2014, the bankruptcy court entered an amended final judgment in favor of the Trustee in the amount of $239,143.14. Gowdy filed his notice of appeal on April 16, 2014 and appealed the bankruptcy court's judgment. The district court affirmed the bankruptcy court's judgment. This appeal followed.

II.

In a bankruptcy case, the Eleventh Circuit Court of Appeals "sits as a second court of review and thus examines independently the factual and legal determinations of the bankruptcy court and employs the same standards of review as the district court." *In re Fisher Island Invs., Inc.*, 778 F.3d 1172, 1189 (11th Cir. 2015) (quoting *In re Brown*, 742 F.3d 1309, 1315 (11th Cir. 2014)). "Where the district court [sitting as an appellate court] affirms the bankruptcy court's order," the Eleventh Circuit "review[s] the bankruptcy court's decision." *Id.* In doing so, the court "review[s] the bankruptcy court's factual findings for clear error and its [—8—] legal conclusions *de novo*," *id.*, and its imposition of sanctions for an abuse of discretion, *In re Walker*, 532 F.3d 1304, 1308 (11th Cir. 2008). A lower court's decision to impose sanctions will be affirmed unless the court "made a clear error of judgment, or has applied the wrong legal standard." *In re Walker*, 532 F.3d at 1308 (quoting *Amlong & Amlong, P.A. v. Denny's Inc.*, 500 F.3d 1230, 1238 (11th Cir. 2007)).

A.

Gowdy initially contends that the bankruptcy court abused its discretion by failing to conduct an evidentiary hearing on disputed issues of fact regarding his civil contempt. Appellees counter that the bankruptcy court conducted an evidentiary show-cause hearing on December 8, 2011. Having reviewed the record, it is clear that Gowdy received notice of the civil contempt allegations against him and that the bankruptcy court gave Gowdy the opportunity to testify, submit evidence, and rebut the allegations of civil contempt at his show-cause hearing. Gowdy failed to disclose any information as to why he could not purge the civil contempt. For these reasons, the bankruptcy court did not err in holding an evidentiary show-cause hearing, which satisfied due process requirements. *See F.T.C.*

v. Leshin, 719 F.3d 1227, 1235 (11th Cir. 2013) ("It is by now well-settled [—9—] law that due process is satisfied when a civil contempt defendant receives notice and an opportunity to be heard . . . .").

B.

Gowdy next argues that his due process rights were violated when the bankruptcy court threatened incarceration for contempt and he lacked counsel at the show-cause hearing. Appellees reply that the show-cause hearing met the due process requirements and that Gowdy was not entitled to counsel at his civil contempt hearing. The United States Supreme Court has made clear Gowdy was not entitled to counsel at his civil contempt hearing because he faced no jeopardy of incarceration. *See Turner v. Rogers*, 564 U.S. 431, 443 (2011) (interpreting prior Supreme Court cases as "pointing out that the Court previously had found a right to counsel '*only*' in cases involving incarceration, not that a right to counsel exists in *all* such cases . . . ."). As the district court noted in its May 31, 2015 order, at Gowdy's show-cause hearing the bankruptcy court stated: "[W]e're not going to incarcerate you . . . . This is a civil contempt motion here notwithstanding that you were arrested on the criminal contempt motion . . . ." Thus, the [—10—] bankruptcy court did not violate Gowdy's due process rights by conducting a show-cause hearing on his civil contempt without appointing Gowdy an attorney.[2]

---

[2] The bankruptcy court did not indicate an intention to incarcerate Gowdy at the show-cause hearing or in the order calling for the hearing. The bankruptcy court's May 4, 2012 order, however, indicated the court would "consider the imposition of sanctions," including incarceration until the contempt was purged, if Gowdy did not purge the contempt within 90 days. Even if that order suggests Gowdy might in the future face the possibility of incarceration, the bankruptcy court met the due process requirements at Gowdy's show-cause hearing and eventually concluded Gowdy was not indigent on March 7, 2014. *See Lassiter v. Dep't of Soc. Servs. of Durham Cnty, N.C.*, 452 U.S. 18, 26–27 (1981) ("[T]he Court's precedents speak with one voice about what 'fundamental fairness' has meant when the Court has considered the right to appointed counsel, and we thus draw from them

C.

Gowdy contends that the bankruptcy court had no authority to punish him for contempt and that the bankruptcy court's sanction amounted to a criminal sanction. Appellees reply that the bankruptcy court had authority to impose civil contempt sanctions.

"Civil contempt power is inherent in bankruptcy courts since all courts have authority to enforce compliance with their lawful orders." *Alderwoods Grp., Inc. v. Garcia*, 682 F.3d 958, 967 n.18 (11th Cir. 2012) (citation omitted). Distinct from the bankruptcy courts' inherent contempt powers, 11 U.S.C. § 105 creates the bankruptcy courts' statutory civil contempt power. *See* 11 U.S.C. § 105(a) ("The [—11—] court may issue any order, process, or judgment that is necessary or appropriate to carry out the provisions of this title."). "Civil penalties must either be compensatory or designed to coerce compliance." *In re Evergreen Sec., Ltd.*, 570 F.3d 1257, 1280 (11th Cir. 2009) (quoting *In re Dyer*, 322 F.3d 1178, 1192 (9th Cir. 2003)).

In this case, the bankruptcy court had subject matter jurisdiction to hold Gowdy, the president and agent of Ocean Warrior, liable for civil contempt. Gowdy did not comply with the bankruptcy court's orders in 1991 and 1992 because he failed to keep the F/V Janice in U.S. waters, failed to maintain insurance on it, and failed to deposit money into the registry of the court. At the show-cause hearing on December 8, 2011, the bankruptcy court determined Gowdy was in civil contempt and sought to coerce Gowdy to return the F/V Janice: "So the Court, based on what you have to say here, determines you are in civil contempt and directs that you have, let's say, 14 days to either deliver the boat or the amount due [Mitchell's] judgment." After Gowdy failed to purge his civil contempt, on

---

the presumption that an *indigent litigant* has a right to appointed counsel only when, if he loses, *he may be deprived of his physical liberty.*" (emphasis added)). Nowhere else in the record does the bankruptcy court mention incarceration. We need not consider whether Gowdy would have been entitled to counsel at a future hearing if the possibility of incarceration had actually arisen.

March 7, 2014, the bankruptcy court imposed sanctions to compensate the aggrieved parties—Mitchell and others—for the costs incurred because of Gowdy's contempt. [—12—]

Further, the sanctions were not punitive. *See In re McLean*, 794 F.3d 1313, 1323 (11th Cir. 2015) ("Punitive sanctions . . . take the form of a fixed fine and have no practical purpose other than punishment; it is immaterial to a court imposing such sanctions that a contemnor might be fully in compliance with the order in question at the time the sanctions are imposed."). Moreover, as the district court noted in affirming the bankruptcy court's orders, "The bankruptcy court never contemplated incarceration or punitive sanctions and it acted within its jurisdiction to find Gowdy in civil contempt." Thus, the bankruptcy court did not err by imposing coercive and compensatory civil contempt sanctions. *See In re Evergreen Sec., Ltd.*, 570 F.3d at 1280; *see also Leshin*, 719 F.3d at 1234 (discussing the distinctions between coercive civil contempt sanctions and compensatory civil contempt sanctions).

D.

Gowdy claims that the bankruptcy court lacked jurisdiction because the civil contempt proceeding was not a "core proceeding." Relying on *Stern v. Marshall*, 564 U.S. 462 (2011), Gowdy argues that the bankruptcy court should have proposed a judgment instead of entering a final order. Appellees disagree, arguing that the civil contempt proceedings relating to the F/V Janice and Gowdy's [—13—] violation of the bankruptcy court's orders are "core proceedings" over which the bankruptcy court has jurisdiction to enter a final order.

Bankruptcy courts may "enter final judgments in 'all core proceedings arising under title 11, or arising in a case under title 11.'" *Stern*, 564 U.S. at 474 (quoting 28 U.S.C. § 157(b)(1)). There are 16 different types of core proceedings set forth by section 157(b)(2), including, in relevant part, "matters concerning the administration of the estate" and "orders to turn over property of the estate." 28 U.S.C. § 157(b)(2)(A), (E). If a proceeding is "not a core proceeding but . . . is otherwise related to a case under title 11 . . . the bankruptcy judge shall submit proposed findings of fact and conclusions of law to the district court." *Id.* § 157(c)(1).

Here, Gowdy violated the bankruptcy court's 1991 and 1992 orders involving the F/V Janice. As a result, following Gowdy's show-cause hearing, the bankruptcy court found Gowdy in civil contempt and ordered him to turn over the F/V Janice or pay damages. The court's orders concerned "the administration of the estate" and "turn[ing] over property of the estate." Therefore, the matters were "core proceedings" under the text of 28 U.S.C. § 157(b)(2). *See* 28 U.S.C. § 157(b)(2)(A), (E). [—14—]

In addition, "[c]ivil contempt proceedings arising out of core matters are themselves core matters." *In re Skinner*, 917 F.2d 444, 448 (10th Cir. 1990); *see In re White–Robinson*, 777 F.3d 792, 795–96 (5th Cir. 2015) (per curiam) (noting post-*Stern* that a contempt order was a "core proceeding" because it was a "matter[ ] concerning the administration of the estate" pursuant to 28 U.S.C. § 157(b)(2) (alteration in original)). Thus, the bankruptcy court had subject matter jurisdiction over the allegations of civil contempt against Gowdy and the authority to enter a final order, not merely a proposed judgment, finding Gowdy in civil contempt. *See In re Skinner*, 917 F.2d at 448.

E.

i.

Lastly, Gowdy argues that the bankruptcy court erred in disbursing his money to pay the Trustee fees pursuant to the July 17, 2013 order. On appeal, Gowdy raises the same argument that he raised at the district court: he contends that, if sanctions were appropriate, fees should have been "paid out of the judgment, not fees awarded from [his] property first, and then a judgment entered on top of the fees." As the district court correctly noted, Gowdy fails to cite case law or statutes to support his argument. In making his

argument, Gowdy also fails to fully explain the details of his critique of the bankruptcy court's sanction and fee [—15—] orders. Appellees counter that Gowdy's appeal of the fee orders was untimely and that the bankruptcy court has wide discretion in fashioning an equitable remedy.

Notwithstanding the foregoing, we are compelled to reverse as to the quantity of the fee award. First, we conclude Gowdy's appeal is not untimely. And second, we conclude the fee award cannot include fees beyond those reasonably related to litigation and asset recovery efforts surrounding the contempt litigation. *See Abbott Labs. v. Unlimited Beverages, Inc.*, 218 F.3d 1238, 1242 (11th Cir. 2000) ("[A]ttorneys' fees in a civil contempt proceeding are limited to those reasonably and necessarily incurred in the attempt to enforce compliance."); *see also Jove Eng'g, Inc. v. I.R.S.*, 92 F.3d 1539, 1557 (11th Cir. 1996) (noting that one purpose of civil contempt sanctions is to "compensate the complainant for . . . expenses it incurred because of the contemptuous act."). Further, on remand, the district court must decide whether to permit the Trustee to pursue its adversary proceeding against Gowdy—a proceeding that never actually took place in light of the transfer of the substantial sums from Texas.

ii. [—16—]

Under Bankruptcy Rule 8002, Gowdy had 14 days from the "entry of the judgment, order, or decree being appealed" to file a notice of appeal. The timely filing of a notice of appeal "is jurisdictional." *In re Williams*, 216 F.3d 1295, 1298 (11th Cir. 2000). Gowdy timely moved to stay and reconsider the July 17 fee disbursal order, but did not file a notice of appeal until April 16, 2014, after the final sanctions judgment was entered and the court ordered the remainder of the fees disbursed to Mitchell. While the language of the rule suggests that Gowdy should have filed a notice of appeal within 14 days of the bankruptcy court's order denying his motion for reconsideration of the fee disbursal order, we conclude he was not required to do so in the circumstances of this case. In the July 17 order, the bankruptcy court characterized the disbursal being authorized as an "interim" award and declined to finally resolve the Trustee's disbursal motion until it held a hearing and entered a final judgment regarding the contempt sanctions. Rule 8002(a)(1) does not require a party to a bankruptcy proceeding to file a separate notice of appeal for each interim fee disbursal at least where, as here, the interim order reserves decision on a substantial intertwined portion of the disbursal motion. The Trustee's motion for the disbursal of the settlement funds was not substantially resolved until the court granted the portion of the order requesting disbursal of the fees to Mitchell and simultaneously entered final judgment in Mitchell's favor. Gowdy timely appealed from that order. [—17—]

iii.

Regarding the actual sanction award and the absence of any resolution of the conversion claim, we believe it is necessary to recount in additional detail what occurred after the Trustee received $224,818.63 from the Texas court registry on May 29, 2013. Instead of continuing to pursue the adversary proceeding, the Trustee filed a motion to summarily disburse Gowdy's settlement funds in the following manner: $135,167.95 to Mitchell; $80,465.78 to Trustee's Counsel; and $9,184.90 to Trustee's Local Counsel in Texas. On July 17, 2013—even though the bankruptcy court had not entered a sanctions award against Gowdy and the adversary proceeding had not been resolved—the court ordered allocation of the Trustee's and attorneys' fees and scheduled a hearing to consider disbursement to Mitchell. The bankruptcy court did not identify the fees as "reasonable and necessarily incurred in the attempt to enforce compliance." *Abbott Labs*, 218 F.3d at 1242. Instead, the court explained the fees were reasonable in light of the work performed during the entire 20-year bankruptcy proceeding.

Finally, on March 7, 2014, the bankruptcy court imposed the sanction award in favor of Mitchell, which was a judgment "in favor of Mitchell in the amount of $372,209.02." The court ordered the Trustee to transfer to Mitchell the [—18—] $133,433.75 remaining from Gowdy's settlement, and then entered a final judgment against Gowdy for the rest of the sanction award, $238,775.27.

Bankruptcy courts have broad discretion in awarding professional fees in bankruptcy proceedings. *Howard Johnson Co. v. Khimani*, 892 F.2d 1512, 1519 (11th Cir. 1990) ("District courts have broad discretion in fashioning civil contempt sanctions."). And, in awarding sanctions for civil contempt, a court "ha[s] numerous options, among them: a coercive daily fine, a compensatory fine, attorneys' fees and expenses." *Citronelle–Mobile Gathering, Inc. v. Watkins*, 943 F.2d 1297, 1304 (11th Cir. 1991). A fee award in relation to a civil contempt sanction, however, is not without limit, and we conclude the bankruptcy court abused its broad discretion because it possessed no legal basis to require Gowdy to pay the full Trustee's fee. *In re Red Carpet Corp. of Panama City Beach*, 902 F.2d 883, 890 (11th Cir. 1990) ("An abuse of discretion occurs if the judge fails to apply the proper legal standard or to follow proper procedures in making the determination, or bases an award upon findings of fact that are clearly erroneous.").

We reach this conclusion because Gowdy was never adjudged liable to the bankruptcy estate for converting the JANICE. Rather, he was found liable for contempt pursuant to Mitchell's motion. Therefore, the fee award should have [—19—] been limited to an amount necessary to "compensate the complainant"—Mitchell—"for losses and expenses . . . incurred because of the contemptuous act [or to] coerce the contemnor into complying with the court order." *Jove Eng'g*, 92 F.3d at 1557. The bankruptcy court could have required Gowdy to compensate the Trustee for the efforts in obtaining the personal injury settlement funds from Texas, which were costs reasonably incurred in enforcement of the court's sanction order. But before being required to bear the full Trustee's fees, Gowdy was entitled to a jury trial in an Article III tribunal on the Trustee's conversion claim. *See Stern*, 564 U.S. at 503.

III.

For the reasons above, we affirm the judgment of the district court in all respects other than the amount of the fee award. We remand for the bankruptcy court to award a fee based on the work the Trustee performed pursuant to Mitchell's motion for contempt. The lower court also shall determine whether the Trustee may pursue its adversary claim at this late date.

AFFIRMED in part, **REVERSED** and **REMANDED in part**.

United States Court of Appeals
for the Eleventh Circuit

No. 14-13754

UNITED STATES
VS.
CRUICKSHANK

Appeal from the United States District Court for the
Middle District of Florida

Decided: September 20, 2016

Citation: 837 F.3d 1182, 4 Adm. R. 472 (11th Cir. 2016).

Before **MARCUS** and **W. PRYOR**, Circuit Judges, and
DAVIS,* District Judge.

* Honorable Brian J. Davis, United States District
Judge for the Middle District of Florida, sitting by
designation.

[—1—] **MARCUS**, Circuit Judge: [—2—]

On February 11, 2014, the U.S. Coast
Guard recovered 171 kilograms of
cocaine from a vessel known as the
"Venus" in international waters in the
Caribbean Sea. Carlington Cruickshank, one
of two men aboard the vessel, was later
convicted and sentenced to 324 months'
imprisonment for one count of conspiracy to
possess with intent to distribute five
kilograms or more of cocaine while aboard a
vessel, in violation of 21 U.S.C.
§ 960(b)(1)(B)(ii) and 46 U.S.C. §§ 70503(a),
70506(a) and (b), and one count of aiding and
abetting possession with intent to distribute
five kilograms or more of cocaine while aboard
a vessel, in violation of 18 U.S.C. § 2, 21
U.S.C. § 960(b)(1)(B)(ii), and 46 U.S.C. §§
70503(a), 70506(a). On appeal, Cruickshank
argues that: (1) jurisdiction did not exist to
prosecute him under the Maritime Drug Law
Enforcement Act ("MDLEA") and, moreover,
the MDLEA is unconstitutional; (2) the
district court erred in denying his motion for
judgment of acquittal based on insufficient
evidence of mens rea; (3) the district court
erred by establishing jurisdiction under the
MDLEA by relying on a United States
Department of State certification, and by
removing from the jury the factual question
concerning jurisdiction; and (4) the district
court clearly erred in denying him a minor-

role reduction under U.S.S.G. § 3B1.2(b). After
careful review of the parties' briefs and the
record, and having had the benefit of oral
argument, we affirm in part, and vacate and
remand in part. [—3—]

I.

First, we reject Cruickshank's claims that
jurisdiction did not exist to prosecute him
under the MDLEA and that the MDLEA is
unconstitutional. We review a district court's
interpretation and application of a statute
concerning its subject-matter jurisdiction *de
novo*, but we review factual findings with
respect to jurisdiction for clear error. *United
States v. Campbell*, 743 F.3d 802, 805, 2 Adm.
R. 543, 544 (11th Cir.), *cert. denied*, 135 S. Ct.
704 (2014). We review the legal question of
whether a statute is constitutional and
constitutional objections *de novo*. *Id.*, 2 Adm.
R. at 544. Under our prior precedent rule, we
are bound to follow a prior binding precedent
unless and until it is overruled by us sitting
en banc or by the Supreme Court. *United
States v. Vega-Castillo*, 540 F.3d 1235, 1236
(11th Cir. 2008).

The MDLEA prohibits knowingly or
intentionally possessing a controlled
substance, with the intent to distribute,
onboard any vessel subject to the jurisdiction
of the United States. 46 U.S.C. § 70503(a)(1)
("While on board a covered vessel, an
individual may not knowingly or intentionally
. . . possess with intent to manufacture or
distribute, a controlled substance."). It was
enacted under Congress's authority provided
by the Felonies Clause, U.S. Const. Art. I, § 8,
cl. 10, to define and punish felonies committed
on the high seas. *Campbell*, 743 F.3d at 805, 2
Adm. R. at 544. Pursuant to the MDLEA, "a
vessel without nationality" is "subject to the
jurisdiction of the United States" and it
defines a stateless vessel as including "a
[—4—] vessel aboard which the master or
individual in charge makes a claim of registry
that is denied by the nation whose registry is
claimed." 46 U.S.C. § 70502(c)(1)(A), (d)(1)(A).

In *Campbell*, the United States Coast
Guard had intercepted the defendant while
aboard a vessel in the international waters off

the eastern coast of Jamaica. 743 F.3d at 804, 2 Adm. R. at 543. The vessel lacked all indicia of nationality: it displayed no flag, port, or registration number. *Id.*, 2 Adm. R. at 543. Although one of the individuals aboard the vessel claimed it was registered in Haiti, the government of Haiti told the Coast Guard that it could neither confirm nor deny the registry. *Id.*, 2 Adm. R. at 543. Campbell, the defendant, argued that Congress had exceeded its authority under the Felonies Clause of the Constitution when it enacted the MDLEA. We disagreed, recognizing that "[w]e have always upheld extraterritorial convictions under our drug trafficking laws as an exercise of power under the Felonies Clause." *Id.* at 809-10, 2 Adm. R. at 548 (quotation omitted). As we explained, a criminal act does not need a nexus to the United States in order to be criminalized under the MDLEA "because universal and protective principles support its extraterritorial reach." *Id.* at 810, 2 Adm. R. at 548. In other words, because the Felonies Clause empowers Congress to punish crimes committed on the high seas, and because "the trafficking of narcotics is condemned universally by law-abiding nations," we rejected the argument "that it is fundamentally unfair for Congress to provide for the punishment of persons apprehended with narcotics [—5—] on the high seas." *Id.*, 2 Adm. R. at 548 (quotations omitted). This is especially true, we explained, when vessels on the high seas "are engaged in conduct that has a potentially adverse effect and is generally recognized as a crime by nations that have reasonably developed legal systems." *Id.*, 2 Adm. R. at 548 (quotations omitted).

We also explained in *Campbell* that the "Due Process Clause of the Fifth Amendment does not prohibit the trial and conviction of an alien captured on the high seas while drug trafficking." *Id.* at 812, 2 Adm. R. at 550 (citing *United States v. Rendon*, 354 F.3d 1320, 1326 (11th Cir. 2003)). In our view, the MDLEA "provides clear notice that all nations prohibit and condemn drug trafficking aboard stateless vessels on the high seas." *Id.*, 2 Adm. R. at 550.

In this case, all of Cruickshank's arguments concerning the MDLEA are foreclosed by our prior precedent. In *Campbell*, we reaffirmed that Congress did not exceed its authority by enacting the MDLEA; we determined that no jurisdictional nexus was required under the MDLEA; and we concluded that convictions under the MDLEA do not violate the Due Process Clause of the Constitution. *See id.* at 809-10, 812, 2 Adm. R. at 548, 550. Because we are bound by our prior precedent concerning all of Cruickshank's challenges to the MDLEA, his arguments necessarily fail. [—6—]

II.

We are also unpersuaded by Cruickshank's claim that the district court erred in denying his motion for judgment of acquittal based on insufficient evidence of mens rea. We review *de novo* whether sufficient evidence supports a conviction, drawing all reasonable factual inferences from the evidence in favor of the verdict. *United States v. Beckles*, 565 F.3d 832, 840 (11th Cir. 2009). Evidence is sufficient if a reasonable trier of fact could have found that it established guilt beyond a reasonable doubt. *Id.* In rebutting the government's evidence, a defendant must do more than put forth a reasonable hypothesis of innocence, because the issue is whether a reasonable jury could have convicted, not whether a conviction was the only reasonable result. *Id.* at 840-41.

To establish a conspiracy, the government must prove beyond a reasonable doubt that two or more persons entered into an unlawful agreement to commit an offense, that the defendant knew of the agreement, and that he voluntarily became a part of the conspiracy. *United States v. Tinoco*, 304 F.3d 1088, 1122 (11th Cir. 2002); *United States v. Alvarez*, 837 F.2d 1024, 1027 (11th Cir. 1988). The defendant's presence on a vessel, though not determinative, is a material factor supporting his participation in a conspiracy relating to that vessel. *Tinoco*, 304 F.3d at 1122-23. "A defendant's presence becomes more significant when the value of the contraband is high, as it is highly improbable that drug smugglers [—7—] would allow an outsider on board a vessel filled with millions of dollars worth of contraband." *Id.* at 1123 (quotation omitted). When we review a conspiracy or a possession-with-intent-to-distribute conviction involving a vessel laden with narcotics, we consider, among other things: (1) the probable length of the voyage; (2) the size of the contraband shipment; (3) the necessarily close relationship between captain and crew; (4) whether the contraband was in plain view, could be smelled, or was in a place where a person on a vessel would ordinarily discover it; and, (5) other factors, including diversionary maneuvers designed to evade detection and apprehension, attempts to flee, inculpatory and false exculpatory statements made after apprehension, witnessed participation as a crewman, and the absence of supplies or equipment necessary to the vessel's intended use. *Id.*; *United States v. Cruz-Valdez*, 773 F.2d 1541, 1546-47 (11th Cir. 1985).

"In order to convict a defendant for possession with intent to distribute a controlled substance, the government must prove knowing possession and an intent to distribute." *United States v. Camacho*, 233 F.3d 1308, 1317 (11th Cir. 2000). The law recognizes that a defendant may constructively possess a controlled substance if he exercises some measure of control over the contraband, either exclusively or in association with others. *Tinoco*, 304 F.3d at 1123. The defendant's intent to distribute may be inferred from a variety of factors, including whether the government seized a large quantity of controlled substances. *Id.* In [—8—] order to prove that the defendant aided and abetted an offense, the government must establish that: (1) someone else committed the substantive offense; (2) the defendant committed an act that contributed to and furthered the offense; and (3) the defendant intended to aid in the commission of the offense. *Camacho*, 233 F.3d at 1317.

After thoroughly reviewing this record, we are satisfied that the evidence was sufficient to establish beyond a reasonable doubt Cruickshank's criminally culpable mens rea or state of mind to convict him on both charges— conspiracy to possess with intent to distribute five kilograms or more of cocaine while aboard a vessel, and aiding and abetting possession with intent to distribute five kilograms or

more of cocaine while aboard a vessel. Among other things, Cruickshank's co-defendant, Carlos Acosta, testified that Cruickshank was one of two individuals who had been hired to transport drugs on a vessel from Colombia to Jamaica. Acosta said that, when he met Cruickshank and told him drugs were on the boat, Cruickshank stated that he was comfortable with that. The other individual who was supposed to show up to assist with the operation did not, leaving only Acosta and Cruickshank to transport the drugs. Acosta admitted that Cruickshank arrived after the cocaine had been loaded onto the Venus, so Cruickshank had nothing to do with loading the cocaine onto the vessel, reconstructing the Venus to carry the drugs, fueling, or attending any of the meetings leading up to the trip. Acosta said, [—9—] however, that Cruickshank programmed the vessel's GPS devices with Acosta's help. In so doing, they configured the GPS devices to transport the ship and the contraband across the Caribbean Sea from Colombia to Jamaica, with waypoints near Jamaica. According to Acosta, once they reached the waypoint closest to Jamaica, someone was going to meet them and take the drugs.

As for their capture, Acosta said that he and Cruickshank had become concerned during the trip when they realized a Coast Guard helicopter was flying above the Venus. They eventually stopped the vessel when the Coast Guard fired warning shots. Before a Coast Guard officer from a nearby vessel boarded the Venus, they threw grocery items, garbage, and clothes overboard in an attempt to get rid of evidence that they were coming from Colombia, and one of the men took off articles of clothing and washed. Cruickshank suggested that they tell the Coast Guard that he and Acosta were searching for another vessel, but they did not decide who would admit to being in charge.

Ian Groom, a lieutenant with the U.S. Coast Guard, and Andre Trinidad, a machinery technician specializing in counter-drug enforcement with the Coast Guard, also testified. Lieutenant Groom explained that in the pre-daylight hours of February 11, 2014, he had been co-piloting a Coast Guard helicopter when he acquired visibility of a vessel operating without navigational lights. Groom noticed the vessel stopping and starting, and, after spotting the helicopter, the [—10—] vessel increased its rate of speed and the two people onboard began throwing overboard unidentified objects, which appeared to be clothing, a bucket, and a jug of water. Officer Trinidad, who was aboard a vessel that Lieutenant Groom had directed to the Venus, testified that he then boarded the Venus to question the occupants. Trinidad relayed that, in response to his questions, Cruickshank said that he was in charge and that the vessel was Jamaican. Trinidad asked for documentation to support that the boat was Jamaican, but there was no supporting documentation. Cruickshank also told Trinidad that they had left Jamaica to assist a friend who had run out of gas, and were planning to return to Jamaica. Cruickshank said that they had not found the friend, and he did not identify the friend or the name of his vessel. Trinidad contacted his supervisor, and Trinidad was eventually informed that Jamaica was not accepting the claim of nationality. At that point, Trinidad's supervisors made a request to assimilate the vessel without nationality, which meant U.S. law would be imposed and the vessel would be subject to all U.S. laws.

Trinidad testified that the captured vessel was the Venus, and that Cruickshank and Acosta were on board. Trinidad also said that a scan performed on the Venus tested positive for cocaine, and that he found hidden kilogram-size packages of cocaine after drilling a hole in a bench on the vessel. Ultimately, [—11—] authorities found a handheld GPS device, a handheld two-way radio, and approximately 171 kilograms of cocaine on the Venus.

As the evidence at trial showed, while Cruickshank was on the Venus, it was operated without lights, it attempted evasive maneuvers when the Coast Guard helicopter was overhead, and the occupants threw items overboard to conceal their starting point. Evidence also revealed that Cruickshank had said he was comfortable with the drugs being on the boat, he programmed the vessel's GPS

devices, he came up with a cover story for the authorities, and he ultimately told the Coast Guard that he was in charge and gave the false statement about why they were at sea. There was more than sufficient evidence to establish Cruickshank's guilt beyond a reasonable doubt on both charges.

III.

We are also unpersuaded by Cruickshank's claims that the district court erred by establishing jurisdiction under the MDLEA in two respects: (1) by relying on a United States Department of State certification, in violation of the Confrontation Clause of the Constitution; and (2) by removing from the jury the question of fact concerning jurisdiction, in violation of *Alleyne v. United States*, 570 U.S. ___, 133 S. Ct. 2151 (2013). Normally, we review whether hearsay statements are testimonial *de novo*. *United States v. Caraballo*, 595 F.3d 1214, 1226 (11th Cir. 2010). But if a defendant (like Cruickshank) did not raise an [—12—] objection based on his confrontation right at trial, we review a confrontation claim for plain error. *United States v. Charles*, 722 F.3d 1319, 1322 (11th Cir. 2013). To show plain error, the defendant must establish (1) an error, (2) that is plain or obvious, and (3) that affected his substantial rights. *United States v. Turner*, 474 F.3d 1265, 1276 (11th Cir. 2007). And, if a defendant satisfies these three conditions, we may exercise our discretion to recognize the error only if it seriously affects the fairness, integrity, or public reputation of judicial proceedings. *Id.* An error is plain when it contradicts precedent from the Supreme Court or our Court directly resolving the issue. *See United States v. Lejarde-Rada*, 319 F.3d 1288, 1291 (11th Cir. 2003). "Errors [] affect a substantial right of a party if they have a 'substantial influence' on the outcome of a case or leave 'grave doubt' as to whether they affected the outcome of a case." *Turner*, 474 F.3d at 1276 (quotation omitted). But "where the effect of an error on the result in the district court is uncertain or indeterminate," the defendant has not met his burden of demonstrating prejudice for purposes of plain error review. *United States v. Rodriguez*, 398 F.3d 1291, 1301 (11th Cir. 2005). And, finally, as we said earlier, we review constitutional issues *de novo*. *Campbell*, 743 F.3d at 805, 2 Adm. R. at 544.

The Sixth Amendment's Confrontation Clause prevents the admission of a witness's testimonial statement when the witness does not appear at trial, unless he is unavailable to testify and the defendant had a prior opportunity to cross-examine [—13—] him. *Id.* at 806, 2 Adm. R. at 545. However, a United States State Department certification of jurisdiction under the MDLEA does not implicate the Confrontation Clause because it does not affect the guilt or innocence of a defendant. *See id.* at 806–09, 2 Adm. R. at 545–48.

In *Alleyne*, the Supreme Court revisited two of its prior cases: (1) *Apprendi v. New Jersey*, 530 U.S. 466 (2000), which requires that, other than the fact of a prior conviction, any fact that increases the penalty for a crime beyond the prescribed statutory maximum be submitted to a jury and proved beyond a reasonable doubt; and (2) *Harris v. United States*, 536 U.S. 545, 567-68 (2002), which held that judicial factfinding that increased the applicable statutory mandatory-minimum sentence was permissible under the Sixth Amendment. *Alleyne*, 133 S. Ct. at 2157-58. In *Alleyne*, the Supreme Court expressly overturned *Harris* because it was inconsistent with its decision in *Apprendi*, and held that any facts that increase the applicable statutory mandatory-minimum sentence for a crime must be submitted to a jury and found beyond a reasonable doubt. *Id.* at 2155, 2163.

The MDLEA expressly provides that the United States's jurisdiction over a vessel is not an element of the offense, and that jurisdiction is a preliminary question of law to be resolved by the district court. 46 U.S.C. § 70504(a) ("Jurisdiction of the United States with respect to a vessel subject to this chapter is not an element of an offense. Jurisdictional issues arising under this chapter are [—14—] preliminary questions of law to be determined solely by the trial judge."). In *Tinoco*, we asked whether the MDLEA jurisdictional requirement raised "factual questions that traditionally would have been treated as elements of an offense under the common law, thereby triggering the constitutional safeguards provided by the Due Process Clause and the Sixth Amendment right to a jury trial." 304 F.3d at 1107-08. Analyzing the common law, we held that the MDLEA's jurisdictional requirement does not raise a factual issue that, under the common law, would have been considered an element of the offense. *Id.* at 1108. This is because the jurisdictional requirement is intended to act as a diplomatic courtesy, and does not bear on the individual defendant's guilt. *Id.* at 1108-09. Therefore, because the jurisdictional requirement under the MDLEA is not an element of the offense, neither the Due Process Clause nor the Sixth Amendment to the Constitution are implicated when the jurisdictional requirement under the MDLEA is not proven to the satisfaction of a jury. *Id.* at 1111-12.

As an initial matter, we review Cruickshank's Confrontation Clause argument for plain error because he failed to raise it at any time before the district court, although we review his *Alleyne* argument *de novo*, since he raised that one in the district court. But under any standard of review, plain or otherwise, there was no Confrontation Clause violation. A United States Department of State certification of jurisdiction under the MDLEA does not implicate the [—15—] Confrontation Clause because it does not affect the guilt or innocence of a defendant. *Campbell*, 743 F.3d at 809, 2 Adm. R. at 547. Nor did the district court err by rejecting Cruickshank's *Alleyne* argument, since we've squarely held the jurisdictional requirement is not an element of the offense, need not be determined by a jury, and does not violate the Due Process Clause or the Sixth Amendment. 46 U.S.C. § 70504(a); *Tinoco*, 304 F.3d at 1108, 1111-12. These claims are without merit.

IV.

As for Cruickshank's last claim, however—that the district court erred in denying him a minor-role reduction under U.S.S.G. § 3B1.2(b)—we are compelled to vacate and remand for resentencing. We review a district court's denial of a role reduction for clear error. *United States v. Bernal-Benitez*, 594 F.3d 1303, 1320 (11th Cir. 2010). Clear error review is deferential, and "we will not disturb a district court's findings unless we are left with a definite and firm conviction that a mistake has been committed." *United States v. Ghertler*, 605 F.3d 1256, 1267 (11th Cir. 2010) (quotations omitted). The district court's "choice between two permissible views of the evidence" as to the defendant's role in the offense will rarely constitute clear error "[s]o long as the basis of the trial court's decision is supported by the record and does not involve a misapplication of a rule of law." *United States v. De Varon*, 175 F.3d 930, 945 (11th Cir. 1999) (en banc) (emphasis and quotation omitted). The defendant bears the burden of establishing his minor **[—16—]** role in the offense by a preponderance of the evidence. *Bernal-Benitez*, 594 F.3d at 1320.

The Sentencing Guidelines provide for a two-level decrease to a base offense level if a defendant was a minor participant in the criminal activity. U.S.S.G § 3B1.2(b). A minor participant is one "who is less culpable than most other participants in the criminal activity, but whose role could not be described as minimal." *Id.*, cmt. n.5. Our leading case concerning the minor-role reduction—*De Varon*—has long instructed sentencing courts analyzing a claim for a minor-role reduction to consider "first, the defendant's role in the relevant conduct for which [he] has been held accountable at sentencing, and, second, [his] role as compared to that of other participants in [his] relevant conduct." 175 F.3d at 940. As the en banc Court explained in *De Varon*, "[t]hese principles advance both the directives of the Guidelines and our case precedent by recognizing the fact-intensive nature of this inquiry and by maximizing the discretion of the trial court in determining the defendant's role in the offense." *Id.* at 934.

In *De Varon*, the defendant was a drug courier—she had ingested and smuggled 70 heroin-filled pellets into the United States from Colombia. *Id.* We recognized that "when a drug courier's relevant conduct is limited to her own act of importation, a district court may legitimately conclude that the courier played an important or essential role in the importation of those drugs." *Id.* at 942-43. **[—17—]** However, we declined to "create a presumption that drug couriers are never minor or minimal participants, any more than that they are always minor or minimal"; rather, we held that "the district court must assess all of the facts probative of the defendant's role in her relevant conduct in evaluating the defendant's role in the offense." *Id.* at 943. We offered examples of relevant factors for the court to consider, including the "amount of drugs, fair market value of drugs, amount of money to be paid to the courier, equity interest in the drugs, role in planning the criminal scheme, and role in the distribution." *Id.* at 945. We stressed that this is "not an exhaustive list," nor is "any one factor . . . more important than another," especially since the determination is highly fact-intensive and "falls within the sound discretion of the trial court." *Id.* The en banc Court in *De Varon* ultimately concluded that it was well within the sentencing court's discretion to deny the minor-role adjustment to the defendant, after it determined that De Varon was central to the importation scheme, that she had carried a substantial amount of high-purity heroin on her person, that it was unclear from the record that she was less culpable than the other described participant in the scheme, and that De Varon had furnished $1,000 of her own money to finance the smuggling enterprise. *Id.* at 945-46.

The Sentencing Commission, through Amendment 635 to the Sentencing Guidelines, adopted our approach in *De Varon* that "§ 3B1.2 does not **[—18—]** automatically preclude a defendant from being considered for a mitigating role adjustment in a case in which the defendant is held accountable under § 1B1.3 solely for the amount of drugs the defendant personally handled." *See* U.S.S.G. App. C, Amend. 635, Reason for Amendment. As the Commission explained, "[i]n considering a § 3B1.2 adjustment, a court must measure the defendant's role against the relevant conduct for which the defendant is held accountable at sentencing, whether or not other defendants are charged." *Id.*

More recent amendments to the Sentencing Guidelines—that went into effect after the sentencing hearing in this case—further clarify the factors for a court to consider for a minor-role adjustment, and still continue to embrace the approach we took in *De Varon*. In November 2015, the Commission added the following language to Application Note 3(C) for § 3B1.2:

In determining whether [a defendant warrants a minimal or minor participant] or an intermediate adjustment, the court should consider the following non-exhaustive list of factors:

(i) the degree to which the defendant understood the scope and structure of the criminal activity;

(ii) the degree to which the defendant participated in planning or organizing the criminal activity;

(iii) the degree to which the defendant exercised decision-making authority or influenced the exercise of decision-making authority;

(iv) the nature and extent of the defendant's participation in the commission of the criminal activity, including the acts the [—19—] defendant performed and the responsibility and discretion the defendant had in performing those acts;

(v) the degree to which the defendant stood to benefit from the criminal activity.

For example, a defendant who does not have a proprietary interest in the criminal activity and who is simply being paid to perform certain tasks should be considered for an adjustment under this guideline.

The fact that a defendant performs an essential or indispensable role in the criminal activity is not determinative. Such a defendant may receive an adjustment under this guideline if he or she is substantially less culpable than the average participant in the criminal activity.

U.S.S.G. Supp. App. C, Amend. 794. Not surprisingly, this non-exhaustive list of factors includes many of the same factors we delineated in *De Varon*, including the defendant's role in planning and carrying out the scheme, as well as the amount the defendant stood to be paid. *De Varon*, 175 F.3d at 945.

Although this Court applies the version of the Guidelines in effect on the date of sentencing, when reviewing the district court's application of the Guidelines, we consider clarifying amendments retroactively on appeal regardless of the date of sentencing. *United States v. Jerchower*, 631 F.3d 1181, 1184 (11th Cir. 2011). As we've explained, an amendment to the commentary, and not the text, of the Guidelines "suggest[s] that it clarifies" the guideline "rather than substantively alters it." *Id.* at 1187. Thus, the government in this case argues correctly that Amendment 794 merely clarified the factors to consider for a minor-role adjustment, and did not substantively change § 31B.2. *Accord United States* [—20—] *v. Quintero-Leyva*, 823 F.3d 519, 523 (9th Cir. 2016) (holding Amendment 794 was intended as a clarifying amendment and it therefore applies retroactively on direct appeal). The Sentencing Commission, moreover, did not describe Amendment 794 as making a substantive change, but stated that it provides "additional guidance to sentencing courts." *See* U.S.S.G. Supp. App. C, Amend. 794, Reason for Amendment. In other words, Amendment 794 merely explains the meaning of the terms in the original guideline. *See Jerchower*, 631 F.3d at 1184.

Our task, therefore, is to review the district court's ruling in light of the Guidelines, our case law, and clarifying Amendment 794. For starters, we note that the evidence at trial painted a fairly full picture of the role that

Cruickshank took in the offense—among other things, he was involved in programming the vessel's route, in evading authorities, and in obstructing the Coast Guard's inquiry. Moreover, the record makes clear that the district court discussed many of the factors our Court and the Sentencing Commission have laid out as important to the minor-role determination. These factors included the quantity of drugs Cruickshank transported, Cruickshank's expectation of "premium pay," Cruickshank's role as one of only two people on board to take the vessel from Colombia to Jamaica, and the dangerousness of the offense of "transport[ing] a large cargo of contraband in a transoceanic voyage from one continent to another"—a "voyage [that] necessitate[d] the intervention of the United States military to [—21—] defeat it," and that intentionally or unintentionally endangered many lives. DE101 at 17-19.

However, one portion of the district court's decision gives us pause—its suggestion that the quantity of cocaine being transported on the Venus was so large that no participant in the scheme could ever have been eligible for a minor-role reduction. At one point the court said that the quantity of drugs was "so large that any participant in [the case] can't be said to be engaged in minor activity." DE101 at 14. Later, it reiterated that "171 kilograms of high-quality cocaine, almost pure cocaine in this circumstance, that will be, as the druggies say, stepped on two or three or four times is *not even available for a minor role* under the language of *Rodriguez De Varon*." DE101 at 18 (emphasis added). But *De Varon* stressed the fact-intensive nature of the inquiry, and the sentencing court's role in assessing the totality of the circumstances, where no one factor is "more important than another." 175 F.3d at 945; *id.* at 943 ("[T]he district court must assess *all of the facts* probative of the defendant's role in her relevant conduct in evaluating the defendant's role in the offense.") (emphasis added).[1]

Moreover, Amendment 794 [—22—] clarified that a defendant could be considered for a minor-role adjustment in many circumstances, none of which turn on drug quantity. *See, e.g.,* Amendment 794 (A defendant who does not have a proprietary interest in the criminal activity and who is simply being paid to perform certain tasks "*should be considered* for an adjustment under this guideline.") (emphasis added); *id.* (A defendant who performed an essential or indispensable role in the criminal activity "*may receive* an adjustment under this guideline if he or she is substantially less culpable than the average participant in the criminal activity.") (emphasis added).

Indeed, although nothing in *De Varon* or Amendment 794 precludes a district court from considering the drug quantity with which the defendant was involved as an indicator of his role, we think it was legal error for the district court to say that this is the *only* factor to be considered in a case like this one. While it is possible that the district court did not rely solely on drug quantity in making its minor-role determination, the consequences for Cruickshank's advisory sentencing range could be significant—a potential six-level reduction to his offense level, *see* U.S.S.G. §§ 2D1.1(a)(5), 3B1.2(b). Thus, we think the wisest course of action is to vacate the district court's decision and remand for resentencing. On remand, the district court should perform an inquiry based on the totality of circumstances, [—23—] taking into account the variety of factors laid out in *De Varon* and Amendment 794.

---

[1] While the Court indicated in *De Varon* that we would not "foreclose the possibility" in a drug courier case "that amount of drugs may be dispositive—in and of itself—in the extreme case," we allowed for that possibility because "the amount of drugs in a courier's possession—whether very large or very small—may be the best indication of the magnitude of the courier's participation in the criminal enterprise." 175 F.3d at 943. *De Varon* involved a defendant who had swallowed the contraband to transport it, so the amount in her possession was actually on her person and perhaps was more likely to be indicative of her relative role in the offense. But this is not that kind of case. Here, there is nothing in the record to suggest that the amount of drugs was [—22—] indicative of the magnitude of Cruickshank's participation in the crime—to the contrary, he did not load the drugs on the vessel, reconstruct the vessel, fuel the vessel, attend the planning meetings for the trip, or otherwise appear to have any role concerning the quantity of drugs aboard.

AFFIRMED IN PART, VACATED AND
REMANDED IN PART.

United States Court of Appeals
for the Eleventh Circuit

No. 14-13228

CHANG
vs.
CARNIVAL CORP.

Appeal from the United States District Court for the
Southern District of Florida

Decided: October 6, 2016

Citation: 839 F.3d 993, 4 Adm. R. 481 (11th Cir. 2016).

Before **HULL, MARCUS,** and **CARNES,** Circuit Judges.

[—1—] PER CURIAM: [—2—]

This action involves a single maritime negligence claim. Plaintiff Gracita Chang alleged that she slipped and fell on Defendant Carnival Corporation's cruise ship. More than a year after the incident, Plaintiff filed suit in federal court. Defendant moved for summary judgment based on the one-year limitation period for filing such suits set out in Plaintiff's cruise ticket. Plaintiff acknowledged that she missed this deadline, but argues that this limitation period should be extended based on the doctrine of equitable tolling. The district court rejected this argument and agreed with Defendant that Plaintiff had untimely filed suit. The court entered judgment for Defendant. Plaintiff now appeals that order. We affirm.

BACKGROUND

For purposes of this appeal, the undisputed facts of this action are as follows. On December 9, 2012, while aboard Defendant's cruise ship, Plaintiff slipped and fell. Plaintiff's cruise ticket contains several restrictions governing Plaintiff's right to sue Defendant. Most importantly, the ticket contains a time limitation within which to file suit and a forum-selection clause. The time-limitation provision disallows a suit filed more than one year after the date of the injury. The forum-selection clause requires Plaintiff to file suit in federal court—and specifically in the Southern District of Florida—so long as there is subject matter jurisdiction in federal court over Plaintiff's claim. Only if subject matter jurisdiction is lacking in [—3—] federal court may Plaintiff file suit in state court, and then suit can be filed only in a court located in Miami-Dade County, Florida.[1]

Plaintiff retained a California attorney to litigate her slip-and-fall claim against Defendant. Aware of the impending litigation, Defendant twice informed Plaintiff's attorney (both on September 4, 2013, and on October 22, 2013) that it would not waive its rights under the forum-selection clause.[2] Less than a month later, on November 20, 2013, Plaintiff substituted Florida counsel for her California counsel. Then, on December 4 or 6, 2013—just a few days before expiration of the one-year deadline—Plaintiff filed her slip-and-fall claim in a Florida state court, not federal court, as she was required to do.

On January 28, 2014, Defendant moved to dismiss the state-court action, asserting Plaintiff's violation of the forum-selection clause. While this motion to dismiss was pending in state court, Plaintiff switched gears, and on March 4, 2014, [—4—] before the state court resolved Defendant's motion, Plaintiff filed this parallel federal action. The federal action, however, was filed almost three

---

[1] The ticket's one-year limitation states, "Suit to recover on any [personal injury] claim shall not be maintainable unless filed within one year after the date of the injury . . . ." The ticket's forum-selection clause states that any personal injury action must "be litigated, if at all, before the United States District Court for the Southern District of Florida in Miami, or as to those lawsuits to which the Federal Courts of the United States lack subject matter jurisdiction, before a court located in Miami-Dade County, Florida, U.S.A. to the exclusion of the Courts of any other county, state or country."

[2] Both communications stated:

All rights in equity, law, and those contained within the guest cruise ticket contract are expressly reserved, including the forum selection / venue provision requiring all passenger lawsuits against [Defendant] to be filed in the United States District Court for the Southern District of Florida in Miami, Florida. [Defendant] will not waive its contractual defense if a lawsuit is filed in the wrong court. (Emphasis added).

months after the one-year limitations period had elapsed.

Defendant moved for summary judgment in federal court based on Plaintiff's failure to file suit within the time limitation set out on the cruise ticket. Plaintiff agreed that the one-year limitation binds her, but argued that, by filing the state court action within a year of her injury, the limitation period had been equitably tolled. The district court concluded that Plaintiff had failed to justify any equitable tolling and therefore had run afoul of the limitation period. The court entered summary judgment for Defendant. Plaintiff appeals that ruling.

DISCUSSION

Plaintiff agrees that the one-year limitation binds her and that more than a year elapsed between her injury and the filing of this action.[3] Nonetheless, Plaintiff argues that she should be deemed to have satisfied the one-year limitation because she filed suit in state court within a year and that filing equitably tolled the limitation. Defendant responds that Plaintiff's filing of the state-court action failed to equitably toll the limitation because Plaintiff's ticket contained a clause requiring the selection of a federal forum so long as there was federal jurisdiction; [—5—] there clearly was federal jurisdiction over the claim; and Defendant had made clear to Plaintiff that it would insist on her compliance with the forum-selection clause. We agree.[4]

---

[3] The one-year limitation arises from a contract, not a statute, but that makes no difference here. *Bailey v. Carnival Cruise Lines, Inc.*, 774 F.2d 1577, 1579 n.3 (11th Cir. 1985) ("There is 'no essential difference between contractu[]al and statutory limitations.'").

[4] The parties agree that "the question of whether equitable tolling applies is a legal one subject to *de novo* review." *Booth v. Carnival Corp.*, 522 F.3d 1148, 1149 (11th Cir. 2008). Our opinions on the standard of review however, are inconsistent. *See, e.g., Arce v. Garcia*, 434 F.3d 1254, 1260 (11th Cir. 2006) (reviewing the district court's application of equitable tolling for an abuse of discretion). However, our earliest opinions on the issue engaged in *de novo* review. *See, e.g., Bailey v. Carnival Cruise Lines, Inc.*, 774 F.2d 1577, 1578 (11th Cir. 1985). We must follow those opinions.

As to Plaintiff's effort to excuse her untimely filing by invoking equitable tolling, "[t]he Supreme Court has made clear that tolling is an extraordinary remedy which should be extended only sparingly." *Justice v. United States*, 6 F.3d 1474, 1479 (11th Cir. 1993). To be in a position to advance a tolling argument, due diligence is a necessary, though not sufficient, prerequisite that a plaintiff must satisfy. *Id.* Further, a late filing based on "garden-variety" negligence is not sufficient to warrant tolling. *Id.* at 1480. In addition, the interests of justice on which a tardy plaintiff relies do not support a plaintiff who has "not file[d] her action in a timely fashion despite knowing or being in a position reasonably to know that the limitations period is running." *Id.* at 1479. Finally, it is the plaintiff's burden to show that equitable tolling is warranted. *Id.* [—6—]

Notwithstanding the above, we have on, at least one occasion, found equitable tolling where a plaintiff subject to a forum-selection clause filed a federal suit late, having earlier filed, in the wrong forum, a timely state court action. In *Booth v. Carnival Corporation*, 522 F.3d 1148 (11th Cir. 2008), a cruise passenger who was subject to the same forum selection clause present here timely filed his negligence action in state court (sixteen days prior to expiration of the limitations period) before later filing an action in the federal court dictated by the forum-selection clause; the federal action was filed past the one-year deadline. *Id.* at 1149–50.

The district court denied the defendant's motion to dismiss. *Booth*, 522 F.3d at 1149. We affirmed that court's ruling, finding applicable equitable tolling on the particular facts before us. *Id.* at 1150–53. In doing so, we focused on a combination of four factors. First, the "state court . . . possessed subject matter jurisdiction concurrently with the federal courts." *Id.* at 1153. Second, "the state suit was dismissed solely on grounds of improper

---

Morrison v. Amway Corp., 323 F.3d 920, 929 (11th Cir. 2003) ("[W]hen circuit authority is in conflict, a panel should look to the line of authority containing the earliest case."). In any event, a more deferential abuse-of-discretion standard would produce the same result in this appeal.

venue." *Id.* Third, the defendant was aware prior to expiration of the limitation period that the plaintiff intended to file suit. *Id.* Fourth, the plaintiff "was entitled to believe that his state filing might be sufficient given the fact that defendants can, and often do, waive their defense of improper venue." *Id.*

[—7—]

From all of the above, *Booth* concluded that the plaintiff had prosecuted his claim with the diligence necessary to warrant consideration of an equitable tolling claim and therefore the limitations period was properly tolled from the date on which he filed his state-court action. *Id.*.at 1158. Although the parties seemingly agree that the first three factors identified above are present here, clearly the fourth factor is not. That is, prior to expiration of the limitations period, Defendant twice notified Plaintiff of its insistence that Plaintiff adhere to the forum-selection clause—that is, that Plaintiff file suit in the federal district court in the Southern District of Florida. Instead of complying with a provision of the contract that Defendant had explicitly and timely brought to Plaintiff's attention, Plaintiff instead chose to file her suit in the wrong forum. This was not the conduct of the plaintiff in *Booth*. And, unlike in *Booth*, Plaintiff here could have been under no misapprehension that Defendant would decline to hold her feet to the fire.

Specifically, before the district court, Defendant submitted an affidavit from its Senior Claims Representative, who averred (1) that "[o]n September 4, 2013, [he] drafted and mailed" the first communication to Plaintiff's California attorney and (2) that "[o]n October 22, 2013, [he] drafted, telefaxed and mailed" the second, similar communication to Plaintiff's California attorney. Defendant attached to the affidavit both communications, which clearly explain that Defendant would not [—8—] waive its forum-selection defense. There is no evidence that the letters were not mailed to the proper address.

In response to the above evidence, Plaintiff provided nothing other than unsupported assertions suggesting the possibility that her California attorney might have failed to receive the communications or might have failed to advise Plaintiff or her Florida counsel of Defendant's warning. But such assertions are not evidence. *Travaglio v. Am. Exp. Co.*, 735 F.3d 1266, 1270 (11th Cir. 2013) ("Statements by counsel in briefs are not evidence . . . .").[5] Moreover, "the burden is on the plaintiff to show that equitable tolling is warranted." *Booth*, 522 F.3d at 1150. With no evidence in opposition to that presented by Defendant, Plaintiff clearly failed to shoulder her burden. *See Pines v. Warnaco, Inc.*, 706 F.2d 1173, 1178 (11th Cir. 1983) (rejecting a plaintiff's similar arguments[6]); 10B Charles [—9—] Alan Wright & Arthur R. Miller, *Federal Practice and Procedure* § 2734 (3d ed. 2015) ("[W]hen a summary-judgment motion is based on the running of the applicable statute of limitations and defendant shows that the prescribed period has elapsed, plaintiff may be able to defeat summary judgment by introducing facts, by affidavits or other evidence, raising a genuine issue whether the statute should be suspended. . . . But the motion should not be denied on the mere chance that there might be facts that would toll the statute.").

---

[5] Even those unsupported assertions fail to squarely state that Plaintiff's California attorney did not timely relay Defendant's communications. Nor is it clear that it would make a difference if Plaintiff had offered such evidence. *See Irwin v. Dep't of Veterans Affairs*, 498 U.S. 89, 92 (1990) ("Under our system of representative litigation, 'each party . . . is considered to have notice of all facts, notice of which can be charged upon the attorney.'").

[6] *Pines* held that a one-year limitation barred the plaintiff's fraud claim because the plaintiff should have known of the underlying fraud more than a year before he sued. The *Pines* plaintiff had argued against summary judgment by asserting that the limitation should begin later. The *Pines* court rejected that contention.

> Although [the plaintiff] argues that there was a factual dispute whether he should have discovered the fraud more than a year before filing suit, mere allegations cannot defeat summary judgment. And [the plaintiff] can point to no evidence supporting his allegation that he was prevented from obtaining information [about the fraud].

706 F.2d at 1178 (citation omitted).

Here, Plaintiff was specifically warned by Defendant that the latter intended to enforce the forum-selection clause, but Plaintiff chose to ignore that warning by filing suit in an incorrect forum, which decision directly led to the need to file suit late in the correct forum. If, on these facts, a plaintiff could circumvent the forum-selection clause, the forum-selection clause would lose much of its force, leading to the unnecessary expenditure of resources by courts and litigants. *See Carnival Cruise Lines, Inc. v. Shute*, 499 U.S. 585, 593–94 (1991) ("[A] clause establishing *ex ante* the forum for dispute resolution has the salutary effect of dispelling any confusion about where suits arising from the contract must be brought and defended, sparing litigants the time and expense of pretrial motions to determine the correct forum and conserving judicial resources that otherwise would be devoted to deciding those motions.") **[—10—]**

CONCLUSION

After having been warned by Defendant that it intended to enforce the forum-selection clause, Plaintiff nonetheless sued Defendant in the wrong forum. Plaintiff finally sued Defendant in the correct forum, but did so after expiration of the limitations period. We find that equitable tolling does not apply under these circumstances. Accordingly, we **AFFIRM**.

United States Court of Appeals
for the Eleventh Circuit

No. 15-15803

GIRARD

vs.

M/V "BLACKSHEEP"

Appeal from the United States District Court for the
Southern District of Florida

Decided: November 3, 2016

Citation: 840 F.3d 1351, 4 Adm. R. 485 (11th Cir. 2016).

Before **HULL** and **MARTIN**, Circuit Judges, and
WRIGHT,* District Judge.

* Honorable Susan Webber Wright, United States District Judge for the Eastern District of Arkansas, sitting by designation.

[—2—] MARTIN, Circuit Judge:

Arnaud Girard is a marine salvor, who works to rescue ships in peril. In December 2013, he undertook a rescue mission for a 125-foot yacht known as the M/Y Blacksheep. Afterward, he filed this action *in rem* against the Blacksheep, seeking a salvage award for services he provided to the yacht. After a two-day bench trial, the District Court found that Mr. Girard failed to show that his services were necessary to the rescue of the Blacksheep, and entered judgment against him. Because a claim for a salvage award does not require such a showing, we reverse and remand for proceedings consistent with this opinion.

I.

On December 28, 2013, the Blacksheep was under the command of Captain Alan Wooldridge. The vessel was located a few hundred feet offshore near the Galleon Marina in Key West, Florida. While testing the port engines' controls, Captain Wooldridge heard a "clunk." Captain Wooldridge instructed the vessel's engineer to investigate. The engineer discovered that the port propeller shaft had dislocated from the gear box coupling and the yacht was taking on water. [—3—]

Captain Wooldridge then made a radio distress call to the U.S. Coast Guard. He said: "I've got an emergency here. I'm just in the front of the Galleon Marina. My prop shaft's come out. I'm anchored. Could someone give me some assistance with some pumps please." In response to Captain Wooldridge's call, the Coast Guard announced over the radio:

Coast Guard received a report of a vessel BLACKSHEEP taking on water near Galleon Marina. All vessels are requested to keep a sharp lookout and assist if possible. The United States Coast Guard sector Key West Florida out. Break.

Again, Mr. Girard is a professional maritime salvor and heard the call come over the radio. He responded within four minutes. When Mr. Girard arrived at the scene, Captain Wooldridge made clear that he wanted Mr. Girard's help and asked if Mr. Girard had a pump. At this point, there was about two feet of water in the bilge (the lowest internal part of a ship). Mr. Girard first deployed his highcapacity pump to dewater the bilge. Then, Mr. Girard, along with his co-salvor, Eric Denhart, dove under the Blacksheep. They repositioned the propeller shaft, bringing it closer to its proper location. Mr. Girard also installed a temporary patch to limit the amount of water coming into the boat. The Coast Guard assisted by placing a patch on the inside of the Blacksheep. Eventually, the Blacksheep was towed to the dock by Towboat U.S. Captain Wooldridge recorded the incident in his logbook, explaining that he had "coordinated safety [—4—] procedures to prevent any sinking of [the] vessel."

Mr. Girard brought a claim seeking a salvage award for the marine salvage operation. This type of action is an *in rem* action, meaning it is brought against the ship and any recovery would necessarily be limited by the value of the ship. The District Court held a two-day bench trial in December 2014 and ruled in favor of the Blacksheep. This appeal timely followed.

II.

A salvage award is "the compensation allowed to persons by whose voluntary assistance a ship at sea or her cargo or both have been saved in whole or in part from impending sea peril." *The Sabine*, 101 U.S. 384, 384, 25 L. Ed. 982, 982 (1879). In *Klein v. Unidentified Wrecked & Abandoned Sailing Vessel*, 758 F.2d 1511 (11th Cir. 1985), this court stated that, in order to obtain a salvage award, the salvor must prove three elements:

(1) A maritime peril from which the ship or other property could not have been rescued without the salvor's assistance.
(2) A voluntary act by the salvor—that is, he must be under no official or legal duty to render the assistance.
(3) Success in saving, or in helping to save at least part of the property at risk.

Id. at 1515. The first prong of *Klein*'s three-prong test requires two distinct showings: first, that the vessel was in "maritime peril" (or "marine peril") and, second, that the vessel "could not have been rescued without the salvor's assistance." *Id.* The District Court applied *Klein*. The court found that the [—5—] Blacksheep was in "marine peril." But, as to the second showing, the court found that Mr. Girard failed to show "what would have happened to the Vessel had [he] not arrived on-scene." The court then found that "Plaintiff's efforts were not necessary to rescue the Vessel" and that "[t]he Vessel would not have submerged or sustained additional damage without the assistance of Plaintiff." Because Mr. Girard failed to meet his burden under *Klein* by proving that the ship "could not have been rescued without the salvor's assistance," the District Court found Mr. Girard was not entitled to a salvage award.

Mr. Girard argues that this second showing required under the first prong of *Klein*—that the ship "could not have been rescued without the salvor's assistance"—is not a proper element of a salvage award claim. Rather, Mr. Girard argues, a plaintiff satisfies the first element of a marine salvage claim by establishing only "marine peril." Under binding precedent, his argument prevails.

The elements of a salvage award claim were articulated by the Supreme Court over a century ago. *See The Sabine*, 101 U.S. at 384, 25 L. Ed. at 982. In *The Sabine*, the Supreme Court held that "[t]hree elements are necessary to a valid salvage claim: 1. A marine peril. 2. Service voluntarily rendered when not required as an existing duty or from a special contract. 3. Success in whole or in part, or that the service rendered contributed to such success." *Id.* See also *Legnos v. M/V Olga Jacob*, 498 F.2d 666, 669–71 (5th Cir. 1974) (citing and applying the [—6—] *The Sabine* standard for a salvage award claim).[1] Neither *The Sabine* nor *Legnos* requires a plaintiff to show that the vessel could not have been rescued without the salvor's assistance to satisfy the first prong. Rather, all a plaintiff must show to establish the first element is that the ship was under a "marine peril." As the former Fifth Circuit explained in *Legnos*, it is a "mistaken notion that for salvors to establish peril they must prove that their actions were necessary to eliminate or alleviate such condition. The law of salvage makes no such demand." *Id.* at 671. *Klein*'s requirement that the ship "could not have been rescued without the salvor's assistance" is in clear conflict with this precedent.

Klein's "necessity" requirement in the first prong also undercuts the policy interests that the salvage award is intended to further. The law of salvage is rooted in a public policy to encourage mariners to come to the aid of a ship in distress. *See The Sabine*, 101 U.S. at 384, 25 L. Ed. at 982; *Mason v. Ship Blaireau*, 6 U.S. (2 Cranch) 240, 266 (1804); *Int'l Aircraft Recovery, L.L.C. v. Unidentified, Wrecked & Abandoned Aircraft*, 218 F.3d 1255, 1261 (11th Cir. 2000). Specifically, the law of salvage aims to induce "*all* to render aid in the face of marine peril," *Legnos*, 498 F.2d at 671 (emphasis added), and to do so "*before* it is a do-or-die wager with high risks." *Miss. Valley Barge Line Co. v. Indian Towing*

---

[1] Under *Bonner v. City of Prichard*, 661 F.2d 1206 (11th Cir. 1981) (en banc), we are bound by all decisions of the former Fifth Circuit handed down before October 1, 1981. *Id.* at 1209.

[—7—] *Co.*, 232 F.2d 750, 755 (5th Cir. 1956) (emphasis added). A rule that limits compensation to those who can prove that the ship "could not have been rescued without the salvor's assistance" is at odds with these principles. *Legnos*, 498 F.2d at 671; *see also Mason*, 6 U.S. (2 Cranch) at 266 (describing the law of salvage as a "liberal and enlarged" compensatory system).

Because the added requirement in the first prong of the *Klein* test is inconsistent with both Supreme Court and binding circuit precedent, it cannot govern here.[2] To satisfy the first element of a salvage award claim, the salvor must show "marine peril," but need not make the additional showing that the ship "could not have been rescued without the salvor's assistance." Because the District Court found that the Blacksheep was in "marine peril"—a finding we do not disturb— Mr. Girard has established the first element of his salvage award claim. [—8—]

III.

Because the District Court found that Mr. Girard failed to satisfy the first prong of the *Klein* test, the District Court ruled against him without reaching the second or third prongs of the test. The second prong—that the salvor's services were rendered voluntarily—is not disputed. The third prong requires a showing that the salvor succeeded "in saving, or in helping to save at least part of the

property at risk." *Klein*, 758 F.2d at 1515. The District Court's findings and some facts from the record could support the conclusion that Mr. Girard's actions contributed to saving the Blacksheep. Mr. Girard deployed his high-capacity dewatering pump; dove below the ship where he successfully pushed the propeller shaft twelve inches closer to its intended position; and applied packing material to prevent further flooding. But we will leave it to the sound judgment of the District Court, in its role as the factfinder, to decide whether Mr. Girard contributed to saving the Blacksheep and, if he did, the value of any salvage award.

REVERSED AND REMANDED.

---

[2] "Under the well-established prior panel precedent rule of this Circuit, the holding of the first panel to address an issue is the law of this Circuit, thereby binding all subsequent panels unless and until the first panel's holding is overruled by the Court sitting en banc or by the Supreme Court." *Smith v. GTE Corp.*, 236 F.3d 1292, 1300 n.8 (11th Cir. 2001).

While the first prong of the *Klein* test conflicts with our prior panel precedent, the same is not true of the second and third prongs of *Klein*'s test. They closely track the second and third elements of a salvage award claim as set forth by the Supreme Court in *The Sabine* and by our prior panel in *Legnos*. Compare *Klein*, 758 F.2d at 1515, *with The Sabine*, 101 U.S. at 384, 25 L. Ed. at 982, *and Legnos*, 498 F.2d at 669–71. The second and third prongs of the *Klein* test thus remain good law.

This page intentionally left blank

United States Court of Appeals for the District of Columbia Circuit

United States Court of Appeals
for the District of Columbia Circuit

No. 14-7162

DISTRICT NO. 1, PAC. COAST DIST., MARINE
ENG'RS BENEFICIAL ASS'N
VS.
LIBERTY MARITIME CORP.

Appeal from the United States District Court for the
District of Columbia

Decided: February 26, 2016

Citation: 815 F.3d 834, 4 Adm. R. 490 (D.C. Cir. 2016).

Before **HENDERSON** and **TATEL**, Circuit Judges, and
EDWARDS, Senior Circuit Judge.

[—2—] **HENDERSON**, Circuit Judge:

Liberty Maritime Corporation (Liberty) appeals a district court order compelling it to arbitrate its ongoing labor dispute with District No. 1, Pacific Coast District, Marine Engineers' Beneficial Association, AFL-CIO (MEBA or the Union). For years, Liberty and MEBA were parties to successive collective bargaining agreements (CBAs) under which Liberty exclusively employed MEBA members as supervisory personnel on several of its bulk-carrier ships. The parties' relationship eventually soured, leading Liberty to replace its MEBA member-employees with those who belonged to a rival union. MEBA asserts that Liberty violated the parties' CBA in doing so. In response, Liberty claims that the parties' CBA had already expired before it switched unions. The parties' dispute thus boiled down to a principal inquiry: *When* did their CBA expire?

The district court determined that under the CBA, this question had to be submitted to arbitration; it therefore granted MEBA's request for an order compelling Liberty to arbitrate. *See Dist. No. 1, Pac. Coast Dist., Marine Eng'rs' Beneficial Ass'n, AFL-CIO v. Liberty Mar. Corp.*, 70 F. Supp. 3d 327, 350 (D.D.C. 2014). On appeal, Liberty claims that the court erred in doing so. As a threshold matter, it claims that the court lacked subject matter jurisdiction over MEBA's suit. On the merits, it argues that the contract-duration

question is not arbitrable; it maintains that the court, not an arbitrator, must decide when the CBA expired. We believe Liberty is wrong on both counts and, accordingly, affirm the district court. [—3—]

I.

Liberty is a maritime shipping company with a fleet of vessels engaged in global trade. For over two decades, Liberty had a series of CBAs with MEBA, a union representing, *inter alia*, officers and engineers working in the United States maritime industry, both at ports and on ocean-going vessels. The most recent was slated to expire in June 2010. Negotiations over a successor CBA stalled and, on August 25, 2010, Liberty and MEBA signed a Memorandum of Understanding (MOU) extending the CBA to September 30, 2011.[1] Specifically, the MOU provided that the then-current CBA, along with the provisions of the MOU itself, constituted a "New Agreement."

Three provisions of the New Agreement are relevant. First, like its predecessors, the New Agreement provided that Liberty could employ *only* MEBA-represented engineers as supervisory personnel[2] aboard certain vessels. Second, the New Agreement included a grievance-and-arbitration provision establishing a detailed procedure to address disputes arising between Liberty and MEBA. Specifically, it required [—4—] that "*[a]ll disputes* relating to the interpretation or performance of this Agreement shall be

---

[1] Although the CBA was to expire on June 15, 2010, it remained in effect per its terms until the MOU was signed, at which point the MOU applied retroactively to July 1, 2010. Thus, at no time from June 15 to August 25, 2010 did the CBA between Liberty and MEBA lapse.

[2] Under the most recent CBA, carried over into the New Agreement, the Liberty personnel to whom the agreement was applicable were deemed supervisors. As the district court noted, this meant that the protections of the National Labor Relations Act, 29 U.S.C. §§ 151 *et seq.*, did not generally apply to them; they could, however, secure and enforce terms and conditions of employment through a CBA, which is what they did here. *See Liberty Mar.*, 70 F. Supp. 3d at 334 n.2.

determined" by an arbitration board consisting of two MEBA representatives and two Liberty representatives. District No. 1, Pacific Coast District, M.E.B.A., Tanker Agreement § 2, at 10 (1986–1990) (Tanker Agreement) (emphasis added).[3] In the event the board could not resolve the grievance by mutual agreement or majority vote, an agreed-upon arbitrator was authorized to render a final, binding decision. Third, and most relevant, the New Agreement included a "Duration of Agreement" provision as follows:

> [The New Agreement will] continue in full force and effect *until midnight, September 30, 2011* and shall continue from year to year thereafter unless either the Company or the Union shall give written notice to the other of its desire to amend the agreement, which shall be given at least sixty (60) days, but no sooner than ninety (90) days, prior to the expiration date. In the event either the Company or the Union serves notice to amend the Agreement, the terms of the Agreement in effect at that time of the notice to amend shall continue in effect until mutual agreement on the proposed amendments *or an impasse has been reached.*

Mem. of Understanding (MOU) § 1 (emphases added). [—5—]

In March 2011, the parties began negotiating a successor to the New Agreement. Liberty's primary issue was the Union's pension plan. MEBA operated under a defined-benefit plan but Liberty insisted that the Union shift to a defined-contribution plan—a change MEBA opposed. Several work-rule changes were also on the table. On July 5, 2011, Liberty notified MEBA that it intended

to terminate the CBA on September 30, 2011,[4] and on July 8, MEBA responded by giving Liberty notice to amend, consistent with the Duration of Agreement provision. With MEBA's notice to amend, the New Agreement's expiration at midnight on September 30, 2011 then became contingent on the parties reaching "impasse" before that date.[5] *See* MOU § 1. [—6—]

Whether Liberty and MEBA in fact reached impasse before September 30, 2011 is the underlying dispute in this case; Liberty claims they did and MEBA claims they did not. The dispute arises from a flurry of last-minute negotiations in the four days leading up to September 30. On September 27, MEBA told Liberty it was not able to accept the defined-contribution pension plan Liberty demanded. Liberty expressed its regret that the parties were unable to reach a deal and began taking steps to bring on another union, the American Maritime Officers (AMO), to fill the MEBA positions beginning at 12:01a.m. on October 1. On September 28, however, MEBA reversed course; its president first contacted Liberty's CEO by phone and then confirmed in writing

---

[3] Both the exclusivity and grievance-and-arbitration provisions were incorporated into the New Agreement by reference to the original CBA. Both parties submitted the 1986–1990 "Tanker Agreement" to the district court to establish the CBA's governing provisions, and we assume the provisions included therein were those applicable in 2010.

[4] Counsel for Liberty acknowledged at oral argument that, although the New Agreement did not contain a "notice of termination" provision, Liberty considered its notice of termination to fall within the "notice to amend" language in the MOU. *See* Oral Arg. Recording at 18:55–19:13.

[5] Although Liberty's answer denied MEBA's allegation that "[b]ased upon the Union's timely notice to amend, the terms of the Agreement in effect at the time of the Notice continue to remain in effect pursuant to the terms of the parties' MOU," Answer ¶ 15, neither party seriously disputes that the contract's expiration at midnight on September 30 was contingent upon impasse. Rather, counsel for Liberty acknowledged that "[t]he durational language does contain reference to impasse; that's why . . . we believe the parties were at a bargaining impasse and no longer able to agree, thus the expiration on September 30." Oral Arg. Recording at 13:52–14:07. Moreover, Liberty maintains that the contract remained in effect until midnight on September 30 at the *earliest*; that is, even if the parties reached impasse before September 30, the contract did not expire until then. *See* Oral Arg. Recording at 14:09–14:22 ("We could not assert the contract expired September 27 because the durational clause . . . carried out [until] the end of the month.").

that MEBA *would* accept the defined-contribution plan Liberty had proposed and invited Liberty back to the negotiating table to work out the remaining issues. On September 29, citing a lack of confidence in MEBA, Liberty rejected the invitation and maintained that the New Agreement was set to expire at midnight the following day, September 30, in accordance with its terms.

Early on September 30, MEBA submitted a formal grievance to Liberty, using the grievance-and-arbitration procedure set out in the New Agreement. The grievance alleged that Liberty had violated the New Agreement in three ways: (1) by "failing and refusing to recognize MEBA as the sole representative of its licensed engineers and deck officers"; (2) by ordering "duly authorized representatives of the MEBA illegally removed from the Company vessels"; and (3) by authorizing "the assignment of the customary work and supervisory jurisdiction of the officers to be performed by other non-vessel and non-union personnel." Ltr. from Bill Van Loo, MEBA Sec'y-Treasurer, to Philip Shapiro, Liberty President & CEO 1–2 (Sept. 30, 2011). In its grievance, MEBA demanded that Liberty cease and desist from these [—7—] actions. Liberty did not immediately respond; rather, that afternoon, its CEO notified its supervisory personnel that MEBA and Liberty "were unable to agree on terms for a new . . . labor agreement." Ltr. from Philip Shapiro, Liberty President & CEO, to Liberty Officers 1–2 (Sept. 30, 2011). At 12:01a.m. on October 1, 2011, MEBA members left Liberty's vessels and AMO members came on board.

MEBA subsequently filed additional grievances related to the New Agreement, which grievances Liberty refused to arbitrate; MEBA then filed this action to compel Liberty to do so. The district court granted MEBA's motion for summary judgment, holding, first, that it had jurisdiction to hear the suit, and second, that the question of impasse was arbitrable under the New Agreement's broad arbitration provision. *See Liberty Mar.*, 70 F. Supp. 3d at 350 ("This Court concludes that it properly may exercise subject matter jurisdiction over MEBA's claims because they arise under section 301 of the LMRA.

Moreover, whether the parties' CBA was still in place at the time of all of the alleged violations is a question that arises under the durational provision of the contract, and is therefore a question for the arbitrator to decide."). Liberty timely appealed.

II.

"We review a grant of summary judgment *de novo.*" *Hairston v. Vance-Cooks*, 773 F.3d 266, 271 (D.C. Cir. 2014). "Summary judgment will be granted when 'there is no genuine dispute as to any material fact and the movant is entitled to judgment as a matter of law.'" *Id.* (quoting FED. R. CIV. P. 56(a)). On appeal, Liberty contends that MEBA was *not* entitled to judgment as a matter of law on the issue of arbitrability. Before reaching that issue, however, we must [—8—] address Liberty's challenge to the district court's jurisdiction to compel arbitration in the first place.

A. Subject Matter Jurisdiction

The National Labor Relations Act of 1935 (NLRA), 29 U.S.C. §§ 151–169, establishes a federal regime for managing labor relations and generally authorizes the National Labor Relations Board (NLRB) to resolve disputes between labor organizations and employers. *See generally Vaca v. Sipes*, 386 U.S. 171, 178–79 (1967). The United States Supreme Court has held that the NLRB's jurisdiction is in general exclusive; that is, if a claim falls within the purview of the NLRB, state and federal courts are preempted from hearing it. *See San Diego Bldg. Trades Council v. Garmon*, 359 U.S. 236, 245 (1959). As the Court put it, "[w]hen an activity is arguably subject to § 7 or § 8 of the [NLRA], the States as well as the federal courts must defer to the exclusive competence of the [NLRB]." *Id.* This rule is referred to as "*Garmon* preemption." *Wash. Serv. Contractors Coal. v. District of Columbia*, 54 F.3d 811, 815 (D.C. Cir. 1995).

The Labor Management Relations Act of 1947 (LMRA), 29 U.S.C. §§ 141 *et seq.*, "carve[s] out" an exception to the NLRB's "exclusive jurisdiction." *Vaca*, 386 U.S. at 179. Specifically, section 301(a) of the LMRA grants a federal district court jurisdiction over "[s]uits for *violations of contracts* between an employer and a labor organization." 29 U.S.C. § 185(a) (emphasis added). Thus, if a labor dispute is contractual, *Garmon* preemption does not apply; instead, the aggrieved party can sue on the contract in federal court.

Some claims, however, can be *both* contractual and representational; that is, a claim that alleges that conduct violates a collective bargaining agreement and also constitutes an unfair labor practice or otherwise violates the NLRA. [—9—] Instead of forcing courts to shoehorn a hybrid claim into one category or the other, the Supreme Court has held that they retain jurisdiction to hear a contractual claim even if the claim is also representational. *William E. Arnold Co. v. Carpenters Dist. Council*, 417 U.S. 12, 16 (1974) ("When [conduct allegedly subject to the NLRA] also constitutes a breach of a collective-bargaining agreement, the [NLRB's] authority 'is not exclusive and does not destroy the jurisdiction of the courts in suits under § 301 [of the LMRA].' " (quoting *Smith v. Evening News Ass'n*, 371 U.S. 195, 197 (1962))). In that event, the "labor case [falls] within the concurrent jurisdiction of the NLRB and the federal courts." *Mack Trucks, Inc. v. Int'l Union, UAW*, 856 F.2d 579, 585 (3d Cir. 1988); *accord Mullins v. Kaiser Steel Corp.*, 642 F.2d 1302, 1316 (D.C. Cir. 1980) ("[F]ederal courts have independent jurisdiction to decide cases alleging the breach of collective bargaining agreements, even though that very breach may also be an unfair labor practice."), *rev'd on other grounds*, 455 U.S. 72 (1982).

In many circuits, a party's mere assertion that a claim is contractual is not an automatic ticket to federal court; rather, the court must "examin[e] the major issues to be decided" and determine "whether they can be characterized as primarily representational or primarily contractual." *Local Union 204, Int'l Bhd. of Elec. Workers v. Iowa Elec. Light & Power Co.*, 668 F.2d 413, 419 (8th Cir. 1982); *accord, e.g., Paper, Allied-Indus., Chem. & Energy Workers Int'l Union v. Air Prods. & Chems., Inc.*, 300 F.3d 667, 675 (6th Cir. 2002) ("simply referring to the claim as a 'breach of contract'

[is] insufficient for purposes of § 301 federal courts' jurisdiction"; instead test is whether claim is "primarily representational"); *Pace v. Honolulu Disposal Serv., Inc.*, 227 F.3d 1150, 1156 (9th Cir. 2000) ("[An] end run around [the NLRA] . . . under the guise of contract interpretation . . . cannot be countenanced, [—10—] and we have drawn the jurisdictional line by asking whether the major issues to be decided . . . can be characterized as primarily representational or primarily contractual." (internal quotation marks and citations omitted) (ellipses in original)); *United Food & Commercial Workers Union, Local 400 v. Shoppers Food Warehouse Corp.*, 35 F.3d 958, 961 (4th Cir. 1994) (court is without jurisdiction if "a dispute is so primarily representational, that it falls solely within the Board's jurisdiction" (internal quotation marks omitted)); *Copps Food Ctr., Inc. v. United Food & Commercial Workers Union, Local 73-A*, No. 90-1905, 1991 WL 135508, at *2 (7th Cir. 1991) (unpublished) ("In answering the question of whether the federal court has jurisdiction to hear a contract-based dispute between a union and an employer, the court generally has to employ a difficult process of determining whether a particular dispute is primarily contractual—hence suited for § 301 federal court jurisdiction—or representational, requiring preliminary NLRB determination of the matter."); *see Trs. of Colo. Statewide Iron Workers (ERECTOR) Joint Apprenticeship & Training Trust Fund v. A & P Steel, Inc.*, 812 F.2d 1518, 1526 (10th Cir. 1987). If the court decides that the dispute is "primarily representational" even if framed as a breach of contract, the court defers to the NLRB's exclusive jurisdiction. *See, e.g., Int'l Bhd. of Elec. Workers, Local 71 v. Trafftech, Inc.*, 461 F.3d 690, 695–97 (6th Cir. 2006).

Although we have not decided the parameters of a claim that is "primarily representational" as opposed to "primarily contractual," several of our sister circuits have done so. The Sixth Circuit has "identified two scenarios in which a dispute will be treated as 'primarily representational.'" *DiPonio Constr. Co., Inc. v. Int'l Union of Bricklayers & Allied Craftworkers, Local 9*, 687 F.3d 744, 750 (6th Cir. 2012) (quoting *Trafftech*, 461 F.3d at 695).

The first occurs if the [—11—] NLRB "has already exercised jurisdiction over [the] matter and is either considering . . . or has already decided" the claim. *Id.* (quoting *Trafftech*, 461 F.3d at 695); *see also Int'l Bhd. of Boilermakers, Iron Ship Builders, Blacksmiths, Forgers & Helpers, AFL-CIO v. Olympic Plating Indus., Inc.*, 870 F.2d 1085, 1089 (6th Cir. 1989) ("In such cases where the Board's resolution of non-contractual issues could also resolve the controversial breach of contract claims brought under § 301, the federal courts should decline to exercise jurisdiction over the contractual allegations."). The second is "where the issue is an initial decision in the representation area," *DiPonio*, 687 F.3d at 750 (quoting *Trafftech*, 461 F.3d at 695); for example, where the court must decide whether the union was properly elected by the employees, *id.* (citing *Amalgamated Clothing & Textile Workers Union v. Facetglas, Inc.*, 845 F.2d 1250, 1253 (4th Cir. 1988)). At least one circuit contemplates a third scenario: a case in which the "center of the dispute" is a representational question, such as whether workers are "employees" or "supervisors" under the NLRA, but the NLRB has not yet taken up "the representation question at issue." *Morello v. Fed. Barge Lines, Inc.*, 746 F.2d 1347, 1349–50 (8th Cir. 1984) (internal quotation marks omitted).

Here, MEBA asserts that the district court's jurisdiction arises under section 301 of the LMRA. It argues that Liberty violated the parties' CBA and that its suit alleges a "violation of [the] contract[]" as section 301 requires. *See* 29 U.S.C. § 185(a). Liberty challenged that assertion in district court and does so again on appeal. Although somewhat garbled, Liberty's argument that the court lacks jurisdiction under section 301—or, at the very least, lacks jurisdiction unless the court determines the disputed impasse question—appears to be two-fold. [—12—]

First, Liberty claims the existence of impasse *vel non* is a jurisdictional fact. As Liberty apparently sees it, if the parties did not reach impasse, the court had jurisdiction

of the claim under section 301[6] but, if the parties did reach impasse, the court did not.[7] Liberty faults the district court for construing its jurisdictional challenge as a facial attack and for *assuming* MEBA's view that impasse was not reached in determining its jurisdiction under section 301; according to Liberty, the district court should have first *resolved* whether or not impasse occurred, a fact it dubs "jurisdictional." If the court had [—13—] resolved the question in Liberty's favor (that is, impasse occurred), then the court would have been obligated to dismiss the case for lack of jurisdiction. Although a court must generally resolve a disputed jurisdictional fact if a so-called factual attack on the court's subject matter jurisdiction is made, *see, e.g., Herbert v. Nat'l Acad. of Scis.*, 974 F.2d 192, 197 (D.C. Cir. 1992), impasse *vel non* is not a jurisdictional fact. Section 301 of the LMRA grants the district court jurisdiction of "[s]uits for violation of contracts between an employer and a labor organization." 29 U.S.C. § 185(a). For a

---

[6] Liberty admits it employed AMO-represented officers and engineers beginning at 12:01a.m. on October 1, 2011. If the parties' CBA remained in effect past midnight on September 30, as MEBA contends, there can be no question that MEBA's suit would be for a violation of the contract and the court would have jurisdiction under section 301.

[7] Liberty starts with the premise that a court cannot exercise section 301 jurisdiction of a claim arising from conduct that took place *after* the contract expired. *See, e.g., Derrico v. Sheehan Emergency Hosp.*, 844 F.2d 22, 25 (2d Cir. 1988) ("When a complaint alleges a claim based on events occurring after the expiration of a collective bargaining agreement, courts have held that section 301 cannot provide a basis for jurisdiction."). Liberty maintains that it abided by the contract until midnight on September 30 and that the conduct MEBA complains of and seeks to arbitrate in this suit—namely, Liberty's replacing MEBA workers with AMO workers—occurred *after* that time. In Liberty's view, *if* the parties reached impasse before September 30, then (1) the contract expired at midnight; (2) the conduct MEBA seeks to arbitrate occurred after the contract expired; and therefore (3) the court cannot exercise jurisdiction over the "contractual" claim because it did not in fact arise under the parties' contract at all. Thus, Liberty concludes, for the court to determine if it has section 301 jurisdiction, it must necessarily determine whether the parties reached impasse.

district court to exercise jurisdiction, then, there need not be a valid contract but only a suit for violation of a contract. The existence of the contract is instead an element of the cause of action. *See Winnett v. Caterpillar, Inc.*, 553 F.3d 1000, 1005–06 (6th Cir. 2009) (section 301's "contract requirement is non-jurisdictional" and instead constitutes "an element of a cause of action"); *Pittsburgh Mack Sales & Serv., Inc. v. Int'l Union of Operating Eng'rs, Local Union No. 66*, 580 F.3d 185, 189 (3d Cir. 2009) ("It is unnecessary for us to resolve whether or not the CBAs were terminated [before the alleged breach] because . . . the existence of a contract is not a jurisdictional element of a section 301 claim."). *See generally Arbaugh v. Y & H Corp.*, 546 U.S. 500 (2006) (court must determine whether statutory requirement is jurisdictional or instead describes elements of cause of action).

Second, Liberty attempts to argue that even if MEBA's suit is nominally contractual, it is in fact "primarily representational" because MEBA's goal in bringing the suit is to replace AMO as the bargaining representative of the officers and engineers aboard Liberty vessels. According to Liberty, "MEBA's objective in this case is to displace its rival union . . . and establish MEBA's representational rights over the supervisors working aboard Liberty's ships"—action that [—14—] violates section 8 of the NLRA and thus triggers the NLRB's jurisdiction. Appellant's Br. at 34.

Liberty relies on the Eighth Circuit's opinion in *Morello v. Federal Barge Lines, Inc.* to support its argument. 746 F.2d 1347. There, two employers had CBAs with one union, which CBAs were set to expire on a date certain provided one party notified the other of its intent to terminate. *Id.* at 1348. The employers provided the required termination notice and the union responded by attempting to begin negotiations. *Id.* The employers ignored the union on the ground that they had no duty to negotiate because the union members were "supervisors" rather than "employees" under the CBAs' terms. *Id.* The union sued, alleging that the employers had breached the CBAs by refusing to

negotiate; specifically, it argued that the employers did in fact have a duty to negotiate because the union members were employees, not supervisors. *Id.* at 1348–49. Although the case was not pending before the NLRB, the Eighth Circuit held that the question at the center of the dispute was whether the union members were supervisors or employees—and that question was "one of representation," not contract. *Id.* at 1349. Accordingly, it held that the district court lacked jurisdiction. *Id.* at 1351.

Liberty claims that here, as in *Morello*, the center of the dispute is a representational question—which union, MEBA or AMO, has the right to represent Liberty's supervisors. According to Liberty, the court "cannot reach the central issues in MEBA's complaint and grant relief without coercing Liberty to accept MEBA-represented supervisors." Appellant's Br. at 39. Because such relief involves a "representational issue" and would, according to Liberty, violate the NLRA, Liberty argues that the claim is "primarily representational." [—15—]

We disagree. Liberty's argument on this point suffers from a fatal flaw: it conflates the type of claim with the effect of a claim's enforcement. *Garmon* preemption is designed to prevent a court from deciding a claim that can only be characterized as representational; to resolve such a claim, a court must decide a representational question. *Morello* is a perfect example. To resolve the dispute, the court would have had to decide whether certain individuals were "employees" or "supervisors" under the NLRA. *Morello*, 746 F.2d at 1349. The court correctly ruled that, even if framed as a "contractual" dispute, that question is one squarely within the NLRB's province. *See id.*

On the other hand, resolving MEBA's suit requires deciding plainly contractual matters—what constitutes "impasse" and whether Liberty's conduct breached the parties' agreement. The decision may ultimately have a representational effect in that MEBA could, under the terms of the contract, be reinstated as the representative of Liberty's officers and engineers. But that effect results from the enforcement of the

CBA, not from the resolution of any representational question. Thus, *Morello* offers Liberty little support.

Moreover, MEBA's suit does not fit into the other two categories of "primarily representational" claims recognized by other circuits. The case is not currently pending before the NLRB, *see DiPonio*, 687 F.3d at 750; in fact, the opposite is true. Liberty initially filed an unfair labor practice charge with the NLRB, claiming that MEBA's lawsuit to compel arbitration violated the NLRA, but the NLRB's Office of the General Counsel (OGC) recommended dismissal because it involved a "bona fide contractual issue," *Marine Eng'rs Beneficial Ass'n (Liberty Mar.)*, Case 05-CB-077851, NLRB Advice Mem. at 6, Aug. 31, 2012; Liberty subsequently [—16—] withdrew its charge. In addition, there is no "initial" representational question at issue, *see DiPonio*, 687 F.3d at 750; in fact, no representational question is presented at all. Rather, the dispute boils down to a contractual one—whether the New Agreement remained in effect as of 12:01a.m. on October 1 and whether Liberty violated it. Accordingly, we conclude that the district court properly exercised its jurisdiction under section 301 of the LMRA.

B. Arbitration

Having concluded that the district court had jurisdiction to compel arbitration generally, we turn to the specific merits inquiry in this case: is *when* the contract expired—*i.e.*, whether the parties reached impasse—an arbitrable issue? The district court answered in the affirmative, *see Liberty Mar.*, 70 F. Supp. 3d at 350, and we agree.

The Supreme Court has set out "the proper framework for deciding when disputes are arbitrable." *Granite Rock Co. v. Int'l Bhd. of Teamsters*, 561 U.S. 287, 296 (2010). "Under that framework, a court may order arbitration of a particular dispute only where the court is satisfied that the parties agreed to arbitrate *that dispute*." *Id.* (emphasis in original); *see also AT&T Techs., Inc. v. Commc'ns Workers of Am.*, 475 U.S. 643, 648 (1986) ("[A]rbitration is a matter of contract and a

party cannot be required to submit to arbitration any dispute which he has not agreed so to submit." (quoting *United Steelworkers of Am. v. Warrior & Gulf Navigation Co.*, 363 U.S. 574, 582 (1960))).

In considering how to apply this framework, we have used "[a] trichotomy among the disputes that arise in arbitrability cases." *Nat'l R.R. Passenger Corp. v. Bos. & Me. Corp.*, 850 F.2d 756, 761 (D.C. Cir. 1988). There are (1) "disputes over the formation of an agreement to arbitrate"; (2) "disputes over [—17—] the breadth of an arbitration clause, where the parties disagree over whether a certain issue falls within or without the subject matter coverage of an undoubted agreement to arbitrate"; and (3) disputes that "relate[] to the length, rather than the breadth, of an arbitration clause." *Id.* at 761. In other words, three types of arbitrability disputes typically arise: (1) formation disputes; (2) breadth disputes; and (3) duration disputes.

It is settled that a formation dispute is "generally for courts to decide." *Granite Rock*, 561 U.S. at 296; *Nat'l R.R.*, 850 F.2d at 761 ("[I]f the parties disagree as to whether they ever entered into any arbitration agreement at all, the court must resolve that dispute."). Similarly, a breadth dispute is "generally for the courts to determine" but "parties may agree to arbitrate questions of breadth" so long as they do so plainly. *Nat'l R.R.*, 850 F.2d at 761.

A duration dispute is a different animal. We have articulated a rather detailed set of "general rules" for "resolving disputes . . . over the expiration or termination of an arbitration clause":

If the arbitration clause is a narrow one, covering only specified types of disputes . . . , then we must presume that the parties did *not* intend for disputes over contract duration to be referred to arbitration. In such a case, the court will decide the question of duration unless the party seeking arbitration makes a clear showing that the contracting parties intended such disputes to be arbitrated. Faced with a somewhat broader arbitration clause, however, such as one providing generally (perhaps with certain specified exceptions) that disputes "arising under" or "concerning" the contract are [—18—] to be arbitrated, we will *presume* that disputes over the termination or expiration of the contract should be submitted to arbitration. Of course, this presumption also attaches where the arbitration clause is broader still, such as one requiring arbitration of "any grievance affecting the mutual relations of the parties."

Id. at 762 (citation omitted) (emphases added). The presumption, however, is not absolute.

[E]ven in cases involving very broad arbitration clauses, the presumption in favor of arbitrating disputes over contract duration can be overcome by a *clear showing* that the parties intended for the underlying contract to expire, or separately agreed to terminate it, before the relevant dispute arose. For example, if a contract provides that "all disputes between the parties shall be arbitrated," but with equal clarity provides that it will expire on a date certain, then any dispute over whether the contract actually expired or was extended by the parties must be decided by the court rather than by the arbitrator.

Id. at 762–63 (emphasis added).

Liberty argues that the dispute in this case is more akin to a formation dispute than a duration dispute; accordingly, it asserts that, before compelling arbitration, the court must decide whether the New Agreement was "in existence" at the time MEBA filed its grievances. Appellant's Br. 50. In support of this argument, it relies heavily on the Supreme Court's statement in *Granite Rock* that if "any issue . . . calls into question the formation or applicability of the specific [—19—] arbitration clause that a party seeks to have a court enforce," the district court must resolve that issue "[t]o satisfy itself" that the parties did indeed intend to arbitrate. 561

U.S. at 297. According to Liberty, its claim that the New Agreement expired "calls into question the . . . applicability" of the arbitration clause. *See id.*

Liberty also relies on *Granite Rock*'s analogous facts. In that case, a union and an employer were parties to a CBA that expired. *Id.* at 292. When the parties reached impasse in negotiating a new CBA, the union went on strike. *Id.* Negotiations continued and eventually the parties reached agreement on a new CBA that included both an arbitration provision and an anti-strike provision. *Id.* at 292–93. The new CBA did not address the employer's damages arising from the strike and the parties attempted to reach a separate "back-to-work" agreement holding workers harmless as to those damages. *Id.* at 293. They were unsuccessful, the union remained on strike and the employer sued the union for damages for violating the anti-strike provision of the new CBA. *Id.* at 293–94. The parties disputed the new CBA's ratification date. *Id.* at 294–95. The union argued that the ratification issue should be resolved via arbitration. *Id.* at 295. The Supreme Court disagreed, holding that ratification determined the date on which the parties agreed to begin arbitrating disputes. *Id.* at 303–05. The district court, not the arbitrator, was required to decide the question. *Id.* at 304.

Liberty's attempt to analogize its case to *Granite Rock* rings hollow. *Granite Rock* falls squarely within the formation-dispute category of the "trichotomy" we identified in *National Railroad*, 850 F.2d at 761. The issue was when the contract went into effect—a formation issue that, in that case, was central to determining whether the parties had agreed to arbitrate *any* dispute. *Granite Rock*, 561 U.S. at 303–05. [—20—] This case has nothing to do with formation. Both parties acknowledge they entered into an enforceable CBA. It thus falls into a different category from *Granite Rock*—it is without doubt a dispute over the agreement's duration. Liberty contends that the New Agreement expired at midnight on September 30, 2011; MEBA contends no impasse was reached and it remained in effect. As a result, *National*

Railroad instructs that *who* decides the duration question—the court or an arbitrator—depends upon the *breadth* of the arbitration provision. 850 F.2d at 762–63 ("[W]e believe that the breadth of the arbitration clause does bear on the question of who must determine its length."). If the arbitration provision is broad, the court presumes that the parties intended to arbitrate the duration dispute; and unless a party can overcome the presumption with "a clear showing" that the parties intended the contract to expire, the duration question is reserved to the arbitrator. *Id.* at 763. Conversely, if the arbitration provision is narrow, and thus does not appear to cover duration, the court determines whether the contract remained in effect. *Id.*

Here, the arbitration clause is quite broad: "All disputes relating to the interpretation or performance of this Agreement shall be determined in accordance with the provisions in this [Arbitration-and-Grievance Procedure] Section." Tanker Agreement, at 10. "All disputes relating to the interpretation . . . of this Agreement," *see id.*, includes a dispute as to the interpretation of the duration provision—including the word "impasse." As the district court pointed out, "[e]ven if this Court were to read the instant arbitration clause to suggest that the parties only intended to arbitrate issues of contract interpretation . . . , the question of whether the parties' otherwise valid agreement expired *is* precisely such an issue—it requires interpretation of the agreement's duration provision." *Liberty Mar.*, 70 F. Supp. 3d at 347 (emphasis in original). As the court further noted, the New Agreement's **[—21—]** arbitration clause is similar to the "broad" arbitration clause to which the Supreme Court found the presumption of arbitrability "particularly applicable." *Id.* at 348 (quoting *AT&T Techs.*, 475 U.S. at 650). As a result, unless Liberty can make a "clear showing" that the parties intended the New Agreement to expire, the duration question is for the arbitrator, not the court.

This Liberty fails to do. The duration provision does not with abundant "clarity" provide a fixed expiration date, *see Nat'l R.R.*,

850 F.2d at 763; rather, the September 30, 2011 deadline gives way as soon as one party gives notice of its intent to amend the agreement. At that point, the New Agreement remains in effect until the parties reach "impasse." *See* MOU § 1. Although Liberty has a plausible argument that the parties reached impasse, MEBA has an equally plausible argument that they did not. Because expiration turns on impasse—and Liberty cannot make a clear showing that impasse occurred—the issue is plainly arbitrable under the terms of the CBA.

For the foregoing reasons, the judgment of the district court is affirmed.

So ordered.

United States Court of Appeals
for the District of Columbia Circuit

No. 15-1035

MAHER TERMINALS, LLC
vs.
FEDERAL MARITIME COMM'N

On Petition for Review of Final Memorandum
Opinion and Order of the Federal Maritime
Commission

Decided: March 22, 2016

Citation: 816 F.3d 888, 4 Adm. R. 499 (D.C. Cir. 2016).

Before **GARLAND,** Chief Judge, **TATEL,** Circuit Judge,
and **SILBERMAN,** Senior Circuit Judge.

[—2—] **SILBERMAN,** Senior Circuit Judge:

Petitioner Maher, a marine terminal operator, challenges a decision of the Federal Maritime Commission authorizing preferential lease terms to a competitor, APM-Maersk. We grant the petition and remand because we think the Commission provided an inadequate explanation.

I.

In the late 1990s, the Port Authority began negotiating new leasing terms for maritime terminal operators servicing the Port of New York and New Jersey. This was a part of an overall effort to modernize the port's facilities and make it an attractive location for shipping into the future. Among the companies the Port Authority negotiated with were Maher and APM-Maersk. Maher is an independent marine terminal operator, which means that it has no affiliated carrier fleet, and services only third party carriers and shippers through its rented terminal. APM-Maersk, on the other hand, is affiliated with the largest ocean carrier-fleet in the United States, Sea-Land, though it also services third party cargo through its terminals.[1] [—3—]

Lease negotiations between Maher and the Port Authority began in 1995. Maher sought an agreement that would make it competitive with other terminal operators, and tentative terms, including an effective annual rate of $68,750 per acre, were reached in late 1997. Negotiations with Maher were suspended in 1998, however, when the Port Authority began negotiating with APM-Maersk. That larger terminal operator had found the initial terms offered by the Port Authority too expensive, and threatened to go to Baltimore. APM-Maersk's business was critical to the Port of New York and New Jersey because of the high volume of container business it could bring through its affiliated carriers. Indeed, Maher's CEO expressed great concern over the potential departure, writing a letter to the Governor of New Jersey warning of the "grave" risk to the port.

The Port Authority opened negotiations with APM-Maersk in July by offering a 350-acre terminal at a rate of $63,000 per acre, per year. That was rejected. Later, in September, the offer was reduced to $36,000 per acre, but again rebuffed. APM-Maersk made clear that it would require as much as $120 million in cost reduction in order to make the port as attractive as other options. The Port Authority finally agreed, and submitted terms that included $30 million in capital and structural improvements paid for by the Port Authority at the terminal, as well as $90 million in basic rent reduction. Those concessions, of $120 million total, reduced APM-Maersk's effective base rent to $19,000 per acre, per year.

Since the purpose of the concessions was to keep APM-Maersk, because of its affiliated carrier fleet and the promise of additional tonnage of cargo, the Port Authority got a "port guarantee," requiring APM-Maersk to actually bring cargo from its affiliated carriers through the port. The Port Authority hoped [—4—] that meant APM-Maersk would not entice third party carriers away from other terminal operators, like Maher. A deal was reached at an effective annual base rent of $19,000 per acre, with certain penalties designed to increase the rent where the port guarantee was not met.

---

[1] What we refer to as APM-Maersk now, as a result of mergers and acquisitions over the period in question, includes both Sea-Land [—3—] and Maersk shipping companies.

With APM-Maersk secured as a tenant, the Port Authority turned back to negotiations with Maher. Maher sought parity with APM-Maersk, but the Port Authority was unwilling to offer the same terms. Lacking the bargaining power enjoyed by APM-Maersk, Maher ultimately agreed to an initial base rent of $39,750 per acre, with an escalator, such that the average base rent over the life of the lease would amount to $53,753 per acre. While the exact annual base rent charged to APM-Maersk may be somewhat variable over the period of the 30-year lease (due to the possibility of penalties for failure to meet cargo guarantees), it is undeniable that Maher was forced to pay substantially more than APM-Maersk.

Maher was purchased by Deutsche Bank in 2007. As the global recession hit in 2008, the port's total container traffic fell for the first time in almost 15 years. Maher lost nearly 15% of its business, while APM-Maersk failed to meet its port guarantees in 2008, 2009, and 2010.

On June 3, 2008, nearly 8 years after executing its lease, Maher filed a complaint against the Port Authority, alleging that the differential terms between its and APM-Maersk's leases violated the Shipping Act. It alleged that the Port Authority had violated 46 U.S.C. § 41106(2) in offering an "unreasonable preference" to APM-Maersk. [—5—]

After some dispute regarding the applicable statute of limitations for the claims,[2] the merits came before an ALJ, who issued a decision on April 25, 2014, denying the claims. Maher appealed, and the Federal Maritime Commission affirmed on December 17, 2014.

The Commission did not deny that the Port Authority had treated Maher and APM-Maersk differently, but the Commission explained the difference was justified, on three counts. First, APM-Maersk had threatened credibly to abandon the port. Maher could make no such threat. Second, APM-Maersk was able to make a port guarantee, relying on its affiliated carrier fleet, that Maher was not. Finally, Maher's terminal was of a higher quality than was APM-Maersk's, thus justifying a higher rent. The Commission similarly dismissed a separate unreasonable practices claim, explaining that Maher had not met its assigned burden under the applicable regulations.

II.

It is common ground in this case that differences between similar entities contracting with Port Authorities must be based on "transportation factors." That term goes back to the Interstate Commerce Act and was extended into the earliest Shipping Act.[3] It is not clear whether it was originally [—6—] articulated as an interpretation of the statutory term "undue or unreasonable preference"[4] or whether it was a policy choice. Perhaps that is why petitioner conflates its challenge as both a statutory claim and an arbitrary/capricious one. And the dispute is further limited by the Commission's concession that neither the port guarantee nor Maersk's supposed superior terminal quality would justify the lower rent. The Commission's decision thus rises or falls on APM-Maersk's credible threat to leave the Port of New York and New Jersey—which the Commission claims is a "transportation factor," justifying the distinction in the treatment of APM-Maersk and Maher.

---

[2] Shipping Act claims, as relevant here, have a statute of limitations of three years. On that basis, summary judgment was requested against Maher. The FMC ultimately held that Maher's request for a cease-and-desist order was not time-barred, and that in the event a violation was found, Maher was entitled to reparations for the full three-year period, though not for the period before that running back to the execution of the lease.

[3] See generally, Distribution Services, Ltd. v. Transpacific Freight Conference of Japan, 24 S.R.R. 714, 719-21 (FMC 1988).

[4] 46 U.S.C. § 41106(2) instructs that a "marine terminal operator" may not "give any undue or unreasonable preference or advantage or impose any undue or unreasonable prejudice or disadvantage with respect to any person...".

Before considering the issue on which the dueling briefs concentrate—whether a large terminal operator's threat to leave can be legitimately regarded as a "transportation factor"—the more obvious question raised by petitioner is why the same rates were not offered to it, which would avoid the issue of discrimination altogether. In that regard, the Commission's explanation in its Order is circular. It said, "The Port's decision *not* to give Maher certain [the same] lease terms cannot be divorced from its decision to give those terms to APM-Maersk." (Emphasis added.) In other words, we understand the Commission to be saying that the reasons APM-Maersk were given new terms somehow necessarily implies that petitioner should not be given the same terms. But that is a *non sequitur*. Whatever the reason the port determined to give lower rates to APM-Maersk, it doesn't at all follow that those same or similar rates should not be offered to petitioner. After all, the [—7—] Commission has previously ordered that same remedy.[5] (Indeed, APM-Maersk sought lower lease rent for itself; it did not seek preferential rates *vis-a-vis* competitors in the Port of New York.)

To be sure, the intervenor, the Port Authority, argued that it would be commercially irrational for it to extend the same terms to Maher. Even if we could accept intervenor's explanations for that of the Commission—which, of course, we cannot— that terse comment is hardly adequate. There are all sorts of factors that might bear on that issue, including economic conditions in the port and the competitive impact of the preference.

Assuming *arguendo* that the Commission adequately responded to petitioner's contention that the same rates should be extended to it, the Commission's explanation as to why APM-Maersk's preference was based on a "transportation factor" was hopelessly convoluted, particularly in light of its precedent. The two cases upon which petitioner relies are *Ballmill Lumber v. Port of New York*, 10 S.R.R. 131 (FMC 1968) and

Ceres Marine Terminal v. Maryland Port Administration, 27 S.R.R. 1251 (FMC 1997).

In *Ballmill*, Port Newark granted an exception to the largest lumber wholesaler, Weyerhauser, from a general policy previously applied to Ballmill. That policy obliged lumber wholesaler tenants to contract for logistical services with either the Port Authority itself or certain approved vendors. Weyerhauser was instead permitted to provide these services from its own in-house entity. The port sought to justify the preference based on Weyerhauser's bargaining position. The [—8—] wholesaler was threatening to leave the Port of Newark if it didn't get the terms it wanted. The Commission rejected that justification, and thus held it was an "unreasonable preference." Interestingly, the Commission never even referred to the term "transportation factor."

Then, more recently, in *Ceres*, the Commission rejected the preferential rates the Maryland Port Authority granted Maersk at the Port of Baltimore for dockage, crane rental and land rental charges. The port presented a strikingly similar argument to that presented in our present case; that Maersk, then operating its own shipping line, threatened to switch to Norfolk, Virginia, which was seeking additional Maersk business.[6] The Commission was told Maersk's loss would be a devastating blow to Baltimore. The Commission, nevertheless, held that the cargo guarantees Maersk offered, and its size, did not justify the differential *vis-a-vis* Ceres. Put succinctly, the Commission said, "status alone is not a sufficient basis by which to distinguish between lessees."

The Commission did not overrule these cases. Instead, it offered rather lame distinctions we find quite unpersuasive. It stated that in *Ballmill*, the Commission did not *in hoc verba* reject the threat to leave the port as a legitimate justification. Therefore, it supposedly could have thought the threat was not credible (even though that was not even argued). And the Commission "interpreted"

---

[5] *See Ballmill Lumber & Sales Corp. v. Port of N.Y. Auth.*, 10 S.R.R. 131 (FMC 1968).

[6] That was prior to its affiliation with Sea-Land.

Ceres as holding only that preferential rates could not be based on status alone (a terminal operator's affiliation with a carrier), even though the port's argument had been squarely based on Maersk's threat to leave—with its affiliated carrier. [—9—]

We express no views on whether the Commission could overrule or modify its previous decisions, but it must do so in a forthright manner. The distinctions the Commission offered were utterly unpersuasive. *See Bush-Quayle '92 Primary Committee, Inc. v. FEC*, 104 F.3d 448, 454 (D.C. Cir. 1997) ("Without adequate elucidation, this court has no way of ascertaining whether cases are indeed distinguishable, whether the Commission has a principled reason for distinguishing them, or whether the Commission is refusing to treat like cases alike.").

We note that in *Ceres*, although at the outset of its opinion the Commission describes the governing law as permitting discrimination based on "transportation factors," its following discussion only asked whether the discrimination was "reasonable." This "reasonableness" standard was also applied in our case; the Commission said Maher had not "met its burden of showing that the Port's reasons ... [were] unreason-able." Does that mean the term "transportation factor" is simply a synonym for reasonable? If so, how does the Commission distinguish between reasonable and unreasonable preferences?

In sum, we must remand this case to the Commission for an adequate explanation of its decision and its policy. It is obvious the underlying problem is competition between ports for a larger share of carrier traffic. We wonder if there is not a regulatory solution to the problem.

***

For the foregoing reasons, the Order is remanded back to the Commission.

So ordered.

Tables of Authority

This page intentionally left blank

Table of Cases

This page intentionally left blank

TABLE OF CASES[1]

---

[1] Cases named solely after ships, *see, e.g., The Pennsylvania*, 86 U.S. (19 Wall.) 125 (1873), are alphabetized under the letter "T." Cases where the United States is the plaintiff are alphabetized by defendant under the letter "U."

B

C

D

E

F

G

H

I

J

K

L

M

N

O

P

R

S

T

U

V

W

Y

Z

Table of Statutes and Rules

This page intentionally left blank

TABLE OF STATUTES AND RULES [1]

PAGE

---

[1] As cited in the opinions reported.

STATUTES

RULES

REGULATIONS

STATE

Index

This page intentionally left blank

INDEX

A

D

E

G

H

I

J

L

M

N

O

P

Q

R

S

T

U

V

W

www.ingramcontent.com/pod-product-compliance
Lightning Source LLC
Chambersburg PA
CBHW081215220326
41598CB00037B/6788